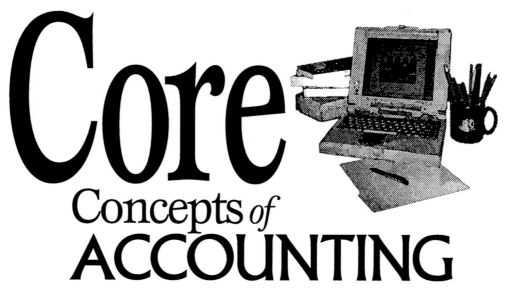

Core
Concepts *of*
ACCOUNTING

INFORMATION

1997/1998 Edition

Theme I

The Users/Uses of Accounting Information

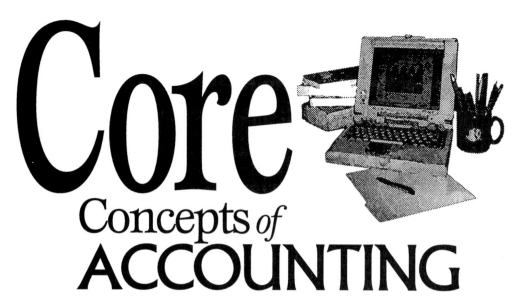

Core
Concepts *of*
ACCOUNTING

INFORMATION
1997/1998 Edition

Karen V. Pincus, Ph.D.
University of Arkansas

Theme I

The Users/Uses of Accounting Information

The McGraw-Hill Companies, Inc.

New York St. Louis San Francisco Auckland Bogotá
Caracas Lisbon London Madrid Mexico Milan Montreal
New Delhi Paris San Juan Singapore Sydney Tokyo Toronto

McGraw·Hill

A Division of The McGraw·Hill Companies

Acknowledgements:

2-45 Quotation from *Be Data Literate—Know What to Know* by Peter Drucker. Reprinted by permission of *The Wall Street Journal*. Copyright © 1992 by Dow Jones & Company, Inc. All rights reserved worldwide.

2-46 From *Management Accounting* by William Ihlanfeldt. Copyright © 1989 by *Management Accounting*, Montvale, NJ. Reprinted by permission of the publisher.

2-75, 3-87 From *Coidentification of Standards for the Professional Practice of Internal Auditing* by The Institute of Internal Auditors, Inc. Copyright © 1993 by The Institute of Internal Auditors, Inc., 249 Maitland Avenue, Altamonte Springs, Florida 32710-4201 USA. Reprinted by permission.

2-79 From *Definitions of Five Components of the COSO Report*. Copyright © by Committee of Sponsoring Organizations of the Treadway Commission. Reprinted by permission.

2-80 From *The Art of Communicating* by Shirley Orechwa Maxey. Copyright © 1989 by California Society of CPAs, Los Angeles, CA. Reprinted by permission.

2-85 From *Standards of Ethical Conduct for Management Accountants*, Montvale, NJ. Reprinted by permission of the publisher.

2-86, 87 From *Thinking Ethically: A Framework for Moral Decision Making*. Copyright © 1996 by Santa Clara University Center for Applied Ethics, Santa Clara, CA. Reprinted by permission of the publisher.

2-41 Quotation from *Internal Auditing Guideline #6*. Copyright © by American Institute of Certified Public Accountants, New York, NY. Reprinted by permission of the publisher.

3-61 Quotation from interview with William McGowan. Reprinted by permission, *Inc. Magazine*, August 1986. Copyright © 1986 by Goldhirsh Group, Inc., 38 Commercial Wharf, Boston, MA, USA 02110.

3-66 Quotation from article by Jaye Scholl. Reprinted by permission of *Barron's*. Copyright © 1990 Dow Jones & Company, Inc. All rights reserved worldwide.

3-90 From William D. Hall. Copyright © 1987 by Arthur Andersen & Co., Chicago, IL. Reprinted by permission of the publisher.

5-1 Quotation from *Statement on Accountability*. Copyright © 1988 by Society of Management Accountants of Canada, Hamilton, Ontario. Reprinted by permission of publisher.

5-3 Quotation from John Case, "A Company of Business People", *Inc. Magazine*, April 1993. Copyright © 1993 by Goldhirsh Group, Inc., 38 Commercial Wharf, Boston, MA, USA 02110.

5-6 Quotation from Michael Cieply, "They Freeze Death if not Taxes". Copyright © 1990 by Los Angeles Times, Los Angeles, CA. Reprinted by permission of the publisher.

5-7 Quotation from William Hackworth, *Inc. Magazine*, May 1990. Copyright © 1990 by Goldhirsh Group, Inc., 38 Commercial Wharf, Boston, MA, USA 02110.

5-24 Quotation from Dan Rubenstein article. Reprinted by permission from the *CPA Journal*, March 1992. Copyright © 1992 by Dan Rubenstein.

Core Concepts of **ACCOUNTING** Information, 1997/1998 EDITION
Theme 1, The Users/Uses of Accounting Information

1 2 3 4 5 6 7 8 9 0   BBC BBC   9 0 9 8 7 6

ISBN 0-07-027627-7

Editor: Julie Kehrwald
Cover Design: Maggie Lytle
Printer/Binder: Braceland Brothers, Inc.

CORE CONCEPTS OF ACCOUNTING INFORMATION
THEME I: The Users/Uses of Accounting Information
Karen V. Pincus

Theme Contents

Note: Detailed tables of contents for each module appear at the front of the modules.

ACKNOWLEDGEMENTS

Core Concepts of Accounting Information was developed by Karen V. Pincus (currently Chair, Department of Accounting, University of Arkansas) as part of the Year 2000 Curriculum Project at the University of Southern California School of Accounting. The project was initiated in 1987 with a goal of creating an accounting curriculum that would prepare students for careers in the 21st century. During the project's early years, the generous funding of the Coopers & Lybrand Foundation and the support of Dean Michael A. Diamond and Project Director Theodore J. Mock were critical to the development of *Core Concepts of Accounting Information.*

A number of people provided helpful advice for the initial design and teaching of the course, reviewed the original materials while they were in process, or contributed appendix materials, including: Douglas Andrews, Jerry L. Arnold, Michael A. Diamond, Michael L. Duffy, Richard Eastin, Dan Elnathan, Lourdes D. Ferreira, John E. Fleming, Patricia Hughes, John Y. Lee, Thomas W. Lin, James Manegold, Theodore J. Mock, Shirley C. Maxey, J. David Pincus, O. J. Vandermause, Ron Wangerin, Paul A. Watkins, Stan Weingart, Doyle Z. Williams, and Jean C. Wyer and Mark Young.

Lawrence Siulagi and Patrick Blasa creatively produced many of the graphics, turning my rough sketches and ideas into eye-appealing art. René Gay, Maggie Palmer, and Milli Penner were enormously helpful in getting the pilot version produced. Julie Kehrwald of McGraw-Hill provided much assistance in making the transition to custom-published course materials. Alan Sachs and a host of people at McGraw-Hill deserve thanks for their efforts to create an electronic database to allow instructors more flexibility in their choice of course materials.

Since the original version of the course materials, numerous people have contributed innovative assignment materials based on their own classroom experience. Those people are acknowledged at the head of the appropriate assignments. Now that *Core Concepts of Accounting Information* is being used at many schools in the United States and Canada, the list of people who have provided helpful comments seems to grow daily--while I cannot name you all, I appreciate your contributions. You will see them reflected in this edition.

To these people and organizations--and especially to the students and teachers now using *Core Concepts of Accounting Information* who provide valuable feedback on many parts of the materials--I express my heartfelt thanks.

FEEDBACK ON COURSE MATERIALS

Comments, corrections, and suggestions for future topics and assignments are greatly appreciated. Address any feedback to:

Dr. Karen V. Pincus
Chair, Department of Accounting
College of Business Administration
University of Arkansas
Fayetteville, AR 72701

A FEW WORDS ABOUT COPYRIGHTS, THE PRICING OF COURSE MATERIALS AND PHOTOCOPYING

Core Concepts of Accounting Information includes material from other authors (such as members of the business press) as well as original material. The authors of these materials have the right to be compensated for the use of their work. Permission has been sought for the use of all copyrighted materials and fees for use, if any, are willingly paid. [Note: If any interests have been unwittingly overlooked, please contact the author and necessary acknowledgements will be made.]

Students should realize that the fees paid to reprint copyrighted materials are part of the cost of the course materials for *Core Concepts of Accounting Information*. The copyrighted materials contribute to your education, and, in turn, you contribute to the livelihood of the copyright holders. This is why it costs more to purchase course materials than it would cost to photocopy them. Photocopying copyrighted materials without permission (and without payment of fees, if any) is prohibited by law and is unfair to the people who originally developed the materials.

ORGANIZATION OF COURSE MATERIALS

Core Concepts of Accounting Information is organized into 4 broad themes:

Theme I: *The Users/Uses of Accounting Information*
Theme II: *Accounting Issues Involving Income and Cash Flows*
Theme III: *Accounting Issues Involving Economic Resources*
Theme IV: *Accounting Issues Involving Capital*

Each theme looks at a variety of topics that cut across the major functional areas of accounting--financial accounting, managerial accounting, systems, tax and auditing. Examples from business, non-profit and government organizations--both domestic and international--are used throughout the themes.

Each theme is further divided into modules that follow the same organizational pattern across the themes:

♦ The first module of each theme provides an introduction to the theme, describing the key points to be covered and presenting needed terminology.

♦ The remaining modules explore the topics of the theme from the perspective of a particular user group for accounting information: management, owners and creditors, government and other users.

♦ Theme I also contains a final module on the environment of accounting that introduces the body of technical rules, laws, standards and guidelines in the 5 major functional areas of accounting and discusses how to research accounting questions and problems.

Instructors may choose to use full themes or may prefer to select one or more modules to cover in a course. The page numbers tell you which theme and module you are reading. Pagination is of the form **I-2-3**, where the initial roman numeral indicates the theme, the middle number indicates the module within the theme, and the final number indicates the page within the module. Thus, page I-2-3 indicates Theme I, Module 2, page 3.

PREFACE FOR STUDENTS: THE STUDY OF ACCOUNTING

Education bewildered me with knowledge and facts in which I was only mildly interested.
-- Charles Chaplin, <u>My Autobiography</u>

Why are accounting courses required for students of business? Why are they recommended for many non-business students? What are you doing here? Chances are, you're not really sure. In fact, chances are you can come up with a few reasons why you'd rather *not* be here. So, before describing what *Core Concepts of Accounting Information* is about, let's start by considering some of the doubts you might have about studying accounting.

ACCOUNTING: THE RUMOR MILL

Rumour is a pipe
Blown by surprises, jealousies and conjectures.
-- Shakespeare, <u>Henry IV</u>, Act 2

Rumor #1: Accounting isn't relevant to most majors. It's not of much interest if you're not majoring in Business or if you plan a career in a non-quantitative area of business like Marketing or Human Resource Management.

This rumor is easy to deal with--it doesn't have a shred of truth. Suppose you are interested in some area of business other than accounting. You still will find yourself relying on accounting information to help you make decisions.

Suppose, for example, you plan a career in marketing. Marketers care a lot about product pricing. Pricing decisions require accounting information. Should an airline lower its fares to increase business? Should an automobile manufacturer offer rebates on its cars to encourage sales? You will need to understand accounting information to help you answer these questions.

Or, suppose you plan a career in human resource management. Human resource managers need information for hiring decisions and performance evaluation. How do you decide how many people to hire for the holiday season in a department store? How do you design a pay scheme that will reward your sales force for helping the company meet its sales targets? Planning for hiring needs requires accounting information, and so does performance evaluation.

There's virtually no area of modern business that doesn't use accounting information for decision-making. Moreover, even if your chosen career path is outside of business, accounting remains relevant to many social decisions, such as deciding on the appropriate tax policy for a nation or drawing up a budget for a state or local government. How much money is needed to improve roads? How does the amount of money spent to educate each student in one country compare to spending levels in other nations? Will the local performing arts center be able to operate if audiences decrease by 10% next year? To answer all these questions, accounting information is needed.

Rumor #2: Accounting is highly specialized and requires extensive technical training. So, it's best to leave accounting for accountants.

There's some truth to this rumor--a few accounting courses won't turn you into an accountant. If you want to be an accountant, you must commit to an extended program of study and mastery of a complex technical body of knowledge. For students who are considering careers in accounting, this course will provide a basis for assessing whether it's worthwhile to pursue that path. But, remember, for most students the goal isn't to become an accountant.

For most students, the goals of studying accounting are to:

♦ understand enough about accounting information to recognize when such information could be *useful* to you,

♦ understand the advantages and limitations of accounting information you are using in decision making; and, of course,

♦ know when you need to hire or work with an accountant to help you fulfill your needs.

Furthermore, if you ever do hire or work with an accountant, you need to know enough about accounting to understand what your accountant is saying. Accounting is often termed "the language of business." You need to speak this language at least well enough to understand what is going on around you.

Rumor #3: Accounting is boring--it's all rules and calculations. If you hated math, you'll hate accounting.

This is an interesting rumor. It's not correct, but it's easy to see how students could get this impression. Mostly, it comes from a confusion between bookkeeping and accounting.

In the past, many students began their study of accounting by being thoroughly indoctrinated into the record-keeping fundamentals of accounting (known as bookkeeping). Because bookkeeping can be repetitive and tedious at times, students easily got the impression that accountants spend their days "crunching numbers," with little need for contact with other human beings and little need for judgment or creative thinking. Only those students who continued to take accounting beyond the introductory level found out otherwise. It turns out that accountants deal a lot with people, and they don't deal as often as you might think in "black-and-white" calculations determined by a cookbook of rules.

Fortunately, times have changed. You will not have to become an accounting major to get a complete picture of the role of accountants in society. Thanks to the automation of bookkeeping, which the computer revolution of the late twentieth century brought about, it's no longer necessary to spend six months to a year dwelling on the record-keeping process. You'll learn enough about bookkeeping to understand the basic process, but you'll get to spend the bulk of your time learning about accounting, rather than bookkeeping. The focus of this course will be on the use of accounting information in decision-making.

Accountants do, of course, deal with numbers and good quantitative skills are valuable in accounting. If you decide to major in accounting, a strong mathematics background will be very useful for some specializations. For example, an accountant for a manufacturing firm that produces many different products on the same production line may find it useful to understand mathematical models that can help determine what it costs to make each individual product. However, the only math that you'll need to know for this course is addition, subtraction, multiplication and division--which really shouldn't be intimidating.

Rumor #4: Accounting courses are hard--there's lots of work to do in a short time.

Oops. There's a lot of truth to this one. However, hard work shouldn't be a turn-off if the payoff for your work is large enough. So, the next logical thing to think about is what benefits you will derive from studying *Core Concepts of Accounting Information*.

ACCOUNTING: WHAT'S IN IT FOR ME?

There's only one corner of the universe you can be certain of improving, and that's your own self.
-- Aldous Huxley, Time Must Have a Stop

As you probably suspect, or at least hope when you pay your tuition, most college courses are designed to provide you with tools for life. Studying accounting should help you develop certain skills and abilities. *Core Concepts of Accounting Information* was designed to help you:

♦　　　　understand the nature of various types of accounting information.

- be able to apply accounting information to a variety of decisions/uses.

- understand the limitations of accounting information.

- be able to recognize problems where accounting information might be useful.

- be able to research relevant professional accounting and business literature to help make decisions/solve problems.

- be able to express accounting-related ideas both orally and in writing, and communicate these ideas well in one-on-one or team situations.

- be aware of the importance of ethics and values in dealing with accounting issues.

All this sounds pretty nice, but very abstract. So, how will you be able to apply your knowledge? You should see a difference, between today and the end of this course, in your ability to read and understand accounting-related articles in the business press. As you progress through the course, you should find it easier to determine what kind of accounting information you can use when facing particular decisions such as whether to buy a stock, or whether to vote for a new bond issue, or whether to donate money to a particular charity.

You'll also be able to read and interpret basic accounting information, such as that found in corporate annual reports and auditors' reports. You'll be able to recognize basic control issues and systems design issues and understand their significance to an organization. You'll recognize why taxes play a crucial part in business decisions. You'll understand some of the accounting issues that will be important in the next several decades as business becomes increasingly international. In short, you should find yourself feeling comfortable speaking the language of business.

LEARNING ABOUT ACCOUNTING INFORMATION: KEYS TO SUCCESS

Plans get you into things, but you got to work your way out.
-- Will Rogers, The Autobiography of Will Rogers

What does it take to succeed in an accounting course? There *is* a lot of material to cover and most of it will be unfamiliar to you. It's rare that a student has extensive business experience before taking an accounting course, so often you will be struggling to understand basic business concepts as well as basic accounting concepts. There are a half dozen keys to success in learning about accounting information:

♦ **Hint #1: Budget Your Time.** Organize your work efforts to cover the scheduled readings and assignments on a timely basis. When learning *Core Concepts of Accounting Information*, you'll find that it's very inefficient--and ineffective--to try to do assignments or follow class discussions without first putting in your reading and thinking time. You'll find that most of the assignments build on the readings, but don't rehash them. They involve thought more than memorization. Since the class meetings and assignments often focus on *applying* the concepts you will learn about in your readings, it helps a lot to do the reading *beforehand*. Each module provides an estimated time budget to serve as a guide. But these numbers are only averages, not promises. You need to adjust the estimates, as needed, to accommodate your own learning style. Early in the course, keep track of the amount of time it takes you to complete scheduled readings and assignments. Use these estimates to budget your time for later sections of the course.

♦ **Hint #2: Be an Active Learner.** Be prepared to be an active participant in the class discussions. When it comes to discussions, you won't benefit much by just listening. You need to take the risk of trying to apply the concepts you've read about to the new situations being talked about in the classroom. Don't be afraid that what you say will be wrong. Lots of times it will be, but remember one important thing: if you could already get the right answer most of the time, there wouldn't be much point in taking a course. Sometimes we learn more from mistakes than from getting things right in the first place. Remember that the classroom is a safe place to make mistakes; take advantage of that safety.

♦ **Hint #3: Use a Business and Accounting Dictionary.** Often, when a passage or homework assignment is unclear, it's because you don't have a clear understanding of an accounting or business term. For example, if an assignment is talking about a manufacturing company that uses bar codes to identify its products and you don't know what a bar code is, you're bound to be frustrated. Do yourself a favor, look it up. Sometimes a problem or reading will assume that you have everyday knowledge of a business term--for example, assuming you know about bar codes from going to the grocery store. If the assumption is incorrect, protect yourself by looking up the term you don't understand.

♦ **Hint #4: Follow Current Business News.** You'll find that following the business news will reinforce what you are learning. Develop the habit of reading the business section of a daily newspaper. Try a trial subscription to a major business periodical-- either in print or on the Internet. Catch the business segment of a television or radio news broadcast. The more you follow the business news, the easier it will be for you to see how accounting information can be used in decision making.

- ◆ **Hint #5: Form a Study Group.** Two or more heads are often better than one--at school as well as in the workplace. Unless you are doing an assignment that is to be graded as individual work, there's no reason to work alone. What one student doesn't understand, another might. In effect, you can pool your resources to make your learning process easier. Since group assignments are a part of this course, it should be pretty easy to convert your work group into a study group to work together on readings and studying for exams, as well as the group assignments.

- ◆ **Hint #6: Ask Questions When You Don't Understand Something.** Ask your instructor, ask other students, ask people you know who know something about business and accounting--just ask. Don't sit on your questions waiting for understanding to hit you. Be aggressive in seeking out help.

Will you do well in accounting? If you take advantage of these hints, there's no reason why you shouldn't. Accounting is difficult, but not impossible. If you take control of your own learning, you should be amply rewarded. As one final hint to get you started off right, you'll find a sample assignment on the next page.

Pagination

Core Concepts of Accounting Information is divided into themes and modules, which different schools put together in a variety of ways.

How do you find material within your bound text? After this preface, pagination is of the form **I-2-3**, where the initial roman numeral indicates the theme, the middle number indicates the module within the theme, and the final number indicates the page within the module. Thus, page I-2-3 indicates Theme I, Module 2, page 3.

SAMPLE ASSIGNMENT: <u>Course Overview</u>

<u>SETTING</u>

You are a student facing your first day in your first accounting class. You need to know as much information as possible about the course--when assignments are due, how the course will be graded, when the exams are scheduled, and so on.

<u>ASSIGNMENT</u>

Review the syllabus for the course. Make sure you note any questions you need to ask your instructor in class or during office hours.

<u>HINTS</u>

This obviously isn't much of an assignment as you probably read the syllabus as soon as you got it. But, it does give you a chance to see how assignments for *Core Concepts of Accounting Information* are set up.

Each assignment begins with a "**SETTING**" that describes the problem situation for you and tells you what role to play. The assignments will usually ask you to apply concepts you have read about to new situations.   They ask you to think like someone in the "real world" role you are playing. They give you a chance to "learn by doing."

The "**ASSIGNMENT**" section tells you what your task is. Some of the assignments are designed to be done individually; others are designed to be done in small groups. Some of the assignments may be discussed in class or handed in for grading; others will be self-corrected. Solutions to self-corrected problems will appear at the end of the module.

Finally, each assignment contains some "**HINTS**" for how to proceed. Before you read the hints, quickly try to think about how you will approach the assignment. Then, read the hints and compare them to your plan to see if your approach makes sense. By using the hints this way, you will not only get information about how to handle the specific assignment, you will also be learning about how to structure approaches to problem-solving and decision-making.

1

MODULE I:

INTRODUCTION: WHAT IS ACCOUNTING?

1997-1998 edition

Table of Contents

MODULE I:

INTRODUCTION: WHAT IS ACCOUNTING?

Estimated Time Budget

Task	Time Estimate
Reading INTRODUCTION: WHAT IS ACCOUNTING?	60 - 90 minutes
Reading APPENDIX: WORKING ON GROUP ASSIGNMENTS	10 - 15 minutes
Assignments	
Assignment I-1-1	15 - 30 minutes
Assignment I-1-2	15 - 30 minutes
Assignment I-1-3	15 - 30 minutes
Assignment I-1-4	15 - 30 minutes
Assignment I-1-5	15 - 30 minutes
Assignment I-1-6	45 - 60 minutes
Assignment I-1-7	30 - 45 minutes
Assignment I-1-8	30 - 45 minutes
Assignment I-1-9	15 - 30 minutes
Assignment I-1-10	45 - 75 minutes
Assignment I-1-11	60 - 90 minutes
Assignment I-1-12	60 - 90 minutes
Assignment I-1-13	ongoing

Note: *These time estimates, like all the time budgets for this course, should be adjusted to suit your own learning style. Time estimates for assignments assume that readings were completed before attempting the assignments.*

MODULE I:

INTRODUCTION: WHAT IS ACCOUNTING?

Great things are done when men and mountains meet...
-- William Blake, Epigrams

Imagine, if you will, a party of explorers that has no tools. They come upon a mountain range. The mountains are both wide and high. Many of the faces are sheer, many of the slopes slippery. The explorers can dream up a multitude of uses for the mountains. If they could get to the top, they might see beyond where they now stand. If they could get to the interior, they might find gold nuggets, or other things of value. But without tools to help them climb the mountains or mine their interior, the explorers' needs go unfulfilled.

Now consider an analogy. For every entity, there is a mountain of raw data about its economic transactions. Consider, for example, General Motors, one of the largest industrial companies in the world. Over the course of a typical week, a company the size of GM will record millions of financial transactions, including sales, payments from customers, payments to suppliers, payroll checks to employees, and so on. By the end of a year, the amount of accumulated financial data is mind-boggling.

For every entity, there are also interested parties (explorers) who can dream up potential uses for the mountain of raw data. At General Motors, management might find it useful to know which products are the most profitable, or which are selling in accordance with expectations. Stockholders, who own a share of the company, could find it useful to know whether they are earning a reasonable return on their investment. Creditors, who lend the company money, would want to know if General Motors is generating enough cash to keep making the required loan payments. The federal government might want to know if General Motors has paid its fair share of taxes. The employees (or their labor unions) could find it useful to know if any segments of the business are doing so poorly that some plants might be closed down in the future. The list goes on and on.

Without tools to mine the mountain of raw data, it's not likely that any of the users will have their needs fulfilled. Accounting is a tool that lets interested parties get the information they need from the mountain of raw data.

Accounting is a system for developing and communicating information needed for economic decision-making. It is a tool, invented by man, to fulfill social needs. This course is about why society needs accounting information and how accounting can be used to fulfill those needs.

Right now, in this module, we'll begin by going back in time when society was simpler and primitive accounting tools were first invented. Then we'll take a brief look at the evolution of accounting over time. In the final portion of this module, we'll talk about who the primary users of accounting information are today.

ACCOUNTING: HOW IT BEGAN

Man is a tool-using animal...Without tools he is nothing, with tools he is all.
        -- Thomas Carlyle, Sartor Resartus

When you think of the Stone Age, you probably don't have an image that includes accounting. Yet, rudimentary accounting tools were part of the Stone Age. In fact, some accounting methods were invented before either written language or numbers existed.

Prehistoric Accounting

The Stone Age, which began about 2.5 million years ago, can be divided into 2 periods. The "old stone age," or Paleolithic period, lasted until about 8000 B.C. The old stone age encompasses the long time span during which people evolved from the earliest human-like creatures to the more familiar *homo sapiens*. People of the old stone age lived in the most primitive conditions. Yet, they were tool-users. The first tools were made of stone (rocks), and later also of wood and bone. While the first tools were very crude and barely distinguishable from other rocks, later tools of the period had more well-defined shapes, such as arrowheads. During the old stone age, man also began to form social units (that is, groups of people organized to help achieve common goals), such as hunting parties.

Moving from the Paleolithic to the Neolithic ("new stone age") period, the rate of progress accelerated. The new stone age lasted from about 8000 B.C. to about 3500 B.C. During this period, humans domesticated animals (such as dogs, sheep, horses and cattle), cultivated food plants, ground and polished their tools, made pottery and ate cooked cereal grains, plowed with animals, built small boats, and developed a village culture. By the end of the new stone age, people were living in social units that shared many characteristics with today's cities, including monumental buildings, government units, taxation, and flourishing trade. Remarkably, all of this occurred without written language or numbers.

The development of writing is commonly used to define the imaginary dividing line between "prehistoric man" and "civilization." Written language and numbers were developed in the period following the new stone age. This period began in about 3500 B.C. with the Bronze Age, so named because of the reliance on tools made of bronze. The 2 largest centers of population at that time were in the Nile Valley (in the area now known as Egypt) and Mesopotamia, the plain between the Tigris and Euphrates rivers (in the area now known as the Middle East, centered in what is now Iraq).

With the development of trade and the growth of villages and cities, the need for accounting information arose. People, even in the Stone Age and the Bronze Age, needed information to conduct trade and run governments. Just as prehistoric people developed tools to help them hunt, they also developed tools to help them account for things of value (**assets**) and debts owed (**liabilities**), and to aid in the collection of taxes.

Once people had more than the minimum needed for subsistence, they were faced with the need to keep track of their assets. How much of each item of value (animals, grains, jars, and so on) belonged to each individual? How much belonged to the rulers or government?

It also became necessary to keep track of debts owed. Which trader, for example, had not yet delivered promised goods? Who was owed wages? Since money did not yet exist, records also had to indicate the nature of the debt. In what goods were the debts to be paid?

Where taxes were collected (again, payable in goods), people needed to keep track of taxes due and paid. Early tax systems were very simple. For example, every farmer owed the ruler a quantity of grain in payment of taxes. Thus, the rulers needed to know both how many farmers there were and how much grain had been paid or was still owed.

How could records be kept without written language or numbers? Archaeologists have discovered several examples of prehistoric accounting record-keeping. In Mesopotamia, records were kept using clay tokens. Archaeologists have found clay tokens that are over 10,000 years old. The tokens vary in shape and size. In 1969, Denise Schmandt-Besserat, then a graduate student researching the uses of clay in the Middle East, made an extensive study of these tokens. Professor Schmandt-Besserat's work over the next several decades revealed much about the meaning of the tokens and gave us our first picture of prehistoric accounting in Mesopotamia.

Take a look at a picture of the tokens (Figure I-1-1, next page) and try to imagine what they mean. You'll find an answer in the following section.

Figure I-1-1

Clay Tokens and Envelopes: A Prehistoric Accounting System

"Envelope" (clay ball) and tokens from Susa, Iran, c. 3300 BC.

Detail of complex tokens. The incised ovoid on the bottom right represents a jar of oil.

Source: Photos courtesy of Musée du Louvre, Département des Antiquités Orientales, Paris. For additional information and photos, see Denise Schmandt-Besserat, <u>Before Writing</u>, Volumes 1-2, The University of Texas Press, Austin, Texas, 1992.

Accounting With Clay Tokens

The shape and size of the tokens communicated information. For example, cones and spheres were used to symbolize grain. The cone shape denoted a deep bowl used to hold grain, so 1 cone token represented about 6 liters of grain. Flat triangles represented a smaller measure of grain; spheres represented a measure 6 times larger than the cone. A cylinder shape indicated an animal. Markings on the cylinders could give information about the animal's sex and age. By combining the right number and shape of tokens, people could keep track of what was owned or owed, even without written language or numbers.

Early tokens were sometimes found grouped in containers or strung together. These containers or strings may represent the **assets** (resources) or **liabilities** (obligations) of particular individuals. However, from a modern viewpoint, this "accounting system" is weak. We would say that control in the system is poor because tokens could be surreptitiously added or removed from a string or container, making it easy to manipulate the records. However, it seems that even prehistoric people recognized how important control is in an accounting system. Dating from around 3250 B.C., groups of tokens enclosed in baked clay balls have been discovered. The tokens can't be removed without breaking the ball. Professor Schmandt-Besserat refers to the balls as sealed "envelopes." She thinks the envelopes were used to segregate tokens for a particular purpose, like a sales contract or a shipper's "bill of lading" (a modern document that railroads, trucking companies or other carriers give to people who ship goods to describe the goods being shipped and serve as a receipt for the goods being transported).

From a modern point of view, the clay balls (or sealed envelopes) represent an improvement in the accounting system's control as you could not tamper with the tokens without breaking the ball. On the other hand, this degree of control may create other problems. Suppose you had a legitimate need to know what was in the sealed envelope. How could you check on the contents without breaking the ball? Prehistoric people seem to have recognized and answered this question, and improved their answer over time. The initial response was to create 2 identical sets of tokens for each envelope. One was sealed inside the ball, the other was attached to the outside to make it easy to determine the ball's contents. Later, perhaps recognizing that it took twice the labor to make 2 sets of tokens for the same ball, a second response arose. Instead of attaching a second set of tokens to the outside of the ball, impressions of the original set of tokens were made in the clay before it was baked. Thus, the outside of the ball showed an image of the tokens contained inside its shell.

This early accounting system was a precursor to writing. As the system evolved, the token-filled balls were replaced by clay tablets with images of tokens impressed on the tablet. Later, instead of using tokens to impress an image on the tablets, the shapes of tokens were drawn on the tablets. With this evolution of accounting tools, the stage was set for the development of writing. Once man had the insight that images drawn on tablets could be used to express all the concepts included in spoken language, the human race moved from prehistory to civilization.

OTHER EARLY ACCOUNTING SYSTEMS

Men think differently who live differently.
-- Harold Laski, quoted in Dorothy Pickles, Introduction to Politics

As you can imagine, accounting did not evolve in the same way or at the same time all across the globe. The tokens and balls of Mesopotamia represent one way to perform rudimentary accounting. Other cultures developed other methods. To give just one example, Incan accountant-historians kept records with knotted strings called **quipus**.

Figure I-1-2 (on the next page) shows a picture of a quipu. Can you figure out how it was used? Imagine how a string could be the basis for an accounting system. The following section briefly describes the Incan system.

Accounting With Quipus

The Incas, renowned for their culture and economic sophistication, created a vast empire in the Andes of South America between 1100 and 1500 A.D. The Incas did not use money, so their accounting records were kept in physical quantities rather than monetary units. The data captured on the quipus included records of births and deaths. Birth and death records were needed to keep track of the tribute (taxes) owed or paid to the Emperor. Quipu records were also kept for inventories of food, clothing and armaments kept in warehouses, and for transfers of goods between warehouses. The performance of the governors (managers) responsible for the royal food warehouses was periodically evaluated based on the quipu records.

The knotted strings were of different lengths and colors. Much like the Mesopotamian use of different token shapes to communicate information, the lengths and colors were used to distinguish one type of record from another. A decimal system of knots along the string indicated quantities.

The quipu records were kept by quipu-camayocs, roughly translated as accountant-historians. Since the quipu-camayocs traveled throughout the empire to record accounting information, their quipus also provided a natural place to store other historical information, like the dates of important events. Thus, quipus became both economic and historical records for the Incas. The quipu-camayocs were considered so important that they were exempt from all payments of tribute.

Two examples illustrate the strong controls built into the Incan accounting system to insure that the quipus would be reliable and accurate. First, only

Figure I-1-2

An Incan Quipu

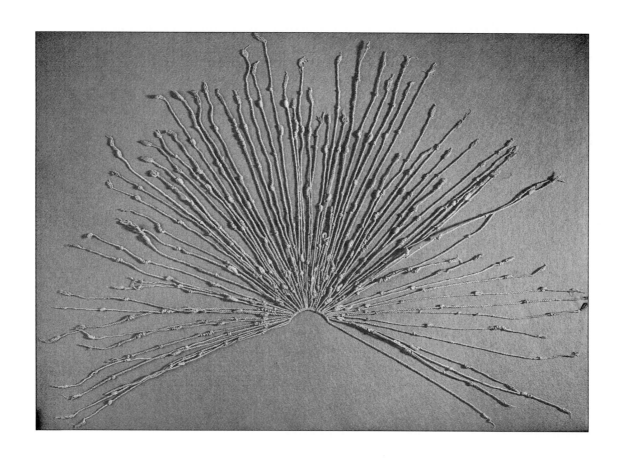

Source: © The British Museum.

quipu-camayocs were taught the system of colors, lengths and knots used in the recording process, which made it difficult for anyone else to read or manipulate the records. In the later stages of the empire, the quipu-camayocs' education took place in formal schools. Second, important quipus were kept in duplicate. Thus, the system had a built-in mechanism for checking records--comparing the 2 quipus and reconciling differences. The duplicate quipu system was an early recognition of something modern users of accounting information are well aware of: **information which has been verified is considered more reliable, and therefore more valuable, than unverified information**. Modern users of accounting information also value timeliness, and so did the Incas. A network of couriers, like the much later Pony Express, transported the quipus from city to city. Thus, information could be quickly dispatched throughout the empire.

Cultural Variations in Modern Accounting Systems

Just as early accounting systems varied, depending on the culture in which they developed, even today accounting systems are not the same throughout the world. As accounting researcher Dr. Stephen Zeff pointed out in his 1971 book, *Foreign Accounting Principles in Five Countries: A History and Analysis of Trends*, the development of accounting is influenced by a variety of economic, political and social factors--such as the type of industry, the form of government, and the distribution of power in the society.

Dr. Gerhard Mueller was one of the first accounting researchers to study the different accounting systems that arise in different environments. In a 1968 article in the *International Journal of Accounting*, he examined "Accounting Principles Generally Accepted in the United States versus Those Generally Accepted Elsewhere." Dr. Mueller, and other researchers who built on his work, found that accounting practices around the world could be classified into distinct groups that are related to environmental differences. For example, as you would expect, countries with centrally-controlled economies (where the state owns most land and production facilities) tend to have very different accounting systems than countries with market-oriented economies (where most land and production facilities are privately held). Where different cultures have different information needs, different accounting systems will arise.

As we approach the twenty-first century, many futurists predict that economic, political and social influences will become increasingly internationalized. Already, much business is conducted by multinational corporations. Even small companies, like high-technology firms in the computer industry, trade globally. As the world becomes more global, accounting should also become more global. More so today than ever before, accountants from many nations are actively involved in efforts to develop international accounting standards. If world cultures meld and nations become more "borderless" in the future, accounting can be expected to evolve in response to these changes just as clay tokens and quipus evolved into more modern accounting systems as the cultures of their users developed.

The Importance of Accounting History

If modern accounting has evolved beyond clay balls and quipus, why do modern accountants and users of accounting information find it valuable to know a little about the history of accounting? Does accounting history have any practical value for modern students of accounting? Accounting history will not tell you how to operate a computerized accounting system, or read a modern annual report, or make a production or investment decision. However, thinking about early accounting systems can yield several important lessons for today. Before continuing to read this section, see if you can discover for yourself some lessons from prehistoric accounting that will help you understand modern accounting. Then, continue reading below to find descriptions of 3 important lessons that can be learned from thinking about early accounting systems.

First, when you think about prehistoric accounting it becomes clear that **accounting information is a basic social need**. When people organize into social units to conduct business for a profit, or to run governments, or to conduct other not-for-profit enterprises (such as educational or social welfare activities), they quickly discover the need for all manner of accounting information.

Second, **accounting tools are developed to fill those human information needs and accounting evolves over time as human information needs change**. The accounting profession plays an important social role. Accountants help identify information needs, design systems to capture data, and analyze captured data to provide information needed by users of the system.

Third, **as accounting information systems evolve, like all human tools, they improve**. As the systems improve, they become capable of providing more and better information to users and they build in increasingly more sophisticated controls to help ensure the efficient, effective operation of a particular social unit (business, government, or not-for-profit enterprise). The next 2 sections discuss a few examples of these improvements and their impact on modern accounting.

THE CONTINUING EVOLUTION OF ACCOUNTING TOOLS: PHYSICAL TOOLS

> ...[T]he computer is not really a tool-in hand; it is designed to extend the human brain rather than the hand, to allow the manipulation of mathematical and logical symbols at high speed. Yet it can be used with a kind of mental dexterity and reminds us of the craftsman's hand.
> -- David J. Bolter, *Turing's Man*, 1984

Some human tools, like writing, are abstract or conceptual tools. Other human tools, like bows and arrows, have a concrete physical existence; collectively, these physical tools are known as technology. As you can imagine, there are accounting tools of both types.

You are probably already familiar with some of the physical tools of accounting--tools like calculators and computers and cash registers--because you see them around you every day in places like department stores, groceries and university cashier's offices. What may surprise you as you learn more about these tools is the full range of power they bring to accounting.

The Computer as an Accounting Tool

Take the computer as an example. What has the computer done for accounting? One change is obvious. Just as paper records eventually replaced clay token and string records, computerized records today are supplementing or replacing paper records. Replacing paper records with computer records has several advantages, including:

♦   easier access to accounting information,

♦   increased accuracy of accounting information, and

♦   improved quality of accounting information.

Easier Access to Accounting Information. First, keeping records on computers can ease access to accounting information (more people can simultaneously access a computerized databank of information than could read a written accounting record). For instance, customer credit records can be centrally stored for access by any authorized user in the system, wherever they are located. With computerized credit records, a clerk at a store in Los Angeles can easily find out that a customer who wants to write a check for a purchase has a history of bounced checks at stores in San Francisco (or Chicago or New York).

Increased Accuracy of Accounting Information. Second, using computers for accounting calculations can improve mechanical accuracy (computers make fewer mistakes adding up long columns of numbers than people do). The age-old image of an accountant, wearing a green eye-shade, sitting on a stool for hours on end trying to get the books to add up is an anachronism in the modern era. The tedium of record-keeping that has existed for many centuries can today be virtually eliminated by computerization.

Improved Quality of Accounting Information. Another, possibly less obvious, change is even more important. Computers present new opportunities for accountants to provide better information to users. For example, whereas noncomputerized accounting systems serve merely to hold data until a human can interpret it, computers provide the possibility of adding some "artificial intelligence" to the accounting system to help users interpret the data and make decisions.

Consider, for example, a noncomputerized system that keeps track of sales made and goods being held for sale ("**inventory**"). The noncomputerized system requires a human to interpret the sales and inventory patterns to decide such things as when to order or produce a particular product. Suppose the system is for a bakery. The bakery owner must monitor the weekly sales and inventory figures to determine which products are selling well or poorly, to decide how much raw materials (flour, eggs, butter, and so on) to order for the next week, and to decide how much of a particular item to bake each day. If, as is common, the noncomputerized system tracks only business transactions, the bakery owner will need to supplement the accounting system information with additional relevant information. For instance, if the baker knows that weather predictions for next week forecast heavy snowfalls, it would be reasonable to predict that next week's cookie sales will drop as people cut back on shopping trips.

By contrast, in a computerized sales and inventory system, the computer can be programmed to automatically review past sales and inventory patterns, as well as other relevant information, and project exactly what should be purchased or produced during a particular time period. The computer system at Mrs. Fields Cookies, for instance, uses past data and current information (such as weather information) to project how many cookies can be sold at a particular store on a particular day. The computer output to the store manager then suggests the amount of dough to be prepared and baked each hour for the day. The manager's job is made much easier because the computerized system provides more complete and timely information than the noncomputerized system. Better information means the store should experience fewer problems with **stock-outs** (where customers are ready to buy, but no cookies are ready to be sold) or **excess inventory** (where too many cookies are left over at day's end and can't be sold).

The Evolution of Computers

Most college students can hardly remember a time when computers were not widely used. But, their parents and grandparents tell a different story: For most of their careers, computers were the exception, rather than the rule. The first patent for a computer, the UNIVAC, was granted in 1951. The UNIVAC, like its experimental predecessor the ENIAC, filled a large room. It consumed huge amounts of power, worked at a pace that would now be considered maddeningly slow, and could operate only when conditions, such as the room temperature, were near perfect. Its cost placed it out of reach for all but the wealthiest organizations. In short, it was a far cry from the world of computers today.

The rapid evolution of computer technology has opened new doors for accounting. Only a small portion of the ultimate power of computers for accounting systems has yet been harnessed. Over the next few decades, advanced computer technologies will provide the opportunity for greatly enhanced accounting information systems. The accountant of the near future may find the accounting of the mid-twentieth century to be as quaint as clay tokens and quipus.

THE CONTINUING EVOLUTION OF ACCOUNTING TOOLS:
CONCEPTUAL TOOLS

Human history is in essence a history of ideas.
-- H. G. Wells, The Outline of History

In most human endeavors, physical tools and conceptual tools work together and enhance each other's value. The farmer's plow gains value when used in concert with agricultural concepts such as crop rotation. Plows are of little value on land made barren by continual planting of the same crops. At the same time, crop rotation is made more feasible by labor-saving tools like the plow.

The technological tools of accounting--from the ancient abacus, a counting device using a system of rods and beads, to the modern computer--work in concert with the conceptual tools of accounting. You will learn about many of the conceptual tools of accounting in this course, but for the moment a single example will serve to illustrate the importance of conceptual tools to modern accounting. The example is double-entry accounting systems.

To understand the example of double-entry accounting systems, you will first need to learn some basic accounting terminology. So, it will take a while to explain this example. But the conceptual tool (double-entry accounting) is important and the vocabulary terms are part of the language of business today. So, take a break if you need it now and then come back and dig into the example.

Double-entry Accounting Systems and Duality

If David Letterman were to create a list of the top ten reasons why accounting has progressed, the number-one spot on the list might well go to a conceptual tool: double-entry accounting systems. Like most good tools, the idea behind double-entry accounting systems--duality--is beautifully simple.

Long ago, accountants realized that **every economic transaction has 2 sides**. This is true in a literal sense as there are 2 parties to every transaction. For every loan, there is a lender and a borrower. For every sale, there is a seller and a purchaser. For every salary paid, there is an employer and an employee. For every transfer of inventory between warehouses, there is a receiver and a sender.

Moreover, transactions also have 2 sides in a second sense. In a transaction, each party both gains something and gives up something. A lender gives up cash, and receives in return a **"note receivable,"** the borrower's promise to repay the debt with interest. The borrower gains cash, but must give up future resources to repay the debt plus interest, which is called a **"note payable"** on the borrower's side of the transaction.

The concept of **duality** recognizes that all transactions have 2 sides. In some ways, the accountant's notion of duality is akin to Newton's third law of motion: for every action, there is an equal and opposite reaction. There is, in effect, a natural balance to accounting.

Even the early accounting systems of Mesopotamia and the Incan empire were capable of capturing simple aspects of the dual nature of economic transactions. Incan quipu-camayocs, for example, could tell from their quipus both who had lent food, clothing or armaments, and who was owed in return.

In Mesopotamia, for another example, specialized terminology reflecting the inflows and outflows possible in economic transactions was already part of the vocabulary of accounting. Terms existed to distinguish **assets** (things of value), **liabilities** (debts owed) and **equity** (ownership interests). The concept of **profit** (income created when revenues exceed expenses) also existed since even then trade was conducted with a goal of increasing wealth.

Modern Accounting Terminology

Today's accountants still make use of the same basic concepts found in much older accounting systems. The chart on the next several pages (Figure I-1-3) gives modern definitions of some basic terms used in accounting for **business enterprises** (entities established with an objective of earning profits).

As you will see from the chart, the modern definitions of these basic concepts are quite sophisticated (you'll know this right away when you see how hard they are to read!). For example, the definition of assets recognizes that while all assets are things of value, not all things of value are accounted for as assets. An organization may value the good public schools and parks in the community where it operates because these services make it possible to attract workers. But, these items of value do not qualify as assets for accounting purposes because they do not meet the technical definition of an asset.

Take a few minutes now to carefully study the technical definitions of these basic accounting terms as they will be used frequently during this course and in your dealings in the business world. While you do not need to memorize technical definitions, you do need to have a good feel for the key points that the technical definitions embody.

Figure I-1-3
Accounting Terms Used For Modern Business Enterprises

CONCEPT	MODERN DEFINITION & EXAMPLES	KEY POINTS TO NOTE
Assets	Probable future economic benefits obtained or controlled by a particular entity as a result of past transactions or events Examples: Cash, Land, Inventory, Patents, Buildings, Equipment	Assets are economic resources that are expected to benefit an entity in the future-- that is, they are items that have value to the organization. However, not all items of value are considered assets. To be treated as an asset, the item of value must be: (1) controlled by the entity--thus, the good highway access that leads customers to a grocery store is valuable, but not accounted for as an asset. (2) the result of a past identifiable event or transaction-- thus, customer loyalty built up over the life of a business is valuable, but not accounted for as an asset.
Liabilities	Probable future sacrifices of economic benefits arising from present obligations of an entity to transfer assets or provide services to other entities in the future as a result of past transactions or events Examples: Wages payable, Mortgage notes payable, Warranties payable	Liabilities are debts owed in either money or other assets (e.g., rent payable) or via services (e.g., warranties payable). Like assets, liabilities result from identifiable past events or transactions --thus, a sense of obligation to support the community in which a business operates is not accounted for as a liability.

CONCEPT	MODERN DEFINITION & EXAMPLES	KEY POINTS TO NOTE
Owners' Equity	Residual interest in the assets of an entity that remains after deducting its liabilities Examples: Common stock, Retained earnings	Whereas liabilities are what is owed, equity is what is owned: the owners' or shareholders' interest in the entity. Ownership interests may arise from the investment of capital (e.g., common stock) or from reinvestment of past profits kept in the business rather than paid out to owners as dividends (i.e., retained earnings).
Revenues	Inflows or other enhancements of assets of an entity or settlement of its liabilities (or both) during a period, based on the production and delivery of goods, provision of services, and other activities that constitute the entity's major operations Examples: Sales revenue, Rent revenue	Revenues are inflows of new resources that come from doing business. It's what you bring in from what you do. A department store will have sales revenue when it sells merchandise. An apartment complex owner will earn rent revenue from tenants. Revenue doesn't always mean immediate cash inflow. Revenues can also involve other inflows of resources (like a credit sale where the customer promises to pay later) or reductions of liabilities (like a sale to an employee where payment is deducted from wages due). To be revenues, inflows must relate to normal business operations. An automobile sold by a car dealer results in sales revenue, but an auto sold by a pizza restaurant that used the car for pizza delivery results in a "gain" or "loss".

CONCEPT	MODERN DEFINITION & EXAMPLES	KEY POINTS TO NOTE
Gains and Losses	Gains are **increases** in equity or "net assets" (net assets = assets - liabilities) resulting from peripheral or incidental transactions of an entity and from other events and circumstances affecting the entity during a period, except those that result from revenues or investments by owners	Revenues and expenses relate to a business's normal operations. Gains and losses arise from <u>other</u> business activities (like selling equipment you no longer need) or from events that are not within the control of the business at all (like earthquake or flood damage).
	Losses are **decreases** in equity or net assets resulting from peripheral or incidental transactions of an entity and from other events and circumstances affecting the entity during a period, except those that result from revenues or investments by owners	If a pizza restaurant sells a car it used for pizza delivery, it has a gain (if the car sells for more than the firm has invested in it) or a loss (if the car sells for less than the firm has invested in it).
	Examples: Gain on sale of equipment, Loss on sale of equipment, Earthquake loss, Fire loss, Gain on settlement of lawsuit, Loss on settlement of lawsuit	On the other hand, if a car dealer sells a car, it has revenue (for the amount of the sale) and expense (for the dealer's cost to obtain the car).
Expenses	Outflows or other use of assets or incurrences of liabilities (or both) during a period as a result of delivering or producing goods, rendering services, or carrying out other activities that constitute the entity's major operations.	Expenses are the costs incurred by an entity in order to produce revenues. Expenses either use up resources (like cash used to pay wages) or create new liabilities (like warranty obligations for products sold during the period).
	Examples: Wages expense, Utilities expense, Cost of goods sold	Expenses, like revenues, must relate to normal operations. Thus, if a store sells merchandise, its cost is treated as an <u>expense</u> (called "Cost of goods sold"). But, if, instead, the goods are stolen, their cost is treated as a <u>loss</u>.

CONCEPT	MODERN DEFINITION & EXAMPLES	KEY POINTS TO NOTE
Net Income	The difference which results from adding all revenues and gains for a period and subtracting all expenses and losses for the period.	This is the famous "bottom line" -- the profit (if net income is positive) or loss (if net income is negative) that the entity has earned in a given period of time. Net income is not the same thing as an increase or decrease in cash. Since revenues or expenses need not all involve immediate cashflows, there will often be a difference between a period's net income and the net increase or decrease in cash.

Note: The modern definitions of assets, liabilities, equity, revenues, expenses, gains, and losses are based on the Financial Accounting Standards Board's Statement of Financial Accounting Concepts #6: Elements of Financial Statements. Copyright © 1986 by Financial Accounting Standards Board, 401 Merritt 7, P.O. Box 5116, Norwalk, Connecticut 06856-5116, U.S. A. Reprinted with permission. Copies of the complete document are available from the FASB.

The definition of net income is consistent with the FASB's definition of earnings in their 1985 Statement of Financial Accounting Concepts #5: Recognition and Measurement in Financial Statements. A variety of terms are used for net income or earnings in current practice.

Duality and the Accounting Equation

Even though early accounting systems included some recognition of **duality** (the 2-sidedness of transactions) and many basic accounting terms, the early systems were very unwieldy in comparison to modern systems. For example, knotted string records, like the Incan quipus, were also used in the Hawaiian Islands. Some of the Hawaiian knotted string records were 400 to 500 fathoms long, about the length of 8 to 10 football fields. Imagine trying to find an error in a string that long! Later, accounting systems were improved by a clever exploitation of the notion of duality: **double-entry accounting**. A double-entry accounting system is a method of recording economic transactions that makes it much easier to prevent, detect and correct recording errors.

Double-entry accounting was made possible by fully recognizing the potential of what is now known as **the accounting equation** or **accounting identity**:

Assets = Liabilities + Owners' Equity

That is, *the total of all the items of value to an organization (its assets) is balanced equally by the total of its obligations to creditors (its liabilities) and its ownership interests (its equities).* Here is the notion of duality again: the 2 sides of the equation must be exactly in balance.

The owners' equity portion of the accounting equation can be expanded to recognize that there are 2 basic ways owners may invest in a company:

♦ **Contributing capital**. In for-profit enterprises, equity is usually initially established by owners or investors providing capital for seed money to start the business. Equity may later be increased by additional capital investments. In return for invested capital, owners or investors gain the right to share in wealth created by the enterprise.

♦ **Reinvesting profits**. If the organization operates at a profit, the owners' equity is increased beyond their capital investment. If losses are incurred, owners' equity is reduced. Additionally, owners' equity may also be decreased by paying out business assets (usually cash) to the owners as dividends--in effect distributing some of the previously earned profits to the owners. Over the lifetime of the organization, the accumulated net income (profits and losses) of the entity, less dividends paid, is called "**retained earnings**." Retained earnings represents the amount of past profits reinvested in the business, rather than paid out as dividends. Thus:

Owners' Equity = Capital + Accumulated Net Income – Dividends

or, since the term *retained earnings* means
accumulated net income less dividends paid,

Owners' Equity = Capital + Retained Earnings

Because owners' equity comes from 2 sources--contributed capital and reinvested profits--the accounting equation (Assets = Liabilities + Owners' Equity) could also be expressed as:

Assets = Liabilities + Capital + Retained Earnings

Whatever form the accounting equation takes, the duality concept still holds: the 2 sides of the equation must be in balance. The concept of duality, as expressed in the accounting equation, is at the root of double-entry accounting systems.

While history does not record the first use of double-entry accounting systems, it is clear they were in use at least by the 15th century, and probably earlier. In 1494, a Venetian friar, Fra Luca Pacioli, achieved lasting accounting fame by writing the first known book about double-entry accounting. The book was soon translated into every major European language and accountants throughout Europe began to work on refinements to the system Pacioli described. An oft-cited quote by economist-historian Herbert J. Muller notes that Pacioli "probably had more influence on human life than has Dante or Michelangelo."

How a Double-Entry System Works With the Accounting Equation

One of the most basic information needs of any entity is keeping track of 2 things: (1) the entity's **"financial position"**--its assets, liabilities and owners' equity, and (2) the **"results of operations"**--the entity's periodic net income. To obtain this information, accounting records of every economic transaction are needed.

The data from each economic transaction are recorded in **"the books"** of the entity in a series of **"accounts"**--one for each type of asset, liability, equity, revenue, expense, gain or loss. For example, there will be separate accounts for each type of asset--such as cash, inventory, notes receivable, land, automobiles, and patents. The double-entry system that Pacioli described is a clever way to record (or **"enter"**) transactions in these accounts because it provides built-in checks that the books are **"in balance"**-- that is, the books reflect 2 equal sides for each recorded transaction.

The double-entry system is based on the concept of duality expressed in the accounting equation: **Assets = Liabilities + Owners' Equity**. Each transaction must keep the accounting equation in balance. Increases to items on one side of the equation must equal increases to items on the other side. Or, decreases to one side of the equation must equal decreases to the other side.

As an example, suppose you form a new business, contributing $60,000 of your own money to start the company. The company is organized as a corporation, so the owner's capital contribution is represented by shares of "stock" in the company. The business now has an asset ($60,000 cash) and an ownership interest ($60,000 of stock):

Assets	Liabilities	Owners' Equity
$60,000 Cash	None	$60,000 Stock

As you can see, the $60,000 of total assets equals the total liabilities and owners' equity ($0 liabilities and $60,000 owners' equity = $60,000).

Next, suppose the business buys a new automobile worth $25,000. This is an increase in assets. An increase of the asset account "automobiles" can be balanced in the accounting equation in any one of several ways, depending on the way the automobile was purchased:

- ◆ on credit,

- ◆ in exchange for stock in the company,

- ◆ for cash, or

- ◆ a combination of the above.

Let's take a look at each of these options.

An Example: Buying an Automobile on Credit. Suppose the business takes advantage of a special "no money down offer" and pays for the car by taking out a loan for the full $25,000 purchase price. Then, the business has gained a car in exchange for an obligation to pay back the loan:

Assets	Liabilities	Owners' Equity
$60,000 Cash $25,000 Automobile	$25,000 Loan Payable	$60,000 Stock

Now, $85,000 total assets equals $25,000 liabilities plus $60,000 owners' equity.

An Example: Buying an Automobile in Exchange for Stock. Now consider another payment option. Suppose, instead of taking out a loan, the business paid the car dealer by issuing the dealer $25,000 of stock in the company. The dealer is willing to accept the stock in exchange for the car because the dealer believes the new business has the potential to be very profitable, making the stock increase in value. Now, there is a total of $85,000 contributed capital ($60,000 from the owner's original investment and $25,000 invested by the car dealer). The business has gained a car in exchange for an ownership interest:

Assets	Liabilities	Owners' Equity
$60,000 Cash $25,000 Automobile	None	$85,000 Stock

Once again, total assets of $85,000 equals total liabilities plus equity of $85,000.

An Example: Buying an Automobile with Cash. Now consider another option: the business pays for the car with cash. Suppose, instead of taking out a loan or issuing stock, the business used $25,000 of its cash to purchase the car. The business would now have $35,000 of cash left [calculation: $60,000 original cash – $25,000 used for car = $35,000] plus a $25,000 car, for total assets of $60,000. The business has gained a car in exchange for reducing its cash, in effect exchanging one type of asset (cash) for another type of asset (automobile):

Assets	Liabilities	Owners' Equity
$35,000 Cash $25,000 Automobile	None	$60,000 Stock

Again, assets of $60,000, still equal total liabilities ($0) plus equity ($60,000).

An Example: Buying an Automobile with a Combination of Credit and Cash. Of course, it's also possible that the business could pay for the car using a combination of methods. Suppose, for instance, the business makes a 10% cash down payment ($2,500 on the $25,000 car) and takes out a loan for the remaining $22,500. This would leave the business with $57,500 cash [calculation: $60,000 original cash - $2,500 used for downpayment on car = $57,500] and a $25,000 automobile. The business would also have a loan payable for the $22,500. The business has gained a car in exchange for reducing its cash and taking on a loan:

Assets	Liabilities	Owners' Equity
$57,500 Cash $25,000 Automobile	$22,500 Loan Payable	$60,000 Stock

In this case, total assets of $82,500, still equal total liabilities ($22,500) plus owners' equity ($60,000).

Summary of the Example. Think about this example in more general terms. The example illustrates that an increase in an asset account (for example, adding an automobile) can be balanced in the accounting equation by:

- ♦ an increase of equal amount in liabilities (such as a loan taken out for the full amount of the car), or

- ♦ an increase of equal amount in equities (such as stock issued to the car dealer in exchange for the car), or

- ♦ a decrease of equal amount in another asset account (such as paying for the car with cash, since cash is another asset account), or

- ♦ a combination of the above (like paying for part of the price of the car in cash, and signing a loan for the remainder of the purchase price).

This example illustrates an important concept of duality: the accounting equation must always remain in balance. No matter how the automobile is purchased, when you add up the total of all the asset accounts, the total assets should always equal the total of all the liability and owners' equity accounts.

Double-Entry Systems: Two Sides to Each Account

An "**account**" is simply a place to record economic transactions and events-- whether on a page in a book or in a portion of a computer database. Another important conceptual contribution of the notion of duality is looking at each account as if it had 2 "sides"--one to record increases and the other to record decreases. To see why this notion is so valuable, consider the complications that can occur when an account is kept without 2 sides. In other words, compare a "single-entry system" to a double-entry system.

A Single-Entry System. Suppose you were keeping the "books of account" for an entity. You could record both increases and decreases in a particular account in the same place, like in a single column (thus, a single-entry system). That's what, in effect, a quipu did. An account was represented by a particular group of knotted strings. If the account was increased or decreased, knots were added or undone to reflect the change. The balance in any particular account could easily be determined by reading the knots.

To see if the quipu as a whole was in balance, it would be necessary to add up all the asset accounts and compare this total to the total of all the liability and equity accounts. If the 2 totals were equal, you could find this system very satisfactory. However, if the accounts did not balance, it could be a daunting task to look for the source of error as you would have no clue as to where to begin.

A Double-Entry System. Now instead, think about a system that keeps the increases and decreases in each account separate and also computes a running balance for the account (the difference between all the increases and all the decreases to the account). In this system, each account is viewed as having *2* *sides*--1 for increases and 1 for decreases (thus, a double-entry system). As a mental picture of an account, you could think of an account as looking like a capital letter T (a visualization accountants aptly named "T-accounts"):

Now here is where the double-entry system described by Pacioli gets very clever. Look at the accounting equation:

Assets = Liabilities + Owners' Equity

Assets are on the *left-hand side* of the equation; liabilities and equities are on the *right-hand side*. Duality tells us that any change to one side of the equation must be reflected in an equal change to the opposite side--sort of like a mirror image. So, reflecting duality, we record **increases** on the *left-hand side* of an **asset** account, but we record **increases** in **liability** and **equity** accounts on the *right-hand side* of the account--a mirror image. Thus, asset accounts will normally show a balance on the left side of a T-account, whereas liabilities and equities will normally show a balance on the right side:

Asset accounts		=	Liability accounts		+	Owners' Equity accounts	
increase on left	decrease on right		decrease on left	increase on right		decrease on left	increase on right

Accounting entries on the *left* side of an account--regardless of whether they are increases or decreases--are called **debits**. Accounting entries on the *right* side of an account--also regardless of whether they are increases or decreases--are called **credits**. Our picture of the accounts now looks like this:

Asset accounts		=	Liability accounts		+	Owners' Equity accounts	
increase by debits	decrease by credits		decrease by debits	increase by credits		decrease by debits	increase by credits

Using this double-entry system, it is much easier to spot and correct errors. In the recording of any single transaction, the **total debits must equal the total credits**. Thus, there is a built-in warning if an individual transaction doesn't balance. This warning makes it easier to catch recording errors early. You can find individual errors much more quickly in a double-entry system than you can in a quipu.

Of course, some errors may still escape attention. For example, a double entry system cannot give you an early warning if you forget to record a transaction or if you record a transaction in the wrong account (like recording the purchase of a car in an account for office equipment). The double-entry system isn't foolproof, even though it does have a significant advantage over other recording methods.

Double-entry Accounting: A Summary

Now that you have the necessary vocabulary, a much shorter explanation of double-entry accounting systems is possible. A double-entry accounting system is a conceptual tool based on the concept of duality expressed in the accounting equation: Assets = Liabilities + Owners' Equity. A double-entry accounting system is a means to record economic transactions. Every transaction has 2 sides, which means it involves 2 parties who each receive something and give something up, so each transaction affects at least 2 accounts for each party. The key feature of a double-entry accounting system is that each recorded transaction consists of an equal amount of debits and credits. The equality of debits and credits provides an early warning system for catching recording errors--a transaction cannot be correct if the debits do not equal the credits.

By this time, you'll probably be relieved to know that this course doesn't dwell on debits and credits. In modern times, recording transactions is the province of bookkeepers, rather than accountants. And computers have taken much of the drudgery out of recording transactions. For example, to record the purchase of an automobile for $25,000 cash, some accounting software packages simply require the bookkeeper to fill out an on-screen image of a check. The software takes the information from the filled-out check and creates the required debits and credits, recording them in the appropriate accounts. With such advances in technology, accountants focus their efforts more on the management and interpretation of data, rather than on the initial recording.

Also, the computerization of accounting records means that the constant checking to be sure that each transaction (as well as the entire set of accounts) is in balance can be done by machine. But think about this. Without a conceptual tool like double-entry accounting, it would be difficult, if not impossible, to efficiently computerize records. The organized nature of double-entry accounting systems has a clear logic that can easily be translated to a computer program. The conceptual tool and the physical tool work together.

So why is it important to understand what double-entry accounting is? Just as you should understand how to multiply, but can rely on calculators to do the actual computations, you should understand the basic idea of double-entry accounting systems, but can rely on bookkeepers and computer software to conduct the actual transaction recording. If you decide to become an accountant, you need to understand the basic process of "keeping books" in a double-entry accounting system so that you can learn such things as how to design accounting systems and how to check the quality of the results of accounting systems.

If you don't become an accountant, but choose a career in business, a nonprofit organization or government, somewhere in your organization there will be a double-entry accounting system that holds information you need to make decisions. Understanding how the data are recorded will help you understand the strengths and limitations of accounting information.

WHAT DO ACCOUNTANTS DO?

People who work sitting down get paid more than people who work standing up.
-- Ogden Nash

Let's go back to the analogy that started this module. Remember that we began with a mountain and a party of explorers that used tools to help them get what they needed from the mountain. Analogously, organizations today have mountains of data, which a variety of interested parties (user groups) would like to explore to help them meet their needs. Accounting is a tool that allows users to mine the mountain of data for information they need to make decisions.

Many different kinds of accountants are involved in helping user groups get the accounting information they need. Most accountants work in 1 of 5 functional areas:

- ◆ systems,
- ◆ financial accounting,
- ◆ managerial accounting,
- ◆ auditing, or
- ◆ tax.

Systems accountants help design information systems to capture reliable data that are relevant to users' needs. Using advanced technologies, systems accountants can even build some artificial intelligence into the system, so that the system will be able to help users make decisions.

Some data can be automatically entered into the information system. For example, scanners built into grocery store checkout counters read the bar codes on items being purchased and automatically record data about the sale. Other data must be manually entered into the system by bookkeepers. After the data are entered into the system, financial accountants, managerial accountants, operational auditors and tax accountants summarize, analyze and verify the data to create needed information. All of these groups rely heavily on computers.

Financial accountants direct their efforts to fulfilling the information needs of external users of accounting information, primarily owners and creditors. **Managerial accountants** direct their efforts to fulfilling the information needs of internal users, primarily management. **Operational auditors**--also known as internal auditors--test their organization's information and control systems to make sure they are working the way they are supposed to work. Operational auditors also recommend changes needed to make the systems operate more effectively and efficiently. And **tax accountants** direct their efforts to helping users understand the impact of taxes on their decisions and help entities figure out how to minimize the taxes they must pay to various government agencies.

Once information has been created, it must be reported to users. The credibility of these reports is strengthened if the information is verified by independent parties. **External auditors**--also known as **financial auditors**--examine accounting records and other evidence supporting an entity's financial statements. The external auditors then report their professional opinion as to whether or not the financial statements fairly present the entity's financial position, results of operations and cashflows to external users.

Another type of verification is performed by **compliance auditors**, who examine accounting reports to determine whether the entity has complied with appropriate laws. For instance, some compliance auditors work for the Internal Revenue Service examining taxpayers' returns to determine if they followed appropriate tax laws.

Figure I-1-4 (on the following page) presents an overview of the accounting process. By and large, accountants enjoy their work. A survey of accountants by the newspaper *Accounting Today* found accountants using words such as "variety," "challenging," "independence" and "problem-solving" to be the best descriptions of the rewarding aspects of their work. Moreover, accountants tend to rank among the better-compensated groups in the United States.

There are many people (about a million) working as accountants in each of the 5 functional areas described above--systems, financial accounting, managerial accounting, tax and auditing--and over 50,000 U.S. college graduates each year receive either Bachelor's or Master's degrees in accounting. Forecasts for future job prospects indicate that accounting jobs overall will continue to grow at a faster rate than most other job categories over the next decade.

Figure I-1-4
An Overview of the Accounting Process

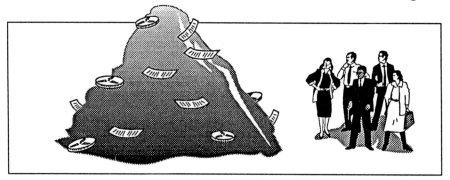

Step 1:

Chaos

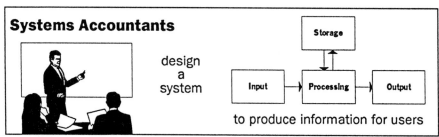

Step 2:

Systems
Design

Step 3:

Recording
Data

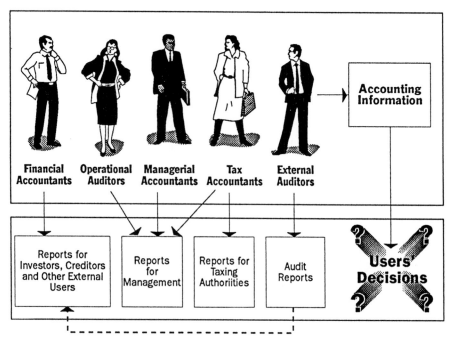

Step 4:

Tranforming the Data
into Useful Information
for Decision-Making

Step 5:

Communicating
Information to Users

One of the major reasons for this continued growth is the movement of the U.S. economy, and many economies across the globe, from an industrial age to an **"information age."** In an industrial age, wealth is created primarily by manufacturing things. In an information age, wealth is created primarily by collecting, interpreting and disseminating information. Aided by the advanced technology of computers, businesses are becoming more dependent on the rapid creation and communication of information.

The success of an organization comes increasingly to depend on the quality of the information it uses. As an advertisement for Dow Jones Information Services, an organization which collects and sells information about businesses, put it: "Business runs on information. Shouldn't you be using premium?"

In an information age, there will be increased opportunity for people who can help impose order on data and communicate information needed to help users make decisions. While the role of accountants is likely to undergo much change with the introduction of increasingly advanced technologies, the basic skills of accountants-- analytical skills, problem-solving and decision-making skills, technological skills, and communication skills--will always be in demand.

WHO ARE THE USERS OF ACCOUNTING INFORMATION?

[U]sers is a term people never apply to themselves; it is given them by people on the other--that is, technical--side.
-- Gerald and Daniella Weinberg,
Journal of Information Systems Management, Winter 1985

Who are the users of accounting information? Think back again to the mountain and explorers analogy and the discussion of accounting information for General Motors. Several user groups were identified in this discussion:

- ♦ management,

- ♦ owners and creditors,

- ♦ government, and

- ♦ other users.

Management

Business organizations exist to make a profit. Other **non-business organizations**--such as nonprofit hospitals, charitable associations, and government entities--do not regard profits as their primary goal. Both business and non-business organizations must be managed well in order to attain their goals.

In both business and non-business organizations, management uses accounting information to make day-to-day operating decisions and plans for the future. Is a product or service profitable? Has a fund-raising brochure produced donations that exceed its cost? Should a particular product be bought or manufactured? Which contractor should be chosen to build a new municipal building? Is there going to be enough cash on hand to meet obligations? Should money be borrowed? Should stock be sold? These management decisions, and many others, involve the use of accounting information.

Owners and Creditors

Businesses may be owned by individuals (**sole proprietorships**), partners (**partnerships**), or stockholders (**corporations**). In each case, owners are interested in determining what the return on their investment has been. They also are interested in deciding whether to invest additional capital, or sell their investment, or hold their current ownership share steady. Potential investors need to decide whether to make an initial investment. Financial analysts, who advise investors on making investment decisions, use the accounting information of many companies to help them decide what investments to recommend to their clients. To make these and other decisions, owners/investors and their investment advisors need accounting information.

Creditors, who lend the company money, are interested in evaluating the safety of their loans and assessing the risk of default on the loan. Potential creditors are interested in assessing the risk of making a new loan to an entity. Does the organization have enough cash to make the required loan payments? What is the chance the entity will go bankrupt before the loan is paid back? Creditors need accounting information to make decisions like these.

Government

In addition to using accounting information to help make day-to-day management decisions, government bodies rely on accounting information to help determine taxes owed by corporations and individuals. Governments also use accounting information to track the health of the economy and make economic policy decisions.

Moreover, many regulatory activities of government involve accounting information. Do utilities charge a fair price for their services? Are companies that publicly trade stock disclosing all that is necessary to current and potential investors?

Legislators also use accounting information to help make public policy decisions. What will it cost if companies are required to provide health insurance to every employee? How much will it cost to close down some military bases? Do tax breaks offered to encourage particular economic activities really work? The necessity of answering questions like these make government bodies frequent users of accounting information.

Other Users

There are many other potential users of accounting information. **Employees**, or their **labor unions**, may make use of accounting information in contract negotiations. Is the pension plan adequate to meet their future needs? Should the employees exercise options to buy a share of the company? Is any segment of the business operating so poorly that there is a danger jobs will be lost? Prospective employees can make use of accounting information to get a feel for the company that has offered them a job.

Suppliers and potential suppliers of a business may want to assess the financial stability of the company before entering into contracts to provide the company supplies. Will they get paid? If the company should encounter cashflow problems, how much will have to be paid to other creditors with stronger claims (such as lenders who have secured their debts with collateral, like a car loan that is secured by the car) before the supplier will be next in line to be paid?

Competitors may be interested in the accounting information of their industry rivals. How much inventory are competing companies holding? Are their profits rising or falling? Have they made any large investments in plant, property and equipment which might indicate they plan to expand? Some businesses buy a few shares of stock in each of their publicly-held competitors just to be able to receive their financial reports. Or, industry trade associations may collect and summarize accounting information about member companies. Trade associations often distribute summarized industry information to their members to aid them in assessing the financial health of the industry.

Citizens can also be users of accounting information. **Voters** may use accounting information to help them make decisions about supporting or voting against ballot propositions that call for new taxes to finance road improvements or new bond issues to finance school construction. How much will these things cost? How will the bonds be repaid?

Likewise, **consumers** may find some accounting information relevant to social decisions they must make. How much more will products cost if they are delivered in recyclable containers? How much money has a company spent on devices to eliminate pollutants created in manufacturing its products? Are donations made to not-for-profit organizations being spent as promised? Once again, answering these and other questions calls for accounting information.

Because of the wide variety of user groups for accounting information, there is much media coverage of newly released accounting information. The financial press (newspapers like *The Wall Street Journal* and magazines like *Forbes* or *Business Week*) and broadcast networks (like CNBC, the Consumer News and Business Channel) frequently focus on accounting information. Business sections of the general press also report such accounting information as the operating results of local (or major national or international) companies. So, **the financial media** themselves become a user group for accounting information.

Accounting researchers--academics who study accounting phenomena and accountants--also are users of accounting information. Financial accounting researchers might examine the accounting information from many companies to determine whether changes in accounting methods affect a company's stock price. Auditing researchers may conduct experiments to determine which factors influence auditors' judgments about the risk of fraud at a company. Managerial accounting researchers may interview management at many companies to determine which reward systems are most likely to achieve desired performance results. Tax accounting researchers may analyze accounting information to determine whether a change in tax policy had the desired effects. Systems accounting researchers may investigate the best ways to represent knowledge in a computerized expert system.

In this information age, there are few physical mountains man has not conquered, but there are an increasing number of mountains of information to explore. The user groups for accounting information include a broad spectrum of people. If you aren't already a member of any of these user groups, it's likely you will be one soon. The unexplored mountains of information that lay before you can be mastered with the tools of accounting. The more you understand core concepts of accounting information, the more successful your exploration will be.

APPENDIX: WORKING ON GROUP ASSIGNMENTS

In a Gallup Organization survey performed for the American Society of Quality Control, eight out of ten full-time workers reported being involved in some kind of team activity in their workplace. Two-thirds of them said their work with teams is part of their normal job, not additional duties. Eighty-four percent said they are involved in more than one team project at a time.

Organizations of all types are finding that efficiency and effectiveness can be greatly improved when people work as teams. However, organizations are also finding that it takes practice to develop the interpersonal skills needed to build effective work teams. Thus, one of your objectives in obtaining a college education should be to develop the interpersonal skills that will help you survive and prosper in team-oriented workplaces. The more practice you have working in groups, the more chance you will have to develop these skills.

This course includes group assignments because of the growing importance of teams in the workplace. The following advice, written by the late Stanley Weingart, is based on years of research and experience with building effective work teams. Use it now to help your group start thinking about the best way to approach working on group assignments. You may also find it helpful to occasionally use it to do a quick "performance check" on how well your group is functioning.

BUILDING EFFECTIVE WORK TEAMS
Stanley Weingart
University of Southern California

Whether you are leading or being a member of an effective work team, there are several essential criteria for your team's success. A successful team is one that achieves its goals in a manner that results in the members having a high level of satisfaction and where growth takes place.

Six criteria for team success are as follows:

1.   Measurable, Mutually Agreed-Upon Goals.

Team members need to agree upon a clear picture of the tasks that they are going to perform and the desired outcome. They also need to define how they will measure their progress. This will provide the team members with a vision and unity of purpose to work together to achieve the team's goals.

Arriving at clear, measurable goals may be difficult. However, without this first step, the team may never bond together and the final outcome may be less than desired.

With clear and measurable goals, the team may continuously check on their progress and take actions necessary to complete their task on time and with the desired quality.

2.   Clear Roles and Expectations.

Members of effective work teams recognize and accept their mutual interdependence. Everyone on the team brings to it certain skills or talents that can contribute to the overall effort. Each can perform a specific role or job to meet the stated goals. Frequently, team effort is hampered when these roles or jobs are not well-defined.

Therefore, one of the first tasks of a newly formed team is to systematically examine its human resources and to clarify roles, responsibilities and job expectations for each team member. The role of the team leader should also be discussed in depth.

When each person on the team understands and accepts what the team expects of them, and what is expected of other members, it is easier to discuss how the team will operate. This will help eliminate potential conflict and misunderstanding and focus the team's creative energy where it belongs--on following the process and achieving maximum results.

3.   Trust and Open Communications.

Successful work teams are characterized by an atmosphere of trust and open communications. In such an atmosphere, team members can speak freely, their ideas and opinions are valued and listened to without ridicule, they are accepted and supported by the other members, and they can take risks and grow professionally.

There are several key elements to development of trust and openness:

a.   **Free Flow of Information** -- brainstorming sessions, frequent meetings with two-way communications, structuring meetings so that each member presents their progress and problems.

b.   **Good Communication Techniques** -- open two-way

communications, speaking clearly and to the point, and active listening.

c. **Constructive Feedback** -- both positive and negative feedback, stated specifically, focusing on behavior not on the person, descriptive not judgmental, timely, accurate, and intended to be helpful.

4. Productive Conflict Resolution.

In an effective team, conflict is addressed openly. Conflict is normal and should be expected from time to time on any team. However, conflict should not be ignored. Valuable exchanges of information and ideas can result from constructive conflict.

To make conflict constructive, the following guidelines are helpful:

a. Confront in a direct, supportive, calm manner.

b. Consider the conflict as a team problem.

c. Clearly identify and describe the source of the conflict.

d. Use problem-solving techniques, not emotional arguments, to reach a solution.

5. Decision-Making by Consensus.

Teams that strive for consensus and develop well-defined decision-making procedures tend to be most effective. Consensus occurs when all members of the team accept the decision with no reservations. Any inability to accept the decision means that the issue is not closed, and the team must continue to use good communications to work on the issue until consensus is achieved. This is especially true for important team decisions related to tasks, roles and goals.

6. Operating Ground Rules.

The most productive teams establish basic ground rules for team operation at the first meeting. These are the accepted norms and standards for member behavior, interaction, participation, and how team meetings will be conducted.

ASSIGNMENTS FOR MODULE 1

ASSIGNMENT I-1-1: <u>Early Accounting Systems</u>

This is an in-class assignment. A description of the assignment will be handed out during the first class.

ASSIGNMENT I-1-2:   <u>**The Conceptual Tools of Accounting:**</u>
                                            The Accounting Equation

<u>SETTING</u>

Your roommate, Lee, tends to be more organized and neater than you are. For example, Lee studies for exams with an index card system. Lee's most recent set of index cards--prepared for an accounting exam taking place tomorrow morning at 8:00 a.m.--consists of a set of 3x5 cards with an "account" listed and defined on each card. Before going to sleep, Lee sorted the cards into 3 piles--(1) assets, (2) liabilities, and (3) owners' equity--to use the next morning for a last-minute review.

About an hour after Lee falls asleep, you accidentally knock all the index cards to the floor, jumbling them together (see next page).

<u>SELF-CORRECTED ASSIGNMENT</u>

Save your relationship with your roommate. Rearrange the cards into the appropriate piles.

<u>HINTS</u>

1.   Review the definitions of assets, liabilities and equity found in Figure I-1-3. Check the "Key Points to Note" column of Figure I-1-3 for guidance.

2.   Use a dictionary of business terms, if needed.

3.   When you've categorized the cards, you can check your work with the solution at the end of this module.

Lee's Cards:

I-1-37

ASSIGNMENT I-1-3:   <u>**The Conceptual Tools of Accounting:**</u>
         Assets = Liabilities + Equities

SETTING

You are a college student (named Lee) who studies for exams with an index card system. Your most recent set of index cards--prepared for an accounting exam taking place today--consists of a set of 3x5 cards with an "account" listed and defined on each card. Before going to sleep last night, you sorted the cards into 3 piles--(1) assets, (2) liabilities, and (3) equity. Early this morning, you used the cards for a last minute review. Now, feeling well-prepared, you are looking at the first exam question:

<u>Question 1</u>: Categorize the following 10 accounts of a magazine publisher as assets, liabilities or equity:

1. Advertising receivables	6. Preferred stock
2. Bonds payable	7. Prepaid insurance
3. Magazine subscriptions paid in advance	8. Printing equipment
4. Magazine subscriptions receivable	9. Retained earnings
5. Paper inventory	10. Taxes payable

ASSIGNMENT

Answer the exam question.

HINTS

1.   Review the definitions of assets, liabilities and equity in Figure I-1-3. Check the "Key Points to Note" column of Figure I-1-3 for guidance.

2.   Use a dictionary of business terms, if needed.

3.   The trickiest part of the question is distinguishing between the 2 similar sounding accounts, "Magazine subscriptions receivable" (money owed by customers for subscriptions they have ordered) and "Magazine subscriptions paid in advance" (money already paid by customers for subscriptions that haven't yet expired). In the first case, the customer owes the publisher something. In the second case, the customer doesn't owe the publisher, but the publisher is obligated to deliver the magazines.

ASSIGNMENT I-1-4:   <u>**The Conceptual Tools of Accounting:**</u>
                                       Duality #1

SETTING

Your friend took an introductory financial accounting course last year and gave you the course exams in case you wanted to study from them. You come across two exam questions about the effects of different transactions on assets, liabilities and equities and remember that the concept of duality comes into play in analyzing these transactions.

SELF-CORRECTED ASSIGNMENT

Answer the first exam question which appears on the next page.

HINTS

1.   Review the definitions of assets, liabilities and equity in Figure I-1-3. Check the "Key Points to Note" column of Figure I-1-3 for guidance.

2.   Review the example discussed in the module in the section entitled *Double-Entry Systems: Two Sides to Each Account.*

3.   When you have completed your work, check it against the solution at the end of this module.

Exam Question #1

Using the form provided below, analyze the following transactions to show their impact on assets, liabilities and equity. The solution for the first transaction has been recorded for you on the form to indicated the desired format. When all 7 transactions are recorded, calculate the final amount of total assets, total liabilities, and total equity. All the transactions are for a book store that is just opening for business.

1. The 3 owners invested $10,000 each of their savings into the business; in return, they each received 10,000 shares of stock.

2. Purchased, for $5,000 in cash, all the books from a book store in another city that is going out of business.

3. Purchased on credit, $2,000 more books from a wholesaler of books.

4. Purchased for $1,000 down and the rest on credit, $10,000 of bookshelves and other furnishings for the store.

5. Paid the first three months rent in cash, $3,000

6. Made the store's first sale to a customer for $30 cash.

7. Paid the $2,000 due to the book wholesaler.

	Assets	Liabilities	Owners' Equity
1	Cash, + $30,000		Stock, + $30,000
2			
3			
4			
5			
6			
7			
Final Total			

ASSIGNMENT I-1-5:   **The Conceptual Tools of Accounting:**
    Duality #2

SETTING

Your friend took an introductory financial accounting course last year and gave you the course exams in case you wanted to study from them. You come across two exam questions about the effects of different transactions on assets, liabilities and equities and remember that the concept of duality comes into play in analyzing these transactions.

ASSIGNMENT

Answer the second exam question which appears on the next page.

HINTS

1.   Review the definitions of assets, liabilities and equity in Figure I-1-3. Check the "Key Points to Note" column of Figure I-1-3 for guidance.

2.   Review the example discussed in the module in the section entitled *Double-Entry Systems: Two Sides to Each Account.*

Exam Question #2

Using the form provided below, analyze the following transactions to show their impact on assets, liabilities and equity. The solution for the first transaction has been recorded for you on the form to indicated the desired format. When all 7 transactions are recorded, calculate the final amount of total assets, total liabilities, and total equity. All the transactions are for a restaurant that is just opening for business.

1. The 2 owners invested $15,000 each of their savings into the business; in return, they each received 10,000 shares of stock.

2. Borrowed $25,000 from a local bank to provide additional operating capital.

3. Purchased for $2,000 down and the rest on credit, $22,000 of furnishings and kitchen equipment for the restaurant.

4. Purchased for $1,500 in cash, food to stock the restaurant's kitchen.

5. Paid the first month's rent in cash, $1,600

6. Hired the cook, who will be paid $800 a month once the restaurant opens.

7. Had the grand opening with the first day's cash sales totaling $1,400.

	Assets	Liabilities	Owners' Equity
1	Cash, + $30,000		Stock, + $30,000
2			
3			
4			
5			
6			
7			
Final Total			

ASSIGNMENT I-1-6:   <u>**The Conceptual Tools of Accounting:**</u>
Marcia's Vet Practice

<u>SETTING</u>

Your sister, Marcia, has just opened up her own veterinary practice, which is being operated as a business corporation. She has purchased computer software to help her keep accounting records for the practice. Marcia plans to use the accounting information she will develop to help her apply for a bank loan to purchase additional equipment and to fill out her tax returns.

Even though the accounting software your sister bought is supposed to be "user-friendly," Marcia is somewhat wary of her ability to create accounting records because she never had an accounting course in vet school. Knowing that you are enrolled in an accounting course, and firmly believing that several heads are better than one, your sister asks you and your group to help her decide how to enter her first set of business transactions into the accounting system:

INITIAL TRANSACTIONS FOR MARCIA'S VETERINARY PRACTICE

1. Marcia uses $10,000 of her own savings and $20,000 borrowed from your father to provide initial seed money for her business. She deposits the money in a business checking account.

2. Marcia writes her first business check, for $6,700, to pay for medical equipment she will use in her business.

3. Marcia orders medications from a veterinary supply house. The supply house sends the drugs and a bill for $370, due in 10 days.

4. Marcia moves into her new office, after writing a business check for $4,000 to pay the current month's rent ($2,000) plus a $2,000 security deposit (which will eventually be used as the last month's rent on a 24-month lease).

5. Marcia writes another business check for $40 to have the office cleaned before her practice opens.

6. Marcia treats her first patient and receives cash payment of $50 from the animal's owner.

7. Marcia pays the bill for the medications.

SELF-CORRECTED ASSIGNMENT

Get your group together and decide how Marcia's first set of business transactions should be recorded.

HINTS

For each transaction, ask the following questions:

1. What does the veterinary practice get? What does the veterinary practice give up? This will tell you what accounts you need to use.

2. For each account: Is the account an asset, a liability, or a part of owners' equity? Does the account increase or decrease? Use the accounting equation to check whether your analysis of the transaction is possible: does the change in total assets equal the change in total liabilities and equities?

3. Once you are sure your analysis of the transaction is in balance, figure out which accounts need to be debited and which accounts need to be credited. Check your logic by making sure that total debits equal total credits.

4. As you finish recording each transaction, check your answer by reviewing the solution provided at the end of this module. Discuss any questions you may have with each other before attempting the next transaction. Remember to make note of any questions you cannot resolve among yourselves to bring up at the next class or during office hours.

5. Extra hint: The fourth transaction is a little harder than the others because it involves an expense account. You need to think about how an expense is related to owners' equity. Additional help on this point is provided in the solution.

ASSIGNMENT I-1-7: **The Conceptual Tools of Accounting:** **Putting Together Accounting Information**

SETTING

You have just completed recording the business transactions for the first month of your sister Marcia's newly-opened veterinary practice (see solution to Assignment I-1-6 at the end of this module). Marcia is grateful to you for your assistance and asks you to help her out once again. She is trying to figure out how the business has done to date and how well it is situated financially for the future.

ASSIGNMENT

Prepare some simple reports for Marcia that show:

♦ her business's financial position (assets, liabilities and owners' equity) at the end of the first month of her practice;

♦ the cash activity (inflows, outflows and ending cash on hand) for the month; and

♦ her "bottom line" (profit or loss) to date.

HINTS

1. Look at the solution to Assignment I-1-6. Here, you have the names of all of Marcia's accounts, as well as a list of debits and credits to the accounts so far. You should begin by figuring out the balance (the difference between all the debits and credits to an account to date) for each account. For example (note: this example is not from Marcia's accounts), suppose you had an asset account called "Prepaid insurance" that had a debit of $1,200 (remember: debits show increases in asset accounts) and a credit of $100 (remember: credits show decreases in asset accounts). The balance in the Prepaid insurance account would be $1,100, computed as $1,200 - $100. Many of Marcia's accounts have only 1 debit or credit, so the balance is obvious. However, you will need to compute a balance for the veterinary practice's Cash account.

2. You'll probably find it easiest to start with a report about the veterinary practice's cash activity. To do this, look at the debits and credits to the Cash account. What were the sources of cash during the month? What were the uses? What should the cash balance be at the end of the month? Prepare a short report (the exact format is up to you) summarizing this activity.

3. Next, figure out the veterinary practice's profit or loss for the month. To do this, look at the balances in the revenue and expense accounts. What were the revenues? What were the expenses incurred to produce those revenues? If revenues were greater than expenses, Marcia's vet practice operated at a profit. If expenses exceeded revenues, the business operated at a loss. This profit or loss is the "bottom line," which is more formally termed "net income (loss)." Prepare a short report summarizing the revenues, expenses and net income (loss) for the month. (The exact format is up to you; if you're curious, you can learn more about formats for this type of report by reading Module 3 of this theme, *Owners and Creditors as Users of Accounting Information*).

4. Finally, prepare a simple report showing the financial position of Marcia's veterinary practice at the end of her first month of practice. This report mirrors the accounting equation, Assets = Liabilities + Owners' Equity, showing the economic resources of the business, the debts owed by the business, and the equity (or "net worth") of the business. You will need the balances in the asset, liability and equity accounts to prepare this report. You will also need a Retained Earnings (or Retained Deficit, if the business has experienced only a loss to date) amount. The Retained Earnings (Deficit) balance for this case is easy since Marcia's business has only been in operation for a month and Marcia has not yet withdrawn any money from the business: the balance will be the total profit or loss to date. The business's Retained Earnings (Deficit) will be part of the Equity section of your report.

ASSIGNMENT I-1-8: **The Conceptual Tools of Accounting: Dan and Betty's Appraisal Business**

SETTING

Your brother Dan and his wife, Betty, have just opened up their own property appraisal business, which is being operated as a business corporation. They have purchased computer software to help them keep accounting records for the business. Dan and Betty plan to use the accounting information they will develop to help them eventually apply for a bank loan to purchase additional office furniture and equipment and to fill out their tax returns.

Even though the accounting software Dan and Betty bought is supposed to be "user- friendly," they are somewhat wary of their ability to create accounting records because they never had an accounting course in school. Knowing that you are enrolled in an accounting course, Dan and Betty ask you to help them decide how to enter their first set of business transactions into the accounting system:

ASSIGNMENT

Decide how Dan and Betty's first set of business transactions should be recorded. The transactions are listed on the following page.

HINTS

For each transaction, ask the following questions:

1. What does Dan and Betty's business get? What does the business give up? This will tell you what accounts you need to use.

2. For each account: Is the account an asset, a liability, or a part of owners' equity? Does the account increase or decrease? Use the accounting equation to check whether your analysis of the transaction is possible: does the change in total assets equal the change in total liabilities and equities?

3. Once you are sure your analysis of the transaction is in balance, figure out which accounts need to be debited and which accounts need to be credited. Check your logic by making sure that total debits equal total credits.

INITIAL TRANSACTIONS FOR YOUR BROTHER AND SISTER-IN-LAW'S PROPERTY APPRAISAL BUSINESS

1. Dan and Betty use $20,000 of their own savings to provide the initial seed money for the business. They deposit the money in a business checking account under the business's name, Prime Property Appraisal. They also give the business the accounting software they purchased earlier for $150.

2. Dan orders office supplies from an office supplies warehouse. The office supplies warehouse sends the supplies and a bill for $125, due in 10 days.

3. Dan and Betty move into their new office, after writing a business check for $1,600 to pay the current month's rent ($800) plus an $800 security deposit (which will eventually be used as the last month's rent on a 24-month lease).

    > (Extra hint: This transaction is a little harder than the others because it involves an expense account. You need to think about how an expense is related to owners' equity.)

4. Dan writes another business check for $200 to pay the first month's charges on a lease for office furniture and equipment.

5. Dan and Betty complete and deliver their first appraisal. The client gives them a check for $300 as payment in full, which they deposit in the business checking account.

6. Betty pays the bill for the office supplies.

7. Dan and Betty complete and deliver their second appraisal. Per a previous agreement, they bill the client $350, to be paid in 30 days.

ASSIGNMENT I-1-9: <u>What Do Accountants Do?</u>: Reading the Job Ads #1

SETTING

It is 5 years from today and you have completed college and received a degree in (surprise!) accounting. After graduation, you moved to another city to take an interesting managerial accounting job.

Now, you are thinking about returning back to the environs of your alma mater. You have been happy with your career choice, so you still want a managerial accounting job.

ASSIGNMENT

Check a national financial newspaper or the Sunday *Business* section of the local newspaper for job advertisements that involve accounting. Read the ads and determine which jobs offer opportunities to continue your career in managerial accounting. Clip the ad which describes the managerial accounting job that sounds most interesting to you.

HINTS

Check the job title first. If you cannot tell which functional area of accounting the job involves from the title, read the brief job description in the advertisement.

ASSIGNMENT I-1-10: <u>What Do Accountants Do?</u>: Reading the Job Ads #2

SETTING

You are taking the first accounting course you have ever taken and wonder what the employment market is like for accountants. Your advisor tells you about 3 Internet sites you can check out for information about jobs in a number of fields:

The Online Career Center: **http://www.occ.com**

E-Span Interactive Employment Network: **http://www.espan.com**

The U. S. Government's job listings **http://www.usajobs.opm.gov**

ASSIGNMENT

Check out these sites and do a search for accounting jobs. Print a copy of your search list to hand in.

Select 2 jobs from each search and investigate further to determine what functional area of accounting the jobs are in and what the duties and responsibilities of the job are. Prepare a brief writeup of your findings and hand in the writeup with copies of the job announcements attached.

HINTS

Since you will have many jobs to choose from, pick the ones you are most curious about to investigate further. Remember that the jobs you choose need not be entry-level jobs. If you want to look at a job announcement for a Chief Financial Officer, go ahead and do so.

You may construct your search to either look for jobs in a particular functional area (e.g., tax) or to list all accounting jobs open. If you use the broader search, you will then need to determine the functional area of accounting for the positions you choose to investigate. Check the job title first. If you cannot tell which functional area of accounting the job involves from the title, read the brief job description included in the position announcement.

Use your own words in the write-up; do not merely copy the listings.

ASSIGNMENT I-1-11: <u>**Who Are the Users of Accounting Information?**</u>**: Finding the Information You Need #1**

SETTING

You have recently joined a team of students who will be spending the next few months learning about the users and uses of accounting information. You want to know what information resources are available to you on campus.

ASSIGNMENT

Choose 1 representative from your team to meet with a member of the library's staff and find out what resources are available in the campus library, including :

- ♦ resources to help you find information about specific companies or specific industries,

- ♦ general resources (print or electronic database) to find news and articles about accounting issues and problems, and

- ♦ resources that can help you locate accounting rules, laws, standards and guidelines (such as financial accounting standards and tax laws).

The team's representative should then brief the rest of the team on what's available in the library.

HINTS

Your instructor will provide you with additional information about when and where the library visit should take place. Your instructor will also provide you with additional information about how this assignment will be evaluated.

ASSIGNMENT I-1-12:   <u>**Who Are the Users of Accounting**</u>
<u>**Information?**</u>: **Finding the Information You**
Need #2

SETTING

You have recently joined a team of students who will be spending the next few months learning about the users and uses of accounting information. You want to know what information resources are available to you on the Internet.

ASSIGNMENT

Do a search of the Internet for information resources related to one of the following topics:

Group 1:   information about financial reports of U. S. public companies
Group 2:   information about financial reports of non-U.S. companies
Group 3:   information about nonprofit organizations in the U.S.
Group 4:   information about taxes in the U.S.
Group 5:   information about taxes in countries other than the U.S.
Group 6:   information about ethics in business and accounting
Group 7:   information about careers in accounting
Group 8:   information about accounting issues for the U.S. federal
                 government

Review the resources you find and choose the 5 sites you think will be the most helpful for this class. Then, prepare a **single-page typed handout** describing these resources and bring enough copies to class for all the enrolled students, plus 2 copies for your instructor.

HINTS

You are likely to find far more than 5 sites for each of these topics. To choose the best 5, it will help if you think about some criteria to use in your evaluation. For example, one thing to consider might be the amount of information available at a site.

To be useful to other students, your handout should include the name of each site, how to reach the sites and the key features of each site.

ASSIGNMENT I-1-13: **Who Are the Users of Accounting Information?: Finding the Information You Need #3**

SETTING

You have recently joined a team of students who will be spending the next few months learning about the users and uses of accounting information. You want to know what information resources are available to you on the Internet. You have heard about electronic mailing lists and are interested to discover that you can sign up for a free subscription to a variety of mailing lists concerning government financial management.

ASSIGNMENT

Sign up for one of the Internet mailing lists available through FinanceNet and monitor the messages throughout the course. You can find descriptions of the available mailing lists and directions for subscribing and unsubscribing at the following address:

http://www.financenet.gov/financenet/start/email.htm

Your instructor will tell you how to report what you find to the rest of the class.

HINTS

When you subscribe to an Internet mailing list, you will receive messages on that topic through your electronic mail. When you no longer wish to receive messages, you should "unsubscribe" from the list.

Read the brief descriptions of the currently available electronic mailing lists closely to find one that includes topics that you would like to learn more about.

Do not expect to understand everything you receive. Some topics discussed will be too complex for you to follow completely. Read each message and try to determine what the key issue is and why it is important to members of the mailing list. Think about how the concepts you are learning in this course apply to these issues.

THE FOLLOWING PAGES

CONTAIN THE SOLUTIONS FOR

THE SELF-CORRECTED ASSIGNMENTS

IN THIS

MODULE.

SOLUTION TO ASSIGNMENT I-1-2

The Accounting Equation: Sorting Lee's Cards

ASSETS (ECONOMIC RESOURCES)

Accounts receivable
Buildings
Cash
Inventory
Land
Marketable securities
Office supplies inventory
Prepaid rent

LIABILITIES (DEBTS OWED TO CREDITORS)

Accounts payable
Mortgage loan payable
Taxes payable
Wages payable

OWNERS' EQUITY (OWNERSHIP INTEREST)

Common stock
Retained earnings

SOLUTION TO ASSIGNMENT I-1-4

The Conceptual Tools of Accounting: Duality #1

	Assets	Liabilities	Owners' Equity
1	Cash, +$30,000		Stock, +$30,000
2	Cash, −$5,000 Inventory, +$5,000		
3	Inventory, +$2,000	Accounts payable, +$2,000	
4	Cash, -$1,000 Furniture, +$10,000	Accounts payable, +$9,000	
5	Cash, −$3,000		Rent expense (Retained earnings), −$3,000
6	Cash, +$30		Sales revenue (Retained earnings), +$30
7	Cash, −$2,000	Accounts payable, −$2,000	
Final Total	$36,030	$9,000	$27,030

Note: If you want more practice, try self-corrected Assignment I-1-6.

SOLUTION TO ASSIGNMENT I-1-6

The Double-Entry System: Marcia's Veterinary Practice

Transaction #1: Marcia uses $10,000 of her own savings and $20,000 borrowed from your father to provide the initial seed money for her business. She deposits the money in a business checking account.

What does the veterinary practice get?

	Account Involved
-- money to put in the bank:	Cash

What does the veterinary practice give up in return?

	Account Involved
-- a promise to repay borrowed money:	Loan Payable
-- ownership interest:	Owner's Capital

Note: The practice is giving up some ownership interest, even though, at this point, there is only 1 owner. At some future date, Marcia may decide to sell part of her ownership interests to another veterinarian. The ownership rights are hers to sell because of her investment in the business.

For each account affected: Is the account an asset, a liability, or a part of owners' equity? Does the account increase or decrease?

-- Cash is an asset. It increases.
-- Owner's Capital is an owners' equity account. It increases.
-- Loan Payable is a liability account. It increases.

Check: Does the change in total assets equal the change in total liabilities and owners' equity?

-- Cash, the only asset, increases by $30,000.
-- Liabilities increase by $20,000 plus Owners' Equity increases by $10,000 for a total of $30,000.

Which accounts need to be debited and which accounts need to be credited?

-- Cash is an asset account. It increases, so it should be debited.
-- Loan Payable is a liability account. It increases, so it should be credited.
-- Owner's Capital is an owners' equity account. It increases, so it should be credited.

Asset accounts		=	Liability accounts		+	Owners' Equity accounts	
increased by debits	decreased by credits		decreased by debits	increased by credits		decreased by debits	increased by credits

Check the logic: Do total debits equal total credits?
Total debits = $30,000   Total credits = $30,000

<u>Transaction #2</u>: Marcia writes her first business check, for $6,700, to pay for medical equipment she will use in her business.

What does the veterinary practice get?

-- medical equipment:

Account Involved
Medical Equipment
(or any similar title)

What does the veterinary practice give up in return?

-- $6,700 from the checking account:

Account Involved
Cash

For each account affected: Is the account an asset, a liability, or a part of owners' equity? Does the account increase or decrease?

-- The medical equipment will be used to produce future business. Therefore, the Medical Equipment is an asset. It increases.
-- Cash is an asset. It decreases.

Check: Does the change in total assets equal the change in total liabilities and owners' equity?

-- There is no change in total assets because the increase in 1 asset is exactly offset by the decrease in another asset.
-- There is no change in total liabilities and owners' equity.

Which accounts need to be debited and which accounts need to be credited?

-- Medical Equipment is an asset account. It increases, so it should be debited.
-- Cash is an asset account. It decreases, so it should be credited.

Check the logic: Do total debits equal total credits?
Total debits = $6,700   Total credits = $6,700

Transaction # 3: Marcia orders medications from a veterinary supply house. The supply house sends the drugs and a bill for $370, due in 10 days.

What does the veterinary practice get?

```
                                        Account Involved
   -- medications:                      Drug Inventory
                                        (or any similar title)
```

What does the veterinary practice give up in return?

```
                                        Account Involved
   -- a promise to pay $370 in 10 days: Accounts Payable
```

For each account affected: Is the account an asset, a liability, or a part of owners' equity? Does the account increase or decrease?

```
   -- The medications will be used to produce future business.
      Therefore, the Drug Inventory is an asset.  It increases.
   -- Accounts Payable is a liability.  It increases.

   Check:  Does the change in total assets equal the change in total
           liabilities and owners' equity?

   -- Only 1 asset changes, for a total increase of $370.
   -- Only 1 liability changes, also a total increase of $370.
```

Which accounts need to be debited and which accounts need to be credited?

```
   -- Drug Inventory is an asset account.  It increases, so it should
      be debited.
   -- Accounts Payable is a liability account. It increases, so it
      should be credited.

        Check the logic:  Do total debits equal total credits?
              Total debits = $370   Total credits = $370
```

<u>Transaction #4</u>: Marcia moves into her new office, after writing a business check for $4,000 to pay the current month's rent ($2,000) plus a $2,000 security deposit (which will eventually be used as the last month's rent on a 24-month lease).

What does the veterinary practice get?

		Account Involved
--	1 month's office space now:	Rent Expense
--	1 month's office rent later:	Prepaid Rent or Rent Deposit (or any similar title)

What does the veterinary practice give up in return?

		Account Involved
--	$4,000 from the checking account:	Cash

For each account affected: Is the account an asset, a liability, or a part of owners' equity? Does the account increase or decrease?

-- The current month's rent is used to produce revenues during the current period, so it is an expense. It increases. An expense, in turn, reduces net income for the period, which reduces retained earnings. So, Marcia's equity will decrease.
-- Remember:

Owners' Equity = Capital + Retained Earnings

Retained Earnings = Accumulated Net Income - Dividends

Net Income = Revenues (and Gains) - Expenses (and Losses)

-- The security deposit will benefit future periods rather than the current period, so it is an asset. It increases.
-- The cash is an asset. It decreases.

Check: Does the change in total assets equal the change in total liabilities and owners' equity?

-- Assets increase by the amount of the security deposit, $2,000, but decrease by the amount of cash used, $4,000. So, the change in total assets is a $2,000 decrease.
-- Owners' equity decreases $2,000 (because of the rent expense), and liabilities are unchanged, so total liabilities and owners' equity decreases by $2,000.

Which accounts need to be debited and which accounts need to be credited?

-- Rent Expense is an expense account. The effect of an expense is to reduce owners' equity. Since owners' equity is decreased by debits, the expense must be recorded by a debit to the Rent Expense account. (See next page for more help, if needed.)
-- Prepaid Rent is an asset account. It increases, so it should be debited.
-- Cash is an asset account. It decreases, so it should be credited.

Check the logic: Do total debits equal total credits?
Total debits = $4,000   Total credits = $4,000

Additional help for #4, if needed:

Why are expenses increased by debits?

(also helpful for #5 and #6)

First: recall that debits decrease Owners' Equity, while credits
           increase Owners' Equity:

                    Owners' Equity accounts

decreased	increased
by	by
debits	credits

Second: Think about the 2 ways Owners' Equity can be increased:

           -- owners invest Capital
           -- accumulated profits are reinvested in the business
                (Retained Earnings)

           So, both Capital and Retained Earnings accounts are
           increased by credits (they are just 2 types of equity
           accounts.)

Third: Think about the accounts that are part of Retained Earnings:

           -- net income: Net income *adds* to Retained Earnings.
           -- dividends: Paying dividends *reduces* Retained Earnings.

           So, net income is increased by credits, and decreased by
           debits.

           [Also, dividends paid are indicated by debits because they
           are reductions in retained earnings.]

Finally: Remember that revenues and gains *increase* net income,
           but expenses and losses *decrease* net income.

           So, if an expense reduces net income, it also reduces
           retained earnings. Consequently, an expense is indicated by
           a debit.

           On the other hand, revenues increase net income and also
           increase retained earnings. Consequently, a revenue is
           indicated by a credit.

Summary: You can break down retained earnings into accumulated net
           income, less dividends. You can further break down net
           income into (Revenues and Gains) - (Expenses and Losses).
           Thus:

                         Retained Earnings

decreased by expenses	increased by revenues
decreased by losses	increased by gains
decreased by dividends	

Transaction #5: Marcia writes another business check for $40 to have the office cleaned before her practice opens.

What does the veterinary practice get?

                                                Account Involved

-- a clean office: Office Cleaning Expense
                                                   (or any similar title)

What does the veterinary practice give up in return?

                                                Account Involved

-- cash from the checking account: Cash

For each account affected: Is the account an asset, a liability, or a part of owners' equity? Does the account increase or decrease?

-- Cleaning the office is a cost of doing business in the current period. The Office Cleaning Expense will reduce Net Income, and therefore will also reduce Retained Earnings, an equity account.
-- Cash is an asset. It decreases.

Check: Does the change in total assets equal the change in total liabilities and owners' equity?

-- Only 1 asset changes (cash), for a total decrease of $40.
-- Liabilities are unaffected, but the increased expense will cause owners' equity to decrease by $40, so the total change in liabilities and owners' equity is a $40 decrease.

Which accounts need to be debited and which accounts need to be credited?

-- Office Cleaning Expense is an expense account. It increases, so it should be debited.
-- Cash is an asset account. It decreases, so it should be credited.

Check the logic: Do total debits equal total credits?
Total debits = $40   Total credits = $40

Need additional help? See the previous page.

Transaction #6: Marcia treats her first patient and receives cash payment of $50 from the animal's owner.

What does the veterinary practice get?

	Account Involved
-- cash payment for services rendered:	Cash

What does the veterinary practice give up in return?

	Account Involved
-- veterinary services:	Sales Revenue or Service Revenue (or any similar title)

For each account affected: Is the account an asset, a liability, or a part of owners' equity? Does the account increase or decrease?

-- Cash is an asset account. It increases.
-- Sales Revenue is a revenue account. It increases.
   Increases in revenue increase net income, which in turn increases Retained Earnings, a part of Owners' Equity. So owners' equity increases.

Check: Does the change in total assets equal the change in total liabilities and owners' equity?

-- Only 1 asset (cash) changes, for a total increase of $50.
-- The revenues have the effect of increasing owners' equity, also by $50, and liabilities are unchanged. So, total liabilities and owners' equity increase by $50.

Which accounts need to be debited and which accounts need to be credited?

-- Cash is an asset account. It increases, so it should be debited.
-- Sales Revenue is a revenue account. It increases, so it should be credited.

Check the logic: Do total debits equal total credits?
Total debits = $50   Total credits = $50

Transaction #7: Marcia pays the bill for the medications.

What does the veterinary practice get?

	Account Involved
-- removal of the debt owed the supplier:	Accounts Payable

What does the veterinary practice give up in return?

	Account Involved
-- cash from the checking account:	Cash

For each account affected: Is the account an asset, a liability, or a part of owners' equity? Does the account increase or decrease?

-- The Account Payable was a liability. It decreases (to zero).
-- Cash is an asset. It decreases.

Check: Does the change in total assets equal the change in total liabilities and owners' equity?

-- Only 1 asset changes, for a total decrease of $370.
-- Only 1 liability changes, also a total decrease of $370.

Which accounts need to be debited and which accounts need to be credited?

-- Accounts Payable is a liability account. It decreases, so it should be debited.
-- Cash is an asset account. It decreases, so it should be credited.

Check the logic: Do total debits equal total credits?
Total debits = $370   Total credits = $370

MODULE INDEX

2

MODULE 2: MANAGEMENT AS USERS OF ACCOUNTING INFORMATION

1997-1998 edition

Table of Contents

MODULE 2: MANAGEMENT AS USERS OF ACCOUNTING INFORMATION

Estimated Time Budget

Task	Time Estimate
Reading PART A: THE ROLE OF MANAGEMENT	45 - 75 minutes
Assignments for PART A	
Assignment I-2A-1	40 - 60 minutes
Assignment I-2A-2	45 - 70 minutes
Assignment I-2A-3	45 - 70 minutes
Assignment I-2A-4	45 - 70 minutes
Assignment I-2A-5	45 - 70 minutes
Reading PART B: BASIC CONCEPTS OF INFORMATION SYSTEMS	45 - 75 minutes
Assignments for PART B	
Assignment I-2B-1	25 - 35 minutes
Assignment I-2B-2	15 - 20 minutes
Assignment I-2B-3	30 - 45 minutes
Assignment I-2B-4	40 - 60 minutes
Assignment I-2B-5	40 - 60 minutes
Assignment I-2B-6	60 - 90 minutes
Assignment I-2B-7	60 - 90 minutes
Assignment I-2B-8	30 - 45 minutes
Assignment I-2B-9	40 - 60 minutes
Reading PART C: BASIC CONCEPTS OF INTERNAL CONTROL SYSTEMS	90 - 120 minutes
Assignments for PART C	
Assignment I-2C-1	120 - 180 minutes
Assignment I-2C-2	40 - 60 minutes
Assignment I-2C-3	45 - 75 minutes
Assignment I-2C-4	120 - 180 minutes
Assignment I-2C-5	20 - 30 minutes
Assignment I-2C-6	60 - 90 minutes
Assignment I-2C-7	60 - 90 minutes
Assignment I-2C-8	20 - 30 minutes
Assignment I-2C-9	120 - 180 minutes
Assignment I-2C-10	120 - 180 minutes
Assignment I-2C-11	20 - 30 minutes
Reading APPENDIX: PREPARING ORAL PRESENTATIONS	10 - 15 minutes

Note: *These time estimates, like all the time budgets for this course, should be adjusted to suit your own learning style. Time estimates for assignments assume that readings were completed before attempting the assignments.*

MODULE 2:
MANAGEMENT AS USERS OF ACCOUNTING INFORMATION

PART A: THE ROLE OF MANAGEMENT

The manager does not handle decisions one at a time; he juggles a host of them, dealing with each intermittently, all the while attempting to develop some integration among them.
-- Henry Mintzberg, <u>The Nature of Managerial Work</u>, 1973

Management is the group of people responsible for running an organization. They are the people responsible for achieving the organization's goals. They are the decision-makers who move the organization forward--or back. Napoleon Bonaparte said it best: "Nothing is more difficult, and therefore more precious, than to be able to decide." Making decisions is the daily task of management.

Making decisions requires information. Without information, you are guessing, not deciding. Many of the decisions managers make are based, at least in part, on accounting information. Accountants play important roles in helping design and maintain organizational information systems. They also play a key role in establishing and supporting the organization's internal control system--the set of methods and procedures which help management efficiently and effectively achieve the organization's objectives.

In the second and third parts of this module, basic concepts of information systems (Part B) and internal control systems (Part C) are described. However, to understand these concepts, you first need to know something about the role of management in an organization. What are the organizational goals that drive managers? What part does management play in the governance of the organization? What kinds of environmental factors affect management?

ORGANIZATIONAL GOALS

The secret of success is constancy to purpose.
-- Benjamin Disraeli, speech, June 24, 1870

All organizations have goals. They exist to pursue those goals. They measure their success against the goals. But, not all organizations share the same goals. Business organizations and non-business organizations pursue different goals.

Goals of Business Organizations

The primary goal of business organizations--from the smallest sole proprietorship to the largest corporation--is economic: **businesses are organized to make a profit for their owners.** This doesn't mean seeking profits is the only goal of business. Many businesses profess to have some social goals, such as contributing to the welfare of the community. Many businesses also have ethical goals. For example, Gannett Co., Inc.--a company that publishes newspapers (including *USA TODAY*), operates radio and television stations, and sells outdoor advertising space--includes among its goals protecting the editorial integrity of the company's news products. Business organizations often have multiple goals, but seeking profit remains their primary purpose.

The owners invest their resources in a business because they expect to receive economic benefits if the business succeeds. In turn, the profit motive and the need to create returns for shareholders drives businesses. Coca-Cola's Chairman Roberto Goizueta once told a *Fortune* interviewer that he worries about improving shareholder returns "from the time I get up in the morning to the time I go to bed. I even think about it when I'm shaving. But I use an electric razor, so I think I'm safe."

MANKOFF 108

"Did you ever have one of those days when the profit motive just wasn't motive enough?"

DOLLARS AND NONSENSE.

Goals of Non-Business Organizations

Non-business organizations include **nonprofit** (or not-for-profit) organizations and **government** entities. **The primary goal of non-business organizations is social**: to fill a social need of the organization's constituents. While all business organizations seek profit as their primary goal, there is more variety of goals among non-business organizations. For example, museums, opera companies, or theater groups have cultural goals. Colleges, universities and educational television companies pursue educational goals. Nonprofit hospitals and missions for the homeless are examples of non-business organizations with health and welfare goals. Political and religious organizations have yet other social goals.

Some non-business organizations do sell products (like Girl Scout Cookies) or services, but seeking profit for owners is not their purpose. Non-business organizations do *not* have defined ownership interests that can be bought or sold in the marketplace. You can't buy or sell stock, for example, in the United Way. Moreover, non-business organizations often receive significant contributions of resources from people who do not expect to receive any personal returns, such as donors who make bequests from their estates to support cancer research.

Government entities are a unique type of non-business organization. Like other non-business organizations, governments do not seek to make a profit. Instead, the primary goal of government entities is to provide public goods and services (such as public schools and highways) for their constituents. However, unlike other non-business organizations, governments have the power to tax their constituents in order to raise the funds needed to sustain operations.

The Line Between Business and Non-Business Organizations.
Business and non-business organizations differ in their goals, but not necessarily in their activities. Hospitals, for example, can be set up as either business organizations (owned by shareholders and seeking profit) or non-business organizations (without owners and not seeking profit). Educational services provide another example of an activity that can be performed by either a business or a non-business organization.

You can't always tell from the name or nature of an organization whether it is a business or a non-business entity. To make this distinction, you need to know what the organization's goals are. Alternatively, you can distinguish a business organization from a non-business organization by looking at its financial records.

Businesses have owners' equity accounts. The owners' equity represents the owners' invested capital and the accumulated profits of the business that have not been returned to the stockholders as dividends. Rearranging the accounting equation (Assets = Liabilities + Owners' Equity) to solve for Owners' Equity shows that in a business organization the equity is equal to the difference between assets and liabilities:

Assets – Liabilities = Owners' Equity.

Non-business organizations do not have owners--their "equity" belongs not to owners, but to constituents. This equity--representing the net resources ("**net assets**") available for future expenditures to serve the organization's social goal--is accounted for as a "**Fund Balance**." Thus, the difference between a non-business organization's assets and liabilities equals its fund balance:

Assets – Liabilities = Net Assets
or
Assets – Liabilities = Fund Balance.

ORGANIZATIONAL GOVERNANCE

To govern is to make choices.
-- Duc de Levis

How do business and non-business organizations go about trying to achieve their goals? First, they must choose a form of organization. This choice has many consequences for the organization: it affects the taxes of the owners, the personal liability of the owners, the number of potential owners, and the organization's financing opportunities.

Once the form of organization is chosen, a mechanism for running the organization must be established. How will the owners' interests be represented? Who will make the day-to-day operating decisions?

Choosing A Form of Organization

There are 3 basic choices for structuring business enterprises:

♦ the sole proprietorship (one person both owns and runs the business),

♦ a partnership (two or more people share ownership and management responsibility), or

♦ a corporation (a government-chartered entity that is legally recognized as being separate from its owners).

Nonprofit organizations, which have no owners as such, are generally structured as corporations.

Sole Proprietorships. Sole proprietorships are the simplest (and most common) form of business organization: one person retains all the power and responsibility for the business. As of the 1990 census, 7 out of 10 U.S. businesses were sole proprietorships. The major drawback of this form of business is that the owner has **unlimited liability** for the debts of the business. Unsatisfied business creditors can force payment from the owner's personal assets.

There are 2 primary advantages of operating as a sole proprietorship. The first is simplicity. For example, there is little or no formal paperwork needed to start a sole proprietorship--although sometimes a local license may be required, or published announcements may be needed if the proprietor wants to operate under a business name (rather than the proprietor's own name). The second advantage is the "pass-through" of business income to the owner. That is, the income of a sole proprietorship is not subject to any business income tax. Instead, the income is treated as part of the individual owner's earned income.

Partnerships. Two or more people may share ownership and/or management responsibility by operating in **partnership**. As of the 1990 census, 10% of U.S. businesses operated as partnerships. Partnerships, like sole proprietorships, are relatively simple to set up, although it is important that all the owners agree in advance what the role of each partner will be. Ordinarily, this agreement will be written down as a contract (called, not surprisingly, "**the partnership agreement**"). Partners need not be equals--the partnership may be structured to reflect different amounts of power, responsibility and profit-sharing for different partners. For example, some partners may be "**general**" or "**full**" **partners**, who both participate in running the company and share in the company's profits or losses in proportion to their investments and management contributions. Alternatively, "**silent**" (or "**dormant**" or "**sleeping**") **partners** invest resources in the partnership and share in its profits or losses, but don't actively participate in running the business.

Willard N. Thornost and his silent partner.

Partnerships, like sole proprietorships, do not pay business income taxes. Instead, the partners each pay taxes on their share of the income through their personal tax returns. The partnership merely files an "**information return**" reporting its partnership income or loss to taxing authorities. Sole proprietorships and partnerships also share another characteristic. Except for the special case of a "**limited**" **partner** (whose liability is legally limited to the amount of his or her investment), sole proprietors and partners bear personal responsibility for any debts of their business.

Partnerships and sole proprietorships differ mainly in number of owners. All sole proprietorships have only 1 owner. Partnerships have at least 2 owners, and may have many more. For instance, professional partnerships, such as CPA firms or law firms, may have thousands of partners in a national or world-wide organization. Having multiple owners can be advantageous. For example, it can be easier to put together the resources needed to start a business with multiple owners contributing funds, as opposed to the sole proprietorship's reliance on a single owner. However, having multiple owners also increases complexity. Sole proprietors are free to unilaterally make important business decisions; partners must come to an agreement.

Corporations. Finally, both business and nonprofit organizations may be structured as corporations. A corporation is recognized under law as a separate entity from its owners (the stockholders in a business) or founders (for a nonprofit organization). To become a corporation, organizations must file formal documents, known as their "**articles of incorporation**" or "**charter**," with the government entity that authorizes the corporation.

State law governs U.S. corporations; in other countries, federal governments may charter corporations. A corporation operating in a particular state is referred to as "**domestic**" in the state where it incorporated, as "**foreign**" if incorporated in another state, and as "**alien**" if incorporated in another country.

Corporations generally must choose a name which reveals their legal status. U.S. corporations, for example, must use the word "Incorporated" (or the abbreviation "Inc.") or a similar term in their legal name to indicate corporate status. In the United Kingdom, corporations use the term "Limited" (or the abbreviation "Ltd.") or a comparable term in their legal name.

Each owner of a business corporation is said to own "**stock**" in the company. When people buy a company's stock, they are buying a share of the company's ownership. In the U.S., shares of stock are represented by paper "**stock certificates**" telling how many units ("**shares**") of a particular company are owned by the stockholder. Stock certificates are usually printed on special paper with intricate engravings to make the certificates difficult to forge. The certificates also bear the stockholder's name (or a broker's "**street name**" if the investor prefers that the certificates be held for safekeeping by a brokerage firm) and must be surrendered whenever the stock is sold. In other countries, such as Japan, paper stock certificates are a thing of the past. In these countries, stock ownership is shown in accounting records, but no paper certificates are issued.

The unique advantages and disadvantages of the corporate form of organization are an outgrowth of its special legal status. Because it is a separate legal entity, the corporation's debts are its own--stockholders cannot be held personally liable for the debts of the corporation (their liability is limited to fully paying for their stock). On the other hand, as a separate legal entity, the corporation itself may be taxed, although U.S. nonprofit corporations are generally exempt from taxation. Thus, for a business corporation, income is eventually taxed *twice*: first, when the corporation earns it and pays corporate income tax, and later, when accumulated profits are distributed to stockholders as dividends, which are subject to individual (personal) income tax.

In addition to **limited liability** for stockholders, the corporate form of ownership offers other advantages. Since shares of stock can be transferred from one person to another without affecting the legal status of the corporation, ownership is relatively easy to transfer without disrupting the organization. In contrast, when a sole proprietor sells his or her business, the business itself is affected: it is dissolved and replaced by a new business. If a partner dies or wants to leave a partnership, the partnership itself changes.

Moreover, as a separate legal entity, a corporation can own other businesses. For example, a corporation can be a "partner" in a business venture or a stockholder in another corporation. This can be particularly advantageous in international business. For example, Anheuser-Busch Cos., the U.S.'s largest brewer, and Kirin Brewery Co, Japan's largest brewer, formed a **joint venture** (a business alliance) to distribute Budweiser beer in Japan. Taking the stockholder route, Canada's John Labatt Ltd. bought shares of stock of FEMSA Cerveza, Mexico's largest brewer (and maker of Tecate and Dos Equis brands).

Improved access to sources of capital is another advantage of incorporation. Because sole proprietorships and partnerships are generally more dependent on particular individual owners than corporations are, it can be easier for corporations to obtain long-term financing. Business corporations can, if they choose, sell debt instruments (like bonds) or stock to the public at large. To do this, however, corporations must become "**public companies**" which, in turn, subjects them to additional regulation, including state and federal securities laws. At the start of the 1990s, there were over 3 million business corporations in the United States and slightly under 15,000 public companies.

Corporations, then, face yet another form-of-business decision: should they "go public" or be privately held? The answer depends on how the corporation values the mix of advantages (like ease of access to capital markets) and disadvantages (like public disclosure requirements) of being publicly held. U.S. public companies must register and periodically file financial statements and other reports with the Securities and Exchange Commission. These statements and reports are then available to anyone who wants to read them, including competitors. Alternatively, a corporation--even a large one--may be **privately held**, with ownership restricted to a relatively small number of shareholders who cannot buy or sell their stock in public securities markets (like the New York Stock Exchange). Mars (yes, the manufacturer of all those best-selling candies) and United Parcel Service are examples of large privately held corporations. Privately held corporations need not disclose (unless they want to) any information to the general public, not even the names of their corporate officers.

New Forms of Organization. As economies and legal systems evolve, new forms of organization sometimes arise. Recently, most of the states in the U.S. have enacted laws to create a new form of organization called a **limited liability company** (LLC), which combines some of the advantages of the corporate form with some of the advantages of a partnership. As its name implies, an LLC has the advantage of a regular corporation's limited liability. Yet, it is taxed as a partnership, yielding the opportunity for tax savings to LLC owners.

The disadvantages of a limited liability company include a variety of restrictions imposed by the state laws governing LLCs. For example, some states limit the life of an LLC or restrict the owners' ability to transfer their interests to someone else. In addition, a few states do not recognize the limited liability of LLCs formed elsewhere, which makes LLCs impractical for some businesses that want national or multinational operations.

Running The Organization

Except for sole proprietorships or very small partnerships, it is not practical for all the owners or constituents to directly participate (other than by occasionally voting on major issues) in the governance of the organization. Too many cooks, as the saying goes, can spoil the broth. Imagine the chaos that would result, for instance, if Toys R Us had to consult all of its owners--over 30,000 stockholders--before making a business decision. To avoid the practical problems of direct participation, most organizations establish a governance mechanism that consists of a Board and a management team.

The Board. Generally, the owners or constituents are represented by a governing body known as the **Board of Directors** (or Trustees, or Governors, or similar title, such as Partners' Council in a large partnership). The board sets overall policies for the organization and serves as the voice of the owners (of a business organization) or the constituents (of a non-business organization).

In business organizations, the board is generally elected by the owners. Thus, partners in large partnerships, such as law firms or CPA firms, often elect a governing body of partners. In the United States, corporate stockholders elect a board of directors to oversee their interests.

Some non-business organizations also have constituent-elected boards. For example, the members of a professional association or a club may elect their board. Other non-business organizations are set up to allow the current board members to appoint new board members, as needed. For example, museum boards are usually appointed, rather than elected, as it is impractical to identify and solicit votes from all the museum's constituents.

The board includes among its responsibilities:

♦ establishing overall policies for the company,

♦ appointing and overseeing top management executives, and

♦ monitoring operating results.

For example, the board of Zenith Electronics Corp. monitors management by tracking data on 20 variables, including production volume, market share by product line, sales in dollars and by units, pretax profits, cash balances, bank borrowings, and productivity measures. In between regular board meetings, 3 outside (non-management) directors meet monthly with the CEO to assess progress. But, the board doesn't run the company on a day-to-day basis: that task falls to management.

Management. Management bears the day-to-day responsibility for making decisions about how to achieve organizational goals, making sure that the decisions are implemented, and evaluating how the organization is performing. The Bureau of Labor Statistics has estimated that just over 10% of the jobs in the U.S. economy are management positions.

What do all these managers do? This can be a hard question to answer because the duties and responsibilities of managers cover a lot of ground. They develop plans for achieving organizational goals. They install and utilize information systems, which provide the information needed for planning, decision-making, and obtaining feedback about how the organization is performing. They establish internal control systems--policies and procedures designed to provide reasonable assurance that the organization's objectives will be accomplished. They make the decisions--pricing decisions, production decisions, spending decisions, investment decisions, hiring decisions, and so on--that must be made. They evaluate performance: how much progress has been made in achieving organizational goals? As Harold Geneen, former Chairman of International Telephone and Telegraph, succinctly stated in his book on *Managing*, "Management must manage!"

Obviously, unless the organization is a sole proprietorship or a very small partnership, all the roles and responsibilities of management cannot be filled by one person. A management team is needed. Leading this team is the job of the **"chief executive officer"** (CEO), who has general responsibility for the management of the organization.

The CEO will delegate some authority and responsibility to other members of the management team. While positions and titles vary among organizations, typically the team might include a **"chief financial officer"** (CFO) who has general responsibility for obtaining and controlling the organization's financial resources, and a **"chief operating officer"** (COO), who has general responsibility for overseeing daily operations of the organization. Depending on the nature of the organization, other important functions may also be represented at the "top management" level. For example, an organization's top management team may include a chief marketer or a chief internal auditor. Reflecting the growing importance of information to organizations, many large corporations now also have a **"chief information officer"** (CIO), whose responsibilities include managing the company's computers and information services.

In turn, the top management group will delegate some of its authority and responsibility to a "middle management" group, such as departmental managers, plant (factory) managers, product managers, and so on, who report to individual members of the top management team. For example, in larger companies, two managers--the Treasurer and the Controller--might report to the chief financial

"As plant manager, what did you *think* you were going to be doing?"

By permission of Paul F. Swan.

officer. The **Treasurer** is responsible for the organization's financing activities (borrowing money or issuing stock) and investing activities. The **Controller** is responsible for the accounting activities of the organization (financial accounting, managerial accounting, systems and tax). Usually, though not always, the internal audit function in the organization will be *separate* from the other accounting activities. This is because the internal audit group must be able to take an objective look at the organization's accounting system. It would be difficult for the internal auditors to maintain their objectivity if their boss was responsible for the accounting system.

Of course, the titles of management positions may vary among organizations. In one organization the CFO may be called the "Chief Financial Officer," in another the "Controller," in another the "Vice President--Finance." Some titles are more descriptive than others. For example, Mrs. Fields Cookies came up with a particularly creative job title for a manager responsible for helping develop and troubleshoot the company's computer software: "Senior Computer Geek."

MANAGEMENT IN DIFFERENT ENVIRONMENTS

Influence is neither good nor bad in an absolute manner, but only in relation to the one who experiences it.
-- André Gide, 1903

Organizations do not exist in a vacuum. They operate in a complex environment that influences the organization and its management needs. Political, legal, economic, sociological and technological factors in the environment will influence the organization's needs, including its need for accounting information. It is also vital to monitor information about the organization's critical success factors.

Political and Legal Factors

The form of government and the laws governing business and non-business organizations influence the organizations and their management needs. How much freedom do organizations have to make decisions about their activities? How stringent are the tax laws? the bankruptcy laws? the environmental laws? the labor laws? Differences in political systems and laws will affect the decisions managers have to make and the information they need to make their decisions.

Consider the case of Russia. For most of this century, Russia operated under a communist system. The government controlled the banking system and most economic activity. Production goals were set by the state in physical quantities only. Meeting production targets, rather than making profit, was the primary goal. Under this system, management did not need (or create) timely and accurate accounting information about such things as product costs or asset values.

In the early 1990s, Russia began to restructure as a capitalist economy. The banking system was revised and state-controlled businesses were converted into private enterprises. Because of this change, Russian managers now require different kinds of information to make decisions and seek capital from investors and creditors. For example, Russia's biggest manufacturing company, Avtovaz, produced 580,000 cars in 1994 but still didn't have the accounting information needed to prepare basic financial reports. In 1995, a team of 30 accountants from Price Waterhouse, an international public accounting firm, worked 7 days a week to help Avtovaz create the necessary accounting information.

Economic and Sociological Factors

Economic and sociological factors also influence organizations and their management needs. How readily available are natural resources? Is the monetary unit (currency) stable? Are prices stable? Are interest rates stable? How large a work force is available? What is the work ethic of the labor force? What are the ethical standards for business? Differences in economic and sociological environments can influence the kinds of decisions managers need to make and the kind of information they need.

Consider the example of businesses operating in countries threatened by hyperinflation (extremely rapid and continuing increases in the general price level that drive the value of currency down sharply). For more than a decade, Brazil suffered from high inflation. In 1984, the general price level rose by about 229%. By 1989, the annual inflation rate reached 1,765%. Prices rose so rapidly that the amount of money needed to buy a stove at the start of 1991 wasn't even enough to pay for a toaster by the end of the year. Prices went up another 2,567% in 1993, which meant wages paid at the end of a month lost about 30% of their value between the time they were earned and the time the paychecks went out. In 1994, an economic stabilization plan cut the monthly inflation rate from 50% in June to 1.25% by December--a remarkably lower rate, but one that is still high by the standards of developed nations. In 1996, prices rose by "only" 12%.

Timely, accurate accounting information becomes vital to survival under these circumstances. High inflation can actually increase demand for goods as people try to buy things today before they become more expensive tomorrow. Businesses always want to sell their products, but in inflationary times managers need to make almost continual pricing and credit decisions. For example, in 1993, if a Brazilian seller received a payment 6 months late, the money was worth less than 10% of its value when the bill first came due.

Managers in inflationary environments need to pay close attention to their cash flows, particularly if the business is international. For example, one Brazilian company, Moinho Pacifico, SA, a flour mill, coped with inflation by buying flour from other countries on credit, with 180 days to make payment. The company then promptly milled the flour and sold it for cash, putting the cash in the bank to earn interest until the bill for the flour came due. By carefully managing cash flows, the company managed to make a profit in difficult times.

Technological Factors

The state of technology and the rate of change in technology will also influence organizations and their management needs. Where the rate of technological change is rapid, managers face many critical decisions. Consider the impact of changing computer technology on business decisions.

Suppose you were in the business of manufacturing typewriters. Think about the decisions you would need to face when the first personal computers were introduced: Will the market for typewriters be affected? Should you continue in the typewriter business? diversify? sell the business now? To make these decisions, managers need to consider several different possible scenarios about future sales patterns for typewriters and estimate the potential revenues, expenses and profits under each scenario.

Suppose you were in another industry that was not competitive with computers. Say you were a retail clothing store. Does the new technology offer you any business opportunities? Could it help you keep track of your stock of clothing and your customers' buying patterns in a way that would improve your business operations? Should you buy a personal computer to keep your own accounting and payroll records that you now have done by an outside service? Do you need state-of-the-art technology? Can you afford it? To make these decisions, managers need information that compares the cost of purchasing the computer now with the estimated future cost savings from computerization.

Critical Success Factors

For each organization, there are some things the organization must do right to be successful. For instance, for a computer manufacturer, these **critical success factors** might include the ability to design and produce new products in a short time, maintaining a reliable distribution system for getting products to retailers, keeping an adequate spread between the cost of producing a computer and its selling price, and achieving high rates of customer satisfaction. If the computer manufacturer fails to attain these critical success factors, long-term value and profitability will suffer.

Management will want to collect information, both financial and non-financial, about these critical success factors. For instance, the computer manufacturer will want to monitor financial information such as the company's **profit margin** (the difference between selling price and cost of goods sold), as well as non-financial information such as the number of customer complaints. This information can help management to highlight areas where the company is falling short of or exceeding its goals and find ways to improve performance.

LEARNING MORE ABOUT THE MANAGEMENT PROCESS

Obviously, you can't learn everything you'd like to know about the management process from this brief discussion. Where else in your college education can you learn more about management?

Business courses are the natural place to start. Explore the business offerings in your course catalog. No matter what area of business (or non-business pursuit) your career plans entail, management skills will be valuable.

You may also be interested in taking some industrial psychology courses. Psychologists have conducted many interesting studies of the management process and the psychology of organizations. Your business courses will expose you to the results of these studies, but you may also find it interesting to supplement your work with one or more psychology courses.

THE ROLE OF ACCOUNTANTS IN MANAGEMENT

How do accountants contribute to the management process? In most organizations, accountants play a key role on the management team, including filling chief financial officer, controller, treasurer and chief internal auditor positions. From these positions, accountants also may advance to become the CEO of some organizations. Moreover, throughout an organization, systems accountants, managerial accountants, tax accountants, internal auditors and financial accountants help identify information needs, design systems to capture data, analyze and interpret the data to provided needed information, and prepare reports to support the managerial decision process:

- ◆ **Systems accountants** can help design the organization's information system and the internal control system.

- ◆ **Managerial accountants** can help determine the kind of information needed to make decisions (such as whether to buy or make a product) and can interpret that information for management.

- ◆ In business organizations, **tax accountants** help management consider the impact of taxes on decisions (non-business, or not-for-profit, organizations are usually exempt from taxes).

- ◆ **Internal (or operational) auditors** help verify whether management policies and procedures are being carried out as intended and suggest ways to increase operational effectiveness and efficiency.

- ◆ **Financial accountants** help management develop the information needed to report back to stockholders and other external parties (such as creditors) the current financial condition of the organization, the results of recent operations, and the cash flows of the entity.

Salaries and career advancement for management accountants are influenced by career preparation. According to a 1995 survey of about 2,400 Institute of Management Accountants' members of all ages, average compensation is higher for people who are **Certified Management Accountants** (CMA, $70,684), or **Certified Public Accountants** (CPA, $74,637), or both ($76,667), compared to management accountants who are neither CMAs nor CPAs ($58,556). The **CMA** and **CPA** designations are professional certifications earned by passing a uniform national exam and fulfilling certain education and experience requirements. Average salaries are also higher for people with Master's degrees compared to those with Bachelor's degrees.

To get an idea of the financial opportunities for accountants in industry and government, review the charts on the next 3 pages. Figure I-2-1 shows recent average starting salaries for entry-level jobs in industry and government. Figure I-2-2 reveals the average annual base salary (before bonuses and other incentives) paid for the type of top management positions typically held by accountants. Finally, the typical "career ladder"--the amount of time it takes to move from entry-level to top positions--is illustrated in Figure I-2-3. As you can see, there is the opportunity for rapid career advancement.

While less data is available on salaries for nonprofit organizations, *The Nonprofit Times* reported in a February 1996 article that the median salary for CEOs of 264 non-profit organizations ranging in size from less than $500,000 to more than $50 million of annual revenues was $54,095 in 1995; non-profit CFOs had a median salary of $38,000. Once again, factors such as size of the organization affect salary. For example, half the CEOs of non-profit organizations with revenues of $50 million or more earned over $85,000 in 1995.

The career skills needed for accountants in business and non-business organizations have been greatly influenced by technological change and the movement toward globalization. In the September 1991 issue of *Across the Board*, Nathaniel Gilbert reported on the "New Hero on the Block: The CFO," noting that chief financial officers of the 1990s and beyond need a much broader set of skills than their predecessors of the past few decades. Gilbert observed that "the CFO has been thrust into a leadership role, becoming an active participant in the design of overall business strategy, sending and sourcing money around the world, and sallying forth to do battle with global competitors." This means that CFOs must have not only strong technical skills, but also a broad-based business education and excellent people skills.

Technological advances and globalization affect organizations of all sizes. For example, a 1996 survey by Arthur Andersen's Enterprise Group and National Small Business United revealed that 23% of small and mid-sized businesses use the Internet in their operations and 18% export products or services. As business becomes more international and technology-dependent, it will be increasingly important to have good information systems and sound internal control systems. These topics are covered in Parts B and C of this module.

Figure I-2-1

National Averages: Entry-Level Salaries for Accountants in Industry

	Less than 1 year experience	1-3 years experience
Cost Accounting	$29,000	$29,000 - $33,500
General Accounting	$28,000	$28,500 - $31,500
Internal Auditing	$30,000	$31,500 - $34,000
Tax Accounting	$29,000	$31,500 - $37,000

DATA: Creative Financial Staffing, *1997 Accountant's Salary Guide*

Entry-Level Salaries for Accountants in the Federal Government, 1997

Qualifications	Starting annual salary
Bachelor's degree	$19,520
Bachelor's degree, 3.0 GPA or better	$24,178
Master's degree	$29,577

DATA: U. S. Office of Personnel Management

Note: In 1994, the average salary of accountants employed by the Federal Government in nonsupervisory, supervisory and managerial positions was $48,500; the average salary of Federal Government auditors was $51,300.

Figure I-2-2

Average Annual Base Salaries for Executive Positions for Accountants in Industry

Chief Financial Officer (CFO)	$194,700
Chief Corporate Information Officer (CIO)	$130,700
Corporate Treasurer	$121,400
Corporate Controller	$113,700
Top Corporate Tax Executive	$106,000
Top Corporate Audit Executive	$92,600

DATA: **William M. Mercer, Inc., 1992.** For a detailed discussion of top management pay see "The New Pay Game...and How You Measure Up," *Fortune*, October 19, 1992, p. 116-119.

Note: When reading this table, bear in mind that salary levels also depend on company size, industry and geographic region. For example, while the average CFO base salary is reported as $194,700, the base salary of CFOs at very large companies (more than $3 billion in annual revenues) averaged $314,100.

Figure I-2-3
Schedule for Climbing the Corporate Ladder

A national survey of private sector accounting-related departments looked at the time spent at each job level before a promotion. Following are the averages for various positions.

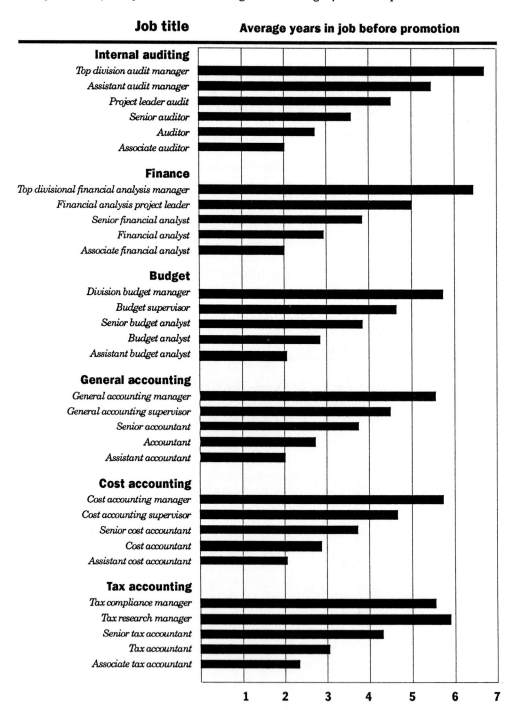

Job title   **Average years in job before promotion**

Internal auditing
- Top division audit manager
- Assistant audit manager
- Project leader audit
- Senior auditor
- Auditor
- Associate auditor

Finance
- Top divisional financial analysis manager
- Financial analysis project leader
- Senior financial analyst
- Financial analyst
- Associate financial analyst

Budget
- Division budget manager
- Budget supervisor
- Senior budget analyst
- Budget analyst
- Assistant budget analyst

General accounting
- General accounting manager
- General accounting supervisor
- Senior accountant
- Accountant
- Assistant accountant

Cost accounting
- Cost accounting manager
- Cost accounting supervisor
- Senior cost accountant
- Cost accountant
- Assistant cost accountant

Tax accounting
- Tax compliance manager
- Tax research manager
- Senior tax accountant
- Tax accountant
- Associate tax accountant

1   2   3   4   5   6   7

Source: *William M. Mercer Meidinger Hansen in* **Journal of Accountancy, July 1990, page 17.** Reprinted with permission from the <u>Journal of Accountancy</u>, ©1990 by American Institute of Certified Public Accountants, Inc.

MODULE 2:
MANAGEMENT AS USERS OF ACCOUNTING INFORMATION

PART B: BASIC CONCEPTS OF INFORMATION SYSTEMS

> *It is best to do things systematically, since we are only human, and*
> *disorder is our worst enemy.*
> *-- Hesiod, Works and Days, 8th century B. C.*

To achieve organizational goals, managers need a system to provide the information used in decision-making. If you look up "system" in a dictionary, you will find that a system is a combination of parts to form a complex whole. An **"information system"** is a combination of people, equipment, policies and procedures that work together to capture data and transform the data into useful information. In Part B of this module, we'll discuss the transformation of data into information, providing a basic overview of information systems. Then, we'll talk about how accounting information systems have evolved. Finally, we'll take a look at advanced technologies and information systems and consider the challenges and opportunities the dawning of the Information Age presents for the design of information systems both now and in the future.

TRANSFORMING DATA INTO INFORMATION

> *Some day, on the corporate balance sheet, there will be an entry which*
> *reads, "Information"; for in most cases, the information is more valuable*
> *than the hardware which processes it.*
> *-- Grace Murray Hopper, speech, 1987*

While all information systems transform data into information, there are many ways systems may vary. This section begins with an example illustrating the difference between data and information; provides an overview of information systems; discusses the importance of flexibility in information systems; and describes the primary differences between manual and computerized systems.

Data Versus Information: An Example

What is the difference between data and information? **Data** are raw facts and figures. Raw facts and figures are the starting point (the input) for creating information. **Information** is created by an information system that manipulates data into a form useful for decision making.

For example, suppose you are trying to decide if you should buy a ticket to the Rose Bowl at a cost of $50. To make this decision, you need information about your current financial position, particularly about how much cash you have. So, you look at your checking account book. It contains lots of data: records of every deposit you ever made, every check you ever wrote, every interest payment you ever received, every service charge you ever paid. But, you don't need all this data, you just need a single piece of information: what is your current balance?

If you've kept your checkbook properly, it also contains *information* about your balance. This information was developed from the data by adding all the deposits and interest receipts and subtracting all the checks written and service charges. In effect, your checkbook is an information system. You input data about deposits, checks, interest and service charges. You transform the data into information by calculating a new balance after each transaction (or set of transactions).

Now, suppose you find that you have $120 as your current checking account balance, more than enough to buy the ticket. But, is the price a reasonable one? To answer this question, you would like to know how the price compares to what you paid for Rose Bowl tickets over the past 2 years. Again, the data in your checkbook can be transformed into the desired information. You simply look for the 2 checks you wrote for the prior years' Rose Bowl tickets, add up the amounts and divide by 2. If your ticket 2 years ago cost $40 and your ticket last year cost $45, the average price was $42.50. Notice that the checkbook still contains the same data set as before, but you have now used it to create different information.

An Overview of an Information System

The transformation of data into information, which is referred to as **data processing** or **information processing**, may involve many different activities. These activities include recording, classifying, merging, sorting, summarizing, analyzing and verifying data, as well as retrieving, reporting and transmitting information. Thus--as shown in Figure I-2-4 on the next page--an information system consists of 4 main functions:

- ◆ input,
- ◆ storage,
- ◆ processing, and
- ◆ output.

The information system takes data as an input, stores it in a database, processes it, and outputs information for users. All information systems--from something as simple as a personal checking account system to something as complicated as a highly automated system for a department store--share these 4 functions.

Information systems may vary according to the amount and type of information they contain. A simple system like a personal checking account

Figure I-2-4

Functions of an Information System

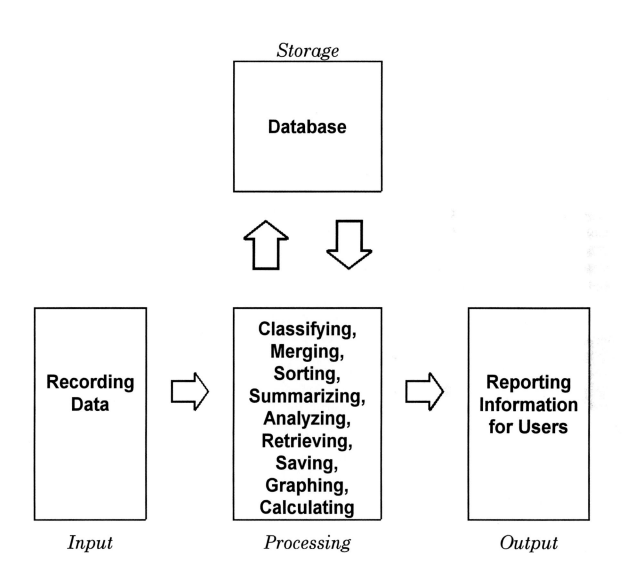

system may contain only a few items of data about each transaction--such as the check number, the date and amount for each check or deposit, and the payee for each check--and a few pieces of information (such as the account balance). A more sophisticated system, like the cash receipts and disbursement records for a large department store, might include additional data (such as the identity of the cashier for each receipt) and produce more information (such as a monthly summary of each type of disbursement--rent, salaries, office supplies expense, and so on.)

Flexibility as a Hallmark of Information Systems

Think about the Rose Bowl tickets example. In this example, the same data set was used to create two different pieces of information--the current checking account balance and the average price paid for past Rose Bowl tickets. The *flexibility* to create different information from the same data set is one of the hallmarks of an information system. The more flexible an information system is, the better it will be able to provide information for a variety of decisions--routine and non-routine, structured and unstructured.

Some decisions are **routine**--they occur repeatedly over the normal course of operations of the organization. For example, a manager responsible for purchasing raw materials for a manufacturing process (like the leather used to make shoes) must regularly decide how much raw materials to order and when to place the order. Other decisions are **non-routine**, occurring only occasionally. For example, most organizations do not regularly need to make a decision about whether to liquidate (wind up operations and dissolve the organization).

Some decisions, including most routine decisions, are **structured**--that is, it is clear what information is needed, when it will be needed, and how it will be used. For example, universities know that each year they will face decisions about how many new professors to hire. Information about enrollment levels and current faculty positions will be needed to make this decision. The relationship of the information to the decision is predictable: as enrollments increase and the number of current faculty decreases (e.g., due to retirements), the university will need to hire more new professors.

Other decisions, including many non-routine decisions, are **unstructured**--that is, it is hard to prespecify what information will be needed, let alone when it will be needed and how it will be used. For example, suppose a university experiences an unexpected significant decline in student enrollments, with an accompanying sharp drop in tuition revenues. What should the university do to counteract the decline: increase mailings to high school students telling them about the university? increase its offerings of financial aid? change course offerings? To make a decision about what to do, the university needs information to help pinpoint the cause of the decline. The more flexible an information system is, the better it will be able to handle information needs for unstructured decisions.

Manual Versus Computerized Information Systems

Different information systems afford different degrees of flexibility. One key difference among information systems is the degree of computerization. Today, information systems can be completely **manual** (all kept by hand--like your checkbook in the Rose Bowl example), or completely **computerized** (with computers used for input, processing, storage and output), or somewhere in between. The major advantage of computerization is that computerization greatly enhances a system's flexibility. With the proper programming, data in a computerized system can be manipulated in an almost endless number of ways.

In addition to the advantage of increased flexibility, computerized systems generally have the advantage over manual systems when it comes to speed and accuracy. Compared to a manual system, a computerized system can transform data into information more quickly and, if properly controlled, with fewer errors. Because of these advantages, and because the price of computing power is decreasing as technology improves, it is not surprising that many organizations have either partially or completely computerized their information systems. Today, even small organizations are likely to be at least partially computerized.

HOW ACCOUNTING INFORMATION SYSTEMS HAVE EVOLVED

[Information technology] is creating a wave of change that is crashing over accounting's shoreline. It crashed across industry in the 1970s. Then it crashed across services in the 1980s. And it will crash across accounting in the 1990s.
--Robert K. Elliott, The Third Wave Breaks on the Shores of Accounting

By now, you have probably figured out 2 common-sense conclusions about information systems. First, if you don't collect the data, you won't have the information you need for decision-making. This is why a company like Federal Express expends the resources to collect data on the company's more than 20 million transactions a day. Second, data accumulates. You can drown in a sea of unprocessed data, but transforming data into information provides a life raft. Thus, managers at Federal Express aren't deluged with detailed data on 20 million daily transactions; instead, they receive information culled from the data.

Accountants help organizations decide what data to collect and what information to produce. As technology changes, accounting information systems also evolve. Today, many companies are experiencing the transition from traditional accounting information systems to more modern systems.

Traditional Accounting Information Systems

The traditional accounting information system--which is overviewed in Figure I-2-5 on the following page--was designed in a world before computers. In this

Figure I-2-5
Overview of a Traditional Accounting Information System

ECONOMIC TRANSACTIONS AND EVENTS

Examples: Sell goods
                    Receive customer payments

produce data that are *initially collected on*

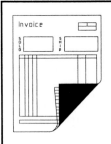

SOURCE DOCUMENTS

Examples: Sales invoice (to customer)
                    Remittance advice (from customer)

from which debits & credits *are recorded in*

JOURNALS

Examples: Sales journal
                    Cash receipts journal

then transferred to accounts *and summarized in*

LEDGERS

Examples: General ledger
                    Accounts receivable subsidiary ledger

and communicated *to users in*

REPORTS

Examples: Financial statements
                    Tax returns

world, it was too difficult and too expensive to record all available data about an organization's activities and events. Thus, traditional accounting information systems were designed to input data only from economic transactions and events that cause a change in assets, liabilities or equities. For example, a manufacturing firm's accounting information system would record data about sales made or customer payments received, but would *not* record any data about sales force calls on customers or complaints handled by customer services.

For many hundreds of years, traditional accounting information systems were manual systems. Today, many organizations still use traditional accounting information systems, but now they are computerized. When computerization became possible, the first wave of accounting applications closely mimicked the manual system--creating electronic versions of the same input, storage structure, processing functions and output reports. Thus, even though computers make it feasible to accumulate larger databases, computerized traditional accounting information systems still concentrate on collecting data about economic transactions and events that affect assets, liabilities and equities.

Data from these economic transactions and events are stored in a multi-layered database that begins with **source documents** (pieces of paper or computer screens where the impact of economic transactions or events is first written down). For example, a sales order form is a source document for recording sales transactions. A customer remittance advice (such as the stub you return when paying your electric bill) is a source document for recording customer payments.

Data from the source documents are recorded in the next layer of the database, the "journals." **Journals** are the accounting books--whether paper or electronic--where debits and credits related to the transactions and events are recorded. [Note: A basic explanation of debits and credits may be found in Module 1 of this theme.] For example, to record a customer payment, the journal will include a debit to cash (showing an increase in this asset) and a credit to accounts receivable (to show a reduction in the amount due from the customer). According to the principles of double-entry accounting, each entry in the journal must balance--that is, the debits must equal the credits. Small companies might have just a single journal, called the **general journal**, where all transactions would be recorded. Larger companies may have one or more **subsidiary journals** (such as a sales journal or a cash receipts journal) for recording common types of transactions, as well as a general journal for other transactions.

Finally, data from the journals are entered in the "ledgers." **Ledgers** are the manual or computerized books where: (1) the debits and credits recorded in the journal are transferred ("**posted**") to each appropriate account--such as Cash, Accounts receivable, or Sales revenue, and (2) account balances are calculated. Once again, smaller companies might have just a single ledger, called the **general ledger**, where all account information would be kept. Larger companies might have one or more **subsidiary ledgers**, such as a subsidiary accounts receivable ledger, as well as a general ledger. The subsidiary accounts receivable ledger would contain an account for each credit customer, showing all that customer's transactions and balance. The general ledger would have a *summary* accounts receivable account only, showing the total debits, credits, and balance from all customers listed in the subsidiary ledger, but no details.

Typically, in traditional systems, only the accountants have access to the database (the source documents, journals and ledgers). The source documents, journals and ledgers act as a sort of data warehouse that customers (users) cannot enter by themselves. Users receive information only through reports-- such as financial statements and tax returns--prepared by the accountants at the end of each accounting period, or when otherwise required.

One major disadvantage of traditional accounting information systems is the "one-size-fits-all" nature of the reports these systems produce. Because the reports are intended to meet the needs of multiple users, they may provide more information than any one user needs and thus be difficult to interpret. As one wag put it, accounting may be the language of business, but sometimes it seems as if the language is Aramaic, a tongue not readily understood by many people. Traditional accounting information systems are also relatively inflexible about report structure. The format of most of these reports is controlled primarily by the preparer; users have little choice in how the reports are formatted.

Different Users Have Different Information Needs

Until very recently, most accounting information systems were very expensive to set up and maintain. Data gathering took small armies of clerks who would then input data into either a manual or mainframe computer-based system. Processing data on mainframes or by hand was costly and, when the processing was done, printed reports had to be distributed to users both within and outside the organization.

Under these circumstances, most organizations could not afford to produce all the information they might want; the costs of doing so exceeded the benefits. When priorities had to be set, the needs of major groups of external users-- stockholders, creditors and government tax authorities--tended to dominate. Secondary user groups (such as potential employees) had to make do with whatever was reported for the primary user groups whenever it was reported.

It's easy to understand why this happened. If a company wants to be able to raise money by selling stock or borrowing, it needs reliable financial accounting reports to show current and potential owners and creditors. If a company wants to stay in business, it needs to pay its taxes promptly, so it has to produce information for its tax returns. It is not surprising, then, that the bulk of effort historically devoted to the accounting information system went to preparing the financial reports needed to obtain financing and the tax returns needed to fulfill tax reporting obligations.

Yet, one of the biggest disadvantages of traditional accounting information systems is that only a subset of data relevant to organizational decisions is captured. Consider, for example, a company that manufactures wood furniture. The company makes a sale to a new retail customer for $50,000 of assorted styles of oak desks. Some of the different information needs related to this transaction are shown in Figure I-2-6 on the following page.

Top management would need to know the impact of this sale on revenues and profits for the year. This financial information *would* be produced by the accounting information system. However, consider some of the information needs the accounting information system would *not* meet. To help target future sales and advertising plans, the sales/marketing manager needs non-financial information to answer questions such as: Did this order come from a sales call or from a response to a print advertisement? To help plan production schedules, the plant manager would need order details to answer questions such as: When is the order due to be delivered? How many different styles must be produced? Since these information needs cannot be met by the traditional accounting information system, other information systems will arise within the company.

The sales and marketing department might start its own information system for sales orders. This system would duplicate much of the data in the accounting information system (such as the number of units sold and selling prices), but would exclude some accounting data not considered immediately relevant for sales and marketing decisions (such as the date the customer was billed or the date the customer paid the bill). The sales/marketing information system would also include some data not captured by the accounting information system (such as the source of the order). Similarly, the plant manager might set up a system to fulfill production scheduling information needs.

This web of systems may be both inefficient and, in some circumstances, ineffective. While the existence of multiple information systems helps the organization function, there is much duplication of effort (such as each system recording the number of units sold), which is inefficient. Furthermore, since none of the systems provides access to *all* the available data, it can be hard to access information for non-routine decisions, which limits effectiveness.

More Modern Information Systems

Computer technology has advanced rapidly over the past few decades, significantly increasing the amount of data which can be stored and the speed of processing and retrieval. Consider that the first computer, ENIAC, filled an entire room but could hold only 20 digits in memory. Today, a single CD-ROM disk provides enough memory to hold the equivalent of a small library of books. By 1989, integrated circuits (the electronic components that provide a computer's power) were 10,000 times more efficient than the first integrated circuits of 1959. Costs have also changed dramatically. By 1995, the cost of processing a million instructions per second was just over $100, compared to over $10,000 in 1980.

Figure I-2-6

Example: Different Information Needs from the Same Event

Evaluation of sales and marketing efforts

Marketing/Sales manager's information needs

EVENT:

SALE OF FURNITURE

Plant manager's information needs

Impact on production schedules

Top management's information needs

Impact on revenues and profits

With advances in technology comes the opportunity to design information systems that are not subject to the disadvantages of traditional accounting information systems. Much of the input function can now be automated, making it possible to increase both the scope and accuracy of organizational databases, as well as the speed of data entry and retrieval. At KMart, for example, clerks now wave scanners over bar codes to electronically gather far more data about items sold than clerks used to be able to input into simpler cash registers. Moreover, store data are sent each night by KMart's own satellite network to huge mainframe computers that hold the company's databases. By early the next morning, KMart's merchandise buyers can access detailed information about how well individual products are selling throughout the country. Merchandising decisions, such as pricing decisions, can be made much quicker than before and can be tailored to particular regions of the country. KMart has also connected its major suppliers (such as Mattel, Inc.) to its network so that the vendors can access KMart's databases, check how their products are selling, and arrange to ship any additional items needed directly to the stores that need them.

Preparation of financial statement information and tax return information can also be extensively automated. As a result, in many organizations, the time and effort accountants devote to financial accounting and tax reporting has been reduced, and the time and effort devoted to preparing managerial accounting information for internal users has increased. In addition, advanced technologies have made company databases accessible to far more people than ever before, increasing the need for accountants to focus on systems design issues and operational audits. As Peter Drucker has observed, the impact of advanced technology on accounting is far-reaching:

> People usually consider accounting to be "financial." But that is valid only for the part, going back 700 years, that...is only a small part of modern accounting....Indeed, accounting is being shaken to its very roots by reform aimed at moving it away from being financial and toward becoming operational....Accounting has become the most intellectually challenging area in the field of management, and the most turbulent one.

Figure I-2-7 (on the following page) provides an overview of a more modern information system. The more modern system differs from the traditional accounting information system in 3 ways:

♦ **More data are captured.** The more modern system includes a greater variety of data--both financial and non-financial--about a broader set of organizational activities and events.

♦ **The database focuses on organizational processes rather than accounts.** For example, a manufacturing company might categorize its database into 3 key operating cycles (repetitive processes): acquisition and payment, production, and sales and collection. The **acquisition and payment cycle** includes the organizational activities and events needed

Figure I-2-7

Overview of a Modern Information System

BUSINESS ACTIVITIES AND EVENTS

Examples: Call on customer
Receive order
Ship goods to customer
Receive customer payments

produce data that *are captured in*

ACTIVITIES/EVENTS DATABASE

Examples: Acquisition/payment cycle data
Production cycle data
Sales/collection cycle data

from which USERs may *choose or generate*

INFORMATION & REPORTS

Examples: Sales activity reports
Financial statements

to obtain and pay for the labor, supplies and raw materials the company needs to create value for customers. For example, obtaining bids from vendors for materials needed is an activity in this cycle. The **production cycle** includes activities and events involved in using the labor, materials and supplies to create products that will be valued. Setting up machines to produce a particular product design is an activity that falls into this cycle. The **sales and collection cycle** includes those activities and events related to selling the products and receiving payments from customers. Sending a customer a bill for a credit sale is part of the sales and collection cycle.

♦ ***Users have direct access to the database, allowing choice about the information and reports to be received.*** While the database in a traditional accounting system is akin to a warehouse that customers (users) may not enter, the database in a more modern accounting system is closer to a library where users have direct access to many sources of information, although they may be restricted from some areas. For example, Federal Express's information system allows employees and major customers to directly access the database to track packages being shipped. However, as you might expect, most employees and all customers are restricted from some areas of the database, such as payroll data.

The next section explores some ways advanced technology has been used to create more modern information systems.

ADVANCED TECHNOLOGIES AND INFORMATION SYSTEMS

Any sufficiently advanced technology is indistinguishable from magic.
-- Arthur C. Clark, The Lost Worlds of 2001

Given the rapid pace of technological change, it is not surprising that many organizations have yet to take full advantage of the opportunities to improve their information systems. But, over the next few decades, many organizations will find ways to use available technology to improve their information systems. Already, some organizations have found ways to take advantage of technology to create more sophisticated information systems, including decision support systems and knowledge-based systems.

Decision Support Systems

Consider the example of Frito-Lay, Inc., the snack food division of PepsiCo Inc. The Frito-Lay system begins with computerized input. For example, Frito-Lay's more than 10,000 sales people--who make more than 400,000 sales calls a week--use hand-held computers to record customer orders, which amount to millions of snack items a week.

Frito-Lay's information processing includes a "**decision support system**" (DSS). All management information systems are designed to provide prespecified information to help users make routine, relatively structured decisions (like deciding how much raw material to order for the manufacturing process). In addition, a decision support system lets users interact with the system to request information needed to make non-routine, relatively unstructured decisions (like deciding how to counteract an unexpected drop in revenues).

For example, the Frito-Lay system is programmed to use color codes to warn users of potential problems. The color red is used to highlight products where market share has dropped in the current period as compared to the previous period. Once the system identifies a problem, the manager needs to make a decision about what to do to counteract the decline--increase advertising? offer discount coupons? replace a weak salesperson? lower prices?

To make this decision, more information is needed. The manager can query the system to find relevant information. For example, the manager can ask if market share is declining in every region, or only in some regions. If the problem is confined to one region, the manager can ask if the problem is at all stores, or only at some stores. By asking enough questions, the manager can locate the source of the problem. This information helps the manager decide what to do.

Advantages of a Decision Support System. The major advantage of a decision support system is that users can directly query the system to get quick answers to their questions. How does this affect an organization? Robert H. Beeby, who was president and CEO of Frito-Lay when its system was initiated, observed many positive effects of using a DSS. He described them in a *Wall Street Journal* article that is reprinted in Figure I-2-8, on the next page.

One of Beeby's themes is speed. As he noted, "you need to know quickly, or the competition will kill you." In organizations of all types, management's need for quick information is increasing as the United States and other countries move from an industrial economy to an information economy. In an industrial economy, increasing productivity and profits are outgrowths of improvements in the design and utilization of machinery and equipment. In an information economy, increasing productivity and profits are more likely to be outgrowths of better use of information than of better use of machinery and equipment.

The increasing need for speed extends to non-business organizations, too. For example, consider the case of the Internal Revenue Service (IRS).

DSS and Non-Business Organizations: The Case of the IRS. The IRS first computerized its tax return processing system in the early 1960s. The system, still largely in place, is only partially computerized. It functions as a traditional management information system, rather than a decision support system. The information system consists of 2 main parts: "pipeline processing" and "support system processing."

Figure I-2-8
Decision Support: Computer Chips and Corn Chips

How to Crunch a Bunch of Figures

Every business manager I know shares one frustration: the difficulty obtaining fast, accurate and comprehensive market information. Whether selling mouthwash, disk drives or, in our case, snack foods, a manager needs to know whether a product is giving the competition fits, or if it's a clinker. And you need to know quickly, or the competition will kill you.

Until recently, Frito-Lay had a centralized decision-making structure common to many corporations. Product information crept upward through the organization on what I thought was a timely basis. I soon discovered it wasn't timely enough.

It did not, for example, provide Frito-Lay enough time to respond quickly to its rapidly changing and complex markets or to fine-tune its inventory. It also did not allow us to shorten our business cycle enough to stay ahead of the competition. And it did not allow me, the CEO, to have the latest sales and profit information on the 14 million snacks sold weekly through our 400,000 sales calls.

So we changed—radically.

The catalyst was our Decision Support System, brought on line last year. DSS kicks back to 200 managers detailed sales and inventory information fed into it by 10,000 route salespeople equipped with hand-held computers.

For example, one of our sales people who handles more than 50 stores for us in New Jersey no longer spends hours writing orders, invoices and sales reports. With his palm-sized computer, he now completes his "paper work" in a minute or two at each stop, running through a programmed product list complete with prices. At the end of each day, his sales report is transmitted in seconds to headquarters in Dallas. Even conservatively, if we estimate that our route salespeople save just

Manager's Journal

By Robert H. Beeby

three hours a week, that's 30,000 hours a week for the entire sales force, and untold savings in clerical, postage and forms costs.

Here's how the system serves us:

• *Helps in tracking new products.* In this area, DSS is invaluable. This spring, for example, Frito-Lay launched its new "Light" line of snack foods. DSS allows me to see if this new line is cannibalizing other Frito-Lay brands—and I get the information in a matter of days, not weeks as was previously the case. I also have easy access to data showing our performance vs. competitive brands'. For Ruffles Light Potato Chips, I can determine: total sales from the previous week; supermarket sales vs. smaller accounts; average sales on a particular route; and the success of our promotions. Most important, the data allow me to make mid-course corrections to ensure the success of the Light line.

• *Facilitates faster, more accurate decisions.* Recently, I noticed red numbers (indicating reduced market share) for tortilla chips in our central business region. I punched up another screen display and located the problem: Texas. I kept punching up new screens and tracked the red numbers to a specific sales division and, finally, the chain of stores. The numbers pinpointed the problem area and, after additional research, revealed the culprit: the introduction of a generic store-branded product. We quickly formulated a counter-strategy and sales climbed again. Time invested: a couple of weeks. Before DSS, finding such a problem and correcting it took the better part of three months.

Through information technology, even cardboard cartons used to transport our products become a business opportunity. Last year, 88% of all cartons shipped to our distribution centers were returned by our sales force for re-use. If we push the percentage up a single point, it saves Frito-Lay $700,000. So, through DSS, we are now tracking cardboard returns by individual sales route, and by store, and hope to push returns above 90%.

• *Assists in "management by walking around."* When Tom Peters coined that phrase he wasn't thinking of a computer tour of operations by the CEO. But that is what DSS allows me and other senior executives to do. I can, at a glance, view the performance of each of our managers and

salespeople around the country. If I see something I don't like, I can fire off an electronic-mail memo. Conversely, if there is good news, I'm likely to contact the manager and congratulate him.

• *Helps us to decentralize.* I never thought a computer would be responsible for a total reorganization of Frito-Lay, but it has been. Last year we decentralized, breaking the company into four geographic business areas, each with its own business plan, structure and profit-and-loss responsibility. We did so because DSS, and the detailed information it provides, allows middle managers to have a complete picture of what is happening in their regions. Now approximately 60% of the decisions that used to be made by top management are made by regional managers, leaving the decisions affecting the company as a whole at corporate headquarters.

As a result, top management can see within a few days which products are hot and which are not, enabling it to devise its strategy on the spot. But most important, DSS gives us the information we need—not what someone wants to give us after it has been massaged and sanitized. And we get it when we want it, which is usually immediately. While DSS currently operates through 200 terminals, it will reach 600 managers before fall, many of them via satellite transmission.

A note of caution, however: When incorporating an information technology system, do so step-by-step. Computers as a strategic marketing tool may still be unfamiliar to lower and middle management, and may require a breaking-in period. Let your people feel the impact of the system, so that as additional programs are incorporated, the process will seem evolutionary. The results will be revolutionary.

Mr. Beeby is president and CEO of Frito-Lay, a division of PepsiCo Inc.

Pipeline processing covers the initial receipt of paper tax returns and the input of data. Data from the returns are used to create a set of master files stored on computer tapes located in Martinsburg, West Virginia. Master files provide tax records covering the most recent 3 years for every individual and business taxpayer. The files contain only key information from each return; paper copies of the returns are stored to preserve the complete information set.

The support system processing deals with the use of taxpayer information once it has been input into the system. Numerous smaller information systems, each containing some information duplicated from the pipeline, are used to conduct investigations and answer taxpayer questions.

This information system has relatively little flexibility. The information that can be retrieved from the system is relatively fixed; IRS workers cannot query the system concerning non-routine information. Moreover, IRS workers can only access limited amounts of taxpayer information electronically. For the rest of the information, they must request paper documents and wait for information from the system to be retrieved and transmitted to them. It takes up to a week or more to retrieve each requested paper document from the vast files of the system.

When the IRS system was installed in the 1960s, its speed and flexibility was comparable to that of many other organizations. The costs of computerization were high--approximately $20 million to process a million instructions per second on a mainframe--so only the most essential data were stored in the computerized portion of the information system. It was more cost-effective to hire small armies of workers to maintain storage warehouses full of paper documents.

But, by the start of the 1990s, it only cost about $80,000 to process the same million instructions per second on a mainframe computer that had cost $20 million in 1960. Then, personal computers rapidly dropped the cost of a million instructions per second to less than $1,000. While the IRS still struggled with a partially-computerized system, other organizations, like banks and department stores, significantly improved the speed and flexibility of their information systems. Taxpayers, used to the more advanced systems of other organizations, complained that the IRS system was too slow to answer their questions or resolve their problems. When IRS Commissioner Lawrence Gibbs left office, he acknowledged in an interview that taxpayers were experiencing a "frustration of expectations" when dealing with the IRS.

Moreover, the situation was worsening as the volume of tax returns to be processed increased steadily over time. Approximately 208 million returns were processed in 1990 and an estimated 224 million returns will be processed in 2001. In 1990, the Information Management and Technology Division of the U.S. General Accounting Office described the IRS system as "slow and unreliable" and noted that "modernizing its tax processing system is critical if IRS is to operate in a world of increasing workloads and limited resources."

The IRS has begun a multi-billion dollar plan to modernize its tax processing system. The plans for the new system include greatly increased flexibility, allowing IRS employees to directly access databases. As part of the tax system modernization, in 1985 the IRS started to computerize data input by allowing taxpayers to file returns electronically, rather than on paper. By 1990, about 4 million returns were filed electronically; by 1997, there were over 13 million electronic filings. In 1997, the National Commission on Restructuring the IRS recommended that electronic filing be required for all taxpayers by the year 2007.

While the IRS is having more than a few difficulties implementing its tax system modernization plan, and progress in converting taxpayers to electronic filing has been slower than planned, there are still some clear benefits from modernization, including:

♦ **increased accuracy**--By 1994, electronic input had cut the error rate to under 1%, compared to 15% to 17% errors with paper filing.

♦ **increased processing speed**--A refund for an electronically filed return in 1996 was processed in about 21 days, compared to about 40 days for a paper tax return. Since the IRS must pay interest on refunds that take over 45 days to process, speeding up processing can reduce interest costs, as well as please taxpayers.

♦ **labor cost savings**-Labor savings with electronic filing are substantial. In 1996, for instance, at the IRS service center in Covington, Kentucky, it took 2,500 people to process 10.5 million paper returns. At the same center, only 50 people were able to process 4.5 million electronic returns.

The taxpayer system modernization plan illustrates some of the advantages that decision support systems provide over traditional information systems. Decision support systems are designed to allow decision makers, like the managers at Frito-Lay or the IRS, to query the system's database to discover information needed for the decision at hand. Decision support systems can also highlight situations where decisions may be needed (such as highlighting a drop in sales for a particular snack food item at Frito-Lay). Yet, the evolution of technology does not stop with decision support systems. In the next section, we will consider even more advanced "knowledge-based systems" which go beyond providing decision support to actually recommending or making decisions.

Knowledge-Based Systems

"**Knowledge-based systems**" (KBS) are computer systems that offer not just data and information, but also *advice* based on facts and relationships stored in a "**knowledge base**." For example, suppose an insurance company wants to build a knowledge-based system to provide advice about the legitimacy of medical insurance claims. In order to provide this advice, the system would need to contain both facts (like the limits of a particular policyholder's insurance coverage) and relationships (like the knowledge that the surgeon's charge for an operation is generally higher than the assistant surgeon's charge). Additionally, the system must include a set of rules for making **inferences**--that is, the system must include software (known as the "**inference engine**") for using the data and knowledge to identify and solve problems.

Some knowledge-based systems, often dubbed "**expert systems**," offer advice of such high quality that they mimic the advice of human experts. An expert system goes beyond accumulating data and providing information to support human decision making: an expert system *automates* complex decisions.

An Example: Travelers Corp.. An example of an expert system is the electronic fraud detection system used by Travelers Corp., an insurance company that has one of the largest managed health care networks in the U.S., serving well over 1 million people in over a hundred cities around the country. Travelers, as well as other insurers, faces a substantial problem when it comes to paying health care claims: it is estimated that somewhere between 3% and 10% of all money spent on health care in the U.S. is paid for fraudulent claims. At that rate, U.S. insurance carriers are being cheated out of about $40,000 per minute.

In this environment, audit verification of claims is particularly important. Even before the electronic fraud detection system was developed, Travelers had a staff of claims auditors, internal auditors who checked the accuracy of thousands of claims each year. Auditors help detect mistakes or fraud in claims, leading to potentially large cost savings.

However, it isn't practical or cost effective to audit every claim. So, the claims auditors' first task is deciding which claims to audit. One possibility is to choose a random sample of claims to audit. However, given that only a minority of the claims are expected to be overbilled or fraudulent, a random audit would probably result in the auditors spending most of their time looking at claims that were *not* problems. It makes more sense for the auditors to deliberately focus their efforts on claims where the risk of overbilling or fraud is relatively high.

How can auditors assess the risk that a claim is overbilled or fraudulent? To do this, auditors look at the characteristics of current claims compared to past claims from the same patients and billing organizations (doctors, hospitals, and so on). They also evaluate the claims against their own knowledge of typical medical billing patterns. They look for patterns that appear suspicious. For example, an auditor may compare two bills from a surgeon and an assistant surgeon for the same surgery. There should be a reasonable relationship between the two. If not,--say, for example, if the assistant surgeon's bill is greater than the surgeon's bill--the possibility of overbilling exists. Part of the auditors' expertise lies in knowing how to recognize suspicious patterns.

Travelers Corp.'s electronic fraud detection system was designed to identify claims that are good audit targets. The system takes claim data and checks for abnormal patterns in order to predict--much as human claims auditors would-- which claims are likely to be overbilled or fraudulent. For example, the system checks treatment dates and flags non-emergency services provided on Sundays or holidays when the provider's office would normally be closed. While there may be reasonable explanations for these claims, it's also possible they indicate fraudulent overcharging. Once the system flags a claim as suspicious, human investigators take over. Travelers finds there are legitimate explanations for some of the claims, but about 4 out of 5 flagged claims do turn out to be fraudulent. Travelers claims that using the system adds about 2% to the health insurance profit margin.

Costs Versus Benefits of Expert Systems. Expert systems are still an emerging phenomenon. The cost of developing expert systems is high, at least in part because it takes a lot of effort to develop a knowledge base and an inference engine. Moreover, the knowledge base must be updated as needed. Likewise, the inference engine must be maintained. As human experts develop new insights into complex decisions, their insights must be transferred to the expert system or the system will lose its value.

You can get an idea of the cost and complexity of developing an expert system by considering another IRS example: an expert system to help "assistors" answer taxpayers' questions. Each year, several thousand assistors answer millions of questions by telephone at toll-free sites across the country, using paper copies of IRS forms and publications for reference. The assistors work in 2 groups: "frontline" assistors who answer calls, and more experienced "backup" assistors, who handle questions the frontline can't answer. The assistance program has come under strong criticism in the press and from Congress because of the relatively low rate of "correct" answers given to taxpayer questions. For the 1991 filing season, for instance, assistors gave technically correct answers to 84% of taxpayer questions, which means they gave bad advice to 16% of the callers.

For several years, the IRS' Research Division has been working on the development of an expert system to help improve the accuracy of assistors' responses. With the expert system, an assistor uses a computer to enter a key word or phrase related to a taxpayer's question. The expert system uses the key word to determine the nature of the problem, and responds by displaying on the assistor's computer screen a question to ask the taxpayer. When the response is entered, a new display appears, until the computer has all the information needed to define the problem. The result is an answer to the taxpayer's query.

The expert system was tested in 1990 and 1991 at the Boston, Philadelphia and Los Angeles call sites. The tests were supposed to help the IRS determine whether it would be worthwhile to install the system nationwide between 1992 and 1994. During the test, all the frontline assistors used the expert system, without referring to any paper copies of forms and publications. In addition, even if they knew the answer to a question themselves, the frontline assistors were asked to refer all questions the system couldn't answer to the backup assistors, so the IRS could measure the efficiency and effectiveness of the expert system.

The test results were inconclusive. The good news was: the expert system gave correct answers to 100% of the questions it could handle. The bad news was: the system couldn't answer about 38% of taxpayer questions because it lacked essential knowledge. Moreover, for simple questions, the expert system was slower than working with paper documents. Plans to install the system nationwide were put on hold until further development work and testing could be done.

The potential savings from using an expert system must be high enough to justify the development and maintenance costs--or, in other words, the benefits of the system must exceed its costs. Thus, expert systems applications currently are found primarily in large organizations which handle huge volumes of transactions, like the millions of claims a year processed by Travelers or the millions of questions a year received by IRS telephone assistors.

Smaller Companies and Expert Systems. Organizations too small to develop their own expert system can sometimes use systems developed by others. For example, companies can hire consultants to review the medical and dental claims paid during the year by their insurance carrier. Coopers & Lybrand, a public accounting firm, uses an expert system called *Dr. Claim*™ to review the claims of its client companies. In one case they found an overbilled claim where the physician used "fee unbundling" (billing multiple surgical procedures for 1 operation) to raise the bill from $900 to $3,500. In another case, a test for duplicate payments found 1,700 duplicate payments totaling over $100,000. Since insurance premiums are based in part on a company's claims experience, identifying billing errors or fraud can be a potent means to control costs.

INFORMATION SYSTEMS IN AN INFORMATION AGE

One thing is certain: The information revolution is changing our lives,
and we need to prepare ourselves to cope with its promise and potential.
-- Albert Gore, Jr.

Information systems are truly evolutionary. Prehistoric man used iron oxide to communicate via cave paintings. Today, the same material--iron oxide--is used to store magnetic signals. But, the pace of change in information systems in the late 20th century accelerated so rapidly that it became revolutionary.

Just like the Industrial Revolution, which occurred slowly and peacefully, the Information Revolution, born in the twentieth century, will likely extend well past the year 2000. Progress takes time to assimilate. For example, while Thomas Edison invented the light bulb and central generating stations in 1879 and 1881, it took about 20 years before the use of electric power began to affect everyday life and it was another 20 years before the full impact of Edison's inventions were felt. At the turn of the century, only about 5% of U.S. manufacturing plants used electric motors; by 1920, the majority did.

Adapting to Technology

Over that 40-year period, people had to adapt their thinking from a world lit by candles and powered by steam to a completely new technology. Not only did people need to change their thinking, they also needed to change the way they worked. Economic historian Paul David notes that in the age of steam-powered manufacturing equipment, factories were typically several stories tall because the steam produced by a coal-fired engine in the basement could more efficiently travel up vertical pipes than across horizontal pipes. Consequently, goods being manufactured had to be moved from floor to floor at various stages of the production process. To take full advantage of the new technology, manufacturers not only replaced their steam engines with electric motors, they replaced their multi-story factory buildings with single-story plants that reduced the labor needed to make a product. Changes of this magnitude take time to implement.

Now consider that the **microprocessor**, an integrated circuit containing the central processing unit of a computer on a small silicon chip, was invented in 1971. This led to the invention of the **microcomputer**, or **personal computer** (PC), creating the opportunity for organizations of all sizes to computerize. Before the invention of the microcomputer, computer use was restricted to those few organizations that could afford to buy an expensive mainframe computer and pay the technical staff needed to program and run the mainframe. In 1960, before the microprocessor, there were a total of 60,000 computers in use world-wide; by 1994 there were 176 million microcomputers in use.

Just as happened with electric power, it took organizations some time to adjust to the new technology of the microcomputer. People had to change their attitudes, as well as the way they worked. IBM, for example, found that one reason executives resisted microcomputers was because they didn't know how to type! Moreover, when computers can provide instant electronic access to information throughout an organization, the traditional multi-level management hierarchy designed for a paper-based information system becomes more cumbersome than helpful; "flattening" the organization (removing some of the old middle management layers) takes time.

Computer experts mark the 1990s as a turning point when many organizations made (or are making) the switch from the old centralized mainframe-based computing system to the more powerful network computing of "**client/server**" systems. In a client/server system, legions of desk-top PCS (the "clients") have access to one or more central computers (the "servers") holding databases and software that can be used by anyone on the system. The client microcomputers can also operate as stand-alone machines. For example, someone using a client PC can download data from the server and then independently use a spreadsheet software package to create charts or graphic displays of the data.

According to surveys by Deloitte & Touche, the percentage of business applications running on client/server systems grew from 5% in 1991 to 50% by 1996. Aetna Life and Casualty provides a good illustration of the switch to network computing. Before the 1990s, Aetna's data on insurance claims were stored on 2 huge mainframe computers--one for personal insurance, the other for commercial insurance--that were only directly accessible to a small group of specialists. Others in the company received most of their claims information in the form of printed reports. Since Aetna switched to a client/server system, service representatives--by merely "clicking" an icon on the screen of their laptop PC--can directly access the claims information stored on the mainframes. The network system had immediately apparent advantages in terms of efficiency and customer satisfaction. Within 3 years, Aetna was able to consolidate 65 claim centers needed to manage the paper flow under the old system to a more efficient group of 22 regional claim centers. By 1995, Aetna estimated cost savings would mount to $100 million.

A Look Into The Future: 2001

In *Murphy's Law, Book Three* Arthur Bloch provides a humorous "law" describing the dilemma of trying to keep up with rapidly changing technology. He cites the eloquently labeled "Bitton's Postulate on State-of-the-Art Electronics": *If you understand it, it's obsolete.* Yet, it is important to keep pace with technology that can affect your organization. So, many organizations expend significant efforts keeping up with the state-of-the-art and looking toward the future of information technology.

The next several decades should bring significant increases in the application of current advanced technology, as well as new technological innovations. Electronics industry experts predict that by the year 2001, a 256-megabyte silicon chip will be available, significantly increasing the power of a microcomputer. It's also conceivable that by 2001, the silicon chip will be an old technology, replaced by the emerging technology of "optoelectronics," where chips are made up not of electronic circuits, but of microscopic light-emitting lasers that receive and transmit data by flashing on or off. As reporters John Carey and Neil Gross noted in the May 10, 1993 issue of *Business Week*'s cover story on optoelectronics ("The Light Fantastic"), optical fibers and optical storage devices (such as optical CD-ROMs, the technical name for the familiar compact disc) can enormously increase the amount and speed of data transmission:

> *The...approach could make today's computers the equivalent of Model Ts. At IBM, AT&T, Martin Marietta, and Honeywell, engineers are building hybrid systems in which beams of light replace wires that connect chips and computers. Big advances also lie ahead for computer-memory technology, says Scotty R. Neal, president of AT&T's CommVault Systems, which makes optical storage devices. "Revolution is an overused word, but it's happening. You'll be able to put more information than all the world's books contain in a box and have it accessible in seconds."*

Deciding What Information to Produce

The availability of abundant, relatively cheap computing power makes possible information systems that could only be dreamed of even 25 years ago. But the appropriate use of this power is not as simple as it may first appear. Older information systems--from the clay tokens of ancient Mesopotamia and quipus of the Incan Empire to the hand-kept double-entry bookkeeping systems of the middle ages and the machine-aided systems of the early twentieth century--were limited in the amount of information they could produce. The limits were practical limits--information that took too long to generate or cost too much to generate wasn't generated. For example, factory owners estimated the number of labor hours used to manufacture each of their products because it wasn't feasible to keep track of the exact labor costs for every individual item made. Systems designers worked within these practical limits, which forced them to prioritize the information needs of users.

But now, technological advances make it possible to collect more data than ever before, and to produce more information than ever before. You can, in effect, produce almost anything you want. Do you want to know the exact amount of labor costs of every individual item you manufacture? Employees can wear identification badges that can be sensed by machines, creating a data set that allows your system to compute an exact amount of labor costs for each individual item manufactured.

A new question now comes into prominence: if you can produce an almost unlimited amount of information, where do you draw the line? The information you can produce will vary in quality. So, the logical answer to this question is: you draw the line when the quality of the information being produced is too low for it to be valuable. This, of course, brings to the forefront another question: how do you assess the quality of the information? This question is addressed in the following section.

Characteristics That Determine the Quality of Information

Somewhere along the line, someone (probably your mother or father) introduced you to the cliche that you *can* get too much of a good thing. Or, as Eric Johnston put it: "The dinosaurs eloquent lesson is that if some bigness is good, an overabundance of bigness is not necessarily better." So it is with information. If some information is good, it does not always follow that more information is better.

Several characteristics define the qualities that make information valuable:

- ♦ costs-versus-benefits,
- ♦ understandability,
- ♦ reliability, and
- ♦ relevance.

These factors, along with considerations of comparability and materiality, determine the value of information. They should be considered when designing an information system.

Costs-versus-benefits. We've already discussed one reason more information isn't always better: sometimes, it costs more to get additional information than the information is worth. Cost-benefit considerations provide an overall constraint on the amount of information a decision maker will get.

Understandability. Now let's suppose for a moment that generating additional information is relatively cheap. Even in this case, there are several reasons why it may not be wise to generate the information. First, the information isn't worth generating if the particular user group doesn't understand it. For example, if a teacher gives a multiple-choice test, there is computer software that can generate lots of statistical information measuring the validity of the test. But most of this statistical information--things like tetrachoric correlation measures--is unfamiliar to students, so reporting the information to students wouldn't make much sense. The information isn't useful if it isn't understood.

Reliability. Second, the information must be reliable--you must be able to count on its being what it purports to be (this is known, more formally, as "**representational faithfulness**") and on its being reasonably free from error and bias (this is known, more formally, as "**neutrality**"). Additionally, for information to be reliable, it ought to be true that if several different people (or systems) set out to derive the information from the data, they would all come to the same conclusion (this is known, more formally, as "**verifiability**"). Information that is not verifiable, or not neutral, or not representationally faithful can't be relied on for decision-making.

Relevance. Finally, the information must be relevant to the user's decision. That is, the information must be clearly related to the decision at hand. Suppose, for instance, that you don't swim and you are trying to decide whether it's safe for you to wade across a stream. Information about the average depth of the stream is irrelevant to your decision--what you really need to know is the depth at the deepest point of the crossing.

There are three primary ingredients that make a piece of information relevant: **timeliness**, **predictive value**, and **feedback value**. Timeliness is important because decision makers need information *before* they make their decisions, not after. Information that doesn't arrive on time quickly loses its value. In addition to timeliness, information also should have either predictive value or feedback value. Information has predictive value if it helps the user to predict the future (like helping a bakery predict customer demand for cookies on the next rainy November day). It has feedback value if it confirms (or disconfirms) the user's expectations. For example, if your car is hesitating and you look at the gas gauge and see that it is on empty, this information confirms your expectation that you are running low on gas. It helps you decide that you should head for a gas station immediately.

Comparability and Materiality. Two other factors interact with relevance and reliability to determine the value of information: comparability and materiality. These 2 factors aren't qualities of the information itself (like relevance and reliability), but they are related to assessing the information's value.

Comparability means that the value of information increases when it can be compared to a benchmark. Thus, information about an organization becomes more useful if it can be compared to information about other organizations or other time periods. For instance, Frito-Lay's information about sales in Texas becomes more valuable when it can be compared to information about sales in other areas. For benchmarks to be most valuable, the measurement of the information and the benchmarks should be consistent. Thus, for example, if sales are going to be compared across geographic regions, the comparison is more meaningful if the same mix of products is offered for sale in each region.

Materiality refers to a threshold below which even relevant, reliable information isn't likely to make any difference in a user's decision. For example, think about how the Frito-Lay expert system highlights products with a declining market share. Clearly, a drop in market share is relevant to managers' marketing decisions and the information is reliable as long as the sales data were properly input into the system. But, suppose the drop in market share is of a very small magnitude--say a $1,000 drop from a $500,000 market. This drop might be too small to be worth investigating--the drop is said to be "**immaterial**."

A materiality threshold can be built into a decision support system or expert system. Thus, for example, the managers at Frito-Lay can decide what they would consider to be a material drop in market share. The system then is programmed to highlight only those drops which are larger than the materiality threshold.

Summary: A Hierarchy of Information Qualities. The qualities that make information valuable are summarized on the next page in Figure I-2-9, taken from *Statement of Financial Accounting Concepts #2*, "Qualitative Characteristics of Accounting Information".

Trade-offs Between Information Qualities

Ideally, information should possess all these qualities--but the qualities may be present in varying degrees. Often, decision makers have to make trade-offs among the qualities. For example, sometimes very relevant information has poor reliability.

Consider the case of a manufacturing company operating in a

Figure I-2-9
A Hierarchy of Accounting Information Qualities

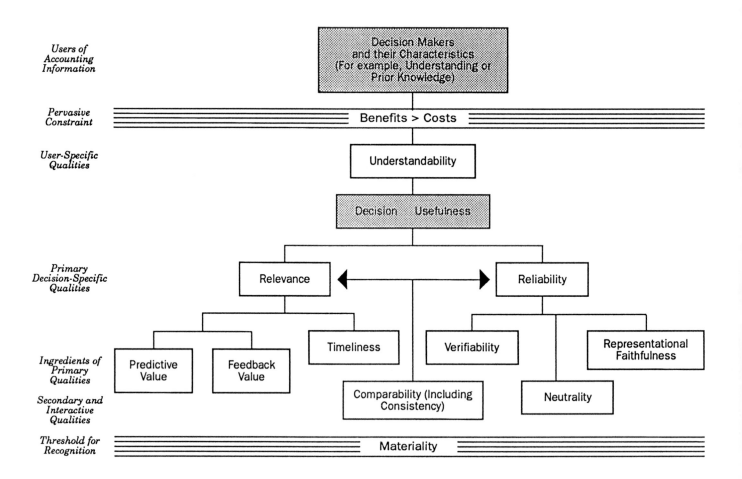

Source: FASB Statement of Concepts #2: *Qualitative Characteristics of Accounting Information.* Copyright by Financial Accounting Standards Board, 401 Merritt 7, P. O. Box 5116, Norwalk, Connecticut, 06856-5116, USA. Reprinted with permission. Copies of the complete document are available from the FASB.

hyperinflationary environment. The company needs to decide how to price its goods for sale today to customers who will not pay for the goods until 30 days later. The price needs to be set high enough to allow the company to replenish its stock of goods ("inventory") and still clear a profit.

The company can get reliable information on what it cost in the past to make the item of inventory it is selling--but this information isn't highly relevant. In a hyperinflationary environment, prices of raw materials and labor are rising constantly--there is no way the replacement inventory could be manufactured in the near future for the same cost as before. On the other hand, the company could estimate what it will cost to make the replacement item thirty days hence. In a hyperinflationary environment, this estimate won't be very reliable--but it is very relevant.

Very few decision makers have the luxury of dealing with perfect information sets. Sound judgments can't be made if information has *no* relevance or reliability--in that situation, you are forced to guess, rather than use judgment. But, short of the zero point, decision makers often need to make tradeoffs among the information qualities they would like to have. How much of one quality you can trade off against another (like relevance versus reliability) depends on the nature of the decision and the decision maker's personal preferences. One of the accounting profession's most important jobs is helping design systems that make information of the *right quality* available to the *right people* at the *right time*.

Accountants as Knowledge Workers

Management theorist and researcher Peter Drucker wrote in the December 1, 1992 *Wall Street Journal* about the impact of changing technology on management. In his piece, titled "Be Data Literate--Know What to Know," Drucker pointed out that "Executives have become computer literate....But not many executives are information literate. They know how to get data. But most still have to learn how to use data." Managers at all types of organizations must learn to become more sophisticated users of information, including accounting information.

Accountants, as you probably realize by now, are really information specialists, or "knowledge workers." Their jobs involve identifying information needs, finding ways to capture data about an increasingly broad range of organizational activities and events, helping design systems that will transform the data into information needed for decision-making, and helping users interpret information. Advanced technologies are changing both the jobs and educational needs of accountants (as well as those of others in business).

What kind of educational preparation do accountants need to face the challenges brought about by advanced technologies? First, and most obviously, accountants today, as always, need strong quantitative skills. Much of the information, and most of the data, in a computerized information system will be quantitative. This is why accountants need good quantitative skills and good analytical and problem-solving skills.

In addition, since accountants must interact with different user groups to find out their information needs, accountants need to understand how organizations work and understand the major kinds of decisions management faces. They must also interact with other information specialists (like computer experts) to determine the best conceptual and technological tools to use to capture data and transform it into information. To work with all these different groups, accountants need good people skills--especially communication skills and interpersonal skills.

Also, as the world becomes increasingly computerized, accountants need to understand available technologies and keep pace with changing technology. Most importantly, accountants--like many others as we approach the 21st century--need to know how to continue to learn and cope with change throughout their careers. The Accounting Education Change Commission (AECC), formed to act as a catalyst for improvements in the education of accountants, issued a 1990 position statement on the *Objectives of Education for Accountants*. According to the AECC, the most important part of education for accountants is "learning how to learn:"

> *The overriding objective of accounting programs should be to teach students to learn on their own....Students should be taught the skills and strategies that help them learn more effectively and how to use these effective learning strategies to continue to learn throughout their lifetimes.*
>
> *Students must be active participants in the learning process, not passive recipients of information. They should identify and solve unstructured problems that require use of multiple information sources. Learning by doing should be emphasized. Working in groups should be encouraged. Creative use of technology is essential.*

Learning how to learn is what prepares accountants for a future that may sometimes seem overwhelming. But, as Marcus Aurelius wrote long ago, "Never let the future disturb you. You will meet it, if you have to, with the same weapons of reason which today arm you against the present." Learning how to learn provides a weapon of reason for the future.

MODULE 2:
MANAGEMENT AS USERS OF ACCOUNTING INFORMATION

PART C: BASIC CONCEPTS OF INTERNAL CONTROL SYSTEMS

Control circumstances, and do not allow them to control you.
       -- Thomas A. Kempis

Management's first task is to set goals--that is, to identify the ends the organization wants to achieve. Then, management is responsible for making plans, specifying strategies the organization will use to achieve the goals. But goals and plans by themselves are unproductive. There needs to be a mechanism to ensure that the plans are carried out as intended and that progress toward goals is regularly reviewed. For business and nonbusiness organizations, this mechanism is the internal control system (or, more generally, the management control system).

Internal control is an elusive concept because it encompasses just about everything management must do to achieve the organization's goals. It's one of those concepts, like love, that's important to understand, but difficult to define. Here, for example, is a typical attempt to define internal control:

> *Internal control is the sum of many diverse procedures instituted by management to insure effective administration of the company: to develop and maintain a functional line of authority among the various departments within the company; to clearly define duties and responsibilities of the various units and activities of the company so that there are no overlapping areas; to develop a system of accounting that provides prompt, complete, and accurate information about the company and its various departments; to set up a system of reporting to line and administrative management based upon accounting and other records; and to set up internal checks for protection against fraud within the company. [From NEW AMERICAN DICTIONARY OF BUSINESS AND FINANCE by Jay M. Shafritz and Daniel Oran. Copyright © 1983, 1990 by Jay M. Shafritz and Daniel Oran. Used by permission of New American Library, a division of Penguin Books USA Inc.]*

When you read this definition you can't help feeling a bit like Alice in Wonderland. One passage in Lewis Carroll's *Through The Looking Glass* perfectly expresses the feeling of bewilderment that one seemingly simple term can mean so much:

> *"When I use a word," Humpty Dumpty said, in a rather scornful tone, "it means just what I choose it to mean--neither more nor less." "The question is," said Alice, "whether you can make words mean so many different things."*

But, internal control does mean many different things. An **internal control system** is a combination of people, equipment, policies and procedures that work together to help ensure that an organization obtains and uses resources efficiently and effectively to accomplish its goals.

Since it's sometimes hard for students with little business experience to imagine an internal control system, we'll start by trying to help you draw a few mental pictures of some of the key steps organizations must take in trying to achieve their goals. To accomplish goals effectively, the internal control system must include steps to:

- ♦ assign responsibility,
- ♦ establish standards,
- ♦ motivate and reward performance,
- ♦ monitor performance, and
- ♦ communicate progress and take corrective action, if needed.

To accomplish goals efficiently, the internal control system must safeguard assets against waste, loss, unauthorized use and misappropriation. Figure I-2-10 (on the next page) summarizes these steps, which are discussed in more detail below.

Once we've described these steps, we'll have come full circle, back to the question of how to define an internal control system. We'll finish this part of the module by talking about a collaborative effort known as "COSO" that has given us a comprehensive definition of internal control and an integrative framework to explain the fundamental components of an internal control system.

ASSIGNING RESPONSIBILITY

The only way to get rid of responsibilities is to discharge them.
-- Walter S. Robertson

No organization expects to achieve all its goals immediately. In fact, most goals are only expected to be attained in the long-run. Long-run goals may be stated in general terms (like "maximize returns to shareholders" or "help find a cure for AIDS") and progress toward those goals may be reviewed over long periods of time. To achieve their long-run goals, organizations establish short-run objectives covering a set period of time (such as a month, a quarter, or a year). Short-run objectives tend to be more specific than long-run goals. Often,

Figure I-2-10

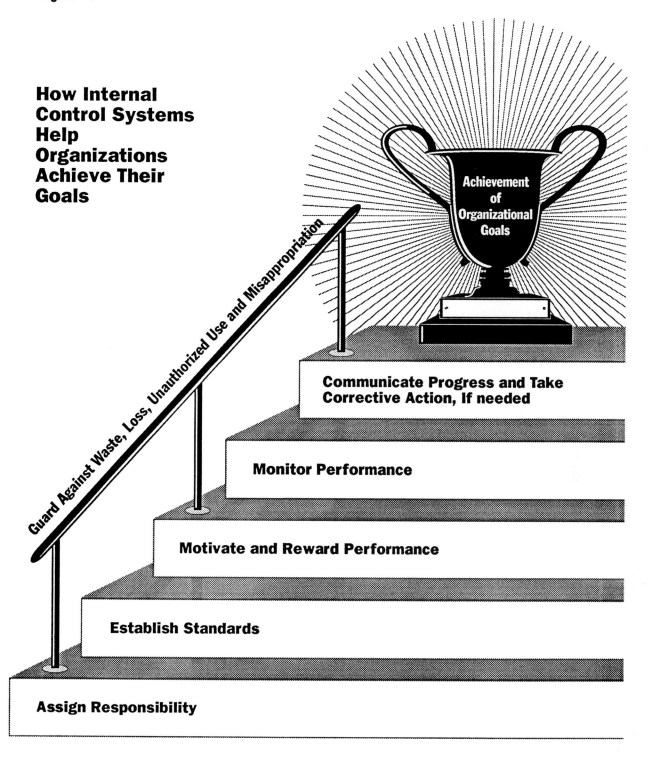

**How Internal
Control Systems
Help
Organizations
Achieve Their
Goals**

Guard Against Waste, Loss, Unauthorized Use and Misappropriation

Achievement
of
Organizational
Goals

**Communicate Progress and Take
Corrective Action, If needed**

Monitor Performance

Motivate and Reward Performance

Establish Standards

Assign Responsibility

they can be stated quantitatively, which means accountants can *measure* how well actual results compare to the objectives.

Some examples might help clarify the relationship between goals and objectives. Suppose a manufacturing firm has a long-run goal of being the leading firm in its industry. To help achieve this long-run goal, the firm may develop short-run objectives related to product design, manufacturing quality, market share, and other factors the firm considers critical to success. A sample objective for the manufacturing firm might be: increase market share in the South by 2% next year. As another example, consider a non-profit university with a goal of being a leader in the education field. To help achieve this goal, the university may have a number of specific short-run objectives dealing with student recruitment, instructional quality, research productivity and community service. An objective for the university could be: increase the average SAT score of the incoming freshmen class by 10 points this year over the previous year.

To help ensure the achievement of organizational objectives, management delegates authority and responsibility for implementing each specific objective to a particular organizational unit (e.g., a department or division) or individual. Assigning responsibility establishes accountability. **Accountability** means the organization can trace its successes and failures to the responsible units or people.

In a sound internal control system, authority and responsibility are matched: one should not be held responsible for something one has no authority over. Also, all organization members must know what is expected of them and what they will be held accountable for. Authority and responsibility can be made clear in several ways, including:

- job descriptions,
- codes of conduct,
- policies and procedures manuals,
- organization charts, and
- the creation of responsibility centers.

Job Descriptions

Figure I-2-11 on the following page shows a job description for an entry-level internal auditor position. **Job descriptions** are formal statements describing the qualifications needed to hold a position, as well as the specific duties, reporting responsibilities, and limits of authority of the position.

Codes of Conduct

Whereas job descriptions define what the organization expects of you when you hold a particular position, codes of conduct establish the standards the organization expects of all employees, regardless of the positions they hold.

Figure I-2-11

Example of a Job Description

University of Southern California

Auditor

Job Code: (14 16) 019022

Department: Audit

---

14 16 1010LO	Conducts or assists in performing various audit assignments or special projects.
14 16 1011LO	Tests, verifies and analyzes data using established audit standards, procedures and techniques.
14 16 1012LO	Reviews transactions, documents, records and operational methods to determine adequacy of control and efficiency of operations.
14 16 1013LO	Conducts preliminary discussions of apparent deficiencies with operating personnel to verify facts and obtain explanations for deficiencies.
14 16 1014LO	Assists in identifying deficiencies and recommends corrective actions to strengthen controls, improve operations and reduce costs.
14 16 1015LO	Makes oral reports and/or prepares formal written reports as requested on the results of assigned audits or special projects.
14 16 1016LO	Maintains effective working relations with operating personnel.
14 16 1018LO	Requires general knowledge of accounting principles and practices and auditing procedures and techniques. Basic knowledge of fund accounting and basic understanding of automated systems and computer capabilities.

Performs other related duties as assigned or requested.

JOB QUALIFICATIONS:

Minimum education:
Bachelor's degree
Equivalent experience in lieu of education

Minimum experience:
2-3 Years
Equivalent education in lieu of experience

Preferred experience:
3-5 Years

Skills, Other:
Analysis; Assessment/evaluation; Conceptualization and design; Communication; Interpretation of policies/analyses/trends/etc.; Interviewing; Knowledge of applicable laws/policies/principles/etc.; Organization; Planning: Problem identification and resolution; Research

Supervises: Level:
May oversee student, temporary and/or casual workers.

SIGNATURES:

Employee: Date:

Supervisor: Date:

The above statements are intended to describe the general nature and level of work being performed. They are not intended to be construed as an exhaustive list of all responsibilities, duties and skills required of personnel so classified.

Codes of conduct (sometimes also called **ethics codes**) delineate organizational values and standards for proper behavior and practices. For example, the code of conduct of BellSouth Corporation sets forth the ethical principles the company stands by, including upholding obligations to customers and shareholders, fair competition when dealing with vendors and suppliers, and nondiscriminatory treatment of employees.

The Importance of Putting Codes of Conduct in Writing. Without a written code of conduct, top management must assume that all employees know what the organization's standards are and understand what steps they are to take if violations occur. These assumptions may be false. Recently, many organizations have come to appreciate that putting a code of conduct in writing makes it more likely that organizational values are clearly communicated to all organization members. For example, KPMG's 1997 *Business Ethics Survey* of Canada's top 1,000 public and private companies found that 66% had a written code of conduct. In the U.S., a 1994 survey found that about 60% of companies had ethics codes.

Moreover, it is important to make sure, even with a written code of conduct, that all organization members are *aware* of the code and understand its importance. Many organizations ask employees to read their code of conduct annually and sign a statement indicating their acceptance of the code. Other companies hold regular ethics awareness training workshops. A story reported in *Management Accounting* illustrates the potential problems that can occur if you assume that policies are known and understood throughout an organization:

> *[A company]...realized it had various components of a written code of conduct and these components should be compiled into one document. The document was completed and reviewed at the top management level. Everyone was very satisfied with it. At the last minute, however, someone suggested that it should be shown to a select group of lower level employees to hear any suggestions that should be considered. They were shocked when these employees said, "Top management must have sent us a code of conduct for some other company, because this is not the way we operate at all!"*

Establishing the "Tone at the Top". Codes of conduct also help communicate the proper **"tone at the top"**--a concern at the highest levels of the organization that ethical standards be maintained. The tone at the top is an important factor in the organization's efforts to maintain a strong internal control system. If organization members do not perceive strong support at the top for ethical behavior, they may view the ethics code as something that need not be taken seriously. Consequently, many organizations devote substantial efforts to establishing the appropriate tone at the top. For instance, a 1992 Conference Board survey found that 1 in 10 companies helps communicate the tone at the top by having an ethics committee of their Board of Directors. Some companies also have ethics officers. For example, BellSouth has a Vice President--Corporate Responsibility and Compliance among its top management group.

Policies and Procedures Manuals

Policies and procedures manuals provide written reference materials to help organization members determine what they should do in given circumstances. **Policies** are *general* rules indicating a course of action that should be taken under particular circumstances. **Procedures** are *more detailed* rules that state how policies will be carried out. In large organizations, there may be multiple policies and procedures manuals as each organizational unit may have a separate manual.

For example, suppose you are a purchasing agent for a large organization. A purchasing agent is responsible for buying whatever materials (such as office supplies or raw materials for a production process) the organization needs. What might you find in the policies and procedures manual for your department?

One thing you might find is your organization's policy concerning the acceptance of gifts from suppliers. For example: May you accept meals or entertainment (like World Series tickets) from a supplier? If so, is there a dollar limit beyond which acceptance would be improper?

Another thing you might find is a description of the normal procedure you should follow in making a purchase. Who is authorized to request that you buy something? Does the request have to be approved by anyone before the order is placed? Do you need to get multiple bids from suppliers before placing an order? What delivery and payment terms are acceptable?

Organization Charts

Organization charts diagram the relationship of units in an organization. Usually, each unit appears in a box, connected to other boxes by lines of authority and responsibility. Additionally, each unit may have its own organization chart showing how each position in the unit relates to the other positions.

Organizational units can be created in many ways. Some organizations may create functional units. For example, a manufacturer might divide its organization into units such as Production, Personnel, Marketing, and Finance. Other organizations may create units according to product lines. For instance, a public accounting firm may create separate units for Auditing and Accounting Services, Tax Services, and Management Consulting Services. Other organizations may create units according to major market segments, such as a computer software company that creates separate organizational units for Business, Government and Education markets. Or, units may be created for particular geographic areas, as might be appropriate for an organization operating in several different countries.

Whatever form an organization takes, the organization chart provides a picture of how the parts interrelate to form a whole. Figure I-2-12 (on the following page) shows an organization chart for the Institute of Management Accountants (IMA), a nonprofit organization that provides educational and other services to its members.

The IMA's organization chart is cast in the traditional form, reflecting the association's hierarchical structure. But as many organizations develop more flexible structures--where managers and employees work together in a variety of interdisciplinary teams, some temporary, others more permanent--new forms of organization charts have been created. For example, Eastman Chemical Co., which uses many cross-functional teams, has an organization chart that looks like a pepperoni pizza--employees even call it the "pizza chart."

Imagine a circular pizza, marked into equal slices, with smaller circles of pepperoni sprinkled all over and one pepperoni dead center. In Eastman Chemical Co.'s organization chart, the President is the center pepperoni. Each of the other pepperoni represents a cross-functional team that may cross over geographic areas or lines of business (or another slice of the pie) in performing its work. The spaces between the pepperoni indicate the area where collaboration needs to take place. Regardless of the form an organization chart takes, the key thing to remember is that it helps each unit see how it fits into the organization.

Creating Responsibility Centers

All organizations, whether business or nonbusiness, exist to produce goods or services. A variety of resources and a sequence of activities goes into producing these goods and services. This linking of resources and activities is sometimes called the **"value chain,"** reflecting the notion that each link in the chain should add something the end-users (such as the customers for a business or the constituency served for a non-profit organization) value.

When an organizational unit is given responsibility for achieving specific objectives, it can be treated as a **"responsibility center"**--that is, it can be held accountable for a specific set of activities and resources (value chain inputs--such as labor costs) or a particular set of results (value chain outputs--such as sales revenues for businesses). Responsibility centers can be classified into 4 groups that vary in their accountability for costs, revenues and investments:

Type of responsibility center	Accountable for		
	Costs	Revenues	Investments
Cost center	✓		
Revenue center		✓	
Profit center	✓	✓	
Investment center	✓	✓	✓

Figure I-2-12

INSTITUTE OF MANAGEMENT ACCOUNTANTS, INC.

Management Organization Chart -- Revised Oct. 1995

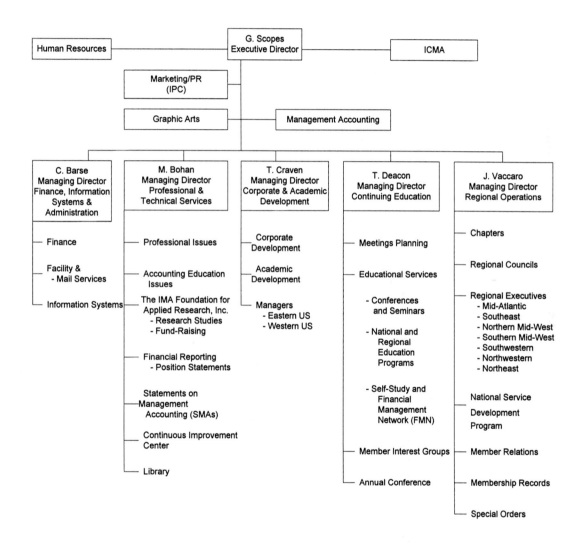

Cost Centers. Cost centers' responsibilities are restricted to certain inputs to the value chain; they are accountable for attaining specific cost control objectives. Staff (advisory) and administrative units--such as the public relations or the legal department of an organization--are often treated as cost centers. Their objective is to provide a certain level of service (at a certain quality) for the minimum possible cost. Units contributing to the general operations of the organization--such as maintenance, EDP (electronic data processing), and security--are also good examples of cost centers. Or, the individual operating departments in a production plant may be treated as cost centers.

Revenue Centers. Revenue centers are responsible for achieving specific outputs, such as revenue targets. Marketing departments, sales departments and fundraising departments (such as the Development office of a university) are examples of organizational units that may be treated as revenue centers.

Profit Centers. Profit centers have responsibilities for both input (expenses or costs) and output (revenue) objectives. Examples of possible profit centers include an individual restaurant in a restaurant chain, or an individual department in a retail department store.

Investment Centers. Investment centers are responsible for making investment decisions, such as the decision to expand to new locations or invest in new equipment, as well as for achieving revenue and expense objectives. They are evaluated based on whether the profits they generate provide an acceptable return on the investments they manage. In many organizations, especially smaller ones, only top management has investment responsibility. However, in large divisionalized organizations, a division may have investment authority. For example, in a large conglomerate (a corporation composed of companies in a variety of businesses), each business may be treated as an investment center.

Once responsibility centers have been established, each center can be evaluated according to how well it carries out its specific role in the organization. Assuming the specific objectives of each responsibility center have been well designed, if each center succeeds in achieving its objectives, the organization's overall goals will be attained.

The Benefits of Accountability

When people know they are responsible for an objective, they know where to put their efforts. When no one "owns" an objective, the objective may go unmet. For example, all organizations want to control costs. But, if responsibility for controlling a specific cost isn't assigned to anyone, excessive costs may be incurred. At one time, Dennison Manufacturing Company felt that its workers' compensation costs (costs of time lost from work due to injuries) were excessive and began a campaign to better control these costs. Part of the campaign included holding managers accountable for controlling workers' compensation costs for employees in their unit. Within 5 years, costs had been reduced by 43%.

ESTABLISHING STANDARDS

In the long run men hit only what they aim at.
-- Henry David Thoreau, Walden

If organizations want to encourage achievement of long-run goals and short-run objectives, it helps to establish standards that allow performance to be measured. For example, to help achieve a long-run goal of maximizing return to shareholders, an organization might develop a short-run objective "to increase sales by 10% over last period." The performance standard related to this objective may set up a range of acceptable performance based on the results management thinks are attainable. For instance, the range could include 10% sales growth as the target, 8% sales growth as the minimum acceptable performance, and 13% or more sales growth as outstanding performance.

Every organization needs some means to communicate standards to its members. Very often, standards are expressed in **budgets**, which are quantified financial plans for a particular time period. For example, a hospital may set monthly budgets for revenues from different types of patient services and for the costs of providing those services. Budgets set standards against which actual performance may be compared; these standards give organization members something to aim at.

In government organizations, budgets take on particular importance as control devices because government budgets take on the force of law. Budgeted costs for government units become absolute maximums, rather than merely performance goals. For example, a state may give a school district a budget authorizing it to spend a certain amount of funds on instructional materials, a certain amount on teaching salaries, and so on. The school district cannot use funds earmarked for one budget purpose (e.g., instructional materials) for another purpose (e.g., salaries)--they *must* keep costs within each of the budget targets.

Budgeted targets for revenues and costs are the most common way of setting performance standards, but they are rarely (if ever) the *only* standards needed. While bringing in enough revenues and controlling costs are almost always critical to the success of an organization, there are also other critical success factors--such as product safety or customer satisfaction--that are not adequately addressed by financial performance standards. While all standards must be *measurable*, not all standards need be expressed in financial terms. Companies that want a "**balanced scorecard**" (a set of performance standards that considers all an organization's key goals and objectives) will need to include some *non-financial* targets among their standards.

Non-financial standards are often useful to set productivity targets (e.g., How many telephone calls should the order desk be able to take in an hour?). Non-financial standards may also be used to set quality targets (e.g., How many defective products are acceptable in a production run of 1,000 units? How many customer complaints are acceptable for each 100 service calls?).

Well-designed internal control systems include a *combination* of financial and non-financial standards. For example, it would not make much sense to set financial targets for revenues without also setting customer complaint targets. A business can harm its reputation--and its chances for long-run success--by aggressively pushing customers to buy too many items that they don't want or like. Similarly, a nonbusiness organization can harm its reputation by using fund-raising tactics that are too aggressive, trading off short-run increased contributions for long-run ill will.

MOTIVATING AND REWARDING PERFORMANCE

A man must love a thing very much if he not only practises it without any hope of fame and money, but even practises it without any hope of doing it well.
-- G. K. Chesterton

Both assigning responsibilities and establishing standards help organizations motivate their members to work toward what the organization wants to achieve. People naturally want to do their jobs well and want to perform up to expectations. But, people also need to feel that the organization supports them in their work and will reward them when their efforts contribute to organizational success. So, strong internal control systems will include measures designed to provide employees with the tools they need to fulfill their responsibilities. Strong internal control systems will also include compensation programs that reward employees for successfully directing their efforts toward organizational goals.

Training and Supervision

Employee training programs are one way that organizations give employees the tools they need to perform their jobs. For example, an organization might offer (or pay for) courses designed to develop management skills. On-the-job training is another means to give employees the tools they need to perform their jobs. New employees may be assigned to work with more experienced employees to help them learn the procedures they need to use on the job. Finally, ongoing supervision contributes to employees' ability to do their jobs well.

Compensation Tied to Performance

Compensation programs can be designed to tie personal goals to organizational goals--the more an organization member does to help the organization meet its goals, the greater the rewards to the member. Most compensation schemes involve monetary rewards, such as salary increases or bonuses, for good performance. Non-monetary compensation, such as merit awards or special recognition, are also possible. For example, a nonprofit association may use special recognition awards to compensate its volunteers for extraordinary efforts. Compensation schemes may also include penalties for failure to meet organizational standards. The penalties might be monetary (such as fines for a baseball player who doesn't show up for a game) or non-monetary (such as the loss of a desirable assignment or a reduction in rank when performance is substandard).

Compensation programs that are explicitly tied to performance standards are known as "**incentive plans**." A Conference Board survey of 2,700 large U.S. companies found that by 1996, incentive plans were used by over 90% of the firms in every major industry sector. Incentive plans can be used at all levels of an organization. Workers on a factory production line can receive extra pay for meeting or exceeding production targets. Sales people can receive commissions on each sale made. Waiters and waitresses can receive tips for good customer service (the word "tip" is an acronym for "to insure promptness"). Top management can receive bonuses for meeting or exceeding profitability goals.

Assigning responsibilities, setting performance standards, and creating incentive compensation plans can be very effective ways to motivate performance. In 1995, Hewitt Associates, a consulting and actuarial firm, released a study of incentive plans comparing 205 companies that used incentive plans with 232 that did not tie compensation to performance. The companies that used incentive plans had significantly higher profitability, better cash flows and stock market performance, and higher productivity. For example, the companies with incentive plans averaged $169,900 of sales per employee compared to an average sales per employee of $126,100 for companies without incentive plans.

On the other hand, poorly designed motivating devices can lead to disastrous consequences. Since compensation tied to performance focuses efforts on the incentives, goals not in the incentive plan may be ignored. For example, merchant banks and brokerages often pay their traders (people who buy and sell stocks for customers) large bonuses based on the volume of their trades. If trading volume is the *only* thing rewarded, the banks and brokerages risk creating "rogue traders"--traders who buy and sell shares on their clients' behalf simply to run up volume or who make very risky trades simply to run up volume. After the 1995 collapse of Barings, a British merchant bank that went bankrupt after a rogue trader caused $1.2 billion of losses, the financial services industry began to take a hard look at incentive schemes. In the U.S., the Securities and Exchange Commission published "best practices" guidelines that suggested at least some part of brokers' rewards should be tied to their record of complying with securities regulations and company internal controls.

Even when money is not involved, poorly designed incentive schemes can cause problems. For example, if an organization places too much emphasis on budgeted targets for revenues and costs and too little emphasis on other standards, managers and employees may resort to "cooking the books"-- manipulating results to make it appear as if targets have been achieved even when they haven't been. In 1994, Woolworth Corp. found it had to restate its 1993 financial results due to inaccurate reporting. An investigation by a special committee of the company's board of directors found that one reason for the problem was that managers perceived a certain pressure to produce short-term results. The special committee's report pointed out that a number of employees felt it was a "tradition" to show a profit each quarter, no matter how small, and noted that top management often urged employees to produce "another good quarter." The short-term pressures and incentives were one reason managers doctored the figures to avoid reporting poor quarterly results.

Care must be taken to create incentives that are congruent with the appropriate organizational goals--to be sure that the organization is asking for the performance it really wants. A key element in creating incentives is choosing the best accounting measure of performance on which rewards will be based. For example, suppose a restaurant wants to create an incentive plan for its waiters and waitresses to help improve profitability. Some menu items, like drinks or desserts, are more profitable than others. In a well-designed plan, bonuses will be attached to selling these particular menu items, rather than to total sales.

MONITORING PERFORMANCE

As soon as the boss decides he wants his workers to do something, he has
two problems: making them do it and monitoring what they do.
-- Robert Krulwich

Bill Bradley, a U.S. Senator from New Jersey from 1979 to 1996, began his career as a professional athlete. Even before his days in the NBA, Bradley was recognized for his basketball prowess as a college player. Reporters marveled at the ease with which he seemed to control a basketball court. When asked what it took to have this control, Bradley responded: "a sense of where you are."

Part of being in control--for organizations as well as basketball players--is having a sense of where you are. Organizations must continually monitor their performance to see how they are doing in relation to their objectives. Thus, performance measurement is an important part of an internal control system. Additionally, organizations will want to monitor the internal control system itself to see if management's policies and procedures are being carried out as intended and if controls are adequate and effective.

Performance Measurement

Accounting information directed towards performance measurement--for example, comparisons of actual performance to budgeted targets--gives organizations a sense of where they are. This information can be created for particular product lines, or particular responsibility centers, or particular regions of the country--or in whatever manner management feels would be useful.

Performance measurement is not a simple task. Consider what happens when an accountant does a **variance analysis**--an examination of the causes of differences (variances) between actual performance and predetermined standards, such as budget targets. First, the accountant must recognize that the implications of variances depend on whether observed differences are **favorable** (performance better than expectations) or **unfavorable** (performance worse than expectations). An example of an unfavorable variance would be actual revenues lower than target, or actual costs higher than target. But actual revenues *exceeding* the target or actual costs *below* the target would create favorable variances.

Second, the accountant must recognize that variances can have multiple causes. For example, suppose a construction company budgeted labor costs for part-time help of $10,000 for a period, calculated as 1,000 hours of labor at $10 an hour, but its actual costs were $12,000. Actual costs could differ from budgeted costs either because the number of labor hours differed from 1,000, or because the cost per hour differed from $10, or both. The accountant needs to isolate the reason(s) for the variance, not just the amount of the difference.

Third, performance measurement must recognize that not all variances are controllable--that is, forces outside the control of the organization may sometimes cause failure to meet targets. For example, unusually bad weather might cause an uncontrollable reduction in revenues for a restaurant. If budget targets were set based on normal weather conditions, performance measurement must be sophisticated enough to take the unusual conditions into consideration.

Operational Auditing

In addition to measuring results, monitoring performance includes observing operations to be sure that management's policies and procedures are being carried out as intended and that controls are adequate and effective. This type of monitoring, which is known as "**operational auditing**," tells management whether the internal control system is working as planned. In cases where the system could be improved, an operational audit provides a means to identify potential problems and suggest improvements.

For example, suppose management has a policy requiring that 3 bids be obtained before materials costing over $1,000 are purchased. The intent of this policy is to control costs by making sure purchases are made at the best available price. Management realizes, however, that having a policy and implementing a policy are different things. An operational audit of the purchasing operations might uncover a problem. For example, the audit could disclose that production departments are regularly requesting materials delivery on an emergency basis, not allowing enough time for bids to be obtained. An occasional emergency is understandable, but regularly recurring emergency purchases indicate that the control system is not working as intended. Unless the system is monitored, management would not know about this potential problem.

Most operational auditing is performed by **internal auditors**--auditors who work exclusively for the organization. For instance, General Motors has several hundred internal auditors world-wide and the U.S. Government has its own internal audit agency, the General Accounting Office (GAO), with over 4,500 auditors. If an organization does not have an internal audit staff, it is possible to hire an external auditor (a member of a public accounting firm that has many different clients) to perform an operational audit.

Independence and Operational Auditing. For operational auditing to be effective, the people conducting the audit need to be free to make impartial judgments about the operations they are reviewing. This freedom, which is termed "**independence**," depends on the auditors' own mental attitude (their personal objectivity) and on their organizational status. An internal auditor, whose paycheck comes exclusively from one organization, is subject to greater threats to independence than an external auditor (who has many clients and reports directly to the board of directors). This makes it all the more important that internal auditors have enough status in their organization to be able to perform their work without interference.

An internal audit staff needs to have the support of--and free access to--the board of directors and top management. The internal audit department should have a place in the organizational hierarchy that protects it, as far as possible, from facing the conflict of interest inherent in having to report on the activities of peers or superiors. This is why many organizations place their internal audit department directly under their CEO or CFO, rather than reporting to their Controller or COO.

The Institute of Internal Auditors' *Standards for the Professional Practice of Internal Auditing* recognize the need for independence as the first standard, noting that independence requires both organizational status and objectivity:

> *100.*   ***INDEPENDENCE** -- Internal auditors should be independent of the activities they audit.*
>
> > *110 **Organizational Status** -- The organizational status of the internal auditing department should be sufficient to permit the accomplishment of its audit responsibilities.*
> >
> > *120 **Objectivity** -- Internal auditors should be objective in performing audits*

The standards also offer more specific guidelines--which may be found in Figure I-2-13 on the following 2 pages--for obtaining and maintaining appropriate organizational status and objectivity. The thoroughness of the standards indicates how important the concept of independence is to auditors. As you read the detailed guidelines, think about how each suggestion helps maintain independence.

Figure I-2-13
Independence Standards for Internal Auditors: Organizational Status and Objectivity

110 *Organizational Status*
The organizational status of the internal auditing department should be sufficient to permit the accomplishment of its audit responsibilities.

.01 Internal auditors should have the support of senior management and of the board so that they can gain the cooperation of auditees and perform their work free from interference.

   .1 The director of the internal auditing department should be responsible to an individual in the organization with sufficient authority to promote independence and to ensure broad audit coverage, adequate consideration of audit reports, and appropriate action on audit recommendations.

   .2 The director should have direct communication with the board. Regular communication with the board helps assure independence and provides a means for the board and the director to keep each other informed on matters of mutual interest.
      a. Direct communication occurs when the director regularly attends and participates in those meetings of the board which relate to its oversight responsibilities for auditing, financial reporting, organizational governance, and control. The director's attendance at these meetings and the presentation of written and/or oral reports provides for an exchange of information concerning the plans and activities of the internal auditing department. The director of internal auditing should meet privately with the board at least annually.

   .3 Independence is enhanced when the board concurs in the appointment or removal of the director of the internal auditing department.

   .4 The purpose, authority and responsibility of the internal auditing department should be defined in a formal written document (charter). The director should seek approval of the charter by senior management as well as acceptance by the board. The charter should (a) establish the department's position within the organization; (b) authorize access to records, personnel, and physical properties relevant to the performance of audits; and © define the scope of internal auditing activities.
      a. The director of internal auditing should periodically assess whether the purpose, authority, and responsibility, as defined in the charter, continue to be adequate to enable the internal auditing department to accomplish its objectives. The result of this periodic assessment should be communicated to senior management and the board.

   .5 The director of internal auditing should submit annually to senior management for approval and to the board for its information a summary of the department's audit work schedule, staffing plan, and financial budget. The director should also submit all significant interim changes for approval and information. Audit work schedules, staffing plans, and financial budgets should inform senior management and the board of the scope of internal auditing work and of any limitations placed on that scope.
      a. The approved audit work schedule, staffing plan, and financial budget, along with all significant interim changes, should contain sufficient information to enable the board to ascertain whether the internal auditing department's objectives and plans support those of the organization and the board. This information should be communicated, preferably in writing.
      b. A scope limitation is a restriction placed upon the internal auditing department that precludes the department from accomplishing its objectives and plans. Among other things, a scope limitation may restrict the:
        -- Scope defined in the charter.
        -- Department's access to records, personnel, and physical properties relevant to the performance of audits.
        -- Approved audit work schedule.
        -- Performance of necessary auditing procedures.
        -- Approved staffing plan and financial budget.
      c. A scope limitation along with its potential effect should be communicated, preferably in writing, to the board.
      d. The director of internal auditing should consider whether it is appropriate to inform the board regarding scope limitations which were previously communicated to and accepted by the board. This may be necessary, particularly when there have been organization, board, senior management, or other changes.

Source: From Standards for the Professional Practice of Internal Auditing, © 1995 by the Institute of Internal Auditors, Inc., 249 Maitland Avenue, Altamonte Springs, FL 32701. Reprinted with permission.

.6 The director of internal auditing should submit activity reports to senior management and to the board annually or more frequently as necessary. Activity reports should highlight significant audit findings and recommendations and should inform senior management and the board of any significant deviations from approved audit work schedules, staffing plans, and financial budgets, and the reasons for them.

a. Activity reports should be communicated, preferably in writing.

b. Significant audit findings are those conditions which, in the judgment of the director of internal auditing, could adversely affect the organization. Significant audit findings may include conditions dealing with irregularities, illegal acts, errors, inefficiency, waste, ineffectiveness, conflicts of interest, and control weaknesses. After reviewing such findings with senior management, the director of internal auditing should communicate significant audit findings to the board, whether or not they have been satisfactorily resolved.

c. Management's responsibility is to make decisions on the appropriate action to be taken regarding significant audit findings. Senior management may decide to assume the risk of not correcting the reported condition because of cost or other considerations. The board should be informed of senior management's decision on all significant audit findings.

d. The director of internal auditing should consider whether it is appropriate to inform the board regarding previously reported, significant audit findings in those instances when senior management and the board assumed the risk of not correcting the reported condition. This may be necessary, particularly when there have been organization, board, senior management, or other changes.

e. The reasons for significant deviations from approved audit work schedules, staffing plans, and financial budgets that may require explanation include:
-- Organization and management changes.
-- Economic conditions.
-- Legal and regulatory requirements.
-- Internal audit staff changes.
-- Management requests.
-- Expansion or reduction of audit scope as determined by the director of internal auditing.

110 Objectivity
Internal auditors should be objective in performing audits.

.01 Objectivity is an independent mental attitude which internal auditors should maintain in performing audits. Internal auditors are not to subordinate their judgment on audit matters to that of others.

.02 Objectivity requires internal auditors to perform audits in such a manner that they have an honest belief in their work product and that no significant quality compromises are made. Internal auditors are not to be placed in situations in which they feel unable to make objective professional judgments.

.1 Staff assignments should be made so that potential and actual conflicts of interest and bias are avoided. The director should periodically obtain from the audit staff information concerning potential conflicts of interest and bias.

.2 Internal auditors should report to the director any situations in which a conflict of interest or bias is present or may reasonably be inferred. The director should then reassign such auditors.

.3 Staff assignments of internal auditors should be rotated periodically whenever it is practicable to do so.

.4 Internal auditors should not assume operating responsibilities. But if on occasion senior management directs internal auditors to perform nonaudit work, it should be understood that they are not functioning as internal auditors. Moreover, objectivity is presumed to be impaired when internal auditors audit any activity for which they had authority or responsibility. This impairment should be considered when reporting audit results.

.5 Persons transferred to or temporarily engaged by the internal auditing department should not be assigned to audit those activities they previously performed until a reasonable period of time has elapsed. Such assignments are presumed to impair objectivity and should be considered when supervising the audit work and reporting audit results.

.6 The results of internal auditing work should be reviewed before the related audit report is released to provide reasonable assurance that the work was performed objectively.

.03 The internal auditor's objectivity is not adversely affected when the auditor recommends standards of control for systems or reviews procedures before they are implemented. Designing, installing, and operating systems are not audit functions. Also, the drafting of procedures for systems is not an audit function. Performing such activities is presumed to impair audit objectivity.

COMMUNICATING PROGRESS AND TAKING CORRECTIVE ACTION, IF NEEDED

The trouble with progress is that it can be progress in any direction.
-- W. A. Ireland

Communication is a vital part of an internal control system. Responsibilities and authority must be communicated to organization members. Performance standards and performance incentives must be communicated. And, finally, progress in achieving organizational objectives must be communicated. The information gleaned from performance measurements (such as budget versus actual comparisons) and operational audits (such as suggestions for improvement) needs to be communicated so it can be acted upon.

A well-designed internal control system includes communication policies and procedures that give adequate attention to:

♦   who should be receiving information (the audience),
♦   what information they should be receiving (the content), and
♦   how the information should be sent (the medium).

The Audience

For information to be valuable to an organization, it needs to come to the attention of the appropriate parties. So, it is important to determine who within an organization needs information about the entity's plans and performance. Suppose, for example, an organization has information comparing actual gasoline expense to budgeted expense for the delivery department. Who needs this information? Some parties who need the information are obvious. The manager of the delivery department, who will be held responsible for the costs, clearly needs to have this information. But, what about the drivers of the delivery trucks? the sales force? the CEO? the board?

The answer to the question "Who should be receiving information?" is simple in theory: whoever needs it to make a decision. The trick comes in anticipating the types of decisions organization members may need to make. For example, if the delivery department is part of a chain of retail stores that have fixed locations where customers come to purchase goods, it is unlikely the sales force would need information on delivery costs. But, suppose the delivery department is part of a wholesaler where the sales force travels to customer sites to solicit orders. In this situation, the sales force might use delivery cost information to help them decide whether to approach a customer in an area where no other customers are located.

The Content

Knowing who needs information is only part of the battle. It's easy to determine, for example, that the CEO needs information on how new products are performing, how each responsibility center is performing, and so on. But, the information system contains an enormous amount of information about these issues. Even if all the information is relevant and reliable, it does not follow that it all should be communicated to the CEO. If it were, the CEO would likely suffer from "**information overload**"--otherwise known as too much of a good thing.

Even lower-level managers can suffer from information overload. Kathleen Mocniak, research and analysis director at Planters Lifesavers Co., once noted to a *Business Week* reporter that marketers frequently find themselves inundated with too much information about product performance. The result, as she put it, is like "trying to get a drink of water from a fire hydrant."

A well-designed system will select the appropriate amount and type of information to communicate to users. To what extent should the information be summarized versus detailed? Can the information be classified into categories (like reporting product sales by region) to help users absorb it quickly? Also, a well-designed system will include procedures that allow users to get additional information, as needed, on a timely basis. If the summarized information raises a question, it should be possible to quickly find an answer. In Frito-Lay's decision support system (described in Part B of this module), managers first receive sales information summarized by broad product categories. If no anomalies are noted, the manager may not need any additional information. But, if potential problems are identified, the manager has the ability to access additional information, such as sales breakdowns by region, or by type of store.

The Medium

In the modern world, communication can take many forms. Information can be communicated in written reports--such as a written internal audit report. Or, information can be communicated personally, as in a conference between the CEO, the CFO and the executive committee of the Board to discuss the quarterly operating results. Or, information can be communicated electronically, as in the Frito-Lay decision support system where the color red on a computer screen is used to communicate a drop in market share.

A well-designed internal control system uses the appropriate medium for each communication. For example, suppose an internal auditor is reviewing the purchasing department. The company's internal control policies require that all purchase requests be authorized by a manager before the item is purchased. The auditor finds multiple examples of purchases being made without the appropriate authorizing signature. Further investigation reveals that each purchase was made for a necessary business purpose. However, the auditor realizes that if the purchasing department makes purchases without appropriate authorization, the company is vulnerable to possible theft from inside the organization. This is a dangerous weakness in the internal control system. A written audit report would be used to convey the seriousness of the matter to the appropriate audience.

Now, suppose instead that the auditor had examined a large sample of purchases and found only a single isolated example of a purchase made without the appropriate authorizing signature. Further investigation revealed that the purchase needed to be made quickly and was authorized by telephone. The auditor feels the telephone authorization should have later been documented in writing, as company policy requires. In this case, the auditor could choose to tell the head of purchasing about the incident in an exit conference (a meeting held at the end of the audit to review the auditor's findings with the auditee), without including a recommendation in the auditor's written report.

Taking Corrective Action, If Needed

Once information about progress and potential problems has been effectively communicated to the appropriate parties, corrective action can be taken, if needed. Discovered weaknesses in the internal control system can be remedied. Good performance can be rewarded, poor performance penalized. Standards can be adjusted if new information indicates a need for change.

In some situations, the appropriate corrective action is to change the organization's plans and objectives. Organizations are not static; the organization's plans and objectives, as well as the control system, evolve over time. Sometimes, the failure to achieve an objective means the objective or plan wasn't reasonable. In this case, information from the control system helps an organization determine how the plans and objectives should be changed. For example, Frito-Lay might learn that its actual sales of a new product are much lower or higher than planned. If further investigation reveals that the difference is due to lower or higher than expected consumer interest in the new product, the sales objectives should be revised to take into account this new information. Plans--such as marketing plans--might also be changed based on the new information.

SAFEGUARDING ASSETS

Protection is not a principle; but an expedient.
-- Benjamin Disraeli

The steps organizations take to achieve internal control--(1) assigning responsibility; (2) establishing standards; (3) motivating and rewarding performance; (4) monitoring performance; and (5) communicating progress and taking corrective action, if needed--help ensure that the organization's goals will be accomplished. But it is not enough just to accomplish goals. It is also important to accomplish the goals efficiently--that is, in the best way possible.

Every organization struggles against inefficiency. For example, for 1995, the Luxembourg-based Court of Auditors estimated that about $11 in every $100 of the European Union Commission's multi-billion dollar budget was lost that year due to inefficient management and fraud. To accomplish goals efficiently, the internal control system must safeguard assets against **waste, loss, unauthorized use and misappropriation** (theft). Waste and loss are usually unintentional; whereas unauthorized use and theft are intentional acts.

Waste and Loss

The *Internal Auditor*, a magazine published by the Institute of Internal Auditors (an international professional association for internal auditors), regularly publishes descriptions of how internal auditors discovered cases of waste and loss in their organizations. Two examples the magazine reported are typical.

In the first example, an internal auditor in India was reviewing controls in the purchasing department. Company policy required that all purchases be shipped to the company in corrugated paper cartons weighing 150 GSM (grams per square meter). The company paid shipping costs based on the 150 GSM weight.

The auditor collected several corrugated paper samples from suppliers and had them tested. No sample met the 150 GSM requirement; they all weighed between 131 and 135 GSM. Further investigation revealed that the company had not experienced any problems with burst cartons. As a result of the audit, the company was able to recover some of their past shipping charges from the suppliers (the difference between the shipping costs of the 150 GSM cartons paid for and the 133 GSM average weight received). Additionally, the company realized that the 150 GSM standard was wasteful and reduced the standard to 133 GSM for future shipments--which resulted in an annual savings of $186,000.

In the second example, an internal auditor for a U.S. city reviewed the city's collection of fees. While the city code provided for collection of penalties on delinquent fees (late payments), the auditor found the penalties had never billed or collected. The uncollected penalties amounted to an average of $300,000 per year. The city was able to recover the lost revenue from $828,000 of past delinquent fees that could still be billed under the law.

Unauthorized Use and Theft

Unauthorized use of assets can occur in many ways--from clerical employees making personal long-distance calls on company telephones to hospital workers making unauthorized use of pharmaceuticals. A 1996 estimate in a study by the Association of Certified Fraud Examiners put the loss from theft, embezzlement and other white collar crime in the U.S. at more than $400 billion annually . A 1997 estimate put the amount of "shrinkage" (inventory that disappears) at U.S. retailers at $27 billion a year. Similar theft problems occur throughout the world. In 1997, for example, the U.K.'s National Audit Office reported to Parliament that £3.5m (one pound then equaled about $1.65) worth of inventory had been lost at an Army warehouse in Germany due to "staff shortages."

Policies and Procedures to Safeguard Assets

Many internal control policies and procedures are designed to safeguard assets, including:

- ♦ limiting physical access to assets,
- ♦ separation of duties,
- ♦ mandatory vacations and bonding,
- ♦ numbering and controlling documents, and
- ♦ independent checks of accounting records.

Limiting Physical Access to Assets. Locks on doors to storerooms, combination safes for storing cash and valuable documents, and security guards at building entrances are examples of control procedures which limit physical access to assets to authorized personnel. Computer passwords are another example of a control that limits physical access: only personnel who know the password can gain entry to restricted software or databanks.

Even simple limitations on access to assets can sometimes have dramatic effects. For example, during 1992, the University of Southern California bookstore changed its internal control policies and procedures in response to continuing annual losses of between $750,000 and $1,000,000 from bookstore thefts. Beginning with the Fall 1992 semester, a secure area for shoppers to check their belongings was opened and a new policy requiring all bags to be checked was instituted. At the end of the semester, the bookstore director reported that sales of textbooks--the most often stolen merchandise--increased significantly as theft losses went down.

Separation of Duties. Access to assets can be indirect--through the preparation or processing of documents--as well as direct. Strong internal control systems limit indirect access to assets, as well as direct access.

For example, suppose an employee of a small retail store has two responsibilities: (1) issuing credit memoranda (pieces of paper that say the store owes the customer money) to customers who return goods, and (2) keeping the accounting records. Even if this employee has no physical access to the cash or returned goods, the employee could steal from the firm by issuing false credit memoranda to friends or cohorts for merchandise that was never returned. This person, who can "steal and conceal", is said to have 2 "**incompatible functions**."

As far as possible, responsibilities should be assigned so that no person has incompatible functions. This principle is called **separation (or segregation) of duties**. Operating and system design responsibilities are incompatible with recordkeeping responsibilities. Therefore, the person who designs the computer system for an organization should not be allowed to input accounting data or run the accounting software. Similarly, physical custody of assets is incompatible with recordkeeping responsibilities. Thus, the person who receives cash payments from customers in the mail should not also keep the bank account records. Also, physical custody of assets is incompatible with authorizing responsibility. So, the person who authorizes shipments of goods to customers should not also be responsible for inventory storage.

Mandatory Vacations and Bonding. People who have access to cash or custody of other assets (like inventory) are in a position to steal from the organization. To reduce the chance of theft, organizations should establish a policy of mandatory vacations. This policy discourages employees from stealing as someone may discover the misappropriation when the employee is on vacation. The Los Angeles Dodgers once learned about this control the hard way. The manager who handled the payroll for stadium employees was so "diligent" that he never took a vacation and never took a sick day. When a major illness finally caused the manager to miss a few days of work, the Dodgers discovered that he had been putting fictitious employees on the payroll for years and pocketing the money. Additionally, to protect the organization against loss, **fidelity bonds**--insurance policies that reimburse the company for theft losses--may be carried on employees who have access to cash.

Numbering and Controlling Documents. Documents used to process economic transactions (like sales order slips, purchase orders, and checks used to disburse cash) should be numbered, and the numerical sequence of the documents should be periodically accounted for to make sure no documents are missing. Without numerically controlled cash sales receipts, a cashier could pocket the cash and the receipt from a sale without the company knowing that anything was missing. But, if a numerically-controlled cash sales receipt is used, the company can determine when something is amiss. The clerk could not pocket the receipt without leaving a gap in the numerical sequence of the sales receipts. The gap would be a "red flag" (a warning) that something was missing. If the clerk tried to pocket the cash without pocketing the receipt as well, then the theft could be discovered by comparing the total of the sales receipts to the total cash on hand.

Independent Checks of Accounting Records. Accounting records indicate the amount of assets--such as cash, inventory, securities held as investments, and so on--on hand. Periodically, these records should be compared with the actual assets to make sure that: (1) all recorded assets exist, and (2) all existing assets have been recorded. Thus, periodically, internal (or external) auditors will count the cash (or inventory or securities) on hand and compare their counts to the recorded amounts. When possible, the recorded amounts should be checked against independent (outside-party) records. For example, the recorded checking account balance should be periodically reconciled to the bank statement for the account.

These and many other internal control policies and procedures help protect assets against waste, loss, unauthorized use, and misappropriation.

THE IMPORTANCE OF INTERNAL CONTROL SYSTEMS

*Those who are too lazy and comfortable to think for themselves and be
their own judges obey the laws. Others sense their own laws within them.*
-- Hermann Hesse

Obviously, it makes good sense for management to design and implement an effective internal control system. In addition to being good business sense, internal control systems are also required by law for U.S. public companies and for the federal government.

Laws Concerning Internal Controls for U.S. Public Companies

In 1977, federal securities laws were amended (as part of the **Foreign Corrupt Practices Act**) to require that all publicly-held U. S. companies maintain adequate records and an appropriate system of internal accounting control. The law decrees that the control system must be adequate to provide reasonable assurance about 4 things:

♦ **Proper authorization**. All transactions must be either specifically or generally authorized by management. An example of general authorization is a price list which authorizes salespeople to sell goods to customers at a particular price.

♦ **Complete and accurate recording**. All transactions must be recorded as needed to permit preparation of financial statements and preserve accountability for assets.

♦ **Limited access**. Access to assets must be limited to authorized parties.

♦ **Periodic checks**. There must be periodic checks comparing recorded assets to existing assets, with appropriate follow-up actions, if needed. For example, periodic physical counts of inventory should be made and the counts should be compared to the quantity of inventory recorded on the books. Differences between physical counts and recorded counts may indicate errors or theft.

The judiciary has also urged that steps be taken to deter white-collar crime. The U.S. Sentencing Commission, an independent agent of the judiciary, recommends stiff penalties for corporations when their employees commit white-collar crimes. For example, under the sentencing guidelines, if an employee commits a $1 million fraud without senior management involvement, the company could be fined from $1 million to $2 million. The penalties can be substantially reduced (to between $50,000 and $200,000 in our example) if a corporation cooperates with federal investigators and can show there was a control system in place to help deter crime.

Laws Concerning Internal Controls for U.S. Federal Government

Federal law also emphasizes the importance of a sound internal control system for the government. The **Federal Managers' Financial Integrity Act** of 1982 requires each executive agency of the government to establish an appropriate internal control system. The law provides that government internal control systems must be adequate to provide reasonable assurance about 3 things:

- ◆ **Compliance with laws**. Any obligations incurred or costs expended by a government agency must comply with applicable laws.

- ◆ **Safeguarding of assets**. All assets must be safeguarded against waste, loss, unauthorized use or misappropriation.

- ◆ **Complete and accurate recording**. All expenditures and revenues must be recorded to permit preparation of financial and statistical reports and preserve accountability.

The Federal Managers' Financial Integrity Act also requires an annual evaluation of every agency's internal control system, with the results reported to the President and Congress.

In addition, the **Chief Financial Officers Act of 1990** included several provisions designed to improve government management and control systems. The CFO Act:

- ◆ created the position of federal CFO, a controller (appointed by the President) to head the Office of Federal Financial Management within the Office of Management and Budget (OMB);

- ◆ requires the OMB Director to prepare, implement and update annually a government-wide 5-year financial plan;

- ◆ requires that major federal departments and agencies have a CFO and a deputy CFO; and

- ◆ requires certain federal agencies to develop and issue audited financial statements.

Two other federal laws extended these efforts to improve government management and control systems. In 1993, the **Government Performance and Results Act** required government agencies to develop strategic plans and measure and report their performance against these goals. A year later, the **Federal Financial Management Act of 1994** extended the audit requirements of the Chief Financial Officers Act of 1990 to a larger number of agencies and also required that there be an audited government-wide financial statement starting with fiscal year 1997.

As you can see from the dates these laws were enacted, it was only relatively recently that the federal government turned its attention to improving internal controls. Unfortunately, there are long-standing significant internal control problems that are yet to be taken care of in many areas of government. In 1995 testimony before Congress, the Comptroller General of the United States bemoaned the fact that the federal government runs the world's largest financial operation without adequate controls and without reliable information for decision-making:

> *[W]idespread weaknesses in financial systems are crippling our government's ability to monitor and manage its $1.3 trillion in annual revenue, $1.5 trillion in net outlays, and over a trillion dollars of assets....The shortcomings of poor financial accountability are alarming. Our audits have identified hundreds of billions of dollars in accounting mistakes and omissions that render information provided to managers and the Congress virtually useless. More often than not, the information needed to measure agency performance and costs is either unavailable or unreliable.*

The need to improve government internal control systems and information systems is well-recognized; some even view the problems as having reached crisis proportions. As an example of the problems, consider some errors uncovered by an audit of the National Park Service, as described in 1995 congressional testimony by the deputy inspector general of the Interior Department:

> *Examples of inaccurate data...were a vacuum cleaner worth $150 that was listed at over $800,000, a dishwasher worth $350 that was listed at over $700,000, a fire truck worth $133,000 that was listed at 1 cent and a mobile radio worth $793 that was listed at over $79 million.*

As Congress struggles to reduce the government's deficit, many difficult decisions about program cuts and taxes will need to be made. Without adequate internal controls and reliable information, this task becomes even more difficult.

The Concept of "Reasonable Assurance"

Both the Foreign Corrupt Practices Act and the Federal Managers' Financial Integrity Act use the words "reasonable assurance" to describe the degree of comfort an internal control system should provide. The concept of "**reasonable assurance**," which is also found in the accounting and auditing literature, recognizes that no internal control system--no matter how well-designed--can provide *absolute* assurance that all its goals will be achieved. There will always be inherent limitations to an internal control system. Two key limitations are the human factor and the cost-benefit tradeoff.

The Human Factor

People play a large part in internal control systems--and people are rarely perfect. Even in a well-designed internal control system, occasional mistakes will occur. People can get tired, or distracted, or make errors in judgment. Moreover, even with adequate separation of duties, the possibility always exists that people can collude (join forces) to circumvent a system. Or, at a high enough level of management, people can override the system.

The Cost-Benefit Tradeoff

In the design of any system, there is a cost-benefit tradeoff which must be recognized. At some point, it costs more to improve an internal control system then can be justified by the additional benefits which result. For example, most internal audit reviews look at only a sample of the transactions processed in an area. Why don't they audit every transaction? One reason is that the costs of a 100% examination would likely exceed the potential savings from audit findings. Another reason is that audit findings lose value unless they are timely--a 100% audit could take longer to complete than is reasonable.

These inherent limitations cannot be avoided. Thus, some occasional failings should be expected in any internal control system. However, in a good internal control system these failings will be occasional, rather than regular. Moreover, the system will include monitoring to detect failings (like internal audit reviews) and detected failings will be promptly corrected.

THE BIG PICTURE: AN INTEGRATED FRAMEWORK FOR INTERNAL CONTROL

> *"The question is," said Alice, "whether you <u>can</u> make words mean so many different things." "The question is," said Humpty Dumpty, "which is to be master--that's all."*
> -- Lewis Carroll, <u>Alice's Adventures in Wonderland</u>

Now that you have mental pictures of some of the steps organizations take in setting up an internal control system, let's return to the question we began with: How do you define internal control? In 1992, a report published by a coalition of 5 professional associations--the Committee of Sponsoring Organizations (COSO)--provided a new answer to this question. The COSO members included the American Institute of CPAs, the Institute of Internal Auditors, the Financial Executives Institute, the Institute of Management Accountants, and the American Accounting Association.

The COSO answer was based on a landmark 3-year study, which included, among other things, seeking the input of chief executives, board members, legislators, regulators, lawyers, and accountants to try and come up with a framework that would integrate all the various things people meant when they said "internal control." The COSO framework is fast becoming the new standard by which organizations can assess their internal control systems.

A New Definition of Internal Control

The COSO report, formally titled "Internal Control--Integrated Framework" offers the following definition:

Internal control is broadly defined as a process, effected by an entity's board of directors, management and other personnel, designed to provide reasonable assurance regarding the achievement of objectives in each of the following categories:

- *Effectiveness and efficiency of operations.*

- *Reliability of financial reporting.*

- *Compliance with applicable laws and regulations.*

The definition has a broad focus on achieving objectives, but also specifies 3 categories of objectives--(1) operational efficiency and effectiveness, (2) financial report reliability, and (3) legal and regulatory compliance--to help clarify the broad definition. Other key elements of the definition are that internal control is a process--a means to an end, not the end itself--and that it is brought to life by the organization's people--the board, management and other personnel. The definition also recognizes that any internal control system has limits and can provide only reasonable, not absolute, assurance.

The COSO report (as it is commonly called) goes on to define 5 interrelated components that are essential to an internal control system:

- the control environment,
- risk assessment,
- control activities,
- information and communication, and
- monitoring.

In the sections below, we'll take a brief look at each of these components. As you read the COSO report's explanations of the 5 components, think about how well they describe the different steps organizations take to achieve their objectives.

The Control Environment

The first component is the **control environment**, from the "tone at the top" to the integrity and ethical values of each individual in the organization:

- ***Control Environment**--The control environment sets the tone of an organization, influencing the control consciousness of its people. It is the foundation for all other components of internal control, providing discipline and structure. Control environment factors include the integrity,* *ethical values and competence of the entity's people; management's philosophy and operating style; the way management assigns authority and responsibility, and organizes and develops its people; and the attention and direction provided by the board of directors.*

The people of an organization are what makes an internal control system work or fail. A weak or negative control environment--for example, a control system that isn't well supported by top management or one that relies excessively on penalties, rather than rewards--increases the chance that the control system will break down.

Risk Assessment

The second component is **risk assessment**, the notion that an organization must always be aware of the risks it faces and must consciously plan how to deal with these risks:

> ■ *Risk Assessment--Every entity faces a variety of risks from external and internal sources that must be assessed. A precondition to risk assessment is establishment of objectives, linked at different levels and internally consistent. Risk assessment is the identification and analysis of relevant risks to achievement of the objectives, forming a basis for determining how the risks should be managed. Because economic, industry, regulatory and operating conditions will continue to change, mechanisms are needed to identify and deal with the special risks associated with change.*

One of the keys to a strong internal control system is establishing ways to identify and manage risk. This aspect of internal control is particularly important in times of significant change. One of the greatest threats to achievement of organizational objectives is the inability to manage change--that is, failure to identify and react to environmental and technological changes that will affect the organization and *should* affect the control system.

Control Activities

The third component is **control activities**, all the policies and procedures that are the nuts and bolts of the control system:

> ■ *Control Activities--Control activities are the policies and procedures that help ensure management directives are carried out. They help ensure that necessary actions are taken to address risks to achievement of the entity's objectives. Control activities occur throughout the organization, at all levels and in all functions. They include a range of activities as diverse as approvals, authorizations, verifications, reconciliations, reviews of operating performance, security of assets and segregation of duties.*

This component should be the rational result of thinking through what it will take to meet organizational objectives, given the risks faced. For example, when the University of Southern California bookstore considered its objective of minimizing costs and the related risk of theft of its merchandise, policies and procedures about checking students' bags at the door were the result. Failure to link control activities to objectives and risks increases the chance of an internal control system breakdown.

Information and Communication

The fourth component is **information and communication**, an integral part of every internal control system:

> ■ *Information and Communication--Pertinent information must be identified, captured and communicated in a form and timeframe that enables people to carry out their responsibilities. Information systems produce reports, containing operational, financial and compliance-related information, that make it possible to run and control the business. They deal not only with internally-generated data, but also information about external events, activities and conditions necessary to informed business decision-making and external reporting. Effective communication also must occur in a broader sense, flowing down, across and up the organization. All personnel must receive a clear message from top management that control responsibilities must be taken seriously. They must understand their own role in the internal control system, as well as how individual activities relate to the work of others. They must have a means of communicating significant information upstream. There also needs to be effective communication with external parties, such as customers, suppliers, regulators and shareholders.*

As is obvious from this component, the five components are interrelated, not sequential. Information and communication are needed throughout the internal control process. Poor communications--that is, not letting organization members know what is expected of them or how they are doing--decreases an organization's chances of attaining its objectives.

Monitoring

The fifth component of internal control is **monitoring**, obtaining and maintaining a "sense of where you are:"

> ■ *Monitoring--Internal control systems need to be monitored--a process that assesses the quality of the system's performance over time. This is accomplished through ongoing monitoring activities, separate evaluations or a combination of the two. Ongoing monitoring occurs in the course of operations. It includes regular management and supervisory activities, and other actions personnel take in performing their duties. The scope and*

frequency of separate evaluations will depend primarily on an assessment of risks and the effectiveness of ongoing monitoring procedures. Internal control deficiencies should be reported upstream, with serious matters reported to top management and the board.

Monitoring is essential because sound internal control systems are dynamic. Monitoring helps determine what modifications to the system are needed as conditions change.

How The Pieces Fit Together

As you can see, the COSO report offers a comprehensive definition of internal control that covers a lot of ground. In addition, the complete report--which consists of 4 volumes--provides a detailed discussion of the framework, a set of evaluation tools that companies can use in assessing their own internal control systems, and guidance to organizations that want to publicly issue reports on internal control.

How do the pieces of the COSO view of internal control--the 3 objectives, the 5 components, and all the detailed policies and procedures established for different organizational activities or units--fit together? The COSO report suggests a good model to consider how the objectives and components interrelate across the various activities and units of an organization. Their model, which may be seen in Figure I-2-14 on the following page, looks much like a Rubic's cube puzzle--a puzzle that fascinates many with its endless combinations.

The point of the model is clear: internal control is relevant to all parts of the organization and its activities. Moreover, as the entire organization strives to meet the 3 objectives--effectiveness and efficiency of operations, reliability of financial reporting, and compliance with applicable laws and regulations--each of the components will come into play.

Like the Rubic's cube in Figure I-2-14, we've looked at internal control from a variety of perspectives, but come finally back to a simple picture. An internal control system is a system of people, equipment, policies and procedures that work together to help ensure that an organization obtains and uses resources efficiently and effectively to accomplish its goals.

Figure I-2-14

Relationship of Objectives and Components

There is a direct relationship between objectives, which are what an entity strives to achieve, and components, which represent what is needed to achieve the objectives.

Internal control is relevant to an entire enterprise, or to any of its units or activities.

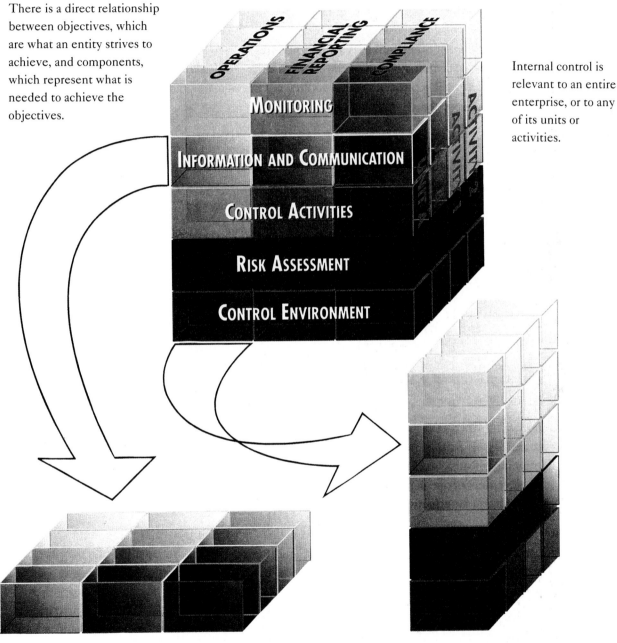

Information is needed for all three objectives categories — to effectively manage business operations, prepare financial statements reliably and determine compliance.

All five components are applicable and important to achievement of operations objectives.

APPENDIX - PREPARING ORAL PRESENTATIONS

The ability to present your thoughts and ideas orally is an essential career skill. Consequently, while you are in college, you should seek out opportunities to hone your oral presentation skills.

How should you prepare for an oral presentation? Below, you will find some advice adapted from The Art of Communicating, developed by Shirley Orechwa Maxey as part of the California Society of Certified Public Accountants' LEADERSHIP Curriculum--a continuing education program designed for professionals as they advance into leadership roles. © 1989, California Society of Certified Public Accountants Education Division.

EIGHT STEPS TO EFFECTIVE ORAL PRESENTATIONS

by
Shirley Orechwa Maxey

1. Analyze the Audience and the Situation.

Even a good presentation can go wrong if it's delivered to the wrong audience. Begin preparing a presentation by determining who will hear it. If you aren't sure who will attend the meeting, ask several people for an "audience profile." If you can identify the members of the audience, analyze them by reviewing their:

- Occupations
- Education
- Positions
- Convictions
- Loyalties
- Experience
- Expertise
- Expectations

Gear the content, organization and delivery of your presentation to the expected audience. Audience analysis also helps you evaluate the situation surrounding your presentation.

2. Determine the Purpose of the Presentation.

To streamline your presentation and increase its effectiveness, determine what you want the audience members to do based on your presentation. If your primary purpose is to inform, be able to state what you want them to know after listening to you. If your primary purpose is to motivate, be able to state what action you want them to take after listening to you.

3. Isolate the Main Idea of the Presentation.

In 1 to 3 sentences, summarize the message you want to leave with your audience. This "main idea" should encapsule the content, tone, and purpose of your presentation.

4. Identify the Key Topics that Relate to the Main Idea and Combine Them to Form the Body of Your Presentation.

Whether a presentation is short or long, you should be able to organize the body into two, three, or four key topics. These key topics should tie directly to the main idea, and they should be somehow related to each other. If the links are not obvious, you should explain their relationships as you unfold the presentation.

5. Develop Facts, Arguments, Support, and Examples to Sell Your Ideas and Make the Presentation Concrete to Listeners.

If an audience is going to tune you out, it usually occurs during the middle of the presentation. To keep their interest and to drive home your point, you need to use colorful detail to support each of the key topics. This support can come in the form of statistics, stories, analogies, expert testimony, and examples.

6. Plan and Create Visual Aids to Strengthen Your Presentation.

Depending on the size of the audience, the room, and the desired effect, you can increase your presentation effectiveness by using flipcharts, transparencies, charts, slides, video films, computer displays, or props. The more complex the visual aid, the earlier you should begin planning and preparing it.

7. Rehearse Until You Are Comfortable With the Content and Organization of the Presentation.

Using an outline or note card, practice your presentation until you are comfortable with the topics you are covering and the organization of the material.

Do not memorize the presentation word for word. Do not think you can "wing it."
Each time you practice the entire presentation, run through the beginning three
times and the closing twice. Those two sections are what the audience will
remember most clearly.

8. Practice Effective Delivery Techniques.

What's inside the package should be more important than the package itself. The
content of your message should matter more to the audience than your delivery
style. But because humans are so visually oriented, the delivery skills of a
speaker are highly noticeable. Once you are comfortable with the content and
organization of a presentation, concentrate your efforts on effective delivery
techniques. Delivery techniques involve these related issues:

> ◆ Posture, stance, and movement
> ◆ Hands and arm gestures
> ◆ Facial expression
> ◆ Eye contact
> ◆ Voice inflection, rate, volume, and quality
> ◆ Filler words and noises
> ◆ Energy

Excellent presenters are those who combine significant content, clear
organization, and enthusiastic delivery into a single package of effective
communication.

ASSIGNMENTS FOR MODULE 2 - PART A

ASSIGNMENT I-2A-1: <u>Organizational Goals</u>: When Goals Conflict

<u>SETTING</u>

You head the accounting group for a division of a large manufacturing business. Your company has a written mission statement that expresses its goals. The primary goal of your company, as for all businesses, is "to earn a profit for shareholders." Additionally, one of the stated goals is "to treat all suppliers, customers and employees fairly and honestly."

You are faced with a dilemma related to these two goals. Because of your position, you are aware that a marketing person, who is one of the sales leaders of the division, is submitting very high expense reports for reimbursement. You are concerned because the total expenses seem excessive and there are indications that the marketer may be claiming personal (non-business) expenditures on his expense reports.

The president has been approving all the requested expense report reimbursements, even when the expenses seem very high.

You feel you have a decision to make: should you tell the board of directors about your concerns? Since the audit committee of the board (a committee that provides a liaison between the board and the external and internal auditors and accountants) has invited you to its next regular meeting, you will have an opportunity to bring the matter up should you decide to do so.

You have sought the advice of a colleague on this matter; he advises you to do nothing as long as sales are going well and the president is approving the reimbursements.

<u>ASSIGNMENT</u>

Rethink your dilemma: Should you tell the board about your concerns?

<u>HINTS</u>

Your dilemma is an ethical question. Don't expect the answer to be easy. As Nobel prize-winning economist Herbert Simon once said: "Ethical questions are the ones where your left side says one thing and your right side says another."

The Institute of Management Accountants, a professional organization for management accountants, has a set of *Standards of Ethical Conduct for Management Accountants* which appears on the following page. Reading these standards will help you understand the professional responsibilities of management accountants and provide a framework for your decision process.

Don't jump immediately to an answer to the question. Think about it first. Answer the following questions to help you think through your position:

What are the important facts?

Who are the "stakeholders"--the people who are affected by your decision? One stakeholder is the marketer. Another is you. Is anyone else affected besides you and the marketer?

Think about this as broadly as you can--who could be helped or hurt by this situation? by your decision?

What are your alternatives? One alternative is to do nothing. Another alternative is to tell the board about your concerns. Are there other alternatives? Generate as many alternatives as you can before you go on to the next step.

What are the pros and cons of each alternative? How will each alternative affect the stakeholders? This is the toughest part because for most ethical questions every alternative will have pros and cons. If you need some help thinking about possible pros and cons, read the short article on the following pages, "Thinking Ethically."

Now try to answer the ultimate question: What should you do?

Standards of Ethical Conduct for Management Accountants

Management accountants have an obligation to the organizations they serve, their profession, the public, and themselves to maintain the highest standards of ethical conduct. In recognition of this obligation, the Institute of Management Accountants has promulgated the following standards of ethical conduct for management accountants. Adherence to these standards is integral to achieving the *Objectives of Management Accounting.*[1] Management accountants shall not commit acts contrary to these standards nor shall they condone the commission of such acts by others within their organizations.

COMPETENCE

Management accountants have a responsibility to:

- Maintain an appropriate level of professional competence by ongoing development of their knowledge and skills.
- Perform their professional duties in accordance with relevant laws, regulations, and technical standards.
- Prepare complete and clear reports and recommendations after appropriate analyses of relevant and reliable information.

CONFIDENTIALITY

Management accountants have a responsibility to:

- Refrain from disclosing confidential information acquired in the course of their work except when authorized, unless legally obligated to do so.
- Inform subordinates as appropriate regarding the confidentiality of information acquired in the course of their work and monitor their activities to assure the maintenance of that confidentiality.
- Refrain from using or appearing to use confidential information acquired in the course of their work for unethical or illegal advantage either personally or through third parties.

INTEGRITY

Management accountants have a responsibility to:

- Avoid actual or apparent conflicts of interest and advise all appropriate parties of any potential conflict.
- Refrain from engaging in any activity that would prejudice their ability to carry out their duties ethically.
- Refuse any gift, favor, or hospitality that would influence or would appear to influence their actions.
- Refrain from either actively or passively subverting the attainment of the organization's legitimate and ethical objectives.

[1] Institute of Management Accountants, *Statements on Management Accounting: Objectives of Management Accounting,* Statement No. 1B, New York, NY, June 17, 1982.

- Recognize and communicate professional limitations or other constraints that would preclude responsible judgment or successful performance of an activity.
- Communicate unfavorable as well as favorable information and professional judgments or opinions.
- Refrain from engaging in or supporting any activity that would discredit the profession.

OBJECTIVITY

Management accountants have a responsibility to:

- Communicate information fairly and objectively.
- Disclose fully all relevant information that could reasonably be expected to influence an intended user's understanding of the reports, comments, and recommendations presented.

RESOLUTION OF ETHICAL CONFLICT

In applying the standards of ethical conduct, management accountants may encounter problems in identifying unethical behavior or in resolving an ethical conflict. When faced with significant ethical issues, management accountants should follow the established policies of the organization bearing on the resolution of such conflict. If these policies do not resolve the ethical conflict, management accountants should consider the following course of action:

- Discuss such problems with the immediate superior except when it appears that the superior is involved, in which case the problem should be presented initially to the next higher managerial level. If satisfactory resolution cannot be achieved when the problem is initially presented, submit the issues to the next higher managerial level.

    If the immediate superior is the chief executive officer, or equivalent, the acceptable reviewing authority may be a group such as the audit committee, executive committee, board of directors, board of trustees, or owners. Contact with levels above the immediate superior should be initiated only with the superior's knowledge, assuming the superior is not involved.
- Clarify relevant concepts by confidential discussion with an objective advisor to obtain an understanding of possible courses of action.
- If the ethical conflict still exists after exhausting all levels of internal review, the management accountant may have no other recourse on significant matters than to resign from the organization and to submit an information memorandum to an appropriate representative of the organization.

Except where legally prescribed, communication of such problems to authorities or individuals not employed or engaged by the organization is not considered appropriate.■

Thinking Ethically:
A Framework for Moral Decision Making

Developed by Manuel Velasquez, Claire Andre,
Thomas Shanks, S.J., and Michael J. Meyer

Moral issues greet us each morning in the newspaper, confront us in the memos on our desks, nag us from our children's soccer fields, and bid us good night on the evening news. We are bombarded daily with questions about the justice of our foreign policy, the morality of medical technologies that can prolong our lives, the rights of the homeless, the fairness of our children's teachers to the diverse students in their classrooms.

Dealing with these moral issues is often perplexing. How, exactly, should we think through an ethical issue? What questions should we ask? What factors should we consider?

The first step in analyzing moral issues is obvious but not always easy: Get the facts. Some moral issues create controversies simply because we do not bother to check the facts. This first step, although obvious, is also among the most important and the most frequently overlooked.

But having the facts is not enough. Facts by themselves only tell us what *is*; they do not tell us what *ought* to be. In addition to getting the facts, resolving an ethical issue also requires an appeal to values. Philosophers have developed five different approaches to values to deal with moral issues.

The Utilitarian Approach

Utilitarianism was conceived in the 19th century by Jeremy Bentham and John Stuart Mill to help legislators determine which laws were morally best. Both Bentham and Mill suggested that ethical actions are those that provide the greatest balance of good over evil.

To analyze an issue using the utilitarian approach, we first identify the various courses of action available to us. Second, we ask who will be affected by each action and what benefits or harms will be derived from each. And third, we choose the action that will produce the greatest benefits and the least harm. The ethical action is the one that provides the greatest good for the greatest number.

The Rights Approach

The second important approach to ethics has its roots in the philosophy of the 18th-century thinker Immanuel Kant and others like him, who focused on the individual's right to choose for herself or himself. According to these philosophers, what makes human beings different from mere things is that people have dignity based on their ability to choose freely what they will do with their lives, and they have a fundamental moral right to have these choices respected. People are not objects to be manipulated; it is a violation of human dignity to use people in ways they do not freely choose.

Of course, many different, but related, rights exist besides this basic one. These other rights (an incomplete list below) can be thought of as different aspects of the basic right to be treated as we choose.

- *The right to the truth:* We have a right to be told the truth and to be informed about matters that significantly affect our choices.
- *The right of privacy:* We have the right to do, believe, and say whatever we choose in our personal lives so long as we do not violate the rights of others.
- *The right not to be injured:* We have the right not to be harmed or injured unless we freely and knowingly do something to deserve punishment or we freely and knowingly choose to risk such injuries.
- *The right to what is agreed:* We have a right to what has been promised by those with whom we have freely entered into a contract or agreement.

In deciding whether an action is moral or immoral using this second approach, then, we must ask, Does the action respect the moral rights of everyone? Actions are wrong to the extent that they violate the rights of individuals; the more serious the violation, the more wrongful the action.

The Fairness or Justice Approach

The fairness or justice approach to ethics has its roots in the teachings of the ancient Greek philosopher Aristotle, who said that "equals should be treated equally and unequals unequally." The basic moral question in this approach is: How fair is an action? Does it treat everyone in the same way, or does it show favoritism and discrimination?

Favoritism gives benefits to some people without a justifiable reason for singling them out; discrimination imposes burdens on people who are no different from those on whom burdens are not imposed. Both favoritism and discrimination are unjust and wrong.

The Common-Good Approach

This approach to ethics assumes a society comprising individuals whose own good is inextricably linked to the good of the community. Community members are bound by the pursuit of common values and goals.

The common good is a notion that originated more than 2,000 years ago in the writings of Plato, Aristotle, and Cicero. More recently, contemporary ethicist John Rawls defined the common good as "certain general conditions that are...equally to everyone's advantage."

In this approach, we focus on ensuring that the social policies, social systems, institutions, and environments on which we depend are beneficial to all. Examples of goods common to all include affordable health care, effective public safety, peace among nations, a just legal system, and an unpolluted environment.

Appeals to the common good urge us to view ourselves as members of the same community, reflecting on broad questions concerning the kind of society we want to become and how we are to achieve that society. While respecting and valuing the freedom of individuals to pursue their own goals, the common-good approach challenges us also to

recognize and further those goals we share in common.

The Virtue Approach

The virtue approach to ethics assumes that there are certain ideals toward which we should strive, which provide for the full development of our humanity. These ideals are discovered through thoughtful reflection on what kind of people we have the potential to become.

Virtues are attitudes or character traits that enable us to be and to act in ways that develop our highest potential. They enable us to pursue the ideals we have adopted. Honesty, courage, compassion, generosity, fidelity, integrity, fairness, self-control, and prudence are all examples of virtues.

Virtues are like habits; that is, once acquired, they become characteristic of a person. Moreover, a person who has developed virtues will be naturally disposed to act in ways consistent with moral principles. The virtuous person is the ethical person.

In dealing with an ethical problem using the virtue approach, we might ask, What kind of person should I be? What will promote the development of character within myself and my community?

Ethical Problem Solving

These five approaches suggest that once we have ascertained the facts, we should ask ourselves five questions when trying to resolve a moral issue:

- What benefits and what harms will each course of action produce, and which alternative will lead to the best overall consequences?

- What moral rights do the affected parties have, and which course of action best respects those rights?

- Which course of action treats everyone the same, except where there is a morally justifiable reason not to, and does not show favoritism or discrimination?

- Which course of action advances the common good?

- Which course of action develops moral virtues?

This method, of course, does not provide an automatic solution to moral problems. It is not meant to. The method is merely meant to help identify most of the important ethical considerations. In the end, we must deliberate on moral issues for ourselves, keeping a careful eye on both the facts and on the ethical considerations involved.

This article updates several previous pieces from Issues in Ethics *by Manuel Velasquez - Dirksen Professor of Business Ethics at Santa Clara University and former Center director - and Claire Andre, associate Center director. "Thinking Ethically" is based on a framework developed by the authors in collaboration with Center Director Thomas Shanks, S.J., Presidential Professor of Ethics and the Common Good Michael J. Meyer, and others. The framework is used as the basis for many programs and presentations at the Markkula Center for Applied Ethics.*

Reprinted from ISSUES IN ETHICS, published by the Santa Clara University Center for Applied Ethics, Vol. 7 Number 1 (Winter 1996).

ASSIGNMENT I-2A-2: <u>**Management in Different Environments**</u>**:**
Changing Political Factors #1

SETTING

It is the early 1990s and you are one of the top managers of a large aerospace and weapons company. For decades, your company's largest customer has been the Defense Department. In addition, you manufacture commercial aircraft. Your company has operations in 4 different states, but the majority of your defense contract employees work at plants in California.

Defense contracts contribute over a billion dollars a year to your revenues. Your defense contract business includes mostly long-term contracts entered into in the middle to late 1980s. While the defense contract business is declining industry-wide, many of your contracts will continue to be in force until the late 1990s.

Ever since the collapse of the former Soviet Union and the end of the "cold war," you have been aware that the U. S. Congress is trying to cut the federal defense budget, particularly given the need to bring the country's budget back into balance after years of deficits. In this morning's newspaper, you read a government prediction that the current defense budget will shrink by more than 25% to about $200 billion a year by the end of the decade.

ASSIGNMENT

Consider the implications for your business of the recent political changes and the planned reductions in the defense budget. Focus on these 3 questions:

1. What is the potential problem for your company?

2. What options do you have for solving this problem?

3. What accounting information do you need to help you decide which option to pursue?

HINTS

The "potential problem" is not "political factors are changing." This is the cause, not the problem. The problem is the potential negative impact this change could have on your business. You need to think about what specific problem this change poses for your business before you can think about options and information needs.

If you get stuck for ideas about options and information needs, try comparing this situation to the example cited in the module's section on "Management in Different Environments." The example concerned businesses facing a technological change when the personal computer was first introduced. Think about how the options and information needs discussed in that example followed from the nature of the change. Then apply the same logical approach to thinking about this political change.

Remember the old maxim: "The best opportunities in life often come brilliantly disguised as problems."

ASSIGNMENT I-2A-3: **Management in Different Environments:**
Changing Demographics

SETTING

You are one of the top managers of a Japanese subsidiary of a U.S. manufacturing company. You have regular meetings with the other members of the management team. At today's meeting, one of your colleagues passes out copies of an article from a leading business magazine concerning the coming world labor shortage.

The article notes that as the world's population ages, labor is expected to be in short supply. Japan is mentioned as one of the world's fastest aging countries. By the year 2000, the Japanese population will have the highest proportion of elderly people of any nation. The article quotes a report by the Japan Federation of Employers calling this "the most difficult problem facing Japanese companies."

You are also aware of the following facts about your company:

1.   Slightly over 15% of your employees will be 65 or older next year. Although there is no mandatory retirement age, you expect retirements to increase over the next few years.

2.   The younger generation does not have the same work ethic as the older generation. Those workers nearing retirement spent most of their work lives working 60 hours per week. Younger workers prefer more leisure time and less overtime.

3.   You have relatively few women employees (which is not unusual in Japan). Also, you have experienced a problem recently: a number of female employees have left the company to care for their dependent parents (Japan has no government-sponsored retirement plans for the elderly and most senior citizens live with their children).

4.   Given recent technological advances, it is now possible to automate a large portion of your manufacturing process. However, it would be very expensive to buy the industrial robots you would need to automate the process.

ASSIGNMENT

Consider the implications for your business of the coming demographic change. Focus on these 3 questions:

1. What is the potential problem for your company?

2. What options do you have for solving this problem?

3. What accounting information do you need to help you decide which option to pursue?

HINTS

The "potential problem" is not "the population is aging." This is the cause, not the problem. The problem is the negative impact this change could have on your business. You need to think about what specific problem this change poses for your business before you can think about options and information needs.

If you get stuck for ideas about options and information needs, try comparing this situation to the example cited in the module's section on "Management in Different Environments." The example concerned businesses facing a technological change when the personal computer was introduced. Think about how the options and information needs discussed in that example followed from the nature of the change. Then apply the same logical approach to thinking about a demographic change.

ASSIGNMENT I-2A-4:   <u>**Management in Different Environments**</u>:
                                            Changing Technology

SETTING

You are one of the top managers of a check printing company that produces almost half of all checks used by individuals and small businesses in the United States. You have regular meetings with the other members of the management team. At today's meeting, one of your colleagues passes out copies of an article which predicts that within 10 years the use of checks will be virtually eliminated as more and more consumers and businesses will pay their bills via electronic transfer of funds.

The electronic funds transfer industry (the industry that produces the hardware and software for electronic transfers) is not yet well-established, but industry leaders are beginning to appear. In fact, several small companies which sell software for automatic teller machines and electronic funds transfer are considered ripe for acquisition (purchase) or merger as they are being dominated in the market by larger firms in the industry.

You are also aware of the following facts about your company:

1.   Currently, your company sells many billions of checks annually to financial institutions. Depending on the style of check and the volume of their orders, your customers pay $8.00 to $15.00 for a box of 200 checks. The financial institutions then resell the checks to their depositors, usually at a markup of approximately 25% to 30% greater than their cost.

2.   Security is a major selling point for the check printing business. Customers for check printing are not highly price sensitive. A recent marketing survey revealed that very few, if any, customers would consider changing check printers if you raised your prices by 5% to 8%, although many would consider changing check printers if prices were raised 10% to 15%.

3.   Your company is in strong financial shape, with a large amount of ready cash (well over $100 million) and minimal debt.

ASSIGNMENT

Consider the implications for your business of the coming technological change.

Focus on these 3 questions:

1. What is the potential problem for your company?

2. What options do you have for solving this problem?

3. What accounting information do you need to help you decide which option to pursue?

HINTS

The "potential problem" is not "technology is changing." This is the cause, not the problem. The problem is the negative impact this change could have on your business. You need to think about what specific problem this change poses for your business before you can think about options and information needs.

If you get stuck for ideas about options and information needs, try comparing this situation to the example cited in the module's section on "Management in Different Environments." The example concerned businesses facing a technological change when the personal computer was first introduced. Think about how the options and information needs discussed in that example followed from the nature of the change. Then apply the same logical approach to thinking about this technological change.

ASSIGNMENT I-2A-5:   **Management in Different Environments:**
Changing Political Factors #2

SETTING

You are one of the top managers of an American company that manufactures blue jeans. You manufacture and sell jeans in several dozen countries throughout the world. Currently, your most profitable market is in Europe, where U.S. brand jeans are so popular that they sell at almost twice the selling price in the United States. Your jeans sell out of European stores shortly after arrival, so you would like to increase your production capacity.

Recently, many Eastern European nations have undergone major political changes, including a policy change to abandon socialist economic systems (where the state controls most production facilities) and move toward a free market economy. Due to these political changes, trading barriers with many nations are being relaxed and many Eastern European governments are now willing to rent or sell some state-owned manufacturing facilities.

You have just received information about a state-owned textile plant in Hungary that is available for sale or rent. The facility is large enough to allow a significant increase in the amount of blue jeans you could produce for European markets.

You are also aware of the following facts:

1.   The Hungarian factory currently houses a sweater-knitting cooperative that employs 1,200 people. The cooperative never met its state-determined production goal and never made a profit in its 15 years of operations. The government is now willing to sell the factory or to rent out 40% of the plant building. You would be allowed to bring equipment and a small top management team into the country, but you would be required to employ primarily Hungarian workers in the plant. The government will allow you freedom to establish your own hiring needs, production targets and pay scales.

2.   The factory's advantages are its location and the ready supply of labor at about $476 a month for production workers and about twice that amount for supervisors. The disadvantages are that the factory's equipment is outdated (you would not be able to use it), and the work force is substantially larger than that needed for efficient production.

3.   Since profit was not the aim of the state-owned cooperative, work force efficiency at the factory was not strongly managed. As many as one-third of the jobs may be unnecessary. Moreover, the line workers are not accustomed to working in a profit-oriented company and are not trained to operate the newer, more technologically advanced equipment used in American blue jean production, such as special machinery for automatically sewing on pockets. Most of the sewing done in the plant to date has been by hand or with simple sewing machines.

ASSIGNMENT

Consider the implications for your business of the recent political changes in Eastern Europe. Focus on these 3 questions:

1.   What is the potential problem for your company?

2.   What options do you have for solving this problem?

3.   What accounting information do you need to help you decide which option to pursue?

HINTS

The "potential problem" is not "political factors are changing." This is the cause, not the problem. The problem is the potential negative impact this change could have on your business. You need to think about what specific problem this change poses for your business before you can think about options and information needs.

If you get stuck for ideas about options and information needs, try comparing this situation to the example cited in the module's section on "Management in Different Environments." The example concerned businesses facing a technological change when the personal computer was first introduced. Think about how the options and information needs discussed in that example followed from the nature of the change. Then apply the same logical approach to thinking about this political change.

Remember the old maxim: "The best opportunities in life often come brilliantly disguised as problems."

ASSIGNMENTS FOR MODULE 2 - PART B

ASSIGNMENT I-2B-1: <u>**Transforming Data Into Information:**</u> **An Example**

SETTING

You are an accountant who has a consulting practice. You have just been hired by the President of a company that sells and services a full line of industrial audiovisual equipment. The company has revenues of approximately $5 million a year.

The President has hired you because she is concerned that the company's marketing efforts are not as productive as she would like. The marketing efforts rely on direct-mail pieces. Each year, 4 direct-mail pieces are sent to a mailing list of 3,000 current and potential customers.

The President would like to be able to increase the number of mailings. For example, the head of marketing wants to do an extra mailing to promote a $16,000 Sony video projection system.

However, each additional mailing is quite expensive. So, before expanding the mailings, the President would like to know if there is a way to make the mailings more efficient. In particular, she wants to know if any data in the company's information system can be used to help target the mailings to the appropriate customers--those who are most likely to buy a product. This is why she hired you.

SELF-CORRECTED ASSIGNMENT

You find that the company's information system contains the following data about past sales transactions:

1. Date of sale
2. Customer name
3. Customer address
4. Customer phone number
5. Product(s) sold
6. Quantity sold
7. Unit price(s)
8. Total price
9. Salesperson

In addition, the information system contains the following data obtained from credit agency investigation reports (the company purchases these reports before granting credit to customers):

1. Customer's line of business
2. Customer size (expressed as either annual revenues or number of employees, depending on the agency issuing the report)

Finally, the costing subsystem of the information system contains information on the gross profit earned on each product (the difference between cost and selling price).

Generate several ways the company can use accounting information and other information in their system to help target the mailings to make them more efficient.

HINTS

Think like a marketer. What information would you like to know about potential customers? Why would you want to know it? Then, think about how this information is related to data in the information system.

Think like a consumer. Consider a product that college students buy a lot of-- something like cassette tapes or CDS. What things about you influence your purchase? [Example: your income probably influences your purchase of cassettes-- your income gives you "buying power."] How could a marketer find out these things about you?

Think like an accountant. Once you have identified the information a marketer would like to have about potential consumers, think about how the accounting information is related to these needs. [Example: the sales revenue information about customers gives you a rough measure of "buying power"--would it make sense to send the mailing for the $16,000 video projection system to a company that had annual revenues of $50,000?]

Don't give up on this problem too quickly. Think about it several times before you look at the solution. Each time you think about it, you're likely to see a new possibility. Try to generate at least 4 to 5 possibilities before you look at the solution.

There are actually many possible solutions to this problem. One good "solution" to consider is the actual set of recommendations that a real consultant and real company President came up with. Their case was written up in *Inc.*, a magazine for entrepreneurs. The *Inc.* article appears in the Solutions section at the end of this module.

ASSIGNMENT I-2B-2: <u>Advanced Information Technologies and Information Systems</u>: The Internal Revenue Service

SETTING

You are an accountant who has a large local tax practice. You are attempting to keep up with the latest technological advances and plan to offer your clients electronic tax return filing at the first possible opportunity. In preparation for this opportunity, you want to develop some materials to explain electronic filing to your clients. To begin with, you would like to be able to show your clients how electronic tax return processing will be different from the Internal Revenue Service's current system for processing paper tax returns. This will help you explain to clients why electronic filing should result in quicker tax refunds and fewer IRS errors.

ASSIGNMENT

Use the graphic of the Internal Revenue Service's current return processing system for paper returns (see next page) as a starting point. Modify the graphic to show which manual processing portions of the system will be eliminated or changed by electronic filing.

HINTS

You need only make a rough draft (hand-drawn) version of your graphic at this point. Your new graphic can use a photocopy of the old graphic as a starting point, if desired.

Think about all the parts of the system--input, processing, output and storage. What will change?

CURRENT IRS TAX RETURN PROCESS

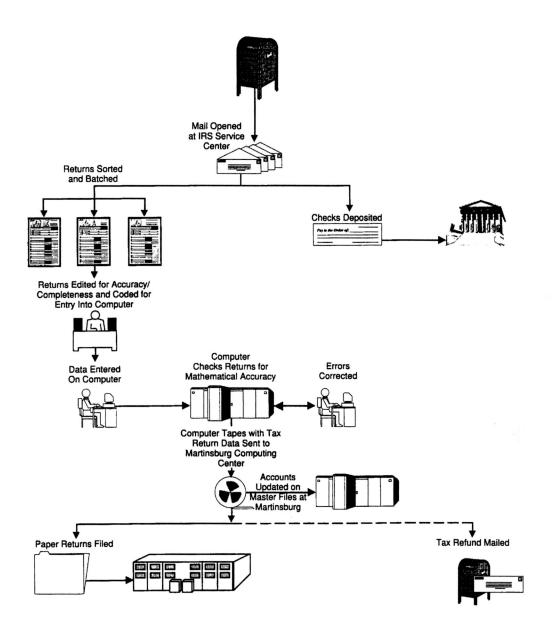

Source: U. S. GAO

ASSIGNMENT I-2B-3: **Advanced Information Technologies and Information Systems: Costs and Benefits of Technology**

SETTING

You are a member of the United States Congress being asked to vote on a proposal to spend billions of dollars improving the information system of the Internal Revenue Service (IRS). The IRS has named the project "TSM" for "tax systems modernization."

As part of the information Congress receives to help make the decision, the U.S. General Accounting Office has gathered information from the Internal Revenue Service about the costs and benefits of modernizing the information system. The information is summarized in 2 charts (see Exhibits 1 and 2).

ASSIGNMENT

Analyze the advantages and disadvantages of voting to approve the spending request. Determine which way you will vote. Prepare a short description of your reasoning for the newsletter you send to your constituents.

HINTS

Use the information in the charts and any other information you have about the proposed new system. Also consider any other information you have which relates to government spending.

Remember that you must not only describe your voting position to your constituents, you must also *justify* it.

Exhibit 1

TSM Costs
(1992) Dollars

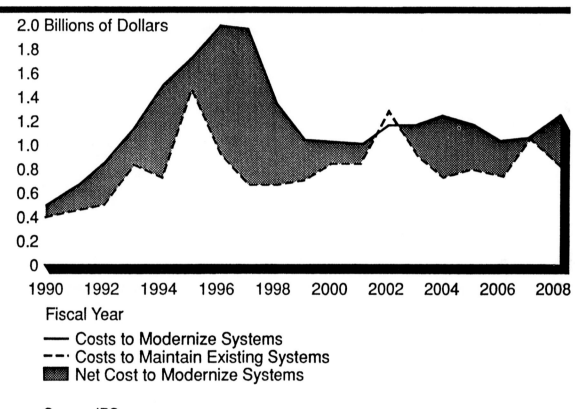

Source: IRS

Exhibit 2

Net Cumulative Costs and Benefits of TSM (1992 Dollars)

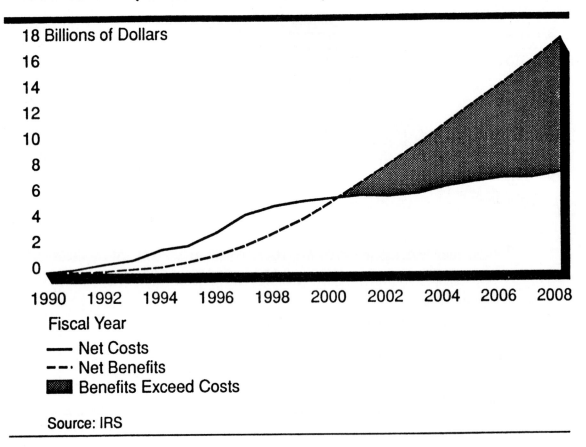

18 Billions of Dollars

Fiscal Year

—— Net Costs

– –· Net Benefits

█ Benefits Exceed Costs

Source: IRS

ASSIGNMENT I-2B-4: <u>Information Systems in an Information Age</u>:
**Qualitative Characteristics of Accounting
Information--Accounting for Real Estate**

SETTING

You are a stockholder in a company that builds, owns and manages housing developments. The major asset of the company is, of course, its buildings.

The company is located in Boston and its buildings are all located in the Boston area. The buildings were constructed during the 1960s, 1970s, and 1980s. The last building constructed was completed in 1985.

The market values of buildings and land in the Boston area appreciated rapidly during the late 1980s. Between 1985 and 1989, for example, the market value of the building completed in 1985 grew by 30%. However, the real estate market then experienced a major downturn. By the end of 1996, the market value of the building was actually slightly less than it cost to build in 1985.

ASSIGNMENT

You receive a survey in the mail asking you the following question about the company you own stock in:

> *What information concerning the company's buildings would you
> like to receive, assuming you can only receive 1 piece of information:
> (a) the cost of the building when constructed, or (b) the market value
> now? Why?*

HINTS

1.   Remember to consider your role as an owner. To what use(s) would you put this information? Once you have a specific use(s) in mind, evaluate the 2 alternatives (cost and market value) using the hierarchy of information qualities summarized in Figure I-2-6: Does one option cost more than the other? Is either option more understandable? more reliable? more relevant? Do comparability or materiality matter here?

2.   Does one option clearly dominate the other? If not, which characteristics of information are more important to you as an owner? Given your priorities, which option is preferable?

ASSIGNMENT I-2B-5: <u>**Qualitative Characteristics of Accounting Information**</u>**: Accounting for Museum Donations**

SETTING

You are a newly appointed member of the Board of Trustees of an historical museum that has a major collection of Chinese urns. At your first board meeting you are pleased to hear that a wealthy patron has donated a new, very valuable urn to the museum. However, when the museum's financial manager presents the financial report, you are surprised to see that the reported value of the collection today is exactly the same as it was a month ago, before the major donation.

You ask the financial manager to explain why the reported value of the collection has not increased. The financial manager explains that most museums, including the largest and finest museums in the country, do not record any revenues or increase in assets for donated items. However, if the same urn had been purchased, the financial reports would have shown the value of the urn as an asset for the amount of the purchase price.

Upon further questioning, the financial manager notes that there are a few museums that do record increases in assets and related revenues for donated items. Also, he tells you that a major financial accounting standard-setting group recommended that all museum donations be recorded at their fair value as revenues and assets, but decided against requiring this treatment after the museum community strongly opposed a change in practice.

ASSIGNMENT

Following the board meeting, you receive a survey from the board's chairperson asking the following question:

> How should the museum handle the financial reporting of donated items:
>
> (a)   continue the current system: disclose donations, but do not record any increase in revenues or assets, or
>
> (b)   change to a new system: increase revenues and

assets by the market value of the donated items?
Why?

HINTS

1.   Remember to consider your role as a board member. To what use would you put this information? Once you have a specific use(s) in mind, evaluate the 2 alternatives using the hierarchy of information qualities summarized in Figure I-2-6: Does one option cost more than the other? Is either option more understandable? more reliable? more relevant? Do comparability or materiality matter here?

2.   Does one option clearly dominate the other? If not, which characteristics of information are more important to you as an owner? Given your priorities, which option is preferable?

ASSIGNMENT I-2B-6:   <u>Information Systems in an Information Age</u>: Alpha Ralpha

***(This assignment was written by Ruben A. Davila,
University of Southern California.)***

SETTING

The Alpha-Ralpha Company has over 200 supermarkets located throughout California, Nevada, and Arizona; 90% of the stores are located in California with the Nevada and Arizona stores being concentrated in the Las Vegas and Phoenix metropolitan areas respectively. California is divided into a Northern and Southern Division.

The store has just completed the installation of scanner systems in all of its stores. These scanners are tied to a mainframe computer at corporate headquarters where all data are stored. The data captured by the scanner system include the following on each transaction:

- specific product data on each sale (i.e., product, brand name, product size, quantity purchased, etc.)

- type of payment (i.e., whether cash, check, credit cards, coupons, or food stamps were used)

- the volume of specific products sold at any time of day or location (region, store, department, checkstand); the data are available by customer if a check-cashing card or credit card is used for payment

In addition, demographic information--such as address, place of employment, yearly wages, and so on--is available on all customers with check cashing cards. Perpetual inventory information (a report of exactly how many units of each product are currently on hand) is also available.

Alpha-Ralpha is literally overwhelmed by the amount of data this scanner system is collecting. The company's management team wants to take advantage of all this available data so they have hired you as a consultant to assist them.

ASSIGNMENT

You have been charged with coming up with ways in which the data can be transformed into information useful in managing the supermarket chain. When making your suggestions, you must specifically address 3 things:

(1) MANAGER NEEDS: Identify the information needs of managers that may be addressed by data held in the scanner system.

(2) USES OF INFORMATION: Indicate how this information can be used by managers to more efficiently run their part of the organization.

(3) REPORT: Briefly describe a report generated from data contained in the scanner database that will fulfill the information needs of the managers identified in (1). The description should include specific references to the type of information in the report, how often it will be made available, and to whom. The information from the scanner system should be easily accessible by the managers. It is possible for one report to meet more than one manager information need. [Note: Do not design the actual report, just describe it.]

Note for Graded Assignments: There are many possible solutions to this problem. **Give your 5 best ideas.** Only the first 5 will be graded. Each idea must specify the manager needs, uses of information and report design.

HINTS

Think like a manager (district, store, department). What would you like to know about customers, products, and customer purchases? Why would you want this information and how would you use it?

Think like an accountant. Develop information that can be easily accessed by managers from the scanner database to meet managers' needs.

ASSIGNMENT I-2B-7:   <u>Information Systems in an Information Age</u>:
<u>Cereal Wars</u>

(This assignment was co-authored by Paul Caster, Fairfield University)

SETTING

You are the Marketing Director for one of the major cereal manufacturers. For the past several years, your company has been engaged in a marketing war with its competitors. One of the chief weapons in the war has been discount coupons. You and your competitors have offered so many "cents off" coupons for your products that more than half of your cereal is being sold well below its list price.

While the cereal wars have been going on, an attack has also come from another direction. Supermarkets have been devoting more shelf space to their "private-label" (store-brand) cereals, which typically sell at anywhere from 30% to 50% less than major brand-name cereals. Even though the cereal wars have kept consumers' costs for brand-name cereals low, the market share for private-label cereals has still been increasing slightly over the past year.

Lately, your CEO and CFO are beginning to worry that the constant use of discount coupons may be training consumers to expect discount pricing...and to buy only when coupons are offered. The CFO has suggested it may be time to end the war, or at least call a cease-fire. The CEO has asked you to prepare a proposal for the next quarter's pricing and discounting policy for your three best-selling cereal brands. Meanwhile, just yesterday, one of your competitors announced it was raising its cereal prices to wholesalers by about 3%.

To prepare your proposal, you need information. You know that there is an information service that gathers data about supermarket purchases for a sample of more than 50,000 households. The information service keeps a complete record of supermarket scanner data for everything these households purchase. The information service then analyzes the data, publishes a few general results (such as the 10 top-selling cereals each quarter) and offers to sell additional information in response to specific questions. For each purchase, the scanner data include the list price of the item (its regular price), the size of the item, the color (if applicable), the net selling price (after coupons), and so on. Scanner data for multiple products can also be combined and analyzed. For example, the information service can tell you how many of the households bought fruit along with their cereal purchase.

There are two important things to note about this service: (1) It can produce just about any information you want to buy, but the information is expensive. (2) You may only purchase information about your own products or about some group of products, including your own and others (e.g., What is the average price of....? What are the best selling cereals in New York City?). The information service refuses to sell detailed information about a particular company's product to anyone except that company.

Your proposal for the CEO is so important that you have decided to spend some of your budgeted funds to purchase information from the service. You telephoned them this morning to get a better idea of the types of information they will sell. Your notes from the conversation are on the next page.

ASSIGNMENT

For each item of information on your telephone conversation list, explain how the information could help you determine whether to continue, end or reduce the cereal wars.

Assuming your budget will only allow you to purchase 2 items of information, which 2 items from the list would you purchase and why?

Think about other information (beyond that on the list) you could request from the service. Name and justify the 1 additional item of information you would most want to purchase.

HINTS

Don't go to the list of available information too quickly. First, think about your situation. What do you really want to know?

When you look at the list of available information, ask yourself: "How can I use this? What does it tell me about pricing policy? What does it tell me about discounting policy?" and so on.

The quality of your explanations is critical. Be sure to clearly explain the reasons for your choices.

 # Memo

Information for sale:

– average base (list) price and percentage change in price over last quarter for top selling cereals (national)

– number of cereals now selling for over $____ or below $____ a box (can specify any amount ...note: our highest priced cereal sells for $5 per box)

– Market shares of the ten best–selling cereals, with prices, current year compared to year ago (or, current quarter compared to same quarter last year)

– Market share for private–label brands, this year vs. last year

– regional info on any of the above (instead of national)

– number of brands being sold currently vs. last year, last five years

– percentage of cereal purchases with coupons

– or, other information requested!!!

ASSIGNMENT I-2B-8: How Accounting Information Systems Have Evolved: Charting the Hits

SETTING

You are the manager of a new rock band that has an album about to come out. You know that you will want to use published industry data to assess the progress of your band's album.

You are aware that in the early 1990s, the music world experienced the impact of advanced technology on information. For generations, music industry sales data were communicated through Top 10 lists, or even Top 100 lists, that simply provided the rank order of albums sold during the previous week based on surveys of music stores. Thus, music industry people could easily find out what the #1 album was in any given week, but they could not find out how many copies of the album had been sold that week.

Advances in computer technology made it possible to automatically collect data on album sales at the point of purchase. A system called SoundScan was developed to collect and summarize the data. Soon, industry magazines like *Billboard* began adding more information--starting with the quantity of albums sold--to their weekly top-seller lists.

Here is one top-seller list for the first year the new system was in operation:

1. Guns N' Roses' "Use Your Illusion II"--770,000.
2. Guns N' Roses' "Use Your Illusion I"--685,000.
3. Garth Brooks' "Roping the Wind"--300,000.
4. Mariah Carey's "Emotions"--155,000.
5. Metallica's "Metallica"--135,000.
6. Natalie Cole's "Unforgettable"--103,000.
7. Ozzy Osbourne's "No More Tears"--80,000.
8. "The Commitments" soundtrack--67,000.
9. Bonnie Raitt's "Luck of the Draw"--66,000.
10. Color Me Badd's "C.M.B."--63,000.

ASSIGNMENT

From your perspective as the band's manager:

♫   What are some of the advantages of expanding the information set to include the quantity of albums sold, as well as the rank order? How could you use this information to analyze how well your band's album is doing in the market?

♫   Are there any disadvantages from your band's perspective?

♫   What additional information would be useful to you?

Bonus trivia question (*Note*: only counts if your instructor agrees to award bonus points for trivia!): Based on this top-seller list, what year was the new system implemented?

HINTS

1.   To determine the advantages of the expanded information set, imagine the top-seller list without the quantity sold information. What do you know from having the information that you wouldn't have known otherwise? Then, think about how you could use the information.

2.   To determine the disadvantages, consider why your band might not want the quantity of albums they sold publicized.

3.   To determine what additional information you might use, think about other information systems, such as the decision support system for Frito-Lay described in this module.

ASSIGNMENT I-2B-9: <u>**How Accounting Information Systems Have**</u> <u>**Evolved**</u>**: Steve's Wood Furniture, Inc.**

<u>SETTING</u>

You have just been hired as an accountant for Steve's Wood Furniture, Inc. The company manufactures wood entertainment centers in a variety of styles. During your first few days on the job, you talked to many of the company's employees to get a sense of what they thought were the key business activities at Steve's. The result of your discussions is an alphabetized "top 20" list:

> add hardware (door handles, etc.)
> clean up scraps
> cut wood
> deliver products to customers
> fasten wood pieces together
> hire workers
> make sales calls
> measure wood
> pay workers
> pay for supplies
> pay for wood
> purchase supplies (nails, screws, glue, etc.)
> purchase wood
> receive sales orders from customers
> receive payments from customers
> sand surfaces of wood
> stain wood
> store wood
> store supplies
> survey customers about satisfaction

You plan to use this list to help the company improve its information system. Steve's has long used a traditional accounting information system. But, the company is interested in moving towards a broader information system. They have hired you to help design the new system. The new system will be organized around operating cycles and will contain a wide variety of financial and non-financial information.

The purchasing manager is particularly interested in the project and has volunteered the purchasing area as the first part of the business to work with you on designing the new system.

ASSIGNMENT

In preparation for your initial meeting with the purchasing manager, complete the following tasks:

1. Determine which of the top 20 business activities would give rise to economic transactions that would be recorded in Steve's traditional accounting information system.

2. Categorize the 20 business activities into 3 cycles: acquisition and payment; production; and sales and collection.

3. Determine which cycle would be of most interest to the purchasing manager. For this cycle, choose 1 of the activities and suggest 1 item of financial information, 1 item of quantitative non-financial information and 1 item of qualitative non-financial information that could be useful to the purchasing manager. Explain why these items of information would be useful.

HINTS

1. Remember that a traditional accounting information system records only transactions and events that affect assets, liabilities or equities.

2. In categorizing the activities into cycles, you may find it helpful to first put the list in chronological order (what happens first? what happens next?). Remember that there is a rough sequence to the operating cycles: acquisition and payment for inputs usually precedes production, which, in turn, comes before sales and collection.

3. Remember that financial information means information measured in money terms--for example, the cost of buying a building is financial information. Non-financial information is not measured in money, but it may be quantitative. For example, the expected useful life of the building in years is quantitative non-financial information. The name of the seller of the building is qualitative (non-quantitative) non-financial information.

ASSIGNMENTS FOR MODULE 2 - PART C

ASSIGNMENT I-2C-1: <u>**Basic Concepts of Internal Control Systems**</u>**:
Steps to Achieving Organizational Goals**

<u>SETTING</u>

You are a student studying *Core Concepts of Accounting Information.* One evening, after a long siege reading about basic concepts of internal control systems, you decide to go to a local fast-food restaurant to take a snack break. When you arrive, you find that you must wait in line for 5 minutes to buy your food. As you wait, you cannot help but observe the process of selling and distributing the food. Almost in spite of yourself, you begin to think about the control process you are observing.

<u>ASSIGNMENT</u>

Use the sale and distribution of food at a local fast-food restaurant to illustrate the steps in an internal control system: assigning responsibility; establishing standards; motivating and rewarding performance; monitoring performance; communicating progress and taking corrective action, if needed. Also consider how the restaurant's control system helps safeguard the cash from sales and food inventories not yet sold.

This assignment should be done as a group project. Your group will have approximately 10 minutes to make a classroom presentation to the other students. Hand in a written outline of your presentation, too.

<u>HINTS</u>

First you need to understand the policies and procedures at a fast-food restaurant. If any group member has worked in a fast-food restaurant, use his or her knowledge of the business as a starting point for your discussion. If no one in the group has ever worked at a fast-food restaurant, interview a current or former fast- food restaurant employee to find out how the sale and distribution of food works. You might also consider some observational research (i.e., visit a fast-food restaurant and watch what goes on). Develop a short description of the system.

Next, analyze the system. What are the goals? Is there a clear assignment of responsibility? What are the performance standards? How is performance motivated? rewarded? How is performance monitored? How do employees find out how they are doing? What kind of corrective action can be taken if problems are discovered (use a particular example--just one will do)? What safeguards are built into the process?

Think about how the internal control system could be described in terms of the COSO report, "Internal Control--An Integrated Framework." What aspects of the system tell you something about the control environment? What are some of the major risks that must be managed? How do the control activities and procedures relate to the organization's objectives and perceived risks? How does the organization provide for information and communication? What kind of monitoring takes place?

Come to class prepared to describe and analyze the system. Think carefully about how to structure your presentation so you can give the class a good picture of the control system in a short time. If you need hints on preparing an oral presentation, see "Eight Steps to an Effective Presentation" in the appendix to this module.

ASSIGNMENT I-2C-2:   <u>**Basic Concepts of Internal Control Systems**</u>**:**
The USFK Ration Control System

<u>SETTING</u>

You are an auditor with the GAO, the federal audit agency. Congress has asked the agency to investigate complaints by the South Korean government about black market sales by U.S. military personnel stationed in Korea. There are about 70,000 active duty military personnel, accompanying dependents (spouses and children), and civilian military employees stationed there. About 88% live on military bases.

You have been assigned to investigate black market sales of rice. A problem is suspected in this area because sales of rice to USFK (United States Forces, Korea) personnel average 170 pounds per person per year. In addition, the Army dining facilities serve 10.6 pounds of rice per person per year. In comparison, average annual per capita consumption of rice in the United States is 13.6 pounds.

Under an agreement with South Korea, U.S. military personnel are allowed to buy goods at commissaries, base exchanges and other retail outlets that are not subject to any Korean taxes. The exemption from import duties and other taxes means that USFK personnel can buy goods at 50% or less of the cost of similar goods purchased elsewhere in South Korea. In return for this privilege, the U.S. armed forces agreed to take steps to prevent the resale of these goods for a profit to unauthorized users ("black market sales"). To do this, the military instituted a "ration control system," an internal control system established to prevent, detect and discipline black market sales by USFK personnel. The system is described on the two pages that follow the "hints" for this assignment.

<u>ASSIGNMENT</u>

Your assignment is to assess the weaknesses in the ration control system, explain the potential negative consequences of each weakness, and include suggestions for improvements that could overcome the weaknesses.

<u>HINTS</u>

There are many weaknesses in the system. Limit your answer to the three weaknesses you feel are the most significant.

Ask yourself: "What could go wrong?" Once you know what could go wrong, you can analyze the "holes" in the system. These are the weaknesses in the system.

Imagine what could happen if someone tried to exploit each weakness. What harm might occur? These are the consequences of the weakness.

Ask yourself: "How could I prevent this problem?" Be imaginative. Your answers will lead to your suggestions for improvements. Bear in mind, however, that your solutions must be cost-effective.

How The Ration Control System Works

The current ration control system consists of three types of controls: monthly monetary limits, monthly quantity limits, and specifically controlled items. A ration control plate (a plastic card similar to a credit card) and a picture identification card are normally required when making purchases. Newly authorized customers use temporary paper ration control cards until they receive their ration control plates.

In addition to goods consumed in military dining facilities, ration control card holders who are single may purchase up to $500 per month of consumable items. The ration control limit is higher for military personnel with families--rising to $700 per month for a family of two, $800 for a family of three, $900 for a family of four, $1,000 for a family of five, and $1,200 for a family of six or more. Certain items--uniforms and accessories, records and other prerecorded items, computer software, clothing and footwear, liquor, cigarettes, beer, wine, soft drinks, water, ice and gasoline--are not subject to the dollar limits. Additionally, any individual item costing over $50 is exempt from the monthly dollar limits, but may be subject to specific quantity limits. Cigarettes and alcoholic beverages are also subject to monthly quantity limits.

Cashiers record purchases of duty-free goods by using the plastic ration control plate. The plate is embossed with raised identification data, such as the individual's name, social security number, rank, sex, family size and expiration date. Purchases under $5 need not be recorded. When an authorized person makes a purchase of $5 or more, the sales clerk makes an impression of the plate onto a three-part form, which is similar to running a credit card through an embossing machine. The temporary paper cards can be checked for authorization, but they cannot be used in the embossing machine. The customer keeps one copy of the form, the retail outlet keeps the second, and the USFK Data Management Division receives the third copy for processing. At the Division, an optical character reader scans the forms and records the information in a database. The database does not contain information on purchases made with temporary control cards.

The database contains an individual's purchases for each month recorded by social security number. Each month's sales data in the database are compared with the control limits to determine if violations have occurred. At the same time, individuals who have exceeded their limits are identified. Since the reports must be timely to be useful, monthly sales data dealing with monetary and quantity limits are not entered into the database or analyzed unless received by the 5th working day of the following month.

Reports of violations are sent to the violator's military unit for appropriate action--for example, counseling, reprimand or court martial. The U.S. Army Criminal Investigation Command and the Air Force Office of Special Investigations investigate violations valued at greater than $1,000. The Army military police and the Air Force security police investigate black market cases involving smaller amounts. During the most recent fiscal year, 531 violations were investigated, including 147 that were over $1,000 each. Sixty-six persons were court-martialed; the rest received lesser penalties, such as losing ration privileges. The largest dollar violations (just over a quarter of a million dollars) involved purchases made with fraudulent ration control plates.

The ration control system costs about $12 million per year, mostly for personnel costs. Responding to increased pressure to reduce costs, the USFK eliminated the jobs of the "ration control monitors" at the end of the most recent fiscal year. The monitors, who were employed at about 25% of the 103 stores in the system, checked identification cards, ration control plates and temporary ration cards at the entrance of each major outlet and verified ration forms and control cards at the exits to the stores. They could also require a person to sign a register of items purchased. Each monitor provided 1 to 3 leads to the Office of Special Investigations and military police per month. During the last fiscal year, the monitors were responsible for all the leads on cases involving fraudulent identification cards or ration control plates.

ASSIGNMENT I-2C-3: <u>**The Importance of Internal Control Systems**</u>**:
What's Wrong With This System?**

SETTING

It is 1990 and you are a member of an internal audit team. Your team has discovered a problem: the federal agency responsible for selling billions of dollars of real estate seized from failed savings and loan institutions does not keep central records showing the properties sold, prices paid, or buyers' identities.

The risks seem obvious to you, but officials of the agency do not see the value of central records. An article in the *Los Angeles Times* (reproduced following this assignment) gives an overview of the problems and arguments.

Your audit team has been asked to prepare a presentation explaining the risks of failing to keep central records. You will also be expected to use your presentation to answer the officials' objections to central records. You will have *10 minutes* for your presentation, after which there will be an open discussion period.

Your presentation will take place at a meeting of agency officials. You anticipate that most of the audience will come to the meeting predisposed to oppose your recommendations. So, your task is to persuade the officials that the failure to keep central records is a serious problem.

There will be 2 or 3 other auditors in the audience, who might be counted on to help you make your case during the discussion period. However, they won't be able to help you during your presentation.

ASSIGNMENT

Your full group should meet and discuss this case. Two key questions must be answered:

(1) What are the potential problems that could occur from the lack of central records to keep track of properties sold, prices paid or buyers?

(2) How would you evaluate the arguments of the officials who say such records are not needed?

Prepare a typed outline of your group's analysis of this case and decide how you would structure a *10-minute* presentation to the meeting of agency officials.

Bring the outline to class to serve as the basis for a presentation, if you are selected. In class, one subgroup will be chosen to make the presentation. The other subgroup in this group will play the role of other auditors in the audience for the presentation (i.e., they will be friendly to your position). Everyone else in the class will play the role of an agency official--that is, they will try to argue against your position and poke holes in your logic.

Class participation points will be assigned to each presenting subgroup member based on the overall quality of the presentation and the contributions of the individual member.

Class participation points will also be assigned to members of the audience (either auditors or agency officials) who make important contributions to the discussion.

After the group discussion, all outlines will be handed in for grading. All students will receive a grade based on their group's outline.

HINTS

1. Potential problems: Identify as many specific risks as possible. To do this, try imagining how you could abuse the system if you were an agency employee and central records weren't kept. Your case will be stronger if you can explain to the officials exactly what could go wrong. Make your arguments personal: how could the internal control weaknesses come back to haunt the officials?

2. Opposing arguments: First, identify each separate objection to keeping central records that is described in the newspaper article. Then, play "devil's advocate" and try to generate possible additional objections.

3. Planning your presentation: Be sure to discuss how you will use the 10 minutes of presentation time if your subgroup is chosen. How will you divide the presentation time? What kind of introduction will you use? What kind of closing will you use? If you need additional hints, read the advice on "Eight Steps to Effective Oral Presentations" in the appendix to this module.

4. Consider preparing some visual aids. You might want to prepare some simple visual aids to help you make your presentation, if chosen. For example, it might be helpful to make a transparency from your outline. If you decide to do this, be sure to use large type when you prepare the outline. You might also want to break the outline up into several pages, one for each potential presenter.

S&L Sales System Record-Keeping Lacks Safeguards

■ **Bailout:** Thrift regulators may be handicapped in detecting potential favoritism, fraud or improper pricing.

By ROBERT A. ROSENBLATT
TIMES STAFF WRITER

WASHINGTON—The federal agency responsible for selling billions of dollars in real estate from failed savings and loan associations lacks a central record-keeping system to keep track of the properties sold, the prices paid or the names of the buyers.

Without such a system, the Washington headquarters of Resolution Trust Corp. may be handicapped in detecting potential favoritism, fraud or improper pricing in the sales of thousands of pieces of property.

The agency's local offices are expected eventually to sell more than $100 billion in real estate from failed thrift institutions, including single-family homes, condominiums, office buildings, shopping centers and land. The corporation's four regional offices are independent in deciding the types of records to keep on purchasers of real estate, The Times has learned.

RTC officials questioned the importance of a central mechanism to identify buyers but added that such a system eventually will be installed.

The agency is not particularly interested in the identity of buyers, said Kevin Shields, spokesman for the Denver regional office, which includes California. "If they have the money and paid in cash, it doesn't matter," he said. "What's the difference to the taxpayer; who cares who buys it?"

He said that agency procedures will prevent fraud and protect taxpayers. "We have policies and guidelines that do not allow us to sell below market value."

S&L: Record-Keeping Questioned

Continued from D1

However, local RTC officials have considerable autonomy, with the authority to cut the price of a property 20% if it hasn't sold in six months.

The agency has 35,000 properties for sale. Buyers can be identified only if the specific address of the property is known. Even then, on sales of specific pieces of property by the 247 thrifts currently operating under Resolution Trust conservatorship, it is usually necessary to go to the S&L involved to search for information.

The agency's 14 local offices should have files on the sales of properties held by S&Ls that have been shut down. However, on a regional level, the compilation of local figures varies.

The Western region in Denver, for example, has no central listing of buyers of real estate assets throughout California, Colorado, Oregon, Washington, Alaska and Hawaii.

In the Dallas region, officials began a complete computer record system in June, insisting that they be notified of the identification of buyers on a routine basis.

Previously in Dallas, RTC regional reports identified buyers only a third of the time.

"The system was spotty at best in tracking buyers," said Teresa McUsic, public affairs officer for the region, which includes Texas and Oklahoma. "The focus at first was on the number of assets and the dollar amount sold," she added. "The focus was not on tracking the buyers."

There is an elaborate set of RTC rules, forbidding officials involved in the cleanup of hundreds of S&Ls to do business with persons who have caused a loss to a thrift institution. The government does not want people who might have contributed to the collapse of an S&L to be able to buy foreclosed properties at bargain prices.

But the lack of a central system makes it difficult for officials in Washington to know precisely who is buying government-owned real estate.

"Washington has decentralized," said Thomas Hamberger, special assistant to Lamar Kelly, director of asset and real estate management. "We in Washington do not keep files on the specific properties."

"The regional directors are in charge of their property, having their people dealing with the purchasers, doing appraisals and selling property," he said. He argued that, because sales take place at a local level, it is unnecessary to have sales records at Washington headquarters.

"It is very difficult for us in Washington to travel to Los Angeles and show a property," Hamberger noted. "We don't have a specific computer base at this time to have the capacity, for example, to keep track of single-family home sales in Los Angeles."

The RTC makes available a list of properties for sale through both printed volumes and computer discs.

However, there is no accompanying list of the properties that have already sold by the agency, which has been in existence since last August.

"They know at the local level who they are selling property to," said Stephen Katsanos, the agency's director of communications. "As far as us in Washington needing to have a five-foot stack of paper listing everyone who bought property, I am not sure how useful that would be."

He added: "If I wanted to go to an S&L and find out everything that S&L has sold, they have the records at the S&L, so I can look at each transaction." And, he said, at local offices of the agency "I can look at what has been sold" from defunct S&Ls.

Katsanos said that his agency eventually will have a central system for identifying asset sales' and buyers. "I can't tell you [when] at this time," he said.

ASSIGNMENT I-2C-4: <u>**Basic Concepts of Internal Control Systems**</u>:
Internal Controls at Music/Video Stores

<u>SETTING</u>

You are a student studying *Core Concepts of Accounting Information*. One evening, after a long siege reading about basic concepts of internal control systems, you decide to go to a local music/video store to take a study break. When you arrive at the store, you spend several minutes browsing until you find something you want to buy or rent. Then, you find that you must wait in line for five minutes to reach the cash register. As you are waiting, you cannot help but observe the internal control system in the store. Almost in spite of yourself, you begin to think about the control process you are observing.

<u>ASSIGNMENT</u>

Use a real music and/or video store to illustrate the steps in an internal control system: assigning responsibility; establishing standards; motivating and rewarding performance; monitoring performance; communicating progress and taking corrective action, if needed. Also consider how the store's control system helps safeguard the cash and inventory (stock held for sale or rental).

This assignment should be done as a group project. Your group will have approximately 10 minutes to make a classroom presentation to the other students. You must also hand in a written outline of your presentation.

<u>HINTS</u>

First you need to understand the policies and procedures at the video/music store. If any group member has worked in a video/music store, use his or her knowledge of the business as a starting point for your discussion. If no one in the group has ever worked at a video/music store, interview a current or former video/music store employee or manager to find out how such a store works. You might also consider some observational research (i.e., visit a video/music store and watch what goes on). Develop a short description of the system.

Next, analyze the system. What are the goals? Is there a clear assignment of responsibility? What are the performance standards? How is performance motivated? rewarded? How is performance monitored? How do employees find out how they are doing? What kind of corrective action can be taken if problems are discovered (use a particular example--just one will do)? What safeguards are built into the process? Come to class prepared to describe and analyze the system.

Think about how the internal control system could be described in terms of the COSO report, "Internal Control--An Integrated Framework." What aspects of the system tell you something about the control environment? What are some of the major risks that must be managed? How do the control activities and procedures relate to the organization's objectives and perceived risks? How does the organization provide for information and communication? What kind of monitoring takes place?

Come to class prepared to describe and analyze the system. Think carefully about how to structure your presentation so you can give the class a good picture of the control system in a short time. If you need hints on preparing an oral presentation, see "Eight Steps to an Effective Presentation" in the appendix to this module.

ASSIGNMENT I-2C-5: **Basic Concepts of Internal Control Systems:**
Read All About It #1

SETTING

You are an entrepreneur who has been working hard on a business plan for a new enterprise. Lately, you've been thinking a lot about the internal control system you will design for your business. To help you think, you've been reading some business books and the financial press.

While doing your reading, you come across 2 stories that relate to basic concepts of internal control (see next page).

ASSIGNMENT

Determine how the stories relate to basic concepts of internal control. What lessons from the stories can be applied to other businesses?

HINTS

Relate the stories to the steps in an internal control system.

Consider how the stories relate to common causes of internal control breakdowns.

Story #1

Source of story: *The Great Game of Business*, by Jack Stack, edited by
Bo Burlingham (Doubleday/Currency, 1992)

Summary of the story:
The Springfield Remanufacturing Corp. is a Springfield, Missouri company that
rebuilds engines from cars, trucks and construction equipment. In 1991, the
company had sales revenue of about $70 million. The company keeps close track
of its costs for materials and labor used in remanufacturing. Other "overhead"
costs (the costs of items such as heating and lighting, toilet paper, paint, and so
on that are necessary for doing business, but are only indirectly related to the
company's products) were less closely monitored. They were recorded in a
"catchall" account. Jack Stack, the company president, noticed that overhead
costs were mounting. On average, overhead expenses had reached $39 for each
hour employees worked on a product. Since the costs weren't closely monitored,
he had no way of knowing why the costs were rising, but he wanted them to be
closer to $32.50 per hour.

To solve this problem, the names of the overhead items (e.g., toilet paper) were
written on slips of paper and put into a pot. Each supervisor and manager drew a
slip from the pot. Each person was then responsible for finding out how big the
budget should be for that item and for following up on the item. By the end of the
year, overhead costs averaged $26.32 per hour.

Story #2

Source of story: *Los Angeles Times*, September 1991

Summary of the story:
The City of Inglewood, California had a checking account at Wells Fargo Bank.
Members of a janitorial service that cleaned the city's offices stole a supply of
blank checks from the finance department when they were cleaning. Over a 5
month period, the thieves filled in the stolen checks with the name of the
janitorial service, made them payable for amounts as large as $374,000, and
signed the checks with a fictitious name that wasn't the name of any authorized
signer.

The bank cashed the checks and the thieves got a total of about $13.5 million.
The theft went undiscovered for months because no one from the city of
Inglewood checked the monthly bank statement. The city's attorney explained
that the city employees thought the bank would never cash a check that wasn't
signed by an authorized person. The bank, in turn, argued that millions of
checks pass through its clearance center each day and it isn't feasible to check all
the signatures. The bank relies on the person or organization whose name is on
the account to verify the returned checks.

ASSIGNMENT I-2C-6: <u>**Basic Concepts of Internal Control Systems**</u>:
Internal Controls at Movie Theaters

(This assignment was written by Paul Caster, Fairfield University; Chris Cornet, University of Southern California; and Will Snyder, San Diego State University)

<u>SETTING</u>

You have just been hired as the part-time afternoon manager of a new "twelveplex" movie theater--called "Campus-12"-- that recently opened across the street from campus. You go to work straight from your accounting class, where you are now studying basic concepts of internal control systems.

At Campus-12, twelve individual theaters are housed within one building. Campus-12 employs 6 ushers, 2 cashiers, a doorperson, a manager, and certain other employees. The theater carries a health insurance plan for its employees, but does not carry a dental insurance plan.

The theater's ticket sales and admissions policies and procedures are as follows:

The cashiers are situated inside a "box office" at the entrance to the building. The cashiers accept cash from a customer and issue a serially-numbered ticket from a ticket machine. The serial number is clearly printed on the end of each ticket. Ticket rolls are placed in the ticket machine as needed and unused rolls are conveniently stored at the cashiers' feet. Occasionally, the cashiers make change for people who need exact change for the bus that stops in front of the building. When business is slow (usually in the afternoon), only one cash register is used, so both cashiers record ticket sales using the same cash register. The cash register has only one money drawer, but each cashier has an individual identification number to log on to the register.

Each movie has 4 showings per day. Six of the movies start at 4, 6, 8, and 10 p.m. each day. The other 6 movies start 30 minutes later than that. Tickets cost $7, but students, children under 12, and senior citizens pay only half price. Bargain matinees (half price) are offered to everyone at the 4 p.m. and 4:30 p.m. showings only; other discounts are not available at those times.

After purchasing a ticket, the customer walks a short distance to the lobby door. At this point, the customer hands the ticket to the doorperson, who tears the ticket in half, depositing one half in a secure container and handing the other half (the stub) back to the customer, who then proceeds into the lobby.

Usher duties include: finding empty seats for late arrivals, covering theater entrances for the first half hour of each movie, and covering theater exits for the last half hour. For a person to be admitted to a specific movie, the ticket stub must be shown to an usher posted outside each individual theater. Additionally, readmission also requires presentation of the ticket stub. At the conclusion of a movie, customers may go directly to the parking lot by using the emergency exits, since these exits do not trigger alarms. Customers may also leave through the lobby, the same way they came in.

Given your current interest in internal controls, you think you see a number of strengths and weaknesses in the theater's internal control system. You mention to the full-time night manager that you might have some good ideas to share.

ASSIGNMENT

The night manager responds to your offer of help with the following list of questions:

1. What are the strengths in Campus-12's internal controls over ticket sales and theater admissions? What is each strength designed to accomplish? [*Grading note*: To be eligible for full credit, your response should list and describe **four** distinct strengths.]

2. What are the weaknesses in Campus-12's internal controls over ticket sales and theater admissions? What is the potential problem with each noted weakness? What corrective action would you recommend for each weakness? [*Grading note*: To be eligible for full credit, your response should list and describe **four** distinct weaknesses, with suggestions for improvement.]

3. What are some specific checks the managers could periodically perform in order to determine whether internal controls over theater admissions are functioning as prescribed? In other words, exactly how could we monitor compliance with our control system over admissions? [*Grading note*: To be eligible for full credit, your response should list and explain **two** specific and distinct tasks the managers should perform to monitor compliance with controls over admissions.]

HINTS

This is a rare opportunity: going out to see a movie may actually help you with your homework. Think about times you have been in a movie theater--what controls were present that may help you identify the strengths and weaknesses at Campus-12?

ASSIGNMENT I-2C-7:   **Basic Concepts of Internal Control Systems:**
                                   The Guaranteed Student Loan Program

SETTING

The U.S. federal government has 2 programs to help students borrow money to finance their post-secondary education. The newer of the programs is the Federal Direct Student Loan Program, which began in July 1994. Under this program, students borrow money from the government itself. The U.S. Department of Education makes loans to students through their schools. The more long-running program is the Federal Family Education Loan Program (FFELP), more commonly known as the guaranteed student loan program (GSLP), which was initiated in 1965.

The idea behind the FFELP is to encourage lenders (mostly banks) to loan eligible students money to finance their education. The incentives to the lenders are that the U.S. Department of Education pays interest subsidies directly to lenders and reimburses lenders for loan defaults. In fiscal year 1993, for example, the Department of Education guaranteed $17.9 billion for about 5 million new student loans and paid about $3.2 billion in interest subsidies and default claims.

You are a member of an audit team of the U.S. General Accounting Office. Your audit team has been assigned to assess the controls over the Department of Education's financial reporting on the guaranteed student loan program. In performing your review you interviewed personnel and tested accounting information at 10 loan guaranty agencies across the country and at the Department of Education headquarters in Washington, D. C. A flowchart of the program, a narrative description of the program, and a description of your audit findings may be found on the pages following the "hints" for this assignment.

ASSIGNMENT

Your assignment is to assess the weaknesses in the GSLP's control system, explain the potential negative consequences of each weakness, and include suggestions for improvements that could overcome the weaknesses.

HINTS

There are many weaknesses in the system. Limit your answer to the 3 weaknesses you feel are the most significant.

Ask yourself: "What could go wrong?" Once you know what could go wrong, you can analyze the "holes" in the system. These are the weaknesses in the system.

Imagine what could happen if someone tried to exploit each weakness. What harm might occur? These are the consequences of the weakness.

Ask yourself: "How could I prevent this problem?" Be imaginative. Your answers will lead to your suggestions for improvements. Bear in mind, however, that your solutions must be cost-effective.

Flowchart of the Federal Family Education Loan Program

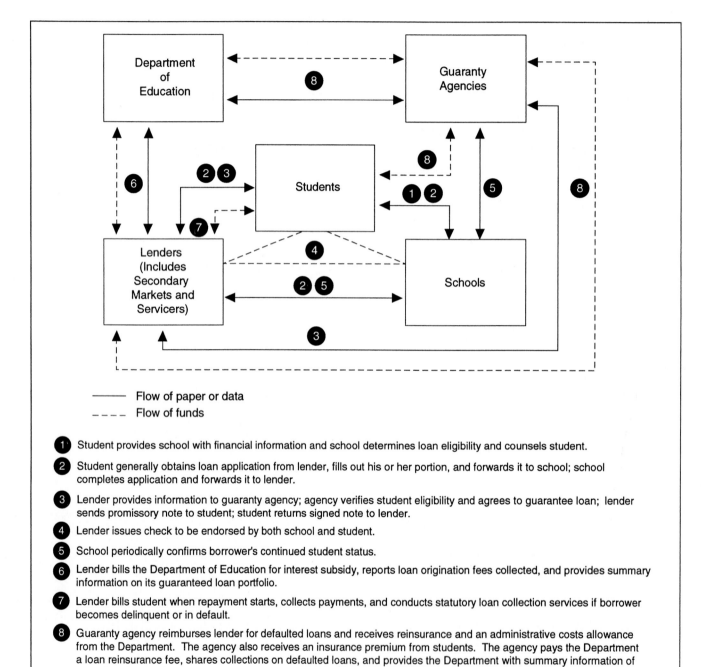

——— Flow of paper or data

– – – – Flow of funds

1 Student provides school with financial information and school determines loan eligibility and counsels student.

2 Student generally obtains loan application from lender, fills out his or her portion, and forwards it to school; school completes application and forwards it to lender.

3 Lender provides information to guaranty agency; agency verifies student eligibility and agrees to guarantee loan; lender sends promissory note to student; student returns signed note to lender.

4 Lender issues check to be endorsed by both school and student.

5 School periodically confirms borrower's continued student status.

6 Lender bills the Department of Education for interest subsidy, reports loan origination fees collected, and provides summary information on its guaranteed loan portfolio.

7 Lender bills student when repayment starts, collects payments, and conducts statutory loan collection services if borrower becomes delinquent or in default.

8 Guaranty agency reimburses lender for defaulted loans and receives reinsurance and an administrative costs allowance from the Department. The agency also receives an insurance premium from students. The agency pays the Department a loan reinsurance fee, shares collections on defaulted loans, and provides the Department with summary information of loans it guaranteed.

Source: GAO/AIMD-94-131 and ACN 17-30302 FFELP's FY 1993 Financial Audit

How The Guaranteed Student Loan Program Control System Works

The guaranteed student loan process is largely automated. Students who participate in the program typically do so by working with their school's financial aid office. A network of guarantee agencies administers the program under the direction of the Department of Education. While some guarantee agencies (e.g., United Student Aid Funds) operate on a national basis, others operate at the level of a single school or a single state. The Department of Education pays guaranty agencies start-up money plus an annual administrative cost allowance. The annual cost allowance is equal to 1% of the principal amount of new loans the agency guarantees in a fiscal year. The Department of Education also reimburses the agencies for any payments to lenders on defaulted loans and allows the agency to keep 30% of any collections it makes on defaulted loans.

Under the guaranteed student loan program (GSLP), borrowers (usually the student) begin the loan process by providing eligibility information to their school and filling out a loan application. If the school verifies a student's eligibility (including verifying that the loan amount does not exceed the cost of the student's attendance) and a guaranty agency approves the loan, the lender disburses the loan amount.

Most students receive below-market interest rates for their loans because of the subsidy paid by the Department of Education to the lender. In order for the lender to continue to receive a market rate of interest throughout the life of the loan, the subsidy is increased or decreased, as needed, on a quarterly basis throughout the loan's life. Students do not become responsible for repayment of the loan until they leave school. Generally, the student pays no principal or interest while attending school or during a short grace period (a specified time after graduation) or deferment period (e.g., verified unemployment). During these times, the government pays the lender not only the interest subsidy, but also the current interest that would be owed by the student.

Over 7,500 schools participate in the GSLP, including 2-year and 4-year private and public colleges and proprietary (for-profit) trade schools. The Department of Education can cancel a school's access to the program if the school has a history of unacceptably high default rates and for various other reasons (e.g., failure to properly verify eligibility requirements).

About 8,000 lenders participate in the guaranteed student loan program. Under the programs rules, lenders are required to exercise proper care in making, servicing, and collecting loans. Lenders are also required to pay an "origination fee" to the Department of Education when the loan is made and an insurance premium to the agency guaranteeing the loan. The premium is usually equal to about 3% of the loan amount. Lenders usually deduct these fees/premiums from the loan amounts disbursed to students.

To encourage the guaranty agencies to make collection efforts and other efforts to prevent default, the Department of Education charges them a reinsurance fee of either ¼% or ½% of new loans made during the year, with the fee amount based on the agency's past default claims experience (the higher the default rate, the higher the fee). To further encourage low default rates, the agencies' reimbursement rate is reduced from 100% if default rates fall below certain "trigger points." Full reimbursement is made if default rates are 5% or lower, but the reimbursement rate drops to 90% if default rates are between 5% and 9%, and drops again to 80% if default rates exceed 9%. The agencies may also receive a payment of $50 per loan for certain default prevention efforts.

Overall responsibility for the GSLP rests in the Department of Education's Office of Postsecondary Education (OPE). As part of its responsibilities, OPE accounts for GSLP operations and reports those results to another arm of the Department of Education: the Office of Management and Budget/Chief Financial Officer. This office is responsible for maintaining the Department of Education's department-level accounting records and reporting the financial results of all of Education's programs to the Office of Management and Budget and the Department of the Treasury.

Lenders bill the Department of Education quarterly for the federal interest subsidy, including the students' share of interest for students who are still in school, a grace period, or a deferment period. Lenders also report the origination fees they owe the Department on these quarterly billings. The Department then pays the lenders the net amount owed (interest subsidies due to the lenders less origination fees due from the lenders). If a lender owes more for origination fees on new loans than it is due in interest subsidies on old loans, the lender must pay the Department of Education when the billing is submitted. Lender billings to the Department of Education often include interest on loans guaranteed by several different agencies. The guaranty agencies periodically review the accuracy of lender billings on the loans they guarantee and report the results of these reviews to the Department of Education.

Lenders make claims for default repayments through the appropriate guarantee agency. Guarantee agencies submit periodic reports to the Department of Education that OPE uses to: (1) reimburse default claims the agencies paid to lenders; (2) calculate its administrative cost allowance to the agencies; and (3) calculate the Department of Education's liability for outstanding guaranteed student loans for Education's financial reports. The liability is an estimate of how much interest subsidies and default repayments remain to be paid in the future on any currently outstanding student loans.

The guaranty agency periodic reports are submitted as follows:

◆ *Monthly reports on default claims and collections*--OPE uses these reports to determine amounts due the agencies and to account for default costs.

♦ *Quarterly reports providing cumulative totals on default claims paid and new loans guaranteed*--By comparing the two most recent quarterly reports, OPE can determine the agency's activity for the quarter. This information is used to calculate the administrative cost allowances owed to the agency, and the reinsurance fees owed by the agency.

♦ *Annual computer tapes (known as "dumps") of selected data on each loan guarantee issued by the agencies during the year*--These reports include each borrower's name and social security number, the net amount guaranteed, the loan status, and the enrollment status. The Department of Education uses the tape dump data for a variety of analyses, including the calculation of its estimated liability.

What Your Audit Uncovered

1.   Guaranty agency reports were often late. Of the 10 guaranty agencies you reviewed, 2 did not submit their final monthly billing for the year on time. This late report resulted in both agencies receiving a higher than appropriate reimbursement for defaults because the 12 month totals, if reported on a timely basis, would have revealed that the agencies' default rates were beyond the trigger point for a reduction in the reimbursement rates for defaults.

2.   Lender billings were often late. For one quarter of the year, 1,693 of 11,294 lender billings were not submitted within the required 90-day time frame and 1,322 of these were not submitted even after 180 days. The Department of Education does not impose penalties for late bills or assess interest on unpaid origination fees, nor does it pay interest subsidies until a lender submits a bill.

3.   The Department of Education often did not perform any tests to see if the various reports reconciled. When your audit team compared the quarterly reports of 10 guaranty agencies to the totals on those same agency's annual tape dumps, you found discrepancies for the same dates ranging from $6 million to $212 million per agency. None of 10 guaranty agencies reconciled their quarterly and yearly data and only 1 reconciled its monthly bills to its quarterly reports.

4.   Your independent reviews of one of the guaranty agencies revealed that the agency did not have many controls to detect clerical errors. There are so many errors that in its most recent quarterly report to the Department of Education, the agency overstated loans made that quarter by more than $30 million (about 60% of the reported loans made during the quarter were, in fact, not new loans). This overstatement could have resulted in the Department of Education overpaying the agency's administrative cost allowance by about $300,000. The errors were corrected by the agency

after your audit team brought them to the agency's attention.

5.   Your independent reviews of the tape dump data consisted of choosing a sample of reported loan information and attempting to verify the information by looking at the appropriate source documents (e.g., loan application forms, school enrollment verification forms, etc.). For 30 randomly selected student loans reported to be in default, you found that 10 had errors in either the reported status of the loan (e.g., the student was still enrolled and hence the loan was not due or in default) or the reported claims paid to lenders.

6.   You reviewed the work of the Department's internal auditors, known as "program review teams." Within the past 24 months, the review teams had audited all of the 10 guaranty agencies you tested. The program review teams' audits concentrated on testing the agencies' procedures for preventing defaults and collecting on defaulted loans. The program review teams also examined financial reports of the agencies to determine the solvency of the agencies.

7.   You reviewed the computer logs for the times when software related to the GSLP was running during the first 9 months of the year. The logs listed over 400 "abnormal processing interruption" events during this time. Abnormal processing interruptions are instances where a software application, such as processing monthly billings, stops running midstream (before the program is finished). No detailed information on these interruptions was maintained.

ASSIGNMENT I-2C-8: Basic Concepts of Internal Control Systems: Read All About It #2

SETTING

You have just been promoted to a management position and will be supervising other employees for the first time. Lately, you've been thinking a lot about how becoming a manager will affect your life. One of the things you realize is that you will now play a different role in the company's internal control system. To help you think about this, you've been reading some business books and the financial press.

While doing your reading, you come across 2 stories that relate to basic concepts of internal control (see next page).

ASSIGNMENT

Determine how the stories relate to basic concepts of internal control. What lessons from the stories can be applied to other organizations?

HINTS

Relate the stories to the steps in an internal control system.

Consider how the stories relate to common causes of internal control breakdowns.

Story #1

Source of story: news reports, August 1994

<u>Summary of the story:</u>
Two Taco Bell customers drove up to the window at the Shirley, New York store and ordered a 7-layer chicken burrito and 2 Meximelts. Moments later, an employee working at the drive-up window turned and saw a small Taco Bell bag had just been placed on her counter. She handed the bag to the customers, who drove away.

Seconds later, the store's assistant manager was alarmed to find the bag missing. It hadn't contained the items ordered; it had contained $1,940 in cash from the store's cash registers that the assistant manager was planning to take to the bank. The assistant manager had prepared the bank deposit, sealed it in a small Taco Bell bag, and placed the bag on the middle shelf of the take-out counter for a few seconds while she got a soft drink to take along on the ride to the bank.

The assistant manager ran out to find the customers, but the car had disappeared from sight; the customers did not return. The assistant manager asked the take-out clerk why she hadn't opened the bag to put in napkins before giving the bag to the customer. The clerk replied that the take-out was very busy, the bag was the right size for the small order, and she had forgotten about the napkins.

Story #2

Source of story: news reports, September 1994

<u>Summary of the story:</u>
The Federal Reserve Bank of Philadelphia operates a program, known as Treasury Direct, that allows direct purchases of government securities by the public. Records of the securities and the interest the securities earn are kept electronically. Investors receive advance notice of interest payments.

In September 1994, a clerk computed the interest due to about 16,000 investors on $800 million of Treasury notes. The clerk made an error: transposing (reversing) 2 digits in the interest rate, changing it from the actual 6.87% to 8.67%. Once the incorrect rate was entered into the computer, all 16,000 interest calculations were done incorrectly--totaling almost $14 million in errors.

Letters signed by the division's director for consumer service were mailed to inform investors of the (incorrect) interest they would be receiving. Some investors who checked their interest using pocket calculators found the error and told Treasury officials before payments were made. The mistake was then corrected.

I-2-138

ASSIGNMENT I-2C-9:   <u>**Basic Concepts of Internal Control Systems**</u>**:
The U. S. General Accounting Office**

SETTING

You have just been hired as a new staff member for the U. S. General Accounting Office (GAO), the investigative arm of the U. S. Congress. You are looking forward to your work as a GAO auditor, which you understand often involves evaluating information systems and internal control systems.

To get off to a good start, you plan to familiarize yourself with some past GAO reports before you go out on your first audit. You are pleased to find that GAO reports are available via the Internet at:

http://www.gao.gov

ASSIGNMENT

Access the GAO home page and choose the link to recent GAO reports and testimony. Review some of the reports to find one that focuses on the review of an information system or an internal control system. Download a copy of the report for your use, and print a copy of the executive summary at the front of the report to hand in to your instructor.

Prepare a brief (5 to 6 minute) oral presentation for the class describing the nature of the GAO's audit and the key findings in the GAO report.

What you must hand in for grading: (1) a printed copy of the summary section of the GAO report; (2) an outline of your oral presentation.

HINTS

1.   There will be many GAO reports listed. Don't pick too quickly. You will have the best chance at making an effective presentation if you choose a report that will be of interest to other class members and one that is not duplicated by other groups. Time spent exploring the databank of reports could pay off in the end.

2.   You may not be able to tell from a report's title whether it has anything to

do with information systems or internal controls. Read the summary at the front of the report to get a better idea of the topic. The body of the report follows the same order as the summary, but with greater details.

3.   A 5 to 6 minute presentation is shorter than you think. The keys to a successful short presentation are planning and practice. Plan ahead to be sure you use your time wisely. Practice your presentation to be sure it sounds polished. If you need hints on preparing for presentations, see the appendix to this module: "Eight Steps to Effective Oral Presentations.".

ASSIGNMENT I-2C-10:   Basic Concepts of Internal Control Systems: Internal Controls at Gas Stations

SETTING

You are a student studying *Core Concepts of Accounting Information.* One evening, after a long siege reading about basic concepts of internal control systems, you decide to take a drive to give yourself a study break. Since your car is low on gas, you stop to fill the tank at a local gas station. While you are there, you decide to buy a soda and candy bar, but there's no attendant in sight to take your cash. While you wait for someone to come back to the cash register, you cannot help but observe the station's internal control system. Almost in spite of yourself, you begin to think about the control process you are observing.

ASSIGNMENT

Use a real gas station to illustrate the steps in an internal control system: assigning responsibility; establishing standards; motivating and rewarding performance; monitoring performance; communicating progress and taking corrective action, if needed. Also consider how the station's control system helps safeguard the cash and inventory (stock held for sale or rental).

This assignment should be done as a group project. Your group will have approximately 10 minutes to make a classroom presentation to the other students. You must also hand in a written outline of your presentation.

HINTS

First you need to understand the policies and procedures at the gas station. If any group member has worked in a gas station, use his or her knowledge of the business as a starting point for your discussion. If no one in the group has ever worked at a gas station, interview a current or former gas station employee or manager to find out how the internal controls work. You might also consider some observational research (i.e., visit a gas station and watch what goes on). Develop a short description of the system.

Next, analyze the system. What are the goals? Is there a clear assignment of responsibility? What are the performance standards? How is performance motivated? rewarded? How is performance monitored? How do employees find out how they are doing? What kind of corrective action can be taken if problems are discovered (use a particular example--just one will do)? What safeguards are built into the process? Come to class prepared to describe and analyze the system.

Think about how the internal control system could be described in terms of the COSO report, "Internal Control--An Integrated Framework." What aspects of the system tell you something about the control environment? What are some of the major risks that must be managed? How do the control activities and procedures relate to the organization's objectives and perceived risks? How does the organization provide for information and communication? What kind of monitoring takes place?

Come to class prepared to describe and analyze the system. Think carefully about how to structure your presentation so you can give the class a good picture of the control system in a short time. If you need hints on preparing an oral presentation, see "Eight Steps to an Effective Presentation" in the appendix to this module.

ASSIGNMENT I-2C-11:   Basic Concepts of Internal Control Systems: Read All About It #3

SETTING

You have just been promoted to a management position and will be supervising other employees for the first time. Lately, you've been thinking a lot about how becoming a manager will affect your life. One of the things you realize is that you will now play a different role in the company's internal control system. To help you think about this, you've been reading some business books and the financial press.

While doing your reading, you come across 2 stories that relate to basic concepts of internal control (see next page).

ASSIGNMENT

Determine how the stories relate to basic concepts of internal control. What lessons from the stories can be applied to other organizations?

HINTS

Relate the stories to the steps in an internal control system.

Consider how the stories relate to common causes of internal control breakdowns.

Story #1

Source of story: *Los Angeles Times*, February 1997

Summary of the story:
In January, 1997 Michael La Motte, Assistant Chief Deputy Clerk of the Pomona Municipal Court pleaded no contest to a felony charge of misappropriation of funds after being accused of stealing about $240,000 from the court system.

La Motte stole the money by periodically asking the Court's mail clerk (who opened the mail) for any checks sent by local cities to reimburse the Court for processing their parking violations. La Motte would then go to the Court's cashier and cash the checks. La Motte would give the cashier a receipt for the money and said he would later deposit the same amount in the Court's bank account, but he never did.

An audit two years earlier had pointed out several internal control problems over cash. La Motte, who headed the Court's auditing division and balanced the Court's bank account, was one of the officials assigned to correct the deficiencies. The theft ended when a bookkeeper happened to balance the bank account one day and found a $7,700 shortage; La Motte immediately confessed his theft.

Story #2

Source of story: U.K. news reports, July 1996

Summary of the story:
A team of scholars at Manchester University was studying manuscripts from the 11th century in England and Wales. In that era, before the invention of any copying machines, scribes would make multiple copies of important records. The scholars found 9 copies--2 in the British Library, 2 in the Bodeleian Library (Oxford), and 1 each in libraries in Cambridge, Canterbury, London and Lichfield--of the records computing taxes owed by church clergymen for 1291-1292.

When they compared the 9 copies, which covered about 9,000 British clergymen, they found that some of the clergy had been overtaxed. The errors occured when scribes who were making the copies mixed up a two monetary units: marks and pounds (a mark was worth two-thirds of a pound. As a result of using the wrong monetary unit, the scribes overstated the clergymen's taxable income. Collecting the overpaymenta after seven centuries is unlikely. But technically, the overpaid taxes--plus interest for 700 years--are now due from the Crown to the churches.

THE FOLLOWING PAGES

CONTAIN THE SOLUTIONS FOR

THE SELF-CORRECTED ASSIGNMENTS IN THIS MODULE.

PAPER TRAIL

To target your best customers, think about digging into your receipt files

BY PAUL B. BROWN

Billy Beer. Dr. Ruth endorsing your product. "The official sponsor of . . ." Most marketing fads are pretty silly. But micromarketing—which shows all the signs of being the next full-blown fad—is an exception. Before your eyes glaze over, keep in mind that micromarketing is nothing more than using mail-order lists, census information, and historical buying patterns to help create the perfect prospect list. Once you have the list, you tailor your sales pitch accordingly.

With a recession circling ever closer like some hungry vulture, wouldn't you love to increase your chance of reaching the right potential customer? Joan V. Silver, president of Reeves Audio Visual Systems Inc., would. And she's figured out a way to do it that strips the concept of micromarketing to its essentials. She looked through her receipts. That's right, her receipts—those slips of paper you give your customers to prove they've paid.

Silver found with a little bit of modification and study, receipts (used broadly here to include invoices and purchase orders) can identify who's likely to buy from you, where you're making the most money, and what product lines or types of business you should drop.

It was necessity, more than any intuitive grasp of selling theory, that led Silver to a more efficient way of marketing.

About four times a year, Silver, who runs a $5-million-plus New York City company that sells and services a full-line of industrial audiovisual equipment, does a mailing to 3,000 customers and potential customers. "Since direct mail is the only advertising we do, other than appearing in the *Yellow Pages,* I'd love to mail more frequently," Silver says. "But mailings are expensive." Yet Silver had a new $16,000 Sony video-projection system in stock that she wanted the world to know about. How could she spread the word—efficiently?

The marketing "experts" would be happy to come in and set up a micromarketing program for tens of thousands of dollars. But Silver, with the help of financial consult-

ant Ted Schlissel of Equity Information Corp., concluded she could get the same information simply by reading her receipts.

Silver came to this conclusion as she tried to figure out ways to market more effectively. Clearly, not all of her customers could afford a $16,000 projection television, but most could, she thought.

After all, weren't 90% of her customers *Fortune* 500 companies? They were when

Joan V. Silver, president of Reeves Audio Visual Systems
Receipts revealed who her customers are—and what they want.

Reeves A/V began in 1973. But as Silver started going through her receipts—trying to figure how to prune the 10% of her mailing list that she thought would be too small to buy a $16,000 video-projection system—she learned an amazing thing. The *Fortune* 500 accounted for just 58% of revenues. The rest came from smaller companies, often with less than $1 million in sales.

Silver continued to explore her records and ranked her top 20 customers by sales, figuring that list would tell her the types of companies that were buying from her. Once she knew who her best customers were, she could then look to see what they were buying. Knowing both things would suggest marketing opportunities.

In compiling the list, Silver found some of

her largest accounts of old had become victims of mergers, cutbacks, or both. No surprise there. But what was surprising were the firms that had taken their place: advertising agencies and insurance companies.

When she examined her receipts she discovered that ad agencies had begun buying custom-designed turnkey editing systems. They were setting up their own editing suites, instead of subcontracting the work out as they had in the past.

And the insurance companies? They were buying television production equipment so they would be able to make training tapes internally.

Knowing all this gave Silver a blueprint for creating a more effective marketing plan. First, she'd look through her receipts for insurance companies and ad agencies who had *not* bought such equipment. The sales pitch to those firms would be simple: "Since your competitors are bringing their production work inside, shouldn't you be thinking about it, too? We can custom-design a system for you."

Second, Silver started classifying the kinds of things her customers were and weren't buying from her. "We found some people knew us for our service work; others just bought equipment from us." She tailored letters to each group, underscoring Reeves A/V's full-service capabilities.

But what of the 42% of her customers for whom a $16,000 purchase is out of the question? They, too, are now the target of focused marketing programs. As a look through Reeves's receipts showed, they were just too important to ignore.

If Reeves A/V is doing a large job for a *Fortune* 500 company, it's not unusual for the work to cost $250,000. But potential new corporate clients tend to put jobs that size out for competitive bidding, which makes it difficult for Silver to maintain pretax margins of an estimated 10%.

Her smaller clients, however, rarely have the luxury of bidding out work. When they need a product, they usually need it immediately. And since most don't have an in-house expert to call on, they need support and service as well. They're willing to pay for the extra service.

As a result, profit on those sales can be higher. To keep that business, Silver is broadening her product line to ensure she has in stock what those customers need, and she's now providing three-hour delivery.

The result of Silver's focused marketing is clear. She can do smaller, more targeted mailings once a month for the cost of the big, unfocused quarterly mailings she used to do. Her response rate is up 10% since beginning this effort.

"We should have done this years ago," says Silver. Perhaps. But having used her receipts as a marketing tool, she's still way ahead of those who are only beginning to talk about the wonders of micro-marketing. ❑

HOW TO CREATE THE PERFECT RECEIPT
A few extra items can reveal a lot about your sales

As a matter of course, you probably have the following nine items on your receipt form: date of sale, customer name, address, phone number, product sold, quantity sold, unit price, total price, and salesperson. And that's fine. Each line by itself can yield loads of information.

But to be truly effective as a source of marketing information, argues consultant Ted Schlissel of Equity Information Corp.—who helped Reeves Audio Visual Systems Inc. analyze its business—a receipt should be able to answer the following four *additional* questions:

What was our profit per unit sold? Clearly, you don't want to print your margins on the receipt. Still, you should be able to tell at a glance if a customer is buying your most profitable items.

How big are they? No need to write "37 employees" after the customer's name. But devise some kind of simple system that can show you that you're serving the *Fortune* 500, mom-and-pops, or companies in-between. A company's size frequently dictates the kind of support it needs.

Intended use of product. Customers have the darnedest habit of coming up with new uses for your product; you should know what they are.

Referred by? This lets you know whom to thank. It also gives you references to check.

MODULE INDEX

-ABC-

-DEF-

-GHI-

-JKL-

-MNO-

-PQR-

3

MODULE 3: OWNERS AND CREDITORS AS USERS OF ACCOUNTING INFORMATION

1997-1998 edition

Table of Contents

MODULE 3: OWNERS AND CREDITORS AS USERS OF ACCOUNTING INFORMATION

Estimated Time Budget

__Task__	__Time Estimate__
Reading PART A: THE ROLE OF CAPITAL MARKETS	70 - 100 minutes
Assignments for Part A	
Assignment 3A-1	10 - 15 minutes
Assignment 3A-2	10 - 15 minutes
Assignment 3A-3	90 - 120 minutes
Assignment 3A-4	90 - 120 minutes
Reading PART B: BASIC CONCEPTS OF FINANCIAL ACCOUNTING	120 - 165 minutes
Assignments for Part B	
Assignment 3B-1	60 - 75 minutes
Assignment 3B-2	15 - 30 minutes
Assignment 3B-3	35 - 50 minutes
Assignment 3B-4	35 - 50 minutes
Assignment 3B-5	35 - 50 minutes
Assignment 3B-6	40 - 60 minutes
Assignment 3B-7	60 - 90 minutes
Assignment 3B-8	35 - 50 minutes
Assignment 3B-9	40 - 60 minutes
Reading Part C: BASIC CONCEPTS OF AUDITING	50 - 75 minutes
Assignments for Part C	
Assignment 3C-1	50 - 75 minutes
Assignment 3C-2	45 - 60 minutes
Assignment 3C-3	45 - 60 minutes
Assignment 3C-4	60 - 90 minutes
Assignment 3C-5	90 - 120 minutes

Note: *These time estimates, like all the time budgets for this course, should be adjusted to suit your own learning style. Time estimates for assignments assume that readings were completed before attempting assignments.*

MODULE 3: OWNERS AND CREDITORS AS USERS OF ACCOUNTING INFORMATION

PART A: THE ROLE OF CAPITAL MARKETS

Money is a singular thing. It ranks with love as man's greatest source of joy. And with his death as his greatest source of anxiety.
-- John Kenneth Galbraith, The Age of Uncertainty

Launching a new venture, whether business or non-business, requires money. In most organizations, the start-up capital is provided by entrepreneurs or founders, who also contribute the ideas that determine the initial organizational goals and plans. If an organization is small enough--or the entrepreneurs or founders are wealthy enough--the organization may be able to carry out its plans without seeking additional sources of capital.

But, many organizations find they need additional resources. They look to sources outside the organization to provide capital. For these organizations, there are 2 choices: borrowing money from creditors (which provides debt capital) or selling a piece of the action to investors (which provides equity capital). Accounting information plays an important role in credit and investment decisions and the functioning of capital markets.

DEBT CAPITAL

If you want time to pass quickly, just give your note for 90 days.
-- R. B. Thomas, Farmer's Almanac

Debt capital is borrowed from creditors or lenders. Lenders are individuals or organizations who loan money to a borrower with the expectation of being repaid with interest. The lender and the borrower enter into a contract specifying the terms of their agreement. A loan may exist for a short or long period of time, but it is not permanent. This section introduces some basic concepts about debt capital including typical characteristics of debt contracts, the need for short-term and long-term borrowing, and the major sources of long-term debt capital.

Characteristics of Debt Contracts

Most forms of debt are described in legal contracts between the lender and the borrower. While variations are possible, the contract typically specifies at least 4 things: (1) the principal amount, (2) the maturity date, (3) the interest rate, and (4) the conditions of lending. The terms of a debt contract are influenced by the degree of risk the lender takes and the return the lender requires.

Principal, Maturity Date and Interest. Suppose a company borrows $50,000 from a bank, promising to repay the loan in 2 years and to pay 10% interest per year while the loan is **outstanding** (not yet paid back). The principal is the amount of money borrowed ($50,000 in our example). The **principal** will have to be repaid by the **maturity date** (the time when the debt becomes due, 2 years from now in our example). As long as any of the principal is outstanding, the borrower must pay **interest** for using the money. Interest is calculated by multiplying the outstanding balance (the portion of the principal not yet paid) by the interest rate, which refers to an annual period unless otherwise specified:

$$\text{Interest} = \text{Principal} \times \text{Rate} \times \text{Time}$$

So, if the interest rate is 10% (per year) on a 2-year loan of $50,000, then $5,000 interest (10% × $50,000) must be paid each year, for a total of $10,000 over the life of the loan:

$$\text{Interest} = \text{Principal} \times \text{Rate} \times \text{Time}$$
$$\$10,000 = \$50,000 \times 10\% \times 2 \text{ years}$$

Conditions of Lending. The conditions of lending (known as "**restrictive covenants**") tell borrowers what they must do or what they cannot do as long as the loan is outstanding. For example, a lender may require the borrower to maintain a certain net worth (another name for total assets less total liabilities) during the life of the loan. Or, the borrower may be restricted from purchasing major equipment or acquiring another company without the lender's approval.

The restrictive covenants protect the interests of the lender. Generally, the covenants are designed to reduce the risk of **default**--the risk that the borrower will not be able to repay the lender. If the borrower complies with the lending conditions, there is a greater chance that the borrower will be able to repay the loan when due. Alternatively, the restrictions may be designed to protect the lender's position in a worst-case scenario--for example, by making sure the lender can compel payment of the loan at the earliest sign of trouble (like falling below minimum net worth) rather than being forced to keep the loan open as the situation deteriorates further. If a borrower violates the restrictive covenants, the lender may demand immediate payment of the loan.

The Risk-Return Trade-off. Lenders may (and should) try to limit their risk, but they can't eliminate it. The lender is willing to accept some risk in order to be rewarded with an appropriate return (profit). For, as A. P. Gouthey once said, "To get profit without risk, experience without danger, and reward without work, is as impossible as it is to live without being born." A conservative lender tries to reduce risk as much as possible and, in turn, will expect a relatively small return. Lenders who accept greater risk, will expect a relatively greater return.

For example, suppose a bank lends $100,000 each to 2 local hospitals. One hospital is able to "secure" its loan by pledging some medical equipment it owns as collateral. If the hospital defaults, the bank can take possession of the medical equipment, sell it, and use the proceeds to pay off the loan. The other hospital rents its medical equipment (so it cannot be used as collateral) and does not have any other collateral to offer; its loan is said to be "unsecured."

Obviously, the unsecured loan is riskier than the secured loan. So, the second hospital can expect to pay a higher interest rate (and, possibly, to be subject to more restrictive covenants) than the first hospital. This risk-return trade-off is one of the fundamental concepts of finance: loans or investments with greater risk must hold the promise of higher returns. Figure I-3-1, on the following page, shows a graph of the relationship between risk and return.

The Need for Short-Term Borrowing

The need for outside capital is not unique to modern organizations. The earliest known records of organizations using outside sources of capital date back to ancient Mesopotamia where a system of agricultural lending (lending to farmers) developed.

Mesopotamian land was fertile and would support more crops than the farmers needed for their own survival. Moreover, there were buyers who wanted to trade other goods for crops if the farmers raised more than they needed. The opportunity to make a profit existed, but first the interested farmers needed to buy seed. A lending system developed. The farmers would borrow at the start of the growing season to buy seeds. At the end of the season--when the crops were harvested--the loans would be repaid with interest. This was the first known example of short-term borrowing.

Even today, businesses have seasonal needs for extra funds. For example, a toy manufacturer must produce goods throughout the year to build up enough stock to meet customer demands for holiday season sales (when more than half of all toy sales occur). The cash-to-cash process that

- ♦ begins with cash being used to purchase raw materials,

- ♦ continues through the manufacture of the toys (or any other product or service), and

- ♦ ends with cash being received for sales

is known as the business's "**operating cycle**." To meet their cash needs, businesses may need to borrow funds at the early stages of their operating cycle, to be repaid at the later stages of the cycle.

Figure I-3-1
The Risk-Return Trade-off

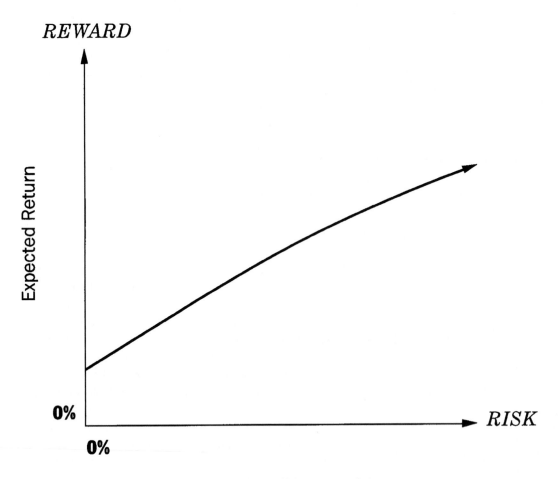

Risk you are willing to take

Short-term borrowing--which lenders today define as borrowing for 1 year or less--is still an important source of capital for business. For example, in 1972, when Nolan Bushnell founded Atari, the first video game manufacturer, he only put in $500 of his own funds to start the company. He borrowed money short-term (on 30-day loans) to buy the parts he needed to manufacture his first games. The games were so popular that he was able to sell them for cash as soon as they were made and repay the loans. Bushnell's effective use of outside capital gave him the ability to create a rapidly growing business. When he sold Atari 3 years later, the purchaser (Warner Communications) paid $28 million for it.

Nonbusiness organizations also engage in short-term borrowing as needed. For example, suppose a charitable foundation collects most of its annual contributions after a once-a-year fundraising event where donors make pledges to send in contributions over a 30-day period. The foundation needs to pay its employees, who work long hours putting together the event, and other costs of the fundraiser, but it may not have enough cash to cover these expenses until the pledges are collected. Short-term borrowing offers a solution.

Beyond Short-Term Borrowing: The Need for Long-Term Capital

Until the twentieth century, most businesses were financed primarily with the owner-entrepreneur's own funds, supplemented by short-term borrowing. Before the Industrial Revolution--which is somewhat misnamed since it occurred slowly and mostly peacefully--the vast majority of businesses were small and unsophisticated by today's standards. Virtually all businesses were operated by their owners and dealt in a simple set of products or services. Some businesses were conducted as "ventures" where owners banded together to engage in a particular business activity (like transporting a shipload of tea from one country to another). Ventures lasted only long enough to complete their purpose and then they were disbanded. Most continuing businesses were agricultural or "cottage industries," home-based businesses that employed only a few people and used little machinery.

The Industrial Revolution changed the nature of business. In Europe, the Industrial Revolution occurred between 1750 and 1850. In the United States, the Industrial Revolution began at about the time of the Civil War. In Japan and Russia, industrialization occurred beginning in the early 1900s. During this period, several important inventions--like the steam engine, the spinning jenny, the power loom, refrigeration and the sewing machine--spurred a move away from small, home-based businesses to large factories employing many workers.

The movement toward industrialization was accelerated by improvements in transportation, communications and power sources. For example, in England, most of the railway lines that exist today had been laid by 1870. Similarly, in the United States, most of the railway lines that exist today had been laid by 1916. In the U.S., both the telephone industry and the electric industry were initiated during the 1880s.

With industrialization came the realization that "economies of scale" could be achieved by larger businesses. For example, when automobiles were first invented, they were manufactured by a small team putting together one car at a time. Henry Ford realized a car could be produced more quickly--and at a much lower cost--by manufacturing with an "assembly line" where workers each performed small tasks and many cars could be worked on at once. By 1925, Ford Motor Company's assembly line was turning out a car every 10 seconds.

As businesses grew more complex and economies expanded, the need for long-term capital arose. Building railways, for instance, required huge amounts of capital, far in excess of most other industries in the 1800s. In the United States, railroads were the first enterprises to depend primarily on outside capital. As another example, financing factory machinery--with its long life and high costs--required more capital for a longer time than financing seeds to grow crops, or raw materials for a cottage industry.

As the need for long-term borrowing grew, the number of lending institutions exploded. For example, by 1913, the U.S. had almost 7,500 national banks, over 14,000 state banks, and over 1,500 loan companies. Today, banks and other lending institutions are still a major source of intermediate-term (1 to 5 years) and long-term (5 years or longer) debt financing. But, lending institutions are not the only source of long-term debt capital. Today, long-term debt financing--funds raised by issuing **bonds** (long-term debt contracts issued by corporations or government agencies), **mortgages** (bonds secured by pledges of property as security for the loan), and other long-term promissory notes--may also be obtained from individual or corporate investors through **public debt offerings**, **government auctions**, or **private debt placements**.

Public Debt Offerings

In a public offering, a company sells its debt securities (such as bonds) in a public securities market (such as the New York Stock Exchange, NASDAQ Over-the-Counter market, or London Stock Exchange). Anyone who can pay the market price may buy these debt securities, thus becoming a creditor of the company. In 1996, $800.7 billion of debt securities were issued in U.S. markets.

The original buyers--who may be individual investors or corporations--do not necessarily intend to remain creditors until the debt matures, which may be decades later. The debt security may be resold to another buyer at any time before maturity. In such a resale, known as "**secondary market**" trading, the only money that changes hands passes from the new creditor to the old creditor. The issuing company is *not* part of secondary market trades and does not receive any funds from the resale. The only thing that changes for the issuing company is the name of the creditor to whom interest (and principal at maturity) is owed.

Issuers of debt securities need information to help them decide what type of security to offer. Then, potential buyers need information to help them make their purchase decision. The market price of the debt security will reflect the market participants' assessments of all the information available about the security.

Deciding What Type of Debt Security to Offer. There are many variations of debt securities in modern markets, from simple bonds with a fixed interest rate and fixed maturity date to more complex instruments such as debt that can be converted to stock at the option of the holder, or debt that can be redeemed (paid off) before maturity at the option of the issuer. There's also an almost endless number of more exotic forms of debt securities such as dual-currency bonds, bonds that pay interest in one currency (like Japanese yen) and repay the principal in another currency (like the U.S. dollar).

With so many options, how does a company decide what type of debt security to offer? Usually, companies rely on their investment bankers, who provide expert advice on the kind of debt security to offer (e.g., what should the interest rate be? when should the maturity date be? what special features should the security have?) and when to offer it. In formulating their advice, investment bankers draw on many sources of information, including accounting information about the company and information about current market conditions.

The investment banker often also acts as an intermediary who buys the debt from the issuer (the borrower) and then resells it in a public securities market. This is called "**underwriting**" the security. The underwriter receives a fee from the issuer and may also profit from the "**underwriting spread**," the difference between what the underwriter pays to the issuer and the price paid by the public.

Obtaining Information About Public Debt Offerings. Companies can sell debt securities in more than one country, as long as they comply with the appropriate laws in each country. For example, debt securities offered for public sale in the United States must be registered with the U.S. Securities and Exchange Commission (SEC), the federal agency charged with regulating public securities markets. The issuer files a "**registration statement**" for the debt securities that discloses information about the company's financial condition and the nature of the debt offering. The registration statement also contains a copy of the "**prospectus**," the document the company uses to inform potential buyers about securities being offered for sale.

Acceptance of a registration statement by the SEC does not mean that the debt security is a good investment: there is no such thing as an SEC seal of approval for a security. Instead, the registration process is designed to make sure the potential buyers have enough information to make their decisions. Potential creditors, or other interested parties, may use the information in the registration statement to help them evaluate the wisdom of purchasing the debt securities. After the initial offering, owners of debt securities may continue to get information about the company through its annual reports and other SEC filings.

Market Prices of Debt Securities. The price of a debt security is set by the market. Each bond has a **face value or par value**, representing the amount of principal to be repaid at maturity, and a stated interest rate. The interest rate is fixed over the life of the bond. However, over that lifetime, interest rates in the world at large will fluctuate with the ups and downs of the economy. So, at any given point in time, the stated interest rate on a particular bond may be less than, equal to, or greater than the prevailing rate of interest (the interest rate buyers would currently be willing to accept for other debt securities of approximately the same risk). The market will see this difference and react to it by bidding the price of the bond up or down. Therefore, while the terms of a bond remain fixed over its lifetime, the market price it sells for will vary as interest rates fluctuate.

Figure I-3-2 (on the following page) shows how the market price of a bond will fluctuate as interest varies. As Figure I-3-2 illustrates, bonds may sell:

♦   **at "par"**: If the stated rate is equal to the prevailing rate of interest, the bond will sell at its face value. In the stock market reports, the bond's price will be listed as 100, meaning that it is selling at 100% of its face value. This is also referred to as selling at "par." Regardless of what a buyer pays for a bond--whether it is par or something other than par--the issuer will repay only the face value of the bond at maturity. Also, interest payments during the life of the bond are based on the face value, regardless of what the buyer paid for the bond or what its market value becomes over time.

♦   **at a "premium"**: If the bond offers a better deal (higher interest) than the prevailing rate, it will become so attractive that many investors will want to buy it. In this case, the increased demand will drive the market price up--as buyers will be willing to offer more than face value to buy the bond. This is known as buying the bond at a "premium." If, for example, buyers are willing to pay 6% more than face value for the bond, its price will be reported as 106, meaning 106% of face value. Generally, buyers will drive up the market price of a bond to the point where the bond is as good a deal--no better, no worse--as other securities of similar risk.

♦   **at a "discount"**: On the other hand, if the bond does not offer as good a deal (i.e., it has lower interest) than the prevailing rate, buyers will only be attracted if it sells at less than face value. This is known as buying (or selling) the bond at a "discount." For example, a bond with a price of 95 is selling at 95% of face value. Again, buyers will drive the market price (in this case, down) to the point where the bond is as good a deal--no better, no worse--as other securities of similar risk.

Figure I-3-2

The Relationship Between Interest Rates and Bond Prices

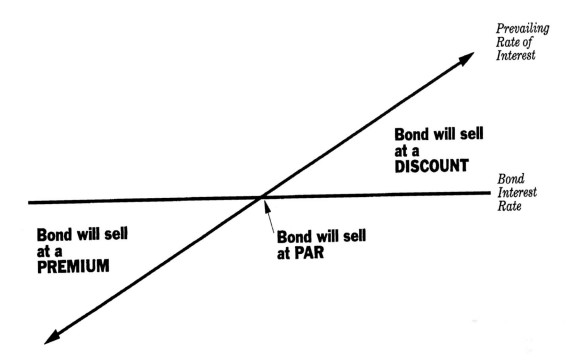

Prevailing
Rate of
Interest

**Bond will sell
at a
DISCOUNT**

Bond
Interest
Rate

**Bond will sell
at a
PREMIUM**

**Bond will sell
at PAR**

Debt Securities: An Example. Figure I-3-3 (on the next page) shows an excerpt from the *Wall Street Journal*'s daily list of "New Securities Issues," which describes the previous day's offerings in both U.S. and non-U.S. capital markets. Look at the first 2 debt securities listed under "Corporate" (AK Steel Holding Corp. and Alltel Corp.) and see if you can determine the principal, interest rate, maturity date and whether they sold at par, a premium, or a discount.

The AK Steel Holding Corp. debt securities have a total principal of $325 million, which--like all corporate bonds--is offered for sale in $1,000 units. The bonds have an interest rate of 10.75%, so each $1,000 bond earns interest of $107.50 per year. The bonds mature on April 1, 2004, 10 years from the date of issue. The bonds sold at par, so each unit cost a buyer $1,000 (plus any commissions paid to the broker who handled the transaction).

The Alltel Corp. bonds have a total principal of $250 million (also in $1,000 units). The bonds have a stated interest rate of 7.25%, so each $1,000 bond earns interest of $72.50 per year. These bonds also mature on April 1, 2004, 10 years after the date of issue. The bonds sold at a discount--they were priced at 99.508. So, each unit cost a buyer $995.08 (99.508 × $1,000) plus broker's commission.

What does the phrase "to yield 7.32%" mean in the Alltel description? Remember that the buyer of each unit receives $72.50 of interest each year, which is calculated on the $1,000 face value of the bond. But, the buyer only paid $995.08, not $1,000. So, the effective interest rate is really a little better than the stated rate of 7.25%. Buying the bonds at a discount made the Alltel bonds as good a deal as buying a bond at par that paid 7.32% interest.

One last question about the AK Steel Holding Corp. and Alltel Corp. bonds. Since both bonds mature on the same date, why aren't the interest rates on the 2 issues the same? The AK Steel Holding Corp. bonds pay almost one and a half times the interest of the Alltel bonds. The short answer is that the 2 bonds do not bear equivalent risk. One way to see this is to look at the credit ratings of the 2 bond issues as assessed by the Moody's Investors Service Inc. and Standard & Poor's Corp rating services. These ratings work much like a report card for risk, with better letter grades indicating lower risk (safer investments). The AK Steel bonds are rated single-B-2 by Moody's and single-B by Standard and Poor's. While these are acceptable ratings for many investors, they are lower than those for the Alltel bonds (single A-2 and single-A-plus), indicating that there is more risk with the AK Steel bonds than with the Alltel bonds. The bonds with the higher risk offer a higher return. Other factors also affect the returns paid. For example, the AK Steel bonds may be called (paid off early at the option of the company) after 5 years, whereas the Alltel bonds cannot be called.

Government Debt Securities

Governments may also issue debt securities. At present, for example, the U.S. federal government has about $4 trillion of outstanding public debt. The

Figure I-3-3
Example Listing of New Securities Offerings--March 30, 1994

NEW SECURITIES ISSUES

The following were among yesterday's offerings and pricings in U.S. and non-U.S. capital markets, with terms and syndicate manager, as compiled by Dow Jones Capital Markets Report:

CORPORATE

AK Steel Holding Corp. — $325 million of senior notes due April 1, 2004, priced at par to yield 10.75%, according to MCM CorporateWatch. The notes, noncallable for five years, are rated single-B-2 by Moody's Investors Service Inc. and single-B by Standard & Poor's Corp. The issue will be sold through underwriters led by CS First Boston Inc.

Alltel Corp. — $250 million of debentures due April 1, 2004, priced as 7.25s at 99.508 to yield 7.32%, according to MCM CorporateWatch. The noncallable issue was priced at a spread of 60 basis points above Treasurys. Rated single-A-2 by Moody's and single-A-plus by S&P, the issue will be sold through underwriters led by Stephens Inc.

Federal Home Loan Bank System — $112 million of notes due April 7, 1997, priced at par to yield 5.73%, according to MCM CorporateWatch. The notes are noncallable for one year and were priced at a spread of 20 basis points above Treasurys. The issue will be sold through underwriters led by Fuji Securities.

Greyhound Financial Corp. — $100 million of notes due April 1, 2001, priced as 7.25s at 99.244 to yield 7.39%, according to MCM CorporateWatch. The noncallable notes were priced at a spread of 88 basis points above Treasurys. Rated Baa-2 by Moody's and triple-B by S&P, the issue will be sold through underwriters led by Citicorp Securities Inc. Greyhound is a unit of **GFC Financial** Corp.

Texas Gas Transmission Corp. — $150 million of notes due April 1, 2004, priced at par to yield 8.625%. The noncallable issue was priced at a spread of 196.5 basis points above Treasurys. Rated Ba-2 by Moody's and double-B by S&P, the issue will be sold through underwriters led by Lehman Brothers Inc. Texas Gas is a unit of **Transco Energy** Co.

EQUITY

Applied Digital Access Inc. — initial public offering of 2.6 million common shares priced at $12 each, according to the company. Alex. Brown & Sons Inc. and Hambrecht & Quist Inc. co-managed the offering.

Cameron Ashley Inc. — initial offering of two million common shares priced at $12 each through underwriters led by Robinson-Humphrey Co.

DPL Inc. — 3.2 million common shares priced at $20.375 each, according to the company. CS First Boston Inc. is the lead manager.

Rouge Steel Co. — initial public offering of seven million shares priced at $22 each, according to the company. Lead manager for the offering is Morgan Stanley & Co.

MUNICIPAL

Honolulu — $150 million of Series 1994A general-obligation bonds priced by a Merrill Lynch & Co. group. Yields range from 4.6% in 1998 to 5.9% in 2013 and 2014. Moody's and S&P have rated the issue double-A. The bonds are noncallable.

Michigan Municipal Bond Authority — $109.8 million of Series 1994A local-government loan program revenue bonds priced by a Goldman, Sachs & Co. group to yield from 2.8% in December to 6.18% in 2018. The bonds are insured by the Financial Guaranty Insurance Co. and carry triple-A ratings from Moody's and S&P.

New York State Environmental Facilities Corp. — $717 million of Series 1994A state water-pollution control revolving-fund revenue bonds priced by a Goldman, Sachs & Co. group. Yields range from 3.55% in 1995 to 6.19% in 2014 and 2015. Moody's and Fitch Investors Service Inc. have rated the bonds double-A, and S&P has assigned a single-A-minus rating. Bonds due in 2008-12 are noncallable. The balance of the securities are callable June 15, 2004, at 102, declining to par in 2006.

MORTGAGE-BACKED

Federal National Mortgage Association — $838.8 million of real-estate mortgage-investment conduit securities offered by Kidder, Peabody & Co. The offering, Remic Trust 1994-75, is backed by the agency's 30-year, 7% mortgage securities. The collateral has a weighted average coupon rate of 7.6% and weighted average maturity of 359 months.

Federal National Mortgage Association — $133.5 million of Remic mortgage securities offered by CS First Boston Inc. The offering, Series 1994-73, is backed by various classes from the agency's Remic mortgage securities, including $21.9 million of Remic 1992-98 Class PK, $74.4 million of Remic 1992-112 Class EB, $18.8 million of Remic 1992-112 Class EC and $18.4 of Remic 1992-126 Class PH.

EUROBOND

Bank Austria AG (Austria) — 170 billion Italian lire of 9.125% Eurobonds due April 29, 2004, at issue price 100.25 via Banca Commerciale Italiana and Banca Nazionale del Lavoro. Bonds yield 9.4% after full fees of two. Callable annually from April 29, 1996, at par.

Deutsche Finance Netherlands BV (German parent) — one billion marks of 5.75% Eurobonds due May 4, 1999, at issue price 101.32 via Deutsche Bank AG. Recommended reoffer price 99.37 to yield 5.9%, a margin of 25 basis points over comparable German government note. Guarantor Deutsche Bank AG. Fees two.

Mitsubishi Corp. Finance PLC (Japanese parent) — 7.5 billion yen of step-up coupon Eurobonds due July 18, 1997, at issue price 100.2 via Mitsubishi Finance International PLC. Coupon 3.15% until July 18, 1996, when bonds callable at par. Thereafter, coupon 3.8%. Keep-well agreement with Mitsubishi Corp. Fees 0.2.

Sweden (sovereign) — 400 million Dutch guilders of 5.75% Eurobonds due April 21, 1998, at issue price 100.28 via ABN Amro Bank NV. Reoffered at 99.53 to yield 5.885%, a margin of 15 basis points over interpolated yield curve between February 1997 and July 1998 Dutch state loans. Fees one.

U S West Communications Inc. (U.S. parent) — 100 million Swiss francs of 4.75% privately placed notes due April 22, 1999, priced at 102.125 via Swiss Bank Corp. Fees 1.5.

OTHER

Royal Bank of Scotland — $200 million of exchangeable capital securities priced with a 8.5% dividend yield. The securities were priced at $25 each, according to MCM CorporateWatch. The securities are exchangeable into U.K. preference shares with a 9.375% dividend yield, at the company's option. The issue is noncallable for 10 years and is rated single-A-3 by Moody's and single-A by S&P. The issue will be sold through underwriters led by Merrill Lynch & Co.

U.S. Treasury regularly issues 3 types of debt securities:

- ♦ **Treasury bills**--short-term debt securities sold in units of $10,000 with maturities of 13, 26 or 52 weeks;

- ♦ **Treasury notes**--issued in $1,000 units maturing in 1 to 10 years; and

- ♦ **Treasury bonds**--issued in $1,000 units, maturing in over 10 years.

The securities are sold at auction to bond dealers, who later resell them to investors.

Besides the Treasury, many other federal government agencies or government-sponsored enterprises--such as the Student Loan Marketing Association--issue debt securities. Some of the government's debt securities **trade actively**--that is, they can be transferred with ease from owner to owner before maturity. Others are restricted to particular owners and do not trade in secondary markets.

State and local governments also issue debt securities, collectively referred to as "**municipal bonds**" or "**municipals**." If you look back at the excerpts from the new securities issues listing from the *Wall Street Journal* shown before, you will see examples of debt securities being offered by the city of Honolulu, the Michigan Municipal Bond Authority (on behalf of local governments in the state), and the New York State Environmental Facilities Corp. (to fund the state's water pollution control efforts).

Municipal bonds generally offer lower interest rates than corporate bonds because the interest on most municipal bonds is exempt from federal, state and local income taxes, whereas interest income received by investors in corporate bonds is subject to tax. In 1996, for example, state and local governments issued $180 billion of tax-exempt bonds.

Private Debt Placements

In a **private debt placement**, debt securities are sold to one institutional buyer (or a limited number of buyers) without a public offering. Pension funds and insurance companies--or other companies with large amounts of cash to manage--are often buyers of private debt issues. The placement is usually handled through an investment banker, who acts as an agent to bring buyers and issuers together. Private placements can be less costly than public offerings because some of the costs of public offerings (like the registration fee and underwriting fees) can be avoided. In 1996, U.S. private debt placements totaled $165.4 billion.

If you look back at the excerpts from the March 30, 1994 new securities listing of the *Wall Street Journal*, you will find a private debt placement listed as the last item under the Eurobonds section: a private placement for 100 million Swiss francs by the American corporation, U.S. West Communications Inc. This sample listing also illustrates the sometimes complex vocabulary of international finance. What is a Eurobond? From the examples in the listing, you might deduce that a Eurobond is a bond issued and traded in countries other than the one in which it is denominated. Similarly, if corporations or national governments deposit money in banks in countries other than their own, they are said to be using Eurobanks. The terms arose when most foreign placements or deposits were in European countries, but now refer to any country other than the corporation's or government's home country.

Other Sources of Debt Capital

Lending institutions and public or private debt offerings are major sources of debt capital, but they are not the only sources of debt capital. In Theme IV of this series, *Accounting Issues Involving Capital*, you can learn about some other sources of short-term and long-term debt capital, such as suppliers who provide credit to their customers.

EQUITY CAPITAL

Don't gamble; take all your savings and buy some good stock and hold it till it goes up, then sell it. If it don't go up, don't buy it.
-- Will Rogers

In addition to creating a demand for long-term debt financing, increased industrialization also led to a demand for long-term **equity financing**--raising funds by issuing common stock, preferred stock or limited partnership units to outside investors.

Partly, the demand for equity capital arose from the need for permanent capital (capital to be invested for an indefinite period of time). Partly, it arose because there wasn't enough debt financing available to fulfill the ever-growing business needs for long-term capital. Investors who might not be attracted by the promise of interest on loans could be attracted by the promise of owning a piece of the business. Partly, the demand for equity financing arose because some businesses found the restrictions of debt financing too binding. They preferred to take in new owners rather than meet the lending conditions.

In contrast to **debt securities**, which are *owed* capital, **equity securities** are *owner* capital. This section introduces some basic concepts about equity capital, including: the types of returns investors may receive, the basic types of equity financing for corporations, public equity offerings, and private placements of equity securities.

Returns To Equity Investors

When a business sells an equity interest, the investors' fortune becomes tied to the company's fortune. If the company does well, the investors do well. If the company does poorly, the investors do poorly.

There are 2 ways investors can expect to receive a return on their investment. First, investors may expect the company to distribute accumulated profits to investors. These payouts are called "**dividends**" for a corporation and "**distributions**" for a partnership. However, dividends (or distributions) are not always paid out when a company is earning profits. Even when a company is doing well, it may be more prudent to reinvest profits in the business to spur future growth. For example, many high-technology companies choose to reinvest profits in research and development in the hopes of creating new or improved products for the future.

Second, the investors may realize a return through **appreciation** (growth in value) of their stock or their share of interest in a partnership as the company's value increases due to successful operations. One of the attractions of ownership is the chance to share in the appreciation in value of the company. For example, consider the history of Berkshire Hathaway, an insurance company that also owns a number of manufacturing, publishing and retailing operations. In 1965, a share of Berkshire Hathaway stock sold for $12 a share. After several decades of success, the 1989 price of a Berkshire Hathaway share hit $8,900.

On the other hand, if the company does poorly, there will be no money to pay dividends or distributions. Whereas a lender is owed interest throughout the life of a loan no matter how the company is performing, dividends need not be paid to shareholders if the company is not doing well. Moreover, if the company has fallen on hard times, the value of the equity investor's stock or share of interest in the partnership will decline. Consider Berkshire Hathaway once more. In the early 1990s, the insurance, manufacturing, publishing, and retailing industries all experienced economic difficulties. Inevitably, the value of Berkshire Hathaway was affected. Within a single year, the price of a share of Berkshire Hathaway dropped over one-third of its value. Owners share the misfortunes of a company, as well as the fortunes.

Types of Equity Financing for Corporations

Corporations can offer 2 basic types of equity financing: **common stock** and **preferred stock**, each with different rights. In 1996, U.S. public companies issued $114.9 billion of common stock and $37.8 billion of preferred stock.

One type of stock is not particularly "better" than the other, but the 2 types are different and thus may appeal to different investors. If a company issues only one type of stock, common stock will be used. But many companies issue both preferred and common stock in order to attract various types of investors. For example, Colgate-Palmolive Company--which manufactures a wide range of consumer products with brand names such as Colgate, Palmolive, Ajax, and Fab-- has both preferred stock and common stock.

Preferred Stock. Preferred stockholders have more rights ("**preferences**") than common stockholders in some areas--usually liquidation rights and dividend rights. A company may design its preferred stock to have various types of preferences, each appealing to particular investors. Some companies even sell multiple classes of preferred stock, each with a different set of preferences.

If a preferred stock has a **liquidation preference**, the preference doesn't come into play until the company goes out of business (**liquidates**). Preferred stockholders with liquidation preferences are typically entitled to get their share of the liquidation proceeds before any payment is made to common stockholders. For example, suppose a preferred stock has a liquidation preference of $100 per share. If the company decides to go out of business, the preferred stockholders would be entitled to $100 for each share owned before the common stockholders could receive anything. However, even the preferred stockholders cannot receive any liquidation proceeds until after debts are repaid to creditors, who have liquidation preferences over all equity investors.

Dividend preferences typically require that a fixed amount of dividends must be distributed to preferred stockholders before any dividends are paid to common stockholders. The Board of Directors is not required to pay dividends at all, but if dividends are **declared** (voted and announced by the board of directors) and the pool of money is limited, preferred stockholders with dividend preferences stand first in line. For the Colgate-Palmolive Company, common stockholders cannot be paid dividends unless the holders of its $4.25 preferred stock first receive annual dividends in the amount of $4.25 per share.

Moreover, because this Colgate-Palmolive preferred stock is "**cumulative**," any year that a dividend isn't paid, the preferred stock dividend accumulates for possible future payment. Suppose, for example, Colgate-Palmolive didn't pay any dividends for 2 years. Then $8.50 of dividends (2 years × $4.25 per year) accumulate. If the company decides to pay dividends the next year, the preferred stockholders must receive $12.75 per share ($8.50 accumulated from 2 years without dividends plus $4.25 for the current year) before the common stockholders receive any dividend payments at all.

Common Stock. While preferred stockholders do have various special rights, common stockholders do not always take a backseat to preferred stockholders. In fact, common stockholders typically have some rights which preferred stockholders do not share--usually **voting rights**. Although there are exceptions possible, common stockholders typically are entitled to vote in elections for the Board of Directors and to vote on other major issues that concern the owners of the company (such as the sale of a division of the business or the hiring of the independent auditors). Preferred stockholders typically do not have voting rights or have lesser voting rights than common stockholders. Moreover, when the company performs extremely well, common stockholders may receive more dividends than preferred stockholders are entitled to receive.

Common stockholders also typically have "**pre-emptive rights**"--that is, whenever additional common stock is issued, they are given priority to purchase the same percentage of the new issue that they owned of the previously outstanding stock. Thus, if a stockholder owns 10% of a company's outstanding common stock and the company makes a new offering, the stockholder is guaranteed a chance to buy 10% of the new shares in order to prevent any dilution of ownership interest.

Public Equity Offerings

Provided they meet the requirements of the securities laws, all corporations and some **limited partnerships** (partnerships where some of the partners have limited liability to creditors) can make public offerings of equity securities.

Public limited partnerships (PLPs) enjoyed a certain vogue in the U.S. during the 1980s because they offered significant tax advantages. Even the Boston Celtics are a PLP. Allan Sloan, a financial columnist for *Newsday* in New York reported that in 1990, the Celtics and their unitholders saved about $2.2 million in taxes by being organized as a public limited partnership rather than a corporation. As Sloan put it, "If the players can learn to dodge defenders the way the owners dodge taxes, the Celtics will have one hell of a team."

By the end of the 1980s, tax law changes removed many of the tax advantages of public limited partnerships. For example, the Celtics will be able to retain their tax advantages only until 1998. After the tax law changed, public limited partnerships continued to trade in the market, but few new partnership public equity offerings were made. In contrast, during 1996, over 500 companies decided to "**go public**" (offered equity securities for public sale for the first time) in the United States and raised about $50 billion of capital.

"Going Public." Companies can "go public" in more than one country, provided they meet the requirements for offering securities in each country. For example, United States companies like Avon Products, Inc. and Levi Strauss & Co. have made public offerings in Japan.

In the United States, equity securities offered for sale in public securities markets must be registered with the Securities and Exchange Commission. Again, the acceptance of an SEC filing does not constitute "approval" of the quality of the investment. The registration process is designed to provide potential investors and other users of the registration statement with the information they need to make decisions, but the SEC does not pass judgment on the merits of the offering. As one SEC staffer once remarked in a *Wall Street Journal* interview, "I'm not going to stop you from buying a company that makes windows for submarines. But I will make sure that you get enough disclosure to know that the company makes windows for submarines."

If a securities offering is for previously unissued (new) shares, it is called a **primary issue**. Companies making primary issues of equity securities typically use the services of an **investment banker**, who provides advice on how the offering should be structured, timed and priced. Additionally, the investment banker helps to publicize the offering and often acts as the **underwriter** (buying the shares from the issuing company and then reselling them to the public).

Equity securities represent a percentage share of ownership, not a particular dollar value. Equity securities may--but need not--have a par value or stated value (like $1 per share). The par or stated value is not the security's price; the price is set by investors in the market. For example, the par value of common stock in Fiat S.p.A., the largest publicly held industrial company in Italy, is 1,000 lire. Yet, in the middle of 1997, the market price of Fiat stock was over 5,700 lire.

What purpose does the par or stated value of a stock serve? For one thing, the par or stated value may be used to express dividend rates. For example, the Board of Directors (which is empowered to declare dividends) may declare a 5% cash dividend on a $1 par value stock. This means a stockholder will receive cash amounting to 5 cents (5% of the stock's par value of $1) for each share owned. If an equity security has no par or stated value, the dividend is merely declared in monetary terms (like 10 cents a share).

Also, in some legal jurisdictions, the par or stated value marks the amount of the stockholder's liability--if the stockholder has paid less than par value and the firm is liquidated, the stockholder may be required to contribute the difference. However, this is highly unlikely to happen as most stocks have par or stated values much lower than their market price--that is, they sell at a premium above par or stated value, like the Fiat stock in the example above. The premium paid above par or stated value is called "**additional paid-in capital**" or "**capital contributed in excess of par (or stated) value.**"

Shares which are **outstanding** (already owned by someone) may be resold by the owner to other buyers. This is known as "**secondary market**" trading. Companies that issue equity securities only receive funds from the primary offering. The money that changes hands in secondary offerings is strictly between the old owner and the new owner. Even though the issuing company only receives money from the initial sale of its securities, the existence of a secondary market is important to publicly held companies. Because the secondary market exists, owners have the freedom to decide whether to increase their stockholdings, sell some of their stock, or stand pat; their investment is said to be "**liquid**" (easily convertible to cash). If investors did not have the freedom to trade their stock at will, they might be less inclined to buy initial offerings of stock.

Private Placements of Equity Securities

Equity securities may also be offered privately to small groups of investors. The private placement market is not open to individual investors; only institutional investors may buy securities through private placements. These institutional investors include finance companies, mutual funds, pension funds, labor unions, insurance companies, and charitable organizations that have large amounts of money to invest. In 1996, $35.9 billion of equity securities were privately placed in the U.S.

THE EVOLUTION OF CAPITAL MARKETS

Among the multitude of animals which scamper, fly, burrow, and swim around us, man is the only one who is not locked into his environment...And that series of inventions, by which man from age to age has remade his environment, is a different kind of evolution--not biological, but cultural evolution.
   -- J. Bronowski, The Ascent of Man

David L. Scott's dictionary, *Wall Street Words*, defines **capital markets** as follows:

> *[Capital markets are the markets] for long-term funds where securities such as common stock, preferred stock, and bonds are traded. Both the primary market for new issues and the secondary market for existing securities are part of the capital market.* [Source: Reprinted by permission from WALL STREET WORDS. Copyright © 1988 by Houghton Mifflin Company.]

Capital markets, like all markets, bring prospective buyers and sellers together. Capital markets play an important role in society: they provide a mechanism for individuals' savings and organizations' excess funds (funds not needed for current operations) to be redirected into debt or equity investments in companies that need funds. This is the role of the primary market.

To attract more capital from outside sources, it helps if debt contracts and stock are easily transferable--that is, potential buyers are more likely to become actual buyers if they know their investment is liquid (able to be sold without difficulty). A market is needed where owners and creditors can sell to other potential investors and lenders. This is the role of the secondary market.

The major stock markets of the world form the backbone of today's capital markets. These stock markets have evolved over time from simple trading centers to highly sophisticated global markets.

The Origin of Stock Markets

Stock markets began in the Middle Ages as outdoor meeting places where merchants came to exchange goods. Many such markets were established in the cities of northern Europe. One of the most successful markets was located in a square in the town of Bruges, where the La Bourse family (whose coat of arms pictured 3 purses, surely an auspicious coat of arms for a trading family) built a large building where merchants could meet daily to trade. Later, stock markets came to be known in French as "La Bourse," in honor of the family who brought them indoors. Today, the stock exchange in France (and some other countries) is still known as the **bourse**.

Coming indoors was an important step in the evolution of stock markets. The Royal Exchange in London, established in the reign of Elizabeth I, operated outdoors on Lombard Street for many years before it moved indoors in 1570. This preceded by several centuries the opening of the first major stock markets in the United States--the New York Stock Exchange and the American Stock Exchange.

Like the European markets, Wall Street began as a place for trading livestock (rather than the kind of stock traded there today) and produce. In the middle of the 19th century, traders came to Wall Street to exchange cows, pigs, dogs, sheep, fruits and flowers, as well as to make and pay loans. The New York Stock Exchange (NYSE) was founded on May 17, 1792 when about 2 dozen brokers met to conduct trades under a buttonwood tree near the present-day building at 68 Wall Street. From the start, the NYSE brokers exchanged corporate securities and governmental bonds, but the volume of trading was far less than it is today.

The stock market we now call the American Stock Exchange began life in the 1850s as the New York Curb Exchange, so named because its members met outdoors to trade on several street corners. The Curb moved indoors to its present location on Trinity Place in 1921.

A similar pattern of development can be found in other industrialized nations. For example, the Tokyo Stock Exchange, now one of the world's largest, is only slightly more than 100 years old. The first Tokyo stock market was opened in 1878. About a century later, there were 150 stock exchanges operating in 54 countries around the globe.

Stock exchanges typically are markets for relatively large volume or frequently traded securities. For securities too small or too infrequently traded to be listed on a stock exchange, a separate trading system developed. A stockholder would bring stock to the front counter of a stockbroker's office to ask the broker to determine the stock's value. The broker would consult with other brokers (either in person or by telephone) to determine what someone else was willing to pay for the stock and then make an offer to buy the stock from the owner for a slightly lower price. This trading system came to be known as "over the counter" trading after the counter where the stockholder sought information.

Today, securities are traded both at **exchanges**, where face-to-face auction style trading--now assisted by computers--takes place, and **"over-the-counter,"** where brokers conduct trades via telephone and computer communications. In the United States there are 8 national securities exchanges: the Chicago Board Options Exchange and the American, Boston, Cincinnati, Chicago, New York, Pacific and Philadelphia Stock Exchanges, with the New York Stock Exchange generating the most trading activity. The major market for over-the-counter trades in the United States is the **NASDAQ** (National Association of Securities Dealers Automated Quotations) System, a computerized network linking brokers and dealers in the U.S. and many other countries.

The Globalization of Modern Capital Markets

Before World War II (the 1940s), most organizations filled their outside capital needs domestically. U.S. firms offered securities to U.S. investors in U.S. markets; U.K. firms offered securities to U. K. investors in U. K. markets, and so on. But World War II had a lasting impact on the world economy.

The war devastated many nations. After the war ended, many international economic assistance programs (one country sending aid to another country) were established at levels never before imagined. These programs strengthened the economic ties between nations and led to an increasingly global economy.

The technological revolution also contributed to the internationalization of world markets. Computers, fiber-optic telephone lines, communications satellites and fax machines brought far-flung countries as close as next door. High-speed airplanes made global business travel feasible for many companies. The Chairman of Price Waterhouse, an international public accounting firm, described the result in a 1986 speech to the Swiss-American Chamber of Commerce:

> *In 1880, the world economy was only 10 percent integrated. In 1950 it was 25 percent integrated. In 1986 the figure is 50%. Some estimates have this integration increasing to as much as 75 percent by the year 2000.*

While this prediction may once have been controversial, by the mid-1990s, few would argue with this statement, other than to suggest that the 75% estimate for the year 2000 may be too conservative.

Businesses have become increasingly multinational. For example, consider The Coca-Cola Company, which was founded in 1886 by an Atlanta pharmacist who had invented a drink he claimed could cure headaches, sluggishness and indigestion. His bookkeeper came up with the product's name (and its now-famous script) based on 2 key ingredients, coca leaves and kola nuts. Until World War II, Coca-Cola's business was primarily domestic. During the war, to help fulfill the CEO's promise that every soldier would have access to a 5-cent bottle of Coke, the U.S. government helped Coca-Cola build 64 overseas bottling plants. After the war, these plants became the nucleus of Coke's internationalization. Today, Coca-Cola earns the majority of its revenues outside its home country.

As businesses become more internationalized, so do capital markets. Since the 1970s, international trading of corporate securities has grown sharply. In 1995, there were $2.75 trillion of cross-border stock purchases, about 7 times the amount in 1975. Companies and investors alike have become accustomed to following market activity around the globe--in Amsterdam, Brussels, Frankfurt, Hong Kong, London, Milan, New York, Paris, Stockholm, Sydney, Tokyo and Toronto. They look for the best financing and investment opportunities available world-wide, not just at home.

With technological advancements, it is now possible to execute financial transactions just about 24 hours a day in some market somewhere around the world. To date, global markets and 24-hour trading are patchwork devices. No truly interconnected market system yet exists. But the technology to support such a system exists--and its creation seems to be the natural next step in the evolution of capital markets.

Challenges On The Horizon

The move towards a global economy and an international capital market presents exciting opportunities and significant challenges for the near future. Two of the most significant challenges are the need for international regulation and the need for international accounting standards.

Currently, each country establishes its own rules for regulating the companies that wish to offer securities in public markets and the public markets themselves (exchanges, investment advisors, and so on). Also, each country establishes its own accounting standards. These accounting standards determine the information which must be disclosed in financial reports to current and potential investors and creditors. Today, there are many examples of country-to-country differences in regulations and standards.

For example, countries differ in the way accounting standards are established and the philosophies underlying accounting standards. In some countries, such as Germany, accounting standards are set by government bodies. Philosophically, German accounting standards are primarily influenced by the need for reliable information for taxation. In other countries, accounting standards are set by private sector bodies, such as the U.S.'s Financial Accounting Standards Board (FASB). Philosophically, U.S. accounting standards are primarily influenced by the needs of capital markets. The FASB's first *Statement of Financial Accounting Concepts* recognized that many user groups for accounting information exist, but acknowledged investors and creditors as the primary external (non-management) users for whom financial reports are prepared.

Country-to-country differences present potential problems for investors, creditors and companies raising funds in international capital markets. For a market to operate well, participants must feel that they are equitably treated--they must trust that the playing field is level. To the extent that country-to-country differences make it difficult to keep the playing field level or erode trust among market participants, buyers and sellers may find it difficult to make the investment and credit decisions they need to make. Or, they may come to regret decisions made without appropriate information.

Currently, several international groups are addressing the regulatory and accounting differences between nations. The International Organization of Securities Commissions and the International Accounting Standards Committee bring together representatives from many nations to grapple with issues that affect harmonization of regulations, accounting standards and enforcement. They are working toward an objective of having similar transactions and events, wherever they occur, be accounted for and reported in similar ways.

INFORMATION NEEDED FOR INVESTMENT AND CREDIT DECISIONS

Select stocks the way a porcupine makes love--very carefully.
-- Robert Dinda

Investors and creditors do not have unlimited resources. There are more investing and lending opportunities available to them than they can accommodate. So, the basic problem investors and creditors face is one of allocation of their limited resources: how do they choose, from all the available alternatives, the best set of investments and loans to commit their resources to?

The answer, in theory, is simple. Both investors and creditors share a common goal: to make as large a return as possible for a given level of risk. Consequently, their decisions depend on their assessments of the riskiness and expected return of the opportunities presented to them. They need information that will help them (or their intermediaries, like financial analysts who make recommendations to investors) to assess the risk and return possibilities inherent in each investment or lending opportunity.

Of course, figuring out what specific information would best suit the needs of investors and creditors is a more difficult task. A few years ago, the American Institute of Certified Public Accountants took a hard look at users' information needs and how well those needs are satisfied by the financial reporting process. A Special Committee on Financial Reporting (also known as the Jenkins Committee, after its chairman Edmund Jenkins) studied users' needs and suggested a new business reporting model with 10 elements essential to users.

Figure I-3-4 (on the following page) shows this model, with the 10 elements grouped into 5 broad categories of users' needs: (1) financial and non-financial data, (2) management's analysis of the data, (3) forward-looking information, (4) information about management and shareholders, and (5) background about the company. Report issuers, standard setters and regulators are now working on many projects that bring us closer to this model.

Figure I-3-4
A Model of Business Reporting

Financial and nonfinancial data

■ financial statements and related disclosures
■ high-level operating data and performance measurements that management uses to manage the business

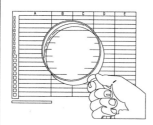

Management's analysis of the data

■ reasons for changes in the financial, operating, and performance-related data, and the identity and past effect of key trends

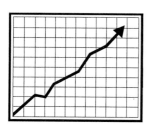

Forward-looking information

■ opportunities and risks, including those resulting from key trends
■ management's plans, including critical success factors
■ comparison of actual business performance to previously disclosed opportunities, risks and management's plans

Information about management and shareholders

■ directors, management, compensation, major shareholders and transactions and relationships among related parties

Background about the company

■ broad objectives and strategies
■ scope and description of business and properties
■ impact of industry structure on the company

Source: The 10 elements were recommended in the AICPA Special Committee on Financial Reporting's *Improving Business Reporting--A Customer Focus*, 1994.

Current and potential investors and creditors have many available sources of information to aid them in making decisions. Much of the information is presented in financial reports. Other important information comes from the financial press (where legions of reporters follow developments affecting particular organizations and entire industries), direct communications with the management of a company, and privately and publicly available databases of information. Each of these sources of information will be examined below, but first we begin by considering the qualities that make information valuable for investment and credit decisions.

What Makes Information Valuable for Investment and Credit Decisions?

Module 2 of this theme discusses the hierarchy of qualities that make information valuable. These qualities include understandability, relevance, and reliability. Moreover, accountants recognize the existence of a pervasive cost-benefit constraint: information must not cost more to obtain than it is worth to decision makers. How do these qualities pertain to the information that is used to make investment and credit decisions?

The Cost-Benefit Constraint. The cost-benefit constraint manifests itself in investment and credit decisions in many ways. For example, investors and creditors might like to have information about companies on a real-time basis (up-to-the-minute reports whenever they are wanted), but generally make do with periodic reports (like annual or quarterly financial reports, or periodic news releases). At least for the present, the cost of obtaining real-time information is too high to justify its production, although advances in technology may one day make access to real-time information feasible.

Another manifestation of the cost-benefit constraint is the reliance on **information intermediaries**--information experts such as financial analysts and credit rating agencies. **Financial analysts** are experts when it comes to investigating the risk and return characteristics of securities. **Credit rating services** are experts when it comes to investigating a borrower's ability to meet debt payments. These intermediaries know how to find the information they need and how to interpret it, using a variety of techniques from simple ratio analysis to complex mathematical models.

For example, institutional investors (such as banks, mutual funds and pension funds) often rely on a bond rating service--including Moody's Investors Service, Inc. ("Moody's") or Standard & Poor's Corp. ("S & P")--to provide risk assessments, which are summarized in a system of letter grades. Institutional investors may, for example, refuse to invest in any bond rated below BBB, which the rating agencies use as the cutoff for an "investment-grade" security.

As another example, lenders may use Dun & Bradstreet's ("D & B") credit reports in making short-term lending decisions. D & B's credit ratings on private and public companies are based on information obtained from companies, their past and current creditors, and other sources (like court records).

Because of the relationship between risk and expected return, credit rating changes can affect an organization's cost of capital. In 1992, Moody's lowered its rating on the general obligation bonds of the State of California from triple-A to double-A1 (note: just as in college, more A's are better) because the state's budget problems increased the risk of default on the bonds. California's treasurer reported that the downgrade would make it more expensive for the state to issue additional bonds, estimating an increase in interest rates of 5 **basis points** (hundredths of a percent) for new bond issues. While a .05% increase sounds small, it adds up quickly when a large amount of bonds is involved. For California, the additional interest costs amounted to about $4 million a year.

Many investors and creditors rely on information intermediaries to help them make investment and lending decisions. It simply costs too much for every individual investor and creditor to go through the entire information assessment process. Information intermediaries can devote their full efforts to this task and share their results with many clients. The use of information intermediaries creates economies of scale that make more sophisticated information analyses available to more users than would be possible with individual analysis. Sometimes, the role that information intermediaries play can be captured in a decision support system or an expert system. For example, several large banks have used a system called The Lending Advisor to help them analyze information and suggest loan decisions. The banks report that the system lets lending officers make quicker and better decisions.

If intermediaries perform their jobs well and information flows freely, the intermediaries can help make a capital market "efficient." The term "efficient" is used in a particular technical sense, but the technical term is in keeping with the common notion that something is efficient if it performs a task quickly. In an **"efficient market,"** security prices reflect all the available information and quickly adjust to any new information that becomes available. This doesn't imply that everyone agrees on what the new information means. Some may interpret the information to mean "buy," others to mean "sell," still others to mean "hold." But, all new information is quickly reacted to and reflected in the market price.

Research indicates that some major capital markets--like the New York Stock Exchange--are remarkably efficient. For example, in an efficient market, stock prices should only react to new information, not to information that is merely repackaged from an earlier form. Suppose much of the information in a company's annual report to stockholders is already known from management's communications (like interviews and press releases) with the financial press or the financial community. The market price of the company's stock should not change--and research shows it generally does not change--unless the annual report contains unexpected news. The fact that information intermediaries follow companies continuously contributes to the efficiency of the market.

Understandability. To be useful for decision making, information must be understandable. Some information about an organization can be directly interpreted. For example, if an established organization is operating at a loss and its liabilities exceed its assets, it is clear that the organization is failing. However, most company-specific information can't be understood in isolation. Suppose a company you are considering investing in had about the same earnings this year as last year. Has the company performed well or poorly? You can't answer this question unless you have a framework for evaluation. To understand the company, you must also understand the industry in which it operates.

Financial analysts, for example, often follow a particular industry, as well as specific companies within the industry. They read the trade press, they learn about the types of problems common in the industry, they follow technological developments that may be important to the industry, and so on. They also follow news concerning political and economic events that could be important to the industry. Industry knowledge provides the crucial context that makes company-specific information more understandable. Industry knowledge also provides benchmarks against which a company can be assessed.

Figure I-3-5 (on the next page) presents a short article taken from the *Wall Street Journal*. When you read the article, consider how industry knowledge was useful in interpreting the "flat" (no improvement over the prior year) earnings performance of Hillenbrand Industries.

Understandability also implies that a certain level of sophistication is needed to use some kinds of information. For example, a naive investor might not understand how to use information about a company's pension liabilities to assess the wisdom of investing in a company. More sophisticated investors (or investment advisors) will be able to make better use of information about pension obligations because they understand its implications for the future of the firm.

Relevance. Investors and lenders are in different positions. Consequently, different information is relevant for investment and credit decisions.

Lenders are looking for 2 things: a return of the principal loaned out, and payment of interest. To a lender, the most important question is: will the borrower have the cash to pay me when interest and principal payments are due? Therefore, the most relevant information concerns a company's **cash flows** (cash coming in and cash going out), **liquidity** (ability to convert assets into cash), and **solvency** (ability to stay in business long enough to pay off the loan).

Investors in equity securities, on the other hand, aren't guaranteed any return on their investment unless the company does well. And, unlike the lender whose return is fixed, the better the company does, the better investors do. So, to investors, the most important question is: what will the future performance of this company be? The most relevant information for investors concerns the company's **quality of management**, **profitability**, and **future prospects**.

Figure I-3-5
Dying in the Burial Business

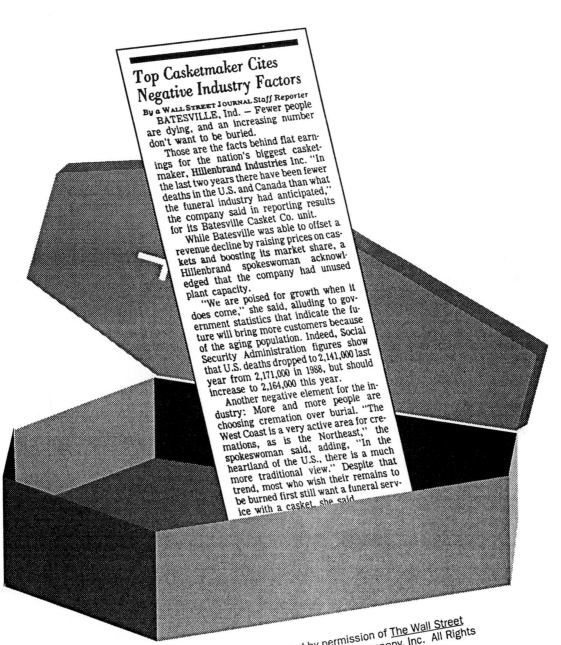

Top Casketmaker Cites Negative Industry Factors

By a WALL STREET JOURNAL Staff Reporter

BATESVILLE, Ind. — Fewer people are dying, and an increasing number don't want to be buried.

Those are the facts behind flat earnings for the nation's biggest casketmaker, Hillenbrand Industries Inc. "In the last two years there have been fewer deaths in the U.S. and Canada than what the funeral industry had anticipated," the company said in reporting results for its Batesville Casket Co. unit.

While Batesville was able to offset a revenue decline by raising prices on caskets and boosting its market share, a Hillenbrand spokeswoman acknowledged that the company had unused plant capacity.

"We are poised for growth when it does come," she said, alluding to government statistics that indicate the future will bring more customers because of the aging population. Indeed, Social Security Administration figures show that U.S. deaths dropped to 2,141,000 last year from 2,171,000 in 1988, but should increase to 2,164,000 this year.

Another negative element for the industry: More and more people are choosing cremation over burial. "The West Coast is a very active area for cremations, as is the Northeast," the spokeswoman said, adding, "In the heartland of the U.S., there is a much more traditional view." Despite that trend, most who wish their remains to be burned first still want a funeral service with a casket, she said.

Reliability. Investors and creditors need to trust the information they base their decisions on. Much of the information investors and creditors use is financial in nature; they receive it as accounting information. Most of the information is produced by the organizations that want financing. Can the information be trusted to present a fair picture of the organization?

Current and potential investors and creditors need some assurance that the information they are receiving in financial reports is credible. This assurance is provided by the independent (or external) auditor. In the U.S., as in most countries, the financial statements of public companies must be audited by licensed independent auditors. The auditors examine the underlying records supporting the financial statements, perform tests of the information in the statements, and, where needed, test the information and control systems of the organization. They make sure that all the information required to be disclosed in the financial statements is there. When the audit work is done, the auditors issue a separate report giving their opinion as to the fairness of presentation of the financial statements. The fact that an outside auditor attests to the fairness of information increases its reliability.

Financial Reports as a Source of Information

Organizations communicate with outside parties through written financial reports. Using words and figures, financial reports document the past performance and current condition of the organization, and often also discuss the organization's future prospects. For most U.S. organizations, financial reporting is accomplished in **annual** (end of the year) **reports**, **interim** (during the year) **reports**, and, for public companies, various SEC filings such as registration statements.

Financial reports provide important information for investment and credit decisions. For example, a 1996 Yankelovich Partners survey of money managers, analysts and investors found that at least 70% of each group view annual reports as a prime source of information for investment decisions. An annual report presents management's view of the organization's performance over the past year and the organization's future prospects. In addition, the annual report presents the organization's annual financial statements.

Financial statements--statements that present accounting information about an organization--are the cornerstone of financial reporting. Throughout the world, public companies are required to publish financial statements at least annually. Although they are not legally required to do so, many privately-held companies also prepare annual financial statements for either internal (e.g., to make decisions about product pricing) or external (e.g., to support a loan application) use. In the United States, the required set of financial statements includes:

♦ a balance sheet,

- an income statement,
- a statement of retained earnings, and
- a statement of cash flows.

These statements are introduced briefly below and are described in greater detail in Part B of this module.

The Balance Sheet. The **balance sheet**, also known as a **statement of financial position**, shows an entity's assets, liabilities and equities at a particular date. It shows the balanced relationship embodied in the accounting equation, **Assets = Liabilities + Equities**. This statement presents information that can be used to assess liquidity and solvency. Consequently, lenders often consider balance sheet information highly relevant to their decisions.

The Income Statement. The **income statement** (also known as an **earnings statement**, **statement of operations**, **profit and loss statement**, or, for nonprofit organizations, a **statement of activities**) shows revenues, expenses, gains, losses and net income for the preceding period and one or more prior periods. This statement, which emphasizes profitability, is often considered highly relevant for investment decisions.

The Statement of Retained Earnings. The **statement of retained earnings** (or fund balances, for a non-profit organization) shows the changes in retained earnings (or fund balances) for the period. Alternatively, companies may present a **statement of stockholders' equity** showing the changes in all equity accounts for the period.

The Cash Flows Statement. The **statement of cash flows** shows how cash came in to the organization (from operations, financing activities, and investing activities) and how it was used.

Other Sources of Information

Published financial reports are not the only source of information for investors and creditors. In fact, much of the information in an organization's annual report might be available before the report is published. This is because the financial reporting process is continuous. The annual report indicates the end of each reporting cycle. It summarizes what has occurred during the period.

During the period, modern managements maintain communications with their major user groups. For example, they may issue forecasts of future earnings or interim (during the period) financial results, like quarterly earnings reports. They may grant interviews to the financial press. If a major event occurs, they are likely to issue a press release and, if public, may be required to file a report (called an **8-K report**) with the Securities and Exchange Commission. Company managements also maintain direct communication with the financial community--for example, by speaking to groups of analysts or investors.

Another potentially valuable source of information exists in private or public databases. Public (free-use) databases include the SEC's database of filings of public companies, which is accessible via the Internet. Many organizations also provide Internet access to their own financial information. Private (accessible for a fee) databases include databases of earnings forecasts made by companies or analysts, databases of economic information, databases that provide a history of the market prices for securities, and so on. These databases, particularly the ones that can be accessed by computer, have made it possible to gather more information much more quickly than was possible a few decades ago.

LEARNING MORE ABOUT CAPITAL MARKETS

The study of capital markets and investment and credit decisions is the major focus of Finance courses. Obviously, since accounting information is relevant for making many investment and credit decisions, the fields of Accounting and Finance have some significant common interests. For example, much of the current academic research in financial accounting has to do with the relationship between accounting information and capital markets. So, you should expect to see a lot of accounting information discussed in Finance classes and, in turn, a lot of discussion of capital markets in more advanced Accounting classes.

Additionally, you can learn more about the economic aspects of markets in Economics classes. Some people, in fact, view Finance as a branch of Economics. A class on money and banking, for instance, can be especially helpful in increasing your understanding of credit markets.

The study of Finance requires a certain amount of mathematical sophistication. For example, the theory of efficient markets is best understood from a mathematical perspective. So, courses in Mathematics can be particularly helpful preparation for increasing your understanding of capital markets.

THE ROLE OF ACCOUNTANTS IN CAPITAL MARKETS

In a 1996 speech, SEC Commissioner Steven M. H. Wallman called accountants the "primary gatekeepers to the integrity of our financial markets." Without the work done by accountants, Wallman said, "the capital markets would be much less efficient, the cost of capital would be higher, and our standard of living would be lower." Accountants are involved in all phases of the financial reporting process: preparing reports, setting financial reporting standards, taking part in the regulatory process, and attesting to the credibility of financial reports.

Report Preparation, Standard Setting, and Regulation

An organization's financial accountants are the primary preparers of financial statements, which form the cornerstone of the financial reporting system. For a discussion of the role of financial accountants in management, consult Module 2 of this theme.

In the U.S., accountants also play a large role in setting financial reporting standards through the Financial Accounting Standards Board (FASB) and various professional associations, like the American Institute of Certified Public Accountants. The role of standard-setters is discussed in Module 6 of this theme.

Accountants in government, through their work with organizations like the Securities and Exchange Commission, play an important role in regulating capital markets. The role of accountants in government is discussed in Module 4 of this theme.

Attesting to the Credibility of Financial Reports

External auditors add value to financial reports by attesting to their fairness of presentation. The term "**attest**" means "to bear witness." An auditor's opinion on a set of financial statements bears witness to the statements' credibility. External auditors bear significant responsibility to the public and, consequently, generally must be licensed by a government body. For example, opinions on U.S. financial statements may only be given by independent **certified public accountants** (CPAs), who must be licensed by the state(s) in which they practice "**public accounting**."

CPA Licenses. CPA licenses are granted by each state to applicants who have completed certain education and experience requirements and passed an extensive uniform national examination. The CPA license is, in effect, a license to perform external audits. However, because of the respect the license engenders, many accountants become certified and maintain active CPA licenses even if they work in areas other than external auditing. For example, many tax accountants have CPA licenses, as do many accounting educators.

Public Accounting Firms. External auditors are employed by public accounting (or CPA) firms. These professional firms may also offer other services to their clients--such as tax services and consulting (management advisory) services. U.S. public accounting firms may be organized as sole proprietorships, partnerships, professional corporations (a special class of corporation that has many of the benefits of the corporate form, but with unlimited liability), or limited liability partnerships.

At the middle of the 1990s, there were 45,000 to 50,000 CPA firms in the U.S. Most of these firms are small businesses that practice in a local or regional area. On the other hand, the public accounting industry also includes a number of very large international and national public accounting firms. Figure I-3-6 (on the next page) contains a list of the 20 largest CPA firms headquartered in the United States.

Figure I-3-6
The 20 Largest CPA Firms in the United States

Firm	Headquarters	1996 Revenues (millions)	1996 Professionals
Andersen Worldwide	Chicago, Illinois	$4,511.0	27,000
Ernst & Young	New York, New York	$3,571.0	14,969
Deloitte & Touche	Wilton, Connecticut	$2,925.0	14,031
KPMG Peat Marwick	New York, New York	$2,530.0	10,020
Coopers & Lybrand	New York, New York	$2,115.0	11,785
Price Waterhouse	New York, New York	$2,020.0	10,512
Grant Thornton	Chicago, Illinois	$266.0	1,798
McGladrey & Pullen	Davenport, Iowa	$251.1	1,793
BDO Seidman	Chicago, Illinois	$211.0	1,103
Crowe, Chizek & Co.	South Bend, Indiana	$86.0	682
Baird Kurtz & Dobson	Springfield, Missouri	$81.9	525
Plante & Moran	Southfield, Michigan	$74.7	513
Clifton Gunderson & Co.	Peoria, Illinois	$68.6	547
Moss Adams	Seattle, Washington	$63.0	392
Richard A. Eisner & Co.	New York, New York	$55.0	269
Geo. S. Olive & Co.	Indianapolis, Indiana	$52.2	339
Altschuler, Melvoin & Glasser	Chicago, Illinois	$49.1	300
Goldstein Golub Kessler & Co.	New York, New York	$44.4	264
Larson, Allen, Weishair & Co.	Minneapolis, Minnesota	$43.1	249

Data From: *The 1997 Accounting Today Top 100 Tax and Accounting Firms* list. ACCOUNTING TODAY, © Lebhar-Friedman, Inc., 425 Park Avenue, New York, NY 10022, USA. (813)-664-6707.

There are several things you may want to note about this list. First, take a look at the largest firms on the list. The first 6 firms on the list are collectively known as the "**Big Six**." Each of these firms has thousands of professionals located in countries throughout the world. Collectively, the Big Six audit about 80% of U.S. public companies, as well as major companies in many other nations.

The size of these firms, which is several times larger than other CPA firms, is not accidental. As large businesses grew more complex and internationalized, public accounting firms needed to expand to keep up with their clients' needs. A large multinational business needs a large multinational auditor. Some CPA firms must also be large enough to provide advice on complex international tax issues and a wide variety of consulting services for multinational organizations.

Second, take a look at the rest of the firms on the list. A few of these firms-- such as Grant Thornton and BDO Seidman--are international, with offices in more than one country. Some are national firms, with offices in many major U.S. cities. Others--such as Baird, Kurtz & Dobson--are regional firms that concentrate their business in a particular area of the country. Still others are large local firms focusing on one metropolitan area.

The largest CPA firms have a wide variety of clients and usually offer a full range of professional services. While the larger firms offer a full range of accounting and auditing, tax, and management consulting services, many smaller firms tend to specialize in a one or a few services, or in small business clients.

Starting Salaries in Public Accounting. More than 1 in every 3 college graduates in Accounting begins his or her career in public accounting. Robert Half International Inc. conducts an annual salary survey for accounting, finance, banking and information systems jobs. The 1997 survey found that the average entry-level (no experience needed) starting salary for public accounting positions ranged from $29,000 to $34,250 for large firms and from $26,500 to $30,000 for medium-sized firms.

Several factors influence starting salaries, including geography and education level. Since economic conditions vary across the country, salaries will vary somewhat depending on geographic area. Additionally, the Robert Half survey finds starting salaries for students with a graduate degree command, on average, a 5% premium, plus an additional 10% for a CPA license.

Remember, however, that professional licensing is possible only after a state's education and experience requirements have been met. Because of the increasing complexity of the business world and the growing body of technical expertise in accounting, many states are increasing the education requirements to sit for the CPA exam. By 1997, 37 states had passed legislation to increase their education requirements from their former standard (which usually required the equivalent of an undergraduate degree in accounting) to a new standard that requires 150 credit hours of education, which must include a baccalaureate. Other states are contemplating increasing their education requirement to the 150-hour standard. The AICPA and some of the major state societies have added a 150-hour education requirement for members beginning in the year 2000.

The 150-hour standard is approximately the number of credit hours in a 5-year professional degree program, such as the Masters of Accounting programs offered at many major universities. But while many aspiring accountants in states with a 150-hour requirement will obtain a Masters degree in Accounting or Taxation, the laws generally do not require a graduate degree in accounting.

There are many alternative ways to fulfill the 150-hour requirement. For example, a student who wishes to specialize in government auditing might choose to fulfill the requirement by obtaining a Bachelors degree in Accounting and a Masters degree in Government and Politics. Or, the student could fulfill the requirement by earning a dual Bachelors degree in Accounting and Government, provided that the program included 150 hours of education and an appropriate selection of accounting courses. Because state laws differ and alternative educational paths are possible, students wishing to become CPAs should consider their state's licensing requirements when planning their coursework.

Salaries Beyond the Entry Level. A 1996 survey by Abbot, Langer & Associates found that the average CPA at the partner level earned $100,000. The range of potential earnings is great, with the highest earnings in a public accounting firm going to the senior partners. While the length of time to become a partner varies depending on the size of the firm and the talents of the individual, CPAs generally look to become partners about a decade after receiving their college degree and passing the CPA exam.

Partners are owners of the CPA firm, so their compensation depends on the performance of the firm. As professionals, CPAs command impressive potential earning power. For example, in 1995, when 2 large CPA firms (Ernst & Young and Kenneth Leventhal) merged, *The Wall Street Journal* reported that Kenneth Leventhal partners had earnings of about $600,000 per year. At the same time, it was estimated that average partner earnings for the largest 6 firms were between $250,000 and $300,000 a year.

Financial Accounting and Auditing

Capital markets help organizations raise money to finance growth. These markets also provide investors and creditors with opportunities to earn returns on their investments or loans. Financial accounting and auditing play important roles in providing reliable information to support investment and credit decisions and, thus, the functioning of capital markets. To learn more about financial accounting and auditing, we'll explore basic concepts of financial accounting in Part B of this module and basic concepts of auditing in Part C of this module.

MODULE 3: OWNERS AND CREDITORS AS USERS OF ACCOUNTING INFORMATION

PART B: BASIC CONCEPTS OF FINANCIAL ACCOUNTING

We need a reason to speak, but none to keep silent.
-- Pierre Nicole, <u>De la paix avec les hommes</u>

"To Offer Shares, Lauder Lifts Veil of Secrecy." That's how the *Wall Street Journal* headlined the story when Estée Lauder Cos. first revealed its financial statements in 1995. The company--a giant in the cosmetics industry that had been privately-held for 49 years by the Lauder family--decided to go public to help raise funds. The financial statements were issued to provide information to potential investors in the company's initial stock offering. To the surprise of analysts, competitors, and retail customers, the financial statements revealed that the company was much more profitable than anyone had previously estimated.

The Estée Lauder story made headlines because the financial statements provided information never before publicly available. Capital markets feed on information, and financial statements offer information the markets crave.

Financial statements are the end product of financial accounting. Financial accountants, following professional standards and guidance that define generally accepted accounting principles, decide which economic transactions (like purchases of assets or sales of goods) and economic events (like the formation of a corporation) should be recorded on the entity's books. They help organizations fulfill their financial reporting responsibilities, deciding when and where particular items of information should be reported in the financial statements, how much detail about the reported items should be included, and what value should be attached to the reported items.

A set of basic financial statements provides information about an entity's financial position at a particular point in time, the results of its operations over a period of time, and the related cash flows and changes in retained earnings, equity or funds over the period. This part of Module 3 introduces you to basic financial statements. It also introduces the notion of "generally accepted accounting principles," including the assumptions, constraints and modifying conventions that underlie financial statements. Finally, we take a look at the typical contents of an annual report, including a discussion of the audit opinion.

BASIC FINANCIAL STATEMENTS

When you have mastered the numbers, you will in fact no longer be reading numbers, any more than you read words when reading books. You will be reading meanings.
        -- Harold Geneen, Managing, 1984

When you first see a set of financial statements for a modern organization, you might find them a bit overwhelming. They seem long and complicated. They are written in a technical vocabulary that you aren't really familiar with yet--words like "depreciation" and "amortization" and "intangible assets" and "deferred taxes" that don't have intuitively obvious definitions. And they have pages upon pages of numbers, followed by pages and pages of footnotes. What does it all mean?

One of the reasons you are learning about *Core Concepts of Accounting Information* is to help you understand more about the information you can find in financial statements. You shouldn't expect to become a sophisticated reader of financial statements overnight, but you can expect to gain a basic understanding of the purpose and formats of financial statements fairly quickly. Then, as you continue your education about accounting, you will gradually come to understand more and more about financial statements. The words and numbers will cease being just words and numbers and become meaningful accounting information that you can use to make decisions.

In the sections below, we'll take a look at the financial statements of 2 businesses (Colgate-Palmolive Company and Hongkong Telecom), and 1 not-for-profit organization (The American Institute of Certified Public Accountants). Before we proceed, here's a little background about these 3 entities:

♦ **Colgate-Palmolive.** Colgate-Palmolive's common and preferred stock is traded on the New York Stock Exchange, as well as on exchanges in Amsterdam, Frankfurt, London, Paris, and Zurich. The company employs about 38,000 people to conduct its business around the world.

The company began in 1806 when 23-year-old William Colgate opened a "Soap, Mould & Dipt Candles" factory and store about 2 blocks from where New York's World Trade Center building stands today. By 1906, the company was making 160 kinds of soap, 625 perfumes and 2,000 other products (including toothcare products). In 1928, the company merged with the Palmolive-Peet Company, manufacturer of a best-selling soap made of palm and olive oil, forming Colgate-Palmolive-Peet Company (shortened to Colgate-Palmolive in 1953).

Today, Colgate-Palmolive has several major lines of business, including oral care (such as Colgate toothpaste), personal care (such as Mennen deodorant sticks), and household care products (such as Ajax cleanser and Fab laundry detergent). The company also produces, through its Hills Pet Nutrition subsidiary, market-leading pet food products (such as Science Diet and Prescription Diet).

♦ **Hongkong Telecom.** Hong Kong Telecommunications Limited's stock is traded on the Hong Kong Stock Exchange. The company, popularly known as Hongkong Telecom, is also listed on both the New York and Pacific Stock Exchanges as **American Depository Receipts** or "ADRs" (negotiable receipts that are traded in lieu of the actual foreign securities to avoid some of the complications of transferring certificates overseas, converting currencies, and so on). The company's two largest shareholders are Cable and Wireless, a U.K. telecommunications company and the Chinese government.

Hongkong Telecom employs over 15,000 people. Most of its operations are in Hong Kong, where its subsidiaries provide local and international telephone services, sell and rent telecommunications equipment, and provide computer, engineering and other services to customers.

♦ **AICPA.** The American Institute of Certified Public Accountants (AICPA) is a national professional organization for certified public accountants (CPAs). At the start of 1996, almost 330,000 CPAs belonged to the organization. About 40% of the members work in public accounting firms, just over 40% work in business and industry, and the rest work in education or government, or are retired.

As a nonprofit organization, the AICPA has different goals than either Colgate-Palmolive or Hongkong Telecom. In addition to serving members, the AICPA recognizes a mission of assuring that CPAs serve the public interest by performing the highest quality professional services. Among its programs, the AICPA prepares and administers the Uniform CPA Examination, a national test used as one of the requirements for licensing in all the states of the U.S. The organization also provides continuing education courses for its members (and others) and represents members' interests on national issues by such activities as testifying before Congress on legislation affecting CPAs.

To begin your study of financial statements, it helps to remember that the basic set of statements is designed to provide information to help answer 4 questions:

♦ What are the results of the organization's operations (or its activities, for not-for-profit organizations) for a particular period?

♦ How have the retained earnings (or stockholders' equity or, for nonprofits, net assets) changed over a particular period?

♦ What is the financial position of the organization at a particular date?

♦ What were the organization's sources and uses of cash over a particular period?

The following 4 sections explore how financial statements help answer these questions.

Results of Operations or Activities

Suppose you are an owner or creditor of an organization. You would like to know what the results of recent operations have been--Is the organization operating at a profit or loss? Are the organization's costs in line with the revenues it brings in? Are one or more segments of the organization more successful than others? How much of the income comes from operating activities that are expected to continue into the future? Answers to these questions may be found in a **statement of operations**, also variously known as an **income statement**, an **earnings statement**, or a **profit and loss statement** (sometimes referred to as "the P&L"). Constituents of a nonprofit organization can find information about operations in a **statement of activities**.

Take a close look at Figure I-3-7 on the next page, where you will find a statement showing the recent results of operations of Colgate-Palmolive Company. As you begin to learn how to read financial statements, there are 4 important things (discussed further below) to note about Colgate-Palmolive's income statements:

♦ they are consolidated,

♦ they are comparative,

♦ they follow a basic format for computing net income, and

♦ they include a measure of earnings per share.

Consolidated Statements. The title of the statement is "Consolidated Statements of Income." The word "consolidated" refers to the fact that the results for all of Colgate-Palmolive's lines of business are combined. Thus, the 1996 reported net sales revenues of $8.8 billion ($8,749.0 million per the top line of the statement) mix together sales of its Softsoap Enterprises, Inc. business in the United States, its Oraltech oral care products business in the British Virgin Islands, its Mennen Company shaving products in the United States, its Cristasol glass cleaners business in Spain, and so on. **Consolidated statements** present accounting information about a related group of legally separate companies (usually referred to as a **parent company** and its **subsidiaries**) that operate as a single economic entity. The parent company is the controlling company; the subsidiaries are the controlled companies.

Given the amount of information aggregated together in consolidated financial statements, investors and creditors might well be interested in a further breakdown of the information. So, for U.S. companies, operating information for each major segment of the business is disclosed elsewhere in the financial report--usually in the management discussion and analysis section, the footnotes, or a separate schedule.

Figure I-3-7

Consolidated Statements of Income

COLGATE-PALMOLIVE COMPANY

Dollars in Millions Except Per Share Amounts	1996	1995	1994
Net sales	$8749.0	$8,358.2	$7,587.9
Cost of sales	4451.1	4,353.1	3,913.3
Gross profit	4,297.9	4,005.1	3,674.6
Selling, general and administrative expenses	3052.1	2,879.6	2,625.2
Provision for restructured operations	—	460.5	—
Other expenses, net	93.8	96.1	82.8
Interest expense, net of interest income of $34.3, $30.6, and $34.2, respectively	197.4	205.4	86.7
Income before income taxes	954.6	363.5	879.9
Provision for income taxes	319.6	191.5	299.7
Income before changes in accounting	635.0	172.0	580.2
Cumulative effect on prior years of accounting changes	—	—	—
Net income	$ 635.0	$ 172.0	$ 580.2
Earnings per common share, primary	$ 4.19	$ 1.04	$ 3.82
Earnings per common share, assuming full dilution	$ 3.90	$ 1.02	$ 3.56

According to U.S. accounting standards, financial information about the major components or **segments** of a business must be reported by business entities. Businesses may define their segments in several ways--for example, by industry, by geographic area or by major customer groups. Colgate-Palmolive defines its segments by both industry and geography. By industry, the company categorizes its many products into 2 segments:

◆ *oral, personal and household care products*, which covers toothpaste and toothbrushes, bar and liquid soaps, shampoos and conditioners, deodorants and antiperspirants, baby products, shaving products, laundry and dishwashing detergents, fabric softeners, and cleansers and bleaches; and

◆ *pet nutrition and other products*, which includes primarily pet nutrition products.

By geographic region, the company further categorizes each of the industry segments into 4 areas: North America, Europe, Latin America, and Asia /Africa.

From the segment disclosures, you can determine the relative profitability of each of Colgate-Palmolive's 2 major industry groups, or each of its 4 regions, or each major industry group in each region. Here, for example, is some of the accounting information about Colgate-Palmolive's 2 industry segments:

	1996	1995[1]		1994
		As reported	Excluding restructuring	
Worldwide Net Sales by Business Segment				
Oral, Personal and Household Care	$ 7,880.3	$ 7,565.7	$ 7,565.7	$ 6,735.8
Pet Nutrition and Other	868.7	792.5	792.5	852.1
Total net sales	$ 8,749.0	$ 8,358.2	$ 8,358.2	$ 7,587.9
Worldwide Earnings by Business Segment				
Oral, Personal and Household Care	$ 1,033.3	$ 551.6	$ 916.5	$ 809.6
Pet Nutrition and Other	125.7	53.0	117.7	162.0
Total Segment Earnings	1,159.0	604.6	1,034.2	971.6
Less: company-wide (shared) items				
Unallocated expenses, net	(7.0)	(35.7)	(4.8)	(5.0)
Interest expense, net	(197.4)	(205.4)	(205.4)	(86.7)
Income before income taxes	$ 954.6	$ 363.5	$ 824.0	$ 879.9

[1] Note: In 1995, Colgate-Palmolive announced a major restructuring to improve efficiency of operations. The restructuring involved closing down or significantly reconfiguring 24 of its 112 factories world-wide and reducing its workforce by about 3,000 people. Although the restructuring won't be completed until 1997, the estimated costs of this restructuring were recognized in 1995. To help users compare 1995 results with other years, the 1995 results are shown both with and without the restructuring costs.

From the segment information, you can easily see that the pet nutrition business is far smaller than the oral, personal and household care business. You can also make performance comparisons such as:

Q: *What is the worldwide segment profit margin (segment earnings as a percentage of sales) for the industry groups for the years reported?*

A: Oral, Personal and Household Care
   1994: $809.6 million ÷ $6,735.8 million = 12.0%
   1995: $916.5 million ÷ $7,565.7 million = 12.1%   (before restructuring costs)
   1996: $1,033.3 million ÷ $7,880.3 million = 13.1%

   Pet Nutrition and Other
   1994: $162.0 million ÷ $852.1 million = 19.0%
   1995: $117.7 million ÷ $792.5 million = 14.9%   (before restructuring costs)
   1996: $125.7 million ÷ $868.7 million = 14.5%

From this comparison, you can see that profitability per dollar of sales is best for the pet nutrition products. However, profit margins are decreasing for this segment while they are growing for the oral, personal and household care segment. Further analysis of the geographic region segment disclosures in the annual report would reveal other interesting information, such as the fact that profitability and growth rates also differ by geographic region.

To assess relative profitability, you needed to perform some simple **ratio** calculations (that is, one number divided by another). Ratios are often used to aid the interpretation of financial statement information because they are "scale free"-- that is, they allow comparisons over different time periods, companies of different sizes, and values measured in different currencies. Ratios are one of the primary tools of financial statement analysis, a topic explored further in Theme II.

Comparative Statements.   The results of operations are presented for several periods (in this case, for 3 years)--this is known as presenting "**comparative financial statements**." Comparative financial statements give the user information about trends, providing another form of financial statement analysis. Comparative statements increase the understandability of accounting information by providing historical benchmarks to use in evaluating the current results.

But while the ratios and trends computed from a single set of financial statements can be helpful, they do not give you a complete picture. To fully interpret the ratios and trends, you need to put them into a more complete context. How, for example, has the organization performed in relation to other organizations in the same industry? For instance, an investor might want to know if Colgate-Palmolive's profit margin trends are better or worse than could be expected, given the business conditions during this period.

External benchmarks--such as performance averages for comparable companies or an industry group--help the user understand the accounting information contained in an organization's financial statements. Performance information about comparable companies can be obtained from other companies' financial statements. There are several computerized databases that provide financial statement information about public companies and a few services that sell information about private companies.

Bear in mind, however, the old warning not to compare "apples and oranges"--in other words, be sure you are using benchmarks for truly similar companies or industry groups. With large companies like Colgate-Palmolive that operate in several lines of business, you're not likely to find truly comparable companies to use as benchmarks for *consolidated* operating results. However, you could find good comparisons for each *segment* of Colgate-Palmolive's business. For example, you could compare the trend for Colgate-Palmolive's pet nutrition segment to the pet nutrition segment of the Ralston Purina Company, the manufacturer of Purina Dog Chow, Tender Vittles cat food, and other pet nutrition products. Or, you might compare the results of the pet nutrition segment to industry averages for all leading companies that make and market pet nutrition products.

When choosing comparison company and industry group benchmarks, you also need to keep the "apples and oranges" problem in mind. For example, since Colgate-Palmolive is a market leader in pet nutrition, the industry performance averages for large companies might be a more meaningful benchmark than the performance averages for the entire industry. Published industry averages usually include a range of norms. For example, Dun and Bradstreet reports industry ratios for the upper and lower quartiles (top and bottom 25%) of the industry, as well as the median for each industry group.

You should also bear in mind that ratios and trends tell you what has happened in the past, which may or may not reflect what will happen in the future. To interpret ratios and trends, you also need information about economic and industry conditions which may affect future performance. Is the economy stable, improving, or declining? Is the industry becoming more competitive or less competitive? You also need information about the organization's future plans. Is the organization planning to expand or contract? Are there any expected changes (such as retirements) in the top management group? Finally, you need to consider whether anything that happened in recent years is unlikely to occur again in the future.

Format of the Statement. Look back again at Figure I-3-7 and you will see that the basic format of Colgate-Palmolive's income statement is:

Net sales
– Cost of sales
Gross profit
– Other operating costs
Income *before* income
– Income taxes
Net income

There are many acceptable variations of the general format of the income statement. For example, companies need not use the identical expense categories and they need not compute the sub-total known as gross profit. There are also multiple terms for some of these items. For example, cost of sales may also be termed cost of goods sold, and gross profit may also be termed gross margin. But if you look beyond these superficial differences, you will find that the underlying structure of most income statements is much like the one used by Colgate-Palmolive.

As another example of a format variation, many companies separately report **operating** revenues and expenses related to their main business activities and **non-operating** results from transactions that are peripheral or incidental to the company's main business activities. For instance, many manufacturing companies would report interest received on their investments in a separate income statement category for non-operating income.

Also, the income statement format will vary if some activities or events of the current period are not expected to continue in the future. In this case, the statement first shows a computation of "income from continuing operations" (which includes deducting taxes related to this income) and then reports the other non-continuing items. These items include any income or loss from **discontinued operations** (such as a subsidiary that was sold during the period) or **extraordinary items** (gains or losses that are both unusual and infrequent, such as a major casualty loss).

Finally, the format may vary if there have been changes in accounting policies. Generally accepted accounting principles are not static. From time to time, the rules of the game may change as new accounting standards are published. Also, even if accounting standards haven't changed, sometimes a company will voluntarily choose to use a different accounting policy from among the set of policies allowed. In either case, there is the potential that net income will be affected in the year of the change.

Whatever its exact form may be, a business's income statement always ends in a "**bottom line**"--the "**net income or loss**." The term "net," which Herbert Casson once called "the biggest word in the language of business," comes to us from a Middle English word which meant "trim" or "clean." In its modern usage, net still means that the number being reported has been trimmed or cleaned of everything but its essentials. Thus, **net income** means income after every revenue, expense, gain, loss and tax has been considered. As another example, "**net sales**" means the sales revenue after deducting **sales returns** (refunds for products brought back by customers), **discounts and allowances** (price reductions given to customers to encourage prompt payment or satisfy complaints). In contrast "**gross sales**" means sales revenues before any adjustments for returns, discounts or allowances.

As you might expect for a major manufacturer, among Colgate-Palmolive's costs and expenses, the largest is its **cost of sales,** also known as **cost of goods sold.** This is the cost of manufacturing the products the company sold to customers. As an intermediate step in calculating net income, Colgate-Palmolive shows a subtotal, known as the as **gross margin** or **gross profit**. The gross profit shows how much the selling price of goods exceeded their cost, and thus how much the sales contributed toward covering the other expenses of the company.

When it comes to other operating costs and expenses, Colgate-Palmolive spent the most on its **selling, general and administrative expenses**. **Selling expenses** are the costs of selling or marketing an organization's products or services, such as advertising costs and sales commissions. **General and administrative expenses** are the costs of operating the overall organization, including such things as the salaries of top management and their clerical staff and other costs of operating the corporate headquarters.

Details about major categories of costs and expenses (or any of the other significant items reported in the financial statements) may be found in the footnotes which are attached to any set of financial statements. In the footnotes to Colgate-Palmolive's statements, for example, you could find that the company spent $565.9 million during 1996 for media advertising costs.

Earnings Per Share. Below the bottom line, the statement also includes 2 figures reporting different measures of "Earnings per common share," otherwise known as **earnings per share (EPS)**. Earnings per share is a ratio that is an important measure of performance for owners of common stock. The ratio reflects the amount of net income attributable to each share of common stock. In its simplest form, earnings per share is computed as follows:

$$\text{Earnings per share} = \frac{\textbf{Net Income - Preferred Stock Dividends}}{\textbf{Weighted Average Number of Shares of Common Stock Outstanding}}$$

Take a look at the first ("primary") EPS figure for Colgate-Palmolive. The 1995 primary earnings per share were $1.04, much lower than the $3.82 in 1994 and $4.19 in 1996. This is largely the result of the 1995 restructuring charges.

Colgate-Palmolive also shows a second EPS measure, one that is calculated "assuming full dilution." When this second EPS number is reported, it will *always* be lower than the first. Fully-diluted EPS reflects the possibility that a stockholder's proportionate share of ownership in the company could be reduced (diluted) in the future. In companies with complex capital structures, there may be some "**common stock equivalents**"--such as stock options, rights or warrants which give holders the right to purchase a specified number of shares of common stock at a specific price and a specified time. Some debt or preferred stock that is convertible into common stock may also be common stock equivalents. If these common stock equivalents are exercised, the current owners will end up with a smaller proportionate ownership share in the company. In Colgate-Palmolive's case, the company has a significant amount of preferred stock which is convertible into common stock, so it must compute *both* EPS numbers:

♦ **primary earnings per share**, which computes the earnings attributable to both common stock and any common stock equivalents that would "dilute" (reduce) EPS by at least 3%, and

♦ **fully diluted earnings per share**, which computes the EPS that would result if every possible convertible security, option, right, warrant or other potential diluter were turned into common stock.

While you need not concern yourself at this stage with the calculation of these 2 EPS figures, you should understand the different information they convey. Fully diluted earnings per share reflects a worst-case scenario, the earnings per share that a current stockholder would have if every possible dilution occurred. Primary earnings per share is a less extreme measure, reflecting the potential effect of only the largest possible diluters.

For years, U.S. companies' EPS reporting has been more complex than international reporting standards require. As part of the effort to harmonize standards, U.S. companies will no longer report primary EPS in financial statements issued for periods ending after December 15, 1997. Instead, consistent with international standards, they will report **basic earnings per share**. Basic earnings per share ignores any dilution from common stock equivalents; it is the simplest form of EPS shown in the formula on the previous page. The presentation of fully-diluted EPS will not change.

Other Examples of Operating Statements: The AICPA. Now that you have had a chance to read one company's income statement, it is time to take a look at how other organizations' operating statements appear. To start, take a look at the **Statement of Activities** of the American Institute of Certified Public Accountants (in Figure I-3-8 on the following page) and see if you can find at least 3 similarities and at least 3 differences between the AICPA's statements of activities and Colgate-Palmolive's income statements.

You should have spotted several similarities, including:

♦ **Consolidated statements**: Like Colgate-Palmolive, the AICPA reports the results for a related group of organizations that operate as a single economic entity. The "*Combined* Statements of Activities" include the revenues and expenses of the national professional organization (the AICPA) and 4 related organizations, including the AICPA Benevolent Fund (an organization that provides financial assistance to needy AICPA members and their families) and the Accounting Research Association (an organization that raises money to support financial and government accounting standard-setting).

♦ **Comparative statements**: Both organizations report several years of results so readers can compare operating performance over time.

♦ **Basic format**: The basic format of revenue (and gains) less expenses is similar, although not identical, for the two organizations.

Figure I-3-8

AMERICAN INSTITUTE OF CERTIFIED PUBLIC ACCOUNTANTS AND RELATED ORGANIZATIONS

COMBINED STATEMENTS OF ACTIVITIES YEAR ENDED JULY 31

	1996	1995
Changes in unrestricted net assets:	($000)	
Revenue and gains:		
Dues	$55,536	$ 55,190
Publications and software	34,860	37,434
Professional development	24,953	25,133
Investment and sundry income	13,418	9,317
Professional examinations	8,052	7,547
Contributions	1,323	1,085
Total unrestricted revenue and gains	138,142	135,706
Expenses:		
Program services:		
Publications and software produced for sale	25,308	27,404
Professional development	25,029	25,266
Member services:		
Regulation and legislation	14,559	14,472
Technical	12,419	11,657
Publications	6,763	6,040
Other	3,350	2,539
Professional examinations	8,294	7,418
Communications and public relations	5,478	4,074
Support and scholarships	5,372	5,250
Assistance programs	1,081	1,055
Supporting activities:		
General management	18,227	18,065
Organization and membership development	6,203	6,343
Total expenses	132,083	129,583
Increase in unrestricted net assets before cumulative effect of changes in accounting principles	6,059	6,123
Cumulative effect of changes in accounting principles:		
Postretirement benefits	(7,493)	—
Marketable securities	3,102	—
Contributions	243	—
Totals	(4,148)	—
Increase in unrestricted net assets	1,911	6,123
Unrestricted net assets, beginning of year	28,917	22,794
Unrestricted net assets, end of year	$30,828	$ 28,917

The accompanying notes to financial statements are an integral part of these statements.

However, you should also have spotted some important differences, including:

♦ **A service-orientation, rather than a profit orientation:** The users of a business's income statement are focused on whether or not the company made a profit during the year. To a business, more earnings are always preferable to less; the business's goal is to maximize profit. But a nonprofit organization isn't trying to maximize profit; it has a service objective, rather than a profit objective. In a sense, the target a nonprofit organization usually shoots for is to have a "bottom line" that is close to *zero*--that is, the organization strives to generate enough revenues to cover operating expenses. The users of a nonprofit's statement of activities want to know whether the organization has been able to operate within its available resources.

For a nonprofit, any "**surplus**" from operations (an excess of revenue over expenditures) may be used to provide a cushion for the future. But, beyond a certain point, too large a surplus is not considered optimum. The organization's constituencies might question why the organization is accumulating funds in excess of its needs, or why it isn't finding a way to make more effective use of its funds. For example, AICPA members might regard too large a surplus as a sign that the organization doesn't really "need" their membership dues. On the other hand, a "**deficit**" from operations (meaning expenditures exceed revenue) usually has the same interpretation for a nonprofit organization as for a business organization. The larger the deficit, the greater the signs of financial difficulty.

Notice that the AICPA doesn't present an earnings per share figure because nonprofit (and government) entities have no shareholders. In fact, the term "net income" isn't even used, reflecting the fact that the AICPA's goals aren't focused on making profits. Instead, the excess of revenue over expenses--which a business would term "income"--is labeled "**increase in unrestricted net assets.**"

♦ **The possibility of donor-imposed restrictions:** In the AICPA's case, the excess of revenue over expenses becomes part of the "unrestricted net assets" and remains available to support the AICPA's operations. The term "**unrestricted**" indicates that the AICPA's management team is free to use the fund balance on whatever projects or activities the management team chooses. In addition to unrestricted funds, many nonprofit organizations have some **restricted** funds--that is, funds which may only be used for a specified purpose. For example, suppose some donors to a college specify that their donations are to be used for scholarships. The college is not free to use the scholarship fund balance for any other purpose. Restrictions on funds may be temporary (after a period of time, the restriction is removed) or permanent. When a nonprofit organization has several types of funds, its financial reports show details for each type of net assets (permanently restricted, temporarily restricted, and unrestricted), as well as a total for the organization as a whole.

♦ **Different revenue and expense classifications:** The AICPA presents a single-step statement, with the simple format:

Revenue and gains — Expenses = Increase in unrestricted net assets

While the basic format of the income statements and activities statements are similar for Colgate-Palmolive and the AICPA, there are some key differences. For instance, the AICPA's statement has no intermediate calculation of gross profit as in Colgate-Palmolive's multi-step income statement. This, of course, is because gross profit is not relevant for a nonprofit organization. The categories of revenue and expenses on the statements also differ because the nature of the organizations differ.

Take a close look at the revenue classifications. Colgate-Palmolive is a business; it gets its revenue exclusively from sales to customers. The AICPA is a not-for-profit organization that gets its revenue from several sources, including membership dues, sales to customers (publications and software), fees for the CPA exam, and contributions from donors.

Now take a look at the expense classifications. Remember that for Colgate-Palmolive's income statement, details were available in the footnotes about *what* kind of expenses were incurred for operations. For example, the reader could find out how much the company had spent on advertising during the year. Accountants call this "**natural classification**" of expenses because the categories tell you the nature of what was bought.

On the other hand, the AICPA's statement does not tell readers *what* expenses were incurred for operations--for example, it doesn't tell the reader how much was spent on things like salaries, advertising, or printing costs. Instead, the expenses are classified by *activity*--such as member service activities, professional examinations, assistance programs, and so on--which tells us *why* the expenses were incurred. Accountants call this "**functional classification**" of expenses because the categories tell you why funds were expended. The "why" information is particularly relevant to constituents of nonprofit organizations; this information helps constituents assess how the organization used its available resources to provide services during the year.

Accounting standards require all nonprofit organizations to report expenses by functional classification. Nonprofits may also disclose information about the natural classification of expenses, but only voluntary health and welfare organizations are required to do so. For these organizations (commonly referred to as "charities"), financial statement users do care about *why* expenses were incurred, but also want some information about *what* the funds were spent on--for example, they are interested in how much of the donated funds were spent on administrators' salaries.

There's one other thing you may have noticed about the AICPA's Statements of Activities--but it isn't unique to nonprofit organizations. For 1996, there is a section after the listing of expenses labeled "**cumulative effect of changes in accounting**

principles." This section might also appear on the income statement of a business. It reports the effects of any changes during the reporting period in the way an organization accounts for its operations. Accounting standards are not fixed, they evolve over time. During the reporting period, several new accounting standards for nonprofit organizations came into effect--for example, there was a change in the standards concerned with recording revenues from donor contributions (accounting for contributions is discussed further in Theme II). When a new standard is first used, or when an organization changes from one acceptable method of accounting to another, any significant effects of these changes are separately reported to help readers make comparisons to prior years.

Other Examples of Operating Statements: Hongkong Telecom. Next, try comparing Colgate-Palmolive's income statement to the way Hongkong Telecom reports its operating results, which you can see in Figure I-3-9 on the next page. Hongkong Telecom's "Consolidated Profit and Loss Account" statement has some similarities and some differences with the income statement of Colgate-Palmolive. In terms of similarities, note that Hongkong Telecom also presents consolidated comparative results and includes an earnings per share figure. In terms of differences, there are a few important format and terminology variations, as well as a difference in reporting period. These differences are discussed below.

Terminology Differences. You should note that there are a few terminology differences between the U.S. and Hongkong systems. In particular, the term "**Turnover**" in the Hongkong system means the same thing as "**Sales Revenue**" in the U.S. system. This specific terminology difference, which extends to many other countries as well, can be especially confusing because the term "turnover" is used in the U.S. to mean the frequency with which an item is replaced during an accounting period. Thus, if a U.S. company reports an **inventory turnover** of 6.0, it means that the inventory is replaced an average of 6 times per year (once every 2 months). So, when you are dealing with international companies, you need to interpret the term "turnover" within the appropriate context.

Minority Interests. When a parent company controls a subsidiary but owns less than 100% of its common stock, the remaining shareholders in the subsidiary are called the "**minority interest**." Consolidated income statements include all the operating results of the subsidiary, but then subtract out the share of the net income or loss that belongs to the other (minority) stockholders. This is the reason for the $24.3 million reduction of Hongkong Telecom's 1996 net income for "minority interests" and the $0.0 million (less than $100,000) reduction for 1995. Colgate-Palmolive also has minority interests, but they are small enough that the company includes them in its "other expenses," rather than separately reporting them.

Fiscal Years. There's one other small difference you might have noted in Hongkong Telecom's P&L statement. While Colgate-Palmolive's income statement covers a calendar-year reporting period (the reporting period ends on December 31), Hongkong Telecom's statement is dated "for the year ended 31 March." Hongkong Telecom, like many organizations throughout the world, uses a "fiscal year" rather

Figure I-3-9
Hong Kong Telecommunications Limited's Income Statement

Consolidated profit and loss *account*
For the year ended 31 March 1996

Note		1996	1995
		$M	$M
3	**Turnover**	**29,405.2**	26,909.6
4	Operating costs	**18,312.5**	17,148.4
	Operating profit	**11,092.7**	9,761.2
6	Net interest and other income	**385.5**	276.2
	Profit before taxation	**11,478.2**	10,037.4
7	Taxation	**1,515.1**	1,338.7
	Profit after taxation	**9,963.1**	8,698.7
	Minority interests	**24.3**	—
8	**Profit attributable to shareholders**	**9,938.8**	8,698.7
	Appropriations		
9	Dividends	**7,619.1**	6,613.6
18	**Retained profit for the year**	**2,319.7**	2,085.1
10	**Earnings per share**	**88.8¢**	78.0¢

than a calendar year to define its financial accounting periods. A **fiscal year** is any 12-month period that an organization consistently uses for accounting purposes.

Why would an organization choose a fiscal year that is different from the calendar year? Sometimes, there may be good practical reasons for choosing a fiscal year-end date other than December 31. For example, department stores often avoid a December 31 reporting date because December is part of their busiest retail season. It's much easier for a department store to go through the process of preparing financial reports at a less busy time of year. So, many department stores have fiscal years ending in late January; others might choose a fiscal year-end in July, at another fairly calm point in their selling seasons. Sometimes there are also tax advantages associated with particular year-end dates.

You may need to take note of the fiscal year-end date when you compare performance results between companies. Suppose you are comparing a company with a 1997 fiscal year that ends March 31 and a company with a 1997 reporting period that ends on December 31. If there were significant economic or political developments between March 31 and December 31 that could affect the companies, you should take them into account when comparing the 2 statements. For example, suppose the 2 companies are airlines and a fare war (deep price-cutting by competitors) broke out in May 1997. The sales pattern for the company with the December 31 year end may be affected by the price cuts, but the sales pattern for the other company will not be affected.

Results of Operations or Activities: A Brief Recap. Now you've seen statements reporting the results of operations for 2 businesses and activities for 1 not-for-profit organization. You know that consolidated statements report on an entire economic entity and that comparative statements include results for multiple periods to help make the accounting information more meaningful. You've been introduced to the importance of ratios, trends and external benchmarks in interpreting financial statements.

You've also learned the basic format for a statement reporting the results of operations or activities, as well as some typical variations. You've seen some differences in statements of business organizations and nonprofit or government organizations--such as the inclusion of earnings per share information for businesses and its irrelevance for nonprofit and government entities. And you've seen some differences in financial statements prepared by organizations in different countries.

Changes in Retained Earnings, Equity or Net Assets

The Statement of Operations (or Income Statement or Statement of Activities) reports the results of an organization's operations for a particular period of time. Financial statement users may also be interested in knowing what has happened to the accumulated earnings of the organization: How much has the organization reinvested in itself? How much has been distributed to owners (if there are owners)? How have the retained earnings (or equity or net assets) changed over this period?

The basic set of financial statements for a business will include a Statement of Retained Earnings or a Statement of Stockholders' Equity. The **statement of retained earnings** reconciles the period's beginning balance and the period's ending balance of a business organization's retained earnings account. Alternatively, a business organization may choose to publish a **statement of stockholders' equity**, reconciling the beginning and ending balances of every equity account.

Nonprofit and government organizations, which have no owners to distribute earnings to, are not required to publish a statement of net assets. However, many nonprofit organizations show a reconciliation of unrestricted net assets at the bottom of their statement of activities.

Format of a Statement of Retained Earnings. The standard format for a Statement of Retained Earnings is simple:

Beginning retained earnings
+ Net income (or – net loss)
– Dividends
Ending retained earnings

Whereas Hongkong Telecom combined its income statement and statement of retained earnings (take a look back at Figure I-3-9 to see this), Colgate-Palmolive's statement of retained earnings follows the standard format exactly:

Consolidated Statements of Retained Earnings

COLGATE-PALMOLIVE COMPANY

Dollars in Millions	1996	1995	1994
Balance, January 1	$2,392.2	$2,496.7	$2,163.4
Add:			
Net income	635.0	172.0	580.2
	3,027.2	2,668.7	2,743.6
Deduct:			
Dividends declared:			
Series B Convertible Preference Stock, net of income taxes	20.9	21.1	21.1
Preferred stock	0.5	0.5	0.5
Common stock	274.8	254.9	225.3
	296.2	276.5	246.9
Balance, December 31	$2,731.0	$2,392.2	$2,496.7

The format of this statement reflects the meaning of retained earnings. Remember that when a business operates profitably, the owners benefit. The profits can either be distributed as dividends or reinvested in the business. The

accumulated profits reinvested in the business are known as **"retained earnings."**
Retained earnings are part of the firm's equity because they are capital indirectly
provided by owners, who forgo dividends today to help the firm prepare for the
future.

On the other hand, when a business experiences a loss, the owners' ability to
receive dividends or reinvest in the business is reduced. Thus net losses are treated
as reductions of retained earnings. If losses ever reach the point where they exceed
accumulated retained earnings, there is said to be a **"retained deficit."** For
example, new companies in the early stages of development may operate at a loss for
several years, leading to a retained deficit. These companies hope to survive long
enough to become profitable. If their future profits are large enough, they will
eventually make up their accumulated deficits.

A retained deficit indicates that a company is experiencing financial difficulty. If
the deficit is large enough, the total equity of the organization may fall into a deficit
position. As Gerald F. Lieberman once observed, "A deficit is what you have when
you haven't got as much as you had when you had nothing." When there is a
negative total equity, the company is in the unfortunate position of having liabilities
greater than its assets. At that point, the company is insolvent.

Changes in Net Assets. Businesses are accountable to their stockholders--who
are, after all, the *owners* of the company. So, it is natural to expect business
financial statements to include a statement of retained earnings. But what about
non-business entities, such as nonprofit and government organizations?

Nonprofit and government organizations recognize their accountability to
different stakeholders by using a form of accounting known as **"fund accounting."**
A **"fund"** represents resources intended to be used for a specific purpose. Each fund
has its own set of self-balancing accounts, including fund assets, liabilities, revenues
and expenses. A non-business organization will typically have several different
funds, each for a different purpose. For example, a university might have several
funds, including a student loan fund to account for resources dedicated to providing
loans to students; a general fund to account for the revenues (e.g., tuition) and
expenses (e.g. faculty and staff salaries) associated with the ongoing educational
mission of the university; and a plant fund to account for resources earmarked for
the expansion or improvement of the university's buildings and other fixed assets
(like laboratory equipment in science classrooms).

 For financial reporting purposes, non-business organizations report a combined
total for all funds. They may also provide details for individually important funds.
Moreover, just as businesses provide a statement showing the changes in retained
earnings, not-for-profit organizations may show the changes in net assets, although
nonprofits do not typically use a separate statement to do this. If you look at the
bottom portion of the AICPA's Statements of Activities, you will find the changes in
net assets reported as follows:

	1996	1995
	($000)	
Increase in unrestricted net assets	**1,911**	6,123
Unrestricted net assets, beginning of year	**28,917**	22,794
Unrestricted net assets, end of year	**$30,828**	$ 28,917

Further details about the changes in net assets are included in the footnotes of the AICPA's financial statements. The footnotes provide information about how much of the net assets belong to each of the related organizations. For example, the Benevolent Fund had a balance of $2,593,000 at the end of fiscal year 1996.

Financial Position: The Balance Sheet

So far, the financial statements we've looked at have focused on what has happened to the organization over a particular recent period of time. But remember that the organization is long-lived. Its current financial position depends not just on the results of its operations in the immediate past, but on all the economic resources and obligations the organization has accumulated up to this point in its history.

The organization's economic resources and obligations also provide the key to its future. Consequently, many users of financial statements will want to know what the financial position of the organization is at this particular point in time--What kinds of economic resources does the organization have? Which of the economic resources are expected to be used up during the coming year? What kinds of obligations does the organization have to pay during the coming year? What is the balance between its debt financing and its equity financing? The balance sheet (also known as **the statement of financial position**) provides information to help answer these questions.

The **balance sheet** reports the assets, liabilities and equities of an entity on a particular date--that is, it gives a picture of the organization at a single point in time. The statement gets its name--and its basic format--from the natural balance that exists in the accounting equation:

$$\text{Assets} = \text{Liabilities} + \text{Equity}$$

Take a look, for example, at Colgate-Palmolive's balance sheet (Figure I-3-10 on the next page) and note that the total assets ($7,901.5 million as of December 31, 1996) equals the total of liabilities and equity at the same date.

Assets. **Assets** are the economic resources of the firm--the things the firm owns that are expected to be of benefit in the future. Take a closer look at the assets section of Colgate-Palmolive's balance sheet. You'll see that it's subdivided into 2 parts, following a format known as a "**classified balance sheet**." The first part reports "**current assets**"--those assets expected to be used or consumed during the

Figure I-3-10

Consolidated Balance Sheets

COLGATE-PALMOLIVE COMPANY

Dollars in Millions Except Per Share Amounts		1996		1995
Assets				
Current Assets				
Cash and cash equivalents	$	248.2	$	208.8
Marketable securities		59.6		47.8
Receivables (less allowances of $33.8 and $31.9, respectively)		1,064.4		1,116.9
Inventories		770.7		774.8
Other current assets		229.4		211.9
Total current assets		2,372.3		2,360.2
Property, plant and equipment, net		2,428.9		2,155.2
Goodwill and other intangibles, net		2,720.4		2,741.7
Other assets		379.9		385.2
	$	7,901.5	$	7,642.3
Liabilities and Shareholders' Equity				
Current Liabilities				
Notes and loans payable	$	172.3	$	204.4
Current portion of long-term debt		110.4		37.0
Accounts payable		751.7		738.7
Accrued income taxes		93.1		76.7
Other accruals		776.8		696.3
Total current liabilities		1,904.3		1,753.1
Long-term debt		2,786.8		2,992.0
Deferred income taxes		234.3		237.3
Other liabilities		942.0		980.1
Shareholders' Equity				
Preferred stock		392.7		403.5
Common stock, $1 par value (500,000,000 shares authorized, 183,213,295 shares issued)		183.2		183.2
Additional paid-in capital		1,101.6		1,033.7
Retained earnings		2,731.0		2,392.2
Cumulative translation adjustments		(534.7)		(513.0)
		3,873.8		3,499.6
Unearned compensation		(370.9)		(378.0)
Treasury stock, at cost		(1,468.8)		(1,441.8)
Total shareholders' equity		2,034.1		1,679.8
	$	7,901.5	$	7,642.3

next year. The second (unlabeled) part reports "**non-current**" (**or long-term**) **assets**.

Current assets tend to be very liquid--they include cash and items which will soon be converted to cash, like **accounts receivable** (amounts due from customers) and **inventories** (stocks of goods held for sale). Some non-current assets may also be quite liquid--for example, long-term investments in securities may be readily converted to cash by selling the securities. Other non-current assets are less liquid-- for example property, plant and equipment. Colgate-Palmolive's **property, plant and equipment** includes the land, buildings and machinery that the company uses in its business--things like the factories that manufacture toothpaste and the office buildings where the corporate headquarters are housed.

Another category of non-current assets is "**intangible assets**"--economic resources that have value, but no tangible, physical existence. Some examples of intangible assets are **patents** (the exclusive right to make or sell a product, like a patent on a drug) and **trademarks** (an insignia or logo that identifies a product) that a company has purchased. Colgate-Palmolive's intangible assets also include "goodwill," which arose from some past acquisitions of other businesses. Sometimes an acquired business is worth more than the market values of its identifiable assets-- perhaps because it has established an excellent reputation that enhances its earnings potential. The excess of the price paid for the business over the market value of its identifiable assets is known as "**goodwill**." According to U.S. accounting standards, purchased goodwill is initially booked as an asset, which is then amortized (allocated to expense) over a period of no more than 40 years.

Liabilities. **Liabilities** are the obligations the entity owes to its creditors. Colgate-Palmolive subdivides its liabilities into a **current** portion (obligations payable in 1 year or less) and a **non-current** portion.

The classification of assets and liabilities into current and non-current portions is useful to creditors who are concerned with liquidity and solvency. As one measure of liquidity, they look at the entity's "**current ratio**," the ratio between its current assets and current liabilities. This ratio shows the organization's ability to pay its current debts out of current assets. As of December 31, 1996, Colgate-Palmolive's current ratio was about 1.25. That is, the organization's current assets ($2,372.3 million) were 1.25 times as large as their current liabilities ($1,904.3 million). To assess how strong their liquidity position was, you would need to know what typical current ratios are like for companies in their industry. The current ratio, like all ratios, can be more meaningfully interpreted if you have external benchmarks for comparison. Additional ratios used to assess liquidity and solvency are discussed in the section on financial statement analysis in Theme II.

Equity. **Equity** is the residual ownership interest in the firm. Colgate-Palmolive's equity section reveals that the company is authorized to issue both preferred and common stock and that the common stock has a par value of $1 per share. You could also have figured this out by noting that the common stock account is valued at $183.2 million for 183,213,295 shares ($1 per share). There is a separate account showing "**Additional paid-in capital**" (also known as "**Capital in excess of par value**") indicating that the stockholders paid more for their stock than its par value.

The equity section also reports the company's retained earnings. Over the course of its life, Colgate-Palmolive has accumulated $2,731.0 million of earnings that have not been distributed to stockholders as dividends. You should note that this retained earnings figure from the balance sheet agrees with the ending balance from Colgate-Palmolive's statement of retained earnings.

Several additional items are reported in the equity section, including:

♦ **Cumulative translation adjustments**: Remember that Colgate-Palmolive does business throughout the world. Its foreign subsidiaries and branches have assets and liabilities valued in the local currency of the countries where they are located. When the consolidated financial statements are prepared, the foreign currency amounts must be translated into U.S. dollars. Since the value of the dollar fluctuates against these foreign currencies, there may be a gain or loss on the translation. As of December 31, 1996, the translation adjustments have amounted to $534.7 million.

♦ **Treasury stock**: The "treasury stock" represents previously issued Colgate-Palmolive stock that the company has repurchased. Companies may either cancel their repurchased stock or hold it "in the treasury" for later resale or use as an award to high-performing employees. The cost of treasury stock is shown as a *reduction* of equity because the shares aren't currently in the hands of stockholders.

International Differences in Balance Sheets. Now, take a look at Hong Kong Telecommunications Limited's balance sheet, which appears in Figure I-3-11 on the following page. You'll note immediately that while the statement reports assets, liabilities and equities, it does so in a very different format. Instead of using the title "Assets," Hongkong Telecom labels its assets section "Employment of Capital." Also, Hongkong Telecom labels its liabilities and equities section "Financed By."

These titles are good descriptions of the distinction between assets, on the one hand, and liabilities and equities, on the other hand. Remember that all organizations need capital, which they either raise from investors (creating owners' capital or equity capital) or borrow from creditors (creating debt capital). Thus, every organization is "financed by" its owners and creditors. The capital the organization raises or borrows is used to acquire economic resources--that is, the organization "employs" its capital to garner assets.

You might also note that Hongkong Telecom presents its balance sheet for both the "Group" and the "Company." The group refers to the economic entity formed by the parent and subsidiaries; the company refers only to the parent corporation. As

Figure I-3-11
Hong Kong Telecommunications Limited's Balance Sheet

Balance *sheets*
At 31 March 1996

Note		Group 1996 $M	Group 1995 $M	Company 1996 $M	Company 1995 $M
	Employment of capital				
11	Fixed assets	22,255.7	19,974.4	—	—
12	Interest in subsidiaries	—	—	5,761.3	6,012.5
13	Other investments	401.3	341.6	85.4	52.1
14	Other non current assets	2,057.9	1,765.6	—	3.7
15	Current assets	11,839.8	7,824.5	8,108.7	4,800.4
		36,554.7	29,906.1	13,955.4	10,868.7
16	Current liabilities	13,666.4	11,437.1	4,495.4	3,958.4
		22,888.3	18,469.0	9,460.0	6,910.3
	Financed by				
17	Share capital	5,654.3	5,576.4	5,654.3	5,576.4
18	Reserves	16,492.9	12,141.6	3,805.7	1,333.9
	Shareholders' funds	22,147.2	17,718.0	9,460.0	6,910.3
	Minority interests	32.1	1.3	—	—
19	Deferred taxation	709.0	709.8	—	—
20	Bank Loans	—	39.9	—	—
		22,888.3	18,469.0	9,460.0	6,910.3

you would expect, the assets (and related liabilities and equities) of the parent company are smaller than those of the entire group. Additionally, if you remember that some of the subsidiaries of Hongkong Telecom were not wholly-owned, you shouldn't be surprised to see a "Minority Interests" value in the equity section for the group. Just as the minority stockholders own a share of the current profits or losses, they also own a share of the equity in the subsidiary.

One final thing to note about the Hongkong Telecom balance sheet: under the heading "Employment of Capital," Hongkong Telecom lists its *least* liquid assets first and then proceeds to the *more* liquid items. Thus, the report starts with fixed assets (its plant, property and equipment), then lists the parent company's investments in the subsidiaries (this only shows up in the "company" columns of the balance sheet as the "group" already includes both the parent and the subsidiaries), then lists its other investments (like investments in securities), its other noncurrent assets, and finally its current assets. The footnotes provide additional information about each of these categories. For example, the current assets include cash, consumable stores (supplies), inventory and trade receivables, among other things.

After the assets are totaled (adding up to $36,554.7 million for the group as of March 31, 1996), the current liabilities are *deducted* from the total, yielding $22,888.3 million of total assets less current liabilities. This figure balances with the total long-term liabilities and equity listed in the "Financed By" section.

Why does Hongkong Telecom subtract current liabilities from total assets instead of including them with the other liabilities and equity? The Hongkong system of financial reporting, like the U.K. system it springs from, has traditionally placed great emphasis on the needs of creditors. To highlight liquidity, current liabilities are **"offset"** against (deducted from) either total assets--as in the Hongkong Telecom balance sheet--or, more frequently, current assets. Thus, Hong Kong and U.K. balance sheets emphasize the creditors' position more than U.S. balance sheets do, although both approaches present the same set of information.

Balance Sheets for Government and Nonprofit Entities. How do balance sheets for government and nonprofit entities compare to those of businesses? They typically follow the same basic format, except that "net assets" (or "fund balances") replace "equities." Thus, the basic format for a not-for-profit balance sheet becomes:

Assets = Liabilities + Net Assets

The balance sheet for the AICPA (see Figure I-3-12 on the following page) follows this basic format. Notice that the total net assets includes $648,000 of permanently restricted funds--these funds are restricted to support of the AICPA's library.

Financial Position: A Recap. In summary, a balance sheet shows the financial position of the organization on a particular date. The statement shows the economic resources (assets) of the entity and the relative positions of the providers of capital: the entity's creditors (to whom the organization owes liabilities) and its owners (who

Figure I-3-12

AMERICAN INSTITUTE OF CERTIFIED PUBLIC ACCOUNTANTS AND RELATED ORGANIZATIONS

COMBINED STATEMENTS OF FINANCIAL POSITION

JULY 31

	1996	1995
	($000)	
Assets:		
Cash	$ 630	$ 165
Marketable securities	70,380	59,390
Accounts and notes receivable (less an allowance for doubtful accounts: 1996, $1,082,000; 1995, $885,000)	11,896	11,346
Inventories	2,385	2,283
Deferred costs and prepaid expenses	3,202	4,054
Furniture, equipment, and leasehold improvements, net	22,850	21,919
Total assets	$111,343	$99,157
Liabilities and net assets:		
Liabilities:		
Accounts payable and other liabilities	$ 14,459	$ 15,381
Advance dues	25,903	23,894
Unearned revenue	12,810	11,400
Long-term debt	1,200	4,000
Deferred rent	14,338	12,789
Deferred employee benefits	11,157	2,128
Total Liabilities	79,867	69,592
Net assets:		
Unrestricted	30,828	28,917
Permanently restricted	648	648
Total net assets	31,476	29,565
Total liabilities and net assets	$111,343	$99,157

The accompanying notes to financial statements are an integral part of these statements.

have an equity interest in the entity). For government and nonprofit organizations that do not have owners, the equity accounts are replaced by net assets (or fund balances). To aid in the assessment of liquidity, the balance sheet may classify both assets and liabilities as current or non-current. Also, the format of the balance sheet may vary between countries, although all balance sheets report how capital was employed to garner economic resources (assets) and how capital was obtained (liabilities and equities).

Sources and Uses of Cash: The Statement of Cash Flows

We've already mentioned that creditors are particularly interested in the liquidity of an organization, which means that creditors are interested in cash flows. Owners tend to be more interested in assessing the profitability of the entity, but they too are interested in cash flow information because it helps them evaluate the entity's prospects for continuing profitability and for paying future dividends. What kind of cash flows does the organization have? Where does the organization's cash come from? How is it used? Do operating activities bring in more cash than they use? Information to answer these questions may be found in a Statement of Cash Flows.

How important are cash flows? In an interview with *Inc.* magazine, William McGowan, cofounder of MCI Communications Corporation, argued that cash flows are critical to an organization:

> *The only thing that matters is cash flow...where it's coming from and where its going and how much is left over. No company has ever gone bankrupt because it had a loss on its P&L.*

McGowan was speaking from experience, having succeeded in a venture that many people thought was impossible. In 1968, McGowan and Jack Goeken started a long-distance telephone company that seemed no match for the giant AT&T system. Yet, today MCI is the second largest long-distance company in the United States, providing service within the U.S. and to over 50 foreign countries. While MCI now operates at a profit, it was not at all profitable at its start. Companies can, and often must, endure without profits, but they cannot endure without cash. This is why McGowan believed so strongly in the importance of cash flow information.

McGowan's point is important. Management's goal may be to make a profit, but management must also control the organization's cash. Profit (or net income) and cash are *not* the same thing. Consider the following example:

> *Jeff is a college student who operates a baseball card business as a way of earning money to pay his tuition. At the beginning of December his inventory of cards includes several Rod Carew rookie cards that he bought for $75 each several years ago.*
>
> *During December, Susan, another student, asks if she can buy one of the Rod Carew cards to give to her friend Paul for a holiday gift. She's willing to pay Jeff's selling price of $450 for the card, but she can't pay him until January. Jeff agrees to the sale and gives Susan the card in December.*

If Jeff were to prepare an Income Statement for his baseball card business for the month of December, he would show a *profit* of $375--the difference between the Rod Carew card's $450 selling price and its $75 cost. But, while the business made a profit in December, it had absolutely *no* cash flow during the month. No cash came in (Susan hasn't paid him yet) and no cash went out (he already owned the cards at the start of the month).

Now, obviously, there is a connection between profit and cash. Jeff's recognition of a December profit hinges on his belief that he will collect the cash from Susan in January. But, the flows of profits and cash are not identical. Profit is what the company earns through its operating and nonoperating activities--it's an economic concept that has no physical existence. On December 31, Jeff has a $375 profit, but nothing in his pockets. Cash, on the other hand, can be put in your pocket: cash is money that can be spent or locked in a safe or saved--it has a physical existence.

The **statement of cash flows** describes the impact on the organization's cash from the period's operating, financing and investing activities. **Operating activities** are the main activities of the organization--like manufacturing and selling toothpaste and other consumer products for Colgate-Palmolive or conducting conferences and preparing the CPA exam for the AICPA. **Financing activities** include raising equity or debt capital, or repaying amounts borrowed, or distributing returns to owners. **Investing activities** include acquiring or disposing of plant, property and equipment and acquiring or selling a business unit (like a subsidiary or division). In short, the statement of cash flows shows the movement of money into and out of the organization. The basic format of a statement of cash flows is:

Cash flows from operating activities
+ Cash flows from financing activities
+ Cash flows from investing activities

Net change in cash during period
+ Beginning cash balance

Ending cash balance

The same basic format is used by business, nonprofit and government entities. According to U.S. accounting standards, statements of cash flows are required for both business and not-for-profit organizations. The statement, however, is not required everywhere in the world.

Look at an excerpt from the AICPA's statement of cash flows (see Figure I-3-13 on the following page) and compare it to the organization's balance sheet (Figure I-3-12) and statement of activities (Figure I-3-8).

First, think about how the AICPA's statement of cash flows relates to its balance sheet. The reported *ending* balance of cash of $630,000 agrees with the cash total reported on the July 31, 1996 balance sheet. The reported *beginning* balance for

Figure I-3-13

AMERICAN INSTITUTE OF CERTIFIED PUBLIC ACCOUNTANTS AND RELATED ORGANIZATIONS	**COMBINED STATEMENTS OF CASH FLOWS YEAR ENDED JULY 31**	
	1996	1995
	($000)	

Increase (Decrease) in Cash:

Operating Activities:

Cash received from members and customers	**$ 128,455**	$131,975
Interest and dividends received	**2,965**	2,777
Cash paid to suppliers, employees and others	**(117,789)**	(120,539)
Interest paid	**(139)**	(290)
Income taxes paid	**(280)**	(144)
Net cash provided by operating activities	**13,212**	13,779

Investing Activities:

Payments for purchase of equipment	**(4,320)**	(8,535)
Payments for purchase of marketable securities	**(142,050)**	(87,364)
Proceeds from sale of marketable securities	**136,423**	83,448
Net cash used in investing activities	**(9,947)**	(12,451)

Financing Activities--payments of long-term borrowings	**(2,800)**	(1,300)
Net increase in cash	**465**	28
Cash, beginning of year	**165**	137
Cash, end of year	**$ 630**	$ 165

The accompanying notes to financial statements are an integral part of these statements.

1996 ($165,000) is, as you would expect, the same as the amount of cash reported at the end of fiscal year 1995.

Now, we'll do something more difficult: consider how the AICPA's statement of cash flows relates to its statement of activities. But first, remember from the baseball card example that profits from a business are *not* the same thing as cash. For example, customers may owe the business cash for items they have purchased on credit. Even though the business can recognize revenue and earn profit on the sale to this customer, the cash has not yet come in. This will help you understand that increases in net assets for a not-for profit organization also are not the same thing as cash. For example, the AICPA might sell publications on credit or might buy some office supplies on credit--in either case, the effect on revenue and expenses would be different than the effect on the organization's cash.

While the AICPA's 1996 Statement of Activities shows a $1,911,000 increase in unrestricted net assets for the year (an *excess* of revenue over expenses), the Statement of Cash Flows reveals that there was only a $465,000 net increase in cash during the year. In Theme II we will return again to this difference between revenue and expenses and cash flows, which is one of the most difficult yet important concepts you need to master to understand accounting information.

Financial Statement Articulation

Now that you've had a chance to look at the set of basic financial statements, you've probably discovered several links between a typical income statement, statement of retained earnings, balance sheet and statement of cash flows. Figure I-3-14 (on the following page) illustrates how this set of financial statements interconnects or "**articulates**." No matter what the format of a particular set of financial statements, the set of statements will always contain important interconnections. The more you become aware of these relationships, the more you will begin to understand the meaning of financial accounting information.

The Importance of Footnotes

There's another aspect of financial statements that also affects your ability to understand financial accounting information. Throughout our discussion of financial statements, there have been regular references to information that is found in the footnotes to the statements. The footnotes are an *integral part* of the statements--the numbers you find in the body of the statements cannot be meaningfully interpreted without the additional information contained in the footnotes.

Reading the footnotes can be a daunting task. The prose can be dense; the notes can be voluminous. Annual reports for government entities, for example, often contain dozens of pages of footnotes. One annual report published in 1990 contained over 70 pages of notes! Yet, if you don't read the footnotes, you may miss important information. In fact, many financial writers, like Jane Bryant Quinn writing on *How*

Figure I-3-14
Building A Set of Financial Statements:
How Financial Statements "Articulate"

To Read An Annual Report, argue that the most important information may be "buried" in the footnotes:

> *So now [the company's] annual report is sitting in front of you ready to be cracked. How do you crack it?*
>
> *Where do we start? Not at the front. <u>At the back!</u> We don't want to be surprised at the end of <u>this</u> story....*
>
> *Stay in the back of the book and go to the <u>footnotes</u>. Yep! The whole profits story is sometimes in the footnotes.*

The complexity of footnotes is one reason why many individual investors choose to rely on investment advisors to help them make decisions. Financial analysts or other professional advisors devote a lot of effort to mining all the information in financial statements and other sources.

There are a few good reasons why footnotes are so hard to read. First, they often contain very complex information. There's no way, for instance, to explain a company's obligations under its complicated pension plan other than to write a complicated note. Second, footnotes often are worded formally or legalistically (and lawyers aren't known for their prose skills). For example, the footnote that describes the organization's potential liability arising from lawsuits is never going to say "We're being sued and we may lose a bundle." That kind of statement may be clearly written, but it could also damage the company's legal case. Consequently, while the footnote may imply that the company might lose a bundle, the wording will be much more technical and delicate.

Suppose you do decide to read the footnotes. What will you find? The first footnote typically describes the accounting policies used by the organization. There isn't always just one right way to account for a transaction; often there are several acceptable accounting methods that might yield different results.

For example, consider the intangible asset "goodwill" that we talked about earlier. For U.S. companies, purchased goodwill is initially recorded as an asset, but it doesn't remain an asset indefinitely. Instead, the cost is "**amortized**" (charged to an expense account) over a period of no greater than 40 years. Yet in some other countries goodwill can be left as an asset indefinitely. Thus, if a U.S. company and a non-U.S. company both have an equal amount of purchased goodwill, they may treat their goodwill very differently. If you read the footnotes, you will find out which accounting method each company is using. This knowledge will help you interpret the reported results. Moreover, even within a single country, there are often multiple acceptable accounting treatments for the same transaction. For example, U.S. companies may value their inventories using one of several different methods-- each of which may yield a different value for their inventory and cost of goods sold.

Other footnotes will contain supplemental information about items reported in the body of the financial statements. The notes will include information about things such as current and potential lawsuits against the company; major acquisitions the company made during the period; the company's pension plan and stock option plans; details about the company's long-term debt obligations; information about financial position and operating results for each major segment of the company, and so on.

GENERALLY ACCEPTED ACCOUNTING PRINCIPLES

> *Figures are not always facts.*
> *--Aesop, <u>The Widow and the Hen</u>*

On first glance, financial statements appear very exact. After all, they focus on numbers--and figures, as Justice Louis Brandeis once said, are "a language implying certitude." But, for the most part, the numbers in financial statements aren't really to-the-penny-exact values. The numbers that appear in the financial statements are the product of a long series of financial accounting judgments.

Financial statements are the end product of financial accounting. To get from the raw data about an entity's economic transactions and events to the financial statements, financial accountants need to make many decisions. How do financial accountants know what events and transactions to measure? how to value them? and when and how to include them in financial reports? Financial accountants are guided in these decisions by a set of professional standards referred to as "**generally accepted accounting principles**" or **GAAP**.

Generally accepted accounting principles provide both detailed rules and standards and general guidance for making judgments in situations where no specific rules or standards exist. GAAP isn't a cookbook; it doesn't include the recipe for handling every conceivable economic transaction or event. Inevitably, the financial accountant must rely on his or her professional judgment, as well as on expert knowledge of the detailed rules that do exist. In Module 6 of this theme, you can learn about how generally accepted accounting principles are established and how they can differ between nations. Here, we'll start to explain GAAP with a brief overview of the important assumptions, principles and constraints that underlie financial accounting.

Basic Assumptions of Financial Accounting

Four basic assumptions (which are summarized in Figure I-3-15 on the following page) underlie financial statements for business, government and nonprofit organizations: economic entity, monetary unit, going concern and periodicity.

<u>The Economic Entity Assumption</u>. The first assumption is that financial statements report on the organization, not its individual members or owners. The organization itself is the economic entity the statements describe.

Figure I-3-15
Four Basic Assumptions of Financial Accounting

ECONOMIC ENTITY

Financial statements report on the organization, not the individuals who own or operate it.

MONETARY UNIT

Financial statements use money as their basic unit of measure. Except under extreme conditions, instability of the unit is ignored.

GOING CONCERN

Unless otherwise stated, financial statements are based on the assumption that the organization will continue to operate into the future.

PERIODICITY

Even though the organization is dynamic, financial statements "stop the clock" and report financial position at a moment in time or financial activities for particular periods of time.

The Monetary Unit Assumption. Second, the statements use money as a unit of measure, which assumes the currency is stable enough to be a reliable measure. Thus, instability in the measurement unit is ignored, except under extreme conditions. An example of an extreme condition that cannot be ignored is the existence of hyperinflation.

Under conditions of high inflation, financial statements presented in monetary units tend to lose meaning because the value of the monetary unit itself is changing rapidly. Under these conditions, a different measurement unit must be used. For instance, to cope with hyperinflation in Brazil, Brazilian accountants use a system of measurement known as "price indexing." With this method, all accounting numbers are converted into a hypothetical stable unit--called a BTN (*bonos do tesouro nacional*) in Brazil's system. Then figures can be reported both in current dollars and in stable units.

The Going Concern Assumption. Third, financial statements assume (unless there is evidence to the contrary) that the organization will continue to operate into the future--that is, financial accounting assumes the entity is a "going concern." This assumption affects the numbers reported in the financial statements. For example, the organization's fixed assets can be reported at cost, not at the price they would bring if the organization were forced to liquidate (dismantle). Consider for example, the difference between cost and liquidation value for a large college. The college probably has a number of plant assets--like a baseball stadium and a practice track-- that are valuable to the school as a going concern, but would have little (or possibly no) liquidation value. Reporting these assets at cost rather than liquidation value implicitly assumes the college will continue operating long enough to make use of them.

The Periodicity Assumption. Fourth, even though an organization operates in a dynamic environment, financial reporting assumes that accountants can "stop the clock" and report on the organization at a particular moment in time, or for a particular period in time. When you try to divide an ongoing dynamic process into discrete time periods, you won't be able to get exact measures of everything--you'll have to make judgments and use estimates for many items.

Consider the example of accounting for the automobiles a company uses for delivery services. When a new auto is purchased, its cost is recorded as an asset because the auto will provide future benefits. As time passes and the auto's services are used up, the cost is allocated to expense in a process known as "**depreciation**." So, if a new $20,000 automobile is expected to have a useful life of 5 years and then be worth nothing, the accountant could allocate one-fifth ($4,000) of the auto's cost to depreciation expense each year for 5 years. At the end of the first year, the income statement would show a $4,000 depreciation expense and the balance sheet would value the auto at $16,000 after depreciation (the original $20,000 cost less the $4,000 allocated to expense already). This is reasonable, but not to the penny accurate.

Figure I-3-16

Four Important Principles of Financial Accounting

FULL DISCLOSURE

Accounting information that is important to users' decisions should be reported.

HISTORICAL COST

Many assets on the balance sheet are valued based on what was paid for them (cost), rather than what they are now worth (market value).

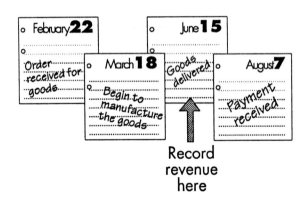

REVENUE RECOGNITION

Revenue should be recorded when it is earned ("realized").

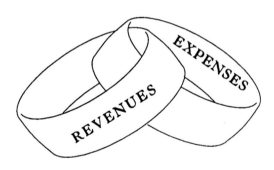

MATCHING

Expenses should be linked (reported in the same period) with the related revenues.

Other depreciation methods--like recognizing a greater amount of depreciation in the early years of auto use and smaller amounts in the later years--might be just as reasonable.

Broad Principles of Financial Accounting

Current U.S. GAAP includes 4 important principles (summarized in Figure I-3-16 on the previous page) that influence all financial statements: these principals concern full disclosure, historical cost, revenue recognition and matching.

Full Disclosure. First, the "disclosure principle" holds that when an entity prepares financial statements for external users, it should report all accounting information that would be important to users' decisions. The disclosure principle is responsible for some of the voluminous footnotes in annual reports. For example, would it make a difference to a reader to know that an organization is doing a lot of business with a supply company that is 50% owned by the CEO and his wife? Most accountants would answer "yes," indicating that this "related party" transaction should be disclosed in the footnotes. The footnote would report the amount of business done with the related party and indicate whether the terms of trade were any more or less favorable than "arms-length transactions" with unrelated suppliers.

Historical Cost. The "historical cost principle" holds that transactions should be recorded at cost and that assets should be reported at their historical cost in the absence of another "exchange" transaction (like a resale). Thus, if Colgate-Palmolive paid $1,250,000 for land that is now worth $3,000,000, the land will be reported on the balance sheet at historical cost, not current market value. This principle is one of the most controversial parts of contemporary U.S. GAAP. Proponents of historical cost praise its reliability; opponents question its relevance. While the principle still stands, there have been compromises. Many detailed standards (specific rules) require exceptions to this principle. For example, one current standard requires that a company's long-term investment portfolio of equity securities should be reported at the lower of cost or current market value. Thus, U.S. balance sheets today include a mixture of costs and market values. Some countries in the world are moving more towards "current value" accounting, while others remain essentially supportive of historical cost.

Revenue Recognition. The "revenue recognition principle" states that revenue should be recognized (reported in financial statements) when it is realized (earned), regardless of when the related cash flow occurs. Thus, if a company receives an order for its products on February 22, begins to manufacture the goods on March 18, delivers the goods (and a bill) to the customer on June 15, and receives payment from the customer on August 7, revenue will be recognized on June 15--when the earnings process has been completed, even though the cash has not yet been received. Conversely, if the customer paid for the goods in advance with the February 22 order, revenue still couldn't be recognized until June 15.

Matching. The "matching principle" is to expenses what the revenue recognition

Figure I-3-17
Four Constraints That Affect Financial Reports

FULL DISCLOSURE

Accounting information will be reported only if the benefits of reporting it exceed the costs of developing and disclosing it.

MATERIALITY

Only information that is potentially important ("material") to users' decisions need be reported. If an item is relatively unimportant ("immaterial"), it can be treated in a simplified manner and it need not be disclosed in financial reports.

CONSERVATISM

Financial reports strive to present realistic figures, but sometimes there is doubt about the appropriate treatment of an item. When in doubt, financial reports should be conservative, choosing the treatment that results in the least optimistic reported net income.

INDUSTRY PRACTICE

Generally accepted accounting practices for a specialized industry may be different than those used by most organizations. Financial reports will follow industry practices, where appropriate.

principle is to revenue. The matching principle holds that expenses should be linked ("matched") to the revenues they help produce. Thus, when the organization buys a $20,000 car that it will use to make deliveries for 5 years, the cost of the car is allocated to expense over the entire 5-year period, rather than being recorded as an expense on the day the car is bought. Taken together, the revenue recognition principle and the matching principle lead to "accrual basis accounting"--a financial accounting process that recognizes a difference between income flows and cash flows.

Constraints That Affect Financial Reports

Accountants, by and large, are practical people. Their practicality helps them deal with the inevitable complexities of the business world. Over time, generally accepted accounting principles have come to acknowledge 4 practical constraints (summarized in Figure I-3-17 on the previous page) that affect financial reports. These constraints involve: costs-versus-benefits, materiality, conservatism, and industry practice.

Cost-Benefit. First, financial accountants recognize a cost-benefit constraint. No matter how much a user might like to have a particular piece of accounting information, the information will be reported only if the benefits of reporting it exceed the costs of developing and disclosing it.

Materiality. Second, if an item is relatively insignificant ("immaterial"), it can be handled in a simplified manner and it need not be disclosed in financial reports. For example, suppose an organization buys a $10 trash can that is expected to be used for 5 years. To be strictly theoretically correct, the cost of the trash can could be allocated to expense at the rate of $2 per year for 5 years. But this allocation is unlikely to make a whit of difference to any financial statement user because the cost of the trash can is minuscule in relation to the cost of other assets purchased. So, because it is immaterial, the $10 cost of the trash can may be treated as an expense when purchased, ignoring its 5-year expected life. However, any material items must be treated in a theoretically correct manner and adequately disclosed.

Conservatism. Third, accountants follow the convention of "conservatism," which holds that "when in doubt, be less optimistic about net income, rather than more optimistic." Conservatism comes into play because of the need to use estimates and judgments in accounting and because there are often multiple acceptable ways to account for the same transaction. If there isn't a clear-cut reason to prefer one accounting choice over another, the rule of last resort is to be conservative and choose the method that will, if wrong, understate rather than overstate net income. Notice that conservatism doesn't mean the accountant will deliberately try to understate net income. Ideally, the accountant strives to report a net income figure that is neither understated nor overstated. Conservatism--also known as "prudence" in the U.K.-- should only come into play as a practical consideration when the choice between competing accounting treatments is otherwise a toss-up.

Industry Practice. Finally, accountants recognize that sometimes an accounting method may be widely accepted in a particular industry even if it would not be accepted generally. For example, industries that have a huge fixed asset base (like utilities or railroads) might use some depreciation methods that are unique to their industry. In the case where industry practices established over long periods of time conflict with general practice, financial reports may follow the industry practice, as long as the practice is disclosed.

These assumptions, principles and constraints underlie and support the more detailed rules (like the standards that delineate the appropriate methods to value investment portfolios or pension obligations, and so on) that make up the bulk of the body of professional standards in financial accounting.

TYPICAL CONTENTS OF AN ANNUAL REPORT

Your company had a very good year in 1982. Some of it was due to luck; some of it was due to good planning and management. We hope you enjoy the numbers and the pictures.
-- Jack Puelicher, letter to shareholders in
1982 annual report of Marshall & Ilsley

Financial statements are the primary reason annual reports are published, but they aren't the only thing in an annual report. This section describes some of the typical contents of an annual report.

Most annual reports for business enterprises begin with a letter to the shareholders from the CEO discussing the past year and prospects for the future. Annual reports of both business and non-business organizations may also include narrative and pictorial descriptions of the organization and its activities. Annual reports present an opportunity for management to communicate directly with far-flung shareholders or constituencies. Consequently, many organizations devote substantial effort to preparing their reports.

The section of the annual report that presents the financial statements may also contain several other forms of financial reporting, including

- an audit committee report,
- a management report,
- management's discussion and analysis,
- an auditor's report on the financial statements,
- an auditor's report on internal controls and/or compliance with laws and regulations, and
- supplementary financial information.

The Audit Committee Report, The Management Report, and MD&A

The *primary* responsibility for the financial statements (and for the internal control structure and financial accounting process which underlie them) belongs to the organization's management. If the organization has an **audit committee**--a sub-group of the board of directors that is concerned with audit issues, the audit committee oversees the financial reporting process on behalf of the board of directors. Both management and the audit committee may include a report in the financial statements that discuss their role in the reporting process.

The National Commission on Fraudulent Financial Reporting recommended that both a management report and an audit committee chairperson's letter should be included in annual reports of public companies. They suggested that the **management report** should:

♦ acknowledge management's responsibility for the financial statements and the system of internal control,

♦ give management's opinion as to the effectiveness of the organization's internal controls, and

♦ discuss other topics management views as important (such as the work of the organization's internal auditors or a change in independent public accountants during the year).

Generally, the **audit committee report** should describe:

♦ the composition of the audit committee;

♦ the audit committee's purpose, objectives and responsibilities; and

♦ the activities of the audit committee during the past year.

Many public companies now include one or both of these reports in their annual report.

Financial reports of U.S. public companies must also include a section known as **"Management's Discussion and Analysis"** (**MD&A**). The Securities and Exchange Commission has established that MD&A should discuss the organization's liquidity, capital resources and results of operations, as well as the future impact of known trends, demands, commitments, events or uncertainties that may affect operations. The MD&A contains *future-oriented* financial information that is not found in the financial statements themselves. For example, the MD&A may include information about upcoming union negotiations, environmental concerns, plans for major capital expenditures, and possible plant closings.

Auditor's Report on the Financial Statements

In August 1990, investors in Hedged-Securities Associates (HSA), a group of limited partnerships that managed the invested funds of 1,500 individual and institutional investors, were shocked to learn that all their money had been lost. The recent unaudited financial statements of the organization had shown a 10.5% gain for their investments through the first half of 1990, and earnings had averaged 23% for the past several years. The financial statements were not required to be audited because James Donahue, the investment manager who headed HSA, had set up the limited partnerships as a series of partnerships that were too small (less than 100 investors each) to be subject to federal securities regulation.

By the end of the 1990, there was growing evidence that HSA's reported earnings had been materially misstated for years. A flurry of lawsuits by investors claiming they had been bilked by the organization followed. In a December 31, 1990 story on the collapse of Hedged-Securities Associates, *Barron's* questioned how the investors had the faith to invest their money in the first place:

> *So bedazzled were they by Donahue's claimed performance record that they chose to violate the first and foremost commandment of investment professionals: Get an audited financial statement before handing over assets. Without one, they had only Donahue's word that he had achieved the remarkable gains for which he was becoming so renowned.*

Audits add credibility to financial statements. The audit report expresses the independent auditor's professional opinion regarding the fairness of presentation of the financial statements. In the United States, 5 types of audit opinions are possible:

- an unqualified opinion,
- an unqualified opinion with modified wording,
- a qualified opinion,
- an adverse opinion, and
- a disclaimer of opinion.

Unqualified Opinion. An **unqualified opinion** states, without any reservations, that the financial statements are fairly presented in accordance with generally accepted accounting principles. The unqualified opinion is sometimes called a **"clean"** opinion, but you should be careful not to misinterpret this term. A unqualified opinion does *not* mean that the organization is performing well; it only means that however the organization is performing, its performance and financial condition are fairly reflected in the financial statements. Thus, even if a company has had a very bad year, it will still receive a "clean" opinion as long as its financial statements follow GAAP and disclose all the necessary information about the past year.

In the United States, there is a standard format for an unqualified opinion that most CPAs follow. While some variations in format are possible, typically if an audit report has more than 3 paragraphs, it's a sign that it is something other than an unqualified opinion. However, since format variations are possible, you should be careful to do more than just count the paragraphs to determine what type of opinion is being given. In the standard format, there are 3 paragraphs:

- an **introductory paragraph** which states that the financial statements are the responsibility of management, that the statements have been audited, and that it is the auditor's responsibility to express an opinion on the statements:

- a **scope paragraph** which states that the audit was performed in accordance with generally accepted auditing standards, gives a brief description of the nature of the audit, and notes that the audit provides reasonable (but not absolute) assurance that the statements are free of material error; and

- an **opinion paragraph**, which, begins with the phrase "In our opinion..." and, for an unqualified opinion, states that the financial statements are "fairly presented in accordance with generally accepted accounting principles".

Unqualified Opinion With Modified Wording. An unqualified opinion with "modified wording" expresses the auditor's opinion that the financial statements are fairly presented overall, but calls the reader's attention to particular matters. Thus, the opinion format looks like an unqualified opinion with extra paragraphs. For example, suppose the organization has changed its method of accounting for a major asset account; the new method is acceptable according to GAAP, but the change means that this year's reported values are no longer comparable with prior reported values. The audit opinion will call the reader's attention to the change.

Qualified Opinion. What if everything is not fairly presented? If a *particular portion* of the financial statements violates GAAP, the auditor will render a **"qualified opinion"** stating that the financial statements are fairly presented according to generally accepted accounting principles,**"except for..."** the particular problem. For example, suppose a business organization publishes financial statements in the United States without separately disclosing information about its major segments. This violates a specific professional standard requiring segment disclosure; the auditor would issue a qualified opinion using the key words "except for." The qualified opinion describes the nature of the problem to the reader.

Adverse Opinion. Sometimes the effects of a violation of GAAP aren't limited to a particular portion of the financial statements. Instead, the violation is **pervasive**, affecting the financial statements overall. In this case, which is rare, the auditor would issue an **"adverse"** opinion, stating that the financial statements **"do not fairly present"** the results of operations and financial position (and cash flows, if appropriate) according to generally accepted accounting principles.

Disclaimer of Opinion. Audit opinions are based on evidence collected by the auditor. Sometimes, the auditor isn't able to find the evidence needed to form an opinion. In this case, the auditors who were associated with the financial statements will issue a **"disclaimer of opinion"**--a statement that they **"do not express an opinion"**--to make it clear that no audit conclusion has been reached.

Figure I-3-18
Types of Audit Opinions

Question: *"Are these financial statements fairly presented?"*
Answer:

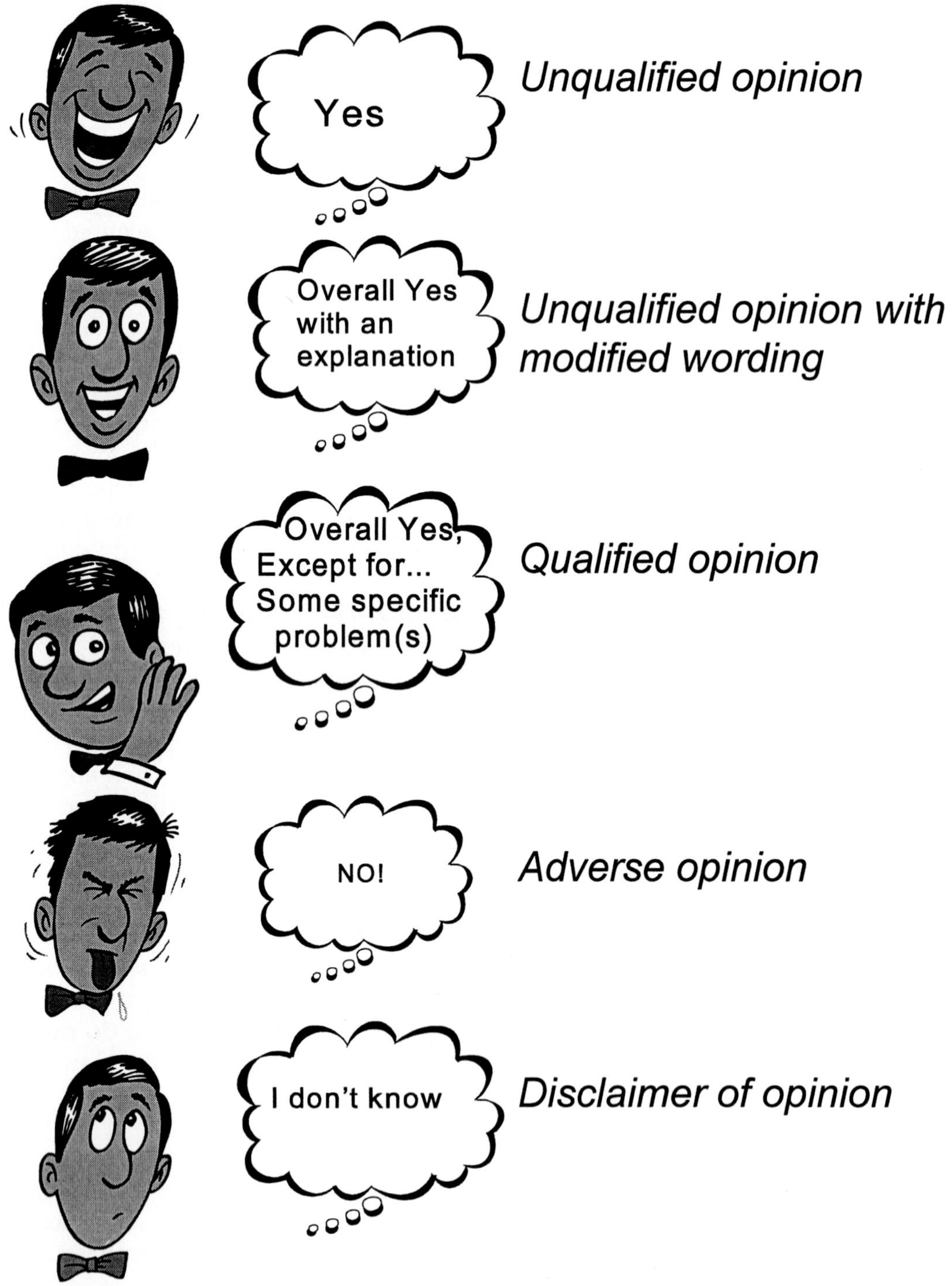

Yes — *Unqualified opinion*

Overall Yes with an explanation — *Unqualified opinion with modified wording*

Overall Yes, Except for... Some specific problem(s) — *Qualified opinion*

NO! — *Adverse opinion*

I don't know — *Disclaimer of opinion*

For example, in 1993 the Internal Revenue Service received a disclaimer of opinion. Ironically, the auditor concluded that the government agency which creates recordkeeping requirements for taxpayers, does not have a good recordkeeping system itself, although it is trying to develop one:

> *Its antiquated systems were not designed to provide the meaningful and reliable financial information needed to effectively manage and report on IRS's operations. Further IRS still does not have supporting information for certain financial statement amounts and has not been able to properly analyze and record certain types of transactions.*

Thus, each type of audit opinion sends a different message to the reader. The basic messages of the 5 types of audit opinions are summarized in Figure I-3-18 on the previous page.

Audit Reports Internationally. The International Auditing Guidelines issued by the International Federation of Accountants recommend the use of essentially the same type of audit reports world-wide as are now used in the United States. Most companies that deal in international capital markets follow these guidelines. There is one important variation in the wording of these reports. Some countries follow the U.S. **"fair presentation"** model ("the financial statements present fairly..."), whereas others follow the British **"true and fair view"** model ("the financial statements give a true and fair view...").

While there is much about the models that is similar, the "fair presentation" model places a greater emphasis on the needs of the investor, while the "true and fair view" model places more emphasis on protecting creditors and dividend-oriented investors. Thus, the recommended wording for an unqualified opinion internationally would be:

> *In our opinion, the financial statements give a true and fair view of (or "present fairly") the financial position of (entity's name) at (date) and the results of its operations for the year then ended in accordance with (the relevant national standards or international accounting standards)...*

Additionally, some international audit reports will also contain an opinion about the entity's compliance with relevant statutes or laws.

While audit reports for companies that deal in international capital markets are substantially similar, there is considerably more variation in audit reports issued exclusively for use within a single country. Some countries, for example, require only a simple audit report about compliance with legal requirements. If the wording of an audit report departs significantly from that recommended by the International Auditing Guidelines, the reader needs to be aware that the objectives of the audit may also be different. Interpreting such reports requires a familiarity with the particular nation's accounting and auditing standards.

Other Kinds of Audit Reports

When public money is at stake, public officials are held accountable not only for what they do with the money, but also for establishing and maintaining a control structure that is adequate to safeguard assets and ensure compliance with appropriate laws and regulations. Consequently, the financial reports of U.S. government entities must include an auditor's report on the entity's internal accounting controls and the entity's compliance with laws and regulations. The **report on internal controls** discloses any material internal control weaknesses observed by the auditor or notes that no material weaknesses were observed. Similarly, the **report on compliance with laws and regulations** either will state that no compliance violations were observed or will disclose observed violations.

Obviously, managements of business and nonprofit organizations are also accountable for establishing and maintaining an adequate control structure and complying with applicable laws and regulations. However, audit reports on controls or compliance are not required for non-government entities under current U.S. standards, although there has been some discussion of doing so in the future.

Supplemental Financial Information

Finally, the annual report of an organization may contain **supplemental financial information** (information outside of the basic financial statements) of interest to users. For example, the AICPA includes balance sheets for several related organizations, such as the AICPA Benevolent Fund, Inc., a charity that raises money to provide financial assistance to needy members of the AICPA and their families. The number and type of additional statements depends on the nature of the organization and the needs of the annual report readers. Such supplemental information may be either audited or unaudited. If the information is audited, the audit report will explicitly state that the opinion applies to these statements.

What's In The Typical Annual Report?: A Recap

Now that you know what you might find in a typical annual report--a set of basic financial statements, a letter from the CEO, narrative and pictorial descriptions of the organization and its activities, a management report, an audit committee report, management's discussion and analysis, an auditor's report on the financial statements, an audit report on internal controls and/or compliance, and supplemental financial information--it's easy to see why annual reports may be as popular as the latest best-selling novel, but aren't as easy to read or understand. You've now taken the first steps to increase your understanding of the reports which result from the work of financial accountants and the related reports of independent auditors. The next part of this module will tell you more about the basic concepts of auditing--including financial, operational and compliance audits.

MODULE 3: OWNERS AND CREDITORS AS USERS OF ACCOUNTING INFORMATION

PART C: BASIC CONCEPTS OF AUDITING

Who hath believed our report?
-- The Bible, Isaiah 53:1

Auditing, like record-keeping, has roots that are very old. The term "audit" comes to us from the Latin word "audire," meaning "to hear." For centuries, auditors were literally "hearers": people who heard oral reports about how other people managed the economic resources in their care.

In medieval times, for example, England's Chancellor of the Exchequer held oral audits twice a year to hear reports about the accounts of estates, manors and the royal family. The chancellor got his title because he met with the auditees (the people being audited) at a table covered by a checkered cloth. The purpose of these audits was to provide assurance to the king that the financial resources of the kingdom were being well cared for. The chancellor bore witness to the king about the financial state of the kingdom. Then, as now, auditors **attested** (bore witness) to the material they audited.

While auditing has a long history, the auditing profession as we know it today is largely a development of the 19th and 20th centuries. The development of modern auditing began in Great Britain during the Industrial Revolution. As the demand for long-term debt capital grew, bankers and other lenders looked for assurance that loan applicants were reliably reporting their financial position. As the demand for equity capital led to increasing separation of ownership and management, absentee (outside or non-management) owners wanted assurance that the managers' financial reports were reliable. As businesses became more complex, management needed assurances that their policies and procedures were being implemented as intended; they also needed an assessment of the efficiency and effectiveness of their organization's operations. As economies became more complex, government regulations also grew in complexity. Regulators needed assurance that laws (like tax laws) and regulations were being observed. The auditing profession grew to meet these needs.

Even today, the auditing profession is still developing in response to social needs for attest services. For example, during the 1980s, auditors began to be called on to attest to the accuracy of computer software--an application of the attest function that wasn't even dreamed of at the start of the century.

Audits are independent (objective) examinations of evidence to determine if the audited material conforms to a set of predetermined criteria or standards. All types of organizations--businesses, not-for-profit organizations, and government entities--make use of audits. Yet few people outside of the auditing profession have a clear understanding of who auditors are or what they do. What types of audits are conducted in modern organizations? What are the characteristics of a good auditor? How is an audit conducted? Who audits the auditor? These questions are explored in this part of Module 3.

WHAT TYPES OF AUDITS ARE CONDUCTED IN MODERN ORGANIZATIONS?

And how his audit stands who knows save heaven?
-- William Shakespeare, Hamlet, Act III

Several basic types of audits are commonly conducted in modern organizations: financial audits, operational audits and compliance audits. Audits are performed because they have value to the users of audit reports. Current and potential owners and creditors are the primary user groups for financial audit reports. Management is the primary user of operational audit reports and regulators are the primary user group for compliance audit reports. For the next few minutes, place yourself in the roles of these user groups. Imagine why you might want an audit and consider the common characteristics of the different types of audits.

Financial Audits

Suppose you are an absentee (outside) owner of stock in a corporation. The company's managers are your agents, legally entrusted with running the corporation on your behalf. Yet, as an owner, you know that the managers are human and must also act in their own self-interest, which may not always be congruent with your interests. Naturally, you and the other outside owners will want to monitor the performance of your agents. So, you will want to receive regular reports about how the company is doing--that is, you will want periodic financial reports. But since management bears the responsibility of keeping accounting records and preparing the financial reports, how do you know if the financial reports are credible?

Many years ago, when ownership and management were first separated, stockholders solved this problem by sending a committee of shareholders to examine the accounting records and verify them. In modern times, this function-- known as financial auditing--is fulfilled by professionals, independent auditors who examine the financial statements and supporting evidence and report back to the stockholders (and other external users--like creditors) whether the statements are fairly presented. The end result of a financial audit is an opinion on the fairness of presentation of the financial statements.

Financial audits play an important part in capital markets. Without audits, potential investors and lenders would be less willing to buy stock or lend funds. In addition, financial audits play an important role in public policy decisions. Audits of government and nonprofit entities that receive public funding provide valuable input to decision makers who must determine how to allocate public funds and monitor the performance of funded entities.

THE WIZARD OF ID   by Brant parker and Johnny hart

By permission of Johnny Hart and Creators Syndicate, Inc.

Operational Audits

Next, suppose you are a member of the top management team of an organization. To help ensure that the organization attains its goals and objectives, you have established a number of policies and procedures for organization members to follow. Yet, as a manager, you know that setting standards does not guarantee that the standards will be followed or that they will work as intended.

How do you know whether the policies and procedures are being carried out? are working as planned? One solution is to send an objective observer to see whether the system is working effectively and efficiently and have the observer report back to you. This is the function of operational auditing. The end result of an operational audit is a report on specific strengths and/or weaknesses of the system, including recommendations for improving operations.

Many operational audit reports are restricted to internal users, primarily management users. However, some types of operational audit reports are more widely disseminated. For example, the General Accounting Office (GAO) publishes its reports of operational audits of government agencies and makes them available free of charge to any interested parties via mail or the Internet.

Compliance Audits

Finally, suppose you are a regulator, responsible for determining whether a particular set of laws or administrative regulations has been complied with. For example, the Federal Communications Commission (FCC) is responsible for enforcing political advertising rules. The rules, designed to help keep elections fair, include a requirement that radio and television stations sell political air time at their lowest advertising rates. In addition, the stations must offer equal opportunity to all political candidates. If one candidate runs an ad, opposing candidates must be able to purchase equivalent air time (i.e., the same amount of time at the same time of day). Also, stations must keep records of their political programming.

How does the FCC know radio and television stations are following federal regulations concerning political advertising? A compliance audit--an audit designed to determine whether a particular set of laws or regulations has been complied with--can provide the FCC with the information it needs. The end product of the compliance audit will be a report concerning the entity's conformance with the laws and regulations. For example, during one election year, the FCC sent auditors to 30 radio and TV stations to audit their compliance with the political advertising rules. The FCC chose to examine 2 TV stations and 4 radio stations each in Cincinnati, Dallas-Fort Worth, Philadelphia, Portland and San Francisco. The cities were chosen to get broad coverage of the nation. The auditors checked the stations' files to determine whether political ads were sold at the lowest available advertising rates and whether all candidates were offered equal opportunity for air time.

Compliance audits are often performed by government agencies. One of the most frequently performed--though not the most popular--compliance audit is the Internal Revenue Service's (IRS) taxpayer compliance audit. The IRS audits taxpayers' returns to determine if the appropriate tax laws and regulations have been followed. Similar compliance audits are performed by taxing authorities throughout the world.

"You're going to meet an intelligent, inquisitive, beautiful girl....she's an auditor for the IRS."

Source: From The Wall Street Journal. Permission, Cartoon Features Syndicate.

Compliance audits may also be performed by public accountants or internal auditors. For example a CPA may be asked to prepare a report for a lender attesting to a borrower's compliance with the restrictive covenants in their loan agreement. Or an internal auditor may be asked to evaluate a company's compliance with fair hiring practices the company has agreed to maintain in conjunction with a government contract.

Characteristics of Audits

All 3 types of audits--financial audits, operational audits, and compliance audits--share certain characteristics:

- ♦ performance by an objective party,

- ♦ examination of evidence, and

- ♦ judgment against predetermined criteria or standards.

First, audits are performed by an objective party. The auditor may be an **external auditor** who works for a public accounting firm and observes professional standards and legal regulations concerning independence from clients. Or, the auditor may be an **internal auditor** who works for one company but is organizationally protected from conflicts of interest with the auditees. Or, the auditor may be a **government or statutory auditor** employed by a government body and authorized to perform financial, operational or compliance audits.

Second, audits involve the examination of evidence--such as looking for support for the figures and disclosures in the financial statements, or looking for evidence that an organization's policies and procedures were followed, or looking for evidence of compliance with laws and regulations. The audit opinion is an expert judgment based on an objective evaluation of evidence.

Third, in each type of audit the auditor has something to judge the audited material against--that is, there are some sort of "rules of the game" the auditor uses to assess the auditee. For a financial audit, the rules of the game are generally accepted accounting principles. For an operational audit, the rules of the game are the company's own preestablished policies, procedures and performance standards. Operational auditors may also make use of other criteria--such as time and motion studies conducted by engineers to establish efficient production rates or industry-wide performance statistics that establish benchmarks for profitability--to evaluate efficiency and effectiveness. For a compliance audit, the rules of the game are the particular laws or regulations.

Since the 3 types of audits share some common characteristics, it's possible to design audit examinations that contain elements of more than one type of auditing. For example, with a few exceptions, state and local governments and nonprofit organizations (like educational institutions) that receive funding from the U.S. Federal Government are required to have periodic audits. These audits combine elements of financial, compliance, and operational auditing.

The requirements for these audits are formalized in 2 circulars published by the Office of Management and Budget, Circular A-128 for state and local government audits and Circular A-133 for nonprofit organizations. As often happens with government regulations, the audits are commonly named by their circular number. The A-128 and A-133 audits must answer 3 questions:

♦ Are the financial statements presented fairly?

♦ Does the entity's control structure provide reasonable assurance that federally funded programs are being managed in compliance with applicable laws and regulations?

♦ Has the entity complied with all applicable federal laws and regulations that directly and materially affect its financial statements and major programs?

The first question is a financial audit question. The second and third questions are compliance audit questions. The second question also has an element of operational auditing as the audit report will discuss observed weaknesses in the internal control structure. Thus, the audit examination contains elements of all 3 types of auditing.

Other Attest Services

In addition to the 3 common types of audits, auditors may be asked to attest to a wide variety of matters such as the adequacy of an organization's control structure, the accuracy of computer software, the presentation of investment performance statistics, and the preparation of financial forecasts or projections. Auditors may express an opinion on all these matters (and many more). These opinions provide assurance to users.

Some applications of the attest function are quite creative. For example, publishers know that new textbooks sometimes face a difficult sales hurdle. Teachers who were "burned" in the past by adopting a new book or piece of classroom software that turned out to be riddled with errors tend to take a "wait and see" attitude towards new texts or software supplements. This creates difficulties for publishers trying to sell the first editions of texts. Several years ago, a publisher hoping to leap this sales hurdle decided to hire a large CPA firm to examine the accuracy of the technical accounting information in a new accounting textbook and to verify the mechanical accuracy of the computations in the solutions manual for the text's assignments. The auditor's opinion that the book and solutions manual were "mathematically accurate and technically correct" was distributed to teachers who were reviewing the new textbook for possible adoption.

Another creative application of the attest function may be found in the gaming industry. Casinos compete aggressively to attract customers. One ingredient of the competition is convincing potential customers that your casino's games offer a good chance to win money. A CPA firm in Las Vegas has been hired to attest to the payout ratio of a casino's slot machines (the percentage of cash put into the machines that is paid out in winnings). The auditor verifies the advertised payout ratios for the casino, adding credibility to the advertising.

However, there are some natural limits to the attest function. For example, auditors cannot attest to something where there are no *preestablished criteria* to judge the material against. Suppose a group of potential creditors or investors wanted to hire an auditor to attest that an organization did not have an "unreasonably small" amount of capital. The auditor could not accept this engagement as there are no criteria against which to judge whether the capital is "unreasonably small." Similarly, an auditor can't attest to an organization's future ability to pay off long-term debts when they mature as it is not possible to determine this ability in advance.

WHAT ARE THE CHARACTERISTICS OF A GOOD AUDITOR?

In times like the present, one who desires to be impartially just in the expression of his views moves as among swordpoints on every side.
-- Herman Melville, Battlepieces and Aspects of the War, 1866

To be an auditor is to be an expert judge: to judge the fairness of presentation of financial statements; to judge the efficiency and effectiveness of operations; or to judge compliance with laws and regulations. The role of an expert judge is not easy. As Socrates noted, "Four things belong to a judge: to hear courteously, to answer wisely, to consider soberly, and to decide impartially." Socrates' 4 things that belong to judges are reflected in the characteristics modern auditors need to possess: people skills, competence, due professional care and independence.

"To Hear Courteously": People Skills

To "hear courteously" auditors must have good "people skills." Auditors obtain evidence from people as well as from inanimate records. Thus auditors need good communications skills and interpersonal skills. The Institute of Internal Auditors' *Standards for the Professional Practice of Internal Auditing* provide a clear statement about the importance of people skills in internal auditing:

> ***Human Relations and Communications:***
>
> *Internal auditors should be skilled in dealing with people and in communicating effectively.*
>
> *Internal auditors should understand human relations and maintain*

satisfactory relationships with auditees.

Internal auditors should be skilled in oral and written communications so that they can clearly and effectively convey such matters as audit objectives, evaluations, conclusions, and recommendations.

These standards are also good descriptions of the people skills needed to perform financial and compliance audits.

Auditors need to know how to ask questions--the right question to the right person at the right time. For example, suppose an auditor is trying to determine whether there are any possible claims against a company that may result in lawsuits. If so, the auditor will want to evaluate whether the matter should be disclosed in the company's financial report. The auditor needs to know who to ask about the possible claims: the President? the in-house counsel? the outside attorney? The auditor also needs to know how to phrase the question to get the appropriate information. Questions that are too broad or too narrow may not evoke the information the auditor needs. Questions must also be phrased in the appropriate language. A question to an attorney about possible lawsuits must use the appropriate legal terms.

Auditors also need to know how to listen. Even today, auditors must be good "hearers" as much evidence begins with hearing something from an organization member or an external party. For example, suppose an auditor is examining the controls over inventory for a hotel's restaurant and bar. Typically, the inventory will include a large amount of liquor. While visiting the hotel to observe the restaurant and bar procedures, the auditor talks to the restaurant's waiters and waitresses. Several of them complain that their tips have been poor lately because their customers are upset that the bar is out of the expensive liquors listed on the menu. If the auditor is a good listener, these complaints will raise questions in his or her mind and prompt a check of the bar's actual inventory against the amounts recorded on the company's books to determine if any liquor is missing, perhaps due to theft. The auditor can also compare inventory levels to sales and purchasing patterns to determine if there are inefficiencies in the hotel's purchasing procedures. Listening to the waiters and waitresses grouse about their low tips can "tip" the auditor to a potential problem.

Auditors also need to know how to communicate the results of their audits. For example, how should an auditor describe a weakness in an internal control system? The auditor must be direct, yet not derogatory or accusatory. The seriousness of the weakness should be made clear, perhaps with an example of the potential harmful effects of the weakness. Moreover, it is usually not sufficient to merely point out the weakness--a remedy should be proposed as well. If the auditor wants to motivate the organization to correct the weakness, the proposed remedy must be worded to make action seem feasible and worth undertaking. The auditor might provide an estimate of the potential dollar savings or labor hour savings or other benefits of the remedy to help motivate the organization to take action.

"To Answer Wisely": Competence

To "answer wisely" auditors must be competent to perform their professional tasks. To be competent, auditors must master the technical body of knowledge of accounting and auditing. In addition, they must understand the nature of the auditee's organization and operations.

As the International Federation of Accountants noted in *International Auditing Standard #3: Basic Principles Governing an Audit*, competence is developed through a combination of education and experience:

> *The auditor requires specialized skills and competence which are acquired through a combination of general education, technical knowledge obtained through study and formal courses concluded by a qualifying examination, and practical experience under proper supervision. In addition the auditor requires a continuing awareness of developments including relevant international and national pronouncements on accounting and auditing matters, and relevant regulations and statutory requirements.*

Education and experience requirements for CPAs licensed to practice in the United States are established by the state boards of public accountancy. Additionally, professional associations may establish education and experience requirements (and qualifying examination requirements) for other certifications. For example, the Institute of Internal Auditors (IIA) establishes education and experience requirements for auditors who wish to become certified internal auditors (CIAs) and the Information Systems Audit and Control Association (ISACA) establishes education and experience requirements for auditors who have the expertise to audit technically complex computerized systems and wish to become certified information systems auditors (CISAs).

The education and experience requirements for CPAs vary from state to state. For example, some states require a bachelor's degree as the minimum education while most require 150 hours of education. Experience requirements also vary widely. Some states have no formal experience requirement to be licensed, while others require several years of experience. However, all the states use the uniform national CPA exam as the qualifying examination for licensing.

Education and experience requirements also vary throughout the world. In Germany, for example, a Master's degree is the minimum education needed for licensing as a "WP" (the abbreviation for licensed auditors or Wirtschaftsprüfer). The United Kingdom has less stringent educational requirements for Chartered Accountants, but requires a good deal of experience before licensing.

Whatever the mix of education and experience required by law, practicing auditors appreciate the need for both. Education provides the technical foundation needed to be a good auditor: a basic understanding of the business, accounting and auditing concepts that are the daily lifeblood of an audit. But experience--gained by working under the supervision of seasoned auditors--is also necessary to deepen understanding of the concepts learned from books and to master the application of those concepts in a dynamic environment. Remember, for example, the difference between what you thought you knew about driving from reading books, listening to lectures and watching movies in driver education classes and the feeling you had when you first sat behind the wheel of a car to drive down a highway.

When William Hall retired from Arthur Andersen & Co. he wrote a book of essays describing *Accounting and Auditing: Thoughts on Forty Years in Practice and Education.* In one of those essays, he talks about his views on the value of experience in developing an auditor's understanding of the concept of materiality:

> *To know how flexible he should be in dealing with differences, the auditor must develop a sound, workable sense of materiality. I would define materiality as an understanding of what is important....An auditor's sense of materiality lies at the heart of his professional judgment. An appreciation of the concept may be innate (we know that it never develops adequately in some people), but experience nurtures, refines and sharpens it. To get a good handle on materiality, one needs broad, diverse business knowledge, an understanding of what is important to management, investors and other users of financial statements. This is, perhaps, the area in which one should not expect too much of new auditing recruits. "Book learning" can only go so far.*

"Good grief! You're both alarmingly young for auditors. I trust you're acquainted with generally accepted accounting principles."

"To Consider Soberly": Due Professional Care

To "consider soberly" auditors must always conduct their audits with "**due professional care.**" Due care is an abstract concept. It does not require the auditor to be perfect, but does hold the auditor to the quality standard of at least the "average" for the profession.

The concept of due professional care comes from the legal concept of a "prudent" or "reasonable" man who acts with average knowledge and average judgment. In any given situation, an auditor should do what other prudent or reasonable auditors would do in the same situation. Due professional care is the level of care a prudent auditor would use in planning and conducting an audit-- that is, it is the standard of care that is maintained by the profession as a whole.

Reprinted with permission of Stan Lee.

Due professional care can't be completely explained because the degree of care required depends on the situation. For example, due care would require more caution and more audit work in cases where fraud is suspected than in cases where there is no reason to suspect fraud. However, due professional care is generally understood to include at least 2 things:

◆ conforming with appropriate auditing standards and guidelines, and

◆ maintaining an attitude of professional skepticism

Conformance With Standards and Guidelines. Due professional care requires compliance with published auditing standards and guidelines. So, for example, a financial audit in the United States would be expected to conform to **generally accepted auditing standards** as published by the Auditing Standards Board and its predecessor bodies. Figure I-3-19 (on the next page) presents the 10 generally accepted auditing standards. In addition to these 10 standards, there are a series of supporting statements that provide additional guidance to auditors. Similar sets of standards and guidelines, established either by law or by private sector bodies, exist in many other countries as well, although the degree of guidance and the details of the guidance vary between countries.

Figure I-3-19
U.S. Generally Accepted Auditing Standards

General Standards

1. The examination is to be performed by a person or persons having adequate technical training and proficiency as an auditor.

2. In all matters relating to the assignment, an independence in mental attitude is to be maintained by the auditor or auditors.

3. Due professional care is to be exercised in the performance of the examination and the preparation of the report.

Standards of Field Work

1. The work is to be adequately planned and assistants, if any, are to be properly supervised.

2. There is to be a proper study and evaluation of the existing internal control as a basis for reliance thereon and for the determination of the resultant extent of the tests to which auditing procedures are to be restricted.

3. Sufficient competent evidential matter is to be obtained through inspection, observation, inquiries, and confirmations to afford a reasonable basis for an opinion regarding the financial statements under examination.

Standards of Reporting

1. The report shall state whether the financial statements are presented in accordance with generally accepted accounting principles.

2. The report shall identify those circumstances in which such principles have not been consistently observed in the current period in relation to the preceding period.

3. Informative disclosures in the financial statements are to be regarded as reasonably adequate unless otherwise stated in the report.

4. The report shall either contain an expression of opinion regarding the financial statements, taken as a whole, or an assertion to the effect that an opinion cannot be expressed. When an overall opinion cannot be expressed, the reasons therefor should be stated. In all cases where an auditor's name is associated with financial statements, the report should contain a clear-cut indication of the character of the auditor's examination, if any, and the degree of responsibility he is taking.

Source: Statements on Auditing Standards, AU 150.02

An audit of a U.S. government entity would be expected to conform to guidance in **"the yellow book,"** the government publication which contains the *Government Auditing Standards: Standards for Audit of Governmental Organizations, Programs, Activities, and Functions.* The performance of other attest services (like attesting to the technical accuracy of a textbook and solutions manual) would be expected to conform to the attestation standards issued by the Auditing Standards Board and the AICPA's Accounting and Review Services Committee.

These guidelines provide standards for the planning and performance of an audit and the reporting of audit findings. For example, all the aforementioned standards specify that less experienced auditors should be adequately supervised.

Professional Skepticism. Due professional care also includes maintaining an attitude of **"professional skepticism"**--a rather tricky balance between not being overly suspicious on the one hand, and not being overly accepting (or gullible) on the other hand. Retired Arthur Andersen & Co. partner William Hall described his view of professional skepticism as follows:

> *An auditor, it has been said, should be skeptical but not suspicious--a fine balance some persons never achieve. If the auditor is too trusting, he will never pursue the warning signals when something seems awry. He will be prone to accept easy answers to hard questions. On the other hand, most managements are honest and prepare reliable financial statements. An auditor who approaches his work with suspicion verging on paranoia, eyeing each transaction as a likely fraud, would never finish his task. He would never see the forest for the trees and would probably antagonize those whose cooperation he most needs.*

> *Alertness and a lively inquisitiveness, I believe, are the answers....[The auditor] must have a natural curiosity about business transactions that leads him to question the whys and wherefores, but without wasting time on inconsequentials--in other words, a sense of balance.*

"To Decide Impartially": Independence

To "decide impartially" auditors must be independent in making their judgments. They must examine the evidence and judge the auditee objectively. **Independence**, often defined as an auditor's ability to act with objectivity and integrity, is the cornerstone of auditing.

Independence is first and foremost a state of mind. Auditors must be **independent in fact**, sure--deep in their hearts and souls--that the judgments they make on audits are impartial. Additionally, because independence is so important, the auditor must be **"independent in appearance."** This means the auditor must be free of any apparent conflict of interest. *International Auditing Standard #3* expresses the general requirements of independence:

> *The auditor should be straightforward, honest and sincere in his*

approach to his professional work. He must be fair and must not allow prejudice or bias to override his objectivity. He should maintain an impartial attitude and both be and appear to be free of any interest which might be regarded, whatever its actual effect, as being incompatible with integrity and objectivity.

<u>International Differences in Independence Rules</u>. Each country also has specific rules and guidelines to prohibit financial auditors from engaging in activities that could impair independence in appearance or in fact. Since different cultures have different views of what constitutes a conflict of interest for auditors, these rules and guidelines vary considerably from country to country. In the U.S., for example, auditors are prohibited from owning any direct interest (or any material indirect interest, such as having a close relative who owns a large block of stock) in a company they audit because stock ownership is viewed as creating a conflict of interest. However, in some countries it is considered acceptable for an auditor to own stock in a client company or to sit on the company's board.

On the other hand, in the U.S., auditors are paid by the companies they audit, whereas in Greece auditors are paid by the state as direct payment by the company is considered a conflict of interest. In France, auditors cannot perform any non-audit services for audit clients, because the additional work is believed to create too close a relationship between client and auditor. But in the United States, although there are some limits, there are still many non-audit services in the tax and management advisory areas that may be performed for attest clients.

Deciding what is and what is not a threat to independence is not a simple task. Because independence is crucial to auditors' reputations, issues about the appropriate ways to preserve independence are often the topic of heated debate. For example, the provision of non-audit services to attest clients has been debated in the United States for decades. This debate over the appropriate "scope of services" that a CPA firm can offer its audit clients has strong voices on both sides. Some argue that current U.S. rules concerning non-audit services are too liberal and threaten independence. These people are concerned that when the audit side of a CPA firm audits a client, they may sometimes examine evidence or evaluate work done by the consulting side of their own firm. Critics question whether auditors can be as zealous as they should be in these circumstances.

Yet, on the other hand, numerous attempts to investigate the impact of non-audit services on audit independence have found little evidence--some say no evidence--of real problems. And proponents of the current U.S. system argue that prohibiting auditors from rendering advisory services to attest clients would be harmful to clients who benefit from the expert advice. Moreover, some argue the financial security provided by fees from non-audit services helps give CPA firms the backbone they need to make the technical and ethical "hard calls" on their audits, even when they know their stands might result in the loss of a client.

The financial press regularly reports news about an auditor refusing to accept a client's desired treatment of a material item on the financial statements. For example, in 1994, the financial press reported stories about a dispute between IDB Communications Group, a telecommunications firm, and its auditors. IDB wanted to record revenue related to the sale of satellite transponder capacity; the auditors argued it was too soon to tell if revenues would be earned. Eventually, the auditors resigned. The fact that auditors regularly take such stands against client positions is positive evidence of their independence.

Independence for Operational Audits and Compliance Audits. While the rules and guidelines discussed above apply specifically to financial auditors, independence is also an important characteristic of operational auditors and compliance auditors. The Institute of Internal Auditors' guidelines for maintaining independence are discussed in Module 2 Part C of this theme. Compliance auditors also must be free in both fact and appearance from any conflicts of interest that could impair their objectivity. For example, it would not be appropriate for an IRS auditor to examine the tax return of a relative. Even if the auditor were able to maintain an independent mental attitude, the family relationship would create a problem with the appearance of conflict of interest.

HOW IS AN AUDIT CONDUCTED?

Take nothing on its looks; take everything on evidence. There's no better rule.
-- *Charles Dickens, Great Expectations*

The specific procedures the auditor performs may vary greatly from audit to audit, depending on the type of audit, the type of auditee, and the particular situation. However, all audits share an underlying common approach. Auditing--whether it be financial auditing, operational auditing, or compliance auditing--is a judgment process that consists of 5 general steps:

- ◆ gain an understanding of the client and audit situation,
- ◆ assess risk and materiality,
- ◆ plan the nature, extent and timing of tests,
- ◆ gather evidence, and
- ◆ interpret the evidence, reach a conclusion and prepare a report.

Gain an Understanding of the Client and Audit Situation

You can't audit in a vacuum. In order to conduct a proper examination, the auditor must have a good foundation of knowledge about the auditee and must understand the industry in which the auditee operates. For example, suppose a financial auditor has 2 clients. One is a savings and loan (S&L) association, the other is a hardware store. The 2 industries are very different and the auditor must understand these differences in order to perform a competent audit. The auditor needs to know how each industry operates in order to know what types of assets and liabilities to expect, what level of profitability is typical, and so on. The auditor also needs to understand any industry-specific laws or accounting principles that could affect the evaluation of the fairness of presentation of financial statements. The S&L client is subject to many industry-specific accounting rules and to many more legal requirements than the hardware store.

Moreover, the auditor must gain an understanding of each individual auditee's situation. Suppose that the auditor in our example gets a third client: another savings and loan association. An audit isn't a "one size fits all" suit. Even 2 clients in the same industry may need very different specific audit procedures. For example, suppose the first S&L client has strong management and a strong customer base and makes only relatively low risk loans, but the second S&L has weaker management and a weaker customer base and makes relatively high risk loans. The auditor needs to understand each client's situation in order to conduct the appropriate audit.

Similarly, the operational auditor must understand the auditee and the audit situation. An operational auditor for a chain of department stores would want to know if the store being audited is newly opened or long-established, whether it is located in a relatively wealthy community or a relatively low-income community, whether the store has many local competitors or few local competitors, and so on.

Of course, the compliance auditor must also understand the auditee and the audit situation. For example, think about the FCC auditor who is examining radio and television stations' compliance with political advertising rules during an election year. The auditor would want to know something about the nature of the elections in the area. How many candidates were running for office? Were any of the candidates unopposed? Were any of the races hotly contested? Were any of the candidates particularly well financed or grossly under-financed?

Auditors bring a lot of general business knowledge with them to each audit. In addition, they develop some industry-specific knowledge and much client-specific knowledge. They gain this understanding in many ways, including reading stories about the client or the industry in the financial press, reading industry publications or taking formal courses about an industry, talking to auditors who have worked on the client previously, reading the "workpapers" that document prior audits, talking to people at the client, and touring the client's operations.

Auditors keep a set of working papers that document all the steps in their audit. Important information about the industry and the client will be entered into the "workpapers" to form a record that helps explain the decisions the auditor makes. The workpapers, which may be printed or electronic, also become a source of information for later audits. New members of audit teams often learn a lot about their clients from reviewing the prior year's workpapers.

Assess Risk and Materiality

Unless the auditee is very small or the audit situation is very specific, it isn't generally feasible for auditors to verify every transaction of the auditee. Imagine, for example, how long it would take to examine all the financial transactions at General Motors, or to test every control procedure at Toyota Motor Company, or to look at every canceled check of every taxpayer the IRS audits. Audits are typically performed on a sample basis because 100% verifications would take too long and cost too much to be worthwhile. An audit report loses value if it isn't timely and it shouldn't be so expensive that its cost exceeds its benefit.

So, given that the auditor can't look at everything, how does the auditor decide where to concentrate his or her efforts? Auditors will focus their efforts on the areas of greatest risk (because that's where problems are most likely to be found) and the areas of greatest importance (areas likely to be material to report users). Consequently, auditors devote a lot of thought and effort to assessing materiality and risk. The workpapers for an audit document the major risks the auditor identified and the auditor's judgments about materiality.

Copyright Neatly Chiseled Features

"ON THE PLUS SIDE WE'VE VIRTUALLY ELIMINATED OUR AUDIT RISK"

As an example, think about a financial auditor testing the inventory at a jewelry store that sells both expensive Rolex watches and low-priced Timex watches. The books say the store has about 100 of each kind of watch. Where would the auditor focus greater effort? Chances are the auditor would focus more on the Rolex watches than on the Timex watches. A small mistake in the number of Rolex watches listed in the inventory could have a large dollar effect on the financial statements, whereas the Timex watches are relatively immaterial.

Risk assessment may be the most important phase of the audit. If an auditor identifies a major risk, the audit can be focused in that area. But, as experienced auditors will tell you, the most dangerous risk of all is the one that goes unnoticed or is underrated. Much of the auditor's expertise lies in the ability to identify and evaluate risks.

Plan the Nature, Extent and Timing of Tests

Once an auditor decides what areas to emphasize, the auditor still must choose the specific procedures to perform (the nature of tests), the amount of testing to be done (extent of testing), and the timing of the tests.

Choosing the Nature of Audit Tests. Auditors have a whole smorgasbord of procedures they can utilize. Each test has its own advantages and disadvantages.

For example, suppose an auditor is trying to test the accuracy of the balance in a Prepaid Insurance account (an asset account containing insurance premiums that have already been paid for future protection). One test the auditor can perform is to examine the auditee's insurance policies and canceled checks for premium payments and calculate the amount that should be in the Prepaid Insurance account. Suppose the company paid $2,400 for an automobile insurance policy that covers the one-year period from January through December. An auditor examining the June 30 financial statements (the half-way point during the policy year) could calculate that half the insurance premium ($1,200) should be listed in the Prepaid Insurance account.

The auditor might also use a different test for the same account balance: sending a letter to the insurance company asking them to confirm the amount of premium paid and the amount that is prepaid. The first test has the advantage of taking less time to get a result, but the evidence it provides isn't as strong as the evidence from the second test. The second test is stronger because the confirmation with the insurance company tells the auditor the policy is still in force. In the first test, the auditor must assume that the auditee hasn't canceled the policy recently.

Choosing the Extent and Timing of Audit Tests. The auditor must also choose the size of the sample to test (the **extent** of testing) and decide when to perform the procedure (the **timing** of the test). As an example of a timing decision, suppose you are the auditor testing the inventory of watches at a jewelry store. Do you want to count the watches at a time close to the financial statement date (a relatively strong test) or count them a few weeks before the financial statement date and estimate the effect of sales and purchases in the remaining time? The second test has the advantage of spreading out your work load (there's a lot of work going on as you get closer to the financial statement date), but the use of estimates for the last few weeks makes the test relatively weaker than a count made close to the financial statement date.

The Link Between Risk, Materiality and Audit Tests. Choices about the nature, extent and timing of tests depend on the auditor's assessment of materiality and risk. The *higher* the risk and/or the *more material* the item, the more likely the auditor is to choose a relatively strong test (nature), a relatively large sample (extent), and/or a relatively tight timing. Auditors devote a lot of effort to making choices about the nature, extent and timing of tests to conduct. Usually, they write down their plans in a step-by-step listing called an "**audit program**" that becomes a part of the workpapers.

Gather Evidence

After the thinking and the planning comes the doing. Evidence is gathered by performing the procedures in the audit program--procedures like counting inventory, confirming insurance coverage, examining canceled checks to support payments, verifying the accuracy of calculations, and so on. Evidence collection continues until the auditor feels there is sufficient competent evidence to support the audit conclusions. That is, auditors continue to gather evidence until they are satisfied (or comfortable) about the judgments they must make.

As evidence is collected, it is recorded in the workpapers and the auditor who performs the work "signs off" the audit program by initialing each audit step when it is completed. At every stage of the audit, the work of entry-level auditors (often called associate or staff auditors) is reviewed by mid-level auditors (often called seniors or supervisors) and any necessary additions or corrections are made. For example, a large financial audit will go through several levels of review from staff to senior, from senior to manager, and from manager to partner. If the company is publicly held, a second partner will also review the work. These levels of review provide a system of quality control within the audit team.

Interpret the Evidence, Reach a Conclusion, and Prepare a Report

At every stage of the audit, judgments were documented in the workpapers and tentative conclusions were offered. Now, when all the evidence has been gathered and the review process indicates that the audit work is completed, final conclusions are drawn and a report is prepared.

The financial audit ends with a report expressing an opinion on the fairness of presentation of the financial statements. The operational audit ends with a report on the specific strengths and/or weaknesses observed by the auditor, with suggestions for improvements. The compliance audit ends with a report stating whether there is evidence that appropriate laws and regulations were complied with and pointing out deficiencies, if any. For example, an IRS audit ends with a report concluding the taxpayer either owes no additional taxes, or is due a refund, or must pay additional taxes (plus accompanying penalties and interest).

Because their objectives differ, the form and content of the report may look very different for financial audits, operational audits and compliance audits. But the general process of the audit has been the same: gain an understanding of the client and the audit situation; assess risk and materiality; plan the nature, extent and timing of tests; gather evidence; interpret the evidence, reach a conclusion, and prepare a report. However, you should be aware that actual audits don't occur in a lock-step fashion where all the steps are discrete and occur only once during an audit.

Sometimes, for example, the evidence an auditor gathers is surprising. Suppose a government auditor is examining a defense contractor's payroll records to determine if the correct amount of labor was charged to government contracts. Based on an initial assessment that the risk of material error is relatively low, the auditor has decided to examine a sample of only 1 month's payroll records. If the auditor discovers more errors than expected, the risk assessment and planning process is revisited and additional tests will be performed. The auditor cycles through the process as many times as needed until he or she is satisfied there is enough evidence to support the final conclusions in the audit report.

WHO AUDITS THE AUDITORS?

"Who will guard the guards?" says a Latin verse,--"Quis custodiet ipsos custodes?" I answer, "The enemy." It is the enemy who keeps the sentinel watchful.
-- Anne Sophie Swetchine, 1782-1857, <u>Old Age</u>

When you stop to think about it, capital markets, the management of businesses and not-for-profit organizations, governments and the public place a lot of trust in auditors. So, the logical question arises: who audits the auditors? That is, how do users of audit reports know that the auditors are competent and trustworthy? that the audit report is a quality product?

Many forces are at work to ensure audit quality. One force is the regulation of the profession by government bodies. Self-regulation through professional associations is a second force. A third force is monitoring by the organizations which employ auditors. And, especially in the case of public accountants, there is the specter of legal liability for failure to perform a quality audit.

<u>Regulation</u>

All countries regulate their licensed professionals. Auditors of publicly held companies in the United States are subject to regulation by the Securities and Exchange Commission (SEC). The SEC is empowered to investigate and discipline auditors who fail to maintain appropriate quality standards. Rule 2(e)(1) of the SEC's rules of practice states that the SEC may temporarily or permanently disqualify an auditor from auditing public companies if the auditor:

♦ lacks the requisite qualifications,

♦ lacks character or integrity, or engages in unethical or improper professional conduct, or

♦ commits (or aids and abets the commission of) a violation of federal securities laws or the related rules and regulations.

The SEC can also impose administrative sanctions, such as restricting a CPA firm from merging with any other firms for a specified period or censuring a firm or requiring a CPA to complete additional continuing education courses.

Moreover, all CPAs--whether they work in public accounting, industry, government, or for a non-profit organization--are subject to regulation by the state or other government body that grants their license. In most jurisdictions, the laws governing public accountancy also prescribe an ethics code and there is a body that enforces the ethics code and conducts disciplinary proceedings. Violations of the ethics code (which include requirements for independence, due professional care, and so on), if serious enough, can result in the loss of the CPA license. Thus, the state boards of accountancy in the United States have the power to remove incompetent practitioners from practice as CPAs.

Self-Regulation

In addition to government regulation, the United States and many other countries also have active professional organizations--such as the AICPA, the IIA, the Association of Government Accountants, the Canadian Institute of Chartered Accountants, the Japanese Institute of Certified Public Accountants and so on-- which promote self-regulation. Auditors who join these organizations agree to abide by their requirements, including ethical standards and continuing education standards.

For example, all members of the AICPA are subject to continuing education requirements in order to maintain their competence. They also agree to abide by the organization's ethics code. Violators of the ethics code are subject to disciplinary action, with revocation of membership being the most severe penalty possible. In addition, CPA firms that belong to the AICPA agree to undergo periodic **"peer reviews"** or **"quality reviews."** As the name implies, these reviews are evaluations of the quality control of an audit organization (a sole practice, partnership or professional corporation) performed by other auditors (peers) from outside the organization.

The reviewers check to see whether the auditors being reviewed have complied with professional quality control standards and the requirements of the professional ethics code, as well as with continuing education requirements. The reviewers examine both the control system the audit organization uses to ensure audit quality and a sample of their audit workpapers. The end product of a peer or quality review is an opinion stating whether the organization has a system of quality control that meets the AICPA standards and whether the organization is in conformity with AICPA membership requirements. If the review team finds any deficiencies, they are discussed with the organization and suggestions for improvements are made. If the deficiencies are material, the organization may be subject to remedial measures or disciplinary action, such as fines, suspension, or expulsion from the AICPA.

Peer review reports for members of the AICPA's SEC Practice Section (the membership division for firms that have publicly held audit clients) are made public. Quality review reports for other CPA firms (those without publicly held audit clients) remain confidential. Public disclosure creates a strong incentive for audit organizations to install and maintain a sound quality control system.

There are many separate professional associations that may have an interest in self-regulatory activities. Without some coordination of efforts, the regulatory process can bog down because a single problem can involve many different associations. Consequently, the AICPA and the state societies of CPAs (the professional association of CPAs in each state) coordinate their efforts to regulate the profession through ethics enforcement and peer reviews.

Monitoring By Organizations That Hire Auditors

Organizations that employ auditors can take steps to evaluate the quality of their auditor's work. The audit committee of a company's board of directors often takes on the responsibility of evaluating the company's auditors, as well as the responsibility for selecting the external auditor to be recommended to the full board and the stockholders. The *Good Practice Guidelines for the Audit Committee* published by the National Commission on Fraudulent Financial Reporting suggest that, among other things, the audit committee should review the external audit firm's latest peer review report and consider the firm's credentials, capabilities, and reputation. Typically, the audit committee will meet with the external auditors to discuss their audit plan and findings. They may also question the auditor and members of management about any potential threats to audit independence (such as the performance of a significant amount of non-audit services) which may exist.

Similarly, the audit committee also may oversee the internal audit function. The Audit Committee provides a direct line of communication between the internal auditors and the board, which helps ensure that the internal auditors are organizationally protected. The Institute of Internal Auditors recommends that the audit committee periodically review the internal audit group's charter (the document which states their purpose, authority and responsibility) and regularly review the internal audit department's objectives, goals and plans for the year, as well as their audit schedules, staffing plans and financial budget. Also, the audit committee might ask the external auditors to assess the qualifications and procedures of the internal auditors.

Legal Liability

Finally, the specter of legal liability creates a powerful incentive to maintain audit quality. In the United States, financial auditors bear substantial legal liability for failure to perform an audit in accordance with generally accepted auditing standards. If there are material undetected errors or omissions in a set of financial statements and the auditor did not comply with generally accepted auditing standards, the auditor's potential liability may be huge--conceivably, the auditor's liability can be far in excess of any audit fees earned from the client. In 1992, for example, CPA firms faced about $30 billion in damage claims.

Auditors can be sued by the users of audit reports if they suffer losses because of their reliance on materially incorrect audited financial statements. If the auditor has failed to conduct an audit in accordance with generally accepted auditing standards, the auditor will be liable for the losses suffered by stockholders (or any other party the audit is being specifically conducted for). Moreover, other users--such as a supplier who decided to extend credit to an organization based on materially incorrect audited financial statements--may be able to recover damages from the auditor under some circumstances. If the auditor's conduct was so poor as to be considered fraudulent (lacking even the minimum required standard of care), then the auditor may be liable to a wide class of users of the financial statements.

In the U.S., which has a reputation as the most litigious country in the world, many accountants believe CPA firms have been too frequently sued when businesses fail--even if their audits were conducted in accordance with generally accepted auditing standards. The theory is that CPA firms were sued because they offer "deep pockets"--one of the few remaining sources of money that stockholders or other parties can look to for relief.

Or, alternatively, the parties that sue may look to the auditor as a guarantor of their investment or loan, rather than as a witness to the fairness of presentation of financial statements. What the users want is what Bertrand Russell said all men want: "not knowledge, but certainty." However, the CPA firms argue that no professional, no matter how expert, can provide certainty--a clean opinion cannot be taken as a guarantee against failure or an endorsement of the quality of management or the business prospects of the organization.

Within the past few years, the profession has moved to accept some extension of responsibility, while asking in exchange for some limits to legal liability. Late in 1995, Congress passed the **Private Securities Litigation Reform Act of 1995.** The law instituted a system of **proportionate liability** designed to reduce "deep pockets" suits (suing parties who are only peripherally involved but have money). Parties who knowingly engage in fraud are still responsible for all losses suffered by plaintiffs, but other defendants will only be responsible for paying their "fair share" of damages. The only exception is that all parties will remain fully liable to plaintiffs with a net worth under $200,000 who lose more than 10% of their net worth. This is a significant limitation in liability for professionals.

In exchange, the law extends auditors' responsibility by requiring them to see that the Securities and Exchange Commission is promptly notified of an illegal act discovered during a public company audit. Auditors must first communicate with the client's board of directors, which has 1 business day to report the illegal act to the SEC. If the report is not filed when due, the auditor must resign from the client and notify the SEC about the situation. Previously, U. S. auditing standards allowed auditors to resign from any clients they found involved in illegal acts, but prohibited auditors from directly notifying any outside parties--including the SEC--due to their confidentiality obligation to the client.

The legal liability of auditors varies throughout the world. Many countries, such as Japan, are far less litigious than the U.S., making it far less likely an auditor will be sued. However, in all countries, regardless of how likely it is for a user to bring suit, auditors are legally responsible for their work. And this liability does serve as a force for maintaining or increasing the quality of audits.

As a percentage of all audits conducted, audit failures (cases where the auditor did not conduct an audit of appropriate quality) are very rare. Some estimates place the audit failure rate at only a fraction of 1 percent of all the audits performed; even the most liberal estimates place the failure rate at only a few percent. Yet, audit failures, when they happen, can be devastating. Thus, while audit failures and law suits are relatively infrequent, they still cast fear into the heart of every audit organization in much the same way that the specter of airplane crashes casts fear into the heart of every airline. Most large CPA firms, given the sizable number of audits they conduct, have on occasion been sued and lost. The memory of those losses (and their negative impact on partners' wealth and reputation) is a powerful force for maintaining and improving audit quality. In effect, it is the enemy who keeps the sentinel watchful.

FUTURE AUDIT, ATTEST AND ASSURANCE SERVICES

The future ain't what it used to be.
-- Yogi Berra

Just as technology and globalization are affecting users' financial reporting needs and the future of financial accounting, these same factors also have implications for the future of auditing. To peer into this future, the AICPA established a Special Committee on Assurance Services (also known as the Elliott Committee, after its chair, Robert K. Elliott of KPMG Peat Marwick).

What did the Committee, which issued its final report in 1997, see as the future? Based on consumer research and an analysis of trends, the committee sees some major changes on the horizon. These changes include potential new CPA services providing assurance about many different kinds of information, only a small portion of which will be presented in financial statements. For example, new directions could include establishing standards for education outcome measurement and teacher evaluation, providing customized measurements and evaluations to investors, and evaluating performance of third-party health care providers, as well as providing Internet assurance services (such as assurances about the privacy and security of electronic commerce).

The changes also include some rethinking of current services. For example, technology is making it possible for a shift in who has the power to decide information content. Today, preparers of information decide the form and content of reports to users. But when users can have access to real-time information in vast electronic databases, one-size fits all financial statements controlled by preparers may no longer be demanded. Users may take on the power of deciding what information to look at and when to look at it. CPAs may also take on new roles, such as helping users be sure the information they choose to view is reliable and appropriate for their decision tasks. While much may change, one thing is constant. From medieval times to the 21st century, auditors provide assurance to users that makes information more credible.

ASSIGNMENTS FOR MODULE 3 - PART A

ASSIGNMENT I-3A-1: <u>Debt Capital</u>: **The Risk-Return Tradeoff**

SETTING

You are a bank lending officer. Two very similar companies (Company A and Company B) have applied for short-term loans. Both companies are small used car dealers doing business in the city of San Francisco.

The 2 companies have about the same amount of total assets, total liabilities and equities. Last year, each company had net earnings after taxes of about $25,000 on sales of about $500,000, which was close to the industry average.

This year both companies expect a slight improvement in earnings. They are optimistic about used-car sales because rising gasoline prices and rising new car prices may increase consumer interest in used cars. Outside of gasoline and car prices, the prices of consumer goods in the San Francisco area are expected to remain fairly stable over the next year.

Company A has invested most of its assets in its inventory of cars, enough to cover about 5 months of sales. It has enough cash on hand to pay about 6 weeks of operating expenses.

Company B has only a small inventory of cars, enough to cover about 6 weeks of sales, but it has enough cash on hand to cover operating expenses for the coming year.

Both companies want to use the loan proceeds to increase their inventory of cars in anticipation of increased demand. Both are applying for unsecured loans.

SELF-CORRECTED ASSIGNMENT

Assume that you decide to make both loans. Your only remaining decision is what interest rate to charge. You may charge the 2 companies different rates of interest, if you feel a rate difference is justified.

Review the information about the loan applicants to determine if the same interest rate should be charged to both companies. If not, which company will have to pay a higher rate of interest?

HINTS

1. Remember that the interest rates will be equal only if the risk the bank is taking is equal. If not, the riskier loan will bear a higher interest charge. Therefore, you need to assess the relative risk of the 2 loans.

2. Much about the companies is the same. What is different? Do these differences result in a different risk for the bank?

When you have completed the assignment, you may check your answer against the suggested solution that appears at the end of this module. Be sure to note any questions you might want to bring up for classroom discussion.

ASSIGNMENT I-3A-2:   <u>**Equity Capital**</u>

(This is an in-class assignment.)

ASSIGNMENT I-3A-3: <u>**The Evolution of Capital Markets**</u>: **Financial Reporting on the Internet**

SETTING

You are a student studying business in preparation for a career as an investment advisor. As you look into your future career, you imagine that much of the information you will use when analyzing companies as candidates for investment will be available to you over the Internet. In fact, according to *The Second Annual Straightline Internet Communications Survey*, 92% of corporate web sites already include financial and investor relation materials and about 1 in 2 corporate web sites includes the company's annual report and/or the company's Form 10-K.

As you surf the Internet, you discover that many corporate web sites update their sites very frequently--some daily, some weekly, and some monthly. This updating includes the financial and investor relation materials. But, you are surprised to learn from the *Internet Communications Survey* that only 11% of the responding companies believe the information on their web site reaches investment analysts. Of the investment professionals who responded to the survey, only 22% prefer receiving financial information over the Internet. The overwhelming majority would rather rely on printed annual reports as their source for receiving financial information.

This information puzzles you as it seems obvious that the Internet is a better medium than printed annual reports for transmitting time-sensitive financial information. You ask an investment advisor you know why investment professionals don't prefer the Internet. The investment advisor's response is: "The big issue with financial information on the World-Wide Web is not how to find it, but how valid it is."

As an example, the investment advisor shows you the financial information that is available on Microsoft's web site (**http://www.microsoft.com/msft/**). It includes not only the company's annual report and SEC filings, but also real-time stock quotes and hyperlinks from the financial statements to a variety of charts and additional information. There's even a "what if" capability--a workbook that helps you manipulate the information in the financial reports and test the impact of alternative assumptions. Not only are the U.S. financial reports on-line, but there are also profit and loss statements for many countries where Microsoft does business. These international statements--which are marked "unaudited"--are prepared in accordance with the particular country's accounting principles and are presented in the country's language and currency.

ASSIGNMENT

Ponder the issues involved in online financial reporting and prepare a brief report describing two significant issues and suggesting possible solutions.

Your instructor will let you know whether your report should be written or oral, as well as any length limitations.

HINTS

Taking a look at the financial information available on Microsoft's web site may help you think about how online financial reporting may differ from printed financial reporting.

You might also try an Internet search to see if you can find any information on the problems and prospects of online financial reporting.

ASSIGNMENT I-3A-4: <u>**The Role of Accountants in Capital Markets**</u>**: Public Accounting Firms**

SETTING

While it is still fairly early in your college education, you are already beginning to think about hunting for a job after graduation. The college placement office advises that you should research companies before you interview with them. Researching a company gives you a better sense of the company's needs and helps you think of questions you might ask during an interview. Moreover, it also helps to research other companies in the industry to provide comparisons.

In your accounting class, you have recently been studying the role of accountants in capital markets, which has introduced you to the public accounting industry. You decide to use this industry to practice your research skills. In particular, you want to see what you can find out about public accounting firms on the Internet.

ASSIGNMENT

Find the web site of your assigned public accounting firm (see the list on the following page), explore the site, and prepare a brief (5 to 6 minutes) oral presentation describing what you learned from the site.

What you must turn in: a printed copy of the home page of your assigned firm and an outline of your presentation.

***Bonus points opportunity*:**

Locate a directory of CPA firms that provides links to firms of all sizes. Choose a firm from your home state (other than the firms listed above) from this directory and describe its web site. How does this web site compare to your assigned web site? To get credit for the bonus points you must turn in a printout of the home page of the directory and a printout of the home page of the chosen firm; you must also briefly describe this site in your oral presentation.

GROUP	FIRM NAME	WEB LOCATION
1	Arthur Andersen	http://www.arthurandersen.com
2	Baird, Kurtz & Dobson	http://www.bkd.com
3	BDO Seidman	http://www.bdo.com
4	Coopers & Lybrand	http://www.colybrand.com
5	Crowe, Chizek & Co.	http://www.crowechizek.com
6	Deloitte & Touche	http://www.dttus.com
7	Ernst & Young	http://www.ey.com
8	KPMG Peat Marwick	http://www.kpmg.com
9	McGladrey & Pullen	http://www.mcgladrey.com
10	Plante & Moran	http://www.plante-moran.com
11	Price Waterhouse	http://www.pw.com
12	Grant Thornton	http://www.grantthorton.com

HINTS

Your presentation should let students know what major categories of information the site contains, but beyond that requirement there are many different ways to structure the presentation. For example, you could focus on a particularly interesting single aspect of the site or you could rate various features of the site. Be creative.

Remember your time limit--the key to a successful short presentation is good planning.

Do you want to show the site during your presentation? In a 5 minute presentation, you should not attempt a live Internet connection as delays could be disastrous. However, it is possible to cache the site for presentation purposes, which gives you better control over your time. If you plan to cache the site for classroom display, be sure to check with your instructor in advance to see if projection equipment will be available. Don't forget lower tech options, too, such as printing a color overhead of the home page.

If your group members are from multiple states, you may choose any 1 of the states for the bonus points portion of the assignment.

ASSIGNMENTS FOR MODULE 3 - PART B

ASSIGNMENT I-3B-1: <u>Typical Contents of an Annual Report:</u> **Reading an Annual Report**

SETTING

You are a college student hoping that your future career will bring you enough wealth to allow you to invest in the stock market. In preparation for that possibility, you are trying to find out everything you can about reading financial reports.

ASSIGNMENT

Obtain a copy of a recent annual report (the more recent, the better, but in no case any older than 2 years old) of a public company (either domestic or foreign) and answer the questions listed in Exhibit 1 on the following page.

Grading note: If this is done as a written assignment, attach a copy of the relevant portions of the annual report to your answers. On the copy, be sure to highlight the information you used to answer the questions. [*Note*: assignment credit will not be given unless a highlighted copy is turned in with your responses.]

HINTS

You can obtain annual reports of public companies in several ways, including:

- ♦ call or write the company's Investor Relations department or use Internet to access the company's information network

- ♦ use an electronic database of annual reports, available in many college or public libraries or your library's file of annual reports

- ♦ check your library to see if it has copies of public company filings with the Securities and Exchange Commission (many larger college libraries have copies of annual report filings to the SEC on microfiche) or access EDGAR at the SEC

Exhibit 1

TEN QUESTIONS TO ANSWER ABOUT YOUR ANNUAL REPORT

1. What is the name of the organization and in what industry does it operate?

2. What title does the company use for the statement that reports the results of its operations? What period does the statement cover? What were the organization's revenues for the most recent period? What was the organization's net income or loss for the most recent period?

3. Does the organization separately report results for any major business segments? If so, what distinguishes the segments?

4. Calculate the profit margin for each business segment (or for the overall organization if there aren't multiple segments) for each year reported on.

5. What title does the organization use for the statement that reports its financial position? What period of time does the statement cover? Is the statement classified or unclassified?

6. What are the total assets of the firm? What are the major types of assets the organization owns? What are the firm's total liabilities and equities? Do total assets equal total liabilities plus equities?

7. How many types of stock does the company have outstanding? Is there any treasury stock?

8. What is the amount of retained earnings at the end of the most recent period? Were any dividends paid in any of the years the financial report covers?

9. How much did cash increase/decrease during the most recent period? Were net cash flows from operating activities greater than, less than, or the same as the net income or loss for the most recent period?

10. Which of the following reports are contained in the annual report: a management report, an audit committee report, an auditor's report?

ASSIGNMENT I-3B-2:   **Basic Financial Statements:** **Financial Statement Articulation**

SETTING

You are a college student working on an assignment for your accounting class. Your assignment was to gather information about a public company from its 1996 annual report and answer a series of questions about the company's financial information for 1995 and 1996. The company you have been assigned is Alberto-Culver Company and Subsidiaries.

Your notes on the company are as follows:

```
Net sales revenue:      1996:   $1,590,409,000
                        1995:   $1,358,219,000
Net earnings:           1996:   $   62,744,000
                        1995:   $   52,651,000
Dividends paid:         1996:   $    9,724,000
                        1995:   $    8,590,000
Total assets:           1996:   $  909,266,000
                        1995:   $  815,086,000
Retained earnings,
    end of year:        1996:   $  390,526,000
                        1995:
```

Late at night, you realize that you forgot to get one of the required pieces of information: the retained earnings at the end of 1995.

SELF-CORRECTED ASSIGNMENT

Without going back to the library or using any other reference source, figure out what Alberto Culver's retained earnings were at the end of 1995.

HINTS

Remember that the end of 1995 is the beginning of 1996. Think about the format of a statement of retained earnings and work backwards. When you are satisfied with your answer, check it against the solution that appears at the end of this module.

ASSIGNMENT I-3B-3:   <u>**Typical Contents of an Annual Report:**</u> **Types of Audit Opinions #1**

SETTING

You are a financial analyst working for a brokerage firm. In today's mail, you receive 4 financial reports of companies that hope you will recommend them for investment. You leaf through the reports quickly, looking at the things that matter most to you. One of the things you look at first is the auditor's report on the financial statements (see the 4 pages following the description of this assignment).

ASSIGNMENT

Prepare a short list that: (1) names each of the companies; (2) tells what type of audit opinion the company received; and (3) explains the reason for any opinions that aren't unqualified.

HINTS

The best way to begin to determine the type of audit opinion is to consider the format of the report. How many paragraphs does the report have? Are there more or less paragraphs than you would expect for a standard unqualified opinion?

Read the report and determine which paragraphs give the introduction, describe the scope of the audit and express the opinion. If there are any additional paragraphs, the opinion must not be a standard unqualified opinion.

Check the opinion paragraph for the key words that help you determine the nature of the opinion.

If the opinion is anything other than a standard unqualified opinion, the extra paragraphs will contain an explanation of the reasons for modified wording, qualification, disclaimer, or adverse opinions.

Auditors' Report to the
Members of Land Securities PLC

We have audited the financial statements on pages 36 to 52 which have been prepared under the historical cost convention, as modified by the revaluation of properties, and the accounting policies set out on page 40.

Respective Responsibilities of Directors and Auditors
As described on this page the company's directors are responsible for the preparation of financial statements. It is our responsibility to form an independent opinion, based on our audit, on those statements and to report our opinion to you.

Basis of Opinion
We conducted our audit in accordance with Auditing Standards issued by the Auditing Practices Board. An audit includes examination, on a test basis, of evidence relevant to the amounts and disclosures in the financial statements. It also includes an assessment of the significant estimates and judgements made by the directors in the preparation of the financial statements, and of whether the accounting policies are appropriate to the circumstances of the company and the group, consistently applied and adequately disclosed.

We planned and performed our audit so as to obtain all the information and explanations which we considered necessary in order to provide us with sufficient evidence to give reasonable assurance that the financial statements are free from material misstatement, whether caused by fraud or other irregularity or error. In forming our opinion we also evaluated the overall adequacy of the presentation of information in the financial statements.

Opinion
In our opinion the financial statements on pages 36 to 52 give a true and fair view of the state of affairs of the company and of the group at 31 March 1996 and of the profit and cash flows of the group for the year then ended and have been properly prepared in accordance with the Companies Act 1985.

PRICE WATERHOUSE
Chartered Accountants and Registered Auditors
Southwark Towers, 32 London Bridge Street,
London SE1 9SY
22 May 1996

Report Of Independent Auditors

Board of Directors and Stockholders
Brightpoint, Inc.

We have audited the accompanying consolidated balance sheets of Brightpoint, Inc. as of December 31, 1996 and 1995, and the related consolidated statements of income, stockholders' equity and cash flows for each of the three years in the period ended December 31, 1996. These financial statements are the responsibility of the Company's management. Our responsibility is to express an opinion on these financial statements based on our audits. We did not audit the 1995 and 1994 financial statements of Allied Communications, which are included in the consolidated financial statements, which statements reflect total assets constituting 33% in 1995, and net sales constituting 36% in 1995 and 45% in 1994 of the related consolidated totals. Those statements were audited by other auditors whose report has been furnished to us, and our opinion, insofar as it relates to data included for Allied Communications, is based solely on the report of the other auditors.

We conducted our audits in accordance with generally accepted auditing standards. Those standards require that we plan and perform the audit to obtain reasonable assurance about whether the financial statements are free of material misstatement. An audit includes examining, on a test basis, evidence supporting the amounts and disclosures in the financial statements. An audit also includes assessing the accounting principles used and significant estimates made by management, as well as evaluating the overall financial statement presentation. We believe that our audits and the report of other auditors provide a reasonable basis for our opinion.

In our opinion, based on our audits and the report of other auditors, the financial statements referred to above present fairly, in all material respects, the consolidated financial position of Brightpoint, Inc. at December 31, 1996 and 1995, and the consolidated results of its operations and its cash flows for each of the three years in the period ended December 31, 1996, in conformity with generally accepted accounting principles.

Indianapolis, Indiana
January 28, 1997

Ernst & Young LLP

REPORT OF CERTIFIED PUBLIC ACCOUNTANTS

Board of Directors

Yes Clothing Co.

We have audited the accompanying balance sheet of Yes Clothing Co. as of March 31, 1996 and 1995 and the related statements of operations, changes in shareholders' equity and cash flows for the years then ended. We have also audited the financial statement schedule for the year ended March 31, 1996, listed under item 14. These financial statements and schedule are the responsibility of the Company's management. Our responsibility is to express an opinion on these financial statements and schedule based on our audits.

We conducted our audits in accordance with generally accepted auditing standards. Those standards require that we plan and perform the audit to obtain reasonable assurance about whether the financial statements are free of material misstatement. An audit includes examining, on a test basis, evidence supporting the amounts and disclosures in the financial statements. An audit also includes assessing the accounting principles used and significant estimates made by management, as well as evaluating the overall financial statement presentation. We believe that our audit provides a reasonable basis for our opinion.

In our opinion, the financial statements referred to above present fairly, in all material respects, the financial position of Yes Clothing Co. as of March 31, 1996 and 1995, and the results of its operations and its cash flows for the years then ended, in conformity with generally accepted accounting principles. In our opinion, the schedule for the year ended March 31, 1996 and 1995 presents fairly, in all material respects, the information set forth therein.

The accompanying financial statements have been prepared assuming that the Company will continue as a going concern. As discussed in Note 1 to the financial statements, the Company has incurred operating losses, has a deficit of working capital and tangible net worth, and other adverse financial indicators. These conditions raise substantial doubt about its ability to continue as a going concern. Management's plans regarding those matters also are described in Note 1. The financial statements do not include any adjustments that might result from the outcome of this uncertainty.

Moss Adams

MOSS ADAMS
Los Angeles, California May 30, 1996 (except for Note 10, as to which the date is June 4, 1996)

2300 North Tower
235 Peachtree St., NE
Atlanta, GA 30303-1499
404 330-2000
FAX 404 330-2047

Report of Independent Certified Public Accountants

Grant Thornton 🥄

GRANT THORNTON LLP Accountants and
Management Consultants

The U.S. Member Firm of
Grant Thornton International

Board of Directors
Vista 2000, Inc.

We were engaged to audit the accompanying consolidated balance sheet of Vista 2000, Inc. and subsidiaries as of December 30, 1995, and the related consolidated statement of operations, stockholders' equity and cash flows for the year then ended. These financial statements are the responsibility of the Company's management.

Sufficient evidential matter supporting the underlying transactions of the operations of Family Safety Products, Inc. and Intelock Technologies, Inc., both wholly-owned subsidiaries of Vista 2000, Inc., could not be provided by the Company. Additionally, sufficient evidential matter supporting the underlying transactions of the operations of Promotional Marketing, Inc., a subsidiary disposed of during 1995, could not be provided by the Company. The carrying value of assets and liabilities attributable to these subsidiaries, which are included in the accompanying consolidated financial statements, are approximately $8,500,000 and $4,500,000, respectively, and sales included in the statement of operations relating to these subsidiaries are approximately $2,500,000. The Company's books and records do not permit the applications of adequate alternative auditing procedures to these activities.

Since we were not able to apply auditing procedures to satisfy ourselves as to the matters discussed in the preceding paragraph, the scope of our work was not sufficient to enable us to express, and we do not express, an opinion on the consolidated financial statements of Vista 2000, Inc. and subsidiaries.

The Company has been named as a defendant in several lawsuits and is the subject of an informal investigation by the Securities and Exchange Commission, as more fully discussed in Note 7 to the consolidated financial statements.

Grant Thornton LLP.

Atlanta, Georgia
May 17, 1996

ASSIGNMENT I-3B-4:   <u>**Typical Contents of an Annual Report:**</u> **Types of Audit Opinions #2**

SETTING

You are a wealthy individual investor. In today's mail, you receive 4 financial reports of companies that hope you will consider investing in their securities. You leaf through the reports quickly, looking at the things that matter most to you. One of the things you look at first is the auditor's report on the financial statements (see the 4 pages following the description of this assignment).

ASSIGNMENT

Prepare a short list that: (1) names each of the companies; (2) tells what type of audit opinion the company received; and (3) explains the reason for any opinions that aren't unqualified.

HINTS

The best way to begin to determine the type of audit opinion is to consider the format of the report. How many paragraphs does the report have? Are there more or less paragraphs than you would expect for a standard unqualified opinion?

Read the report and determine which paragraphs give the introduction, describe the scope of the audit and express the opinion. If there are any additional paragraphs, the opinion must not be a standard unqualified opinion.

Check the opinion paragraph for the key words that help you determine the nature of the opinion.

If the opinion is anything other than a standard unqualified opinion, the extra paragraphs will contain an explanation of the reasons for modified wording, qualification, disclaimer, or adverse opinions.

REPORT OF INDEPENDENT ACCOUNTANTS

**TO THE BOARD OF DIRECTORS AND
SHAREHOLDERS OF SUN COMMUNITIES, INC.**

We have audited the accompanying consolidated balance sheet of Sun Communities, Inc. as of December 31, 1996 and 1995, and the related consolidated statements of income, stockholders' equity, and cash flows for each of the three years in the period ended December 31, 1996. These financial statements are the responsibility of the Company's management. Our responsibility is to express an opinion on these financial statements based on our audits.

**Coopers
&Lybrand**

We conducted our audits in accordance with generally accepted auditing standards. Those standards require that we plan and perform the audit to obtain reasonable assurance about whether the financial statements are free of material misstatement. An audit includes examining, on a test basis, evidence supporting the amounts and disclosures in the financial statements. An audit also includes assessing the accounting principles used and significant estimates made by management, as well as evaluating the overall financial statement presentation. We believe that our audits provide a reasonable basis for our opinion.

In our opinion, the financial statements referred to above present fairly, in all material respects, the consolidated financial position of Sun Communities, Inc. as of December 31, 1996 and 1995 and the consolidated results of its operations and cash flows for each of the three years in the period ended December 31, 1996 in conformity with generally accepted accounting principles.

Coopers + Lybrand L.L.P.

Detroit, Michigan
February 25, 1997

 Peat Marwick

The Board of Directors and Stockholders
Honda Motor Co., Ltd.:

We have audited the accompanying consolidated balance sheets of Honda Motor Co., Ltd. and subsidiaries as of March 31, 1995 and 1996, and the related consolidated statements of income, stockholders' equity and cash flows for each of the years in the three-year period ended March 31, 1996. These consolidated financial statements are the responsibility of the Company's management. Our responsibility is to express an opinion on these consolidated financial statements based on our audits.

We conducted our audits in accordance with generally accepted auditing standards. Those standards require that we plan and perform the audit to obtain reasonable assurance about whether the financial statements are free of material misstatement. An audit includes examining, on a test basis, evidence supporting the amounts and disclosures in the financial statements. An audit also includes assessing the accounting principles used and significant estimates made by management, as well as evaluating the overall financial statement presentation. We believe that our audits provide a reasonable basis for our opinion.

The segment information required to be disclosed in financial statements under United States generally accepted accounting principles is not presented in the accompanying consolidated financial statements. Foreign issuers are presently exempted from such disclosure requirement in Securities Exchange Act filings with the Securities and Exchange Commission of the United States.

In our opinion, except for the omission of the segment information referred to in the preceding paragraph, the consolidated financial statements referred to above present fairly, in all material respects, the financial position of Honda Motor Co., Ltd. and subsidiaries as of March 31, 1995 and 1996, and the results of their operations and their cash flows for each of the years in the three-year period ended March 31, 1996 in conformity with United States generally accepted accounting principles.

As discussed in note 1 (h) to consolidated financial statements, the Company adopted the provisions of Statement of Financial Accounting Standards No.115, "Accounting for Certain Investments in Debt and Equity Securities" in the year ended March 31, 1995.

The accompanying consolidated financial statements as of and for the year ended March 31, 1996 have been translated into United States dollars solely for the convenience of the reader. We have recomputed the translation and, in our opinion, the consolidated financial statements expressed in yen have been translated into dollars on the basis set forth in note 2 to consolidated financial statements.

Tokyo, Japan
May 24, 1996

KPMG Peat Marwick

REPORT OF INDEPENDENT AUDITORS, ERNST & YOUNG LLP

Board of Directors
Paychex, Inc.

We have audited the accompanying consolidated balance sheets of Paychex, Inc. and subsidiaries as of May 31, 1996 and 1995, and the related consolidated statements of income, stockholders' equity, and cash flows for each of the three years in the period ended May 31, 1996. These financial statements are the responsibility of the Company's management. Our responsibility is to express an opinion on these financial statements based on our audits.

We conducted our audits in accordance with generally accepted auditing standards. Those standards require that we plan and perform the audit to obtain reasonable assurance about whether the financial statements are free of material misstatement. An audit includes examining, on a test basis, evidence supporting the amounts and disclosures in the financial statements. An audit also includes assessing the accounting principles used and significant estimates made by management, as well as evaluating the overall financial statement presentation. We believe that our audits provide a reasonable basis for our opinion.

In our opinion, the consolidated financial statements referred to above present fairly, in all material respects, the consolidated financial position of Paychex, Inc. and subsidiaries at May 31, 1996 and 1995, and the consolidated results of their operations and their cash flows for each of the three years in the period ended May 31, 1996, in conformity with generally accepted accounting principles.

As discussed in Note A to the consolidated financial statements, the Company changed its method of accounting for income taxes in fiscal year 1994 and for investments in fiscal year 1995.

Ernst & Young LLP

Syracuse, New York
June 27, 1996

To the Shareholders of ALLTEL Corporation:

We have audited the accompanying consolidated balance sheets of ALLTEL Corporation (a Delaware corporation) and subsidiaries as of December 31, 1996 and 1995, and the related consolidated statements of income, shareholders' equity and cash flows for each of the three years in the period ended December 31, 1996. These financial statements are the responsibility of the Company's management. Our responsibility is to express an opinion on these financial statements based on our audits.

We conducted our audits in accordance with generally accepted auditing standards. Those standards require that we plan and perform the audit to obtain reasonable assurance about whether the financial statements are free of material misstatement. An audit includes examining, on a test basis, evidence supporting the amounts and disclosures in the financial statements. An audit also includes assessing the accounting principles used and significant estimates made by management, as well as evaluating the overall financial statement presentation. We believe that our audits provide a reasonable basis for our opinion.

In our opinion, the financial statements referred to above present fairly, in all material respects, the financial position of ALLTEL Corporation and subsidiaries as of December 31, 1996 and 1995, and the results of their operations and their cash flows for each of the three years in the period ended December 31, 1996, in conformity with generally accepted accounting principles.

Arthur Andersen LLP

Little Rock, Arkansas,
January 31, 1997

ASSIGNMENT I-3B-5: <u>**Typical Contents of an Annual Report:**</u> **Types of Audit Opinions #3**

SETTING

You are a financial analyst working for a pension fund. Your job is to recommend investments for the fund. In today's mail, you receive 4 financial reports of companies that hope you will recommend them for investment. You leaf through the reports quickly, looking at the things that matter most to you. One of the things you look at first is the auditor's report on the financial statements (see the 4 pages following the description of this assignment).

ASSIGNMENT

Prepare a short list that: (1) names each of the companies; (2) tells what type of audit opinion the company received; and (3) explains the reason for any opinions that aren't unqualified.

HINTS

The best way to begin to determine the type of audit opinion is to consider the format of the report. How many paragraphs does the report have? Are there more or less paragraphs than you would expect for a standard unqualified opinion?

Read the report and determine which paragraphs give the introduction, describe the scope of the audit and express the opinion. If there are any additional paragraphs, the opinion must not be a standard unqualified opinion.

Check the opinion paragraph for the key words that help you determine the nature of the opinion.

If the opinion is anything other than a standard unqualified opinion, the extra paragraphs will contain an explanation of the reasons for modified wording, qualification, disclaimer, or adverse opinions.

BDO Seidman, LLP
Accountants and Consultants

720 Olive Street, Suite 2300
St. Louis, Missouri 63101-2387
Telephone: (314) 231-7575
Fax: (314) 621-6891

Report of Independent Certified Public Accountants

To the Board of Directors and Shareholders
of KV Pharmaceutical Company

We have audited the consolidated balance sheets of KV Pharmaceutical Company and Subsidiaries as of March 31, 1996 and 1995, and the related consolidated statements of operations, shareholders' equity and cash flows for each of the three years in the period ended March 31, 1996. These financial statements are the responsibility of the Company's management. Our responsibility is to express an opinion on these financial statements based on our audits.

We conducted our audits in accordance with generally accepted auditing standards. Those standards require that we plan and perform the audit to obtain reasonable assurance about whether the financial statements are free of material misstatement. An audit includes examining, on a test basis, evidence supporting the amounts and disclosures in the financial statements. An audit also includes assessing the accounting principles used and significant estimates made by management, as well as evaluating the overall financial statement presentation. We believe that our audits provide a reasonable basis for our opinion.

In our opinion, the consolidated financial statements referred to above present fairly, in all material respects the financial position of KV Pharmaceutical Company and Subsidiaries as of March 31, 1996 and 1995, and the results of their operations and their cash flows for each of the three years in the period ended March 31, 1996, in conformity with generally accepted accounting principles.

BDO Seidman, LLP

BDO SEIDMAN, LLP

St. Louis, Missouri
July 12, 1996

REPORT OF INDEPENDENT PUBLIC ACCOUNTANTS

To Oneita Industries, Inc.:

We have audited the accompanying consolidated balance sheets of Oneita Industries, Inc. (a Delaware corporation) and subsidiaries as of September 28, 1996 and September 30, 1995, and the related consolidated statements of operations, cash flows and shareholders' equity for each of the three years in the period ended September 28, 1996. These financial statements and the schedule referred to below are the responsibility of the Company's management. Our responsibility is to express an opinion on these financial statements and schedule based on our audits.

We conducted our audits in accordance with generally accepted auditing standards. Those standards require that we plan and perform the audit to obtain reasonable assurance about whether the financial statements are free of material misstatement. An audit includes examining, on a test basis, evidence supporting the amounts and disclosures in the financial statements. An audit also includes assessing the accounting principles used and significant estimates made by management, as well as evaluating the overall financial statement presentation. We believe that our audits provide a reasonable basis for our opinion.

In our opinion, the consolidated financial statements referred to above present fairly, in all material respects, the financial position of Oneita Industries, Inc. and subsidiaries as of September 28, 1996 and September 30, 1995 and the results of their operations and their cash flows for each of the three years in the period ended September 28, 1996, in conformity with generally accepted accounting principles.

The accompanying financial statements have been prepared assuming that the Company will continue as a going concern. As shown in the accompanying consolidated financial statements, the Company has incurred significant losses for the fourth quarter of fiscal 1995 and for the year ended September 28, 1996. Unaudited interim information indicates that losses are continuing for fiscal 1997. As discussed in Note 1 to the accompanying consolidated financial statements, the Company was not in compliance with certain terms of its long-term debt agreements at September 28, 1996. As a result of the covenant violations contained in the Company's long-term debt agreements, the holders of such debt may declare the entire amount of such indebtedness due and payable immediately. These matters, among others, raise substantial doubt about the Company's ability to continue as a going concern. Management's plans in regard to these matters, including plans to restructure its long-term debt are described in Note 1. The accompanying consolidated financial statements do not include any adjustments relating to the recoverability and classification of recorded asset amounts or the amounts and classification of liabilities that might result should the Company be unable to continue as a going concern.

Our audits were made for the purpose of forming an opinion on the basic consolidated financial statements taken as a whole. The schedule listed in the index to consolidated financial statements and schedule is presented for purposes of complying with the Securities and Exchange Commission's rules and is not a required part of the basic financial statements. This schedule has been subjected to the auditing procedures applied in the audits of the basic financial statements and, in our opinion, fairly states in all material respects the financial data required to be set forth therein in relation to the basic financial statements taken as a whole.

ARTHUR ANDERSEN LLP

Columbia, South Carolina,
November 19, 1996.

INDEPENDENT ACCOUNTANTS' REPORT

Board of Directors
Jack Henry & Associates, Inc.
Monett, Missouri

We have audited in accordance with generally accepted auditing standards, the consolidated balance sheets of JACK HENRY & ASSOCIATES, INC. AND SUBSIDIARIES as of June 30, 1996 and 1995, and the related consolidated statements of income, changes in stockholders' equity and cash flows for each of the three years ending June 30, 1996, referred to in the proxy statement for the 1996 annual meeting of the stockholders of JACK HENRY & ASSOCIATES, INC. (not presented herein). In our report dated August 22, 1996, also referred to therein, we expressed unqualified opinions on the aforementioned consolidated financial statements.

In our opinion, the information set forth in the accompanying condensed consolidated financial statements is fairly presented, in all material respects, in relation to the consolidated financial statements from which it has been derived.

Baird, Kurtz & Dobson

BAIRD, KURTZ & DOBSON

August 22, 1996
Joplin, Missouri

To the Stockholders and Board of Directors of
Lindsay Manufacturing Co.:

We have audited the accompanying consolidated balance sheets of
Lindsay Manufacturing Co. as of August 31, 1996 and 1995, and the
related consolidated statements of operations, stockholders' equity
and cash flows for each of the three years in the period ended August
31, 1996. These financial statements are the responsibility of the
Company's management. Our responsibility is to express an opinion
on these financial statements based on our audits.

We conducted our audits in accordance with generally accepted
auditing standards. Those standards require that we plan and perform
the audit to obtain reasonable assurance about whether the financial
statements are free of material misstatements. An audit includes
examining, on a test basis, evidence supporting the amounts and
disclosures in the financial statements. An audit also includes
assessing the accounting principles used and significant estimates
made by management, as well as evaluating the overall financial
statement presentation. We believe that our audits provide a
reasonable basis for our opinion.

In our opinion, the financial statements referred to above present
fairly, in all material respects, the consolidated financial position of
Lindsay Manufacturing Co. as of August 31, 1996 and 1995, and the
consolidated results of their operations and their cash flows for each
of the three years in the period ended August 31, 1996 in conformity
with generally accepted accounting principles.

As described in Note A, the Company changed its method of
accounting for income taxes in fiscal 1994.

Coopers & Lybrand LLP

Omaha, Nebraska
October 9, 1996

Coopers & Lybrand L.L.P.

ASSIGNMENT I-3B-6: <u>Basic Financial Statements:</u> The Balance Sheet

SETTING

You have just taken a job as a financial accountant with the CP Company. To orient yourself to the company, you decide to manually prepare a set of financial statements for the most recent month-end. You decide to start by preparing a balance sheet.

ASSIGNMENT

Given the alphabetical listing of account balances (see the following page) as of September 30 of this year, prepare a Balance Sheet for the CP Company. Be sure to include appropriate headings, sub-totals and totals.

HINTS

1. Remember that the basic format of a balance sheet is embodied in the accounting equation:

    Assets = Liabilities + Equities

    You know your balance sheet can't be correct unless total assets are equal to the total of liabilities and equities.

2. Take a look at the financial statements reproduced in this module to get ideas on how to format the balance sheet. If you need additional examples, seek out your library's files of corporate annual reports.

3. Use your dictionary to check the definitions of any terms which are unfamiliar to you.

ASSET, LIABILITY AND EQUITY ACCOUNTS

FOR THE CP COMPANY

Accounts Payable	$ 80,000
Accounts Receivable	40,500
Accumulated Depreciation on Building	55,000
Accumulated Depreciation on Equipment	20,000
Allowance for Doubtful Accounts	2,000
Building	158,000
Bonds Payable	202,000
Cash	76,300
Common Stock	124,500
Equipment	70,000
Franchises	45,000
Temporary Investments in Marketable Securities	11,750
Inventory	63,250
Land	270,000
Mortgage Note Payable	90,000
Patents	20,000
Premium on Bonds Payable	4,000
Preferred Stock	54,500
Prepaid Expenses	7,700
Retained Earnings, Sept. 30	125,500
Wages Payable	5,000

ASSIGNMENT I-3B-7: **Basic Financial Statements: Preparing Department Store Financial Statements**

SETTING

You have just taken a job as a financial accountant with a department store. To orient yourself to the company, you decide to manually prepare a set of financial statements for the most recent year-end. You decide to start by preparing a balance sheet and a statement of earnings.

ASSIGNMENT

Given the alphabetical listing of account balances (see the following page) as of January 31, the end of the department store's fiscal year, prepare a Balance Sheet and a Statement of Earnings for the company. Be sure to include appropriate headings, sub-totals and totals.

HINTS

1. Remember that the basic format of a balance sheet is embodied in the accounting equation:

    Assets = Liabilities + Equities

    You know your balance sheet can't be correct unless total assets are equal to the total of liabilities and equities.

2. Remember that the financial statements must articulate--that is, the net income reported on the earnings statement must affect the retained earnings reported on the balance sheet.

3. Take a look at the financial statements reproduced in this module to get ideas on how to format the statements. If you need additional examples, seek out your library's files of corporate annual reports or do some research to find annual reports on the Internet.

4. Use your dictionary to check the definitions of any terms which are unfamiliar to you.

ACCOUNTS LIST
(Dollars in thousands)

Accounts Payable	277,584
Accounts Receivable, Net	893,927
Accrued Expenses Payable	47,834
Accrued Income Taxes Payable	14,644
Accrued Salaries, Wages and Taxes Payable	185,540
Cash and Cash Equivalents	24,517
Common Stock	168,440
Cost of Sales and Related Buying and Occupancy Costs	2,806,250
Current Portion of Long-Term Debt	74,210
Deferred Lease Credits and Other Deferred Liabilities	111,601
Dividends and Other Reductions of Retained Earnings	91,046
Income Taxes	107,200
Interest Expense, Net	39,295
Long-Term Debt (non-current portion)	365,733
Merchandise Inventories	626,303
Net Sales	4,113,517
Notes Payable	232,501
Other Assets	16,545
Prepaid Income Taxes and Other Prepaids	68,029
Property, Buildings and Equipment, Net	1,103,298
Retained Earnings, beginning of year	1,180,466
Retained Earnings, end of year	1,254,532
Selling, General and Administrative Expenses	1,120,790
Service Charge Income and Other Income, Net	125,130

ASSIGNMENT I-3B-8   <u>**Basic Financial Statements:**</u> **Preparing Manufacturing Company Financial Statements**

SETTING

You have just taken a job as a financial accountant with a company that manufactures consumer products. To orient yourself to the company, you decide to manually prepare a set of financial statements for the most recent year-end. You decide to start by preparing a statement of earnings and a statement of retained earnings.

ASSIGNMENT

Given the alphabetical listing of account balances (see the following page) as of September 30, the end of the company's fiscal year, prepare a Statement of Earnings and a Statement of Retained Earnings for the company. Be sure to include appropriate headings, sub-totals and totals.

HINTS

1. Remember that the financial statements must articulate--that is, the net income reported on the earnings statement must affect the retained earnings as well.

2. Take a look at the financial statements reproduced in this module to get ideas on how to format the statements. If you need additional examples, seek out your library's files of corporate annual reports or do some research to find annual reports on the Internet.

3. Use your dictionary to check the definitions of any terms which are unfamiliar to you.

ACCOUNTS LIST
(Dollars in Thousands)

Advertising, promotion, selling & administrative expenses	584,856
Cash dividends	8,590
Cost of products sold	682,589
Interest expense, net of interest income	6,532
Net Sales	1,358,219
Property, Plant and Equipment	286,034
Provision for income taxes	31,591
Receivables, less allowance for doubtful accounts	128,482
Retained earnings, beginning of year	293,445
Retained earnings, end of year	337,506

ASSIGNMENT I-3B-9:   <u>**Basic Financial Statements:**</u>
Preparing A City's Financial Statements

<u>SETTING</u>

You have just taken a job as a financial accountant with a municipal government. To orient yourself to the city, you decide to manually prepare a set of financial statements for the most recent six month period. You decide to start by preparing a balance sheet for the city's general fund.

The general fund is used to support most city services except for street maintenance, water and sewer, and solid waste disposal, which are accounted for in other funds, such as the street fund. While a portion of the general fund has already been committed ("reserved and designated") for particular future expenditures, the majority of the fund is unreserved.

<u>ASSIGNMENT</u>

Given the alphabetical listing of account balances (see the following page) as of June 30, the end of the city's most recent 6-month period, prepare a Balance Sheet for the city's general fund. Be sure to include appropriate headings, sub-totals and totals.

<u>HINTS</u>

1.   Remember that the basic format of a balance sheet is embodied in the accounting equation, which, for a single fund of a government body is:

Assets = Liabilities + Fund Balance

You know your balance sheet can't be correct unless total assets are equal to the total of liabilities and fund balance (net assets).

2.   Take a look at the financial statements reproduced in this module to get ideas on how to format the balance sheet. If you need additional examples, seek out your library's files of nonprofit and government annual reports or do some research to find such annual reports on the Internet.

3.   Use your dictionary to check the definitions of any terms which are unfamiliar to you.

ACCOUNTS LIST

Accounts receivable	296,883
Accounts payable	863,045
Accrued expenses payable	741,258
Cash	235,730
Due from other governments	604,539
Due to other funds	71,306
Due from other funds	1,293,513
Escrow deposit liabilities	796,149
Investments	8,134,504
Prepaid expenses and other assets	180,901
Reserved and designated fund balance	1,032,101
Unreserved fund balance	7,242,211

ASSIGNMENTS FOR MODULE 3 - PART C

ASSIGNMENT I-3C-1:   **Types of Audits Conducted in Modern Organizations:**
Operational Audits and Financial Audits

SETTING

You are a member of an audit team examining the inventory records of the RainBroos Company, a company that sells waterproof cosmetic organizers. The product sells best as a holiday gift item (the strongest sales are near Mother's Day) and also sells well during the hottest months of summer when trips to the beach are at their peak. Demand falls considerably at other times of the year.

You have obtained a schedule of RainBroos' purchases and sales of inventory over the past year (see the page following the description of this assignment). You have tested the evidence supporting this schedule and believe that there are no material errors in the number of units listed on the schedule.

This is RainBroos' third year in business. Sales and income have grown each year; demand for the organizers is expected to increase about 5% in units over the next twelve months. After several years in business, RainBroos now has a reasonable cash flow--in fact, the company currently has about $48,000 of excess cash in a bank account that earns 7% interest. Recently--for the first time--Rainbroos' suppliers indicated they are willing to extend credit for inventory purchases (instead of requiring cash payment). The terms require payment within 30 days; after 30 days a finance charge is added at the rate of 18% per year (1.5% per month).

The minimum order RainBroos must place with its supplier to earn a quantity discount (a price break for buying in large numbers) is 5,000 units per order. At this level, each unit costs RainBroos $10. There is no change in the quantity discounts for orders between 5,000 and 9,999 units, but if 10,000 units are purchased at one time the unit price drops to $8.50.

At December 31, the financial statements for RainBroos show 14,000 units in inventory at an average cost of $10 each, for a total inventory value of $140,000. The retail price of the cosmetic organizers is now $20.

ASSIGNMENT

This assignment has 2 parts that differ only in the kind of audit you are performing:

Part 1:   You are a member of an operational audit team.

Part 2:   You are a member of a team of independent auditors examining the year-end financial statements.

Answer the following questions for each assumed role:

♦   What audit conclusions would you reach?

♦   Who would your report be addressed to?

♦   What would your report say?

HINTS

Auditing is a logical process. Even though you have never been either an operational auditor or a financial auditor, you should be able to reason out what the auditors would conclude in this situation.

Think about the objectives of the different types of audits. Then, look at the schedule of information on purchases and sales of units of inventory. Think about how the information on this schedule (and the additional information provided in the Setting section) helps you fulfill your objective. If the information raises any questions or recommendations in your mind, try to explain the problem or recommendation as clearly and specifically as possible. The information provided in the Setting section of the assignment may help you flesh out your ideas. Do your observed problems or recommendations belong in your audit report?

Your report should be addressed to the primary user group. It should clearly state your conclusions and describe any problems you observed that were relevant.

RAINBROOS COMPANY
Schedule of Inventory Purchases and Sales in Units
For the Year Ended December 31

MONTH	PURCHASES	SALES	BALANCE
January 1 beginning balance			8,000 units
January	5,000	400	12,600 units
February	5,000	900	16,700 units
March	5,000	1,600	20,100 units
April	5,000	2,500	22,600 units
May	5,000	15,000	12,600 units
June	5,000	7,800	9,800 units
July	5,000	10,000	4,800 units
August	5,000	9,500	300 units
September	5,000	3,000	2,300 units
October	5,000	1,000	6,300 units
November	5,000	500	10,800 units
December	5,000	1,800	14,000 units
TOTALS FOR YEAR	60,000	54,000	

ASSIGNMENT I-3C-2: <u>**Types of Audits Conducted in Modern Organizations**</u>**:**
Audit Baseball

SETTING

You are a student in an introductory accounting class. You and your group have been working hard to understand basic concepts of auditing. You know that there are 3 types of auditing--financial auditing, operational auditing, and compliance auditing--and you know that there are both similarities and differences between the types of audits.

All you know so far about today's assignment is that it's entitled "Audit Baseball."

ASSIGNMENT

For this assignment, the class will be divided into 2 teams who will be pitted against each other in a game of baseball. The aim of the game is to score "runs" by correctly naming similarities and differences between the 3 types of audits. A run is scored by a player advancing around all 4 points (bases) on a diamond-shaped (♦) playing field.

The game will begin when your instructor randomly chooses a team to come up to bat. The team member who is "at bat" will roll a die to determine what "pitch" he or she must hit (i.e., what question must be answered correctly):

If the die turns up:	You must name:	To get a:
1	a similarity	single (1 base)
2	a difference	double (2 bases)
3	a similarity	triple (3 bases)
4	a difference	home run (4 bases)
5	--	base on balls (1 base)
6	--	hit by pitch (1 base)

If you are unable to correctly name a similarity/difference, your team gets an "out." When one team gets 3 outs, the game is over and the team with the most runs wins.

Unlike the real game of baseball, in this game teams will alternate "at bats" so a separate diamond will be used to keep track of each team's players on base.
The rules for base-running are as follows:

♦   When the player at bat gets a hit, all players already on base advance by the same number of bases earned by the batter.

♦ If first base is occupied when a batter gets a base on balls or is hit by a pitch, the baserunners advance as needed to clear a spot on first for the batter. Otherwise, the baserunners stay put.

♦ Players on base will remain on base until they score or until the team has 3 outs and the game is over.

HINTS

When your team is "at bat," one member must roll the die to determine what pitch he or she must hit. The team member's own regularly-assigned group members can help formulate the answer, but the batter has the final say in what the response will be. Other people who are on the same team may not help the batter. [*Example*: if the odd-numbered groups are playing the even-numbered groups and a member of group 1 is at bat, the other members of group 1 may help formulate the answer, but the members of groups 3 and 5 may not assist the batter.]

Once you have rolled to determine your pitch, you have 1 minute (no more!) to come up with your answer. Otherwise, the batter is out. The instructor (or a neutral observer, if present) will keep track of the time at bat.

The instructor (or a neutral observer, if present) is the final authority for determining which answers are correct. It doesn't pay to argue with the ump.

In case of a tie at class's end, there will be a *sudden-death tie-breaker*. The instructor will roll the die to determine a final pitch. Each individual student will then write down an answer without consulting any other individual. The individual answers will be reviewed by the instructor. The team with the most correct individual answers will win the tie-breaker. [*Note*: if there are more students on one of the teams, the larger team will be asked to have some students sit "on the bench" for the tie-breaker so that the number of players is equal for the final answers.]

ASSIGNMENT I-3C-3: <u>**The Characteristics of a Good Auditor**</u>: **Auditor Independence**

<u>SETTING</u>

You are a taxpayer. You have just received a copy of the audited financial statements for the House Child Care Center, an independent organization that is incorporated under the laws of the District of Columbia for the sole purpose of providing preschool child care for children of Members, officers, employees and support personnel of the U.S. House of Representatives. If space is available, the Center can also provide care for children of Senators, officers and employees of the Senate, and employees of legislative branch agencies.

The auditor's reports appear on the following 3 pages. You note that the auditor reports on fairness of presentation, internal accounting controls, and compliance with laws and regulations. But you are surprised to see that the audit report is signed in the name of Charles A. Bowsher, Comptroller General of the United States, for the General Accounting Office. You did not realize until now that GAO auditors could sign opinions on audits.

<u>ASSIGNMENT</u>

Compare and contrast the relative independence of internal auditors, external auditors, and government auditors (in particular, GAO auditors).

Why are internal auditors not considered independent to perform financial audits for corporations, but GAO auditors--who work for the government--are considered independent to perform financial audits for government entities? Do you agree or disagree with the current independence rules?

<u>HINTS</u>

Review, as needed, from Module 2 of this theme: the standards for independence for internal auditors.

Review, as needed, from Module 3 (this module!): the standards for independence for external auditors.

Consider: How is the GAO similar to an internal auditor? an external auditor?

GAO

Comptroller General
of the United States

B-234458

October 14, 1994

The Honorable Donnald K. Anderson
Clerk of the House of Representatives

Mr. Randall B. Medlock
Acting Director, House Office of
   Non-Legislative and Financial Services

As you requested, we audited the balance sheets of the House of
Representatives Child Care Center (the Center) as of September 30, 1993
and 1992, and the related statements of revenues, expenses, and fund
balance and statements of cash flows for the years then ended. In addition,
as required by section 2(d) of H. Res. 21, 99th Congress, 1st Session (1985),
we audited the balance sheet of the House of Representatives Child Care
Center, Inc. (the Corporation), as of September 30, 1991, and the related
statement of revenues, expenses, and fund balance and statement of cash
flows for the month then ended. As of the beginning of fiscal year 1992, the
Corporation's activities, except for its fund-raising activities, were
transferred to the Center (see note 1). We found

- the financial statements were reliable in all material respects;
- internal controls in effect on September 30, 1993, provided reasonable
  assurance that losses, noncompliance with laws and regulations, and
  misstatements material to the financial statements would be prevented or
  detected; and
- no material noncompliance with laws and regulations we tested.

The following sections outline each conclusion in more detail and discuss
the scope of our audit.

Opinion on the Financial Statements

The financial statements and the accompanying notes of the Center as of
September 30, 1993 and 1992, and the Corporation as of September 30,
1991, present fairly, in conformity with generally accepted accounting
principles, the Center's and the Corporation's

- assets, liabilities, and fund balances;
- revenues and expenses; and
- cash flows.

As discussed in note 10, the financial statements present only the activities funded from tuition and related revenues. The statements also include appropriations received by the Center and the Corporation to cover the costs of employee benefits and employment taxes. They do not include costs relating to office space, building operations, and office furniture and equipment, which are financed by other legislative appropriations and are not readily identifiable.

Internal Controls

The internal controls we considered were those designed to

- safeguard assets against loss from unauthorized use or disposition;
- assure the execution of transactions in accordance with laws and regulations; and
- properly record, process, and summarize transactions to permit the preparation of financial statements and maintain accountability for assets.

Those controls in effect for the Center on September 30, 1993, provided reasonable assurance that losses, noncompliance, or misstatements material in relation to the financial statements would be prevented or detected.

Compliance With Laws and Regulations

Our tests for compliance with selected provisions of laws and regulations disclosed no material instances of noncompliance. Also, nothing came to our attention in the course of our work to indicate that material noncompliance with such provisions occurred.

Objectives, Scope, and Methodology

Management is responsible for

- preparing annual financial statements in conformity with generally accepted accounting principles,
- establishing and maintaining internal control systems to provide reasonable assurance that the control objectives mentioned above are met, and
- complying with applicable laws and regulations.

We are responsible for obtaining reasonable assurance about whether (1) the financial statements are reliable (free of material misstatements and presented fairly in conformity with generally accepted accounting principles) and (2) relevant internal controls are in place and operating effectively. We are also responsible for testing compliance with selected provisions of laws and regulations.

In order to fulfill these responsibilities, we

- examined, on a test basis, evidence supporting the amounts and disclosures in the financial statements;
- assessed the accounting principles used and significant estimates made by the entity's management;
- evaluated and tested relevant internal controls, including those over revenues, expenditures, and payroll; and
- tested compliance with selected provisions of section 312 of Public Law No. 102-90, as amended, 40 U.S.C. section 184g (Supp. IV 1992), and H. Res. 423, 102d Cong., 2d Sess., agreed to April 9, 1992, with respect to the Center; H. Res. 21, 99th Cong., 1st Sess., agreed to December 11, 1985, as enacted into permanent law and amended, 40 U.S.C. sections 184b-184f (1988 and Supp. II 1990), with respect to the Corporation; and federal, state, and District of Columbia regulations on withholding and payment of income and social security taxes.

We limited our work to accounting and other controls necessary to achieve the objectives outlined in the section on internal controls. Because of inherent limitations in any system of internal control, losses, noncompliance, or misstatements may nevertheless occur and not be detected. We also caution that projecting our evaluation to future periods is subject to the risk that controls may become inadequate because of changes in conditions or that the degree of compliance with controls may deteriorate.

We performed our audits in accordance with generally accepted government auditing standards. We completed our audit work on June 18, 1994.

Charles A. Bowsher
Comptroller General
of the United States

ASSIGNMENT I-3C-4: <u>**The Characteristics of a Good Auditor**</u>**: An Auditor's Dilemma**

(This case was written by Professor Paul Caster, Fairfield University.)

SETTING

You are a Certified Public Accountant with your own accounting practice. Your brother-in-law, Harry, asks you for a favor. Harry needs to borrow $1,000,000 to keep his used car business running, and the Hoomdoya Trust and Bank has asked for audited financial statements from Harry's business before it will grant a loan. Although you initially decline, Harry IS your spouse's brother, and your spouse pleads with you to help Harry out...after all, Harry really needs this loan to stay in business, and he cannot afford to pay an auditor, and why should he when he has an in-law (you) who is a CPA? Feeling pressure from your spouse, you agree to at least take a look at his books before you decide.

You arrive at Harry's Used Car Lot the next day and soon discover that Harry has just 3 employees:

♦ Maxine, the salesperson,
♦ Glenn, the mechanic, and
♦ Harry himself, who runs the entire business, including keeping the books.

As you examine Harry's books, you find them to be remarkably well kept. Everything appears to be in order, EXCEPT a charge to Miscellaneous Expense of $9,000 (out of a total of $12,000) that represents payment to Fidel's Smoke Shop. You always wondered how, at family gatherings, Harry was able to afford the most expensive cigars.

One other thing you discover, when examining the Cost of Used Cars account, is several checks paid to an I. M. Suhlees, each check for exactly $1,000. You ask Harry about these checks and he replies:

I. M. is an insurance adjuster for County Farm Insurance and we have worked out a great deal. Whenever I. M. comes across an expensive, late model (no more than 2 years old) car with heavy damage, say, around $4,000, I. M. writes it up as if the car was a total wreck and cannot be repaired. This way, County Farm's customers are happy because they get brand new cars to replace the "wrecks." By writing it up as a total wreck, the market value of the car drops to its junk value, about $3,000. I. M. has the car towed to my lot, and I pay the $3,000 for the car, plus $1,000 "commission" to I. M. Then I have my mechanic fix the car, which usually costs about $4,000 and I end up with a used car I can sell for about $15,000. Since it only costs me a total of $8,000 on average, I nearly double my money on those cars.

You shake your head and Harry continues:

Look...this kind of thing goes on all the time. County Farm is a big outfit. They can afford it, and they want to keep their customers happy. Besides, if I didn't buy these "wrecks" from I. M., I would have been out of business years ago, and I. M. would sell them to one of my competitors anyway.

Since it is late in the day anyway, you leave Harry's Used Car Lot and head for home, ready to contemplate your next action.

ASSIGNMENT

You have gone this far and there is no turning back the clock. Answer the following questions:

- ◆ What are the most important facts in the situation?

- ◆ Who are the stakeholders--the people who may be affected by your decision?

- ◆ What are your alternatives?

- ◆ What are the pros and cons of each alternative?

- ◆ What should you do?

HINTS

If you need some help thinking about this dilemma, read the article "Thinking Ethically" which appears in Module 2 of this theme with Assignment 2A-1.

Think broadly, particularly when identifying the stakeholders and alternatives.

ASSIGNMENT I-3C-5:   **<u>Future Audit, Attest and Assurance Services</u>: The Special Committee on Assurance Services**

<u>SETTING</u>

You have been trying to decide on a career and you are assessing the pros and cons of becoming a Certified Public Accountant and working in the public accounting industry. You are aware that whatever career you choose, the future is unlikely to be exactly like the past. So, you decide to do some research about the future of audit, attest and assurance services. You know that the AICPA had a Special Committee on Assurance Services that published a report on this topic in 1997, so you decide to check out the website at:

http://www.aicpa.org/assurance/sitemap/index.htm

<u>ASSIGNMENT</u>

Prepare a brief (5-6 minute) oral report on one of the following topics addressed by the Special Committee on Assurance Services:

- ◆   Group 1: The Effect of Information Technology on Assurance Services
- ◆   Group 2: Competencies Needed by CPAs in Assurance Services
- ◆   Group 3: The Future of the Financial Statement Audit
- ◆   Group 4: Elder Care Assurance Services
- ◆   Group 5: Electronic Commerce Assurance Services
- ◆   Group 6: Information System Reliability Assessment Assurance Services
- ◆   Group 7: Health Care Performance Measurement Assurance Services
- ◆   Group 8: Risk Assessment Assurance Services

<u>HINTS</u>

This web site has a huge amount of information and it should provide a strong basis for your report. If you are having trouble understanding the topic, you might also want to consult articles in recent professional magazines.

THE FOLLOWING PAGES

CONTAIN THE SOLUTIONS FOR

THE SELF-CORRECTED ASSIGNMENTS IN THIS MODULE.

SOLUTION TO ASSIGNMENT I-3A-1

<u>Debt Capital</u>: The Risk-Return Tradeoff

The companies vary only in how they have invested their economic resources. Company A has placed most of its assets in inventory and has minimal cash. Company B has kept a large portion of its assets in cash and invested relatively less in inventory. In short, Company A is less liquid than Company B.

How does the difference in liquidity affect risk? If the demand for cars drops off, Company A will run out of cash long before company B. Therefore, the loan to Company A is riskier for the bank than the loan to Company B.

If the companies are charged different rates of interest, Company A will pay a higher rate than Company B.

SOLUTION TO ASSIGNMENT I-3B-2

Basic Financial Statements: Financial Statement Articulation

You have all but one element of the Statement of Retained Earnings for 1996:

Beginning retained earnings	???
Plus: net earnings for 1996	62,744,000
Less: dividends for 1996	$9,724,000)
Ending retained earnings	$390,526,000

If you work backwards, you can calculate the retained earnings `at the *beginning* of 1996 (which was the *end* of 1995!):

$390,526,000 + $9,724,000 — $62,744,000 = **$337,506,000**

MODULE INDEX

—ABC—

—DEF—

—GHI—

—JKL—

—MNO—

—PQR—

—STU—

—VWXYZ—

4

MODULE 4: GOVERNMENT AS A USER OF ACCOUNTING INFORMATION

1997-1998 edition

Table of Contents

MODULE 4: GOVERNMENT AS A USER OF ACCOUNTING INFORMATION

Estimated Time Budget

Task	Time Estimate
Reading PART A: THE ACTIVITIES OF GOVERNMENT	50 - 90 minutes
Assignments for PART A	
Assignment I-4A-1	60 - 90 minutes
Assignment I-4A-2	25 - 40 minutes
Assignment I-4A-3	60 - 90 minutes
Reading PART B: BASIC CONCEPTS OF TAXATION	50 - 90 minutes
Assignments for PART B	
Assignment I-4B-1	45 - 90 minutes
Assignment I-4B-2	45 - 60 minutes
Assignment I-4B-3	40 - 60 minutes
Assignment I-4B-4	50 - 75 minutes
Assignment I-4B-5	50 - 75 minutes
Assignment I-4B-6	90 -120 minutes
Assignment I-4B-7	90 -120 minutes
Assignment I-4B-8	20 - 30 minutes
Assignment I-4B-9	90 -120 minutes
Assignment I-4B-10	20 - 30 minutes
Assignment I-4B-11	90 - 120 minutes
Reading APPENDIX: GRAPHIC PRESENTATIONS	10 - 20 minutes

Note: These time estimates, like all time budgets for this course, should be adjusted to suit your own learning style. Time estimates for assignments assume that readings were completed before attempting assignments.

MODULE 4: GOVERNMENT AS A USER OF ACCOUNTING INFORMATION

PART A: THE ACTIVITIES OF GOVERNMENT

No man ever saw a government. I live in the midst of the Government of the United States, but I never saw the Government of the United States.
    -- Woodrow Wilson

As we began the 1990s, approximately 17 million people in the United States were employed by federal, state and local governments--roughly 10 million working for local governments, 4 million for state governments and 3 million for the federal government. What does a government do? Government activities fall into 3 major categories:

- providing public goods and services;

- generating money to pay for public goods and services; and

- administering laws.

In each of these activities, government is a user of accounting information.

PROVIDING PUBLIC GOODS AND SERVICES

The legitimate objective of government is to do for a community of people whatever they need to have done, but cannot do at all, or cannot so well do for themselves, in their separate and individual capacities.
    -- Abraham Lincoln

Kinds of Public Goods and Services

What kinds of public goods and services do governments provide? The answer to this question varies among different political systems and over time. For example, the federal government of the United States provides retirement benefits to its citizens through the Social Security system, which is not true in all countries. Retirement benefits, however, haven't always been provided by the U.S. government. Germany, for instance, had a social security system many decades before the U.S. system was established during the 1930s.

Figure I-4-1

How the U.S. Federal Government Spent Its Money, 1995

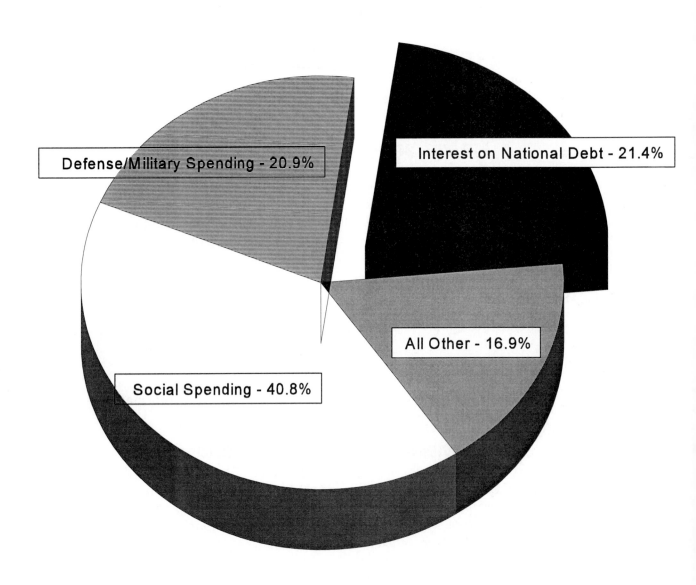

Source: OMB Data

In the United States in the 1990s, federal, state and local governments provide a variety of public goods and services including postal services, roads and highways, national defense, police protection, parks, dams, and education and health services. As can be seen in Figure I-4-1 (on the preceding page), almost half of federal outlays are for social welfare expenditures--including social security payments, public aid, health and medical programs, veterans programs, arts, education and housing. The second-highest category of federal spending is for national defense. For state and local governments, which do not spend money on defense, social welfare expenditures constitute over 60% of all outlays.

The Size of Government Operations

The operations of federal and state governments in the U.S. dwarf the size of most large public companies. In 1995, for example, the federal government had revenues of almost $1.4 trillion dollars to administer, far in excess of even the largest Fortune 500 company, General Motors. With 1995 revenues of approximately $169 billion, GM's revenues were only about 12% the size of the federal government's. Similarly, the state governments are also an impressive size. Even the state with the least revenues to manage has revenues in the billions of dollars.

Local governments are also significant providers of public goods and services. The city of New York, for example, has a multi-billion dollar annual budget, which it uses to provide such services as operating over a dozen large hospitals and maintaining tens of thousands of city-owned apartments for low-income families. The city must service over 1 million people on public assistance.

Uses of Accounting Information in Government Operations

When a governmental unit acts to provide a public good or service, it uses accounting information in much the same way as any other business or nonbusiness (not-for-profit) organization. For example, when the government provides educational services in the form of public schools, each school district faces many management decisions, such as deciding whether to build a new school, deciding how many teachers to hire, and deciding how much to spend on textbooks and classroom materials. These decisions require accounting information.

Accounting information can also be used for performance evaluation. For example, in 1993, an audit of a California county's waste management department yielded dozens of recommendations that could save the county about $1.65 million a year. One recommendation arose from the audit finding that county-operated landfills were too heavily staffed--there were so many attendants that there was usually no waiting time at all for landfill customers. The auditors calculated that 14.5 positions could be eliminated, at a savings of about $100,000 per year, and the extra waiting time for dumping would average only 45 seconds.

GENERATING MONEY TO PAY FOR PUBLIC GOODS AND SERVICES

Blessed are the young, for they shall inherit the national debt.
-- Herbert Hoover

Sources of Government Funds

Where do governments get the money needed to provide public goods and services? Governments have several options to obtain funds: (1) raising money through taxation or by charging user fees for public goods and services; (2) borrowing money by issuing debt; and (3) in the case of national governments, creating new money.

Of these options, taxation is by far the most important source of revenue to fund public spending. In 1995, for example, tax revenues and user fees financed over 90% of all U.S. government outlays. If a government's tax and user fee revenues exactly equal the government's total outlays for a particular period, a **balanced budget** exists. If tax and user fee revenues exceed outlays, there is a **budget surplus**; if they are less than outlays, there is a **budget deficit**.

In the modern United States, the federal government has frequently operated with a budget deficit. During the 1950s, the federal government had a budget surplus in 3 years and a budget deficit in 7 years. During the 1960s, there were 2 surplus years and 8 deficit years. During the 1970s and 1980s, and so far during the 1990s, every year has been a deficit year. The 1992 deficit set a new record at $290 billion; by 1996, the annual deficit had decreased to $107 billion.

These deficits must be covered by either increasing debt, which the federal government can do by issuing Treasury bills, or creating money. Creating new money can cause inflation-- that is, as the money supply expands, the purchasing power of a dollar will tend to decrease. The issuance of debt to meet a budget deficit also has a cost--interest must be paid on the debt while it is outstanding.

Public Debt

The cumulative amount of money owed by the federal government is known as the "**public debt**" or the "**national debt**." As you can imagine, with the recent pattern of federal government budget deficits, the public debt has been growing rapidly, from about $256 million in 1950 to over $3 trillion by 1990 and over $5 trillion by 1997. Figure I-4-2 (on the next page) shows the "per capita" national debt, or the average debt for each taxpayer at the start of every decade since 1950. Given the broad time range, per capita federal tax figures for these same years are provided to help you keep the public debt numbers in perspective. The public debt has grown so high that by 1996, a little less than $1 dollar out of every $6 the federal government spent went to pay interest on the debt.

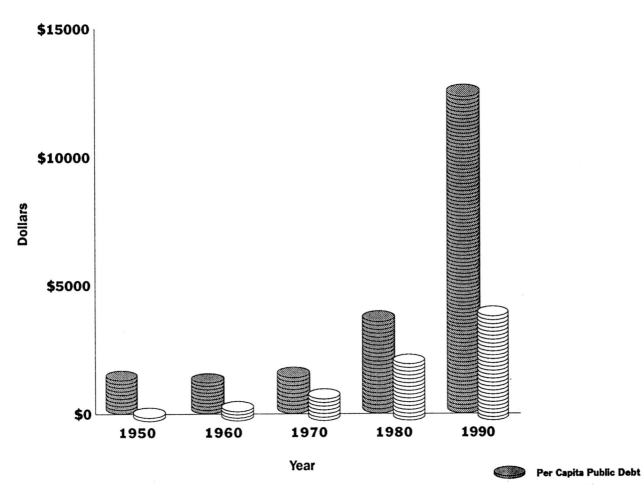

Figure I-4-2
Per Capita Public Debt and Federal Taxes, 1950-1990

Source: *Public Debt:* Department of Treasury, Financial Management Service;
Tax: Internal Revenue Service

Concern over the size of the public debt has led to growing cries for a balanced federal budget and debt reduction. Over the past decade, there have been several unsuccessful Congressional attempts to set targets for bringing the budget into balance. For example, Congress passed a law in 1985 that required incremental reduction of the budget deficit each year until 1991, when a balanced budget would be required. Before 1991 arrived, this bill was superseded by another law that set specific deficit reduction targets aimed at achieving a balanced budget by 1996. In 1997, still without a balanced budget, Congress agreed on a blueprint to balance the budget by 2002. Thus, there is growing pressure to either reduce levels of public goods and services provided by government or increase taxes.

Many state and local governments face similar fiscal pressures. Forty-nine of the 50 states (all but Vermont) are legally required to balance their budgets each year. Yet, some states struggle with deficits. In 1994, for example, the National Governors' Association and National Association of State Budget Officers reported that 10 states faced budget deficits for the year, with the prospect of needing to raise taxes or cut services to bring their budgets into balance. Facing a $7 billion shortfall, Michigan voters went to the polls in 1994 and approved a sales tax increase and other measures to raise funds for school financing.

Uses of Accounting Information in Generating Funds

When governments direct their efforts toward generating money to pay for public goods and services, accounting information often is an important resource. Accounting information can be used to: (1) provide the primary basis for tax assessment, (2) prepare budgets and plan tax policy, and (3) assess the health of the economy.

The most noticeable use of accounting information to help governments generate funds is the use of accounting information to measure the "tax base" (the amount that is subject to tax). For example, individuals and businesses must report accounting information, such as income earned or sales made, to tax authorities as part of the tax assessment process.

Governments at the federal, state and local levels also make use of accounting information in preparing budgets and planning tax policy. Accounting information can be used to help forecast expected future tax revenues and to help estimate the impact of tax changes on future revenues. For example, in 1996, Texas considered several different plans for the state to raise future revenues. One plan was to raise the sales tax rate. Accounting information was used to calculate that if sales taxes were raised from 6.25% to 6.5%, the state would gain additional revenues of $406.9 million in 1999 alone.

Moreover, governments can make use of accounting information to determine the potential costs or savings of program changes. In 1994, for example, California's governor proposed cutting welfare grants by 10% as of July 1, with another 15% drop at year-end. Accounting information was used to estimate that these cutbacks would result in $460 million of cost reductions for a year.

Accounting information also is used in "economic indicators" that help assess an economy's health. For example, in many developed nations, governments monitor the monthly change in business inventories as a leading indicator of the quarterly change in the gross national product (GNP), a measure of the current market value of all final goods and services produced in the economy in a given period. Information about inventories can also be used to provide early warning signals of periods of recession or economic upswings. Very high inventories in relation to sales, for instance, may be an early signal of impending recession. Corporate profits and tax collections are also indicators of economic trends. In 1994, Japan's Finance Ministry forecast an upturn in the economy based on information that revenues from a tax on consumer goods were rising.

Problems With Unreliable Accounting Information

Without good accounting information, it is difficult for governments to generate tax revenues, draw up reliable budgets, or prepare reliable assessments of current and future economic conditions. For example, the quality of accounting information decreases whenever a large portion of business activity takes place "underground" or "off the books"--that is, without being reported to taxing authorities or other government agencies. Off-the-books transactions are typically in cash or barter, which leaves no paper trail once the business chooses not to record the transaction.

All economies have some underground portion, which includes both illegal activities (such as drug trafficking) and otherwise legal activities (such as an unreported construction business). Some countries have large underground economies. It has been estimated that Mexico's underground economy equals almost 40% of the country's GNP. As the underground portion of an economy grows, the accounting information available to decision makers becomes less reliable, so planning, budgeting, and assessing performance become more difficult. For example, a large Mexican cement company used government statistics showing a decline in business in the construction industry to forecast a decreased demand for the company's cement products. Much to the company's surprise, so much construction was being done off the books that an increase in demand occurred instead.

Tax collection also becomes more difficult as the underground economy increases. Those companies and individuals who do pay taxes end up bearing more than their fair share of the burden because tax rates must be set higher than they would be if all income were reported. In December 1989, the Mexican Congress voted to reduce the income tax rate from 55% to 35%. Their theory was that the lower tax rates might induce some underground businesses to report their results. If enough of the underground economy could be induced to report results, government economic planning could be improved and the tax burden could be more equitably distributed.

As expected, Mexico's tax revenues did increase after the tax rates were lowered. However, tax policy alone cannot prevent an underground economy from flourishing. When the Mexican peso was devalued in the mid-1990s, citizens' buying power was cut by more than half. This economic shock resulted in a rapid increase in the underground economy. The Ciemex-Wefa Group, an economic forecasting firm, estimated that about 11.5 million Mexican citizens were in the underground economy the year after the devaluation, a 22% increase from a year earlier.

REGULATION: ADMINISTERING LAWS

Government can exist without law, but law cannot exist without government.
-- Bertrand Russell, Unpopular Essays

Uses of Accounting Information in Administering Laws

Regulation is the act of administering a law. Government is responsible for the enforcement of laws concerning such diverse areas as the operation of securities markets, banking, drug control, white-collar crime , transportation, and health and safety. In a surprising number of these areas, governments make use of accounting information.

In recent years, for example, the primary strategy against drug traffickers has been "assaulting their assets." In the United States, accountants work with such government agencies as the Drug Enforcement Administration (DEA) to follow the trail of drug money as it is "laundered" through a variety of banks and businesses. The Federal Bureau of Investigation (FBI) also makes use of accounting information in white-collar crime investigation. Over a thousand special agent accountants develop financial evidence against white collar criminals, including embezzlers, public officials who accept bribes, defense contractors who make false claims against government contracts, and members of organized crime mobs. Similar use of accounting information in law enforcement occurs at the state and local levels.

Accounting information is also used in the regulation of many industries. For instance, U.S. public utilities provide accounting information to state regulatory commissions to help them evaluate the reasonableness of rate (price) changes. Banks and savings and loan institutions report accounting information to several federal and state regulatory agencies that help enforce banking laws and uphold confidence in the banking system. The state and federal governments in the United States also regulate the offering, sale, and trading of securities.

Securities regulations are particularly important to public companies. The laws governing the offering, sale, and trading of securities affect these companies' ability to raise funds in public capital markets. Securities regulations are such an important part of government regulation that they are the focus of the remainder of Part A of this module.

SECURITIES REGULATION

When signing the Securities Act of 1933, President Roosevelt announced that the old rule of caveat emptor [let the buyer beware] would no longer apply to the sale of securities. A new standard was established--caveat vendor [let the seller beware].
-- Michael F. Barrett, Jr.
The SEC and the Accounting Profession: Issues for Congress, 1984

The most important regulatory agency for U.S. public companies is the **United States Securities and Exchange Commission** (SEC), which was created by the Securities Exchange Act of 1934 to administer and enforce federal securities laws. There are at least half a dozen key questions about the SEC and securities regulation that every business person should be able to answer:

- ♦ Why was the SEC created?

- ♦ What is the SEC's aim?

- ♦ Do securities laws change over time?

- ♦ How is the SEC organized?

- ♦ How does the SEC establish its accounting and disclosure policies?

- ♦ Are there any other important securities regulations?

If you need answers to these questions, you will find them below.

Why Was The SEC Created?

Before the famous stock market crash of 1929, the United States government did not regulate securities markets. During the autumn of 1929, the value of New York Stock Exchange-listed securities plummeted almost 80%, falling from $89 billion to $18 billion. By 1932, the value had fallen further to $15 billion. Following these large losses to investors and the related damage to the U.S. economy, Congress began an investigation of the securities industry. This investigation centered on widespread complaints about fraudulent and deceptive practices in the marketplace--including price manipulation by brokers and dealers, insider trading, and inadequate disclosure of financial information.

What kind of information was available to investors in the 1920s? At first glance, the information set appears to have much in common with the information available to today's investors. In 1926, for example, all New York Stock Exchange-listed firms published balance sheets, and 82% were audited by CPAs. But while balance sheet information was available, little income statement information was published. Only 55% of the New York Stock Exchange-listed firms disclosed sales; only 45% disclosed cost of goods sold. Moreover, the auditing profession in America was far less developed than it is today and the audit report was less informative than it is now. The "adverse opinion," now rendered when the auditor feels the financial statements are *not* fairly presented, did not yet exist as a report option. Although "qualified opinions" existed, audit reports in that era provided no indication of the significance of the auditor's reservations.

In the aftermath of the 1929 stock market crash, Congress enacted the **Securities Act of 1933** (often referred to simply as "the 1933 Act") and the **Securities Exchange Act of 1934** ("the 1934 Act"). These acts provide the basic framework of regulation for **initial public offerings** (new sales of securities to the public) and **secondary market trading** (trading after initial issuance). Additionally, these laws give the SEC regulatory power over securities markets, such as the New York Stock Exchange, and brokers, dealers and transfer agents. These acts also give the SEC the authority to prescribe the form and content of financial statements and auditor's reports for public companies.

Interestingly, the SEC was not created until the 1934 Act. The first federal securities law (the 1933 Act) was originally administered by the Federal Trade Commission (FTC). After the SEC was created by the 1934 Act, the 1933 Act was amended to transfer regulatory responsibility from the FTC to the SEC, where it still rests today.

What is the SEC's Aim?

The preamble of the Securities Act of 1933 states the aim of federal securities regulation: **"...to provide full and fair disclosure of the character of securities sold...and to prevent frauds."** To help achieve this aim, the 1933 Act requires registration of public offerings of securities and the 1934 Act requires a continuing flow of information about public companies.

Public Offerings. The 1933 Act deals with initial offerings of securities for sale to the public. With a few specific exceptions, the 1933 Act requires firms offering securities for public sale to register the securities. Registration is accomplished by filing a registration statement with the SEC.

The basic registration statement used for initial public offerings of securities is known as a **Form S-1**. The S-1 consists of 2 parts. The first part, known as the **prospectus**, includes audited financial statements, a summary of the company's history, a list of company officers and directors, and other pertinent information for potential investors. The issuer must furnish a copy of the prospectus to anyone interested in buying the security. The second part of Form S-1 contains additional disclosures, such as details about some of the financial information in the prospectus. Thus, if a potential investor wants information beyond that in the prospectus, the second part of the registration statement is a good place to look.

Form S-1 is only one of several forms that may be used to register securities under the 1933 Act. Multiple forms exist because the amount of information needed to provide "full and fair disclosure" depends on the circumstances. Suppose, for example, that 2 companies (A and B) are each preparing to offer a new issue of securities for public sale. Company A has never made a public offering before, so it has made no previous SEC filings. Company A will use a Form S-1 to register its securities. Company B has been public for many years, but is now offering additional securities for sale. If Company B has produced annual reports and other required SEC filings for at least 3 years, its new securities can be registered on a Form S-2. The Form S-2 is a streamlined version of the S-1. The simpler form can be used because potential investors already have access to some public information about Company B.

Other types of registration statements include forms for mergers and acquisitions (Form S-4), forms for registering securities offered to a company's own employees as part of an employee benefit plan (Form S-8), and forms for small issues (Form SB-2). In each case, the forms are tailored to the information needs of the potential investors.

Continuing Reports. The Securities Act of 1933 focuses on disclosure for the primary (original issue) market. The Securities Exchange Act of 1934 recognized the need for a continuing flow of information about securities that are traded publicly. This need is particularly strong in modern capital markets where the volume of secondary (after original issuance) market trading far exceeds the volume of new public offerings.

The 1934 Act reporting requirements apply to companies with securities traded on a national securities exchange. In 1964, Section 12-g of the Act extended reporting responsibilities to companies trading in the over-the-counter market. Unlisted companies with at least $5 million of assets and 500 shareholders are also subject to 1934 Act requirements.

Public companies subject to the 1934 Act must file annual registration statements. They also must file periodic reports, such as the **Form 10-K** and **Form 10-Q** annual and quarterly reports. Additional disclosures may be reported on **Form 8-K**, covering such timely disclosure matters as a change in the company's external auditors or the sale of significant business assets. The 1934 Act also sets disclosure requirements for proxy statements. **Proxy statements** describe matters to be voted on at shareholders' meetings, such as the election of new Board members or compensation plans for top management.

Figure I-4-3
What's In SEC Filings

10-K: Official annual business and financial report filed by U.S. public companies.

20-F: Official annual business and financial report or registration filed by non-U.S. registrants.

10-Q: Quarterly statements providing a continuing view of a company's financial position.

8-K: Report of unscheduled material events of importance to shareholders or the SEC.

Proxy Statement: Shareholder meeting statement listing company directors and officers, showing title, age, annual remuneration and describing votable matters.

Registration Statement: Official report containing business and financial information that issuers must file before securities may be publicly offered.

Annual Report to Shareholders: Full text of the management discussion focusing on a company's basic structure, operational results and future outlook.

Tender Offer and Acquisition Reports: Report of ownership or purchase by shareholders holding 5% or more outstanding shares.

Legend

A – always included - included-if occured or significant

F – frequently included

■ special circumstances only

TYPE OF FILING

REPORT CONTENTS	10-K	20-F	10-Q	8-K	10-C	6-K	Proxy Statement	Prospectus	'34 Act F-10 8-A 8-B	'33 Act "S" Type	ARS	Listing Application	N-SAR
Auditor													
☐ Name	A	A	■				F	A	A	A	A	■	A
☐ Opinion	A	A							A		A		A
☐ Changes				A			■						
Compensation Plans													
☐ Equity	■		■	■			F	F	A	F		■	■
☐ Monetary							A	F	A	F			
Company Information													
☐ Nature of Business	A	A				F		A	A	A		■	
☐ History	F	A					■	A	F	A			
☐ Organization and Change	F	F		A	■	F		A		F	A		
Debt Structure	A					F		A	A	A	A		A
Depreciation & Other Schedules	A	A				F		A	A	A			
Dilution Factors	A	A		F		F		A	A	A	A		
Directors, Officers, Insiders													
☐ Identification	F	A				F	A	A	A	A	F		
☐ Background							■	A	A	A	■		
☐ Holdings		A					A	A	A	A			
☐ Compensation		A					A	A	A	A			
Earnings Per Share	A	A	A			F			A		A		A
Financial Information													
☐ Annual Audited	A	A							A		A	A	A
☐ Interim Audited		A					■	■		■	■		
☐ Interim Unaudited	■		A	■		F		F		F			
Foreign Operations	A							A	A	A		F	
Labor Contracts				■					F	F			
Legal Agreements	F			■					F	F			
Legal Counsel								A		A			
Loan Agreements	F								F	F			■
Plants and Properties	A	F						F	A	F		■	
Portfolio Operations													
☐ Content (Listing of Securities)													A
☐ Management													A
Product-Line Breakout	A							A		A		■	
Securities Structure	A	A			■			A	A	A			
Subsidiaries	A	A				■			A	A			
Underwriting				■				A		A			
Unregistered Securities	■					■				A			
Block Movements				F		■			A			■	

TENDER OFFER/ACQUISITION REPORTS	13D	13 G	14D-1	14D-9	13E-3	13E-4
Name of Issuer (Subject Company)	A	A	A	A	A	A
Filing Person (or Company)	A	A	A	A	A	A
Amount of Shares Owned	A	A				
Percent of Class Outstanding	A	A				
Financial Statements of Bidders			F		F	F
Purpose of Tender Offer			A	A	A	A
Source and Amount of Funds	A		A		A	
Identity and Background Information			A	A	A	
Persons Retained Employed or to be Compensated			A	A	A	A
Exhibits	F		F	F	F	F

Source: Disclosure, Inc. • 5161 River Road, Bethesda, MD 20816 • (301) 951-1300

Access to SEC Filings. Each year, over 10,000,000 pages of disclosure documents are filed with the SEC. Figure I-4-3 (on the preceding page) summarizes the types of information that can be found in these documents. Paper or microfiche copies of SEC documents are kept on file in the SEC's public reference rooms and at many public and private libraries throughout the nation.

Additionally, information from SEC filings that have been electronically-submitted are available via the Internet on the SEC's database, known as **EDGAR** (which stands for "Electronic Data Gathering and Analysis"). Electronic filings were phased in between 1994 and 1996; all public companies now file electronically. The SEC's world-wide web site--which may be reached via **http://www.sec.gov**--provides access to EDGAR filings, as well as background information about the SEC, information about SEC enforcement actions (such as recent litigation releases and investor alerts), and information for investors (on-line publications about investing).

The EDGAR database can be searched by company name, ticker symbol, or filing type. The search can be structured to consider only recent filings or to explore the whole archive, which is currently planned to hold two years of filings at all times. All filings in the database may be viewed online, printed, or downloaded. However, the SEC web site does not yet allow for analysis of numeric data or "key word" searches which means you cannot use it to do things like locate filings of all companies with assets over $2 billion or select only companies with qualified audit opinions. Both the SEC and several commercial information providers are working on developing software that will allow key word searches in the future.

Accountants use the EDGAR database for a variety of tasks. For example, a public accounting firm may have a client wondering about how to word footnote disclosures about a particular issue. The CPA firm can use EDGAR to review the footnotes of similar entities to find examples of comparable footnotes for the client to consider. Or, filings of peer companies may provide information for managerial accountants performing a ratio analysis of how their firm compares to others in the industry.

Do Securities Laws Change Over Time?

Over the years, the SEC's regulatory authority has been expanded through amendments and additions to the federal securities laws. Most of the changes to the securities laws reflect changes in the business environment. For example, the Investment Company Act of 1940 and the Investment Advisers Act of the same year extended the SEC's authority to include regulation of investment companies and investment advisers. In 1964, as trading in the over-the-counter market grew, the securities laws were amended to make companies with securities trading in the over-the-counter market subject to SEC regulation.

In 1977, the **Foreign Corrupt Practices Act** amended the 1934 Act to make it illegal for U.S. companies to pay bribes to foreign officials. The Foreign Corrupt Practices Act (FCPA) put foreign bribes on an equal footing with domestic bribes, which had been prohibited by earlier laws. The FCPA also imposed requirements that public companies keep accurate books and records and maintain an adequate system of internal control. While keeping accurate books and records and maintaining a sound internal control system has always been part of good business practice, the FCPA added the specter of civil liability and potential criminal prosecution for failure to maintain appropriate practices.

How Is the SEC Organized?

The SEC is made up of 5 commissioners, each appointed for a 5-year term by the President of the United States, subject to confirmation by the U.S. Senate. The commissioners' terms are staggered, so that each year on June 5, one commissioner's term expires. No more than 3 commissioners at any one time may be members of the same political party.

The President also appoints one of the commissioners to chair the SEC. The chairman (or chairwoman), like the other commissioners, has only one vote on issues before the SEC. However, the chair has greater power than the other commissioners because the chair sets the agenda for the meetings and serves as CEO (chief executive officer) of the Commission. As a result, the Chair controls the budget process and the staff appointments process.

The commissioners are aided by staff at the Washington, D.C. headquarters; regional offices throughout the nation; and district offices in some of the larger cities in each region. The staff is organized into 4 main divisions--Corporation Finance, Enforcement, Market Regulation and Investment Management--and a series of offices.

Corporation Finance. The **Division of Corporation Finance**, sometimes referred to as "Corp Fin," administers the SEC's full disclosure system, including reviewing registration statements and continuing reporting filings. The volume of information filed with the SEC is very large, so the staff reviews only a sample of the filings. In fiscal 1995, for example, the staff conducted full disclosure reviews of 3,930 reporting issuers (about 30.8% of all reporting issuers). As you would expect, the filings which may be perceived to have higher risk--such as filings from first-time issuers--are the most likely to be reviewed.

Enforcement. The **Division of Enforcement** investigates possible violations of the securities laws so that the SEC can bring appropriate enforcement actions. During fiscal 1995, the Enforcement staff analyzed and responded to over 42,500 complaints.

Enforcement activity covers a broad range of legal violations, including insider trading, market manipulations, fraudulent securities offerings and financial disclosure violations. About half the 1995 complaints involved broker-dealers;

the remainder were split between issuing companies, mutual funds, banks, transfer and clearing agents, investment advisors and various financial and non-financial matters. One of the SEC's top enforcement priorities is fraudulent financial reporting. Typical cases might involve premature revenue recognition (e.g., recording a sale when no goods have yet been shipped to the "customer" and no payments have been received) or delayed recognition of losses (e.g., failing to write down the value of inventory which is known to be obsolete), both of which are discussed in Theme II of this series.

Where does the Enforcement division get its leads? Some, of course, come from the reviews conducted by the Division of Corporation Finance. In addition, the securities exchanges and the National Association of Securities Dealers (NASD) have market surveillance programs which provide leads for potential insider trading or market manipulation cases. Tips and public complaints are also sources of leads. For example, the SEC sometimes gets tips from competitors who are concerned about the behavior of others in their industry. Or, an anonymous tip can be received, such as the time someone sent in a copy of a page of an SEC filing with one footnote circled and marked "This is not GAAP [generally accepted accounting principles], it's crap." In 1995, nearly 1 in 5 investigations were prompted, at least in part, by investor complaints.

If a lead looks promising, a **"matter under inquiry"** is opened. The investigation can be done informally, where the contacted parties voluntarily provide information, or formally, where the SEC can subpoena testimony and documents. Formal investigations require approval of the Commission; informal investigations may be conducted without specific Commission authorization.

Each enforcement case is headed by an attorney. For fraudulent financial reporting cases, an accountant will be a member of the enforcement team. The team will also include other appropriate investigators, such as an analyst.

Cases don't always end in enforcement actions. Some may be resolved upon investigation. Others may be dropped for pragmatic reasons, such as a lack of clear-cut evidence. Before an official enforcement action can be taken, the staff needs the Commission's approval; settlement negotiations must also be approved. During 1994 and 1995, the SEC brought almost 1,000 actions against about 2,200 companies and individuals.

Figure I-4-4 on the following page depicts the range of sanctions available to the SEC. Although some cases are referred to the Justice Department for criminal prosecution, most enforcement actions involve either civil or administrative penalties. The SEC's primary civil remedy is an **injunctive action**, which directs the subject to comply with the law in the future. Civil injunctive actions may be accepted by consent or imposed by a United States District Court judge. Failure to comply with an injunctive action can result in fines or imprisonment. The court can also require additional remedies, such as requiring a subject company to undergo a special review by an accounting firm.

Figure I-4-4
The Range of Possible Sanctions
for SEC Enforcement Actions

ADMINISTRATIVE   **PENALTIES**

Examples: permanent or temporary denial to attorneys, accountants or other professionals of the right to practice before the SEC; censure for misconduct; permanent or temporary bar from holding office in a public company.

CIVIL PENALTIES

Examples: an injunction   directing the subject to comply with securities law in the future; money penalties.

REFERRAL FOR   **CRIMINAL PROSECUTION**

Potential penalties   include: jail sentences

The SEC's enforcement powers also include a 3-tiered system of fines for securities law violators and limited authority to issue "**cease and desist**" orders and orders requiring **disgorgement** (giving back) of illegal profits.

Administrative penalties may be agreed to by consent or result from proceedings before an administrative law judge. **Administrative penalties** include a broad range of remedies such as denials, suspensions or revocation of registrations; censure; permanent or temporary denial to attorneys, accountants, or other professionals of the right to appear or practice before the SEC; and temporary or permanent bans from holding office in a public company.

Market Regulation. The **Division of Market Regulation** oversees the operations of U.S. securities markets and market professionals. In 1995, the division had oversight over the 8 U.S. registered securities exchanges, the NASD and over-the-counter markets, and over 8,500 broker-dealers with over 58,000 offices and over 500,000 registered representatives.

Investment Management. The **Division of Investment Management** administers the regulations concerning investment advisers and the mutual fund industry. The division's responsibilities include improving communications to investment company shareholders. For example, in 1995 and 1996, the division pilot tested (with the cooperation of 8 mutual fund companies) a plan to simplify investment company prospectuses and improve risk disclosures.

Other SEC Staff. In addition to these 4 Divisions--Corporation Finance, Enforcement, Market Regulation, and Investment Management--there are several important staff offices, including:

♦ **The Office of Compliance Inspections and Examinations** conducts investigation activities to support the divisions of Market Regulation and Investment Management. During 1995, for example, this office inspected 348 investment company complexes and 1,075 investment advisors.

♦ **The Office of the Chief Accountant** is the primary adviser to the commissioners on all accounting and enforcement matters concerning accountants and auditors. The Chief Accountant also communicates with the accounting profession regarding accounting and auditing standards.

♦ **The Office of the General Counsel** is the SEC's legal adviser and focal point for litigation brought by the commission.

♦ **The Office of Economic Analysis** advises the commission on economic policy matters and supervises economic and statistical research.

♦ **The Office of International Affairs** develops legislation and takes other initiatives (such as implementing information-sharing agreements) to facilitate international cooperation between securities agencies.

How Does the SEC Establish Accounting and Disclosure Policies?

Public companies and their accountants have an ongoing relationship with the SEC. While this relationship may become adversarial during an enforcement action, the normal atmosphere should not be contentious. The SEC's role is to protect investors' interests by requiring full and fair disclosure. The SEC establishes and communicates its position on accounting and disclosure through 2 regulations--*Regulation S-X* and *Regulation S-K*--and 2 series of supplemental guidance, the *Financial Reporting Releases* and the *Staff Accounting Bulletins.*

Regulation S-X prescribes the form and content of financial statements filed with the SEC, while **Regulation S-K** covers the non-financial-statement portions of registration statements and certain periodic filings. Although the securities laws give the SEC broad rule-making authority, the SEC delegates much of the responsibility for setting accounting and auditing standards to private sector authorities, such as the Financial Accounting Standards Board and the Auditing Standards Board. The relationship between the SEC and private sector standard-setting bodies is discussed in Module 6 of this theme.

In addition, when specific accounting, auditing and reporting issues need to be addressed, **Financial Reporting Releases** (FRRs) are published. As official releases of the Commission, the policies stated in the FRRs (other than those which deal with enforcement matters) become incorporated into Regulation S-X and S-K. Also as needed, informal interpretations by the SEC staff are published in **Staff Accounting Bulletins** (SABs). Regulations S-X and S-K, the FRRs, and the SABs thus become part of a database of guidance on proper accounting and disclosure available to companies and their accountants.

In addition to published guidance, the SEC encourages open communication with its staff. Companies and their accountants and auditors are encouraged to discuss significant questions affecting the company's registration statements or other filings with appropriate members of the SEC staff on a consultative basis (before the filings are made) in order to reduce the potential for future problems. Sometimes, an organization asks the SEC staff whether it is acceptable to treat a transaction in a particular way. If the staff thinks the treatment is appropriate, they issue a written response. These letters are often called **"no action" letters** because they state that "the staff will recommend no action to the Commission" if the transaction is treated as proposed.

Are There Any Other Important Securities Regulations?

Securities can be offered in primary markets or traded in secondary markets in multiple states or nations. Each state or nation may regulate securities offerings or trade within its boundaries.

State Securities Laws. In the United States, securities law is established and regulated by the states, as well as at the federal level. Companies and individuals must comply with the laws of each jurisdiction in which they do business. The state securities laws are known as **"blue sky laws"** because a 1917 court case (Hall v. Geiger-Jones Co.) portrayed them as preventing "speculative schemes which have no more basis than so many feet of blue sky."

Although the state securities laws are not uniform, some commonalties exist. Most state securities laws contain antifraud provisions and require registration of broker-dealers and their agents. Also, securities generally (except in a few New England and Mid-Atlantic states) must be registered with a state agency before they can be sold in the state. Thus, if an underwriter intends to distribute a new securities offering nationally, the offering must be "blue-skyed" (registered) in most of the states, as well as with the SEC. A widely-distributed offering could involve over 40 state registrations.

International Securities Laws. On an international level, the regulatory powers of governments vary depending on the country's political system and stage of economic development. Some countries--like Taiwan--have relatively little regulation of publicly traded securities. Other countries--for example, Japan--regulate securities with agencies very similar in authority to the U.S. Securities and Exchange Commission. However, even if the regulatory power in 2 countries is similar, the specific regulations can be different.

As businesses become increasingly international, the number of companies listing their securities on exchanges in more than one country is growing. These companies are subject to the regulatory authority of each country where their securities are traded. For instance, foreign firms trading in U.S. markets must file an annual **Form 20-F**, which is similar to the domestic Form 10-K, but with somewhat relaxed disclosure requirements.

The disclosure requirements for foreign firms are relaxed in some areas where accounting procedures differ across national boundaries. Relaxation of requirements is most likely if conformance with U.S. disclosure requirements could be costly enough to discourage foreign companies from entering U.S. capital markets. For example, U.S. and Japanese disclosure requirements differ concerning segment information. The Form 10-K filing of a U.S. company must report revenue and net income for each major business segment. When filing a U.S. Form 20-F, a Japanese company--which is not required to make segment disclosures by Japanese accounting standards or securities laws--is only required to disclose segment revenues, with some supplemental narrative discussion required if revenue and net income contributions differ substantially.

Even when information is adequately disclosed, international differences in accounting standards can lead to significant differences in reported accounting information. For example, consider the 1993 financial reports of Germany's largest manufacturer, Daimler-Benz AG, a company that includes the Mercedes-Benz automotive subsidiary and Deutsche Aerospace among its divisions. Since Daimler-Benz became the first German company to list shares on the New York

Stock Exchange in 1993, the company now prepares financial reports based on both German and U.S. standards. Under German standards, which are tied heavily to tax laws, Daimler-Benz reported a 1993 consolidated net income of 651 million Deutsche-marks (about $390 million). However, under U.S. standards, which are much less tied to tax laws, the company reported a net *loss* of 1.8 billion DM (about $1.05 billion). Differences of this magnitude complicate decisions based on accounting information.

As more and more companies want access to global capital markets, the calls for harmonization of accounting standards may be expected to mount. Broader access to capital markets has been beneficial to Daimler-Benz. In the first year after the company was listed on the New York Stock Exchange, the company's list of U.S. stockholders doubled from about 4% to close to 8%. The importance of access to capital markets was highlighted by another Daimler-Benz decision in 1995. The company reported well over 1 billion DM (about $720,000) of restructuring costs (e.g., costs related to employee layoffs), which complied with U.S. accounting standards but was not necessary per German standards. The restructuring costs were the major reason why Daimler-Benz reported a large loss. The willingness to voluntarily report bad news is a powerful testimony to the importance of access to capital markets.

As business becomes more global, securities enforcement efforts also must be coordinated internationally. For example, how can the SEC obtain evidence relevant to violation of U.S. securities laws when the evidence may be located outside the United States? At present, the SEC approaches this problem by developing information-sharing agreements with various foreign authorities, including those of Brazil, Canada, France, Italy, Japan, Luxembourg, the Netherlands, Switzerland and the United Kingdom. When no formal information-sharing agreement exists, the SEC cooperates informally with foreign regulators.

LEARNING MORE ABOUT GOVERNMENT ACTIVITIES

Where in your college education will you learn more about government activities than you already know from your prior education and your experiences as a citizen? Courses in public sector economics and macroeconomics can be important contributors to your understanding of the activities of government. Elective courses in political science and government, or political economy and public policy, offer other avenues to expand your knowledge.

Additionally, accounting and finance courses can improve your understanding of the role of taxation in business decisions. Accounting courses also cover the details of U.S. and international tax regulations. Business law courses can improve your understanding of securities law.

If you are planning a career in international business, it is important to understand that all governments do not operate in the same manner as the U.S. government. Courses in the culture and politics of foreign countries (as well as foreign language courses) can help prepare you for productive careers in international business.

THE ROLE OF ACCOUNTANTS IN GOVERNMENT

Government Accounting Jobs

One in 10 accountants in the United States is currently employed in a position within the federal, state or local government.

Government operations require the same types of basic accounting services as any business or not-for-profit organization. So, as you would expect, many government accountants have job responsibilities that involve financial accounting. For example, a large number of accountants are employed by the Department of Defense to keep track of the financial operations of the military services. Many government accountants also have managerial accounting responsibilities, such as keeping track of the actual spending of government agencies in relation to budgeted spending levels.

Auditors play an important role at all levels of government. For example, auditors from the **General Accounting Office** (GAO) examine the operational efficiency of federal departments, agencies and programs. They also perform contract examinations, systems reviews, and special congressional assignments. State and city accountants and auditors fulfill similar roles for other levels of government.

Government accountants also may be involved in jobs with responsibilities that are unique to government. In particular, accountants work in many agencies that are responsible for administering laws. The Securities and Exchange Commission, the Internal Revenue Service and the Defense Contract Audit Agency are examples of agencies where accountants play a role in administering laws.

As you already know, accountants working at the Securities and Exchange Commission may monitor public company reports or investigate potential violations of securities laws. Many accountants in the Internal Revenue Service, the largest federal employer of accountants, are compliance auditors--that is, their job is to audit tax returns to determine if the taxpayers complied with all aspects of tax law. The Defense Contract Audit Agency, as its name implies, is responsible for the review and appraisal of private firms and universities conducting research or manufacturing products under contracts with the Department of Defense.

Accountants are often attracted to government jobs by the opportunity to serve the public. Government jobs also are valued because they offer good benefits and excellent job security. As an indication of the attractiveness of government jobs for accountants, consider that in 1993, the GAO reported having as many as 5,000 to 7,000 applicants for 250 openings, with three-quarters of GAO's new hires having advanced degrees. On the other hand, the major drawback of government jobs is often the salary level. Government jobs tend to pay less than equivalent positions in the private sector.

The Future of Government Accounting

If you read the newspaper, listen to television or radio news broadcasts, or read current events magazines, you cannot go very long without hearing or reading criticisms of government financial management. Federal, state and local governments are criticized for excessive waste and mismanagement of financial resources. Signs of fiscal stress seem to be everywhere. Budget deficits, growing taxes and increasing public debt are the subjects of much local and national concern.

These problems have built up over many years. In part, they reflect an earlier era when the importance of good accounting in government was largely unrecognized. For example, until the 1980s, it was rare for city or state governments to have outside audits. As another example, the federal government has multiple different, and incompatible, accounting systems which were created over time as new departments, agencies and programs were established. The large number of different systems makes it difficult to quickly obtain government-wide accounting information and makes it difficult to compare performance across government units.

Because of the growing recognition of government fiscal problems, the next several decades promise to be a time of great opportunity for accountants to contribute to the operations of government. Both accountants within government, and those outside of government, are actively involved in the ongoing debate about the best ways to improve government operations.

MODULE 4:
GOVERNMENT AS A USER OF ACCOUNTING INFORMATION

PART B: BASIC CONCEPTS OF TAXATION

The point to remember is that what the government gives it must first take away.
-- John Coleman, address to Detroit Chamber of Commerce

Each year, the Tax Foundation calculates "Tax Freedom Day"--the number of days in the work year an average U.S. taxpayer must toil just to pay federal, state, and local taxes. In 1997, for example, Tax Freedom Day came 129 days into the work year, on May 9. The tax burden, of course, varies from state to state. In 1997, citizens of Louisiana had the lowest tax burden, reaching Tax Freedom Day on April 26. At the other extreme, New York taxpayers had the longest haul, not reaching Tax Freedom Day until May 23.

Taxes are required payments of money for the support of governments. Depending on the form of government, taxes may be imposed by fiat or by the consent of the governed. In the United States, the federal government's basic power to tax is embodied in the first article of the U.S. Constitution:

> *The Congress shall have the power to lay and collect taxes, duties, imposts and excises, to pay the debts and provide for the common defense and general welfare of the United States; but all duties, imposts and excises shall be uniform throughout the United States.*

Citizens of the United States are also subject to taxation by state and local governments. Finally, in some states, special districts (such as school districts or water districts) have the power to tax.

In this part of Module 4, we'll take a look at a number of topics that affect taxpayers. While our primary focus will be on taxation in the United States, we'll also consider some issues that affect taxpayers throughout the world. The topics we'll cover include:

♦ the different types of taxes,

♦ how taxes are calculated,

- the goals of taxation,

- how taxes are enacted (particularly in the United States), and

- tax complexity/simplicity.

TYPES OF TAXES

...most colonies imposed a tax on bachelors over the age of twenty-five, while Virginia had a window tax.
-- Robert Kozub, "Antecedents of the Income Tax in Colonial America," *The Accounting Historians Journal*, 1983

How many kinds of taxes are you familiar with? When most people think of taxes, they automatically think of income taxes. This is rational, since income taxes provide a substantial portion of tax revenues. But, there were no federal income taxes until 1862, and some states--for example, Nevada--have no state income taxes to this day, so there are obviously additional kinds of taxes. In fact, there are many kinds of taxes, which generally fall into 4 categories: head taxes, income taxes, wealth taxes and consumption taxes. In addition, user fees (fees charged for the use of public goods or services) can be a form of taxation.

Head Taxes

Head taxes, also known as **poll taxes**, are no longer in use in the United States. In colonial times, when the economy was relatively undeveloped, taxes were imposed directly on people. For example, in 1641, the colony of Maryland raised revenues to support its government by imposing a tax (payable in 15 pounds of tobacco) on every free man or woman and every servant over 12 years old. Head taxes are most likely to exist in undeveloped economies, where distinctions between people based on wealth or income tend to be small.

Income Taxes

Income taxes are levied on the income earned by a person or business. There are 2 major kinds of income taxes--general income taxes (federal income tax and state income tax) and payroll taxes (Social Security and unemployment taxes).

Federal Income Taxes. U.S. federal income taxes first were collected in 1862, as a means to raise the money needed to fight the Civil War. At the same time, a federal office--the Commissioner of Internal Revenue--was established to administer the tax laws passed by Congress. This office has evolved into today's Internal Revenue Service.

After the Civil War, the government's expenses (and need for revenues) decreased dramatically. Consequently, income taxes were abolished in 1872.

They were revived in 1894, but only for a short time, as income taxes were declared unconstitutional in 1895. The U.S. Constitution (in article 1, section 9) specified that any direct taxes imposed on citizens had to be proportional to population--that is, states with a greater population should bear more of the burden than states with a lower population. Since, by the late 1800s (as well as today), income was not distributed proportionally among citizens of the various states, an income tax violated this constitutional requirement. In 1913, the Sixteenth Amendment specifically granted Congress legal authority to tax the income of individuals and corporations:

> *The Congress shall have power to lay and collect taxes on incomes, from whatever source derived, without apportionment among the several States, and without regard to any census or enumeration.*

Today, income taxes are the primary source of revenue for the U.S. federal government, as well as for the governments of many other nations. Multinational businesses are subject to the tax laws of each country in which they operate. As you can imagine, paying taxes to multiple countries can quickly become a complicated process.

While many countries, such as Switzerland, assess income tax only on income earned within their national boundaries, the United States assesses income tax on all *worldwide* earnings of U.S. corporations. In order to prevent double taxation of earnings, the U.S. gives its multinational corporations a "**foreign tax credit.**" This credit reduces the U.S. tax liability of the multinational corporation either by granting the company credit for taxes paid to other nations, or by letting the company deduct its foreign earnings from its U.S. taxable income.

Many nations also enter into **tax treaties** to establish policies on all manner of international tax issues. For example, a tax treaty may specify whether interest earned in one country by a citizen of another country will be subject to tax withholding, and, if it is, will specify the withholding rate.

State and Local Income Taxes. While there are still a few states (for example, Nevada) that are income-tax free, most U.S. state and local governments depend heavily on income taxes for raising revenues. Corporations doing business in multiple states must keep track of the portion of their income earned in each state so they can pay the appropriate state income taxes. Similarly, individuals who work in more than one state over the course of a year must apportion their income between the states for income tax purposes.

Payroll Taxes. Payroll taxes are another example of an income tax. In the United States, payroll taxes are collected to help finance Social Security benefits and unemployment insurance. Unlike general income taxes, which apply to all sources of income, **payroll taxes** are based only on wages and salaries--hence the name "payroll" tax. Thus, for example, interest income is subject to income tax, but not to Social Security or unemployment taxes.

Payroll taxes may also differ from general income taxes in another way. Payroll taxes can be assessed simultaneously on both the employer and the employee. For example, both employers and employees are responsible for payment of **Social Security taxes**--called **FICA** taxes after the **Federal Insurance Contribution Act** that established Social Security taxes and benefits. For 1996, FICA taxes rates were 6.2% on employee wages up to $62,700 plus another 1.45% due on every dollar of wages to cover Medicare. Thus, if an employee's 1996 salary was $70,000, both the employee and the employer would pay $4,902.40 of FICA taxes [calculation: (6.2% x $62,700) + (1.45% x $70,000) = $3,887.40 + $1,015.00 = $4,902.40].

Wealth Taxes

Taxes may also be levied on wealth embodied in assets or property. Common types of **wealth taxes** include real estate taxes, personal property taxes, and gift and estate taxes. Wealth taxes--particularly real estate and personal property taxes--are an important source of revenue for many state and local governments in the United States.

Real Estate Taxes. Real estate taxes are the most common type of property taxes. Taxes on real property (land and items permanently attached to land) may be imposed on privately owned homes, land and business property. They are usually assessed by county governments, special tax districts (such as school districts or water districts), or local governments, although the states generally establish guidelines for local property tax assessment.

Personal Property Taxes. Personal property taxes may be assessed on anything that isn't real property, which is just about anything other than land that you might own--e.g., boats, cars, livestock, or business inventories. Taxes on livestock, for example, were a major source of U.S. federal revenues when the nation's economy depended heavily on agriculture. As the economy became less dependent on agriculture, livestock taxes decreased in importance, but they still exist today.

Estate and Gift Taxes. Estate and gift taxes must be paid on estates or gifts above a certain threshold amount. For example, if a U.S. citizen or resident died in 1996, a federal estate tax return had to be filed if the estate had a gross value of $600,000 or more.

Consumption Taxes

Consumption taxes are levied on expenditures for goods and services. Consumption taxes include sales taxes, use taxes, excise taxes, import and export duties, and value-added taxes.

Sales Taxes. **Sales taxes** are a familiar form of consumption tax that apply to most retail sales. Sales taxes are collected by the retailer from the consumer at the time of sale. The first sales taxes in the U.S. were imposed during the War of 1812. Sales taxes on gold, silverware, jewelry and watches provided funding for the war. At the start of 1997, the U.S. did not have a federal sales tax, but for all but a few states (e.g., Alaska) retail sales taxes were an important source of state revenues. In addition, many county and city authorities also levy sales taxes. For example, in 1995, the average combined sales tax rate was 8.17% (1.61% city, 1.44% county and 5.12% state).

Use Taxes. Use taxes are a variation of sales taxes. **Use taxes** generally apply to the storage, use or purchase of personal property. State use taxes are commonly applied to lease or rental transactions, or to major items (such as cars) purchased outside of the state.

Excise Taxes. **Excise taxes** are taxes on the sale or use of a specific kind of good or service (as opposed to sales taxes, which are imposed on retail sales in general). In the early years of the U.S. federal government, no tax revenues were collected. Government operations were funded by donations from the states. Later, excise taxes became one of the first sources of tax revenue for the federal government, coming into prominence during the Civil War years. From 1791 to 1802, federal excise taxes included taxes on alcohol, carriages, sugar, tobacco and snuff. Today, the primary federal excise taxes cover cigarettes, alcoholic beverages, and motor fuels. Other federal excise taxes are imposed on such items as airline tickets and long-distance telephone calls. Additionally, all 50 states impose a tax on liquid fuels (gasoline and diesel fuels). Other state excise taxes cover a wide variety of goods and services, such as airline tickets, beer, firearms, fishing equipment, liquor, tires, tobacco products and utilities.

Excise taxes differ from sales taxes in several ways. First, unlike sales taxes, which are collected at the point of sale, excise taxes are typically collected at the point of manufacture. They are still a form of consumption tax, however, as consumers bear the ultimate tax burden in the form of increased product prices. Second, whereas sales taxes are **ad valorem taxes** (taxes assessed according to value), many excise taxes are assessed according to quantity. Thus, while the amount of a sales tax on a dress or suit will differ depending on whether you buy the item at full price or on sale, the excise tax on a pack of cigarettes or a six-pack of beer will be the same regardless of the price you pay for the item. For example, in Massachusetts, the tax on a pack of cigarettes is 76 cents, no matter what the price of the pack.

Excise taxes are also known as **"luxury" taxes** or **"sin" taxes**. The "luxury" tax nickname came about because use of some products and services subject to excise taxes, such as airline travel and long-distance telephone calls, may be indicative of a better than minimal standard of living. The "sin" tax moniker arose when excise taxes were imposed on products, such as cigarettes and alcohol, that society somehow frowns on or wishes to discourage.

Import and Export Duties. Import and export duties, also known as **tariffs** or **customs duties**, are a variation of excise taxes which apply to international trade. **Import duties** are taxes on products brought in from foreign countries. **Export duties** are taxes on products shipped out of the country. In the early history of the United States, import duties were an important source of tax revenues. In 1817, for example, Congress revoked all internal taxes. For the next several decades, the federal government was supported by import duties. Now, import and export taxes are only a minor source of revenue for the U.S. federal government and for most developed nations. However, import and export taxes are major sources of revenue for some lesser developed countries because it is relatively easier to value and monitor goods which cross national borders than income earned within the country.

Value-Added Taxes. As its name implies, a **value-added tax** (or **VAT**) is a tax on the value added to a product or service at each stage of the production and distribution process. For example, if a business buys an item of inventory for $50 and sells it for $75, the value added is $25. The major difference between value-added taxes and sales, use or excise taxes is that a VAT is a multi-stage tax. The VAT is collected at each stage of the production and distribution process, whereas the other consumption taxes are collected at a single point in the process.

Value-added taxes, which were first suggested by a German industrialist in 1918, are major sources of revenues in all countries of the European Union (EU) and all but 2 of the world's other major industrialized countries (Australia and the United States). In order to promote trade between member nations, the EU requires member countries to use value-added taxes rather than sales taxes (which are known as turnover taxes in Europe). The logic to this requirement is that the multi-staged VAT allows taxes to be collected at each step of the production and distribution process, so that every country in the chain can receive its fair portion of the tax. Most VAT systems also exempt goods for export, but tax imports. Because the U.S. relies on federal corporate income taxes rather than a VAT, critics argue that U.S. goods are less competitive in international markets than they could be.

The U.S. does not currently use value-added taxes at the federal level and there is little use of VAT at the state level. The U.S. Congress has debated the possibility of adding a federal VAT or a similar broad-based consumption tax for years. However, many state and local jurisdictions that impose sales taxes are against a broad-based consumption tax at the federal level.

User Fees

User fees are just what they sound like--charges for the lease, purchase or use of a particular public good or service. Examples of user fees include tolls paid to cross bridges, campsite fees at a public park, fees paid for a hunting or fishing license, charges paid to obtain a copy of a birth or death certificate, fees to buy stamps for mailing letters, and tuition charges at public colleges and universities.

Economically, a user fee has some of the characteristics of a market price. People who directly benefit from the good or service are asked to pay for it. If the user fee is increased, demand for the good or service may fall. For example, if hunting license fees are raised high enough, hunting may decrease.

However, user fees generally lack many of the characteristics of a market price. Most user fees bear little relation to the fair market value of the good or service. For instance, toll bridges usually charge the same toll during rush-hour as during non-rush hour, whereas market demand during these 2 periods can be very different. Also, many user fees do not even cover the costs of providing the good or service. For example, tuition fees at public universities often cover only a fraction of the cost of educating a student. Fees for campsites at state or national parks do not even approach the rental value of the land.

All taxes are the price we pay for public goods and services. User fees differ from other taxes mostly in that the charges can be attached to a particular good or service received. Thus, economically, user fees can be viewed as a form of taxation, albeit one that may sometimes be perceived as more equitable than most taxes.

In recent years, many state and local governments have turned to establishing or increasing user fees as a way to raise new revenues to help balance budgets. At the federal level, President Clinton's proposed budget for fiscal 1995 included dozens of new and increased user fees to raise $1.5 billion of revenues. One reason for the popularity of user fees is that politicians seem to think the public will accept user fees more willingly than income or sales tax increases. Often, announcements of proposed user fees describe the fees as a "cost reduction" device, rather than a tax.

There is, however, ample evidence that the public views user fees as a form of taxation. Reflecting public sentiment, the Capitol Steps, a political satire troupe made up of current and former congressional aides, crafted a song that recognizes the relationship between user fees and taxes. A Capitol Steps member--pretending to be former President George Bush--sings the song to the tune of "Fifty Ways to Leave Your Lover":

> *You heard my campaign promise I would never raise a tax*
> *And if I try, I know that I would face right-wing attacks*
> *Well, since I got myself elected I have seen those budget facts*
> *But I've got fifty ways to hide new taxes*
> *I've got nifty ways to hide new taxes*
> *Just call it a fee, Lee*
> *A revenue plan, Stan*
> *Just cough up the dough, Mo*
> *An S&L fee*

HOW TAXES ARE CALCULATED

How much money did you make last year? Mail it in.
-- Stanton Delaplane, <u>San Francisco Chronicle</u> column, March 7, 1934

Tax Liability = Tax Rate x Tax Base

All tax calculations follow a very simple formula:

Tax Liability = Tax Rate x Tax Base

For example, if you purchase a tape cassette for $9.98 in a jurisdiction that has a 6% sales tax, your tax liability is calculated as:

Tax Rate x Tax Base = Tax Liability
6%   x $9.98   = $ .60 (rounded to nearest cent)

Once you know the tax rate and tax base, the tax liability calculation is simple. However, complexities can arise in determining the appropriate measure of the tax base, and in some cases, the appropriate tax rate. Moreover, once the tax liability is computed, there may be tax credits which can be used to reduce the liability. Also, it is important to recognize that there may be differences between income for tax purposes and income for financial reporting purposes.

The Tax Base

The **tax base** is the object of taxation--the particular wealth, consumption, income or head total that is being taxed. The tax base in the example above was simple to measure--it was the purchase price of the tape cassette. However, the calculation of the tax base is not always so direct. In arriving at the appropriate tax base, you need to consider possible exemptions (or exclusions) and deductions.

Exemptions or Exclusions. Let's go back to the store where we bought the cassette tape a few minutes ago. Suppose it is a large variety store. The second time you go to the store, you purchase another tape cassette for $9.98 and 4 food items--a loaf of bread, a jar of peanut butter, a jar of jelly and a gallon of milk--for $7.50. Your total purchases now cost $17.48, but when you pay for the items, you find you are still charged only $ .60 sales tax. Why? The reason the sales tax doesn't change is that not all your purchases are included in the tax base. Some purchases, such as food items in many areas, are **exempt** (or free) from tax. Thus, in calculating the tax base for the second example, you must subtract the exempted items.

Exemptions, or **exclusions**, exist for many types of taxes. For example, consider the 1864 federal tax on swine and sheep--livestock owners paid 10 cents tax for a slaughtered swine and 5 cents for a slaughtered sheep (or 2 cents if slaughtered for the pelt), but with an exemption. The exemption was that no tax was charged on a total of up to 20 sheep or swine slaughtered for personal use. As a more modern example, U.S. taxpayers are granted an exemption for a certain amount of their personal income. In 1995, single taxpayers with income of $114,700 or less and no dependents got a personal exemption of $2,500.

Deductions. In addition to considering possible exemptions, some tax bases naturally require multi-step calculations. Consider income as a tax base. The calculation of taxable income begins with gross income (income from all sources), from which exemptions must be subtracted. To complete the calculation of taxable income, allowable expenses and losses must also be deducted. Thus, in calculating **taxable income** (the tax base), you must take into account both **exclusions** (receipts which are exempt from tax) and **deductions** (expenses and losses which may be offset against receipts).

The Tax Rate

The **tax rate** is the percentage charge (or other unit charge) levied on the tax base. Sometimes, the tax rate is simple--like the 6% sales tax rate in the example at the start of this section. Other times, the tax rate may be a bit more complex.

Multiple tax rates may apply to the calculation of a particular tax liability. For example, most countries with value-added taxes use multiple rates--a standard rate, a reduced rate for items deemed to be necessities, and a higher than standard rate for items deemed to be luxuries. In Spain, for instance, there is a standard VAT rate for most goods, but a lower percentage rate applies to necessities (such as food) and a higher percentage rate applies to luxury items.

Graduated (or **progressive**) tax rates may also be used. With a graduated rate, the higher the tax base, the greater the tax rate becomes. For example, for 1996, U.S. corporate income tax was assessed at a graduated rate of 15% on the first $50,000 of taxable income, 25% on the next $25,000 of taxable income, 34% on taxable income between $75,001 and $10 million, and 35% on income over $10 million. Tax rates may also be complicated by the addition of a **surtax**, which is a tax on top of (or in addition to) a basic tax rate. For U.S. corporations in 1996, there was a 5% surtax for corporations with taxable income between $100,000 and $335,000 and a 3% surtax on incomes between $15,000,000 and $18,333,333.

Tax Credits

After the tax liability is calculated, tax credits may be used to reduce the liability. Unlike exemptions, exclusions and deductions, which apply to the calculation of the tax base, a **tax credit** is a direct (dollar-for-dollar) reduction in the computed tax liability.

The **foreign tax credit**, for example, allows multinational firms to reduce their U.S. income taxes by the amount of taxes paid to foreign countries. Another example of a tax credit is the research tax credit. At the start of 1997, for instance, businesses that invested in qualified research and experimentation expenditures received a credit (amounting to 20% of their expenditures beyond a certain base amount) against their tax liability. On personal income tax returns, limited credits are allowed for child care needed due to a parent's employment.

Book-Tax Differences

There may be differences between the way transactions are measured for financial accounting purposes and for tax purposes. This is particularly true for income taxes. These differences are commonly referred to as "**book-tax differences**." Book-tax differences may occur for several reasons.

Different User Groups. One reason for book-tax differences is that, in some cases, tax law specifies different accounting methods for calculating taxable income than generally accepted accounting principles specify for calculating net income for financial reporting purposes. Why do these differences between tax accounting and financial accounting exist?

The answer is simple: differences between tax accounting and financial accounting exist because the needs of the user groups are different. Governments using accounting information for tax purposes have one set of needs--they want to raise revenue and, as we shall discuss more fully in the next section, they may want to encourage or discourage certain activities. Owners and creditors using accounting information from financial reports have another set of needs--they want to make investment and credit decisions. These different needs are sometimes best served by different accounting methods.

Book-Tax Differences: An Example. Thinking through an example may help you understand how different user needs can lead to differences between tax accounting and financial accounting:

> *Suppose a business is being sued because one of its products has injured someone. The company and its attorneys believe that it is <u>probable</u> (though not guaranteed) that the business will be held liable (required to pay damages) to the plaintiff. However, the case has not yet been settled, so the liability is contingent upon settlement or a trial decision at a future date. Nonetheless, a range of potential payments can be estimated based on previous product liability cases.*

The example is summarized in Figure I-4-5 on the following page and discussed in more detail below. There are 2 questions to consider:

♦ How would owners and creditors view this contingent liability for the purposes of computing net income for financial reports?

♦ How would taxing authorities view this contingent liability for the purpose of computing taxable income?

Figure I-4-5
Book-Tax Differences: An Example

The FACTS

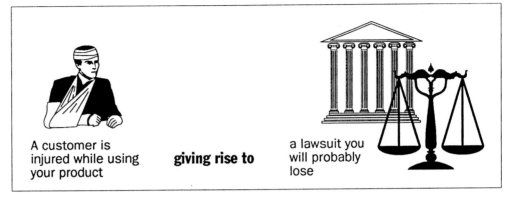

A customer is
injured while using
your product   **giving rise to**   a lawsuit you
will probably
lose

Point of View	**Owners and Creditors**	**Taxing Authorities**
Key Questions for each User Group	*Related to a past transaction?* **(Yes.)** *Loss likely?* **(Yes.)** *Amount reasonbly estimable?* **(Yes.)**	*Already paid?* **(No.)** *Definite obligation?* **(No.)**
Appropriate Accounting Treatment	*Include the estmated loss in the computation of financial accounting income.*	*Ignore the estimated loss in the computation of taxable income.*

"BOOKS" **"TAX"**

First, think about this example from the viewpoint of owners and creditors. Should the estimated loss be taken into account in calculating net income for financial accounting purposes? Generally accepted accounting principles say *yes*--the loss, which relates to a past product sale, is likely to occur and reasonably estimable. The probable liability clearly is relevant information for investors and creditors. So, the loss will be recognized in the amount of the most likely estimate in the range of potential payments (or the smallest estimate in the range if the most likely amount cannot be determined). Net income for financial reporting purposes will be reduced by the amount of the estimated loss.

Next, consider this example from the viewpoint of taxing authorities. Should the estimated loss be deducted in calculating taxable income? Tax law says *no*--the obligation isn't yet definite and will not be until some time in the future. No loss can be deducted in computing taxable income until the settlement is paid.

In this example, all else equal, taxable income will be higher than income for financial reporting purposes. However, "all else" is rarely equal. There are many possible book-tax differences, some which cause tax income to be higher than book income and others which do the reverse.

Different Preparer Goals. The second major reason for the existence of book-tax differences occurs in situations where multiple acceptable methods exist to account for the same transaction. Taxpayers are free to choose among the acceptable methods for both financial accounting and tax accounting purposes. Will they always choose the same method for both purposes? No. In some situations, they will decide to handle a transaction one way for financial reporting purposes and another way for tax purposes.

Why would this happen? Once again, remember that the reason for computing income for tax purposes and for financial reporting purposes differs. The preparer's goal in computing income is different in the 2 settings:

♦ **Tax accounting goal: wealth maximization.** The reason for computing taxable income is to determine the base for computation of tax liability. Taxpayers are neither obliged to, nor expected to, pay more than their legal share of taxes. Thus, taxpayers should be expected to make accounting choices for tax purposes that legally maximize their wealth--which usually means minimizing their taxable income, and thus, their taxes.

♦ **Financial accounting goal: fair presentation.** On the other hand, the reason for computing financial accounting income is to measure operating results fairly for reporting to external users. To be presented fairly, the accounting income reported in financial statements should be neither overly optimistic nor overly pessimistic. It would not be in the best interests of users of financial statements for accounting income to be minimized.

We'll discuss book-tax differences in more detail in later Themes of this series. For now, however, it's important to understand that an organization's taxable income and its financial reporting income need not be the same amount.

GOALS OF TAXATION

The art of taxation consists in so plucking the goose as to obtain the largest possible amount of feathers with the smallest possible amount of hissing.
-- Jean-Baptiste Colbert, 1665

In establishing tax policies, governments have 3 basic goals:

♦ to raise revenues;

♦ to maintain equity in the tax system; and

♦ to achieve social goals.

Raising Revenues

The first and foremost goal of taxation is to raise revenues. Taxes, after all, exist to support the government and fund the provision of public goods and services.

Once a revenue goal is set, tax policy-makers must decide how the goal will be met. Should there be a wealth tax? an income tax? a consumption tax? some combination? What should be included in the tax base? What should the tax rate structure be? The possibilities are almost endless. For example, as Figure I-4-6 (on the next page) illustrates, the same amount of revenue can be raised either by using a high tax rate with a low tax base or by using a low tax rate with a high tax base. More exemptions, deductions and credits can be part of the system for the high rate-low base option than for the low rate-high base option.

Decisions about the best ways to raise revenues will depend on factors such as enforceability and ease of administration. For example, countries with cash-and-barter economies may choose not to use income taxes as they would be difficult to enforce. With cash-and-barter systems, it is difficult for tax collectors to verify how much income has been earned.

On the other hand, one reason for the popularity of value-added taxes in industrialized nations is that they are fairly easy to enforce. Remember that at each stage of a VAT, tax is charged on the difference between the proceeds for the sale of an item and its purchase cost. The seller has a clear incentive to obtain documentation for the purchase price, as the purchase invoices become support

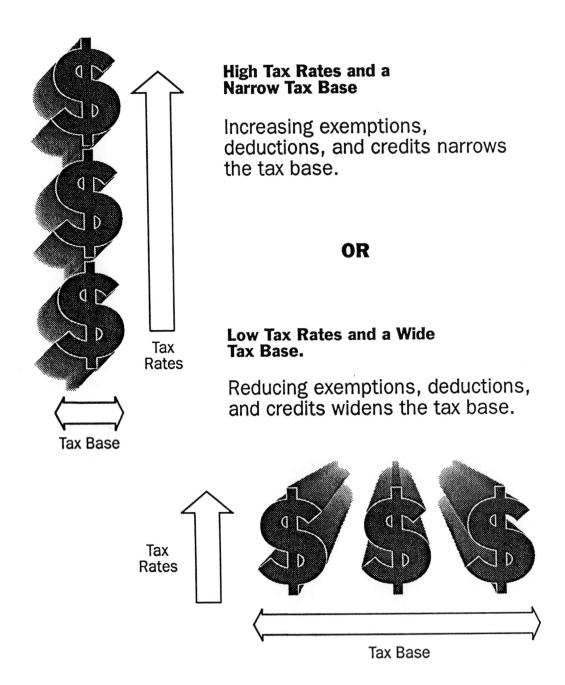

Figure I-4-6
Alternative Ways to Raise the Same Amount of Revenues

High Tax Rates and a Narrow Tax Base

Increasing exemptions, deductions, and credits narrows the tax base.

OR

Low Tax Rates and a Wide Tax Base.

Reducing exemptions, deductions, and credits widens the tax base.

Tax Rates

Tax Base

Tax Rates

Tax Base

Source: *IRS, Understanding How Taxes Evolve: Tax Rates and the Tax Base*

for the value-added calculation. At each step in the production and distribution process, the taxpayer higher in the chain has an incentive to request documentation from the taxpayer lower in the chain. This documentation becomes an audit trail for tax collectors. The chain of invoices allows tax collectors to track the amount of taxes owed the government.

In 1992, for example, when Thailand instituted its first value-added tax, business income taxes were lowered by an average of 12% at the same time the new 7% VAT was imposed. For business taxpayers, the combined income taxes and VAT in the new system could result in lower overall taxes than in the former income-tax-only system. The drop in taxes was substantial enough that Toyota Motor Thailand Co. was able to lower its prices on automobiles by up to 10,000 baht (approximately $395) per car in the first month of the new system.

The government had no intention of reducing tax revenues with the new system. On the contrary, the deputy-general of Thailand's Revenue Department (the Thai version of the IRS), expected the new system to produce at least as much overall revenue as the old system by drawing former members of Thailand's large underground economy into the government's "tax net."

Maintaining Equity

The second goal of taxation is to keep the tax system equitable, or fair, to all classes of taxpayers. Fairness is a laudable social goal, but it also is a pragmatic goal. An equitable tax system enhances the government's ability to raise revenues. Without an equitable system, taxpayers may revolt and tax payments may decline. The story of one such revolt may be found in the Bible in the Book of Kings. The taxpayers asked King Rehoboam (who was Solomon's son) to lower their taxes. Rehoboam, who was not as wise as his father, replied "My father made your yoke heavy, but I will add to your yoke." In other words, he raised the taxes. The result was a tax revolt which split the kingdom into 2 parts, Israel and Judah. King Rehoboam was left to collect taxes only from Judah.

What makes a tax system equitable? It's possible to view tax equity from 3 perspectives:

♦ horizontal equity,

♦ vertical equity, and

♦ the benefit principle.

Horizontal Equity. Horizontal equity exists when taxpayers in the same situation pay the same tax. An excise tax on cigarettes illustrates horizontal equity. Everyone in a city who buys a pack of cigarettes a day pays the same tax.

Vertical Equity. Vertical equity, or **progressivity**, exists when the tax burden is distributed proportionately to ability to pay--that is, taxpayers with greater resources pay higher taxes than those who can afford to pay less. Graduated income taxes are an example of a progressive tax--taxpayers with higher incomes pay a higher tax rate than those with lower incomes.

When vertical equity doesn't exist, taxes are said to be **regressive**. Sales taxes are an example of a regressive tax. Since lower-income people generally must spend most of their earnings on consumption, they end up paying a higher percentage of their income in sales taxes than wealthier taxpayers (who consume proportionately less of their income) pay.

The graphs in Figure I-4-7 (on the following page) demonstrate the difference between progressive and regressive taxes.

The Benefit Principle. According to the **benefit principle**, tax equity exists when those who receive the most benefits from public goods and services pay the most taxes. User fees are equitable from a benefit principle perspective. The person or organization that directly receives a public good or service pays a fee for that service.

Achieving Tax Equity. Tax equity can be difficult to achieve. Think about the following situation involving income taxes. Taxpayer A is a single man with an income of $100,000. Taxpayer B is a family of 4 (husband, wife and 2 children) with a family income of $100,000, all earned by the husband. From the perspective of horizontal equity, both taxpayers earn $100,000, so both should pay the same taxes. But, from a vertical equity perspective, the family must support 4 people on their earnings and so has less ability to pay taxes than the single person. Thus, from a vertical equity perspective, the tax rate for the family should be lower than for the individual. However, it's likely that the family receives more benefits from public goods and services (such as public schools) than the single person. Consequently, according to the benefit principle, the family should be taxed at a higher rate than the individual. So, what is equitable? The different perspectives on equity lead to conflicting answers.

The conflict represented in the above example can't be completely resolved. Moreover, most tax situations present a mix of advantages and disadvantages in terms of horizontal equity, vertical equity, and the benefit principle. However, a tax system as a whole may be perceived as equitable if the advantages and disadvantages of its parts balance out. The United States tax system, as most tax systems, has evolved to include a variety of different kinds of taxes, tax bases, and tax rates. This evolution is a natural way to try to achieve an equitable tax system.

Achieving Social Goals

The third goal of taxation is achievement of social goals. Governments can use tax systems to either discourage socially undesirable behavior or encourage

Figure I-4-7
Regressive and Progressive Taxes

REGRESSIVE

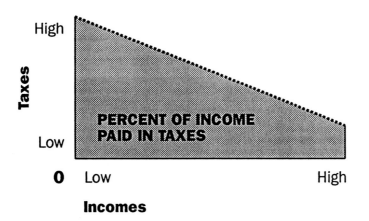

Regressive taxes take a larger percentage of low incomes than high incomes.

PROGRESSIVE

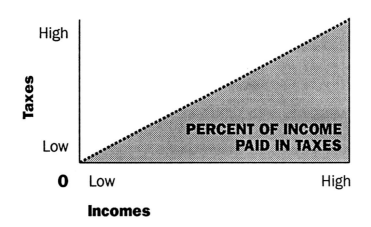

Progressive taxes take a larger percentage of high incomes than low incomes.

Source: *IRS, Understanding How Taxes Evolve*

socially desirable behavior. Excise taxes, tax credits, and tax exemptions are often intended to achieve social goals.

Using Taxation to Discourage Behavior. Excise taxes often have the dual purpose of raising revenues and discouraging consumption of the taxed good. Since excise taxes increase the effective price of a good, they act to decrease demand for the good, particularly among price-sensitive consumers. A U.S. General Accounting Office (GAO) study, for example, examined the impact of raising federal cigarette excise taxes on teen-age smoking. Based on other research that estimated that a 1% increase in cigarette prices prompted between .76% and 1.2% of teen-age smokers to quit, the GAO estimated that a 21-cent-per-pack increase in the federal excise tax on cigarettes would lead to over 500,000 teen-agers quitting smoking.

Another example of an excise tax used to discourage behavior is the excise tax on ozone-depleting chemicals. In 1989, a group of industrialized nations agreed to reduce their production and consumption of chemicals which destroy the earth's ozone layer. In the United States, to help achieve this goal, a 1990 excise tax was placed on ozone-depleting chemicals such as chlorofluorocarbons (CFCs, which work as refrigerants and solvents) and halons (chemicals useful in manufacturing semiconductors and many electronic products). The tax was to keep rising until eventually CFC production would be entirely eliminated. The original target date for no CFCs was the year 2000; but after evidence of growing holes in the ozone layer, the target was revised to 1995.

In 1992, when the CFCs tax had reached $1.67 per pound, the OECD (an international Organization for Economic Cooperation and Development) reported evidence that the U.S. tax had even influenced foreign companies. To avoid simply transferring the CFCs problem to countries without such taxes, the U.S. tax was imposed not just on the chemicals themselves, but on all products bought in the U.S. which were made with or contained CFCs. This made the tax apply to a wide variety of goods, such as computer chips that commonly were cleaned using CFCs. Consequently, Asian electronic firms with major U.S. customers began to look for ways to reduce their own use of CFCs, fearing that competitors might gain market advantages in the U.S. by eliminating CFCs first.

Excise taxes are not the only way to use the tax system to discourage behavior. An activity can be discouraged by disallowing related income tax deductions. California, for instance, disallows any state income tax deductions for business entertainment (e.g., meals to discuss business with potential customers) at social clubs that discriminate on the basis of sex, race, religion or ancestry. Thus, a business meal eaten at an all-male private club is not deductible, although the same meal eaten at a nondiscriminatory social club would be.

Using Taxation to Encourage Behavior. Tax credits often are used to encourage behavior. Tax credits do not raise revenues at all. In contrast, credits give back to taxpayers a portion of their tax liability. This benefit encourages the behavior covered by the credit. For example, the research tax credit was enacted in 1981 in response to Congressional concerns that American business was becoming less competitive in world markets because U.S. businesses were not investing enough in research and experimentation that could lead to new products or technologies.

The research tax credit was intended to stimulate additional investment in research and experimentation, so the credit was designed to apply only to increases in spending over a moving-average base. For every 1995 research dollar spent over the base, taxes were reduced by a 20-cent credit. Thus, in effect, the tax credit reduced the cost of performing research.

A GAO study estimated that for the first 4 years the research credit was available, about $7 billion of research credits were claimed and research spending was $1 billion to $2.5 billion higher than it would have been otherwise. Thus, every dollar in taxes foregone by the government yielded between 15 cents and 36 cents in additional research spending. So, was this credit a good idea or not? If you just look at the cost figures, you might be tempted to say the credit was a bad idea--an investment that returns only 36 cents on a dollar doesn't look very good. However, remember that the real return isn't the amount spent on additional research. Instead, the real benefit is the value of new products or technologies developed as a result of the research. For this case, as for many cases involving social benefits, it is difficult or impossible to measure the benefits achieved.

Tax exemptions may also be used to achieve social goals. For example, in order to promote exports, most countries exempt exports from value-added taxation. The most prominent U.S. example of using tax exemptions to achieve social goals is that not-for-profit organizations are exempt from most taxes. The exemption makes it easier for religious, charitable, educational, civic, and other nonprofit organizations to operate, which encourages their activities. Nonprofit organizations file only **information returns** with the Internal Revenue Service and the states in which they operate. These returns become public information, so the public can monitor the activities of organizations that pay no taxes.

HOW TAXES ARE ENACTED

Politics are almost as exciting as war and quite as dangerous. In war you can only be killed once, but in politics many times.
-- *Winston Churchill*

In the United States, federal taxes are enacted by the U.S. Congress and state taxes are enacted by state legislatures. Figure I-4-8 (on the following page) provides a broad picture of how a federal tax bill becomes a law. Each state and local jurisdiction also has a formal process for enacting tax laws. In many states, certain tax issues are subject to ballot, so individuals can express their own vote on tax policy decisions.

Figure I-4-8
Tax Laws: The Legislative Process

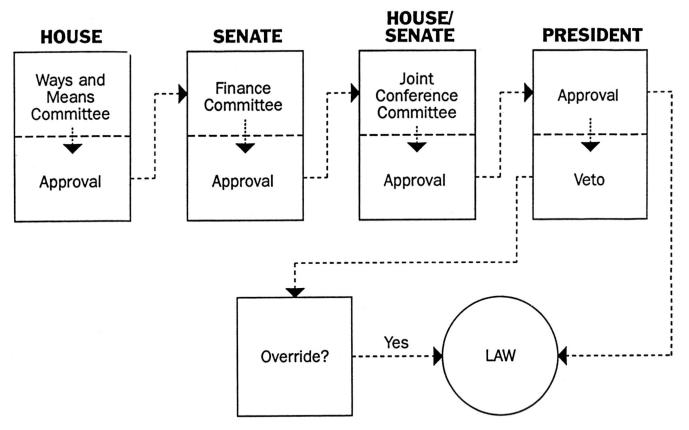

Source: *IRS, Understanding How Taxes Evolve*

What Figure I-4-8 does not show, of course, is the informal process that affects tax legislation. Individuals and businesses can lobby their congressional representatives to express their views on appropriate tax policy. Lobbying can range from an individual taxpayer writing a letter for or against an issue, to a hired lobbyist representing the views of an interest group such as a business or industry, to a public advertising campaign on an issue.

Lobbying arguments often concern issues of tax equity. Constituents can be expected to protest loudly if they feel their share of the tax burden is unfair. Cost-benefit issues are also commonly argued. For example, a proposed 1993 gasoline tax increase created much furor about a predicted devastating impact on the automobile, trucking, and airline industries. Opponents claimed the added 4.3 cent tax per gallon would result in job losses in these industries as people would cut down use of cars, trucks and airplanes as fuel costs rose. Proponents, on the other hand, lauded the proposed tax as a way to reduce gasoline consumption and improve the environment, while raising an estimated $24 billion of revenues between 1994 and 1999.

TAX COMPLEXITY/SIMPLIFICATION

The hardest thing in the world to understand is income tax.
-- Albert Einstein

We've been discussing basic concepts of taxation--and it hasn't been all that simple. If you stop to think about it, there are many factors that drive a tax system to become complex:

♦ Every time the proposed budget of a government unit is out of balance, either costs must be cut or new tax revenues found. Each new government program proposed requires revenues to support it. Thus, there are frequent periodic incentives to look for new taxes or to adjust tax bases or tax rates for taxes already in existence. Between 1986 and 1992, for example, there were about 5,000 changes to U.S. federal tax laws.

♦ Taxpayers can be subject to a variety of taxing authorities. Consider the U.S. multinational firm that is subject to taxation in every country in which it operates, and, possibly, in multiple state or local jurisdictions within every country. Even if each of the tax laws is reasonably simple, the combination can quickly become complex. One multinational company's U.S. federal income tax return consisted of 21,000 pages turned in to the IRS in 30 volumes! For a personal return, imagine the plight of professional athletes who may be subject to taxes in a variety of cities and states where they play.

♦ Tax equity must be maintained, but is difficult to achieve. Efforts to be fair to different taxpayers under different circumstances can lead to a

Figure I-4-9
AICPA Open Letter on Tax Simplification

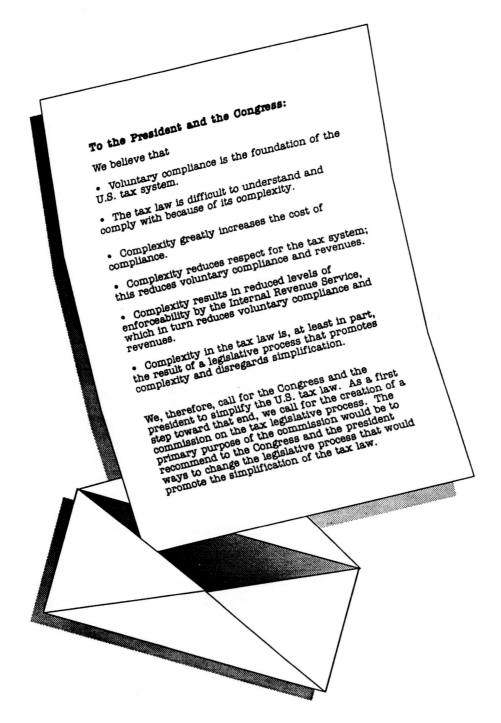

To the President and the Congress:

We believe that

- Voluntary compliance is the foundation of the U.S. tax system.
- The tax law is difficult to understand and comply with because of its complexity.
- Complexity greatly increases the cost of compliance.
- Complexity reduces respect for the tax system; this reduces voluntary compliance and revenues.
- Complexity results in reduced levels of enforceability by the Internal Revenue Service, which in turn reduces voluntary compliance and revenues.
- Complexity in the tax law is, at least in part, the result of a legislative process that promotes complexity and disregards simplification.

We, therefore, call for the Congress and the president to simplify the U.S. tax law. As a first step toward that end, we call for the creation of a commission on the tax legislative process. The primary purpose of the commission would be to recommend to the Congress and the president ways to change the legislative process that would promote the simplification of the tax law.

Source: American Institute of Certified Public Accountants, 1990

patchwork of different taxes, exemptions, credits or deductions, and rates.

♦ The tax system is used to achieve social goals, as well as to raise revenues. The more this is done, the more likely it is the system will grow complex.

So, a certain amount of tax complexity must be expected. But, at some point, if the tax system becomes too complex, taxpayer compliance may decline. A tax system can become so complex that taxpayers grow to resent it, and resentment breeds lack of compliance. Or, even if taxpayers want to pay their fair share of taxes, they may fail to comply with laws that they do not fully understand. Making fun of a sad situation, comedian Dave Barry says just the title of some IRS forms is complicated enough "to cause the ordinary taxpayer's brain to explode."

Also, as a tax system becomes more complex, it becomes more difficult to administer. For instance, as complexity increases, greater administrative resources must be devoted to providing guidance on interpretation of tax laws. Greater resources must also be devoted to compliance audits. On the tax preparer's side, the administrative costs of complying with tax law can be daunting. A Tax Foundation study estimated that it would cost American business and individual taxpayers $235 billion in 1996 just to keep the required tax records and fill out the required forms.

Given the natural tendency of tax systems to become more complex, most tax systems will undergo periods of adjustment when efforts are made to simplify the system. Korea, for example, replaced a very complicated sales tax system with a much simpler single-rate value-added tax system. In the United States, tax simplification was a major impetus of the Tax Reform Act of 1986. The 1986 tax law changes did simplify some aspects of taxation by streamlining tax rates and phasing out some tax deductions. However, the 1986 act in itself was very complex. As U.S. Congressman Delbert Latta commented on receiving his copy of the bill, "I hold in my hand, 1,379 pages of tax simplification." Not surprisingly, the outcry for simplification has increased since the 1986 act was passed.

There are many who feel the current U.S. tax system is overly complex. Even the American Institute of Certified Public Accountants, many of whose members are tax experts, has called on Congress to simplify the tax system. The AICPA campaign for tax simplification included an open letter to Congress, which is reproduced in Figure I-4-9 (on the preceding page). The AICPA's campaign for tax simplification also included developing a "tax complexity index", a simple, multiple-choice question scoring device designed to help legislators measure the potential in any new tax laws for reducing or increasing taxpayer confusion.

Complaints about tax complexity have become so common that they have even been discussed in Ann Landers' advice column. In April 1990, a "frustrated" accountant sent Landers a letter of complaint (shown in Figure I-4-10 on the following page) that included a sample passage from the regulations defining the

Figure I-4-10

Dear Ann. . .

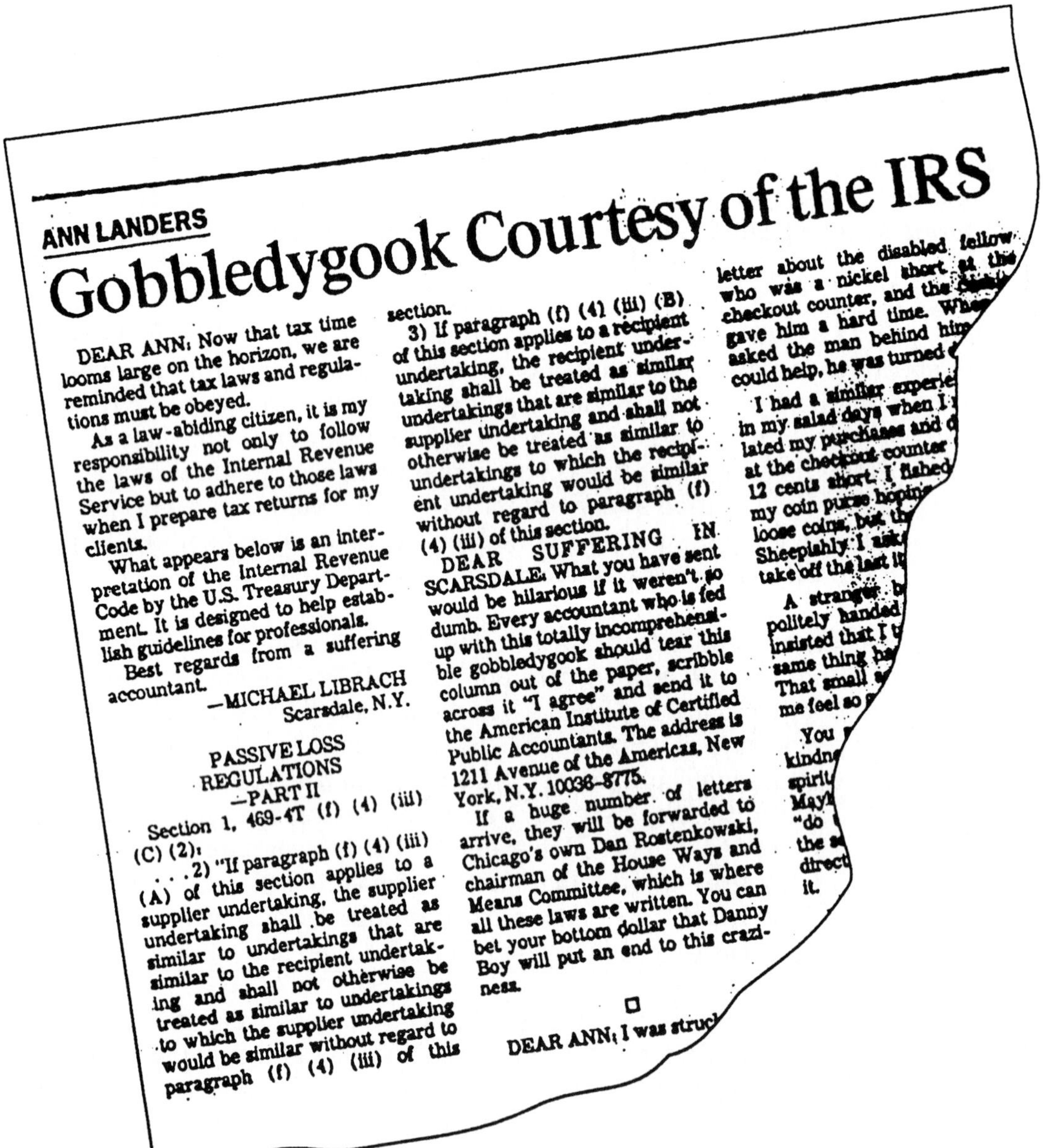

ANN LANDERS

Gobbledygook Courtesy of the IRS

DEAR ANN: Now that tax time looms large on the horizon, we are reminded that tax laws and regulations must be obeyed.

As a law-abiding citizen, it is my responsibility not only to follow the laws of the Internal Revenue Service but to adhere to those laws when I prepare tax returns for my clients.

What appears below is an interpretation of the Internal Revenue Code by the U.S. Treasury Department. It is designed to help establish guidelines for professionals.

Best regards from a suffering accountant
    —MICHAEL LIBRACH
        Scarsdale, N.Y.

PASSIVE LOSS REGULATIONS
—PART II

Section 1, 469-4T (f) (4) (iii) (C) (2):

. . .2) "If paragraph (f) (4) (iii) (A) of this section applies to a supplier undertaking, the supplier undertaking shall be treated as similar to undertakings that are similar to the recipient undertaking and shall not otherwise be treated as similar to undertakings to which the supplier undertaking would be similar without regard to this paragraph (f) (4) (iii) of this section.

3) If paragraph (f) (4) (iii) (B) of this section applies to a recipient undertaking, the recipient undertaking shall be treated as similar undertakings that are similar to the supplier undertaking and shall not otherwise be treated as similar to undertakings to which the recipient undertaking would be similar without regard to paragraph (f) (4) (iii) of this section.

DEAR SUFFERING IN SCARSDALE: What you have sent would be hilarious if it weren't so dumb. Every accountant who is fed up with this totally incomprehensible gobbledygook should tear this column out of the paper, scribble across it "I agree" and send it to the American Institute of Certified Public Accountants. The address is 1211 Avenue of the Americas, New York, N.Y. 10036-8775.

If a huge number of letters arrive, they will be forwarded to Chicago's own Dan Rostenkowski, chairman of the House Ways and Means Committee, which is where all these laws are written. You can bet your bottom dollar that Danny Boy will put an end to this craziness.

□

DEAR ANN: I was struck

letter about the disabled fellow who was a nickel short at the checkout counter, and the clerk gave him a hard time. When asked the man behind him could help, he was turned d

I had a similar experie in my salad days when I lated my purchases and c at the checkout counter 12 cents short. I fished my coin purse hopin loose coins, but th Sheepishly I ask take off the last it

A stranger b politely handed insisted that I t same thing ha That small me feel so

You kindn spirit May "do the s direct it.

term "passive loss." Landers, who agreed that the passage was exceedingly complex, advised her readers to make their feelings on tax complexity known.

Within a week of the advice column's publication, the AICPA received over 10,000 responses which were presented to the chairman of the House Ways and Means Committee. Two years later, in 1992, the tax regulations defining "passive losses" were simplified--7 pages of new regulations replaced the 100-plus pages that prompted the original letter to Ann Landers.

As outcries over tax complexity grow louder, it becomes increasingly likely that tax reform will occur. Thus, you should keep in mind that the tax laws you learn about today are unlikely to be static. Even if major tax reform does occur, you should still not expect the resulting tax laws to remain static as the natural forces that push tax systems toward complexity will always be with us. Tax systems, like any social system, are dynamic. Many forces act to push a tax system out of balance and to bring it back into balance again.

THE ROLE OF ACCOUNTANTS IN TAX PRACTICE

Private accountants, public accountants and government accountants all have a role to play in the tax system.

Private Accountants in Tax Practice

Given the complexity of tax laws, large corporations often employ accountants as in-house tax specialists. These accountants play an important role in tax compliance by helping their companies stay abreast of current tax law and the information demands created by the law. Private tax accountants are usually also responsible for seeing that all the tax forms and tax returns their company needs to file are appropriately prepared.

In addition to their role in tax compliance, private accountants play an important role in tax planning for their companies. In fact, many companies spend more time on tax planning than they do on tax compliance. Why is tax planning so important? Taxes are a cost of doing business and, just as any other cost, they should be controlled. The best way to control tax costs is to take them into account whenever any business decision is made.

Tax planning involves being aware of the tax impact of management's decision alternatives. Taxes can often be important enough costs that they influence decisions. For example, plant location decisions may be affected by differences in tax rates between the sites being considered.

Private tax accountants also acts as advocates regarding tax policy decisions that may affect their companies. Accountants monitor proposed legislation and rule changes, evaluate the impact of the changes on their companies, and recommend to management whether lobbying action should be taken.

Public Accountants in Tax Practice

Public accountants in tax practice perform the same types of roles as private accountants--tax compliance, tax planning, and tax advocacy. However, unlike private accountants, who perform their role only for the company that employs them, these tax accountants serve many clients, both corporate and individual.

Because of their wide variety of experience, public accounting firms also do tax work for many large corporations that have their own in-house tax staffs. In these cases, the public accountants provide expertise to supplement the in-house staff when the company is faced with new or particularly complex decisions.

Government Accountants in Tax Practice

Government accountants in tax practice share a common goal with their counterparts in private and public practice--all want to be sure that taxpayers pay their fair share of taxes. However, the groups approach this goal from differing perspectives. Public and private accountants take the taxpayer's perspective. They focus on helping taxpayers minimize the taxes they pay. In contrast, government accountants take the perspective of the tax assessor. Thus, government compliance auditors (such as IRS auditors) focus their efforts on making sure taxpayers pay all the taxes they owe so the government receives all the revenues it is due.

Government accountants also play a role in tax policy by providing legislators with information on the impact of current and potential tax policies. The U.S. General Accounting Office, for example, conducts many studies concerning the operational effectiveness of tax policies--such as the studies concerning excise taxes on cigarettes and the research tax credit cited earlier. The GAO has also performed many studies to help legislators assess the efficiency of the administration of the tax system. For example, the GAO has issued many reports concerning the Internal Revenue Service's efforts to computerize the filing and processing of tax returns.

Education for Tax Accountants

Given the complexity of tax laws, specialized educational preparation is generally needed for tax accounting careers. While tax accountants can begin their careers after an undergraduate education, many tax accountants find additional education is needed for career advancement. Thus, tax accountants often enhance their educational preparation by obtaining law degrees or master's degrees (usually a Master of Business Taxation or a Master of Accounting with a tax specialization).

APPENDIX: GRAPHIC PRESENTATIONS

Studies have shown that people remember 25% of what they hear, 40% of what they see, and 60% of what they see and hear. Thus, it isn't surprising that when people have quantitative accounting information to communicate, they often try to present graphic images, as well as word images of the numbers.

Not so many years ago, accounting reports depended on graphics prepared by hand. Now, with the cost-saving and labor-saving assistance of computer software, graphics can quickly and easily be prepared for use in annual reports, budget reports, and all manner of accounting reports.

A good graphic simplifies information, makes information easier to grasp and draws your attention. A well-constructed graphic can get the message contained in accounting numbers across more clearly and quickly than words alone could do. When you see a good graphic, it looks so "right" that it seems obvious the information should have been presented in that manner. But as more people come to prepare their own graphics using the graphics capabilities of spreadsheet software or presentation graphics packages, many have come to realize that it takes practice to design good, simple visual images.

In some of the written and oral presentations for this course, you have the opportunity to enhance your presentation by using good graphic images. If you are a novice at preparing graphics, you might find it helpful to read the advice on the following pages about things to bear in mind when constructing simple line charts, bar charts and pie charts. The advice was compiled by Douglas Andrews, head of the Business Communication Department at the University of Southern California School of Business Administration.

If you master the simple design principles in this advice, you will soon find yourself ready to take full advantage of the more sophisticated options of state-of-the-art graphics software.

ADVICE ON PREPARING GRAPHICS

(Compiled by Doug Andrews, Department of Business Communication, University of Southern California)

The Line Graph

The line graph is perhaps the most popular and useful of all graphs. The line graph (or chart) portrays a trend or series of figures, usually over a number of time periods. It is used to illustrate several elements so that the viewer can make easy comparisons. Because of the many useful qualities of the line graph, let's make a closer examination of how it is constructed. Keep in mind that the primary concern here is to demonstrate how to construct ordinary, simple line graphs.

First, the line graph is composed of a vertical axis (the y-axis) and a horizontal axis (the x-axis) that intersect at right angles. The zero point of the graph generally indicates where the two axes meet.

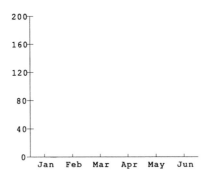

Notice that there are no lines; they're imaginary to avoid a cluttered appearance. Rather than drawing complete grid lines, hash marks appear only on the x and y lines. However, imaginary lines are still there for the points you need to plot along the appropriate intersections.

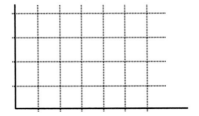

In preparing line graphs, try to choose the axes so that the fluctuations appear vertically. For example, if you want to show the trend in sales over time, the horizontal axis should represent increments in time, which can be divided into fixed periods (such as months), while the vertical axis represents sales, which fluctuate over time.

Let's plot Blooper sales for the first six months of 19X4. The y-axis (vertical) will be the amount or quantity of Bloopers sold. The x-axis (horizontal) will represent the individual months. We have divided the vertical axis information into equal portions from the least amount at the bottom to the greatest amount at the top. The horizontal axis is divided into equal portions/units from the left to the right and it is labeled to show the values.

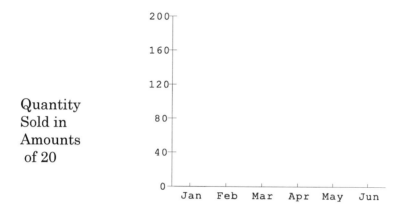

Quantity Sold in Amounts of 20

In January we sold 125 Bloopers; February, 140; March, 150; and so on. Once the values are plotted--the amount sold intersecting with the month that corresponds with the sale, we connect the points to form a continuous line, and the relationship becomes readily apparent.

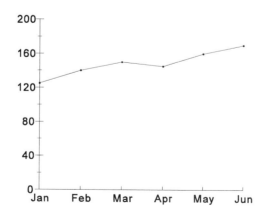

Now we'll show how comparative material lends itself to line graphs. There are two plotted lines in the next example: the two sets of statistics show the comparison between the sales of 19X5 and the sales of 19X6 over the same time period, the first six months of the year.

Blooper Company

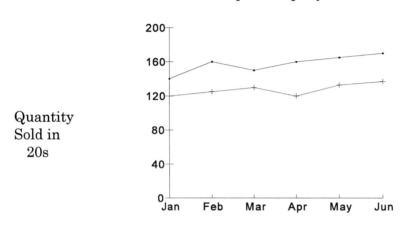

Quantity
Sold in
20s

One very important rule to remember when constructing a line graph is to keep the ratio on the x-axis and the y-axis scales equal. If you don't, different visual impressions will result because the scales are distorted. Even though the same point is shown on each graph below, the scales are not equal, so the visual images differ.

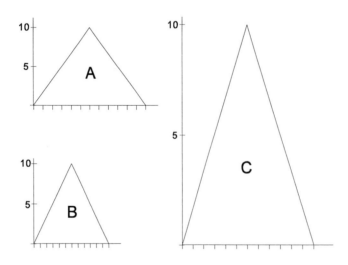

Here is a list of things to keep in mind when preparing line graphs:

Guidelines for Line Graphs

· Avoid distortion by keeping the ratio between the scales constant
· Hold grid lines to a minimum
· Avoid plotting too many lines; three is a good standard limit
· Try to differentiate each line (use color, broken lines, etc.)
· Make sure your title describes the data
· Identify all variables with a legend or a label
· Make all lettering read horizontally (when possible)
· Pick a scale for your variables that you think best shows what you want to show.

The Bar Graph

The bar graph is probably the simplest form of graph. It is composed of a series of either horizontal or vertical bars of varying lengths with each bar representing a relative quantity. The bar graph is best for showing simple comparisons, especially changes in quantity.

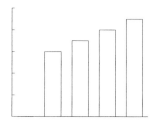 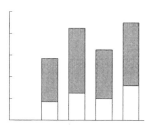 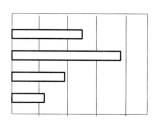

These graphs compare data over a certain time. (The time scale is the x axis.) The bars are also used to represent height.

This graph compares data for a particular point in time or is used to represent distance.

Guidelines for Bar Graphs

· Use gridlines only when necessary to help viewers compare lengths
· Keep all vertical and horizontal scales equal
· Keep the width of the bars and the spaces in between bars equal
· Use color, shading, or crosshatching to emphasize contrast
· Arrange what the bars represent in numerical, alphabetical, chronological, or other logical order for easier comprehension.

Circle Graphs

Circle graphs, or pie charts, partition a whole into various parts or elements.

Book Sales
For the Current Year
19____

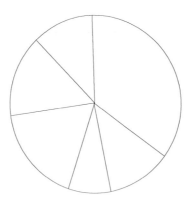

The pie chart makes for ease and accuracy of reading. It shows proportions and the relative size of related quantities accurately.

Guidelines for Pie Charts

- Convert figures into percentages whenever possible
- Put the largest segment beginning at twelve o'clock and proceed clockwise, but always put the "other" segment last no matter what its size
- When possible, identify each segment horizontally within the circle (if room permits)
- Coloring, shading, and crosshatching can be used for emphasis
- Make the size of the pie chart appropriate--the more "slices" the pie has, the larger the circle should be.

ASSIGNMENTS FOR MODULE 4 - PART A

ASSIGNMENT I-4A-1:   **Providing Public Goods and Services: Performance Evaluation**

SETTING

You are part of a team of accountants that has been asked to perform the first-ever performance evaluation of a city's mass transit system. Your performance evaluation will be used to help the city decide how much of its resources should be devoted to the mass transit system and how to change the services offered. Your evaluation is to be restricted to services currently offered--a bus and subway system. The evaluation is to consider 5 general areas:

 (1) Is the transit system reliable?

 (2) Is the transit system safe?

 (3) Does the transit system provide a reasonably comfortable environment for passengers?

 (4) Are adequate information services available to passengers?

 (5) Is the transit system cost effective?

The team has decided to begin by generating *specific* questions related to each of the 5 areas to help determine the exact nature of information that needs to be collected.

ASSIGNMENT

Develop a series of *10 specific questions* which can be used to evaluate 1 of the 5 general areas of the examination. Your instructor will tell you which area to work on. If your instructor does not assign you an area, develop your 10 questions for *reliability* (area 1).

HINTS

Ask yourself what the purpose of this assignment is. If your answer is "to learn about evaluating transit systems," you are missing the point. The goal of this assignment is to give you practice at learning how to ask questions to gather information you need to complete a task. In government as well as industry, accountants often act as business advisors. Therefore, an important skill for accountants to develop is knowing how to ask "good questions." For this assignment, a good question may be defined as a question specific enough that it is easy to see ways to collect the evidence or data needed to answer the question.

How do you know when you have a good question? Put yourself in the place of someone being interviewed by the team of accountants. Ask yourself the questions. Questions which could elicit vague general responses, questions which can easily be avoided by interviewees, or questions which would not lead to any quantifiable response will not be particularly helpful in doing the performance evaluation. In addition, questions must be relevant to the area you are investigating.

Here are some examples of questions concerning system reliability, moving from some weak questions to some stronger questions [*Note*: These questions may not be included in your responses to the assignment.]:

- *Are the buses kept clean?* [Very weak question: The question is not relevant to system reliability; it is more relevant to area 3, a "comfortable environment." Even if the question was relevant, it is worded in a way that would tend to produce vague responses. For example, it would be easy for an interviewee to simply say "yes" and move on to the next question, yielding very little real information.]

- *Is the system reliable?* [Weak question: This question is relevant, but so broad as to be very difficult to answer in anything other than vague terms. The question also allows interviewees to manipulate their responses. For example, interviewees could avoid certain weak spots by interpreting the question to cover other aspects of reliability.]

- *How often do buses arrive on time?* [A good question: This question relates to system reliability and will generate a specific response, such as an on-time percentage.]

- *How often do buses arrive within 5 minutes of schedule?* [A very good question: This question is relevant and designed to generate a specific response. Also, because a common benchmark (specifying 5 minutes as a cut-off) is provided, all interviewees are reporting comparable data. Otherwise, one interviewee might interpret "on time" to mean exactly on schedule, while others could interpret on time to be within 1 to 10 minutes of schedule, and so on.]

How do you come up with topics for questions? Think about your experiences as a user of transit systems. How does the transit system operate (For example, where do you get schedules? What does the bus or subway look like? What makes you, as a passenger, pleased or displeased with the system?) Use your experiences as background to help generate specific questions.

ASSIGNMENT I-4A-2: <u>**Generating Money to Pay for Public Goods and Services**</u>: The 1995 Orange County Ballot

SETTING

You are a first time voter in California for the June 1995 special election. There is only 1 item on the ballot, *Measure R*. You know that this election is important because *Measure R* addresses one way to help solve Orange County's financial problems following the county's unfortunate declaration of bankruptcy late in 1994.

You take your responsibility as a voter seriously. In preparation for voting, you read the sample ballot (see next page) and impartial legislative analysis of *Measure R*, as well as a summary of the arguments for and against each proposition (see excerpts on the pages following the ballot).

SELF-CORRECTED ASSIGNMENT

Look at *Measure R* and determine 3 things:

♦   the nature of the public good or service being considered--what type of social welfare expenditure is at issue?

♦   the expected total cost if the measure is approved

♦   the source of funding--tax revenues or increased debt?

When you have completed the assignment, check your own answers using the solution at the end of this module. If the solution is not clear to you, be sure to note any questions you may want to raise in class or ask your instructor during office hours.

HINTS

The impartial analysis must describe the nature of the issue being voted on and the costs involved. Read the proposition first to see if you can answer the questions directly. If not, seek additional information in the analysis.

SAMPLE BALLOT

A

OFFICIAL BALLOT
COUNTYWIDE BANKRUPTCY RECOVERY
SALES AND USE TAX

COUNTY OF ORANGE

June 27, 1995

This ballot stub shall be torn off by precinct board
member and handed to the voter.

MEASURES SUBMITTED TO VOTE OF VOTERS		
COUNTY OF ORANGE		

R	**COUNTYWIDE BANKRUPTCY RECOVERY SALES AND USE TAX** Shall Ordinance No. 3933 be adopted, which would impose a State administered one-half percent (1/2%) sales and	Yes	+
		No	+

use tax automatically terminating in 10 years, to raise revenue for general County purposes, including, but not limited to, preservation of essential County services and payment of County bankruptcy obligations to schools, cities and other creditors, with a citizens' oversight committee authorized to recommend earlier repeal of the tax?

30-101A   A

VOTE BOTH SIDES

IMPARTIAL ANALYSIS BY COUNTY COUNSEL
MEASURE R
COUNTY OF ORANGE

Measure R is a local ballot measure that proposes adoption of Orange County Ordinance No. 3933, which would raise the retail sales and use tax charged in Orange County by one-half of one percent (1/2%), to 8.25%, for 10 years, beginning January 1, 1996. A "Yes" vote on Measure R is a vote to increase the tax. A "No" vote is a vote against increasing the tax. The tax increase will take effect only if it receives a majority of "Yes" votes.

The increased sales and use tax would be charged on all the retail sales and uses of tangible personal property for which State and other local sales and use taxes are charged. The tax increase would be administered by the State Board of Equalization.

The proceeds of the tax increase would be deposited into the County's General Fund and would be used for general purposes of Orange County, including, but not limited to, preservation of essential County services and payments to schools, cities and other creditors of obligations and debts of the County related to the County's bankruptcy. The Orange County Board of Supervisors would decide how the tax proceeds are spent.

The Measure provides for appointment of a Citizens' Oversight Committee to receive public input, monitor uses of the tax proceeds and advise the Board of Supervisors and Orange County residents about (1) appropriate uses of the tax proceeds, (2) actual and anticipated revenue to the County from the tax and other sources, including lawsuits for damages the County has filed as a result of its bankruptcy, (3) whether the sales and use tax increase continues to be needed, and (4) whether the tax increase is generating more revenue than the County legitimately needs. The Citizens' Oversight Committee may recommend repeal of the tax increase before 10 years if it determines that the legitimate financial needs of the County can be met without the tax proceeds.

The Measure provides for repeal of the tax increase before 10 years by a majority vote of the Board of Supervisors followed by a majority vote of the County electorate, or by any other method of repeal permitted by law.

Measure R is authorized by State law, Revenue and Taxation Code Section 7285.

ARGUMENT IN FAVOR OF MEASURE R
COUNTY OF ORANGE

Former treasurer Bob Citron and his Wall Street accomplices dug a 1.7 billion dollar hole for Orange County taxpayers.

Voters now have two choices. Vote YES on Measure R and climb out of the hole ... or vote NO and get buried in it.

Measure R is part of a bankruptcy recovery plan which includes sales of county assets, privatization of services, litigation awards and substantial budget cuts.

Orange County is cutting 1,590 from the County work force and has reduced its operating budget by almost 50%. The Sheriff and District Attorney have been cut by 13.3 million dollars. Salaries have been reduced ... and more cuts and layoffs are coming.

Even if the County's operating budget is cut to zero, Orange County's financial problems would not be solved.

The County owes hundreds of millions to school districts, cities and other investors. Nearly 400 million is due by June 30.

Orange County residents will suffer for many years if these obligations are not met.

School officials predict layoffs of 2,400 teachers. Local school districts would also face bankruptcy, resulting in a takeover of local schools by Sacramento bureaucrats.

A default on bonds will make us a deadbeat County. We will be unable to borrow money to build schools, jails, hospitals and roads ... or we will pay much higher interest, which is nothing more than a hidden tax.

Measure R will keep our schools out of bankruptcy, stop deeper cuts in law enforcement and prevent default of County bonds.

Public officials made irresponsible decisions which led Orange County into bankruptcy.

The voters must now make a tough, unpleasant, but necessary decision to lead us out of bankruptcy. Vote YES on R, the only responsible solution to Orange County's problems.

Citizens For Economic Progress - YES on Measure R

s/ William J. Popejoy
Chief Executive Officer of Orange County

s/ Brad Gates
Orange County Sheriff-Coroner

s/ Connie Haddad, President
League of Women Voters of Orange County

s/ Reed Royalty,
Executive Vice President
Orange County
Taxpayers Association

s/ D. A. ("Del") Weber
Teacher, Anaheim High School
Instructor, Rancho Santiago Community College
President, California Teachers Association

REBUTTAL TO ARGUMENT IN FAVOR OF MEASURE R
COUNTY OF ORANGE

Like Chicken Little, these fearmongers have consistently tried to frighten voters into tax after tax -- they always claim the sky is falling. Now they threaten us with "burial" if we don't pass this, their new so-called "recovery plan" tax.

More likely, any tax increase would bury us in the recession sure to follow. When the latest recession forced a drastic reduction in private industry jobs, county government continued to overtax, overspend, and recklessly add thousands to its payroll. The current cutbacks barely make a dent in that bloated growth. Planned cuts will be only about 5% of total county spending.

We need real cuts and honest pursuit of other alternatives, such as selling excess county property and reallocating surplus funds from other local public agencies.

OCTA, water and sanitation districts still have billions of tax dollars in reserve, but defy requests to share with schools, public safety, and other essential functions. In fact, the same insiders pushing this tax brokered a closed door bankruptcy settlement that gives MORE to transit and private toll roads than our schoolchildren.

Even if the tax passed, the kids might never see a cent of it. Sure, there's a bogus committee, but they're toothless -- they can only "monitor and advise".

Don't be frightened by Chicken Littles. Orange County has a bright future, if only we can keep excessive taxes and government spending from wrecking our economy.

Vote NO on this irresponsible tax!

No on "R"

s/ Thomas C. Rogers, Former Chairman
Republican Central Committee, Orange County

s/ Sandra L. Genis, Councilmember
City of Costa Mesa

s/ Bruce Whitaker, Chief Spokesman
Committees of Correspondence

s/ H. A. (Hal) Fischer, Past President
Orange County Chiefs' and Sheriff's Association

s/ Teddi Lorch, Vice President
Board of Trustees, Saddleback Community College District

ARGUMENT AGAINST MEASURE R
COUNTY OF ORANGE

Who's spending millions trying to pass this regressive tax? Follow the money! The special interests pushing this tax benefit enough from large county budgets to be able to afford slick, expensive campaigns, leaving the poor and middle class to pay the tab.

Don't be fooled by proposed changes to county government. The elite power brokers who run Orange County from behind closed doors simply want to trick you into strengthening their stranglehold. The public faces might look different, but the money and power behind them would be the same.

Your tax dollars would go to the same arrogant bunglers who gambled Orange County into bankruptcy. There are no guarantees the tax wouldn't be used just to support their addiction to cronyism and high living. They could use it for even higher salaries and pensions.

This irresponsible tax would weaken the economy by driving employers away, costing thousands of taxpayer jobs, and driving us back into recession. Meanwhile, Wall Street bankers, speculators, wealthy land developers and overpaid politicians would reap our tax dollars.

Better alternatives exist. Rather than pursuing cost-cutting alternatives, county insiders focused on raising revenues, and hastily conceived this tax to bail themselves out with your dollars. Force them to reduce expenses by defeating this tax.

This tax would be used to borrow more money. The resulting debt would go on for years, pawning our children's future. County gambling losses should be covered by disciplined cutbacks, not by going further in debt. Excessive debt is what drove the county bankrupt in the first place.

Vote No on Measure R and ask your friends and neighbors to do the same. If this tax isn't defeated by a large margin, the proponents will keep bringing it back.

To contact grassroots taxpayers working to help you keep your hard-earned dollars, **call 714-650-1537**

No on "R"

s/ Thomas C. Rogers, Former Chairman
  Republican Central Committee, Orange County

s/ Sandra L. Genis, Councilmember
  City of Costa Mesa

s/ Bruce Whitaker, Chief Spokesman
  Committees of Correspondence

s/ H. A. (Hal) Fischer, Past President
  Orange County Chiefs' and Sheriff's Association

s/ Teddi Lorch, Vice President
  Board of Trustees, Saddleback Community College District

REBUTTAL TO ARGUMENT AGAINST MEASURE R
COUNTY OF ORANGE

Vote YES and Get Orange County Out of Bankruptcy Now.

Existing county revenues are only 275 million dollars per year. If we shut down county government for six years, we would still not raise the 1.7 billion dollars we need to get out of bankruptcy. Asset sales will help, but Measure R is the key to a fast and complete recovery.

A No Vote Will Cost Taxpayers Much More.

• Measure R is needed to prevent a default on county bonds. A default may cost taxpayers billions in lawsuits and higher interest rates.

• Orange County taxpayers have already spent 25 million on lawyers, accountants and bankers in 5 months. We will spend hundreds of millions more if the bankruptcy problem continues for years.

• New businesses will not locate in a bankrupt county. We must recover quickly to prevent serious job loss.

• Home values have been plunging since the bankruptcy. A half cent sales tax increase is a small price to pay to protect your largest investment.

The Public Is Protected Against the Misuse of Measure R Funds.

The Board of Supervisors must comply with a court approved bankruptcy recovery plan. This protects the public against misuse of the money.

Measure R Opponents Have No Solution.

Years of turmoil, endless lawsuits, higher interest rates and lower home values are the price of a no vote. The opponents might be willing to pay this price -- you should not.

Vote YES on R and Put This Bankruptcy Behind Us.

Citizens For Economic Progress - YES on Measure R

s/ William J. Popejoy
  Chief Executive Officer of Orange County

s/ Connie Haddad, President
  League of Women Voters of Orange County

s/ D. A. ("Del") Weber
  Teacher, Anaheim High School
  Instructor, Rancho Santiago Community College
  President, California Teachers Association

s/ Brad Gates
  Orange County Sheriff-Coroner

s/ Reed Royalty,
  Exec. Vice President
  Orange County Taxpayers Assn.

ASSIGNMENT I-4A-3:   Regulation: Comparison of 10-K and 20-F Disclosures

SETTING

You are a member of the staff of the SEC. You have been invited to attend an investors' club meeting. The club members pool their money to make investments.

The topic for discussion at the meeting is segment disclosures (disclosures concerning major lines of business or geographic areas of an organization). The club chose this topic because some club members noticed a big difference in the segment disclosures of 2 companies they are considering as potential investments.

The club provides you with financial reports from the 2 companies. Both are large, multi-division businesses in the same primary industry (automobile manufacturing). The U.S. company discloses net sales, operating profit, research and development expense, identifiable assets, depreciation and amortization, and capital expenditures for each of its major business segments. The foreign company only discloses sales for each segment.

At the club meeting, you remark that both companies have complied with U.S. securities regulations. The regulations require more segment disclosure from U.S. companies than from foreign companies.

At this point, several club members raise strong objections. (See the page following this assignment for examples of objections raised by club members.) The regulations, in their opinion, are unfair to U.S. investors and U.S. firms.

ASSIGNMENT

Prepare a *4 to 5 minute oral response* justifying the current regulations and answering the objections of the club members.

At the next class meeting, randomly chosen individuals will present their response to the class. The remaining members of the class will play the role of the club members who think the rules are unfair to U.S. investors and U.S. companies. Be prepared to answer questions from the audience after your remarks.

Class participation points will be awarded to presenters and to audience members who ask particularly good questions.

HINTS

1. Remember that you are obliged to take a position supporting the current regulations. You do not necessarily have to argue that the current regulations are perfect, but you do need to argue that they are better than the available alternatives. So, a good first step would be to determine what the available alternatives are.

2. This debate can be viewed as an ethical issue because it concerns fairness. Who are the stakeholders? How would each stakeholder group benefit (or be harmed) by requiring equal disclosure? by allowing differential disclosure?

3. Remember that you must also be ready to play the role of the investment club member--i.e., you need to be able to argue both sides of the issue. The following page presents examples of objections raised by the investment club members. You need to think about these objections and consider other possible objections as well.

4. If you need hints on preparing a short oral presentation, review the advice in the appendix to Module 2 of this theme).

EXAMPLES OF OBJECTIONS RAISED BY THE INVESTMENT CLUB MEMBERS

♦ Why should U.S. investors be provided with less disclosure about a company listed on a U.S. stock exchange just because the company is foreign? Isn't this unfair to investors?

♦ Why should U.S. companies be forced to bear greater disclosure costs than their foreign competitors? Isn't this unfair to U.S. public companies?

ASSIGNMENTS FOR MODULE 4 - PART B

ASSIGNMENT I-4B-1:   <u>Types of Taxes</u>: **Preparing a Briefing Report**

SETTING

You have just started a job with the state government. The state legislature is embroiled in debate on the proposed budget for the next fiscal year. State law requires a balanced budget, but the projected budget shortfall amounts to several billion dollars. The legislators face some difficult decisions as they will need to raise revenues and/or decrease expenditures in order to bring the proposed budget into balance.

In order to help the legislature make these decisions, your office has been asked to prepare a briefing on the sources of tax revenues for the state. You have been assigned to work on this report. You obtain the following information from the Governor's Budget Summary concerning estimated tax revenues:

Personal income tax	$16.363 billion
Sales and use tax	$13.448 billion
Bank and corporation tax	$ 5.585 billion (See Note 1)
Motor vehicle fees	$ 3.362 billion (See Note 2)
Motor vehicle fuel tax	$ 1.330 billion
Insurance tax	$ 1.279 billion
Cigarette tax	$ .863 billion
Horse racing tax	$ .160 billion (See Note 3)
Distilled spirits tax	$ .094 billion

> *Notes:* 1. Paid on net income.
> 2. Paid annually as part of the motor vehicle registration process; based on value of vehicle.
> 3. Paid on admission tickets to race tracks.

ASSIGNMENT

Use a spreadsheet or presentation graphics computer software package to prepare a graphic presentation showing the major sources of state revenues--income taxes, consumption taxes, and wealth taxes. In addition, the graphic should show the specific taxes (e.g., distilled spirits tax) included in each of the categories. Your graphic must be in black and white, as the budget for your department does not allow for color graphics.

HINTS

Points for this assignment will be awarded both for accuracy (are your numbers correct?) and presentation (is the information communicated clearly?).

Accuracy: Remember that good accounting systems make use of independent checks to help ensure accuracy. You can approach the first part of this assignment in a manner that will increase your chances of arriving at an accurate result. Before your subgroup discusses the assignment, each individual member should independently decide on the appropriate categorization of each of the taxes. Then, the subgroup can compare answers and discuss any areas of disagreement.

Presentation: Most of your effort in this assignment will be spent deciding how to best design your graphic so that it will communicate the information quickly and clearly to the legislators. Also, remember that the picture you present graphically must be a clear communication. If your audience looks only at the visuals, everyone should still get a fair sense of the underlying data. When you finish your graphics, ask yourself if the pictures alone communicate what is happening with the taxes.

If you need hints on preparing graphics, read the advice that appears in the appendix to this module.

ASSIGNMENT I-4B-2: <u>How Taxes Are Calculated</u>: Simple Personal Income Taxes

SETTING

You have taken a part-time job while you are attending college. This job will pay you $2,000 by the end of the year, which dwarfs the only other income you earn-- $50 in interest on a savings account.

As April 15 nears, you realize that you must file an income tax return. Since you are a student learning *Core Concepts of Accounting Information*, you are reasonably confident that you can handle this task, even though you realize your course doesn't cover tax return preparation. You check with your instructor, who confirms your ability. Further, your instructor tells you that the Internal Revenue Service has prepared some computer software to help you learn how to calculate simple personal tax liability.

SELF-CORRECTED ASSIGNMENT

Use the *Understanding Taxes!* software to learn how to calculate tax liability for simple personal income tax returns. The software will allow you to prepare the return for your income from your new job and savings account, and will help you correct any mistakes you might make.

HINTS

1. To start the software, simply insert the disk in an IBM-PC or compatible and type "TAXES" and then hit the return (Enter) key.

2. Work through each section of the tutorial in turn. However, if you already are familiar with the material covered in a section, you may skip it and go on to the next section.

3. The tutorial is self-correcting. It includes a self-test for additional practice, too.

ASSIGNMENT I-4B-3: <u>How Taxes Are Calculated</u>: Book-Tax Differences

SETTING

You are an accountant for Dow Corning Corp., a 50-50 joint venture of Dow Chemical Company and Corning, Inc., headquartered in Midland, Michigan. For years, your company was the largest manufacturer in the world of silicone breast implants and also supplied silicone gel to many other implant makers. However, in 1992, after more than a million women had elected to have implants, the U.S. Food and Drug Administration (FDA) halted cosmetic silicone breast implants. The FDA's decision followed a number of lawsuits and other complaints alleging that leaking implants caused serious health problems.

By the end of 1992, Dow Corning discontinued its silicone implant manufacturing business. By this time, the company had been named as a defendant in almost 7,000 suits relating to silicone implants.

Until September of 1993, it was almost impossible to even estimate the potential financial impact of the suits. But then, a group of lawyers representing various plaintiffs met with representatives of Dow Corning and other defendants (other manufacturers, health care providers, raw materials suppliers, and so on) to propose a large class-action settlement. The plan was to create a $4.75 billion fund to compensate women with claims of physical or emotional injury from breast implants. Dow Corning Corp. and the other defendants would each contribute to the fund.

By the end of 1993, settlement negotiations were still going on, but the parties felt an agreement would be reached. However, the parties were still having difficulty reaching a final agreement on the exact terms of the deal. For example, there were disputes among some of the defendants about their relative individual shares of contributions to the settlement fund.

At the end of 1993, Dow Corning estimated that its share of contributions to the fund would be about $1.24 billion. Of this amount, about half would be covered by insurance proceeds, leaving Dow Corning with a before-tax cost of $640 million and an after-tax cost of $415 million (since the settlement costs would, at some point, be tax deductions for Dow Corning).

It is now early in 1994, and you are trying to decide how to handle the estimated settlement cost for book and tax purposes.

ASSIGNMENT

Determine how much of the estimated settlement cost should be included in the calculation of Dow Corning Corp.'s 1993 net income for financial reporting purposes. Justify your decision.

Also determine how much of the estimated settlement cost should be deducted from Dow Corning Corp.'s taxable income on its 1993 federal income tax return. Justify your decision.

HINTS

1. Consider the needs of the user groups for financial reports and tax returns.

2. Remember that generally accepted accounting principles require recognition of a liability and the related loss if: (1) the liability and related loss arose from a past transaction or event, (2) it is probable that the entity will be held liable, and (3) the amount of the liability and related loss are reasonably estimable. Are these criteria met?

3. Remember that tax law typically allows recognition of a deduction when the obligation is definite. Is this criterion met?

ASSIGNMENT I-4B-4: <u>**Goals of Taxation**</u>**: Tax Exemptions for Hospitals**

SETTING

You've come back home to Erie, Pennsylvania on a short break from college, where you are currently taking introductory courses in economics and accounting. As you sit at the breakfast table with Mom and Dad, the conversation turns to a burning local issue--should Erie's Hamot Medical Center continue to be exempt from taxes?

Dad feels strongly that the hospital should not be tax exempt because the exemption gives Hamot Medical Center an unfair advantage over for-profit competitors. Mom feels strongly that the tax exemption is justified because of all the good things the hospital has done for the community, including its recent efforts to revitalize the decaying downtown area.

Looking up from your doughnut, you remark that you have just been talking about taxation in your accounting class. Seeing a chance to break their deadlock, Mom and Dad turn and ask, "So, what do you think about the medical center?"

ASSIGNMENT

Read *The Wall Street Journal* article (on the next page) about the Hamot situation. Decide what your personal position is and come to class prepared to present your position to "Mom" and "Dad." Remember that they may question you and ask you to support your logic.

HINTS

Try to assess the present situation (the hospital is tax-exempt) in relation to the 3 goals of taxation. Then, compare the alternative (the hospital should be taxed) to the same 3 goals.

The debate over tax-exempt hospitals is an important issue in many areas. Many stories about the controversy have appeared in the press. If you feel you do not know enough about hospitals to answer the question, a little library research may pay off well.

Think through your position. Play "devil's advocate" with yourself by trying to tear down your own arguments. Try to anticipate the questions "Mom" or "Dad" will raise.

Challenge to Erie Hospital's Tax Status Gains Attention of Cash-Poor U.S. Cities

By ALECIA SWASY

Staff Reporter of THE WALL STREET JOURNAL

ERIE, Pa.—Past the vacant downtown store fronts and shuttered office buildings sits this depressed city's most lavish developer—the local hospital.

Hamot Health Systems Inc. has spent millions to raze tenements and sleazy bars that once loomed just outside its emergency-room doors. Condominiums, townhouses, perhaps a hotel will soon dot the waterfront overlooking Hamot's marina on Erie Bay. "This used to be the worst part of town," says Dana Lundquist, Hamot chief executive officer. "Now it's the best."

Yet local government officials don't embrace Hamot's benevolence. Despite profits of $6.9 million in fiscal 1989, Hamot doesn't pay taxes on most of its property. The reason: The hospital qualifies as a public charity. "It hardly seems right," says Gerald Villella, deputy solicitor for the city, which along with Erie's school district has sued to force Hamot to pay at least $600,000 in property taxes a year.

It's a legal battle that could have national implications. A court ruling in the non-jury Erie case is expected this spring. A verdict against Hamot could prompt challenges to tax exemptions that nonprofit hospitals claim in scores of cities.

Tax Crunch

Nonprofit hospitals have been targeted by tax collectors to offset a declining tax base in many communities. Not all hospitals are wealthy, of course. But the marinas, restaurants and office buildings of those that are make them a target of public outrage. A recent nationwide survey of hospital administrators showed that roughly 70% of them figure their property-tax exemption is in jeopardy.

"The halo is off health care," says Uwe Reinhardt, a health policy economist. "Sooner or later, all communities will go after their hospitals."

Hospitals were first granted tax exemptions on the theory they deserved them because they treated indigent patients, relieving local governments of that burden.

But the public, which is footing a higher tax bill because of the exemptions, is becoming increasingly critical of such arrangements. In Pittsburgh, for instance, County Solicitor Ira Weiss says the city and the county will this week initiate a legal challenge to the tax-exempt status of Allegheny General, the county's largest hospital. The hospital is exempt from property taxes yet had net income of $36.4 million in 1988, for a net profit margin of about 10%. Properties owned by Allegheny General are among 100 that Mr. Weiss wants on the tax rolls.

Long Lists

In both Pittsburgh and Erie, local officials figure at least one-third of their city properties are exempt from property taxes. The lists include properties held by universities and local government, too.

Giving a profitable hospital such as Hamot a tax break isn't popular in Erie, especially when local folks are smarting from paying higher taxes and a new garbage-collection fee. Police and fire services have been trimmed as the city scrimps to balance its budget. "The city is in pretty bad shape," Mr. Villella says.

Courtroom disclosure of Hamot's financial strength has provided fodder for local newspaper columnists. Particularly irksome to readers was the disclosure of Mr. Lundquist's salary of about $200,000, plus perks. "For a purely public charity, that's really out of line," says John Beatty, attorney for the school district.

Hamot has enjoyed a surplus for several years, allowing the parent company to use about $26 million in health-care profits to buy real estate, such as the marina, and revive the downtown.

Across from the hospital, for instance, a Hamot partnership owns a seven-story office complex, complete with a tony restaurant, Back Bay Lights. "They've turned into their own private redevelopment authority," Mr. Beatty says.

Charity Test

By his measure, even Hamot's medical center flunks the public-charity test because it no longer relies on charitable contributions to survive nor does it donate a substantial amount of its services.

Hamot defends the tax exemption for its hospital grounds, noting that it provides about $16 million in services free of charge each year. "We treat more indigent than any other hospital in Northwestern Pennsylvania," says Stephen Danch, Hamot's vice president of finance. "That balances any pressures in property taxes." Besides, Hamot's for-profit affiliates pay about $200,000 a year in property taxes.

Hamot figures its decision to stay and clean up the neighborhood was charity, because "no other business was capable" of salvaging the area, says Mr. Lundquist. "It was a poor business decision," he adds. "It would've been better to move."

One option to settle such disputes is for the hospital to offer some payment in lieu of taxes. Erie County dropped out of the lawsuit against Hamot when the company agreed to give $300,000 to finance a county 911 emergency system. "We wanted the payments to be related to our health-care mission," says Mr. Lundquist.

Hamot resists a similar pact with the city and schools because it wouldn't have control over how the money was spent. Besides, there's a principle involved, and Mr. Lundquist firmly believes that his and other hospitals should retain their charitable status. "The easiest way is to pay the money and run," he says. "But we're not going to do that."

ASSIGNMENT I-4B-5: <u>**Tax Complexity/Simplification**</u>: **Reading the Internal Revenue Code**

(This assignment was adapted from a problem created by Michael L. Duffy, University of Southern California.)

SETTING

You are a student studying *Core Concepts of Accounting Information.* You have learned about the various goals Congress may have in mind while writing tax legislation. You have also considered different ways to evaluate tax equity (horizontal equity, vertical equity, and the benefit principle). But, you have never seen a section of the Internal Revenue Code.

A senior accounting major offers you a bet. The bet is that you can't understand Section 135 of the Internal Revenue Code. To win the bet, you must be able to explain the provision described in the code section, determine the possible goals of the legislature in enacting this provision, and evaluate the equity of the provision.

ASSIGNMENT

Read Section 135 of the Internal Revenue Code. Then, see if you can accomplish the 3 requirements of winning the bet:

1. Translate the section into simpler language that explains the provision.
2. List the goals of the provision.
3. Evaluate the equity of the provision.

HINTS

1. Don't skip the section title. The Internal Revenue Code provision is summarized in the section title. Don't skip anything else, either. Every phrase means something.

2. Remember that tax laws are written by lawyers. The laws use very specific wording to help ensure that the each law says exactly what it is intended to say. However, "legalese" is hard to read, so you need to translate it into everyday words. Remember that the

underlying ideas in the tax code can be simple even if the words are complex. Look for the simple ideas. Read slowly. Figure out one phrase at a time. For example, the 9 lines of Sec. 135(b)(1)(A) can be broken down as follows:

(1) There's a catch--
    (A) if
  (i) you get more for the savings bond than
  (ii) you pay for tuition and fees
then the income from the savings bond is only tax-exempt up to the total of your tuition and fees; the rest is taxable income.

3.   Don't forget to use your dictionary. For example, if you don't know what a "savings bond" is, look it up.

4.   Be patient. Don't give up. Even if you never need to read a section of the Internal Revenue Code again, there will be lots of occasions in life when you will need to translate complex language into simpler terms. Consider: the rental agreement for an apartment, the propositions on an election ballot, a contract with an employment agent, the insurance policy for your medical coverage...not to mention the rules for pre-registering for college courses!

INTERNAL REVENUE CODE SECTION 135
INCOME FROM UNITED STATES SAVING BONDS USED TO PAY HIGHER EDUCATION TUITION AND FEES.

[Sec. 135(a)]

(a) GENERAL RULE--In the case of an individual who pays qualified higher education expenses during the taxable year, no amount shall be includible in gross income by reason of the redemption during such year of any qualified United States savings bond.

[Sec. 135(b)]

(b) LIMITATIONS.--

(1) LIMITATION WHERE REDEMPTION PROCEEDS EXCEED HIGHER EDUCATION EXPENSES.--

(A) IN GENERAL.--If--

(i) the aggregate proceeds of qualified United States savings bonds redeemed by the taxpayer during the taxable year exceed

(ii) the qualified higher education expenses paid by the taxpayer during such taxable year,

the amount excludable from gross income under subsection (a) shall not exceed the applicable fraction of the amount excludable from gross income under subsection (a) without regard to this subsection.

(B) APPLICABLE FRACTION--For purposes of subparagraph (A), the term "applicable fraction" means the fraction the numerator of which is the amount described in subparagraph (A)(ii) and the denominator of which is the amount described in subparagraph (A)(i).

(2) LIMITATION BASED ON MODIFIED ADJUSTED GROSS INCOME.--

(A) IN GENERAL.--If the modified adjusted gross income of the taxpayer for the taxable year exceeds $40,000 ($60,000 in the case of a joint return), the amount which would (but for this paragraph) be excludable from gross income under subsection (a) shall be reduced (but not below zero) by the amount which bears the same ratio to the amount which would be so excludable as such excess bears to $15,000 ($30,000 in the case of a joint return).

(B) INFLATION ADJUSTMENT.--In the case of any taxable year beginning in a calendar year after 1990, each dollar amount contained in subparagraph (A) shall be increased by an amount equal to--

(i) such dollar amount, multiplied by

(ii) the cost-of-living adjustment under section 1(f)(3) for the calendar year in which the taxable year begins, determined by substituting "calendar year 1989" for "calendar year 1987" in subparagraph (B) thereof.

(C) ROUNDING.--If any amount as adjusted under subparagraph (A) or (B) is not a multiple of $50, such amount shall be rounded to the nearest multiple of $50 (or if such amount is a multiple of $25, such amount shall be rounded to the next highest multiple of $50).

[Sec. 135(c)]

(c) DEFINITIONS.--For purposes of this section--

(1) QUALIFIED UNITED STATES SAVINGS BOND.--The term "qualified United States savings bond" means any United States savings bond issued--

(A) after December 31, 1989,

(B) to an individual who has attained age 24 before the date of issuance, and

(C) at discount under section 3105 of title 31, United States Code.

I-4-73

(2) QUALIFIED HIGHER EDUCATION EXPENSES.--

(A) IN GENERAL.--The term "qualified higher education expenses" means tuition and fees required for the enrollment or attendance of--

(i) the taxpayer
(ii) the taxpayer's spouse, or
(iii) any dependent of the taxpayer with respect to whom the taxpayer is allowed a deduction under section 151.

at an eligible educational institution.

(B) EXCEPTION FOR EDUCATION INVOLVING SPORTS, ETC.--Such term shall not include expenses with respect to any course or other education involving sports, games, or hobbies other than as part of a degree program.

(3) ELIGIBLE EDUCATIONAL INSTITUTION.--The term "eligible educational institution" means-

(A) an institution described in section 1201(a) or subparagraph (C) or (1) of section 481(a)(1) of the Higher Education Act of 1965 (as in effect on October 21, 1988), and

(B) an area vocational education school (as defined in subparagraph (C) or (D) of section 521(3) of the Carl D. Perkins Vocational Education Act) which is in any State (as defined in section 521(27) of such Act), as such sections are In effect on October 21, 1988.

(4) MODIFIED ADJUSTED GROSS INCOME--The term "modified adjusted gross income" means the adjusted gross income of the taxpayer for the taxable year determined--

(A) without regard to this section and sections 911, 931, and 933, and
(B) after the application of sections 86, 469, and 219.

[Sec. 135(d)]

(d) SPECIAL RULES.--

(1) ADJUSTMENT FOR CERTAIN SCHOLARSHIPS AND VETERAN BENEFITS.--The amount of qualified higher education expenses otherwise taken into account under subsection (a) respect to the education of an individual shall be reduced (before the application of subsection (b) by the sum of the amounts received with respect to such individual for the taxable year as--

(A) a qualified scholarship which under section 117 is not includable in gross income.

(B) an educational assistance allowance under chapter 30, 31, 32, 34, or 35 of title 38, United States Code, or

(C) a payment other than a gift, bequest, devise, or inheritance within the meaning of section 102(a) for educational expenses, or attributable to attendance at an eligible educational institution, which is exempt from income taxation by any law of the United States.

(2) NO EXCLUSION FOR MARRIED INDIVIDUALS FILING SEPARATE RETURNS.--If the taxpayer is a married individual (within the meaning of section 7703), this section shall apply only if the taxpayer and his spouse file a joint return for the taxable year.

(3) REGULATIONS.--The Secretary may prescribe such regulations as may be necessary or appropriate to carry out this section, including regulations requiring record keeping and information reporting.

Amendments P.L. 100-647. § 6009(a):

Act Sec. 6009(a) amended Part III of subchapter B of chapter 1 by redesignating section 135 and by inserting after section 134 a new section 135 to read as above.

The above amendment applies to tax years beginning after December 31, 1989.

ASSIGNMENT I-4B-6:   <u>Goals of Taxation</u>: Achieving Social Goals

SETTING

In January 1992, Anheuser-Busch Co., the world's largest brewer, announced its sales results for 1991. The company announced that in 1991 it sold 86 million barrels of beer, a slight decline from the 86.5 million barrels sold in 1990. This was the first sales decline Anheuser-Busch had experienced in 15 years.

Shortly after the results were announced, some analysts suggested that the .5% decrease in sales was caused by the federal excise tax on beer, which had doubled beginning January 1, 1991. The excise tax jumped from about $9 a barrel to $18 a barrel, which works out to about 32 cents per six-pack. The analysts reasoned that the combination of the higher cost of beer and the recession drove beer drinkers to less expensive brands than Anheuser-Busch.

Other stock analysts argued that it was the 1990 sales that were thrown off by the increase in excise taxes, not the 1991 sales. They observed that Anheuser-Busch's 1990 sales included particularly strong sales in December, 1990. They reasoned that restaurant and bar owners who would otherwise have made purchases in January 1991 rushed to make their purchases in December 1990 to avoid having to pay the increased excise tax.

At about the same time that Anheuser-Busch reported its 1991 sales results, Coors Brewing Co. (a subsidiary of Adolph Coors Co.) reported record-breaking 1991 sales of 19.5 million barrels. This was a 1.2% increase over 1990 sales, which had also been a record-breaking year.

You are an investigative reporter for a newspaper that is planning a series of stories on taxation. Your editor has asked you to cover the story: Did increased excise taxes cause a drop in beer sales?

ASSIGNMENT

Assess the facts reported in the press and the logic of the analysts.

In addition to providing your assessment of the evidence, suggest specific ways that accounting information could be used to provide additional evidence about the relationship between excise taxes and beer sales.

HINTS

Unless you are already familiar with the firms in the beer industry, you may find it helpful to do some simple library research on the industry. For example, it might be helpful to know which companies produce relatively low-priced beer and which companies produce relatively high-priced beer.

ASSIGNMENT I-4B-7:   Goals of Taxation: Clinton's Proposals

SETTING

When President Bill Clinton took office in January 1993, he inherited the largest federal budget deficit in history and the highest public debt level in history. Following the 1992 election campaign, there was ample evidence that the public was concerned over mounting deficits and debt and wanted the President and Congress to "do something" about it.

Within the first year of his administration, Clinton suggested several tax proposals that were related to cutting the deficit or finding new ways to fund programs without increasing the deficit. The proposals included:

♦ An increase of 15 cents per gallon to the gasoline tax--Estimated revenues: $15 billion a year.

♦ A new, broad-based energy tax levied on BTUs (British Thermal Units, a measure of heat content in various energy sources, such as oil, gas, and coal)--Estimated revenues: $18 billion a year

♦ An import fee of $5 a barrel on foreign-produced oil brought into the United States--Estimated revenues: $11 billion a year

♦ A value-added tax on goods and services--Estimated revenues: a 5% VAT would raise about $140 billion a year

♦ A 10% investment tax credit, available on business purchases of equipment in excess of 80% of 1992 equipment purchases--Estimated impact: $11 billion of credits (reduced taxes) over 2 years would spur equipment purchases, leading to increased jobs; an estimated 500,000 new jobs would add tax revenues to balance out the cost of the credit within 2 years

♦ Increased taxes on tobacco and alcohol to help pay for a revamped health care system--Estimated revenues: $35 billion

You are a legislative assistant to a new member of the House of Representatives. The Representative has asked you to prepare a brief analysis of these proposals, indicating the nature of each proposed item, and focusing on the pros and cons of each proposal.

ASSIGNMENT

[Note: Your instructor will let you know whether to do 1 proposal or all 6 proposals and will give you additional directions, if any.]

Prepare a briefing report for the Representative. The report should contain *1 clearly-written page* on each proposal. Each page should be organized as follows:

♦ a brief description of the proposal;

♦ a categorization of the proposal by type of tax--for example, consumption tax, wealth tax, and so on; and

♦ an analysis of the equity of the proposals--that is, discuss what group(s) bear the burden and/or the benefits.

HINTS

Remember that your briefing report should be brief, but complete and objective, noting the pros and the cons of each proposal. Bear in mind that the Representative serves voters. Which voter groups are likely to favor or oppose each proposal?

ASSIGNMENT I-4B-8: <u>**Goals of Taxation**</u>**: Two Tax Twists from Texans**

<u>SETTING</u>

When the Republicans swept the 1994 Congressional election, several members of the House of Representatives almost immediately began to suggest new ways to raise tax revenues.

The House Majority leader, Richard Armey of Texas, argued for replacing the income tax--both corporate and personal--with a "flat tax." You know that a flat tax is a tax at a relatively low rate, but that it applies to a relatively broad base. This is true about Armey's suggested flat tax for individuals. Individuals would pay a tax rate of 17% on all wages, salaries and pensions (but not Social Security). No other income (e.g., dividend or interest income) would be taxed. The flat tax plan allows for fixed exemptions for a taxpayer, the taxpayer's spouse and the taxpayer's dependents, but does not allow any other exemptions, deductions or credits. This means that long-standing tax deductions, such as those for paying mortgage interest or making charitable contributions, would no longer be available to taxpayers.

The new chair of the House Tax-Writing Committee, Representative William Archer, is another Texan. Archer has suggested eliminating corporate and personal income taxes entirely. In their place, Archer wants to see a national sales tax.

You are a legislative assistant to a new Congressional Representative. The Representative has asked you to prepare a brief analysis of these proposals, indicating the nature of each proposed item, and focusing on the pros and cons of each proposal.

<u>ASSIGNMENT</u>

Prepare a briefing report for the Representative. The report should contain *1 clearly-written page* on each proposal. Each page should be organized as follows:

♦ a brief description of the proposal;

♦ a categorization of the proposal by type of tax--for example, consumption tax, wealth tax, and so on; and

◆ an analysis of the equity of the proposals--that is, discuss what group(s) bear the burden and/or the benefits.

HINTS

Remember that your briefing report should be *brief,* but complete and objective, noting the pros and the cons of each proposal. Bear in mind that the Representative serves voters. Which voter groups are likely to favor or oppose each proposal?

ASSIGNMENT I-4B-9:   Goals of Taxation: What Do the Voters Want?

SETTING

In election years, politicians tend to listen very carefully to voters. In 1996, what politicians heard from voters--loud and clear--was: "Simplify taxes." Both the Democratic and Republican parties supported tax reform, but, as any voter would expect, they proposed 2 different plans.

Republicans rallied around a "flat tax" proposal sponsored by House Majority Leader Richard K. Armey (R-Texas) and Senator Richard C. Shelby (R-Alabama). Their tax proposal became the focus of its own web set on the Internet, reached via:

http://flattax.house.gov/

The web site includes a detailed summary of the proposal, various endorsements, and the full text of the bill, H.R. 2060.

Democrats preferred a home page touting "The 10 Percent Tax Plan," a tax simplification proposal offered by House Minority Leader Richard A. Gephardt. This site contains a summary of the tax plan, various endorsements, and charts that let taxpayers compare how much they would pay under this plan versus how much they would pay under the Armey/Shelby flat tax proposal or the current tax system. This web site may be reached via:

http://www.house.gov/democrats/taxplan/taxplan.html

Both plans would clearly simplify taxes. For example, the Tax Foundation calculated that the cost of maintaining tax records and filling out tax forms would drop to under $10 billion a year under the flat tax plan, versus over $200 billion a year under the current system.

However, as you are aware because of your accounting education, there are factors to consider other than simplicity when creating a tax system. These factors include the effectiveness of taxes in raising revenues, the fairness of the tax system, and the ability to encourage desirable behaviors or discourage undesirable behaviors.

ASSIGNMENT

As a voter, investigate the 2 tax proposals and prepare a brief report directed toward other voters that:

♦   briefly describes each proposal;

♦   compares the 2 proposed programs in terms of:
- --   simplification
- --   the ability to raise revenues
- --   fairness to taxpayers
- --   the ability to encourage desirable behaviors or discourage undesirable behaviors

HINTS

Remember that your briefing report should be *brief*, but complete and objective, noting the pros and the cons of each proposal. Don't let your party affiliation rule your judgment.

The web sites of the proposal authors are likely to be one-sided in their views. While it is not required to do so, you can find much more information about these tax simplification proposals from other Internet sites, if desired.

ASSIGNMENT I-4B-10:   <u>Basic Concepts of Taxation</u>: Where Have I Heard Something About That?

<u>SETTING</u>

When you began taking a course on the *Core Concepts of Accounting Information,* one of the first things your instructor told you was that accounting provides tools for life and that the course should help you learn to use accounting information. Since that seemed a bit vague, your instructor gave you some examples of how you would be able to apply your knowledge. One of the examples was: "You should see a difference, by the end of this course, in your ability to read and understand accounting-related articles in the business and general press."

Now, you are only a few weeks into the course, but already you are starting to notice newspaper articles that relate to topics you are studying. Just this week you noticed the following 3 press reports:

♦   A financial press story reports an argument within the airline industry. The argument involves what type of taxes to use to raise money to support the Federal Aviation Administration. Seven of the U.S.'s largest airlines (American, Continental, Delta, Northwest, TWA, United and USAir) have been lobbying Congress to charge all airline passengers a "user fee" of $2 per flight ($1 per flight for turboprop and commuter planes). Southwest Airlines and many of the other discount airlines oppose this plan and suggest instead a 10% ticket tax--that is, a tax that rises as the cost of a ticket goes up.

♦   A widely-circulated media story about comedian Dave Barry notes that his favorite IRS tax form is Form 1118-Schedule J, titled: *Separate Limitations Loss Allocations and Other Adjustments Necessary to Determine Numerators of Limitation Fractions, Year-End Recharacterization Balances, and Overall Foreign Loss Account Balances.*

♦   A story in a Florida newspaper reports that the ecology of the Everglades has been degrading over the past few years. In response, environmentalists want a 2-cent per pound tax on all sugar grown in the Everglades Agricultural Area. Much of the proceeds of the tax would be used to help restore damaged areas and protect undamaged areas of the Everglades. Sugar workers are quoted as opposing the tax because they fear the tax will make Everglades-grown sugar more expensive, and that consumers will turn to cheaper imported sugar, causing Florida sugar workers to lose their jobs.

ASSIGNMENT

Tie each of these stories to a something discussed in this module.

HINTS

Consider this a test of whether or not you are getting your tuition's worth of tools from this course. If not, suggest (to yourself or your instructor) some means for increasing the value.

ASSIGNMENT I-4B-11:   Tax Complexity/Simplification: Taxation of Internet Transactions

SETTING

You have an idea for an entrepreneurial venture--a business that sells college textbooks at discount prices over the Internet. Basing your idea on the model of Amazon.com, an Internet bookseller, you have the dream of making a profit while selling textbooks direct to students at prices lower than any college bookstore.

Like Amazon.com, yours would be a virtual business--all your transactions would be conducted over the Internet. At present, you are putting together a business plan, which includes investigating a number of issues that could potentially effect your business. One of these issues is taxation of electronic commerce, which could have enormous implications for your business.

ASSIGNMENT

Find answers to the following questions:

◆ Are there any federal, state, or local taxes on businesses conducted over the Internet?

◆ What is the U.S. Treasury position on taxation of electronic commerce? What policy changes is the Treasury contemplating?

◆ Has the U.S. Congress made any attempts to regulate the taxation of electronic commerce?

Prepare a brief written report on your findings that will become part of your business plan.

HINTS

Some of your research can be conducted via the Internet. For example, the U.S. Treasury has a website (**http://www.ustreas.gov**) that includes a search engine. There are also several websites that will give you access to information about bills in the U.S. Congress, including **http://thomas.loc.gov/**.

THE FOLLOWING PAGES

CONTAIN THE SOLUTIONS FOR

THE SELF-CORRECTED ASSIGNMENTS

IN THIS

MODULE.

SOLUTION TO ASSIGNMENT I-4A-2

Generating Money to Pay for Public Goods and Services:
The 1995 Orange County California Ballot

Measure R:

The measure is designed to provide funds for general operating activities of the County. The funds would help preserve essential County services and keep school funding at pre-bankruptcy levels. Payments due to cities and other creditors for obligations related to the bankruptcy would also be eligible for payment out of the tax receipts.

The money would be raised by a consumption tax. No estimate of the expected total cost is given, but the sales tax rate would increase by 0.5% from 7.75% to 8.25% for 10 years, unless repealed. The tax base would be the same retail sales and uses of tangible personal property under the current sales and use tax. Thus, a curious taxpayer could estimate the total taxes to be raised by multiplying 0.5% times the most-recent year's sales subject to the current tax.

Note: For the 1996 elections, California ballot information was available via the Internet. Voters could download ballot propositions, legislative analyses, and arguments for and against propositions. Election results were available online soon after the votes were counted. California voter information is accessible via the California Secretary of State's home page (**http://www.ss.ca.gov**), which also includes accounting information about campaign financing, including statements detailing contributions and expenses of candidates for public office.

MODULE INDEX

-ABC-

-GHI-

-JKL-

-MNO-

-PQR-

-STU-

-VWXYZ-

5

MODULE 5: OTHER USERS OF ACCOUNTING INFORMATION

1997-1998 edition

Table of Contents

MODULE 5: OTHER USERS OF ACCOUNTING INFORMATION

Estimated Time Budget

Task	Time Estimate
Reading Module 5	60 - 90 minutes
Assignments for Module 5	
Assignment 5-1	90 - 150 minutes
Assignment 5-2	35 - 50 minutes
Assignment 5-3	30 - 45 minutes
Assignment 5-4	90 - 150 minutes
Assignment 5-5	60 - 90 minutes
Assignment 5-6	90 - 150 minutes
Assignment 5-7	60 - 120 minutes
Assignment 5-8	120 - 180 minutes
Assignment 5-9	90 - 150 minutes
Assignment 5-10	40 - 60 minutes

Note: *These time estimates, like all the time budgets for this course, should be adjusted to suit your own learning style. Time estimates for assignments assume that readings were completed before attempting the assignments.*

MODULE 5: OTHER USERS OF ACCOUNTING INFORMATION

When you think about users of accounting information, your first thoughts are likely to be about management (the primary internal user group) and investors and creditors (the primary external user group). You might also think of governments as users of accounting information, particularly in the roles of regulator and taxing authority. Yet there are still many other potential users of accounting information, including employees, suppliers, customers, competitors, donors, the public, reporters and researchers. In this module, we'll consider some examples of how these groups make use of accounting information.

EMPLOYEES AS USERS OF ACCOUNTING INFORMATION

> *Labor is prior to, and independent of capital. Capital is only the fruit of labor, and could never have existed if labor had not first existed.*
> *--Abraham Lincoln*

Employees have a legitimate need for accounting information about their employer and management has a responsibility to provide this information. As the Society of Management Accountants of Canada noted in its *Statement on Accountability*, management is accountable to employees for a variety of information needs:

> *Employee expectations are presenting formidable challenges to management. In addition to pay equity and equitable employment practices, job security and satisfaction, safety and health are common challenges presented by employees. Employees want to participate in the decision making as team members to ensure that their interests are well considered in the future plans for the enterprise.*

The statement goes on to note that management accountants must exercise "active leadership in developing reporting mechanisms and internal standards" for providing accounting information to employees and other stakeholders.

In this section, we'll discuss employees as users of accounting information. Our focus will be on what types of decisions employees need accounting information for, where employees get their accounting information, and why an increasing number of organizations are sharing non-public accounting information with employees.

Employees' Need for Accounting Information

Employees need accounting information for both personal and operating decisions. From the moment a person considers taking a new job to the moment that person retires, accounting information can be useful for all manner of personal decisions:

♦ **Deciding whether to seek or accept a job:** Prospective employees or employees who are thinking about leaving their current job to take another one may use accounting information to help decide whether an organization offers a good place of employment. Is the organization growing or contracting? Is it financially stable? Is its work force expanding? What are the prospects for future compensation and job stability? Is the organization's employee pension plan sound?

♦ **Making decisions about employment contracts:** Current employees (and their labor unions) also have many opportunities to use accounting information. Accounting information can help employees or their unions decide what types of adjustments in employment contracts are feasible goals for individual or collective bargaining. Or, accounting information can help employees or a union decide whether to make wage and benefit concessions to help an employer cut costs in times of fiscal stress. In 1992, for example, Delta Airlines--which had recently disclosed a record-breaking annual loss-- asked its pilots to defer a promised 5% pay increase. Before making their decision, the pilots' union looked at Delta's books to assess the extent of the fiscal problem and the potential contribution of deferring the pay increase.

♦ **Deciding whether to invest in the company:** Many companies provide the opportunity for employees to buy shares of stock in the company at a bargain price. Companies encourage employee stock ownership because employees who are also stockholders tend to be more motivated to help the organization maximize profits. If the employees' efforts help to make the company profitable, the employees who are stockholders share in that success through dividends and stock appreciation. However, employee stock ownership plans, like any investment, put the employees' money at risk-- that is, stocks can lose value, as well as gain value. Accounting information can help an employee decide whether to invest in the organization's employee stock ownership plan.

♦ **Deciding whether to invest with the company:** Some companies also give employees the opportunity to invest for their future in company-sponsored savings or capital accumulation plans. As with any investment decision, employees should monitor the results and the amount of risk they are taking. In 1994, employees of Atlantic Richfield Co. were stunned when the company's Money Market Plus fund for employees suffered a $22 million loss on investments in derivatives. While the company offered to reimburse the losses, the employees still learned a hard lesson: as Jim Kaitz, a vice president of the Financial Executives Institute put it, "People have to ask more questions, and they will."

In addition to needing accounting information for personal decisions, employees often need accounting information to help them make day-to-day operating decisions on their jobs. If, for example, a salesperson is trying to decide which of an organization's products or services to feature, accounting information about profit margins would be useful in reaching that decision. Or, if an engineer is trying to design a new model for the company's product line, information about the costs of various materials or production methods would be useful in designing a cost-effective product.

Sources of Accounting Information for Employees

Employees obtain accounting information from both externally published financial reports and internal (non-public) reports. With varying degrees of success, employees have sought and obtained access to accounting information about their organizations for several centuries. Accounting historians report examples of U.K. and U.S. firms preparing employee-oriented financial reports during the 1800s, although disclosure to employees was not then the norm. In the modern era, employees have become an increasingly important audience for accounting information. For example, many organizations prepare special **employee annual reports** that focus on information about employment statistics, salaries, benefits, safety, education and training programs, as well as on information about the organization's performance, profitability and plans for the future. France even requires by law that large companies publish employee annual reports including specified minimum disclosures.

While organizations rarely balk at sharing publicly-available information with employees, some organizations are reluctant to share non-public accounting information with them. For example, although experts on collective bargaining have long advocated sharing financial information as more advantageous than withholding financial information, organizations are sometimes reluctant to disclose information they fear may be used against them in labor negotiations.

A 1993 poll of *Inc.* magazine's readers (who are mainly entrepreneurs) revealed that 2 out of 3 had some reluctance about sharing financial information with their employees and cited a bevy of reasons for their hesitation:

> *Some feel rather proprietary about financial information. "Employees who know too much become greedy." Some seem concerned with maintaining traditional corporate hierarchy. "Too much information given to too many people will destroy the organizational structure." One major concern is the possibility that sharing numbers would put a company at a competitive disadvantage. "Employees may go to an enemy*

company and bring our info with them." Many think financial information is beyond most employees. "People don't understand overhead or return on investment." Employees, some say, just don't need this information to do their jobs. "It's necessary for employees to understand their own work, but it's distracting and counterproductive for them to understand the entire company."

On the other hand, many organizations have found that there can be substantial benefits to providing non-public, as well as publicly-available, accounting information to employees--a practice that has become known as **"open-book management**." For example, all of Wal-Mart's employees receive both weekly and monthly information about their own store's operations, including some non-public information such as delivery times and profit margins on particular items the store carries. In recent years, an increasing number of organizations have moved to an open-book management system.

The Movement Toward "Open-Book Management"

There are several reasons why organizations are becoming more open in sharing information with employees. Some reasons have to do with the changing business environment. The movement from an industrial age to an information age has made information more of a competitive tool. As managers and employees must react to an increasingly complex and rapidly changing business environment, free flow of information has become increasingly beneficial. Other reasons have to do with the capabilities of accounting systems. As technological advances have allowed the development of more sophisticated accounting systems, it has become more cost effective to produce and distribute detailed cost and profit information on particular products or projects. As benefits increase and costs fall, more information sharing with employees may be expected.

Providing accounting information to employees can help improve the effectiveness and efficiency of an organization because employees need information to help them make sound decisions. John Case, writing in the April 1993 issue of *Inc.* magazine about changes in the workplace ("A Company of Businesspeople"), made note of the growing number of companies choosing to share information--including some non-public financial information--with their employees. Case argues that as the workplace is changing from the traditional system (where managers had all the information and decision-making power) to a more team-oriented environment where employees share in the decision-making, providing accounting information to employees has become a hallmark of "new" (more modern) companies:

> *...[P]eople need the information necessary to make intelligent decisions. That is a truism, and any company that sets up quality teams or any other modification of the traditional system makes sure its employees have some data to work with. But businesspeople--executives and owners--don't just look at weekly production figures or defect rates; they look at the big picture: cash flow, budget projections, cost of capital, on and on. Their*

key tools, the income statement and the balance sheet, prepared by the month (at least), have traditionally been the province of the accounting department and top executives. The new companies make them available to all.

That may be the single biggest difference between the new approach and the old; that's why the system has been dubbed open-book management.

As Bob Argabright, a plant manager at Chesapeake Packaging, told Case, sharing non-public accounting information with employees makes sense because "I've never seen a parade yet that was very impressive where only the drum major had the sheet music."

The movement toward open-book management is not without its risks. When companies share non-public accounting information with employees, there is a risk that the information will leak outside of the organization. Since information has a competitive value, this is not an insignificant risk. Employees have an ethical obligation--and, in many cases, a legal obligation--to keep non-public information confidential. When companies practice open-book management, the ethical environment is critically important.

SUPPLIERS, CUSTOMERS AND COMPETITORS AS USERS OF ACCOUNTING INFORMATION

He who only knows his own side of the case, knows little...
-- John Stuart Mill

Suppliers and Customers

Suppose you are the sales representative for a company that manufactures furniture. You are contacted by the purchasing agent for a large chain of department stores. The chain wants you to supply them with an exclusive line of sofas and chairs for sale in the department stores. The deal will increase your revenues and profits substantially, but it will require that you expand your production capacity considerably. Should you take the deal?

To answer this question, you need accounting information. Is the department store chain in solid financial shape? If you become a supplier to the stores, you will depend on the stores for both profits and cash flows. Does the chain have the necessary liquidity to pay you on a timely basis for deliveries? Moreover, if the chain ceases to do business, you will still have to pay the costs of your expanded capacity, but you may find it difficult to find other buyers for the customized line of sofas and chairs. Is the department store chain clearly solvent?

Now turn the tables and consider this deal from another point of view. Suppose you are the department store chain, looking to be a customer of the furniture manufacturer. You also need accounting information to help you determine whether the furniture company is in sound enough financial position to be a reliable source of goods. Will the company be able to obtain sufficient resources to meet your production needs? Will the company be able to meet the cash flow demands of the increased production?

Whenever long-term supplier-customer relationships are being established, both parties may be wise to use accounting information to evaluate the relationship's chance for continued success. Even a one-shot deal--if the deal is important enough--may still merit the use of accounting information to check the financial health of the participants. A September 9, 1990 story by Michael Cieply in the *Los Angeles Times* described a chilling case where some customers' failure to obtain accounting information about the cryonics company they were doing business with had devastating consequences:

> To date, 26 people have been cryonically suspended--frozen for the future-- in the United States. As it happens, 24 of them are in California, where the urge to live forever is beginning to look like a serious business...[C]ryonics is clearly evolving from cult phenomenon into California's latest--and perhaps most troubled--growth industry...

> The sign-up boom--and the prospect that some groups will receive multimillion-dollar inheritances as the first generation of aging cryonics advocates begins to die--has sparked entrepreneurial vigor, as well as new problems, in the field that itself nearly expired in 1976. That's when the Cryonics Society of California suffered financial collapse...

> In the midst of a financial debacle, four bodies maintained at a Chatsworth storage facility were allowed to thaw, and a Los Angeles jury eventually entered a $1-million fraud award against CSC and its companion Cryonic Interment Inc., both now defunct. That helped to persuade cryonics advocates that nothing--except, perhaps, body-damaging autopsies requested by nosy insurance examiners--was to be feared more than financial instability.

Competitors

Christian Bovee--who lived from 1820 to 1904 and thus never had to make a decision about cryonics--observed, perhaps prematurely, that "Formerly, when great fortunes were only made in war, war was a business; but now when great fortunes are only made in business, business is war." While the "business is war" analogy only goes so far, it is true in at least one way: in business, as in war, it pays to know who you are up against. Competitors want to understand their competition. One way to learn about business competitors is to study their published accounting information. Are your competitors' sales increasing or decreasing? Are their profit margins holding steady or changing? Is any particular segment of the business doing exceptionally well or poorly? Are inventory levels growing or declining? Published financial information can help provide answers to these questions.

Companies considering "going public" must weigh the costs of public disclosure against the benefits of access to public capital markets. The fact that financial information published for the benefit of stockholders and creditors also may be valuable to competitors illustrates a potential indirect cost of financial disclosure. After Cirrus Logic Inc. went public, Joshua Hyatt interviewed CEO Michael Hackworth for *Inc.* magazine about the experience. One part of the experience was discovering that competitors found the information in the prospectus for the offering to be valuable:

> *Competitors, too, panned the prospectus for incriminating nuggets. One of them, delighted to find that one product line represented 70% of the company's revenues, derided Cirrus as a one-product company that wasn't serious about some of its customers. "It created an issue our salespeople had to deal with," says Hackworth with a sigh...."I understand what going public really means," says the 49-year-old. "It doesn't just mean that securities will be held by public shareholders instead of private ones. It means going public with a great deal of information. It's easy to underestimate the amount or detail that will come out."*

Companies that want to go public must balance the costs of disclosure against the benefit of being able to raise funds in public markets.

Accounting information can also be voluntarily shared with competitors in a cooperative effort that preserves confidentiality. Industry trade associations often assist their members in gathering financial information about firms in the industry. For example, the department stores in an area may confidentially report monthly sales data to a trade association that publishes the aggregate (combined) results for all the stores, without revealing the results for any individual store. Individual stores are willing to provide the information about their own results because they benefit from having the aggregate information about their industry. For instance, a store manager can see whether last month's sales decline was unique to the store or part of a larger industry-wide phenomenon. This information helps the manager decide what to do to counteract the decline.

Over the past decade, as many industries have experienced the "double whammy" of intensified competition and rapidly changing technology, one reaction has been to focus on improving operations through "benchmarking." **Benchmarking** is a systematic comparison of the work processes of one organization with those of its peers. Organizations use benchmarking to determine how well they are performing various operations relative to others. In particular, they look to the best in their industry and try to analyze how to change their own operations to reach the benchmarks set by the best performers.

Sometimes, benchmarking even takes place across industries. For example, a hospital might benchmark its admission process against the best practices in hotel registration. One airline benchmarked its turnaround time for aircraft at the gates against Indianapolis 500 pit crews.

Benchmarking often requires a substantial commitment to information sharing. For example, the National Association of College and University Business Officers (NACUBA) began a benchmarking program during the 1992-1993 academic year. Forty academic institutions took part in a detailed survey about operational and administrative costs in several dozen different areas, from bookstore operations to food services operations to the development office (the office responsible for soliciting donations). For example, the survey asked schools to report what it cost, per donor, to run their development office.

The participating schools received a detailed report of the survey data and--to encourage additional participation in future surveys--some summary data are publicly available for non-participants to share. For example, the survey reports the average and range (high to low) of development office costs per donor broken down by school type (public versus private). This helps schools evaluate--particularly when compared to donations received--whether their development efforts are cost-efficient and effective. As Robin Jenkins, director of the Financial Management Center of NACUBA, noted: "Benchmarking gives you a discipline, like when you go on a diet, stepping on a scale gives you a discipline." The survey is repeated periodically to update and expand the set of benchmarks.

DONORS AS USERS OF ACCOUNTING INFORMATION

Philanthropy is almost the only virtue which is sufficiently appreciated by mankind.
-- Henry David Thoreau, Walden

Donors form a major potential user group for accounting information. For example, according to the American Association of Fund Raising Counsel Inc., Americans contributed $150.7 b illion to all kinds of philanthropic (charitable) organizations in 1996. As can be seen in Figure I-5-1 (on the next page), 80% of the contributions came from individual donors; the rest came from foundations, bequests and corporate donors. How do donors know whether an organization seeking funds is a legitimate charity--one that is spending donations for the stated purpose? How do they know if the organization is operating efficiently--so that a reasonable amount of their donated funds will be used for the intended social purpose?

People or corporations with money to donate can use accounting information from tax filings and financial statements to evaluate the wisdom of contributing money to a particular charity. In this section, we'll talk about these 2 sources of information, as well as about information intermediaries who use tax and financial accounting information to help donors evaluate charities' performance. In addition, we'll consider some important financial reporting issues for charities.

Figure I-5-1
Philanthropy: Sources and Destinations, 1996
(Total Contributions: $150.7 billion)

Sources:

Corporations $8.5 billion (5.6%)
Foundations $11.8 billion (7.8%)

Individuals $119.9 billion (79.6%)
Bequests $10.5 billion (6.9%)

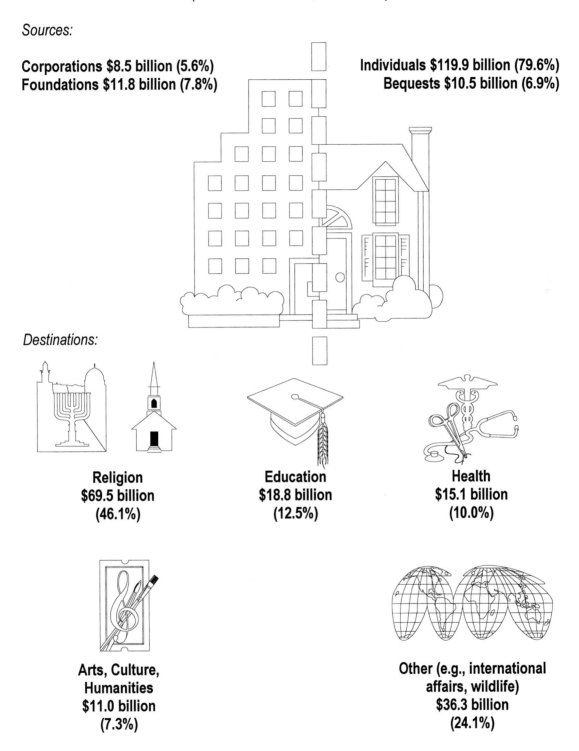

Destinations:

Religion
$69.5 billion
(46.1%)

Education
$18.8 billion
(12.5%)

Health
$15.1 billion
(10.0%)

Arts, Culture,
Humanities
$11.0 billion
(7.3%)

Other (e.g., international
affairs, wildlife)
$36.3 billion
(24.1%)

Data Source: American Association of Fund Raising Counsel, Inc.

Finding Information in "Information Returns"

Even though charities are tax-exempt in the United States, they must still file financial information with the Internal Revenue Service and appropriate state agencies in order to establish and maintain their tax-exempt status. U.S. federal law requires nonprofit organizations to make their annual **information returns** (known as **Form 990**) available for public inspection. Copies of an organization's Form 990 may also be obtained directly from the IRS under the Freedom of Information Act. The Form 990 reports information of various types, including:

♦ **basic operating data**, such as total receipts and total expenditures for the year (or other operating period);

♦ **some details about expenditures**, such as categorizing expenditures into groups, including: (1) program services (expenditures made for the organization's exempt purpose), (2) fundraising (expenditures made to seek contributions from donors), and (3) management and general (expenditures made to administer the organization); and

♦ **information about officers, directors, trustees, and key employees**, including total compensation paid to these people by the organization, its affiliates, and related entities--for example, if a business has a related non-profit charitable foundation and its director also holds a top management position with the business, compensation from both positions must be reported.

Finding Information in Audited Financial Statements

In addition to the Form 990 filings, many charitable organizations publish a full set of audited financial statements, which they supply on request to potential donors. Audited financial statements provide assurance that the organization is spending its funds as reported. This helps the donor distinguish legitimate charities from dubious organizations that prey on people's good intentions.

It is important for donors to determine the legitimacy of a charity because donors can often be targets for fundraising fraud. For example, in 1992, the state of California sued to close down a telemarketing firm, Orange County Charitable Services, accusing the firm of fraudulently raising $8.6 million for three charities. The state charged that the charities were created as "money-making fronts," rather than legitimate charities. One of the charities--United Citizens Against Drugs--raised $3.7 million from donors who thought they were supporting educational programs to prevent drug and alcohol abuse. In fact, less than $170,000 of the donated funds were spent on such programs. While this was a particularly large case that involved donors in several states, the district attorney's office for Orange County, California had previously estimated that the county's residents were being fleeced to the tune of $25,000 a day ($9 million a year) by solicitors for fraudulent charities. Potential donors should be wary of unfamiliar organizations that cannot provide audited financial statements.

Even among legitimate charitable organizations, some may be more efficient than others. Potential donors can use an organization's financial statements to determine how much of the donated funds are expended for the stated purpose, after fundraising and administrative expenses are paid. For example, the statements can be used to calculate the ratio of program expenses to total expenses. The lower the ratio, the smaller the portion of your donation that will be spent on the cause you want to help.

Potential donors may also be interested in looking at the size of the organization's fund balance and cash balance--the balances should not be so large as to spark doubts about whether there is a need to raise additional funds. By one rule of thumb, a charity should have enough funds to cover normal operating expenses for 2 years, but not much more than that.

Or, donors can use accounting information to evaluate the reasonableness of a charity's expenses. A few years ago, for example, donors to the United Way charities learned from the financial press that the group's national CEO was being paid a very high salary and many high-cost benefits, such as first-class air travel. Slowly the picture worsened. In 1995, the CEO and 2 other executives were sentenced to prison terms of up to 7 years for defrauding the United Way of over $1 million.

Reaction to the initial disclosure that the CEO's annual salary and benefits had reached $463,000--which was more than 4 times the average compensation for CEOs of national charities--was swift and strong. Donations to United Way charities across the country suffered. The CEO resigned, and the charity's new CEO quickly began instituting internal controls to prevent future problems. The new controls included improving the "tone at the top" by adding 15 seats to the national organization's board and creating new board committees on budgets, ethics and compensation. The new controls also included policies limiting travel expenses, creating daily meal allowances while on fundraising trips and requiring coach-class, rather than first-class, travel.

Information Intermediaries for Donors

Since there are over 450,000 U.S. charities and individual donations may be for relatively small amounts, donors may not always believe the cost of searching out accounting information about charities exceeds the benefits of protecting oneself from fraud and waste. But, donors need not directly examine a charity's Form 990s or audited financial statements to make use of accounting information. Just as information intermediaries (like financial analysts and credit rating agencies) aid investment and credit decisions, information intermediaries also help potential donors make philanthropic decisions. For example, *Money* magazine publishes an annual efficiency ranking of the 100 largest national charities.

On a larger scale, the National Charities Information Bureau (NCIB) has been monitoring charitable organizations since 1918. The NCIB reviews the financial statements, tax returns and solicitation letters of charities and publishes research reports that evaluate the organizations. Individual donors may request up to 3 reports a year at no charge from the NCIB reported ratings on about 400 groups. In addition, the Council of Better Business Bureau's Philanthropic Advisory Service (PAS) also evaluates charities and publishes free or inexpensive reports to help donors assess effectiveness. The St. Louis-based American Institute of Philanthropy also serves as an information source about charities.

Each of these organizations has guidelines for their ratings. For example, one of the NCIB's guidelines is that nonprofit organizations should spend 60% or more of their revenues on their program, rather than on fundraising or administrative costs. In recent years, about 4 out of every 10 charities have failed to meet NCIB evaluation standards.

It is also important to check the consistency of information disclosed in various sources. For example, the National Association for the Advancement of Colored People (NAACP) had a long track record of receiving "A" ratings, the highest rating given by the American Institute of Philanthropy (AIP). But, the rating abruptly changed to a question mark (indicating inadequate or inconsistent records) in 1994 after the AIP found the NAACP had reported $3 million more expenses to the New York State Office of Charities Registration than it had disclosed on its Form 990 for the same period. The AIP's president commented that such a large discrepancy meant either sloppy bookkeeping or deliberate misreporting. This inconsistency may also have been an early warning signal of cashflow problems developing at the NAACP. Within a month, the NAACP had to furlough most of its staff for 15 days due to a large budget deficit and a severe cash crunch.

Financial Reporting Issues for Charities

The NCIB's 60%-plus guideline for program expenditures indicates how important it is to donors that a substantial portion of their donations be spent to further the main social purpose of the charity, rather than to administer the charity or solicit more donations. Thus, the accounting classification of expenditures as either **program expenditures** or **fundraising costs** is an important issue for charities.

Current financial accounting standards recognize that expenditures may have a dual purpose; thus, costs may be allocated (apportioned) between the two categories (program and fundraising). Suppose, for example, an environmental group pays for a mailing that includes information about the need to protect the environment and a plea for contributions. How much of the cost of this mailing--which helps fulfill the group's educational mission--should be treated as a program expenditure? How much of the cost of the mailing--which is a solicitation for funds--should be treated as a fundraising expenditure?

Up until 1987, a charity had only one option when accounting for dual-purpose expenditures. Generally accepted accounting principles then in effect required the charity to determine the expenditure's *primary* purpose and to use that purpose to determine its accounting classification. If, for instance, a mailing was considered to be 70% for fundraising and 30% educational, the entire cost of the mailing would be treated as a fundraising expenditure.

This method was simple, but not particularly accurate. Many charities count among their social goals informing the public about their chosen mission. The American Cancer Society, for example, includes among its goals educating the public about early detection of cancer. So, a mailing that both provides information about early warning signs for cancer and solicits donations for the charity, is, in reality, partly a program expenditure (the part that fulfills the organization's educational mission) and partly a fundraising expenditure (the part that asks for money). Treating the entire cost of the mailing as just a program expenditure or just a fundraising cost oversimplifies reality.

Consequently, in 1987, the American Institute of Certified Public Accountants issued a *Statement of Position* on "Accounting for Joint Costs of Information Materials and Activities of Not-for-Profit Organizations that Include a Fund-Raising Appeal." This statement of position--which is considered part of the body of generally accepted accounting principles for charities--holds that joint costs of a multipurpose mailing (or any type of dual-purpose activity) may be allocated between fundraising and program expenditures.

The suggested criteria for evaluating a dual-purpose mailing include the nature of the recipients of the direct mail and the contents of the materials. Under the current accounting standards, then, a charity's accountants determine what portion of the mailing relates to the program and what portion relates to fundraising. Next, they allocate the cost of the mailing proportionately between program and fundraising expenditures. Thus, if the mailing is considered to be 70% for fundraising and 30% educational, 70% of the cost would be considered a fundraising expenditure and the other 30% of the cost would be considered a program expenditure. These are judgments that the organization's accountants must make and their auditors must evaluate.

Recently, there has been much controversy over charities' financial accounting for dual purpose expenditures. While the basic idea that expenditures can have multiple purposes is not questioned, critics do question the soundness of judgments about the proportion of expenditures that is program-oriented. In a world where charities compete for donors' dollars, there is an incentive for charities to skew their judgments to understate fundraising expenditures.

Critics have questioned whether the accounting standards are being abused. For example, the National Charities Information Bureau has criticized the National Wildlife Federation for treating the cost of millions of dollars of merchandise it sells--including holiday cards and toys with wildlife conservation themes--as a program expenditure, rather than a fundraising expenditure. The National Wildlife Federation, on the other hand, claims this merchandise helps the organization carry out its mission to get people "excited about nature." Is this compliance with generally accepted accounting principles for charities or is it an "accounting game?"

In responses to concerns over accounting games, in 1997 the American Institute of Certified Public Accountants issued a new *Statement of Position*, effective for fiscal years beginning on or after December 15, 1997, that tightens the standards for deciding when costs may be allocated and requires disclosure when joint costs are allocated between fund-raising and program expenditures. The criteria do not specify or prohibit any particular allocation method, but they do set standards of purpose, audience and content that must be met.

Charities contribute substantially to the quality of life in American society. Yet, according to a 1992 study by the Independent Sector, an association of nonprofit groups and grant-makers, public confidence in charitable organizations has been declining. The association suggests that confidence in financial reporting is critical to maintaining donor confidence. In addition, concern for ethics, internal controls, and full disclosure are important aspects of the management of charities and are essential to keeping the trust of donors.

THE PUBLIC AS USERS OF ACCOUNTING INFORMATION

A business that makes nothing but money is a poor kind of business.
-- Henry Ford

Some people, notably Nobel prize-winning economist Milton Friedman, argue that the only valid goals for business enterprises are economic: to maximize profits and shareholder wealth. In achieving its economic goals, the only social responsibility of a business is to comply with legal requirements. Society benefits indirectly if the business is successful: the economy will be strengthened, better goods and services will be available, and jobs will be provided. But, according to this line of argument, a business has no direct social goals or responsibilities. Any social obligations that society deems appropriate to impose on businesses will be reflected in legal requirements that the company must obey.

Others argue that business entities, like individuals, are responsible to the society that empowers them. In pursuing their economic goals, businesses make use of societal resources--like clean air and water, community schools and police protection--and thus take on an obligation to the public, as well as to stockholders. Under this view, businesses are accountable to society for their efforts to improve the communities in which they operate and for the social costs-- like air pollution and noise pollution--their economic activities create. According to this line of argument, the social obligations of business extend beyond legal requirements (such as equal opportunity laws or pollution control laws) to include an ongoing responsibility to help solve social problems and improve the quality of life. The organization's interest in profits should be balanced by an interest in providing satisfying jobs, preserving the environment for future generations, and so on. Being socially responsible is simply an ethical obligation of business.

Still others argue that the two viewpoints may not be as far apart as it first appears. Being socially responsible, they argue, makes economic sense. Being a good "corporate citizen" creates a positive image for the business that is a valuable asset--customers may be more willing to buy a business's products or services because of the company's positive image. A 1994 poll by Roper Starch Worldwide for Cone Communications, for example, revealed that 78% of respondents felt a company's social responsibility reputation influences their buying decisions--and one-third were more influenced by a company's social activism than its advertising.

Moreover, being socially responsible forestalls further government regulation. Voluntary efforts to address social problems may be less costly in the long run than adding more layers of regulation. Walter Haas, Jr. of Levi Strauss & Co.-- an organization known for its long history of corporate social responsibility efforts, including affirmative action initiatives in the company and the communities where it operates and nation-wide AIDS education efforts-- commented in a speech to small business owners that being socially responsible may be costly in the short-run, but will increase profits in the long-run:

> *Some people argue that doing what's right is somehow contrary to doing what's good for business. I find this view both puzzling and wrong. In my own company, we have learned over and over again that when we do what we believe is proper, the company gains. I don't know how to translate that value into a number that appears on a financial statement, but I do know that we wouldn't want to be in business and we would not be the leader in our industry if we did not enjoy this kind of relationship with our people.*

Reporting on Social Costs and Benefits

Haas's remarks point out an important issue for accountants: how can we account for social costs and benefits? This question is the topic of much discussion internationally. In their book *Accounting for the Human Factor*, three accounting researchers from countries around the globe--Lee Parker (Australia), Kenneth Ferris (United States) and David Otley (England)--review the history and practice of accounting for social impact. They present several examples of actual and proposed accounting reports providing qualitative and quantitative social accounting disclosures. One of the examples they cite, which is based on the cost-benefit approach, is reproduced in Figure I-5-2 on the following page.

As you can imagine, there are profound measurement problems which must be faced in preparing a social accounting report. Primarily, it is difficult to measure

Figure I-5-2
Example of a Social Responsibility Report

PSI Ltd
Social Responsibility Report
Year Ended 30 June 19X8

Social Benefits

To employees

Increases in pay	$14,260	
Increase in company contributions to superannuation, long service leave, holiday pay	9,820	
Employee training	12,265	
Job enrichment program	6,240	
Tertiary course subsidies	4,200	
		$ 46,785

To consumers

Price reductions on sales of products benefitting from increased productivity of new process	3,480	
Decrease in repair charges to consumers (compared with 19X7)	2,970	
		$ 6,450

To community

Wages paid for new jobs created	26,400	
Increased taxes paid by company	5,760	
Donations to charities	1,100	
Equipment and facilities hired for use by outside groups	720	
Training of handicapped workers	4,695	
		$ 38,675

To environment

Cost of landscape gardening around manufacturing plants	13,240	
Cost of painting old building exteriors	9,870	
Cost of initiating air pollution control devices	26,400	
		$ 49,510
		$141,420

    TOTAL SOCIAL BENEFITS

Social Costs

To employees

Work-related injuries and illness	6,580	
Postponed cost of new safety devices	2,820	
Unpaid overtime worked	8,526	
		$ 17,926

To consumers

Reduced resale value on two products now rendered obsolete	26,500	
Cost of additional safety feature not added to one product (for this year's sales volume)	9,280	
		$ 35,780

To community

Increase in public facilities and services used	2,485	
Wages lost through layoffs	24,268	
		$ 26,753

To environment

Cost to local government of detoxifying local water supply	2,526	
Cost of non-renewable resources used	22,326	
Estimated cost of waste dumped	3,397	
		$ 28,249
		$108,708

    TOTAL SOCIAL COSTS

Net social benefits generated by company for year ended June 19X8		$ 32,712

Comprising:	$28,859	
Net Social Benefits to Employees	(29,330)	
Net Social Costs to Consumers	11,922	
Net Social Benefits to Community	21,261	
Net Social Benefits to Environment		$ 32,712

Source: Parker/Ferris/Otley, ACCOUNTING FOR THE HUMAN FACTOR, Copyright © 1989, pages 180-181. Adapted by permission of Prentice Hall, Englewood Cliffs, New Jersey.

the benefits of an organization's efforts to improve the quality of life for employees, consumers, or the community. For example, the social impact report shown in Figure I-5-2 lists employee training and training of handicapped workers as one way the organization benefits society. The dollar amounts attached to these items are the *costs* of the training. Thus, the "total social benefits" of $141,420 listed on the report are not really measuring the value to society, but merely the amount invested for societal benefit.

The difficulties encountered in assigning numerical values to social impact are one reason why many social accounting reports are restricted to qualitative (non-numeric) statements. For example, a company may disclose the existence of its programs to train handicapped workers without attaching a numerical value to the programs. The result is that less information is disclosed (e.g., the reader has no idea whether the training program was small or extensive), but the report avoids giving readers a false impression of precise valuation.

The debate over the appropriate way to measure and disclose social impact has built slowly over the past several decades, but promises to accelerate in the near future. In at least one area--environmental accounting--the debate has begun to move beyond the talking stage to the doing stage. At the start of the 1990s, 650 industry and government leaders who make up the World Economic Forum ranked the environment as the most important challenge facing business. In the U. S. alone, it was estimated that environmental liabilities could mount to between $750 billion and $1.2 trillion by the year 2020. Yet, there were no international standards and few national standards for what is sometimes called **"green accounting"**--the measurement of the impact of organizations on the environment. Since then, there has been a movement toward green accounting.

The Movement Toward "Green Accounting"

Environmental accounting information has many potential uses for making decisions within an organization, about an organization, or about an economy:

◆ **Decisions made within an individual organization**--such as decisions about how to design and manufacture a product, what equipment to invest in, or what to charge consumers for a product--can involve environmental costs. For example, if a company is considering locating a new plant on land that was previously used for a gas station, the costs of removing underground storage tanks and ensuring that the ground is free from hazardous chemicals must be considered. Management accounting information about environmental costs can be useful in making these internal decisions. When companies first begin to track environmental costs, managers are often surprised at their magnitude. For example, when Amoco Oil Company first measured environmental costs they were 7 times higher than managers had expected.

♦ **Decisions made about an individual organization by external user groups**--such as investors' decisions about whether to buy a company's stock, lending decisions by creditors, and decisions by local citizens about whether to move into the neighborhood where an organization operates-- may also make use of environmental accounting information. For example, before moving into a housing development next to an oil company, a homebuyer may want to know if there is any material litigation against the company for creating environmental pollution. Financial accounting information, such as that prepared for annual financial statements, can help with these decisions. External users are concerned with information not only about environmental costs, but also about environmental liabilities (such as a company's estimated future costs of cleaning up sites polluted by past manufacturing operations) and environmental assets (such as a company's investment in pollution prevention equipment).

♦ **Decisions made by national and international policy-makers about entire economies**--such as decisions made by national governments about conservation of natural resources, taxation policies, and how to increase the country's gross national product--may also benefit from information on environmental costs. For example, a government may need environmental accounting information to decide whether to allow more traffic through national parks or to decide whether or not to reduce fuel taxes. Environmental accounting at this level involves the aggregation of information from many individual organizations to create a picture of how environmental costs affect societal well-being.

Within organizations, management accounting for environmental costs is becoming quite common. A 1994 Price Waterhouse survey of a large sample of U.S. companies found that 73% were conducting environmental audits for internal use--an increase of 40% from 2 years earlier. The quality of the information, however, is not yet optimal. A study published in 1995 by the IMA Foundation for Applied Research found that not even 1 in 100 leading manufacturing companies had a complete system for effectively identifying and managing environmental impact. The study's author, Marc J. Epstein of Stanford University, observed that measurement within the framework of accounting and dollars is certainly difficult, but nonetheless necessary for effective decision-making.

What about information available to external decision-makers? A 1993 United Nations survey of 222 transnational companies found that most reported some information about environmental impact, but the information disclosed was inconsistent within industries and inconsistent between countries. Such reporting inconsistencies make it difficult, if not impossible, for financial report users to compare companies, industries and nations. Whether looking at individual organizations or entire economies, they rarely get all the information they would like to have for decision-making.

There are a number of current efforts to improve environmental accounting. Because this issue is so important to so many people, we'll take a look in this section at some of the ongoing efforts in 2 areas of the world--Europe and North America--to develop better methods of accounting for environmental impact.

European Efforts. European countries took the early lead in developing and implementing methods of accounting for environmental impact. For example, in June 1990, the Chartered Association of Certified Accountants in the U. K. published a research report on the *Greening of Accountancy*. The report recommended major changes to accounting and information systems to reflect environmental concerns. The proposals included:

♦ **compliance and ethical audits** to answer the question: Does the organization meet legal requirements and its own code of conduct?

♦ **waste and energy audits** to answer the question: Is the organization making the best use of its inputs?

♦ **environmental budgets** to set "green targets" for every activity center in the organization, and

♦ **environmental and social reporting**, including disclosure of the organization's : (1) environmental policies; (2) environmental spending; (3) emissions statements (measuring known pollutants released into the atmosphere); and (4) environmental contingencies (potential liabilities or losses, such as the danger of oil spills for an oil company).

Rob Gray, the University of Dundee professor who wrote the research report, concluded that "if organisations are to respond to environmental issues, there must be a substantial change in the organisational information systems--an area in which accountants have a great deal to offer."

In 1993, the European Union environment ministers adopted legislation to create a voluntary system of environmental auditing. The EU considered making the system mandatory for many companies, but decided to use a voluntary system since many environmental management standards and measurement tools were still being developed. The incentive for organizations to voluntarily participate is that they will be able to publicize the fact that they meet EU certification standards. This is expected to have a competitive value, such as making stock in these companies more attractive to investors.

Under the EU's voluntary certification program, managements of participating companies prepare environmental statements that describe significant environmental issues the organization faces, present a summary of figures on pollution emissions and other environmental costs, state the organization's environmental policies, and assess the performance of the organization's environmental protection systems. The statements are then audited. As part of the program, the EU has specified training standards to accredit environmental auditors, who may be either external auditors or internal auditors who are organizationally independent from the activities audited.

Even before the EU legislation, some European organizations, such as BSO/Origin, a Dutch information and technology consulting company, began experimenting with different ways of measuring and reporting environmental impact. BSO published its first environmental accounting report along with its 1990 annual report. The company estimated that its consulting business--which is not an industry one normally thinks of as particularly damaging to the environment--created 2.2 million guilders (approximately $1.2 million) of environmental costs (such as pollution) during the year. On the benefit side, the report also tallied the amount BSO spent on things that help improve the environment. The report drew much interest, yet the company's president voiced doubt about whether BSO would continue to prepare such a detailed environmental accounting report in the future. He cited 2 reasons for his doubts:

♦ **Measurement difficulties**: The degree of difficulty of measuring environmental benefits and costs makes report preparation very expensive--BSO spent about $175,000 to prepare their first report.

♦ **The lack of comparative benchmarks**: BSO discovered that much of the company's contribution to pollution came from things BSO purchased from other companies. Until green accounting becomes more widespread, BSO's report could only provide a small piece of the complete picture. Without more complete reporting by other organizations, BSO's report is difficult to interpret.

Despite these doubts, BSO did decide to continue publishing environmental accounting reports annually. Eckhart Wintzen, BSO's president, even suggested that companies should be taxed on their "net value extracted," or net environmental costs.

This raises an interesting question about the role that taxation can play in efforts to improve the environment. Worldwatch, an international environmental research organization, has suggested to the European Parliament in Strasbourg, France that income taxes should be replaced with environmental taxes as a primary source of government revenue. These "**green taxes**" are a form of consumption tax placed on the use of fossil fuels, pesticides, paper and paperboard, and so on. Recognizing the growing use of green taxes, in 1997 the European Commission adopted guidelines for the efficient use of environmental taxes in the EU.

North American Efforts. Relatively few North American companies did much in the way of measuring or disclosing environmental costs before 1990, but this has been changing recently, with Canadian efforts taking a slight lead over

U.S. efforts. For instance, while Dow Chemical had previously published environmental reports for its Canadian and European operations, its first U.S. report was in 1993. Recent and ongoing North American efforts to develop environmental accounting and auditing standards are wide-ranging:

♦ In 1990, the Canadian Institute of Chartered Accountants (CICA) adopted rules on accounting for environmental liabilities for site cleanups. The CICA also sponsored a 1992 research study of environmental accounting and auditing.

♦ In the United States, in 1990, the Emerging Issues Task Force (EITF) of the Financial Accounting Standards Board developed a consensus opinion on accounting for environmental damage **cleanup costs** (also known as **remediation costs**). These are the costs organizations may be legally responsible for if, at any time in the past or present, they failed to adequately dispose of hazardous materials. The basic question the EITF considered was *when* to recognize the expenses associated with removing toxic waste, neutralizing it, and creating protection systems against future environmental contamination.

The essence of the EITF's decision was that *as soon as they are known*, most cleanup costs should be **expensed**--that is, recorded as an expense, thus reducing the current period's net income. For instance, if you know it will take $500,000 to clean up an oil spill, the $500,000 should be reported as an expense in the year of the spill. The one major exception to the general rule is that expenditures to improve environmental safety or efficiency, reduce future contamination, or prepare a contaminated property for sale may be **capitalized**--that is, recorded, at first, as an asset and then allocated to expense over the period of benefit. Thus, $500,000 spent on equipment to make future oil spills less likely should initially be reported as an asset, with a portion of the cost recognized as an expense over each year the equipment is used.

The EITF appears to have had some effect on environmental accounting in the United States. In 1990, according to a Price Waterhouse survey, only 22% of U.S. companies recorded clean-up liabilities upon internal discovery of the contamination. By 1994, 40% of companies did so.

♦ In 1992, the Institute of Internal Auditors published a research report on *The Role of Internal Auditors in Environmental Issues*. The report urged internal auditors to: (1) be alert for potential environmental problems related to their organizations' processes or products, and (2) help their companies create written environmental policies, an environmental management control system, and an environmental auditing program. The report also summarized the approximately 11,000 pages of federal environmental regulations in effect when the report was published.

♦ Also in 1992, the U. S. federal government's Environmental Protection Agency (EPA) began "The Environmental Accounting Project" to encourage and motivate businesses to understand the full spectrum of their environmental costs and pay attention to these costs in their decision-making. The project has produced a series of reports and case studies directed toward improving environmental accounting, such as case studies of environmental accounting at AT&T and Ontario Hydro. The project members also actively participated in the development of Canada's first *Management Accounting Guidelines* on environmental accounting.

♦ In 1993, the Emerging Issues Task Force decided that companies should: (1) evaluate environmental liabilities *independently* of any potential claim for recovery (such as insurance coverage), and (2) disclose the *gross amount* of the liability (rather than the net amount after expected recoveries) in their balance sheets. The EITF took this position because it believed offsetting a liability with expected recoveries could leave financial statement users unaware of the magnitude of the environmental liability.

♦ Also in 1993, the Securities and Exchange Commission issued a *Staff Accounting Bulletin* urging companies not to delay recognition of an environmental liability, even in the presence of measurement uncertainties. The SEC recommended that an estimate of the liability could be based on past experience, existing technology, current laws and regulations, and information published by organizations such as the Environmental Protection Agency. If management believes the liability is within a range, but no one amount in that range is more likely than the rest, then management should recognize the *minimum amount* as a liability. As more information becomes available later, changes in the estimate should be reported in the periods when they occur.

♦ In 1996, the AICPA's Accounting Standards Executive Committee issued a new *Statement of Position* (SOP) on environmental remediation liabilities that provides more specific accounting guidance on estimating these liabilities, timing recognition, and environmental accounting disclosures in financial reports.

As in Europe, the appropriate use of taxation to implement environmental policy is also an issue in North America. Worldwatch has criticized the U.S. Internal Revenue Code as subsidizing excessive energy use and waste, maximizing economic GNP but at too great a cost to the environment and society. For example, a Worldwatch report cited a study by the Congressional Budget Office that found increasing taxes on fuels could reduce energy consumption and emission of pollutants significantly, while only reducing GNP by a small amount. Yet, in the 1996 presidential election year, there was much political support for a *decrease* in the motor fuel tax.

International Efforts: ISO 14000. In 1996, the International Organization for Standardization--a group established in 1947 to develop world-wide standards for goods, processes and services--began releasing a series of standards known as ISO 14000. These standards promote a common international approach to environmental management systems, environmental performance evaluation, life cycle assessment (evaluation of the environmental impact of a product over its lifetime from manufacture to use to disposal), environmental labeling, and environmental auditing.

Among other things, the ISO 14000 standards establish guidelines for keeping track of the materials companies use and their generation, treatment, and disposal of hazardous wastes. In effect, this sets up a common model for environmental bookkeeping that in turn, makes it easier to reach the goal of comparable reporting. The ISO 14000 standards also provide guidance on what should be done in an environmental audit. Companies that adopt the standards can be certified as in compliance with ISO 14000 standards and then are allowed to publicize their compliance.

While compliance with ISO standards is voluntary, previous experience shows that voluntary standards can have a strong impact. Compliance with the ISO 9000 quality-management standards quickly became important to being competitive in international trade; trading parties commonly require vendors to certify their ISO 9000 compliance. A similar pattern could happen with the ISO 14000 environmental standards. For example, the U.S. Department of Energy required that all its suppliers be registered to the standard by the end of 1997.

The ISO 14000 standards create pressure on external and internal auditors to become more aware of environmental auditing. A 1996 survey by the Center for Integrated Auditing at the Henley Management College in the U.K. found that only 17% of internal auditors were actively involved in environmental audits and 80% had no relevant training in environmental auditing. In 1997, the Institute of Internal Auditors and the Environmental Auditing Roundtable (an organization of U.S. environmental auditors) formed a joint venture to train and certify environmental auditors for ISO 14000 audits.

Considering a New Group of Stakeholders. While much effort is now being devoted to accounting for environmental impact, accounting information currently being produced in most organizations for internal use and external reporting does not fully meet the needs of users when it comes to green accounting. Environmental accounting is at the beginning stage of evolution, particularly in comparison to financial accounting:

◆ While financial reporting and financial statement audits are mandatory (required by law), environmental reporting and environmental audits are still largely voluntary.

◆ While there is a large body of established standards for financial accounting measurement and reporting, the standards for environmental measurement and reporting are still in an early phase of development.

♦ While financial reports contain large amounts of quantitative information (mostly measured in money) and qualitative information, most companies that currently prepare environmental reports tend to make primarily qualitative disclosures about environmental matters because of the difficult measurement issues involved in obtaining quantitative estimates.

Many users argue that without quantitative measures, the information is not all it should be. The discussion document for the 1992 "Earth Summit"-- a U.N.-sponsored meeting where world leaders discussed environmental issues--argued that sound environmental policies won't be achieved until environmental costs are measured and reflected in the prices businesses charge for their goods and services. The ISO 14000 standards may be a model for increasing disclosure of quantitative measures.

Organizations also face growing pressure from the courts to find ways to anticipate environmental problems. For example, Occidental Petroleum Corporation was brought to trial during the 1990s to answer for some decisions Hooker Chemical Company (a firm Occidental acquired in the 1960s) made during the 1940s and 1950s. During that period, Hooker buried thousands of steel drums containing dioxin and other chemical waste in a landfill near Love Canal, New York. While this was an accepted method of disposal at the time, the results were horrifying. The community became so contaminated from chemicals leaking from corroded barrels that eventually the area was declared a disaster. Residents suffered health problems and were forced to abandon their homes.

New York State's lawyers argued at the trial that Hooker knew there might be resulting environmental damage. They cited a 1945 memo by a Hooker manufacturing analyst expressing concern about a "potential future hazard." Observers of the court case commented that Hooker may have made a different decision had the accounting system produced information that helped estimate such potential future costs. The difficulty, of course, is that the extent of the damage might not have been easily predicted decades before it occurred. But, as Daniel Rubenstein commented in the March 1992 *The CPA Journal*, the failure to consider future "invisible stakeholders" may have contributed to poor decision-making:

> *The problem here is a failure to recognize the natural capital contributed by society in the form of free goods such as air, water, and other prerequisites for industrial activity, which are lent to businesses for use, rather than consumption. This is the basis of judgments the courts are now handing down....That is, the courts may establish that these hitherto "invisible" stakeholders had an interest in Hooker's operations, even though it went unrecognized during the 1940s and 1950s.*

In 1994, Occidental agreed to pay the state of New York approximately $123 million to settle the 14-year old lawsuit. The "invisible" stakeholders surely had an interest that no one had anticipated in the 1940s.

Green accounting is based on the notion that natural resources are shared by society and that society as a whole becomes a stakeholder in any organization that draws on or damages natural resources. These stakeholders require different kinds of information than now produced by most accounting systems. The challenge to accountants is to develop better methods and measurements to fulfill these information needs.

REPORTERS AND RESEARCHERS

Half my lifetime I have lived my life by selling words, and I hope thoughts.
    -- Winston Churchill

Accounting is a complex human activity that influences the lives of many people and entities. Thus, it is not surprising that accounting information and accounting institutions are the object of human curiosity. We want to understand the information and institutions. What does the information mean? How is it produced? Why is it produced that way? Is there a better way? How does accounting information affect behavior within a company? How does it affect the capital markets? What is the social impact of accounting choices? Inquiring minds, as a famous advertising slogan notes, want to know.

Curiosity about accounting information and institutions leads to efforts to create or add to knowledge. Some of these efforts are very narrow and pragmatic; others are very broad and theoretical; others fall at varying points within that range. Among the many people who attempt to satisfy curiosity about accounting information and institutions, 2 groups are prominent: the financial media and accounting researchers. These groups have become important users of accounting information.

On a daily basis, the financial media report on accounting information and accounting institutions. Print and broadcast journalists offer both descriptive reports of newly available accounting information--such as reporting on the release of quarterly earnings figures for a major company--and investigative and analytical reports--such as examining the potential impact of newly proposed accounting standards or using accounting information to build an argument about the success or failure of a government program. The financial media also report on the development of accounting standards. For example, the activities of the Financial Accounting Standards Board are widely covered in the press.

Accounting researchers, who are primarily academics, study accounting phenomena and accountants. Their work may be "applied research"--research that is directed toward solving a specific current problem--or "pure research"--

research that is aimed at answering a theoretical question that isn't necessarily related to a particular current problem, but is interesting in and of itself. In either case, research attempts to satisfy curiosity and expand knowledge.

Examples of accounting research include financial accounting studies of the stock market's reaction to financial disclosures and managerial accounting studies about the impact of budget goals and compensation schemes on management behavior. Auditing research studies include investigations of the relationship between experience and audit judgment and analysis of the patterns of litigation against auditors. Systems accounting research explores ways to control computerized information systems or construct reliable knowledge-based systems. Tax researchers study topics like the factors that affect taxpayers' compliance with tax laws or the impact of tax policy on economic decisions.

Through their work, the financial media and accounting researchers attempt to satisfy curiosity, expand knowledge and share their findings with others. Throughout this course, you've been exposed to some of the products of reporters and researchers. Their work differs in the scope of their interests, methodology, and style of communicating results. Reporters tend to investigate and analyze specific current issues and problems; academic researchers are more likely to have a broader and more long-run focus. Reporters tend to rely on already published data and interviews with experts to forge their conclusions; academic researchers are more likely to gather new data and to use more rigorous methodologies such as statistical tests of their theory-based predictions. Reporters try to make their arguments and conclusions enticingly readable or easy to listen to; academic researchers are more likely to craft their arguments and conclusions in a technically precise prose that can be difficult for non-researchers to read.

Critics of the financial media sometimes complain that the desire to create stories that entice the reader or listener can lead to biased stories--stories that omit facts or opinions which support different impressions or conclusions than those reported. Critics of academic research sometimes complain that the focus on methodology and esoteric jargon limits the usefulness of research results. Yet, the best evidence of the worth of a product is whether someone will buy it. The financial media are among the most successful of all media. For example, one of the U.S.'s most widely-read newspapers is *The Wall Street Journal,* with almost 2 million daily readers. And prominent academic researchers are among the most sought after and highly-compensated members of university faculties.

As you continue your study of accounting and business, you will find yourself learning from both the financial media and academic research. As you do so, bear in mind the strengths and limitations of these sources of knowledge.

ASSIGNMENTS FOR MODULE 5

ASSIGNMENT I-5-1: **Employees as Users of Accounting Information:** **Looking for Social Impact Information**

SETTING

You and your friends are about to begin your post-college careers. When you entered college, your response to questions about what you were seeking was: "Money. I want to make a lot of money when I graduate." You still want money, so you are job hunting with major companies that offer many career opportunities for you. However, during your college years, you became convinced that you also wanted to make a contribution to society. Now, in addition to making money, you also want to be with an organization that is socially responsible.

You've narrowed your list down to a small number of prospective employers based on career opportunities. Now, you want to find out as much as possible about these companies' social impact.

ASSIGNMENT

Review the social responsibility disclosures in the 1996 annual report (and any other information available) for 1 of the companies listed below [*Note*: unless your instructor provides different directions, your group should review only the single annual report indicated.]:

Group 1:	Atlantic Richfield Company (ARCO)
Group 2:	Emerson Electric Company
Group 3:	Freeport-McMoran Copper & Gold, Inc.
Group 4:	International Business Machines Corporation (IBM)
Group 5:	Pharmacia & Upjohn, Inc.
Group 6:	Philip Morris Companies, Inc.
Group 7:	Phillips Petroleum Company
Group 8:	Sonoco Products Company

Prepare a 10-minute oral presentation describing and evaluating the disclosures. [*Note*: if this assignment is to be graded, hand in an outline of your presentation, plus a copy of the relevant disclosures.]

Bonus points opportunity: Compare the disclosures in the most recent annual report to the disclosures in the same company's 1990 annual report. Has there been any change in the amount or types of disclosure? To receive bonus points credit, you must hand in a copy of the relevant disclosures from the earlier report.

HINTS

Remember that disclosures may be found in several places in an annual report, including the narrative discussion, the MD&A section, and the footnotes to the financial statements. Also remember that 10-K reports filed with the Securities and Exchange Commission may contain disclosures beyond those in the annual report.

Remember that you must *evaluate* the disclosures, not just describe them. One good approach is to decide on and describe your criteria for evaluation and then assess the disclosures against these criteria. For example, if one of your criteria is that there should be some quantitative information and some qualitative information, you can check to see the mix of information actually disclosed.

If you need advice on preparing for oral presentations, review the hints presented in the Appendix to Module 2 of this theme.

ASSIGNMENT 5-2:   <u>**The Public As Users of Accounting**</u>
<u>**Information:**</u> **Do National Accounts Reflect**
How We're Doing?

(This assignment was coauthored with Jack Hanna when he was a Visiting Professor at Curtin University of Technology, Perth, Western Australia.)

<u>SETTING</u>

You are on a visit to Australia and come across an article in the *Australian Financial Review* ("What Price Happiness?" by Trish Carroll, April 15, 1996) that makes you stop and think. The author is a marketing manager for a leading Australian law firm. She argues that the Australian government is measuring the wrong things (or at least not all the right things) in reported measures of success.

You know that governments of countries frequently quote figures like gross national product (GNP) and GNP per capita as indicators of how they are doing. If GNP per capita increased by 3% in a year, it is suggested that a country is doing better because its citizens have 3% more things to share amongst themselves than they did in the previous year.

Assuming the things measured are reasonable (is the work of full-time homemakers included and should it be?) and the measurements are accurate (many estimates are involved), these figures may indeed convey useful information. But, the article questions whether these measures tell us enough.

Carroll points out that policy-makers tend to pay attention to whatever is measured and that most national measures revolve around financial well-being. As she puts it: "Political parties measure their success or failure by what is happening on the economic balance sheet. Little is ever mentioned of their performance on the social balance sheet." Moreover, Carroll argues that the country might be better off if monetary values were attributed to "whole and happy people" as well as material success.

Among things that could be valued, Carroll suggests that the nation could measure the social costs of loneliness (possibly as reflected in teenage suicide) or an inability to accept life's ups and downs (possibly as reflected in the number of drug addicts). She notes that once nations began to measure environmental costs, there was more attention paid to clean water and air and wonders if the same might not be true for other social impact measures.

ASSIGNMENT

This assignment will be done as an in-class exercise using a brain-storming technique that is one of many techniques groups can use to generate ideas. The unique piece of this technique is that the group works together without talking. These are the steps in the technique:

1.   Individually think about desirable things that you believe should be measured and reported so a country can determine how it is doing.

2.   Join the appropriate small group formed by your instructor for this assignment and complete the following steps:

      a)   Each group should gather at a different area of the classroom wall.

      b)   Without any group discussion, generate a list of potential items to consider by the following process: Using a "post-it note" pad provided by your instructor, the first group member should write down something (e.g., neighbourhood safety) that he/she thinks is important to consider in order to know how a country is doing and stick the "post-it-note" up on the wall. *As quickly as possible*, pass the pad to another group member who should do the same--but this person must come up with a different item. Continue to pass the pad to each group member in turn. After a complete round, repeat the procedure until the group runs out of ideas or your instructor calls time. If one member can't think of an idea during any round, that member can pass the pad to the next group member. [Note: Just put the "post-it-notes" up on the wall/board in any random order.]

      c)   When your instructor calls time, move to the next phase: Without any discussion, try to arrange the individual items in terms of importance. To do this, all group members can move any notes on the wall to any new location--but *remember that no group member can talk during this period.*

3.   Individually:

When your group has finished rearranging the "post-it-notes" or when your instructor calls time, each group member should make a list of the things the group believes should be measured and taken into account in order to properly determine how a country is doing. Each person should list the things in order of importance and be prepared to present them to the class in an organized 2-3 minute presentation.

HINTS

Be broad minded and innovative in deciding what you want to measure, but don't forget to consider the things that are commonly included in GNP measures as well.

ASSIGNMENT I-5-3:   <u>**Donors as Users of Accounting Information**</u>:
                                            Dual-Purpose Mailings

SETTING

Each day as you come home from school, the first thing you do is check your mailbox. Today, you find a mailing from Greenpeace asking you to send a greeting to the crew of a Greenpeace ship, answer the "National Marine Mammal Survey," and make a donation to Greenpeace.

Included with the mailing are a 6-page letter, a 1-page survey, a Greenpeace sticker and 6 Greenpeace stamps. (See the following pages.) In addition, the mailing included a "Bon Voyage" card for the crew of a Greenpeace ship, a small postcard-type photo of the ship, and an offer to provide a free copy of a home guide to environmentally safe and hazardous household materials to donors of $20 or more.

You just finished reading in your accounting book that classifying expenditures as either program expenditures or fundraising expenses is an important issue for charities. As you read the mailing, you cannot help but wonder about the appropriate accounting for the cost of the mailing. When the mailing was sent, the AICPA's Accounting Standard Division's *Statement of Position 87-2* would have been the appropriate authoritative standard for accounting for such direct mail costs.

ASSIGNMENT

Read the Greenpeace mailer and determine:

♦   What is the purpose of the mailer? Is it strictly for fundraising? strictly educational? or a combination of both?

♦   If you had to account for the costs of the mailer what percentage of the cost would you assign to fundraising expenses? what percentage would you assign to program expenditures? What basis did you use to develop these percentages? Are there any alternative bases?

HINTS

Remember that generally accepted accounting principles--as expressed in the AICPA *Statement of Position*--hold that the joint costs of a multi-purpose mailing can be allocated between fund-raising and program expenditures.

The suggested criteria for evaluating the mailing include the nature of the recipients of the direct mail (the audience) and the contents of the materials, as well as the purpose of the mailing. Your first task is to decide if the mailing has a dual purpose. If so, you must then determine what portion of the mailing relates to the program and what portion relates to fund-raising.

GREENPEACE

Attention:

The enclosed "Bon Voyage" card

is not for you to keep!

Dear Friend,

This is probably the most unusual "Bon Voyage" card you've ever received.

For two reasons:

First of all: It's not for you. Instead of keeping it, I'm asking you to sign your name to it and then return it to me ...

... so I can convey your message of support to the captain and crew of our Greenpeace ship, the Rainbow Warrior.

Second: this card is unusual because the Rainbow Warrior is not bound for a pleasure cruise.

Far from it.

Actually, the captain and crew of the Rainbow Warrior may be placing themselves at risk.

That's their resolve. And that's why they need all of the encouragement and support we can give them.

As you may know, the original Rainbow Warrior now rests on the ocean floor ...

... a hole blown in the starboard side, and another in the stern. This act of despicable sabotage

(over, please ...)

by French secret agents took the life of one of our crew members.

The current captain of the new Rainbow Warrior, Joel Stewart, from the United States, and his crew know the risks full well. Only recently, baton wielding French commandos boarded and seized our ship as it sailed to protest French nuclear weapons testing in the Pacific.

Fortunately, no one was hurt. And the Greenpeace crew is determined to carry out the original mission of the Rainbow Warrior:

To prevent the needless slaughter of marine mammals, and prevent the contamination of our oceans.

Only recently, another Greenpeace crew was detained by the Russian Navy, while investigating an ocean dump site for nuclear wastes.

One of our ships was also rammed by an armed Japanese escort vessel while tracking a dangerous shipment of plutonium halfway around the world.

And right now yet another Greenpeace ship is in Antarctica to confront the Japanese whaling fleet there.

You see, here at Greenpeace we refuse to bow down in silent acceptance of the destruction of our planet ...

... the oil giants ... the chemical and timber companies ... the pulp and paper mills ... the industrial fishing fleets ...

These powers and superpowers are destroying our Earth.

Who will challenge them? Who will hold them responsible?

And who will, when necessary, even jeopardize their physical safety to put a stop to this senseless destruction?

And that's what the 1993 voyage of the Rainbow Warrior is all about.

Perhaps many years ago you saw the picture in the National Geographic, showing a few Greenpeace campaigners in a small inflatable boat blocking a giant Soviet whaling ship -- truly a "David verses Goliath" confrontation.

And now today the fight goes on.

Japan and Norway's whaling fleets are still killing whales, despite the international moratorium on commercial whaling.

The Steller sea lion is fighting for its existence on Alaska's rugged coast.

And dolphins are still being killed in monstrous industrial fishing nets.

Quite frankly, however, the captain and crew of the Rainbow Warrior realize that the number of ships Greenpeace can send to confront environmental abuse has lessened.

The worldwide economic recession has hurt Greenpeace. We've been forced to take some serious actions:

1. Selling our ship, Gondwana.

2. Drastically cutting back on our budget for the floating laboratory ship, Beluga, and putting its pollution monitoring equipment into storage.

3. Keeping our ships Greenpeace and Moby Dick at dock for several months simply because we did not have the funds to operate them fulltime.

4. Selling two helicopters -- critical to locating renegade whaling fleets at sea.

I regret to inform you of these measures because the fleet has been the backbone of Greenpeace for more than 20 years.

What is happening these days?

Have the giant industrial powers won the battle?
Are we going to surrender the oceans to those who so
callously slaughter hundreds of thousands of dolphins
and sea lions and whales?

Are we going to stop protesting the polluters and
the toxic waste dumpers?

No! Here at Greenpeace we will not surrender!

But we're faced with some practical facts of life:

> In brief, without financial support
> from folks like you, our resources
> will be lessened, our range could
> be reduced, our voice silenced.

All this is why I am, without apology or
reservation, asking you to please help.

Help us! -- by sending a gift to support the crews
of the Rainbow Warrior.

Today, if you possibly can.

We must keep the Rainbow Warrior on the high seas.
Our mission is clear:

... Stop the killing of dolphins, whales and
other marine animals.

... Stop off-shore oil drilling from threatening
our coastlines.

... Stop waste dumping in the ocean.

... Stop radioactive contamination from continued
nuclear weapons testing.

Our planet is running out of time!

So send $25 if you possibly can, or send $50, or
$100. Even $20 will be a tremendous help to us.

We are <u>committed</u>, believe me, to saving the
<u>world's whales, and the</u> sea lions, and the dolphins
from brutal death and extinction.

And we must encourage the captain and the crew of
the Rainbow Warrior to carry on the grand mission of
Greenpeace.

But we need <u>people like you to make our work</u>
<u>possible</u>. We depend entirely upon public support.
<u>We do not</u> solicit grants and funding from the
government or large corporations.

(Most governments and large corporations wish we
would just shut up and go away!)

<u>So please</u>, take just a moment right now and do
<u>four things for me</u>:

    Number 1. Sign your name on the enclosed "Bon
                 Voyage" card. (Your first name will
                 be just fine.)

    Number 2. Return the card to me so I can let the
                 captain and crew of the Rainbow Warrior
                 know that you are with them in spirit.

    Number 3. Fill out the enclosed Greenpeace Marine
                 Mammal Survey. Your opinion is import-
                 ant to us as we confront governments and
                 industry who are destroying the world's
                 ocean and marine life.

    Number 4. Send the best gift you can -- $25, or
                 $50, or $100 -- to support Greenpeace.
                 Even $20 will be a tremendous help.

Then, as a small token of my appreciation for your
support and help with a contribution of $20 or more,
I have <u>two fascinating and helpful gifts to send you</u>.

<u>First</u>: "Stepping Lightly on the Earth -- A
Minimum Impact Guide to the Home". Please remember,
the place to start saving the planet is right in your
own home! This Greenpeace pamphlet tells you about

the toxic risks of many common household products --
and how to avoid them.

Second: I'll send you regular copies of our
special Greenpeace newsletter to keep you up to date on
all our work around the world.

The Greenpeace newsletter is exactly what you need
to learn about all of our work to save marine mammals
and to preserve our environment.

Please respond today.

Thanks so much for reading this letter. I look
forward to hearing from you.

Sincerely yours,

Barbara Dudley
Executive Director

BD:bvf

P.S. Remember, your gift of $25, $50, $100, or even $20
will help us keep the Rainbow Warrior on the high
seas.

We must not be forced to abandon the oceans to the
deadly mercy of commercial greed.

And your signed "Bon Voyage" card will tell the
captain and crew you're behind them as they take
their vessel in harms way.

To the Captain and crew
of the Rainbow Warrior:

Sail On!

I wish you safety and success.
I share your goals for our Earth,
and am with you on your voyage.
Keep up the fight!

Best wishes,

_____
(signed)

Bon Voyage!

NATIONAL MARINE MAMMAL SURVEY

Greenpeace
1436 U Street N.W.
P.O. Box 96128
Washington, D.C. 20090

INSTRUCTIONS:
Your participation in this National Survey on marine mammals is requested. You'll find the questions easy to answer. Estimated time to complete the survey is 2-3 minutes. Please mark your answers in the spaces provided and return to Greenpeace within 10 days. Thank you.

12MMSB   Printed on 100% recycled, unbleached paper.

1. Millions of marine animals will die this year in high-seas driftnets – modern monstrosities of plastic monofilament that trap and kill *any* living creature that enters their paths: dolphins, seals, marine birds, even whales. Would you favor efforts to bring international pressure to bear against countries that use massive driftnets to fish for squid and other species, to insure that these nations stop driftnet fishing by the United Nations deadline of December 31, 1992?

☐ Yes ☐ No ☐ Undecided

2. Japan – the world's foremost whaling nation – exports hundreds of millions of dollars worth of fish to the United States. Would you support the president's imposing an embargo on Japanese fish imports into the U.S., as prescribed under U.S. law (the Pelly Amendment), to put pressure on Japan to stop its killing of whales?

☐ Yes ☐ No ☐ Undecided

3. Huge fishing fleets trawling the Bering Sea off Alaska for pollock, Pacific cod, and other fish are also competing with Steller sea lions for food. The Steller sea lion population is declining so rapidly, its listing may be changed from "threatened" to "endangered" status. Would you support measures to limit commercial fishing in the region in order to allow the sea lion population to return to normal?

☐ Yes ☐ No ☐ Undecided

4. In recent years there have been two major cases of dead bottlenose dolphins washing ashore in U.S. East Coast waters; government officials say they don't know why. Would you support increased government efforts to investigate the reasons behind these catastrophic losses of marine mammals?

☐ Yes ☐ No ☐ Undecided

5. Do you support Greenpeace's nonviolent, direct actions to protect all marine animals and preserve ocean ecosystems?

☐ Yes ☐ No ☐ Undecided

6. Would you be willing to spend just a few cents a day to help Greenpeace expose, confront, and stop the decimation of the world's oceans and marine life?

☐ Yes ☐ No

If your answer to the last question is "Yes," Greenpeace can sure use your help. Please make your contribution payable to "Greenpeace" and return it with your survey answers today!

You can return your survey – and your gift – in the enclosed postage-free reply envelope.

Stopping toxic pollution starts in the home. Greenpeace shows you how to make your own environment safer.

STEPPING LIGHTLY ON THE EARTH
A Minimum Impact Guide to the Home

Many of the cleaners, polishes and sprays you use in your home every day are hazardous to your family's health. And when you throw the cans away, or rinse the chemicals down the drain, you contribute to the toxic pollution of our environment.

Now Greenpeace has put together an easy-to-follow guide to *safe* alternatives—biodegradable cleansers you can prepare at home:

- all-purpose cleaner
- laundry detergent
- oven cleaner
- insecticides for your home or garden

Stepping Lightly on the Earth has recipes for these and many more environmentally sound substitutes. They are safe, effective, and often cheaper to use than commercial products.

Help Greenpeace clean up our environment.

For your contribution of $20 or more, Greenpeace will send you a *free* copy of Stepping Lightly on the Earth, A Minimum Impact Guide to the Home.

The pamphlet will help you create a cleaner, safer environment at home. And you'll be helping Greenpeace fight for a cleaner, safer environment around the world.

Greenpeace 1436 U Street N.W., P.O. Box 96128, Washington, D.C. 20090

Printed on recycled paper

12BTP2

SAFE POLISHES FOR METALS

Gold: Wash in lukewarm, soapy water, dry and polish with a chamois cloth.

Silver: Rub with a paste of baking soda and water.

Brass: Mix equal parts of salt and flour with a little vinegar, then rub.

Paint Thinners · Bug Sprays · Cleaners · Solvents · Aerosols · Polishes

I-5-44

GREENPEACE '93

P.O. BOX 96128 • WASHINGTON, D.C. 20090
RECYCLED PAPER

ASSIGNMENT I-5-4:   **<u>Donors as Users of Accounting Information</u>: Wild Donations**

<u>SETTING</u>

You are a lover of wildlife. You recently won $5,000 in a lottery and wish to donate it to a worthy nonprofit organization that promotes wildlife. There are 4 organizations you are considering:

-   American Society for the Prevention of Cruelty to Animals
-   Humane Society of the United States
-   National Wildlife Federation
-   The Wilderness Society

Not wanting to waste your winnings foolishly, you are willing to spend some time investigating your candidate charities. Therefore, you decide to check out the reports published by the Philanthropic Advisory Service (PAS) of the Council of Better Business Bureau's Inc. before making your choice. You are pleased to learn that these reports may be accessed on the Internet at:

http://www.bbb.org/about/pas.html

<u>ASSIGNMENT</u>

Obtain and read the PAS reports on the 4 wildlife organizations. Based on the information you find (and any other information you choose to search out), rank order the 4 charities according to how likely you are to make a donation (where #1 = most likely and #4 = least likely). Justify your rank orders by explaining *why* you rated each organization as you did.

<u>HINTS</u>

Remember that PAS reports do not make recommendations about donations; they report on how a charity rates according to the guidelines established in the CBBB's "Standards for Charitable Solicitations." You may find it helpful to read these standards before reviewing the 4 reports. Also remember that the guidelines alone may not be sufficient for making your decision. You need to consider whatever other information is important to you as well.

ASSIGNMENT I-5-5: <u>**Donors as Users of Accounting Information**</u>**: Assessing a Charity's Performance and Position**

SETTING

You have recently received an inheritance of $50,000. In a spirit of helping others, you have decided to donate $10,000 of this inheritance to a worthy charity. Realizing how important this donation is to you, you are willing to spend some time investigating your candidate charity.

ASSIGNMENT

Obtain the annual report of the charity of your choice and assess the charity's performance and position. Would you be willing to donate money to this charity? Justify your response.

Bonus point opportunity: Also obtain the charity's Form 990 and use it in your analysis.

HINTS

Consider some of the guidelines suggested by rating agencies as benchmarks for your analysis. You may also want to do some research to find other benchmarks (e.g., comparable measures for other charities).

ASSIGNMENT I-5-6:   **Green Accounting:**
                                 Looking for Green Accounting Information

SETTING

After a recent hazardous waste spill near your community, you are very interested in the debates over environmental issues. Thinking about these issues has made you curious about the quality of information on environmental matters that can be found in annual reports of large public companies. You decide to investigate.

ASSIGNMENT

Review the environmental disclosures in the 1996 annual report (and any other information available) for 1 of the companies listed below [*Note*: unless your instructor provides different directions, your group should review only the single annual report indicated.]:

Group 1:	Birmingham Steel Corporation
Group 2:	Eastman Chemical Company
Group 3:	The Geon Company
Group 4:	Gibraltar Packaging Group, Inc.
Group 5:	Harsco Corporation
Group 6:	Holly Corporation
Group 7:	Safety-Kleen Corp.
Group 8:	Vulcan Materials Company

Prepare a 10-minute oral presentation describing and evaluating the disclosures. [*Note*: if this assignment is to be graded, hand in an outline of your presentation, plus a copy of the relevant disclosures.]

Bonus points opportunity: Compare the disclosures in the most recent annual report to the disclosures in the same company's 1990 annual report. Has there been any change in the amount or types of disclosure? To receive bonus points credit, you must hand in a copy of the relevant disclosures from the earlier report.

HINTS

Remember that disclosures may be found in several places in an annual report, including the narrative discussion, the MD&A section, and the footnotes to the financial statements. Also remember that 10-K reports filed with the Securities and Exchange Commission may contain disclosures beyond those in the annual report.

Remember that you must *evaluate* the disclosures, not just describe them. One good approach is to decide on and describe your criteria for evaluation and then assess the disclosures against these criteria. For example, if one of your criteria is that there should be some quantitative information and some qualitative information, you can check to see the mix of information actually disclosed.

If you need advice on preparing for oral presentations, review the hints presented in the Appendix to Module 2 of this theme.

ASSIGNMENT I-5-7:   <u>The Movement Toward Green Accounting</u>:
The Ceres Principles

SETTING

In 1989, an environmental disaster occurred. The Exxon *Valdez* oil tanker hit a reef and sprung a leak which sent 11 million gallons of crude oil into Prince William Sound, off the shores of Alaska. Damage to water and wildlife was estimated to be in excess of a billion dollars.

After the Valdez oil spill, the Boston-based Coalition on Environmentally Responsible Economics (Ceres) developed a 10-point code of environmental conduct, known originally as the *Valdez Principles*, and later renamed the *Ceres Principles* after the organization which developed the code. The coalition, along with other environmental groups, asked about 500 companies to adopt the code in writing. One of the 10 principles is that the companies accepting the code agree to submit to an annual environmental audit and report their progress on lowering their emissions of pollutants.

You are the accounting advisor to the CEO of a publicly-held company in the retail industry. The company owns and operates a chain of specialty clothing stores located throughout the United States. The company deals with suppliers throughout the world.

Some of the company's shareholders have asked the Board of Directors to adopt the Ceres Principles as company policy. The CEO has asked you to provide advice regarding this proposal, with a particular focus on the accounting issues involved.

Upon investigation, you find that over 70 companies have signed the Ceres code, but many large corporations--including Exxon--refused to sign. The lack of generally accepted accounting and auditing standards for environmental disclosures has been cited as a major obstacle to the acceptance of the *Ceres Principles*. On the other hand, in 1994, General Motors Corp., the world's largest industrial corporation, gave its endorsement to the code.

ASSIGNMENT

Prepare a brief (maximum: 4 pages, double-spaced) report to the CEO evaluating the advantages and disadvantages of adopting the code. Per the CEO's request, focus on the accounting issues involved. The report should recommend a position to the CEO on the stockholders' proposal and provide concise well-argued reasons for that position.

HINTS

While there is no requirement to do so, it may be useful to do some library research to obtain a copy of the *Ceres Principles* and find out why other organizations have accepted or rejected them.

In doing your analysis, consider who the stakeholders are and consider whether any of the stakeholders have conflicting needs. Also consider the quality of the information that can be developed to meet these user groups' needs.

ASSIGNMENT I-5-8: **The Movement Toward Green Accounting:**
Enviroene

SETTING

The U. S. Environmental Protection Agency and the Strategic Environmental Research and Development Program together support an Internet site called Enviroene. The site provides an information exchange forum for all levels of government, researchers, industry and public interest groups concerned with environmental impact. The site may be reached at:

http://es.inel.gov

When you reach this site you discover that it contains a wealth of information about environmental accounting that you can share with your class.

ASSIGNMENT

Use the search facilities provided in Enviroene to find information about "environmental accounting" and print the list of matches to your search query. Count off the number of items on the list and choose the item number that corresponds to your group number for this class (e.g., if you are Group 3, choose the 3rd item on the list). Choose this item to examine further. Print a copy to hand in to your instructor on the day of your presentation.

Examine the selected report to determine what its key points are about environmental accounting. Finally, prepare a brief oral presentation [maximum 10 minutes] for the class describing these points and any interesting facts you learned while reading this report.

What you must hand in: a printed copy of the list of matches to your search and a copy of the report your presentation covers

Note on technical problems: Given the random selection process being used, it is possible that the report you choose may not be suitable for your oral presentation. For example, the report may be a 1-page abstract that doesn't give you enough information for your presentation. Or, you may find a report is inaccessible for technical reasons. If for some reason, the report you are supposed to select is unsuitable, choose as a substitute the item on the list which corresponds to the sum of your group number *plus* the total number of groups in your class. For example, if you are group 3 and the class has 8 groups, choose item 11 on the list (3 + 8 = 11). If that report is also unsuitable, choose the item that corresponds to the sum of your group number plus *twice* the total number of groups in your class (e.g., the 19th item if you are Group 3 in a class of 8 groups.) If you need a 4th try, choose the item number equal to your group number plus *three* times the total number of groups in your class, and so on.

HINTS

Do not expect to understand everything you will read in the report you select. There may be some science and some accounting discussions that are beyond your grasp. Focus on finding a few key items to report that are interesting to you and that helped you understand more about environmental accounting.

If you need help on environmental accounting terms or concepts, there is a report available through Enviroene entitled "An Introduction to Environmental Accounting as a Business Management Tool: Key Concepts and Terms" that can be very helpful. You can download this report from the section of Enviroene that describes the "EPA's Environmental Accounting Project," which, at the time of this writing could be accessed at:

http://es.inel.gov/partners/acctg/acctg.html

You may want to begin your oral presentation by giving your classmates a brief overview of what the report covered. Then, focus on what you learned about environmental accounting in the report. What you learned may include illustrations of applications as well as new concepts.

In doing your analysis, consider who the stakeholders are and consider whether any of the stakeholders have conflicting needs. Also consider the quality of the information that can be developed to meet these user groups' needs.

ASSIGNMENT I-5-9: <u>**Reporters and Researchers as Users of Accounting Information:**</u> **Reading for Self-Education**

SETTING

You are a college student who is considering a career in accounting or business. Consequently, you are making an effort to become well-read in this area.

ASSIGNMENT

Your group should choose 1 article from the financial press or an academic or professional journal that meets the following 3 criteria:

♦ the article deals with an accounting issue;
♦ the article is an in-depth treatment of a topic--that is, the article must involve investigation or analysis, not just news reporting; and
♦ the article was published within the last month.

Read the article and discuss it with your group. Prepare a *5 to 10 minute* oral presentation for the next class meeting which will tell your fellow students:

♦ what the article was about;
♦ how the article relates to something we have studied in this course; and
♦ what accounting issues are raised and why they are important.

Before making your presentation, *you must give a copy of the article and an outline of your remarks to your instructor.*

HINTS

One way to choose an article is to browse the current issues of periodicals in the library. You need to find an article that has some "meat"--the idea of this assignment is that your group will attempt to make a complex article accessible to your fellow students.

You may want to use a short hand-out to summarize your key points for other students. Also, you should consider using audio-visual aids if they will help you get your points across. If you need advice on preparing oral presentations, read the hints in the appendix to Module 2 of this theme.

Presentations will be graded on both content and presentation style. You may divide the presentation among group members as you see fit. You may, if you wish, choose a subset of the group (at least 2 people) to perform the actual presentation, as long as all group members work together on the preparation.

ASSIGNMENT 5-10:   **The Public As Users of Accounting Information: Safe To Drink?**

On the following 3 pages, you will find a case from the American Accounting Association publication, <u>Ethics in the Accounting Curriculum: Cases and Readings</u>, edited by Dr. William W. May.

ASSIGNMENT

Read the "Safe To Drink?" case and consider the two case questions:

♦   What are the ethical issues?

♦   What should Rebecca do?

HINTS

In considering the accountant's dilemma, consider the following questions step by step:

♦   What are the facts?

♦   Who are the stakeholders (affected parties) and what are the ethical issues?

♦   What ethical principles, rules or values come into play here?

♦   What are the accountant's alternatives?

♦   How do these alternatives stack up in comparison to the ethical principles, rules or values?

♦   What are the consequences of each alternative?

♦   What should the accountant do?

SAFE TO DRINK?

Prepared by Professor Suzanne M. Cory, St. Mary's University

Rebecca sat and stared at the glass of water sitting on her kitchen table. She picked it up slowly and rotated the glass so that the water swirled quickly and then set the glass down again.

The water's motion eventually stopped and she again peered at the contents of the glass. She could not see anything other than the crystal clear drinking water her town had provided its inhabitants for years. Yet, the morning paper included a story about dead fish having been found recently in the river that supplied the drinking water for the town. It was time for her to get ready for work, but instead Rebecca thought over the sequence of events which had led her to her suspicions.

Rebecca had been employed by Tomas and Brown, CPAs, for just over two years. She had been very fortunate to secure a position on the audit staff of Tomas and Brown, since very few accounting positions had been available in the university town in which she resided. The job situation in the town had not changed during her two-year period of employment with them. Rebecca's husband, Alan, was trying to complete his graduate degree at the local university and they needed her paycheck until he could complete his education in two more years. He had suffered some setbacks in his education last semester because he had required surgery and had to drop out of school for several months to speed his recovery. Fortunately, the health insurance provided by Tomas and Brown was excellent, and Alan's continuing medical costs were almost completely covered by the insurance.

Rebecca had twice previously participated on the audit of Techno, Inc. Techno, Inc. had been an audit client of Tomas and Brown for many years and represented a healthy percentage of Tomas and Brown's annual audit fees. Techno, Inc., manufactured and repaired airplane parts, and faced tough economic times due to the defense industry cutbacks mandated by Congress. Techno had laid off 20% of its work force two years ago, but seemed to be recovering by diversifying its product line. Techno was developing a new chemical product, Fuelplus. When Fuelplus was mixed with airplane fuel it had the ability to minimize fuel usage while improving performance. In fact, Techno believed Fuelplus would eventually be marketed so successfully that they purchased several acres of undeveloped land near the river as a site for possible future plant expansion for Fuelplus manufacture. However, no construction was yet underway.

Rebecca had audited liabilities and related expenses on the Techno audit this year. Through analytical review, she noticed the toxic waste disposal costs had decreased significantly in relationship to production during the year.

Manufacturing and repairing airplane parts required the parts to be dipped in toxic cleansing chemicals. Due to increased laws protecting the environment, toxic waste disposal costs incurred by Techno had been steadily increasing for several years. While production and repair services had been declining during the last few years, they were not decreasing as rapidly as the associated costs of disposing of the toxic chemical.

When Rebecca asked the controller if she was aware of any reason for the change in this relationship between production and repair activity and toxic waste disposal costs incurred, the controller speculated that since the remaining work force was more experienced, they were simply more efficient in usage of the chemical. Therefore, there was less chemical that needed to be placed into reinforced barrels and shipped to a licensed waste disposal site.

While Techno's waste disposal costs had decreased, purchases of reinforced barrels had remained stable when compared to purchases made over the last three year period. She asked the controller about the usage of barrels and the controller indicated that she thought the barrels might be used for storing Fuelplus, but Rebecca knew that the barrels did not appear on Techno's inventory and that Fuelplus did not require usage of reinforced barrels, which were more expensive than regular barrels.

Rebecca next asked the production foreman about the possible explanation for the variances offered by the controller. The foreman indicated that he was not aware of any increased efficiency on the part of the work force, and while he was not in charge of the separate production of Fuelplus, he could not remember any Fuelplus being stored in a reinforced barrel.

However, he was unable to account for the missing barrels. He suggested that perhaps an enterprising employee had found an alternative use for the reinforced barrels and since they were not well guarded, had somehow managed to load the barrels on a truck and take them home. Rebecca knew that the reinforced barrels were quite heavy, even when empty, and their theft would be difficult.

She discussed the results of her analytical review and the explanations offered by both management and production personnel with the senior on the audit, Ken Ambers. Ken asked her if she believed a liability had possibly been omitted from the balance sheet and its corresponding expense omitted from the income statement. Rebecca replied that she could find no evidence of any unrecorded outstanding liability or expense, but she had an uneasy feeling and distrusted the explanations she had been given for the variances she noted. Rebecca suspected that Techno was not disposing of the toxic cleansing chemical in the same manner as in the past. Ken replied that, in addition to their suspicions, auditors need evidence to draw conclusions.

She replied that if Techno had been dumping the wastes illegally and was caught doing so, the fines levied by the federal government would be severe. In fact, Techno would more than likely be forced into bankruptcy if that were to happen.

Ken asked her about the probability of Techno's possible violation of environmental laws being discovered and reported to the proper authorities. He pointed out that she had no firm evidence regarding her suspicions.

Rebecca told Ken that she thought the auditors had a responsibility for reporting illegal acts performed by their client, but Ken responded that they were not even sure an illegal act had occurred. He told her he had known Techno's management for many years, and had faith in their honesty. Ken then suggested that unless they felt further audit procedures were clearly warranted, Rebecca should accept the explanations given to her. He reminded her that both Techno and the partner-in-charge of the engagement expected the audit to be completed soon. He also asked her to be sure to write an audit memorandum indicating that since several empty reinforced barrels could not be accounted for, better control over them was to be recommended.

Rebecca had a great deal of respect for Ken and knew he had been employed with Tomas and Brown for several years. He had been promoted rapidly by the partners at Tomas and Brown and they seemed to think highly of him. There had been recent rumors in the office that Ken's promotion to manager would be announced shortly.

What are the ethical issues?

What should Rebecca do?

MODULE INDEX

-ABC-

-DEF-

-GHI-

-JKL-

-MNO-

-PQR-

-STU-

-VWXYZ-

6

MODULE 6: THE ENVIRONMENT OF ACCOUNTING

1997-1998 edition

Table of Contents

MODULE 6: THE ENVIRONMENT OF ACCOUNTING

Estimated Time Budget

Task	Time Estimate
Reading PART A: LAWS, RULES, STANDARDS AND GUIDELINES	60 - 90 minutes
Assignments for Part A	
Assignment I-6A-1	30 - 60 minutes
Assignment I-6A-2	60 - 90 minutes
Assignment I-6A-3	60 - 90 minutes
Reading PART B: RESEARCHING ACCOUNTING ISSUES	20 - 30 minutes
Assignments for Part B	
Assignment I-6B-1	30 - 60 minutes
Assignment I-6B-2	20 - 40 minutes
Assignment I-6B-3	30 - 60 minutes
Assignment I-6B-4	30 - 60 minutes
Theme Overview Assignments	
Assignment I-1	150-210 minutes

Note: *These time estimates, like all the time budgets for this course, should be adjusted to suit your own learning style. Time estimates for assignments assume that readings were completed before attempting assignments.*

MODULE 6: THE ENVIRONMENT OF ACCOUNTING

PART A: LAWS, RULES, STANDARDS, AND GUIDELINES

All information is imperfect. We have to treat it with humility.
-- Jacob Bronowski, The Ascent of Man

In the practice of accountancy, many different users, different information needs, and different measurement systems intertwine. Because users' needs vary--and sometimes conflict--there isn't a single accounting measurement system that can satisfy everyone's needs. In developing appropriate accounting practices, trade-offs must often be made. Consequently, good accounting practice is not static. Accountancy is constantly evolving and changing. Its rules are not cast in concrete.

By now, you have grasped some basic concepts of accounting and you have become aware that there is a large body of technical knowledge that delineates good accounting practice. This technical body of knowledge encompasses accounting-related laws (principles and regulations established by governments), such as tax laws and securities laws. The technical body of knowledge also encompasses rules and standards established by authoritative bodies, like the Financial Accounting Standards Board. Such rules and standards have less force than laws, but function similarly to laws because of their general acceptance by the accounting profession.

Where no laws, rules, or standards exist, the accumulated knowledge of accountancy provides guidelines for good practice. For example, no specific law, rule, or standard requires organizations to periodically reconcile the amount of "cash in the bank" shown on their books to the balance shown on their bank statement. Nonetheless, there is ample guidance in the accounting literature advising that bank reconciliations are an important internal control for cash.

What constitutes the technical body of knowledge for tax, financial accounting, auditing, systems and managerial accounting? How are these laws, rules, standards and guidelines developed? Part A of this module addresses these questions. You may be surprised--even overwhelmed, at first--at the number of different sources of laws, rules, standards, and guidelines that define the practice of accountancy. If you find the system complex, remember that modern accountancy reflects the complexity of the world of business, nonbusiness, and government organizations.

TAX

Law must be stable, and yet it cannot stand still.
--Roscoe Pound

If you walk into the office of a tax accountant, you are bound to be impressed with the office's library. One look at the number of volumes--and, most likely, the computer terminal tie-ins to electronic databases of tax information--will convince you of the complexity of the body of knowledge in tax.

U.S. Federal Income Taxes

Consider the sources of authority for federal income taxation:

♦ income tax law,
♦ Treasury Department regulations,
♦ IRS rulings and other publications,
♦ court cases, and
♦ the tax accounting literature.

Let's take a brief look at each of these sources.

The Internal Revenue Code. The first source of authority, of course, is the income tax law legislated by Congress. Like all laws, income tax law is subject to regular revision. Up until 1939, tax practitioners had to look for information about the federal income tax law in each separate piece of legislation passed by Congress. In 1939, all the separate laws were integrated into one "code." The current version of the law is compiled in a multi-volume set known as "**The Internal Revenue Code** of 1986, as amended." The 1986 date refers to the most recent major revision of federal income tax laws, the Tax Reform Act of 1986, with the "as amended" referring to later changes.

Treasury Department Regulations. Many answers to tax questions may be found directly in the Internal Revenue Code. However, Congress sometimes passes generally worded tax legislation, with a provision that the Treasury Department will be responsible for creating more specific interpretations of how the law is to be implemented. To fulfill this responsibility, the Treasury Department publishes **regulations**, which may be found in another multi-volume collection entitled the *Code of Federal Regulations*.

In addition to **"legislative" regulations** (the regulations Congress directs the Treasury Department to design), there are also **"interpretative" regulations** issued by the Treasury Department to provide additional guidance or clarification of points in the tax law. Interpretative regulations are used by both tax preparers and Internal Revenue Service employees to help answer specific questions. For example, tax law grants individual taxpayers tax exemptions for each "dependent" child. The regulations offer guidance on such matters as how to determine whether a student who lives away from home is a dependent.

IRS Rulings. The Internal Revenue Service (IRS), the subunit of the Treasury Department that administers the tax laws, is responsible for designing tax forms, answering taxpayer questions, auditing tax returns, and so on. The IRS issues **Revenue Rulings** in response to taxpayer questions about the interpretation of tax law in particular circumstances.

There are 2 types of Revenue Rulings: published and private letter. **Published rulings** are intended as general guidance applicable to a wide range of taxpayers; **private letter rulings** are intended as a response to a particular individual taxpayer's specific circumstances. The published rulings represent a general policy of the IRS, while the private letter rulings do not--the IRS is not bound by a private letter ruling to anyone other than the specific inquiring taxpayer. Nevertheless, private letter rulings can be a helpful source of information to taxpayers facing similar situations. Both types of rulings become public documents, although any information that might identify the inquiring taxpayer is removed.

Other IRS Publications. The IRS also issues "**Revenue Procedures**" concerning administrative matters such as due dates for tax forms, and other publications, such as **Technical Information Releases** and **Technical Advice Memoranda**. The flow of IRS publications is so heavy that tax practitioners have many choices of subscription services to help them keep up-to-date.

Court Decisions. The law, it is often said, is "gloriously uncertain"--meaning that it is subject to interpretation. As you can imagine, given the complexity of tax laws, there can be disputes between a taxpayer and the IRS over the appropriate treatment of certain items. The disputes can range from the significant to the mundane. For example, in 1988, Cynthia Hess, who worked as a stripper under the name Chesty Love, claimed a $2,088 deduction for depreciation on the surgical implants she had to enlarge her bust to size 56FF. The IRS disallowed the deduction, arguing that spending money to improve health or appearance, even if useful for business, is a non-deductible personal expense. Hess disagreed, arguing that the implants were "stage props" she was carrying solely to make money.

Tax disputes that cannot be settled by mutual agreement of the 2 parties may end up being settled by the judicial system. In 1994, a judge ruled that Cynthia Hess's implants did increase her income and weighed so much (10 pounds each) that there was no personal benefit to carrying them. Hess got her depreciation deduction. Tax disputes may be heard in the Tax Court, in a federal district court, or in the U.S. Claims Court. Appeals from the first 2 courts may be made to the regional circuit courts of appeal; appeals from the Claims Court may be made to the Federal Circuit Court of Appeals. Decisions of a circuit court may be appealed to the U.S. Supreme Court.

Figure I-6-1
The Technical Body of Knowledge for Tax Accountants

 Federal Tax Laws - e.g. The Internal Revenue Code of 1986, as amended

 Treasury Department Regulations

 Published and Private Letter Rulings Other IRS Publications

 Court decisions

 The tax accounting literature - articles on current practice and unsettled issues

 State tax laws

 International tax laws and tax treaties

All these court decisions (except for decisions in small claims cases that are heard in a less formal manner in a special division of the Tax Court) become a part of the public record. These case decisions show how the courts interpreted the tax law under particular circumstances, and thus become important sources of guidance for tax practitioners.

The Tax Accounting Literature. In addition to these authoritative sources of information, there are several other sources of guidance for deciding how to handle a particular tax issue. Tax practitioners often subscribe to tax services that provide compilations and editorial interpretations of laws, regulations, rulings and cases. These services may be delivered in bound volumes, looseleaf volumes, or via electronic media. Finally, guidance for tax practitioners is provided in the tax accounting literature, where practitioners and academics express their views on a variety of tax issues. This literature includes textbooks and other books, practitioner magazines (like the *Tax Advisor*) and research journals (like the *Journal of the American Taxation Association*).

Other Taxes

In addition to understanding federal income taxation, U.S. tax practitioners must also be aware of other tax laws that might affect organizations they work for or clients they serve. Suppose an organization does business in several states of the U.S. and multiple foreign countries. The organization's tax accountants must understand the laws of each state and country where the company operates. They should also be familiar with any tax treaties between their home country and the foreign countries. **Tax treaties** are agreements between countries that establish how income earned in one country by individuals or corporations from the other country will be taxed. Tax treaties, when they exist, take precedence over national laws, such as the Internal Revenue Code.

How Tax Accountants Master Their Body of Knowledge

By now you have a better understanding of why the library in a tax accountant's office looks so impressive. The body of knowledge needed to answer tax questions and formulate plans to minimize taxes is enormous. Figure I-6-1 (on the previous page) summarizes the sources of the technical body of knowledge for tax accountants. How do tax accountants master this body of knowledge?

Obviously, even the most proficient tax accountant can't be expected to know everything in the body of knowledge about tax. Instead, through education and experience, tax accountants learn in detail the subset of the body of knowledge which is most relevant to tax practice in general. They also learn the most important aspects of tax knowledge for the particular job they hold. A tax accountant who works in the public utility industry will learn a lot about the specialized tax aspects of public utilities; a tax accountant who works for a motion picture studio may know little or nothing about public utility taxation, but will know a great deal about tax laws affecting the motion picture industry.

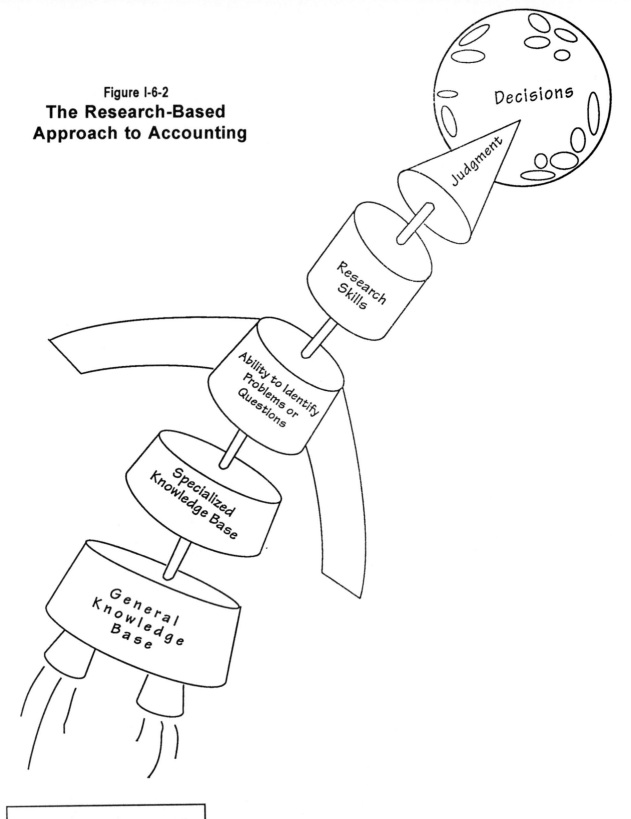

Figure I-6-2
The Research-Based Approach to Accounting

Decisions

Judgment

Research Skills

Ability to Identify Problems or Questions

Specialized Knowledge Base

General Knowledge Base

Launching Pad

Once this base of general and specialized tax knowledge is established, the competent tax practitioner also must know how to identify tax problems or questions and how to use the available guidance to find answers to these problems and questions. Tax practitioners don't have every conceivable tax law, rule, regulation, court decision and treaty memorized. Instead, they know how to perform research to find whatever they need to know in a given situation.

Earlier in the twentieth century, a proficient accountant *could* know everything there was to know about taxes, but that is no longer true. When the number and complexity of tax laws burgeoned, tax practitioners turned from a "know everything" approach to a "know the most important chunk and be able to find the rest" approach--that is, to a research-based approach to tax problems and questions.

The research-based approach to accounting is illustrated in Figure I-6-2 (on the previous page). The accountant's general knowledge base launches the process and the specialized knowledge base adds thrust to the process. The accountant's ability to identify problems or questions controls the direction of the research process and research skills provide maneuverability among the vast reaches of stored information. Finally, the accountant uses judgment to combine the results of the research process and make decisions.

We've already discussed how tax accountants use a research-based approach to accounting. By now, the switch to a research-based approach to an ever-increasing body of knowledge also applies to financial accountants, auditors, managerial accountants and systems accountants. As you will see below, each of these areas has its own increasingly large body of knowledge.

FINANCIAL ACCOUNTING

Principles always become a matter of vehement discussion when practice is at an ebb.
-- George Gissing

At the start of the twentieth century, accountancy was a very old profession that, paradoxically, was still in its infancy. There were few laws, rules or standards to abide by--good practice was determined primarily by the judgment of individual accountants. As businesses and the economy became increasingly complex, and as the number of creditors and outside investors in businesses grew, the need for a common set of criteria to define good financial accounting practice became apparent. This section discusses:

- ◆ the authority to establish U.S. financial accounting standards,
- ◆ U.S. generally accepted accounting principles ("GAAP"),
- ◆ government accounting standards, and
- ◆ international accounting standards.

The Authority to Establish U.S. Financial Accounting Standards

In the United States, the federal securities laws enacted after the stock market crash of 1929 gave the U.S. Securities and Exchange Commission (SEC) the power to set accounting standards for public companies. Widespread recognition of the financial reporting deficiencies that contributed to the crash also sparked private sector efforts to establish financial accounting standards. Rather than exercising its power to directly set accounting standards, the SEC has chosen to operate as an overseer of the private sector standard-setting process, reserving the authority to take action as necessary to resolve specific accounting and reporting problems. The SEC's position was clearly stated in 1973 in *Accounting Series Release No. 150* (ASR #150):

> *Various Acts of Congress administered by the Securities and Exchange Commission clearly state the authority of the Commission to prescribe the methods to be followed in the preparation of accounts and the form and content of financial statements to be filed under the Acts...In meeting this statutory responsibility effectively, in recognition of the expertise, energy and resources of the accounting profession, and without abdicating its responsibilities, the Commission has historically looked to the standard-setting bodies designated by the profession to provide leadership in establishing and improving accounting principles...*

In ASR #150, the SEC recognized that official pronouncements of the Financial Accounting Standards Board (FASB) and its 2 predecessor bodies--the Accounting Principles Board (APB) and the AICPA Committee on Accounting Procedure (CAP)--carry **"substantial authoritative support."** ASR #150 also stated that practices contrary to these standards "will be considered to have no such support." This recognition, along with the requirement that AICPA members must *disclose and justify* any departures from these standards, have made the official pronouncements of the FASB, the APB and the CAP the cornerstone of U.S. generally accepted accounting principles (GAAP).

U.S. GAAP

As you already know, the current "rules of the game" for financial accounting are collectively known as **generally accepted accounting principles** (GAAP). What does GAAP consist of and where does GAAP come from? It may be easier for you to understand the answers to these questions if we start by talking about what GAAP is *not*.

First, GAAP is *not* a comprehensive set of rules for every conceivable circumstance. Economic transactions and events occur in an almost limitless variety. During the 1980s, for example, Wall Street investment bankers helped their clients raise capital by creating many new forms of financial instruments, including some securities that blurred the line between debt and equity. GAAP can't anticipate all the possible economic transactions and events. So, instead of being a cookbook with a recipe for every financial item, GAAP is more like a combination of a self-help book that explains a set of fundamental principles which help accountants evaluate the nature of their accounting problems and a set of detailed rules that determine the appropriate treatment for some of the more common or important economic transactions or events.

Second, GAAP doesn't come from just one source. Instead, there is an entire pool of sources--more formally known as "**the GAAP hierarchy**" that helps practitioners determine generally accepted accounting principles. Figure I-6-3 (on the following page) illustrates the GAAP pool for business and non-profit organizations in the United States. As you can see in the figure, there are several levels to the pool, beginning with official pronouncements on the first level and descending to non-authoritative accounting literature at the lowest level. If you want to find the GAAP for a particular area, you dive into the pool only as deep as you need to go. If, for example, the issue you are concerned about is covered in an official pronouncement, you need go no further into the pool.

Let's take a look at each of the levels of the GAAP hierarchy:

Official Pronouncements. When questions come up that they do not know the answer to, financial accountants begin their search for guidance in the first level of the GAAP hierarchy (*level a* in the pool). This level contains the official pronouncements of the Financial Accounting Standards Board and its 2 predecessor standard-setting bodies, the Accounting Principles Board and the AICPA Committee on Accounting Procedure:

♦ the Financial Accounting Standard Board's *Statements of Financial Accounting Standards* and related *Interpretations*,

♦ the *Opinions* of the Accounting Principles Board that have not been superseded by later standards, and

♦ the *Accounting Research Bulletins* of the AICPA Committee on Accounting Procedure that have not been superseded by later standards.

These official pronouncements cover all manner of financial accounting issues-- from revenue recognition to matching to disclosure to valuation--for most major types of accounting transactions and events.

Because the official pronouncements carry so much weight, the issuance of a new standard occurs only after an established process takes place. Currently, the FASB's "**due process**" includes procedures for:

♦ putting an issue on the FASB's agenda,

♦ appointing a task force of experts to advise the FASB on the issue,

Figure I-6-3
GAAP for Nongovernmental Entities

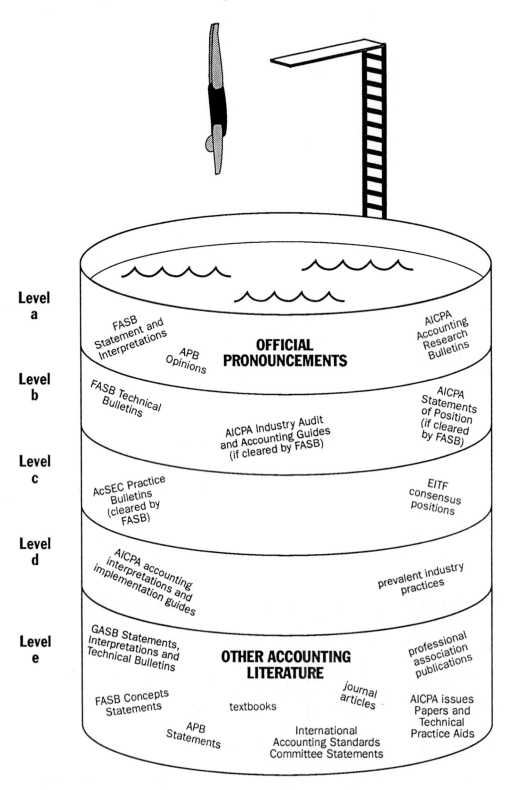

Level a — FASB Statement and Interpretations, APB Opinions, AICPA Accounting Research Bulletins — **OFFICIAL PRONOUNCEMENTS**

Level b — FASB Technical Bulletins, AICPA Industry Audit and Accounting Guides (if cleared by FASB), AICPA Statements of Position (if cleared by FASB)

Level c — AcSEC Practice Bulletins (cleared by FASB), EITF consensus positions

Level d — AICPA accounting interpretations and implementation guides, prevalent industry practices

Level e — GASB Statements, Interpretations and Technical Bulletins, professional association publications, FASB Concepts Statements, textbooks, journal articles, AICPA issues Papers and Technical Practice Aids, APB Statements, International Accounting Standards Committee Statements — **OTHER ACCOUNTING LITERATURE**

♦ having the FASB staff (or external researchers) conduct any needed research on the issue,

♦ publishing a *Discussion Memorandum* or *Invitation to Comment* covering the major points of argument and possible alternative solutions,

♦ holding a public hearing on the issue, if necessary,

♦ deciding on a proposed statement, which is then issued as an *Exposure Draft* for public comment, and

♦ issuing an official *Statement of Financial Accounting Standards*, upon approval of a "super-majority" of the Board members (5 or more positive votes from the 7 full-time Board members).

As the designated body for establishing private sector accounting standards, the FASB has issued over 100 standards and several dozen related interpretations from its inception in 1973 to the present day.

Other Sources of Guidance. What if the accountant's question isn't covered by current official pronouncements? Then the accountant may find potential solutions in one of the other levels of the pool. Let's take a look at some of the major items found at different levels in the GAAP hierarchy.

The second level in the GAAP hierarchy (*level b* in the pool) consists of pronouncements about accounting principles or practices prepared by bodies of technical experts, provided the pronouncements have been exposed for public comment and cleared by the FASB:

♦ **FASB Technical Bulletins**: In addition to its official pronouncements, the FASB also issues periodic *Technical Bulletins.* These bulletins are prepared by the FASB staff to provide clarification or guidance on applying FASB statements or interpretations. The bulletins are not official pronouncements because they do not go through the full due process procedure. They are, however, exposed for public comment and reviewed by the FASB members, so they provide a reliable source of guidance.

♦ **AICPA Industry Audit and Accounting Guides, if cleared by the FASB**: These guides, written by AICPA committees or task forces, describe current good practice for particular industries, such as hospitals or construction contractors. The FASB's *Statement of Financial Accounting Standards No. 32* designated certain AICPA industry guides as preferred practices. The FASB reviews new guides before publication to avoid potential conflicts with current FASB pronouncements or any plans to issue a new standard on the same topic. If the FASB has "**cleared**" an industry guide, it is considered to be in the second level of the GAAP hierarchy.

♦ **AICPA Statements of Position cleared by the FASB**: The AICPA also publishes periodic *Statements of Position* (SOPs) that present the organization's views on unsettled issues. The SOPs--which advocate particular positions--are issued by majority vote of the 15 members of the AICPA's Accounting Standards Executive Committee (AcSec), a senior technical committee that also reviews any new industry guides before they are published. The FASB reviews new SOPs for much the same reason it reviews new industry guides. If the FASB clears a new SOP, the SOP becomes part of the second level of the GAAP hierarchy.

The third level of the GAAP hierarchy (*level c* in the pool) consists of more pronouncements issued by bodies of technical experts. However, these pronouncements are not exposed to public comment before issuance:

♦ **AcSec Practice Bulletins cleared by the FASB**: The AICPA's Accounting Standards Executive Committee (AcSec) also issues periodic *Practice Bulletins* discussing particular technical accounting issues. If cleared by the FASB, these Practice Bulletins become part of the third level of the GAAP hierarchy.

♦ **EITF Consensus Positions**: In 1984, recognizing that its due process procedures made it difficult to rapidly address newly occurring accounting issues, the FASB formed an **Emerging Issues Task Force** (EITF). The EITF consists of 13 representatives from public accounting and key industry groups, including the Financial Executives Institute, the Institute of Management Accountants and the Business Roundtable. The group meets on an as-needed basis (generally once a month) to discuss and vote on the appropriate treatment of particular events or transactions. For example, during the late 1980s, the EITF regularly addressed the accounting treatment of new financial instruments created by Wall Street. An *EITF Consensus Position* is published if agreement on the issue is reached--consensus is considered to be reached when no more than 2 task force members disagree with the position. The Chief Accountant of the SEC participates in EITF discussions, but does not vote. The consensus positions of the EITF took on added importance when the Chief Accountant indicated that SEC registrants need to justify any departures from treatments agreed on by the EITF.

The fourth level of the GAAP hierarchy (*level d* in the pool) consists of various sources of information about current good practice. There are several sources of guidance at this level, including :

- **AICPA Accounting Interpretations and Implementation Guides**: Yet another source of guidance from the AICPA, AICPA *Interpretations* and *Implementation Guides* describe how to apply particular pronouncements in practice.

- **Prevalent industry practice**: Prevalent industry practice refers to specialized accounting practices that have been developed in an industry over time. For example, the oil and gas industry has developed ways to account for its reserves of natural resources that are unique to the industry.

The last level of the GAAP hierarchy (*level e* in the pool) consists of a wide variety of other accounting literature. This level of the GAAP hierarchy is most useful for obtaining guidance on new issues and problems for which no higher level of guidance exists. However, because many of these issues are unsettled, those searching for guidance may find that sources at this level do not always agree with each other. There are many possible sources of guidance in the other accounting literature, including:

- **Books and journal articles discussing current accounting issues**: Textbooks, business books, magazines and research journals provide forums where practitioners and researchers write on financial accounting issues. For example, much of the current guidance on "green accounting" exists only at this level of the GAAP hierarchy.

- **International Accounting Standards**: While domestic standards define the highest levels of U. S. GAAP, practitioners may also seek guidance in the *International Accounting Standards*. These standards will be discussed further later in this section.

- **AICPA Issues Papers and Practice Aids**: The AICPA's publications also include some *Issues Papers,* which present neutral descriptions of current unsettled issues in accounting, and *Practice Aids* (such as disclosure checklists) that help accountants form an organized approach to accounting tasks.

- **FASB Statements of Financial Accounting Concepts**: In addition to publishing standards, the FASB has published works, known as *Statements of Financial Accounting Concepts*, that consider a variety of theoretical issues in accounting. These works can provide a conceptual foundation for viewing accounting issues and problems. For example, a FASB Statement of Financial Accounting Concepts provides the framework for considering the qualitative characteristics (such as relevance and reliability) that make accounting information useful.

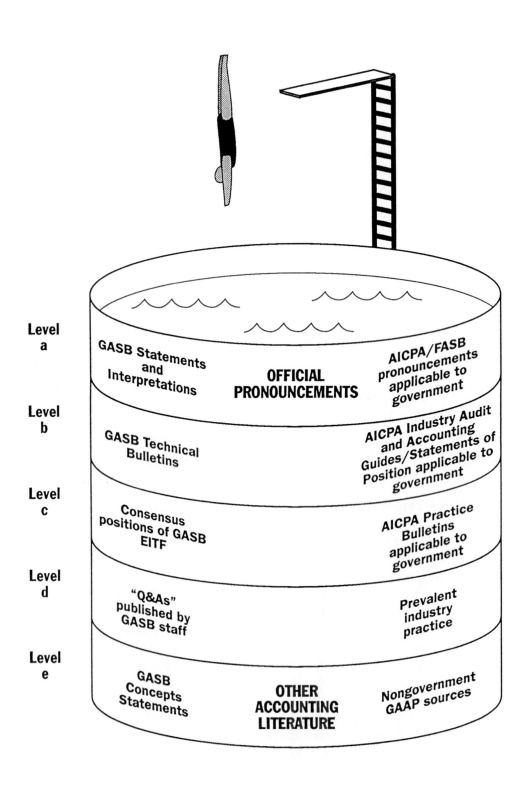

Figure I-6-4
GAAP for State and Local Government Entities

Level a

GASB Statements and Interpretations

OFFICIAL PRONOUNCEMENTS

AICPA/FASB pronouncements applicable to government

Level b

GASB Technical Bulletins

AICPA Industry Audit and Accounting Guides/Statements of Position applicable to government

Level c

Consensus positions of GASB EITF

AICPA Practice Bulletins applicable to government

Level d

"Q&As" published by GASB staff

Prevalent industry practice

Level e

GASB Concepts Statements

OTHER ACCOUNTING LITERATURE

Nongovernment GAAP sources

♦ **GASB Statements, Interpretations and Technical Bulletins**:
While the Government Accounting Standards Board (GASB) is
concerned, obviously, with accounting for government entities,
there is sometimes overlap between accounting issues and
problems faced by government entities and business or non-profit
organizations. Thus, GASB publications can also provide a source
of guidance for business and non-profit entities.

♦ **Other professional association publications**: Many
professional groups--for example, the Financial Executives
Institute, the professional association of corporate financial officers
and other members of top management--devote efforts to
discussing and studying accounting issues. The publications of
these groups provide an additional source of guidance.

As you can see, GAAP comes from *many* sources, official and unofficial.
Generally accepted accounting principles are all the myriad concepts and
methods that form the basis for deciding which events and transactions should be
recorded, how they should be valued, and how they should be reported or
disclosed. Consequently, the financial accountant's library--both print and
electronic-- is as impressive as the tax accountant's library.

Government Accounting Standards

In 1984, the Financial Accounting Foundation (the organization which funds
the FASB) became the parent to a sister organization of the FASB, the
Governmental Accounting Standards Board (GASB). The state
governments and AICPA all recognize the GASB as the authority to establish
financial accounting and reporting standards for state and local government
units. Federal government agencies do not fall under GASB's jurisdiction. The
Federal Accounting Standards Advisory Board (FASAB) recommends
accounting practices for federal government agencies.

The GASB follows an extended due process system that operates much like the
FASB system. The GASB issues *Statements of Governmental Accounting
Standards, Statements of Governmental Accounting Concepts* and *Interpretations.*
In addition, the GASB staff issue *Technical Bulletins* providing timely guidance
on specific government accounting issues.

Just as there is a hierarchy of GAAP for business and non-profit entities, there
is also a hierarchy of GAAP for government entities. Figure I-6-4 (on the
previous page) illustrates the pool of GAAP for government entities.

As you can see, the logic to the hierarchy parallels the logic to the GAAP
hierarchy for non-governmental entities. The official pronouncements of the
GASB and those official pronouncements of the FASB and predecessor bodies
that apply to government entities form the first and most important layer of the

hierarchy. The remaining levels--which are detailed in Figure 6-4--contain the government analogues of the private sector levels of GAAP.

The relationship between standard setting for government entities and non-government entities can be complex. Under the agreement that created the GASB, state and local governments are also obligated to comply with FASB pronouncements that address issues not yet covered by GASB pronouncements, unless the GASB relieves them of the compliance obligation. In the first 5 years of its existence, the GASB denied the applicability of 2 FASB statements--one that required nonprofit organizations to record depreciation expense on their plant and equipment and another that concerned pension accounting. The GASB members felt these standards were of interest to owners and creditors of private sector institutions, but not relevant to the legislative bodies and oversight officials that are the primary users of reports on government-owned entities.

For the most part, the interests of the FASB and the GASB do not overlap. However, there are certain "special entities"--industries like hospitals and colleges--that may be either government-owned or not. The government-owned entities must comply with GASB pronouncements; the non-government entities must comply with FASB pronouncements. Thus, a government-owned hospital need not depreciate its buildings and equipment, while a private sector hospital must do so. This is another example of the trade-offs which must be made in accountancy. To satisfy different needs of different user groups, comparability is sacrificed. The financial statements of the 2 special entities--one government-owned and the other privately held--are not completely comparable due to differences between GASB and FASB standards.

International Accounting Standards

Historically, the United States took the lead in formal standard setting for financial accounting, beginning a movement that spread internationally. Today, many countries have a large and ever-increasing body of financial accounting-related rules, laws and standards. To date, there are many between-country differences, but recently there has been a growing effort to harmonize standards.

International Differences. At present, most nations have less complex accounting standards, with less complete disclosure requirements, than the United States. In many cases, other countries believe the U.S. requirements are overly complex, trading off decreased flexibility for increased comparability. These nations feel that the U.S. system has become inflexible, failing to allow for legitimate alternatives for companies in varying situations. The critics also argue that the U.S. practice of issuing detailed standards for common or important practices is self-defeating. They maintain that more general standards are better suited to quick reactions to a changing environment. On the other hand, the United States is acknowledged to have the world's most successful capital markets; many experts credit the country's accounting standards and SEC enforcement program as instrumental in the success of the U.S. markets.

Even as recently as 1990, globalization of capital markets was more an idea than a reality, so international accounting differences had relatively little impact on access to capital. But as we continue to rapidly move toward true market globalization, the incentive to harmonize standards increases. Unless companies can present their financial reports in terms understandable to a diverse group of foreign investors and creditors, they will limit their access to capital.

Harmonization Efforts. Many organizations have been working on harmonization. In 1973, the professional bodies of Australia, Canada, France, Germany, Japan, Mexico, the Netherlands, the United Kingdom and Ireland, and the United States joined together to found the **International Accounting Standards Committee** (IASC). By 1995, the IASC had expanded to include 114 accountancy organizations from 83 countries.

To date, using a due process system much like the FASB's, the IASC has issued several dozen *International Accounting Standards* (IASs) and a conceptual discussion of the *Framework for the Preparation and Presentation of Financial Statements*. English is the IASC's official language and the IASs are translated into over a dozen additional languages.

The IASC is not legally empowered to enforce standards for its member nations, but encourages voluntary compliance. A 1993 survey on the use and application of international accounting standards found that the majority of countries were in compliance with most of the then-existing standards. However, you should be aware that the IASC has not yet attempted to require a single accounting treatment on issues where significant inter-country differences exist. Instead, in these instances, the IASC has identified certain treatments as preferable, but still allowed the others as alternatives. This, however, is a significant step in narrowing diversity.

For the past decade, the IASC has also been working (as yet with limited success) to convince the international community that all international enterprises should reconcile their reported net income and equity with the figures that *would* have been reported if all the preferable treatments defined in IASC standards had been used. To the extent that harmonization and comparative disclosures are increased, users will find it easier to interpret accounting information internationally.

During the 1990s, the IASC has taken steps to reduce the number of acceptable accounting alternatives under international standards and to increase the acceptance of international standards. A major step occurred in 1995 when the International Organization of Securities Commissions (IOSCO)--the members of which include securities regulators from Canada, China, Japan, the U.K., the U.S. and other world capital markets--agreed to formally endorse a core set of international accounting standards (IASs). Endorsement means the core set of IASs will be considered sufficient to define reporting requirements for cross-border listings on the stock exchanges of all member nations by 1999.

This agreement is contingent on the IASC successfully completing 15 new or revised standards needed to complete the set of core requirements. The 4 new IASs will cover topics--such as interim reporting--on which current IASs are silent. The 11 revisions will narrow choices currently allowed under IAS standards in such areas as accounting for leases and goodwill. The IASC has a work plan to satisfy the IOSCO requirements by the deadline date. Globalization of capital markets provides a strong incentive to do so.

AUDITING

> *It is impossible for all things to be precisely set down in writing; for rules*
> *must be universal, but actions are concerned with particulars.*
> *--Aristotle, Politics*

To financial accountants, financial statements are the endpoint--the goal. To financial auditors, financial statements are the starting point--the entry level. Thus, to perform their audits, financial auditors must be familiar with those portions of GAAP and tax law that potentially affect their clients' financial statements. In addition, the auditor must be familiar with the technical standards of auditing, or **"generally accepted auditing standards"** (GAAS). What GAAP is to financial accounting, GAAS is to financial auditing. This section discusses the technical body of knowledge contained in GAAS, as well as the body of knowledge needed to perform compliance and operational audits.

Financial Auditing

U.S. Private Sector Standards. Financial auditing standards for the U.S. private sector are established by the **Auditing Standards Board** (ASB), which operates under the auspices of the AICPA. The ASB's official pronouncements are known as *Statements on Auditing Standards*, or **"SASs."** The SASs carry considerable force. The financial auditor's report for a U. S. company must state whether the audit was conducted "in accordance with generally accepted auditing standards.". When auditors do not comply with these standards, they are considered negligent and face legal liability for this negligence.

The *Statements on Auditing Standards* are fashioned around the 10 **generally accepted auditing standards (GAAS)** --a sort of 10 commandments for auditors. The GAAS include 3 "general standards" that describe the general qualities required of all auditors (competence, independence and due professional care), as well as 3 standards of performance for "fieldwork" (audit tests performed for a particular client) and 4 standards related to the preparation of audit reports. These 10 standards establish overall guidelines for conducting a quality audit, but leave the details of financial audits to the judgment of the auditors. The SASs require a few specific audit procedures--such as requiring that auditors physically observe the annual count of a client's inventory, if it is material. Otherwise, the specific procedures to be performed on an audit depend on the particular circumstances of the client.

U.S. Government Auditing Standards. In the U.S., government auditing standards are contained in the "**yellow book**" published by the U.S. GAO. The basic auditing standards, which have much in common with GAAS, are known as "**generally accepted government auditing standards**" or GAGAS. Since government audits tend to combine aspects of financial auditing, operational auditing and compliance auditing, GAGAS go beyond private sector auditing standards in some areas. Independent external auditors who perform audits of government entities or government-sponsored entities (like colleges receiving government funding) must comply with both GAAS and GAGAS.

International Auditing Standards. For the first three-quarters of the twentieth century, only the United States, Canada and the United Kingdom had formalized auditing standards. As auditing standards began to be formalized in other countries, these standards were often used as models. Consequently, while country-to-country differences do still exist, there are fewer between-nation differences in auditing standards than in accounting standards.

Today, *International Standards on Auditing* (ISAs)--formerly known as *International Auditing Guidelines* (IAGs)--for the private sector are published by the International Auditing Practices Committee of the **International Federation of Accountants** (IFAC), the body which also oversees the International Accounting Standards Committee. The IFAC also publishes international ethics and education standards, including a model code of ethics. The ethics code is divided into 2 parts--1 for accountants in public practice and 1 for accountants in industry. The IFAC urges adoption of the code by the international business community.

International standards for government audits are published by INTOSAI, the **International Organization of Supreme Audit Institutions**. INTOSAI, which is headquartered in Vienna, Austria, receives funding from the United Nations. Its standards are published in English, and translated into Arabic, French, German, Spanish and other languages. While INTOSAI standards are not mandatory, they do represent a statement of the best practices among supreme audit institutions, such as the United States' GAO.

The Auditing Literature. In addition to published standards, there is a large body of auditing literature, including publications of professional associations, textbooks and other books, and practitioner and academic journals. Many of the ideas which later become formalized in auditing standards begin their life in the auditing literature. For example, most of the ideas behind the use of statistical sampling in auditing were developed in the auditing literature before they were made part of auditing standards.

Compliance Auditing and Operational Auditing

Standards for compliance audits performed by external auditors or government auditors may be found in attest standards issued by the ASB and the

GAO's yellow book. In addition, standards for compliance and operational audits performed by internal auditors may be found in the **Institute of Internal Auditors'** (IIA) *Standards for the Professional Practice of Internal Auditing.* Because of the IIA's international membership, these standards have world-wide influence on internal auditing. For example, Swedish law requires all internal audits of public authorities to comply with the IIA standards and code of ethics.

The IIA standards define the criteria by which the operations of an internal audit department should be evaluated and measured. They include standards on independence, professional proficiency, the appropriate scope of internal audit work, the performance of internal audit work, and the management of internal audit departments. Like the standards for financial auditing, these standards are broad descriptions of desired characteristics, not detailed procedural requirements. The specific procedures to be performed on a particular internal audit are a matter for the auditor's judgment.

Various additional publications of the IIA and other professional associations, like the Information Systems Audit and Control Association, as well as the portion of the auditing literature which deals with internal auditing, also contribute to the technical body of knowledge for compliance and operational auditing. Much of the accumulated wisdom of the profession about specific internal audit procedures may be found in the internal auditing literature.

SYSTEMS AND MANAGERIAL ACCOUNTING

Our knowledge is the amassed thought and experience of innumerable minds.
  -- Ralph Waldo Emerson

The work of tax accountants, financial accountants and financial auditors is directed toward both external (non-management) and internal users of accounting information. It is the presence of external users which creates an incentive to formalize laws, rules and standards.

On the other hand, the work of systems and managerial accountants is directed exclusively toward internal (management) users of accounting information. Their reports are not issued externally. This does not imply that their work is unimportant to external users, but only that the relationship between systems and managerial accountants and external users is indirect. External users are influenced by the work of systems accountants because the information system contributes to the accuracy and reliability of financial statements. They are also influenced by the work of managerial accountants, who are responsible for much of the planning, budgeting, cost control and cash flow management activities that contribute to the organization's continued success. Even so, systems and managerial accountants have no direct external reporting responsibilities.

Thus, it is not surprising that the technical body of knowledge for systems and managerial accounting is primarily literature-based, with less emphasis on formalized laws and standards. Nonetheless, several professional associations for systems and management accountants have issued standards and urged voluntary compliance. For example, there is a committee of the International Federation of Accountants that issues *Statements on International Management Accounting Practice*. In the U.S., the Management Accounting Practices Committee of the Institute of Management Accountants issues periodic *Statements on Management Accounting*. Similarly, in Canada, the Society of Management Accountants issues periodic *Management Accounting Guidelines*. In addition, there are authoritative cost accounting standards for government contractors. This section discusses those authoritative standards and the interdisciplinary literature of systems and management accounting.

Authoritative Standards: The CASB

There is one area where the interests of external users have provided strong incentives for formal standardization: the area of cost accounting for companies that have government contracts. **Cost accounting** is the area of management accounting concerned with attaching specific costs to particular products, services or projects. Cost accounting information is especially useful for internal management decisions, such as deciding how to price products or services.

Cost accounting takes on a particular importance in government contracting, especially with defense contractors. Many defense contracts are for unique products (like jet fighters for the military) that involve high-risk technology development and little opportunity for selling the product to other buyers. Consequently, many defense contracts are negotiated to allow the suppliers to recover their costs plus a reasonable profit. Some of the problems associated with accounting for the costs of defense contracts are discussed in Theme II of this series.

The integrity of the defense contracting system depends on the accurate estimation and reporting of product costs. Several decades ago, Congress established the **Cost Accounting Standards Board** (CASB) to issue cost accounting standards that would apply to federal government contracts. The CASB issued twenty standards over a decade of work before being disbanded in 1980 for lack of funding. Within 10 years, recognizing that there was no mechanism for dealing with new controversies in defense contracting, Congress recreated the CASB.

The CASB standards are mandatory for companies that have government contracts totaling over a certain dollar amount ($25 million). Moreover, a subset of the CASB standards apply to all contractors and subcontractors on negotiated contracts of over $500,000.

The Interdisciplinary Literature of Systems and Management Accounting

The body of knowledge for systems and managerial accountants is inter-disciplinary. It crosses over into the literature of related areas like computer sciences, decision sciences, psychology, and finance.

One good gauge of the interdisciplinary nature of systems and managerial accounting is to look at the prescribed body of knowledge for professional certification in these areas. Consider, for example, the Institute of Management Accountants' **Certified Management Accountant** (CMA) program. The 4 sections of the CMA exam include:

♦ Economics, Finance and Management;

♦ Financial Accounting and Reporting;

♦ Management Reporting, Analysis and Behavioral Issues; and

♦ Decision Analysis and Information Systems.

As another example, the Information Systems Audit and Control Association (ISACA) offers a "**Certified Information Systems Auditor**" (CISA) exam that covers the numerous tasks performed by information systems audit, control, and security professionals. The CISA exam covers such specialized topics as information systems development, acquisition and maintenance, as well as broader topics such as management practices. To be certified as a CISA--as is also true of the CMA--an applicant must not only pass the licensing exam, but must also meet certain education and experience requirements. In addition, CISAs and CMAs agree to comply with the ethics code of their professional organization.

Because of the interdisciplinary nature of their body of knowledge, systems and managerial accountants need a broad educational base as well as specialized technical skills. Like the body of knowledge for tax, financial accounting and auditing, the bodies of knowledge for systems and managerial accounting have become so vast that accountants in these areas are likely to carve out specializations. For example a managerial accountant might specialize in planning and budgeting or in cost accounting or in compensation systems. A systems accountant might specialize in designing information systems, or in auditing information systems. The increasing tendency toward specialization within the functional areas of accounting means that accountants of the future are likely to be doing more of their work in teams of coordinated specialists rather than as individuals.

THE POLITICS OF DEVELOPING LAWS, RULES AND STANDARDS

We need supermen to rule us--the job is so vast and the need for wise judgment is so urgent. But, alas, there are no supermen.
-- Brooks Atkinson, <u>Once Around The Sun</u>, 1951

Given their direct connection to external users, tax accounting, financial accounting and auditing operate in an environment of laws, rules and standards. Accounting information fills social needs and lawmaking and standard setting are social processes.

Lawmakers and standard setters make both intellectual judgments and value judgments. In making laws and setting standards, many trade-offs must be made. For each trade-off, some group "wins" and some group "loses"--some bear the costs, others reap the benefits. Robert Swieringa, a FASB member, once observed that the social nature of standard setting--which equally applies to lawmaking--begets a very complex process:

> *Standard setting is more than making choices. It is a process of preparing people for change and even, perhaps, motivating and committing them to accept and adopt change.*

These thoughts echo earlier reflections by David Solomons, who noted that standard setters--and again, this applies equally well to lawmakers--cannot possibly please all interested parties:

> *Faced with a multitude of different value judgments, satisfying everyone is more than any standards board or committee can hope to do. What it <u>can</u> hope to do is to convince its constituents that they will be better off if they accept its constraints than if they do not.*

Inevitably, there is a political element to lawmaking and standard setting. In this section, we consider some aspects of the politics of developing laws, rules and standards.

Jurisdictional Disputes

When power is vested in multiple lawmaking and standard-setting bodies, jurisdictional disputes may arise in areas where the bodies' interests overlap. For example, consider the ongoing debate over the pros and cons of a U. S. federal value-added tax (VAT), which proponents argue would be an effective, efficient way to raise revenues, as well as to make U.S. goods more competitive internationally. Even so, you could expect any proposed federal VAT to be vigorously disputed by the state governments, who would view the VAT as conflicting with their ability to generate state and local sales taxes.

For another example, recall that the interests of the GASB and the FASB overlap when it comes to industries where some of the enterprises are government-owned and others are in the private sector--such as public utilities, colleges and universities, and hospitals. In 1988 and 1989, there was a jurisdictional dispute between the FASB and the GASB over which board's standards should prevail in these industries.

The initial decision of the Financial Accounting Foundation (FAF), the parent organization for both bodies, was that the FASB standards should take precedence. The FAF argued that the entities in these industries competed against each other in the capital markets; therefore, their financial statements should be comparable. Dana Wechsler, writing in the December 11, 1989 issue of *Forbes* magazine, described the brouhaha that ensued. She reported that the state and local government groups were "furious" because they viewed the decision as "an invasion of their turf." The states even threatened to rethink their traditional support of other FASB standards--to secede, in effect, from the accounting union.

Since the U.S.'s state governments have sovereign rights, they have the right to determine who sets their financial accounting standards. Given this power and the states' apparent intention to use it, the result of the jurisdictional dispute was obvious. Just a few days short of 1 month prior to the state-imposed secession deadline, the president of the FAF issued a proposal to reinstate the GASB's jurisdiction.

This reversal of position was not without its cost. Industry groups that supported the original proposal objected vigorously. *Forbes* cited the case of the National Association of College and University Business Officers, a membership association for the financial officers of over 2,000 schools. According to *Forbes*, quoting the association's Director of Finance as saying she felt "betrayed" by the outcome, the association "would have preferred war" to capitulation on this point.

Jurisdictional disputes may be resolved by avoidance--as they have been so far in the case of the potential federal VAT, or by dint of superior power (one side gives up its position)--as they were in the GASB-FASB dispute, or by negotiated settlements, as is often the case in tax treaties.

Lobbying and Special-Interest Groups

Both lawmaking and standard-setting bodies have constituencies and their constituencies have a voice in the process. In a democratic society, sensitivity to constituencies is a desired goal. The expression of support or opposition to proposed laws and standards is encouraged--even sought. But, given the nature of the process, it isn't generally possible for both sides of the argument-- proponents and opponents--to be simultaneously satisfied.

Consider how taxes are enacted in the United States. Lobbying by special-interest groups is an integral part of this process. For example, in the early 1990s, a tax on the sale of stocks and other securities was proposed, but not enacted. It was estimated that a tax of no higher than 0.5% of the sales price of securities would raise several billion dollars a year in tax revenue. Proponents of the tax argued that in addition to raising needed revenues, the tax would have the added benefit of curbing volatility in the stock markets because the additional trading cost would discourage excessive reactions to small changes in stock market prices. On the other hand, opponents argued that the tax would harm the competitiveness of the U.S. securities industry because investors would move their trading to foreign markets in order to avoid the tax. One side argued that the benefits would exceed the costs; the other side argued the opposite.

Similar arguments often surround proposed financial accounting standards. For example, in the early 1990s, the FASB proposed a new accounting standard for banks: the banks would have to value their portfolio of investment securities at market value, rather than at cost. This "**mark-to-market**" proposal was met with both vigorous support and vigorous opposition. Supporters--including SEC Chairman Richard C. Breeden, who had urged the FASB to issue the proposal-- argued that market values are more relevant to users and pointed out that market-value accounting could provide a better early warning system for banks in danger of failing.

Opponents--including most financial institutions subject to the standard-- argued that even small changes in market prices for their large investment portfolios could lead to large swings in balance sheet values. As a result, bankers might change their strategies to emphasize shorter-term investments to avoid the possibility of excessive volatility. This change in the investment portfolios could lead to a decreased volume of funds available for long-term loans, thus raising the cost of long-term capital to borrowers. One side argues that the benefits will exceed the costs; the other side argues the opposite.

After several years of argument, the FASB voted in 1993 to require a modified form of mark-to-market accounting. The new standard required that securities be reported at market value, but allowed for an exception to the general rule if a financial institution could show the intention and ability to hold a security until it matured. This compromise, however, did little to silence critics. On the day the final vote was taken, the executive vice president of the American Bankers Association told the press, "This is truly a terrible decision they've made today." Meanwhile, supporters were quoted praising the decision as a significant improvement for users of financial reports.

Given the difficulty of actually measuring the costs and benefits of proposed laws and standards, there is generally no clear-cut resolution to these kinds of arguments. While the expression of views of interested parties is sought out as helpful to the process, lobbying by interest groups can have detrimental effects, if carried to extremes. These detrimental effects are not inevitable, but they can pose threats to the process.

One potential threat arises because the ultimate beneficiaries of the process--

the users of accounting information--tend to be more diverse and dispersed, and thus less well-organized politically, than the preparers. This can lead to an imbalance in input to lawmakers and standard setters. For example, in a December 1993 commentary published in *Accounting Horizons*, Dennis R. Beresford, the Chairman of the Financial Accounting Standards Board, noted the lack of input from users when the FASB sets standards:

> *We occasionally receive letters from individual users but that is the exception not the rule. And the few letters from users do not compare favorably with many hundred from corporate preparers and at least a few score from accounting firms and CPA societies on most important projects....*
>
> *An obvious question is why aren't users more active in our process. One possibility is that they don't derive as much benefit from financial reporting as we accountants may have assumed. I think a more logical answer is that they simply aren't as well equipped and as well organized to participate in our process as are some other groups.*

Who speaks for the users? One effort to address users' needs was the AICPA's **Special Committee on Financial Reporting** (commonly called the Jenkins Committee, after its chairman, Edmund L. Jenkins). In 1994, the committee issued a series of recommendations for standard setters about how to make financial reporting more responsive to users' needs. The recommended changes for businesses--which are now being considered in the deliberations of standard-setters and regulators-- include publishing more detailed information about financial results by segment, more operational data and disclosures (such as more information about companies' market share and product quality), and more disclosures about risks and uncertainties.

Another potential threat arises because interest groups sometimes forget that there *are* 2 sides to most issues--and that there would be little need for lawmaking or standard setting if the solutions were obvious. As FASB member James Leisenring observed, the reason FASB proposals spark such heated debate is that "people believe there is a right and wrong answer." When one side or the other eventually "loses" the debate, it is human nature to take the loss personally. With enough losses, interest groups can become bellicose and lose their faith in the process. When a large enough portion of the constituencies lose their faith in the process, the process fails.

There are some people who think the FASB is in danger of failure due to loss of support from some constituencies, primarily the preparers of financial statements. In 1996, the financial press bristled with debate when a committee of the Financial Executives Institute criticized the FASB as unresponsive to business and suggested that a new outside organization should oversee and control the FASB's agenda. John C. Burton and Robert J. Sack, writing in the December 1990 issue of *Accounting Horizons*, suggested there may be a naturally limited life span for standard-setting bodies because of political conflicts:

The Committee on Accounting Procedure lasted about 20 years. The Accounting Principles Board survived for 15.....A self-regulatory system has a certain honeymoon period, because of the consensus which accompanies its creation. A consensus, like a honeymoon, can last a long time, but very long-lived examples are rare....We may have to accept the CAP - APB - FASB - XXXX cycle as the necessary cost of self-regulation.

There is yet another source of threat if lobbying is carried to extremes. Certain interest groups may have so much power that they "capture" the lawmaking or standard-setting body. R. G. Walker, who served as a member of Australia's Accounting Standards Review Board (ASRB), wrote a detailed history of the ASRB during the mid-1980s, which was published in *Accounting and Business Research* during 1987. Walker argues that the ASRB at that time was effectively controlled by certain interest groups. As a result, Walker observes that the ASRB favored the positions of auditors and preparers and did not treat other interest groups in an "even-handed manner."

Game Playing

Laws, rules and standards have a tendency to multiply and grow ever more detailed. This creates the opportunity for game playing. As Irvin Cobb--an American journalist and short-story writer who lived from 1876-1944-- humorously observed, game playing consists of trying to "beat the system":

Learn all the rules, every one of them, so that you will know how to break them.

Some people think that both tax accounting and financial accounting show evidence of game playing. For example, researchers have observed that tax preparers take the most liberal deductions in areas where they know audits are not likely. Researchers and the financial press have also documented cases where businesses structured deals around detailed accounting standards to force the financial reporting treatment they wanted, even if the substance of the deal warranted a different treatment.

On the one hand, such game playing is a rational economic reaction, reflecting human competitive spirit. On the other hand, treating laws, rules and standards as a system to be beaten threatens the integrity of the process. When too much game playing goes on, people lose confidence in the system and a downward spiral begins.

Partly in reaction to this potential threat, there have been many calls for tax simplification and for reducing the "**standards overload**" (the increasing number and complexity of standards) in financial accounting. The debate over tax complexity and standards overload inevitably becomes a political debate, as well as a debate over technical matters in accounting and taxation.

Is This Process Worth More Than It Costs?

Throughout this theme, we've looked at many of the positive social aspects of accountancy. For the last few pages, we've focused on some of the potential negative aspects of developing laws, rules, standards and guidelines for the practice of accountancy. How do the accounting profession's scales balance? Is this process worth more than the cost? We've reviewed the system's assets and liabilities; what is its net worth?

At least in the short run, no one can definitively answer these questions. But most observers--critics as well as supporters--would probably say that the scales tip in favor of the benefits. While accountants and user groups continue to strive for an "ideal" system, they also recognize that this is an inspiring, but unattainable, goal. As Jacob Bronowski eloquently commented in his opus on *The Ascent of Man*, "All information is imperfect. We have to treat it with humility."

MODULE 6: THE ENVIRONMENT OF ACCOUNTING

PART B: RESEARCHING ACCOUNTING ISSUES

Knowledge is of two kinds. We know a subject ourselves, or we know
where we can find information upon it.
-- Samuel Johnson, 1709-1784

Picture this scenario: You are a college student who has just chosen your major. You are sitting in the Student Center mapping out the courses you plan to take when a friend, who is about to graduate, walks by. He stops to chat, tells you about his new job, and hands you a folder of career planning information he found helpful. When he leaves, you pick up the first thing in the folder, a copy of the Fall of 1990 *National Business and Employment Weekly*'s guide, "Managing Your Career." As you are reading an article by Robert Troutwine entitled "Prepare now and succeed later," you come across a frightening fact:

> *Most [students] see college as a means of gathering enough facts,*
> *knowledge and skills to make them employable....Yet most fields of study*
> *have a half-life of knowledge of about four years--50% of what you learn in*
> *college will be obsolete before your five-year reunion.*

While no one has formally measured the half-life of an accounting or business education, accounting and business are dynamic fields. If you choose to pursue a career in these areas, you will find that much will change from decade to decade throughout your career.

Consider, for example, that students who went to college and majored in accounting in the 1960s began their careers in a world that was still dependent on manual accounting systems. The Accounting Principles Board issued financial accounting standards. The version of the Internal Revenue Code they studied was heavily influenced by a major revision of the tax law in 1954. During the 1970s, these students saw businesses of all sizes enter the computer age. They saw the Accounting Principles Board die and witnessed the birth of the Financial Accounting Standards Board. During the 1980s, they saw the microcomputer revolution sweep through the business world and watched as Congress made massive changes in the Internal Revenue Code in 1986. Each decade of their careers, accountants had to adjust to major changes in the body of knowledge.

So, Troutwine's statistic is at least in the ball park--you can expect the knowledge base you will need for a successful career to undergo constant change. How do people cope with this kind of change? Troutwine offered a suggestion by retelling a famous story about Albert Einstein:

> *Use Albert Einstein as a role model. One day a reporter was interviewing him in his office. Toward the end of the interview, the reporter asked for Einstein's home phone number. Einstein reached over for the phone book, looked up his number and gave it to the reporter. The reporter was astounded. "You don't know your own phone number?" he asked. Einstein smiled and replied that he didn't want to clutter his mind with such trivia. The important thing, he said, is knowing where he could find the information when needed.*

In the first part of this module, we talked about how accountants cope with their vast and ever-increasing body of knowledge. Through education and experience, they build a layer of fundamental knowledge and specialized knowledge needed for their particular job. In addition, they know how to perform research to find whatever else they need to know in a given situation.

In the rest of this module, we will discuss how accounting practice issues are researched. There are 3 basic steps in researching an accounting issue:

- ◆   problem identification,

- ◆   selecting sources of information, and

- ◆   searching sources of information.

Each of these steps is discussed below.

PROBLEM IDENTIFICATION

A problem adequately stated is a problem well on its way to being solved.
-- R. Buckminster Fuller

The first step in researching accounting issues sounds deceptively simple: you need to identify the problem. To get to this point in your life as a student, you've invested years in solving homework problems. Think about what that usually involves: first, you look at a box marked "Problem" or "Question" or "Assignment" and read what the problem is; then, you go about trying to solve it. But real-world problems don't come in nicely marked boxes. They don't appear in bold-face type. Real-world problems can be maddeningly ambiguous. You have to define the problem before you can solve it.

An Easy Example

To be able to identify problems, you need a base of fundamental knowledge so you can understand the issue at hand. Consider this example and see if you can identify the problem and the appropriate question(s) to ask to research the issue:

> *Megan is a senior at an American university. In order to graduate in June, she needs to complete 6 required courses and 2 electives. Of the electives, there is 1 course she really wants to take; she is flexible about the second course. For the Fall semester, the registration schedule shows that 3 of the required courses she needs are being offered. The elective she really wants to take is being offered, but the time conflicts with the only section of 1 of the required courses she needs.*

Chances are, you rather quickly identified Megan's problem: should she sign up for the elective course she really wants or for the required course? And chances are you can define the questions she should be researching, such as: (1) Will the required course be offered in the Spring? and (2) Will the elective course be offered in the Spring?

You are able to identify the problem and the questions that need research very quickly because you understand a lot of basic concepts about the way college course offerings work. It's your core of knowledge--which you probably learned with at least some pain during your freshman year--that helps you identify a problem and define the right questions to ask.

A Harder Example

Now, consider this example adapted from the first-year staff training program of Coopers & Lybrand, an international public accounting firm, and see if you can identify the problem and the appropriate question(s) to ask to research the issue:

> *During the current year, Best Marine Corp. traded in its company yacht, the "Titanic," for a new pleasure yacht, the "S. S. Minnow." Best Marine Corp. paid $25,000 (plus the trade-in) for the S. S. Minnow. Three years ago, Best Marine paid $98,000 for the Titanic. Prior to its trade-in, the Titanic had $12,000 in accumulated depreciation. The invoice price listed for the S. S. Minnow was $115,000.*

The facts of the situation are summarized in Figure I-6-5 (on the following page). Before reading any further, take another look at these facts and try to determine the accounting problem or issue.

Chances are, the problem doesn't jump out at you automatically here, although you probably can figure it out. That's because you are still building

Figure I-6-5
What Accounting Issue/Problem
Does Best Marine Face?

Best Marine gives up:	In order to purchase:
 $25,000 Old Yacht: Original Cost: $98,000  Accumulated Depreciation: $12,000	 New Yacht: Invoice Price $115,000

The accounting problem/issue is:

? ? ?

your basic layer of knowledge in accounting--you don't know as much about accounting as you do about being a college student. There are 2 things, however, that will help you identify a problem. First, you understand enough accounting vocabulary by now to follow what has happened--Best Marine purchased a new yacht with a hefty trade-in and some cash. Second, you remember (hopefully) that assets are recorded on the books at cost, not market value.

One of the problems an accountant would immediately identify in this situation is: at what value should Best Marine record the new yacht on its books? If the company had bought the *Minnow* for straight cash (without any trade-in), the answer would be obvious. But Best Marine paid a small amount of cash and traded in an old yacht, so the answer isn't so obvious. Before you read any further, try to answer the question without the benefit of doing any research. What dollar amount would you record for the *Minnow*? In a few moments, we'll see if you were right.

How Research Helps

Now let's say you decide you better do some research. What questions could you ask to help you research this problem? The facts describe a trade-in that doesn't involve much cash. It's primarily a non-monetary exchange. Consider: how are non-monetary exchanges treated in financial accounting? Or: how do you treat the gain or loss on a non-monetary exchange? These questions are researchable.

So, you could start to search for accounting standards concerning "trade-ins" or "non-monetary exchanges." And, it turns out, there is an Accounting Principles Board opinion (*APB Opinion No. 29*, if you're curious) that gives you the answer you need. Paragraph 22 of that opinion says:

> the enterprise...shall record the asset received at the amount of the monetary consideration paid plus the recorded amount of the nonmonetary asset surrendered.

Let's break this down. "The monetary consideration paid" is the cash you paid for the new yacht, $25,000. "The nonmonetary asset surrendered" is the *Titanic*, the yacht you traded in. The "recorded amount" for the Titanic is its original cost of $98,000 less the depreciation of $12,000--that is, $86,000. So, the recorded value of the *S. S. Minnow* will be $111,000 (the combined total of the $25,000 cash paid and the $86,000 recorded value of the traded yacht).

Did you have this answer? Without doing the research, you might easily have made an error. There are several different calculations you could have done that would yield answers other than $111,000. For example, without the benefit of the research findings, you might have thought the new yacht should be valued at its list price of $115,000.

Before we cast off this example, here's one more thing to consider: Was there only 1 problem suggested by the Best Marine situation? The answer is no, at least to an accountant. For example, you might want to know if the trade-in is handled the same way for tax accounting and financial accounting purposes. Research could help you answer that question, too.

Problem Identification: A Summary

What's the point of this example? First, you can't solve a problem that you don't identify. The first task in researching accounting issues is problem identification. Don't expect all problems to be clearly stated. You need to look at the situation and think about what the problems might be. Second, you generally can't identify problems from a point of zero knowledge; a base of fundamental knowledge helps. You need to understand the basic concepts embedded in the situation to be able to define the problem to the point where you know what specific questions to ask.

SELECTING SOURCES OF INFORMATION

He is wise who knows the sources of knowledge--who knows who has written and where it is to be found.
--Archibald Alexander Hodge

Once you have identified a problem and formulated some specific questions, the next step is to select the sources of information to search. In Part A of this module, you learned about the technical body of knowledge in accounting. Understanding the structure of that body of knowledge is the first step in knowing where to search for information about accounting issues.

What Sources Do You Want To Consult?

Once you identified a problem about the appropriate valuation of the *S. S. Minnow*, you knew you were dealing with a financial accounting question. If you remember the figure showing the pool of GAAP, you'd know that the first place to look for an answer would be in the authoritative pronouncements of the Financial Accounting Standards Board and its 2 predecessor bodies. That's where the answer turned out to be--in an opinion of the Accounting Principles Board. If the answer hadn't been there, then you would have proceeded to search the remaining levels in the GAAP hierarchy (deeper in the pool of GAAP).

Or, suppose we had chosen to also research the second identified problem: is the GAAP treatment of trade-ins the same for tax accounting purposes? Where would you start? Again, remembering Part A of this module, the first place you'd look would be in the Internal Revenue Code. If you didn't find the answer there, you'd proceed to look at regulations, rulings, and court cases. There is a strategy to selecting sources: start with the most authoritative sources first.

We've been supposing you were an accountant or a member of management at Best Marine who had to record some value for the *S. S. Minnow*. Now let's change roles. What if you were an investor or creditor trying to assess the merits of buying Best Marine stock or making a loan to the company? What sources of information would you want to research now? You'd probably want a database of company information so you could compare Best Marine with other companies in the industry. You'd also likely want a database of industry news articles so you could assess the overall prospects and risks for the industry. Or, you might want a database of credit ratings or financial analysts' recommendations so you could see how other experts evaluate the company. The databases you choose depend on your information needs.

Where Do You Find These Sources?

Where do you actually find all these sources? At present, the most likely answer is in a library--either your university library or your firm library. Most likely, your library will contain the information you need either in printed reference books or in electronic databases. One other possibility is that you'd have your own personal library that travels with you on the job. Many larger CPA firms now provide an electronic library to their employees. The libraries contain, often on a single CD-ROM disk, the firm's own proprietary policy manuals and the major sources of information for tax, financial accounting and auditing research. If your firm can't afford to develop its own electronic library, you can purchase an *Electronic Body of Knowledge* library from the AICPA.

All of the information we've talked about so far in this module is available on CD-ROM (which stands for compact-disc, read-only memory). CD-ROM databases look like a CD you buy in the music store, but contain documents instead. There can be over a quarter of a million pages of text stored on a single CD-ROM. For example, if you want information about global businesses, you might consult a CD-ROM database called Disclosure/Worldscope™ Global. The database includes 10 years of financial data for over 8,000 international corporations in several dozen industries, as well as country and industry benchmarks for a variety of financial ratios. The database even highlights country-specific accounting practices.

What if you don't have easy physical access to a library? One possibility is to gain access to remote libraries--including many university libraries and the U.S. Library of Congress--via the Internet, an electronic network that interconnects over 100,000 corporate, educational and research networks around the globe. The Internet also provides access to professional associations, standard-setting bodies and regulators, where a wealth of information is available. For example, you can find annual reports for U. S. public companies by accessing the Securities and Exchange Commission's EDGAR (Electronic Data Gathering and Retrieval) database.

In addition, you can find many sources of information by dialing-in to a computer service like America Online or CompuServe. Each of these computer services is like an information supermarket providing access to many databases. For example, CompuServe provides access to *The Accountant's Forum*, which has a library for electronic research, a message center where members can exchange mail, a conference center where public or private interactive conferences can be held, and a catalog for ordering accounting publications or educational services.

As of 1994, there were over 7,500 on-line databases available for searching. There are so many databases now available that often the first place to start your research is in a directory of databases! Or, you might start with an information intermediary that provides an organized set of research resources. On the Internet, for example, there are several sites that provide links to accounting-related sites, as well as discussion groups, including:

♦ The Rutgers Accounting Web (RAW) at Rutgers University in New Jersey, accessed via **http://www.rutgers.edu/accounting/**

♦ The Summa Project, housed at the University of Exeter in the U. K. and financed by the Institute of Chartered Accountants in England and Wales, which may be accessed via http://**www.icaew.org.uk/**

♦ The Accounting Network (ANET), a cooperative international venture housed at Southern Cross University in New South Wales, Australia and accessed via **http://www.scu.edu.au/anet/**

Obviously, since there are so many possible information sources, you needn't try to learn the names of every one. Even if you had a photographic memory, it would be a losing battle as new sources become available constantly. As you work with different sources, you will become familiar with the ones that are most important to your work. The same search techniques that help you make the most of these sources individually will help you explore new sources, as needed.

There's one very important practical issue to be faced when searching for information. Databases provide access to enormous amounts of information. But information, even when freely available, is not usually costless. Many databases will charge user fees. Additionally, there is a personal cost for the time you spend searching for information. Consequently, it's important to learn effective and efficient search techniques.

SEARCHING SOURCES OF INFORMATION

The searcher's eye not seldom finds more than he wished to find.
-- G. E. Lessing, <u>Nathan the Wise</u>, 1779

We are living in the Information Age. As you go through your chosen career, you are likely to have many possible sources of information to use in making decisions and solving problems. Once you select the sources you wish to check, how do you go about searching them?

To search a source efficiently, you need to develop a search strategy. Some of these databases are very large. If you search too narrowly, you risk missing important information. For example, if you searched a database of financial accounting standards using the term "boat trade-in," you wouldn't have located the Accounting Principles Board opinion you needed. The opinion deals with non-monetary exchanges in general; it isn't specifically about boat trade-ins. On the other hand, if you search too broadly, you may find yourself drowning in a sea of information, much of which isn't relevant to your problem. For example, if you searched the financial accounting standards database using the broad term "valuation," you would have retrieved many standards that didn't pertain to your problem at all.

Search strategy is learned partly by practice, but there are a few hints that can help you get started:

♦ Analyze the facts and look for key words.

♦ Use technical jargon, if it exists.

♦ Follow up: when you find a good match, look for more key words.

♦ Seek expert help when needed.

Analyze the Facts and Look for Key Words

First, analyze the facts in the situation. Which ones are key? Use these facts to choose your "key words" for your initial search. For the yacht valuation problem, the trade-in was what made it difficult to answer the valuation question, so starting to plan your search strategy with the word "trade-in" makes sense.

Use Technical Jargon, If It Exists

Second, when searching technical issues, use technical vocabulary terms whenever possible. Looking at the yacht valuation problem again, think about the terminology in the APB opinion. The opinion used the term "nonmonetary transaction" to describe the situation. If the database you searched allowed "**full text search**" (a search that covers every word in each document), then searching with the term "trade-in" might work well. But some databases allow only "**key word search**" (a search that covers a list of descriptive terms about the topics in the database, but not every word in each document). The technical term "nonmonetary transaction" is more likely to be on the key word list than the non-technical term "trade-in."

When You Find a Good Match, Look for More Key Words

Third, when you find a document that is exactly on target, don't quit. Review the document to see if it contains any key words you might not have thought of using. Then, check to see if using the new key words pulls up any more relevant information you might have missed. In the yacht example, suppose you found the APB opinion using just the key word "non-monetary exchange." If you read the opinion, you'd find a new vocabulary term for the $25,000 cash that Best Marine paid along with the traded-in yacht--the money is known as "boot."

If you searched the database again using the term "boot," you would find that there is also an Emerging Issues Task Force consensus position on how to handle trade-in transactions when the boot is more than 25% of the invoice price of the new item--and the treatment is different in these circumstances. In the particular situation Best Marine is in, the boot was less than 25% of the invoice price--but what if it had been more than 25% and you had missed finding the consensus position?

Seek Expert Help When Needed

Pretend for a moment that Best Marine is a business owned by your grandparents, and suppose your grandparents had asked you to research the yacht question for them now that you are studying accounting. At this point, your search skills aren't well developed and your base of fundamental knowledge is still being built. You'd probably be pleased to comply with your grandparents' request, but only if they also had a more experienced accountant verify your answer.

Given the vast body of knowledge and the large number of databases, researching accounting issues can be complicated. Research skills, like other skills, develop with experience--there are different levels of expertise to be reached. Even accounting practitioners sometimes need to consult research experts for particularly difficult questions. Large firms often have a research specialist on staff who is consulted for non-routine searches, or when the search is particularly important. Smaller firms can--for a fee--use the search services of the AICPA. The more critical the search, the more likely you will need to seek expert advice.

In an advertisement for Dow Jones Information Services, a cartoon of briefcase-toting cavemen appeared under the headline, "In the age of information, survival still depends on hunters and gatherers." If you follow the basic steps for problem identification, selecting sources of information, and searching sources of information, your hunt should prove successful.

ASSIGNMENTS FOR MODULE 6 - PART A

ASSIGNMENT I-6A-1:   <u>**Laws, Rules, Standards, and Guidelines:**</u>
A Scavenger Hunt

SETTING

It is Halloween. To celebrate, your accounting professor has developed a "scavenger hunt" list of accounting questions and dared the class to find the answers to these questions by the stroke of midnight. The list of questions appears on the following page.

ASSIGNMENT

Draft a plan for how you would look for the answers to the scavenger hunt questions. Be as specific as possible. [*Note*: Unless your professor directs you to actually look for the answers, you need only develop a search strategy (you need not actually perform the search).]

HINTS

First, determine what functional area of accounting (tax, financial, managerial, systems or auditing) the question pertains to. Then, review the text for information about the sources of laws, rules, standards and guidelines in that area. Always start with the most prominent source--for example, with the official pronouncements of the Financial Accounting Standards Board in financial accounting.

SCAVENGER HUNT

1. You want to buy a special birthday gift for a friend who loves English toffee. You think you may be able to obtain the "real thing" by telephoning in an order to a London candy shop. Will your purchase be subject to the value-added tax?

2. You are concerned about the physical security of your bank account balance, which you usually access through the bank's automatic teller machine. What kind of controls should be built into the automatic teller machine to prevent unauthorized access?

3. You are reading a Statement of Cash Flows in an annual report. You come across a section captioned "financing and investing activities not involving cash." Why are these non-cash activities reported on the cash flows statement?

4. You are reading an auditor's opinion in an annual report. You note that it has 2 dates: "December 21, 1996, except for Footnote G, dated January 2, 1997." Why is the report dual dated?

ASSIGNMENT I-6A-2:   The Politics of Developing Laws, Rules, & Standards: A Current Case

SETTING

You are a student taking your first accounting course. Since you began taking the course, you've noticed a number of articles in newspapers and business magazines that relate to the development of accounting-related laws, rules, and standards.

ASSIGNMENT

Find an article about a proposed or recently passed (within the last 3 months) accounting-related law, rule or standard. The article must discuss the arguments either for or against (or both) the new law, rule or standard.

Analyze the article. Your analysis should cover the following questions:

- ◆ What is the proposed or enacted law, rule, or standard about?
- ◆ What interest groups are covered in the article?
- ◆ What are their positions?
- ◆ Does the article represent both sides of the issue? If not, what is the other side?
- ◆ Are there any errors in the article, such as incorrect definitions of accounting terms or garbled explanations of accounting concepts?
- ◆ What is your overall impression of the article?

Prepare an outline that presents your analysis. At the next class, turn in your outline (and a copy of the article) for grading. Also, be prepared to have 1 member of the group make a brief (maximum time: 5 minutes) presentation to the class about the article. The class will then discuss the issues you have uncovered.

HINTS

While you only need to analyze 1 article, you may find it helpful to look at several articles on the same topic. The other articles may help you understand the positions of various special-interest groups.

ASSIGNMENT I-6A-3: <u>**The Politics of Developing Laws, Rules &**</u>
<u>**Standards:**</u> **The Frustrations of A Standard**
Setter

SETTING

You are a student taking your first accounting course. Since you began taking the course, you've noticed a number of articles in newspapers and business magazines that relate to the development of accounting-related laws, rules and standards. It is becoming obvious to you that the process is a complex one.

In your reading, you find a commentary by the then-Chairman of the Financial Accounting Standards Board on the "Frustrations of a Standards Setter" (see the reprint from the December 1993 issue of *Accounting Horizons* on the following pages). The article raises a number of issues worth considering.

ASSIGNMENT

Choose 1 of the following topics and prepare a 5 to 10-minute oral presentation for the class on this topic:

♦ Why aren't users more involved in the standard-setting process? Under what circumstances would you expect an individual user or a business to respond to a proposed standard? Is there any way to increase user involvement?

♦ How should standard setters resolve conflicts between the competing interests of different user groups and stakeholders? In particular, how should the interests of preparers, auditors and users of financial reports be balanced? Among the user groups, should some user groups be considered more important than others?

Prepare an outline that presents your analysis and turn in the outline on the day of your presentation. The class will then discuss the issues you have presented.

HINTS

Use Dennis Beresford's commentary as a starting point, but also bring in your own ideas.

© 1993 American Accounting Association
Accounting Horizons
Vol. 7 No. 4
December 1993
pp. 70-76

COMMENTARY

Dennis R. Beresford

Dennis R. Beresford is Chairman, Financial Accounting Standards Board.

Frustrations of a Standards Setter

The March 1988 issue of *Accounting Horizons* included my article entitled "The 'Balancing Act' in Setting Accounting Standards." Based on experience gained in my first year at the FASB, I used the "balancing act" terminology to describe how we strive to

1. Make sure we are working on the right issues,

2. Weigh input from our constituents, and

3. Endeavor to reach answers that are as relevant and practical as possible.

I used several of the active accounting issues at that time to illustrate how we'd done our best to accomplish those objectives. But I've found in my years at the Board that there are recurring questions about why we work on projects and why we reach the decisions we do. We obviously need to keep answering these questions. As the former executive director of the Financial Executives Institute once told me, we can *never* communicate too much.

With that in mind, these comments will have a somewhat similar theme to what I said back in 1988. However, based on my experiences over the past five plus years, I've titled my thoughts "Frustrations of a Standards Setter."

WORKING ON THE RIGHT ISSUES

The first point from my 1988 article was the need to make sure that we are working on the right issues. I continue to believe that agenda setting is the single most important decision that we make at the FASB. Yet, for all the care that goes into this process, it may be one of our least understood and least appreciated activities.

Before the Board votes on whether to add a project, our staff has usually spent at least several months developing materials to help us decide if there is enough reason to take on the new challenge. Nearly all of these potential projects are brought to us by others. For example, on the stock compensation project, in 1984 we received a lengthy Issues Paper from the AICPA urging us to reconsider Accounting Principles Board Opinion No. 25. We also received letters from most of the major accounting firms that urged us to deal with this issue, and the SEC and many others also supported our consideration of the topic. I should add that the Board gets many more requests than we can handle with our limited resources, so we turn down most requests.

Recognizing the importance of agenda decisions, in recent years we have enhanced our procedures to evaluate potential projects. For example, before we added the present value and impairment of long-lived assets projects in late 1988, we developed a long list of potential projects based on various requests that had been made. We circulated that list to a number of interested parties and asked for their input.

More recently, we used a so-called prospectus to solicit views on whether we should add a project on accounting for mortgage servicing rights. No matter how careful we are in adding projects, however, two things commonly happen later in a project's life. First, most people forget what caused us to work on the project. Second, support for working on the project often ebbs as people realize we might actually reach an answer that requires some change in accounting.

The first of these phenomena is primarily a communications challenge for the FASB. We need to keep reminding our various audiences of the problems that led us to work on particular projects. This became an issue for us a few years ago when the SEC made an informal review of the FASB's procedures. The SEC asked us to explain why projects like other postretirement benefits and income taxes were being studied. We've also prepared this kind of after-the-fact explanation for our Oversight Committee in connection with their reviews of a couple of our projects.

In each of these reviews our procedures were found to be quite appropriate. But the fact that these questions keep coming up indicates that we need to concentrate much harder on telling people more often the *why* for each project. This is particularly necessary during the research stages of a project—before an Exposure Draft is issued—when our work isn't quite as visible as it is later on.

The second phenomenon—that attitudes change about the need for a project—is more difficult to address. I think our dilemma is best illustrated by a brief story.

In 1988 we were in the middle of considering adding one or two projects to our agenda and had developed a long list of possibilities as I mentioned earlier. I attended a meeting of the AICPA's Accounting Standards Executive Committee at which they were trying to decide which projects to recommend to us. One of the members told me he was having a hard time deciding what his position should be. He finally said, "Denny, I can't really say what project you should work on until you tell me what your answer will be!" That was a very direct and honest statement, but it's also contrary to our unbiased approach to setting standards. It is essential that we avoid starting any project with a preconceived idea of the outcome.

Sometimes we are concerned that initial support for a project is really a means to avoid a more immediate alternative—in effect, a form of stalling technique. Let me illustrate this point with another brief story.

A few years ago the SEC expressed great concerns about the accounting for marketable securities, particularly debt securities held by banks, S&Ls, and insurers. The AICPA tried to deal with the problem but was unable to follow through on a proposed Statement of Position that was strongly opposed. Faced with then-Chairman Breeden's threat of an SEC accounting pronouncement, the AICPA urged us to take on the project and deal with it as a high priority. An AICPA official said at that time, "There is a need for a more objective standard such as one based on mark to market."

And, in an unprecedented action, the Big Six firms jointly signed a letter that endorsed the AICPA recommendation to us, referring to the SEC's call for *market-based* measures of valuation. Yet three of the Big Six firms later urged us to back off from our exposure draft on this issue—a proposal, by the way, that would have called for considerably less change than might have been expected. We understand that positions can change after more thought—after all *our* tentative decisions often are modified. But we also can become concerned about the sincerity of some positions when we see such dramatic switches in attitudes about whether we should even be dealing with an issue.

We do try to challenge our agenda from time to time. For example, on an annual basis our Advisory Council members give us their views on relative priorities of the projects currently on our agenda, whether any other projects are so pressing that we should add them, and whether any current projects should be discontinued. And just because something was important at one time doesn't mean we must work on it forever. We did, for example, discontinue a fairly narrow project on accounting implications of prepayments of financial instruments last year.

But it is also important that we not back away from difficult issues because the "going gets tough." This is part of the balancing act I mentioned earlier. On the one hand, we want to be seen as having the courage of our convictions. We take the mission of the Board very seriously, and we recognize that almost any change will face strong opposition. On the other hand, we really do listen carefully to input on our projects, and we are willing to change direction or even kill a project when a sufficiently persuasive case is made to us. Trying to achieve the right balance requires great judgment, *and* it obligates us to clearly and honestly explain the reasons for our actions.

DOING THE RIGHT THING

So in deciding what to work on and what decisions we ultimately reach, all we really need to do, as Spike Lee would say, is "do the right thing." Of course, what *is* the right thing is undoubtedly "in the eye of the beholder." One way of helping us make this kind of decision may be to try to focus more on who our customers are and what do they want. But it seems to be difficult for us and those who are interested in our work to agree on who our customers are. For example, they include

- The people who buy our publications

- The SEC and AICPA who provide the enforcement mechanism for our standards

- The corporations and other organizations who actually apply our standards and the auditors who attest to their application

- Financial analysts, lending officers, portfolio managers, and others who use the reports based on our standards.

Add in professors, students, shareholders, regulators, and a whole host of others and you soon see that we have an extremely diverse customer population, and their interests are often in opposition to one another.

My best answer to the question of who our customers are comes from the first sentence of our Mission Statement. It says:

> The mission of the FASB is to establish and improve standards of financial accounting and reporting for the guidance and education of *the public*, including issuers, auditors, and users of financial information.

Thus, the Board's customers are almost everybody with any direct or indirect interest in financial reporting! And serving that diverse customer list involves some delicate balancing. In particular, the Board's decisions must balance the benefits of improved reporting against the costs. This is made both difficult and complex because of two facts. First, the benefits and costs of our decisions do not affect each of our diverse constituents in the same proportions. Second, objective and reliable information about benefits and costs is difficult to get.

The Board needs input from each constituent, within the unique areas of their expertise, to make an informed decision. Some are experts on costs, some on benefits, and others on the reliability and auditability of information. Unfortunately, as I will discuss later, we do not get all the input that we would like from one group of constituents—the users of external reporting. My question is, would getting more input from the users help the Board make more informed decisions?

WHO ARE USERS AND WHY AREN'T THEY MORE INVOLVED?

I'll try to answer that last question a little later, but first I should note that, unfortunately, it isn't even clear who fits into the user category. For example, we often receive letters from major corporations who say they are expressing their views as a preparer *and* as a user. They say they use other companies' financial statements as a creditor or as an investor. The flip side of this is where we get a letter from a bank lending officer who purportedly is writing as a user, but who clearly has been influenced by the preparer side of the bank.

Let's make an heroic assumption at this point—which I will challenge later—and agree that we have identified users as our primary customer *and* that we have no problem knowing who they are. I'll assume they are mainly financial analysts and bank lending officers, although I know there are several other user groups such as portfolio managers and rating agencies. Analysts and lending officers are the users that we hear from most frequently through

- The Association for Investment Management and Research—the AIMR—which is the analysts group and

- The Robert Morris Associates—the RMA—which is the lending officers group.

But when I say we hear from analysts and lending officers most frequently, that is a relative statement. In fact, on many projects the only two letters from users we receive are from the AIMR and the RMA. We occasionally receive letters from individual users but that is the exception not the rule. And the few letters from users do not compare favorably with many hundred from corporate preparers and at least a few score from accounting firms and CPA societies on most important projects.

To give a more specific idea of the dearth of input from users, on our controversial 1992 proposal on loan impairment, we received about 150 letters in total. One came from the AIMR and another from the RMA. One came from a credit rating agency and three were from individuals or firms that specialize in analyzing financial statements of banks. Of those six letters, which, based on our experience, is a *very* large number from users, two generally supported the exposure draft and four opposed it.

An obvious question is why aren't users more active in our process. One possibility is that they don't derive as much benefit from financial reporting as we accountants may have assumed. I think a more logical answer is that they simply aren't as well equipped and as well organized to participate in our process as are some other groups.

Financial analysts and bank lending officers should have at least a general knowledge of financial accounting and reporting. But I'm sure most would admit that they aren't technical accountants who are used to speaking in terms of accounting concepts and other FASB jargon. Also, responding to our proposals simply *has* to be a lower priority for users than it is for preparers and auditors. Unless

it's a critical issue like cash flow for lenders or segment reporting for analysts, users seem to be willing to wait for improvements to happen more or less naturally. That may be changing, however, as evidenced by the AIMR position paper that I'll mention later.

I think that another reason for a limited amount of involvement is that at least some users prefer the status quo. They believe that *they* understand the nuances of present financial reporting, and they don't want things to be made simpler for their competitors.

I'm obviously frustrated about the relatively low level of user involvement in our process, because their input is so critical. Users are experts on what information would be most useful to them and why and the relative benefits of the Board's proposals in making capital allocation decisions. While other constituents, and the Board, can only speculate about what would be most beneficial to users, only the users really know.

Any absence of user involvement increases the risk that the Board's decision-making process will become overly cost focused rather than balanced with benefits. The Board already hears plenty about costs from preparers and auditors. Users can add important information about benefits that other constituents cannot provide and help insure that the Board's decision process will be more balanced. We've tried a number of things over the years to get users more involved in our process and we'll continue to discard those techniques that don't work so well and try others. Some recent activities by other organizations seem very promising and I'd like to mention each briefly.

AICPA SPECIAL COMMITTEE AND AIMR REPORT

First is the AICPA Special Committee on Financial Reporting. The scope of that Committee's work is very broad—broader than the scope of the FASB's mission, for example. One of our Board members attends the Committee's regular meetings, and we have loaned a senior staff person on nearly a full-time basis.

Also, we've provided other staff and Board assistance to a subproject referred to as the investor and creditor discussion groups. That is an exciting project that held a series of in-depth meetings with groups of high-level financial analysts, portfolio managers, and creditors of various types. No results are available yet from the AICPA Special Committee, but what we finally see from this thorough study of user needs is likely to significantly influence the FASB's future agenda. It also may help us figure out ways to get users more involved with our process.

The other activity I want to mention is the position paper "Financial Reporting in the 1990's and Beyond" issued late in 1992 by the AIMR. The AIMR paper is impressive—it gives some good insights into the way analysts actually use financial statements and related information. A few of the many provocative recommendations are:

- Companies should *disclose* current value information for all assets and liabilities.

- All executory contracts (e.g., leases) of more than one year should be recognized in the balance sheet.

- Segment data should be improved *and* should be required on a quarterly basis as well as on an annual basis.

The FASB will carefully evaluate these recommendations in due course, along with the recommendations of the AICPA Special Committee.

EVALUATING COMMENTS FROM USERS

Having described some efforts to get more input from users, and having referred to what one important group of users wants, let me move on to *another* of my frustrations, which relates to our difficulties in evaluating comments on some projects. This point is best made by another brief story.

As I mentioned earlier, on our 1992 Exposure Draft on loan impairment, we received a letter from the Financial Accounting Policy Committee of the AIMR. It supported the basic thrust of the proposal to "measure impair-ment of a loan based on the present value of expected future cash flows." But we also received a couple of letters from individual analysts who specifically follow bank stocks. They disagreed with the discounting approach and later told us that we should ignore the AIMR letter because the group that prepared it wasn't sufficiently representative of bank analysts. I was challenged on this project by the CFO of a major bank who said that he heard that we were ignoring the strong views of users on this project. I replied that it depended on which particular users he thought we should listen to!

Now this may be an unusual situation, first because we received this much input from users, and second because there was such basic disagreement among the user community. On some other projects we may find much more agreement among users. For example, we *know* that financial analysts believe that we need to greatly improve segment disclosures, including requiring them on a quarterly basis. But will analysts agree on what specific changes constitute improvement? And even if we get strong, unified support from users, does that mean that corporations and other interested parties will sit quietly and acquiesce to any major changes we propose in this just because users want it?—I doubt it!

While the RMA organization hasn't developed a comprehensive paper like the AIMR, the bank lending officers have *strongly* supported a requirement for all corporations to present their full *consolidating* financial statements. If the Board were to propose this in light of the strong support from RMA, would preparers and others fall in line?—I doubt it.

In fact, if our approach were simply to require all that users wanted instead of to carefully balance their wish list against the views of corporate preparers, auditors, regulators, academics, and other interested parties, why wouldn't we just adopt the AIMR position paper? Would the CFO who told me that we need to adopt the position taken by bank analysts on the loan impairment project agree with capitalizing all leases, disclosing fair values for *all* assets and liabilities, requiring quarterly segment data, etc.?—Again, I doubt it.

Please don't misunderstand these last few comments. I'm not saying we should ignore users—in fact, as I said earlier we need to get them much more involved in our process and listen carefully to what they have to say. But even if they are our principal customers, we have to *balance* their input against others and continue to consider cost-benefit tradeoffs and other factors that make our FASB "scales of justice" particularly sensitive.

BOWING TO POLITICAL PRESSURE

Another issue that continues to cause some frustration is that when challenging some of our positions, many parties assert that we are merely "bowing to political pressure." For example, one letter from a Big Six firm on the stock compensation project said in part:

> . . . some of the intensity of the opposition in corporate America to changing the employers' accounting reflects a perception that too much of the FASB's agenda is being determined by the regulatory authorities.

We received a large number of letters from corporations and others that made the same point. They apparently believe that we are working on this project *only* because of the threat of legislation by Senator Levin or possible accounting rule making by the SEC. We also received many letters on our marketable securities project that similarly charged that we were bowing to the political pressure brought by the SEC.

What these arguments leave out, however, is the fact that we often—if not always—get conflicting signals from our nation's capital. For example, on accounting for stock options, it is true that Senator Levin urged us to consider requiring compensation expense for stock options. But Treasury Department official John Robson was quite outspoken in his opposition—going so far as to author a *Wall Street Journal* editorial page piece on the issue. And President Clinton's campaign materials included a promise that he would oppose the FASB's requiring compensation expense for high-tech and emerging businesses.

On marketable securities, it is true that then-SEC Chairman Breeden urged us in the strongest way to adopt a market value approach. The GAO also weighed in with strong support for market value, in light of their continuing concerns about S&L and bank failures. But Alan Greenspan, other banking regulators, former Treasury Secretary Brady and many other D.C. luminaries pushed strongly in the other direction.

Even if it were clear *which* political pressures we were or were not supposed to bow to, we often can't get a consistent message from specific sources in Washington. For example, remember how just a few years ago the bank regulators, the GAO, and others were up in arms about the understatement of bank and S&L loan loss reserves. The GAO has stayed the course, but the bank regulators are now being told to take it easy on bankers to ease the credit crunch.

In addition to those concerned about our bowing to pressure from politicians, there are other groups equally concerned about our bowing to pressure from the Business Roundtable, the Big 6 accounting firms, or just about any other group. I don't mean to sound cynical, but some might say that when we accept *your* position it is because of your powerful and persuasive conceptual and practical reasoning. When we accept the other guy's position, however, we are obviously bowing to political pressure.

Please understand that I *share* the concern about political pressure. It *is* very important that our process not become politicized. At the same time, it is equally important that we get the reasoned input of government officials, particularly the SEC. After all, the FASB's very existence is largely dependent on our being able to continue to convince the SEC that they should rely on us to set accounting standards.

However, I am convinced that only by retaining our independence and objectivity, and only by continuing to be seen as setting the most neutral financial reporting standards possible, can we retain the trust of the SEC. And only by being independent of political pressures can we also retain the necessary respect of all others who are affected by our standards.

CONCLUSION — FINDING THE RIGHT BALANCE

So far I've discussed why we add projects, the role of users in our process, and the allegations about political pressures. At this point, one might ask what does all this mean in explaining the answers we reach. Someone described the art of compromise as making *everybody* mad, and, given the various conflicts and pressures I've described, perhaps this is what our process leads to in most cases.

At a recent meeting, one of our Board members said that finding the right balance on many of our projects is like the story of Goldilocks. Like Goldilocks' porridge, we can't be too hot or too cold—we must be "just right!" Rather than Goldilocks, I like to refer to one of my favorite philosophers, the late Ricky Nelson. You may recall the line from one of his best selling songs, "you can't please everyone, so you've got to please yourself."

At some level, our standard setting process *has* to follow the Nelson philosophy. We obviously can't please all interested parties—their interests are simply too diverse.

And the answer that might please the largest number who choose to write on a particular project won't always be consistent with our mission.

Also, unfortunate as it may seem, some part of our activity *must* be used to instill discipline in financial reporting. Former FASB chairman Don Kirk noted that "many issues have found their way to the FASB's agenda that were on the border between the responsibility of ethical or regulatory enforcers and the technical accounting standard setter." The result of what Don observed is that occasionally we must issue a standard that merely seems to state the obvious—such as that "straight line means straight line." It is that occasional action, and the threat that we could do it in more cases, that seems needed to assure that accounting literature is followed.

In summary, it will continue to be difficult to find the right balance in our standard setting efforts. And I will no doubt continue to be somewhat frustrated in dealing with some of the difficulties and challenges inherent in the process. Perhaps the most I can promise is that we will continue to perform the FASB's balancing act in the best way we can.

ASSIGNMENTS FOR MODULE 6 - PART B

ASSIGNMENT I-6B-1: <u>Searching Sources of Information:</u>
Using the Internet to Find Tax Information

<u>SETTING</u>

You are working on your tax return. For the first time, you will be filling out a Schedule A for itemized deductions. One category of itemized deductions is charitable contributions. Since you made some donations--both cash and property--to your college this year, you want to know 2 things: (1) if there is a limit to the amount of charitable donations you can deduct, and (2) how you should value the donated property.

<u>ASSIGNMENT</u>

Access the IRS world-wide web site. To start at the "Digital Daily" newspaper that provides entrance to IRS information and forms use:

http://www.irs.ustreas.gov/prod/cover.html

Find the answers to your 2 questions. To document each answer, indicate the name of the publication where the answer was located and hand in a copy of the first page of the section of the publication that answered the question.

<u>HINTS</u>

Before you connect to the IRS, think about the key words you will use to search the database.

Internet connections can sometimes be maddeningly slow. Don't procrastinate. Leave yourself enough time to finish the assignment even if you get a few busy signals.

ASSIGNMENT I-6B-2:   **Searching Sources of Information:
Using the Internet to Find Financial
Information**

SETTING

You have just been reading a copy of Gannett Co.'s most recent annual report and you want to know what has happened since that report. In particular, you know the company issues quarterly earnings reports in April (for the first quarter), July, October and February (for the fourth quarter) each year. Now, you'd like to know Gannett's *most recent* quarterly results.

ASSIGNMENT

Log on to Gannett's on-line information network. You may reach Gannett Co. on the world-wide web via:

http://www.gannett.com

Once you reach Gannett Co., determine the quarterly results for the most recent quarter. Hand in a copy of the screen where you found the quarterly results.

Also find the most recent quarterly results using *a different* database (that is, a database other than Gannett's own information network). This second database may be either paper-based or electronic. Hand in a copy of the page or screen where you found the quarterly results. Describe what you had to do to find the results using this second source. Compare the advantages and disadvantages of the two sources you used.

HINTS

Internet connections can sometimes be maddeningly slow. Don't procrastinate. Leave yourself enough time to finish the assignment even if you get a few busy signals.

ASSIGNMENT I-6B-3:   <u>**Searching Sources of Information:**</u>
An Internet Scavenger Hunt

<u>SETTING</u>

It is Halloween. To celebrate, your accounting professor has developed a "scavenger hunt" list of accounting questions and dared the class to find the answers to these questions on the Internet by the stroke of midnight. The list of questions appears on the following page.

<u>ASSIGNMENT</u>

Find the answers. Prepare a brief summary of the answers (1 page maximum) and attach a printed copy of the Internet "pages" (screens) where you found the answers.

[Note: No credit will be given for a correct answer unless documentation of the source is attached.]

<u>HINTS</u>

None--in the true spirit of a scavenger hunt, you're on your own!

INTERNET SCAVENGER HUNT

1. In what cities in your state will the next CMA (Certified Management Accountant) exam be given?

2. What were the total receipts to the U.S. federal government from corporate income taxes in 1996?

3. What was the topic of GASB (Governmental Accounting Standards Board) Statement No. 29 and when was it issued?

4. What was the amount of total assets at the close of business on December 31, 1996 for Compaq Computer Corporation?

ASSIGNMENT I-6B-4:   <u>Searching Sources of Information:</u> <u>An Internet Scavenger Hunt #2</u>

SETTING

It is getting close to exam week and tension is mounting. To get your mind off exams, your accounting professor has developed a "scavenger hunt" list of accounting questions and dared the class to find the answers to these questions on the Internet by the stroke of midnight. The list of questions appears on the following page.

ASSIGNMENT

Find the answers. Prepare a brief summary of the answers (1 page maximum) and attach a printed copy of the Internet "pages" (screens) where you found the answers.

[Note: No credit will be given for a correct answer unless documentation of the source is attached.]

HINTS

None--in the true spirit of a scavenger hunt, you're on your own!

INTERNET SCAVENGER HUNT

1.   If you want to sit for the Certified Internal Auditor (CIA) exam as a student, what fees must you pay?

2.   If you want to report fraud, waste, abuse or mismanagement of federal funds, what E-mail address can you use?

3.   Where is the Accounting Hall of Fame and who was the first person inducted into the hall?

4.   What was the amount of total stockholders' equity at the end of fiscal year 1997 for Trans Texas Gas Corporation?

THEME OVERVIEW ASSIGNMENTS

ASSIGNMENT I-1: The Users/Uses of Accounting Information: Consider Your Options

SETTING

A student organization is putting together a program to discuss recent criticisms that American executives are overpaid. As part of this program, a panel of students studying business and accounting will answer questions from the audience that relate to executive compensation. You have been asked to be a member of that panel. Your role on the panel will be to answer questions about stock option plans used in executive compensation.

In preparation for the program, you are given some background on compensatory stock options (see Exhibit 1). In addition, you are given a list of seven questions that audience members are likely to pose (see below). The program organizer asks you to prepare answers for these potential audience questions. Your answers must be clear, concise and logical to satisfy the demands of the college student audience.

ASSIGNMENT

Prepare concise, written answers [*Note:* confine your responses to a total of 5 typed, double-spaced pages or less] to the following questions:

1. Why would a company want to pay their executives with stock options instead of additional cash bonuses? [*Note:* need at least 2 good reasons.]

2. Why would executives be willing to accept stock options instead of additional cash bonuses? [*Note:* need at least 2 good reasons.]

3. How can accountants justify not recording any compensation expense on the grant date for stock options with a strike price at market? [*Note:* need at least 2 well-argued justifications.]

4. On what grounds can the current non-recognition method of

accounting for stock options be criticized? [*Note*: need at least 2 well-argued criticisms.]

5. How well does the current non-recognition method of accounting for stock options fulfill the information needs of:
    (a) management?
    (b) labor unions/employees?
    (c) stockholders?
    [*Note*: be specific in your discussion. Discuss each user group separately.]

6. If you want to find out more about accounting standards related to stock options, what research sources could you consult and what search strategy would you use? [*Note*: just describe the sources and search strategy, don't actually do the research.]

7. How does the stock options controversy illustrate the politics of standard setting?

HINTS

This assignment gives you a chance to apply what you've learned in Theme I to a new topic that we've never discussed. Don't panic. Remember that the question isn't really about stock options per se; it's about the needs of user groups and other issues you *are* familiar with. Consider this a test of your ability to apply your knowledge--and of how far you've come since you started this course.

Outside research isn't necessary. Everything you need to know about stock options is in Exhibit 1.

EXHIBIT 1:

BACKGROUND INFORMATION ON COMPENSATORY STOCK OPTIONS

How Are CEOs Paid?

The total annual compensation of CEOs of major U.S. public corporations averages about $3 million, which is about 145 times the pay of a typical factory worker. There is less disclosure about executive pay in other countries, but researchers have estimated the CEO:factory worker pay ratio to be less than 25:1 in Japan.

U.S. CEOs (and other top managers) typically receive 3 forms of compensation:

 (1) a base salary, paid in cash;

 (2) a bonus, paid in cash if certain short-run targets (e.g., profit targets) are met; and

 (3) stock options.

For CEOs of America's largest companies, the total of the first 2 items is typically in the $1 million to $2 million range. Stock options can add substantially to total compensation.

For example, David W. Johnson, Chairman of Campbell Soup Co., received a $987,500 base salary for 1996 plus a $1.16 million bonus. But, he also received stock options for 220,000 shares of Campbell Soup Co. that could be exercised over the next few years. The options had a current value of about $3.4 million at the end of fiscal year 1996.

What Is a Stock Option?

A stock option is a right to buy shares of a company's stock at a specified price (the "strike price" or "exercise price") for a specific period of time (the "life" of the option). Typically, stock options given to executives are granted with certain restrictions, most commonly that the options cannot be exercised until after a certain amount of time (the "holding period") has passed. Other common restrictions are lack of transferability (i.e., the executive cannot sell the option to anyone else) and cancellation if the executive leaves the company before the end of the holding period. Most executive stock options are granted with a strike price equal to the market price at the date of the grant.

Here's an example: A CEO is granted a stock option in 1996 to buy 100,000 shares of the company's stock at a strike price equal to the then-current market price of $7 per share. The options cannot be exercised until 1999 (a three-year holding period). In 1999, if the market price of the stock has fallen to $5, the options are worthless (since the exercise price of $7 is higher than the market price). In this case, the CEO has no gain, but also has lost nothing. On the other hand, if the stock price has risen to $10 a share, the CEO can exercise the options and immediately resell the stock, making a profit of $300,000 ($3 per share x 100,000 shares). If the buy/sell transactions are conducted simultaneously, the CEO need not even put up any cash to do the deal.

What Is The Current Accounting/Tax Treatment of Options?

Accounting for a stock option that has a strike price equal to the market price on the grant date is simple. At the grant date, under current generally accepted accounting principles, the company does not record any compensation expense. However, the existence of the options and the terms of the options must be disclosed in footnotes to the financial statements as long as the option is outstanding. If the options are exercised, the company records the transaction just like any other sale of stock--that is, cash increases and stockholders' equity (e.g., common stock and paid-in-capital) increases. Thus, no compensation expense related to the stock options is ever recorded.

In addition, public companies must disclose the most recent 3 years compensation for the CEO and the 4 highest-paid executives other than the CEO (assuming their total annual compensation is at least $100,000). The disclosure is presented in a table in the company's proxy statement. Other proxy statement disclosures provide additional information, such as the number and terms of outstanding options and their value.

U.S. tax law does not consider the options to affect the executive's taxable income until they are exercised. Any gain on the exercise of a stock option is taxable to the executive.

How Can You Estimate The Value Of An Option?

Academic researchers have created theoretical models for valuing stock options before they are exercised. While complex, these mathematical models can be used to compute a theoretical value for a stock option at the grant date.

The FASB once asked a number of investment banking firms to compute the value of several specific stock option contracts. The investment banking firms came up with estimates that were significantly different from each other for the same option contract. The differences were large enough that most accountants would consider them material.

What's Been Happening Recently?

From 1993-1995, the following series of events related to stock options occurred:

♦ The National Association of Corporate Directors' Blue Ribbon Commission on Executive Compensation issued a 50-page report with recommendations concerning executive pay. Among the recommendations were reducing the proportion of executive compensation coming from base salary and creating truly independent compensation committees to set executive pay levels.

♦ By a 6-1 vote, the Financial Accounting Standards Board decided to issue an *Exposure Draft* calling for compensation expense to be recognized for stock options, beginning in 1997. The amount of compensation expense, to be recognized over the vesting period, would equal the fair value of the stock options at their grant date (as determined by a mathematical model).

- Senator Carl Levin (D-Michigan) proposed that if the FASB failed to adopt its proposed standard, federal legislation should require public companies to recognize compensation expense when compensatory stock options are granted.

- Senator Joseph Lieberman (D-Connecticut) proposed legislation to overrule any FASB decision to impose expense recognition at the grant date. Lieberman stated that the FASB's approach might be defensible from an accounting perspective, but it was "unnecessary and unusually disruptive" from a public policy perspective." He argued that the proposal, if enacted, would lead to a loss of jobs and competitiveness for U.S. companies in many industries, particularly for small, emerging companies.

- Tax laws were changed so that for years beginning on or after January 1, 1994, the amount of executive compensation expense that a company may deduct in determining its taxable income is limited to $1 million per executive per year, unless the compensation is tied to a performance-based incentive plan, such as a plan that ties compensation to shareholder returns or return on equity.

- Representative Martin Sabo (D-Minnesota) introduced an "Income Equity Act," proposing to deny businesses tax deductions for executive pay that exceeds 25 times the pay of other workers.

- The Business Roundtable, a group of CEOs from the largest U.S. companies, urged members to choose the valuation method they would use for proxy disclosures carefully. The Roundtable urged members not to use the method favored in the FASB proposal.

- One of the Big Six public accounting firms issued a study predicting that newer public companies (public for less than 10 years) could see their annual income cut by an average of 26.5% were the FASB proposal adopted; companies public for 10 years or more were estimated to see an average 3.4% income drop.

- The FASB received more than 1,000 comment letters on its proposal. About 90% opposed the standard; the majority of letters recommended dropping the project entirely, rather than changing the proposal.

- By a 9 to 6 vote, the AICPA's Accounting Standards Executive Committee recommended that the FASB drop the proposal and require merely disclosure, not recognition, of stock options when granted. At a January 1994 national conference, SEC Chief Accountant Walter Schuetze responded to this vote by chiding CPA firms for acting like "cheerleaders for their clients."

- In the summer of 1994, the U.S. Senate passed a resolution urging the FASB to abandon the stock options project.

- The Association for Investment Management Research (AIMR) voiced its support for the FASB stock option exposure draft. Raymond DeAngelo, an AIMR vice president, explained: "We do not believe it is appropriate for the Congress or any other government body to get involved in setting accounting standards."

- In October 1994, several members of Congress introduced the *Accounting Standards Reform Act of 1994*, a proposed amendment to federal securities laws to require that all new accounting standards/principles be approved by the SEC.

- In November 1994, after the Republicans swept the elections, incoming Senate Securities Subcommittee Chairman Phil Gramm called for new hearings on the stock option exposure draft and the entire FASB process.

- In December 1994, the FASB voted 5 to 2 against requiring the proposed treatment of stock options. Instead, the FASB decided to "work toward improving disclosures...rather than requiring an expense charge for all options."

- In February 1995, in his last pre-retirement address to the AICPA's National Conference on Current SEC Developments, SEC Chief Accountant Walter Schuetze said: "Given the great degree of opposition to [the FASB's] proposal and the clear danger that Congress would get involved with legislation, I believe that the FASB acted wisely to end the controversy by requiring disclosure instead of formal recognition in expense of the value of stock options."

- In October 1995, the FASB issued *FASB Statement No. 123: Accounting for Stock-Based Compensation*, which requires entities to disclose the fair value of their employee stock options, although they do not have to record the options at fair value in their financial statements.

- In May 1996, the *Wall Street Journal* reported that a survey of 30 major corporations by analysts Pearl Meyer & Partners, Inc., found that executives received 212 times more pay in 1995 than the average U. S. worker--a jump of 500% since 1965.

- In a May 1996 annual meeting, shareholders of Germany's largest company--Daimler-Benz AG--raised questions about 1995 executive bonuses. They asked why, when the company had a large loss (5.7 billion marks, about $3.7 billion) and shareholders received no dividend for the first time in 45 years, executives received bonuses. At the same meeting, shareholders were asked to approve a stock option plan for executives.

Post Script: 1997

- In April 1997, Bear Stearns & Co. released the results of their survey of 1996 Form 10-K filings. Most companies chose to continue accounting for options as in the past: that is, they recorded no compensation expense.

MODULE INDEX

-ABC-

-DEF-

-GHI-

-JKL-

-MNO-

-PQR-

-STU-

-VWXYZ-